SOCIAL ISSUES, JUSTICE AND STATUS

RACE AND ETHNICITY: CULTURAL ROLES, SPIRITUAL PRACTICES AND SOCIAL CHALLENGES

SOCIAL ISSUES, JUSTICE AND STATUS

Additional books in this series can be found on Nova's website
under the Series tab.

Additional E-books in this series can be found on Nova's website
under the E-book tab.

SOCIAL ISSUES, JUSTICE AND STATUS

RACE AND ETHNICITY: CULTURAL ROLES, SPIRITUAL PRACTICES AND SOCIAL CHALLENGES

JONATHAN K. CRENNAN
EDITOR

NOVA

Nova Science Publishers, Inc.
New York

NOTICE TO THE READER

The Publisher has taken reasonable care in the preparation of this book, but makes no expressed or implied warranty of any kind and assumes no responsibility for any errors or omissions. No liability is assumed for incidental or consequential damages in connection with or arising out of information contained in this book. The Publisher shall not be liable for any special, consequential, or exemplary damages resulting, in whole or in part, from the readers' use of, or reliance upon, this material.

Independent verification should be sought for any data, advice or recommendations contained in this book. In addition, no responsibility is assumed by the publisher for any injury and/or damage to persons or property arising from any methods, products, instructions, ideas or otherwise contained in this publication.

This publication is designed to provide accurate and authoritative information with regard to the subject matter covered herein. It is sold with the clear understanding that the Publisher is not engaged in rendering legal or any other professional services. If legal or any other expert assistance is required, the services of a competent person should be sought. FROM A DECLARATION OF PARTICIPANTS JOINTLY ADOPTED BY A COMMITTEE OF THE AMERICAN BAR ASSOCIATION AND A COMMITTEE OF PUBLISHERS.

Additional color graphics may be available in the e-book version of this book.

LIBRARY OF CONGRESS CATALOGING-IN-PUBLICATION DATA

Race and ethnicity : cultural roles, spiritual practices and social challenges / editor, Jonathan K. Crennan.
        xvi, 406 p. : ill. (some col.) ; 26 cm.
Includes bibliographical references and index.
ISBN 978-1-60692-099-2
1. Race. 2. Ethnicity. I. Crennan, Jonathan K.
HT1523 .R25125 2010

2010284100

Published by Nova Science Publishers, Inc. ✛ *New York*

CONTENTS

PREFACE

The term race or racial group usually refers to the categorization of humans into populations or groups on the basis of various sets of heritable characteristics. The physical features commonly seen as indicating race are salient visual traits such as skin color, cranial or facial features and hair texture. Consequently, an ethnic group is a group of humans whose members identify with each other, through a common heritage that is real or assumed. Ethnic identity is further marked in the recognition from others of a group's distinctiveness and the recognition of common cultural, linguistic, religious, behavioral traits as indicators of contrast to other groups. Ethnicity is an important means through which people can identify themselves. This book presents and reviews important data on race and ethnicity.

Chapter 1 - Race and racism are significant factors posing formidable challenges to racialized groups. Historically, race and racism have been implicated in the exclusion of 'people of colour' from full participation in North American society. Some scholars argue that North America has entered a post-race era when race does not matter as a factor in inter-group dynamics. Improvements have occurred in recent times for racialized groups in Canada and America. After centuries of racially motivated discrimination, stereotypes, and exclusionary policies, change came to America in November 2008, when the country elected its first racialized individual as president. Three years prior, in September 2005, Canada had appointed the first black person, remarkably, a woman, as the country's Governor General. Although epoch-making, the extent to which such events bespeak a post-race era in North American history is open to debate. The claim that North America has been ushered into a post-race Shangri-La is seriously challenged by the presence of 'refined' forms of racism, including the emergence of perhaps the newest strains – Islamophobia and Arabiphobia. Unfortunately, very little scholarly work exists on the status and articulations of contemporary racisms in the social work and ethnic relations literature. Almost nothing is known about how race and racism shape current processes such as the 'arabianization' of terrorism, 'islamization' of fundamentalism, 'muslimization' of extremism, or the 'asianization' of gang activity. For social workers, the lack of enhanced understanding of racialization processes impinges negatively on the provision of culturally sensitive social services to racialized clients. This chapter contributes to the social work and ethnic relations literature by presenting a critical analysis of the historical and contemporary statuses of race and racism and their role in shaping the lives and life chances of racialized groups in North American society. The chapter proposes an integrative counter-racism framework for addressing social problems engendered by the twin issues of race and racism. A number of recent events are drawn on to demonstrate that North America is far from being a monochromatic society. Race and racism remain resilient largely because North American society continues to function and individuals continue to behave in ways that suggest race will always matter in inter-group relations and public discourses. Given the complex and multiform nature of racism, an integrative counter-racism framework offers great promise, more so than single methodologies, for detoxifying the harmful doings of racism and other systems of social oppression.

Chapter 2 - This study approaches a topic which is highly germane to the enhancement of foreign/second (L2) language education: the manner in which learners glean cultural perspectives during reading, in this specific case EFL reading (English as a Foreing Language) in Argentina. The importance of cultural perspectives for enhancing the comprehension of L2 texts has been widely acknowledged by theorists and researchers in the field. The chapter reports part of the results of a broader study carried out in 2005, whose specific aim was to describe the comprehension of the cultural content of a literary narrative text through response writing tasks and visual reformulations. About 200 Argentine college students (prospective teachers and translators of English) voluntarily participated in the study. They were Caucasian, mostly female, middle class, Spanish-speaking, between 19-21 years of age, and were enrolled in the course English Language II at the National University of La Plata in Argentina. This is a prestigious, public, access for all university in a developing country. The results corresponding to a culturally loaded text, written in English (a foreign language), are reported here. The selection, a fragment from Desert Wife, describes one Christmas celebration in a Native American context with an outsider perspective, i.e., with a narrator who participates in the celebration described but is not a member of the culture represented in the text. In reaction to this text the participants produced a response writing task in Spanish, a response writing task in English, and a visual reformulation (among other tasks), whose analysis serves as the foundation of this chapter. Data were analyzed in terms of culturally distinctive idea units and textual modifications (reader behaviors). Both measures of analysis (amount of free recall in the form of cultural idea units and the kind of information recalled in the form of reader behaviors) are consistent with Carrell (1984c), Steffensen, Joag-Dev and Anderson (1979), and Sharifian, Rochecouste and Malcolm (2004), among others. Results showed different levels of apprehension of cultural aspects during reading, i.e. different degrees of depth, complexity and details with respect to the cultural reality of the Navajos. In general, the approach to Otherness was limited to the perception of what was exotic or exciting about the Navajo culture, without a genuine effort to become familiar with what was strange. The difficulty this population revealed in approaching Otherness manifested itself in the abundance of stereotyped perspectives about the Native Americans in the written tasks produced.

Chapter 3 - This chapter provides an overview of what is known about content of possible selves and implications of possible selves for outcomes for male and female teens differing in race/ethnicity (African American, Asian American, Latino, Native American, and white teens). Although findings are somewhat ambiguated by heterogeneity in time focus (e.g. 'next year', 'when you are an adult', 'in five years'), it appears that expected possible selves for the near future most commonly focus on academic and interpersonal domains, while fears are more diverse. There is some evidence that number of academic possible selves declines across the transition to middle school and from middle to high school. Low income, rural and Hispanic youth are at risk of having few academic or occupational possible selves, or having such general possible selves in these domains that they are unlikely to promote self-regulation. For a number of reasons, possible selves of girls may function more effectively as self-regulators. Moreover, there is at least some evidence that content of possible selves and especially the existence of strategies to attain these selves is predictive of academic attainment and delinquent involvement.

Chapter 4 - Increasing globalization is forcing a growing number of organization members of different ethnic origins to interact across linguistic boundaries. And since language affects almost all aspects of everyday life, this calls for the attention of researchers and practitioners engaged with multiethnic organizations. Extant research has noted a strong association between ethnic identity and language use. However, while the link between language and ethnic identity is often perceived to be linear, this chapter takes a different approach. By drawing on anthropological theories on ethnicity and ethnic identity it is argued that the relation between language and identity is dynamic and dialectical due to the ways it is negotiated in interaction. In the empirical analysis the chapter focuses on the encounters between expatriates and local employees in two Danish subsidiaries – one in England and one in Saudi Arabia. The author use ethnographic field study methodology relying on longitudinal participant observations and semi-structured interviews to collect data. The findings show that identity-making may be actualized by competition for resources and recognition. This can be done by investing certain objects such as the symbolic application of language with certain identifications. It is finally argued that the processes by which identifications develop can cause both polarization and accommodation in the relation between groups and individuals. It is recommended that the character of language as linked to social strategies is taken into account in expatriate management and management in multiethnic organizations. Ignoring the important role of language in these organizations may lead to loss of resources and hindrances to organizational and managerial development due to lack of communication.

Chapter 5 - In 2007 approximately 38 million immigrants resided in the United States. The large increase in contemporary immigration has given rise to a record number of children who are raised in immigrant families. Since the 1980s, a new generation of immigrants has populated the nation's schools. It is the fastest growing and the most ethnically diverse segment of America's child population. About one of every five individuals under 18 is either an immigrant or has parents who are immigrants. This population is certain to increase. The first section of the paper examines the role social class plays in academic achievement of second generation students. There is a significant debate between schools stressing the socioeconomic vs. sociocultural perspective on educational achievement. The second section of the paper analyzes the sociocultural perspective. Why do Asian children excel in school to a much greater extent than children from Latino families? To what degree is this disparity explained by socioeconomic class as opposed to the factors related to the culture of various ethnic groups? The third section of the paper will critically analyze variants of assimilation theory. What factors condition the adaptation process of second generation youth? The traditional assimilation framework of Gordon (1964) and his followers believe that a "foreign" group will with increasing contact overtime be absorbed in the 'mainstream' of American society. In contrast Portes and Rumbaut (2006) propose that a process of "segmented assimilation" better characterizes the experience of recent immigrants to the US and their children. Finally the last section of the paper will conclude with an examination of some of the major challenges of integrating immigrant and second generation students in the

American mainstream. Factors such as poverty, segregation, and attitudes toward immigration will be discussed.

Chapter 6 - Breast cancer incidence rates are higher among white than African-American (AA) women in the USA, although mortality rates from breast cancer are higher among AA women. Many published studies have shown trends towards younger age at diagnosis, worse prognostic features and lower survival rates for AA and other ethnic minority women with breast cancer compared with white women. Other studies have reported on racial and ethnic differences in patterns of care for women with breast cancer, suggesting that unequal access to care may in part explain the noted disparity in survival. While debate continues as to the relative degree in which tumor biology vs. socioeconomic factors influence racial differences in survival, cultural and behavioral differences play at least some role, and can partially explain the noted disparity in breast cancer survival seen among different racial and ethnic groups. Approximately 5 to 10% of all breast cancer in this country is associated with known hereditary mutations in the BRCA1 and BRCA2 genes, meaning nearly 22,000 breast cancer cases diagnosed per year are due to mutations in these cancer susceptibility genes. Hereditary breast cancer is more common among women with early age at diagnosis and is also more common among certain ethnic groups. While AA women are more likely to develop breast cancer at a younger age than white women, cancer risk assessment and testing for hereditary breast cancer syndromes is underutilized among AA women compared to non-minority women. It is incumbent on health care professionals to help develop solutions to the inequities in access to medical care for women with breast cancer in order to decrease the gap in breast cancer outcomes seen in this country. One way to achieve this is to improve access to screening and cancer risk assessment for all eligible women, and to make state of the art cancer treatment available for all women affected with breast cancer.

Chapter 7 – Context: American ethnic minorities, particularly those of African and Hispanic descent have a greater risk of developing hypertension and type 2 diabetes compared to American Whites. Despite the consistency of the epidemiologic evidence of the racial/ethnic variation for these diseases, relatively little is known with confidence about the causes of the non-White dilemma. Objective: To determine how much of the relative difference in the rates of hypertension and type 2 diabetes between high-risk Blacks and Hispanics and low-risk Whites is attributable to their differences in obesity. Methods: Data (n=5531) from the 1999-2002 U.S. National Health and Nutrition Examination Surveys were utilized for this analysis. Gender-specific proportions of White to non-White differences in odds of hypertension and diabetes that were due to their relative differences in the prevalence of obesity were estimated using relative attributable risk derived from multiple logistic regression modeling. Statistical adjustment was made for age, education, alcohol intake, education, and physical activity. Results: 50.2% and 30.6% of differences in odds of hypertension between White men and Black men and between White men and Hispanic men, respectively, are attributable to their differences in rates of obesity. The analogous values for diabetes were 70.7% and 57.4% for Black men and Hispanic men. Also, 30.6 % and 13.4% of differences in odds of hypertension between White women and Black women and between White women and Hispanic women, respectively, are associated with their differences in rates of obesity. The analogous values for diabetes are 62.2% and 83.7% for Black women and Hispanic women when compared with White women. Conclusion: The magnitude of racial/ethnic differences in hypertension and diabetes due to their differences in obesity provides an encouraging reason to continue to implement public health obesity prevention programs in the United States' minority groups. Aggressive programs to reduce obesity and increase physical activity in Blacks and Hispanics may prove useful in reducing racial/ethnic disparities in hypertension and diabetes.

Chapter 8 - This chapter reviews the empirical literature related to cancer topics among those of racial/ethnic populations and/or low literacy groups. A comprehensive search of databases retrieved 23 relevant articles. These articles were classified into five overall groups of topics pertaining to characteristics of Internet users, attitudes toward Internet use, psychological aspects of Internet use, health attitudes and Internet use, and readability and the Internet. Some points concluded include that those of racial/ethnic populations are less likely to use the Internet than whites. Also, Internet websites would be of greater interest and relevance to those of racial/ethnic populations if there is tailoring of the websites to their cultural interests. Lastly, there are potential mental and physical health benefits for using the Internet. However, among the racial/ethnic group of African Americans, they are unlikely to use the Internet for health information and are less interested in online support groups. Also, the websites are often written at 10th grade or higher levels.

Chapter 9 - Clinical psychology is concerned with the diagnosis and treatment of mental disorder, such as anxiety or depression. Despite some cross-cultural differences in the exact prevalence of psychological disorders, most disorders are common across the world, to all cultures and ethnic groups. A key point is that such disorders cause substantial distress across cultures, and pose a significant social and economical challenge by affecting hundreds of millions of people worldwide. The World Health Organisation Global Burden of Disease Survey estimates that mental disease will be the second leading cause of disabilities worldwide by the year 2020. This calls for a better understanding of the development and maintenance of psychological disorders in order to be able to treat them effectively. Many treatments have been shown to be effective for a range of different psychological disorders, for instance cognitive behavioural treatments (CBT) for anxiety and depression. However, despite their clinical effectiveness, questions remain about dissemination in various contexts, and about a considerable proportion of patients who drop out of therapy or do not benefit from CBT. Hence, there are current efforts to refine CBT and advance further the underlying theory and current practice. Ethnicity and cultural roles are key factors that may play a large role in how psychological disorders are developed, why they are maintained, and, in turn, how patients respond to treatment. More specifically, cultural beliefs, attitudes, values, expectations and assumptions, such as cultural differences in beliefs about psychological health and disorders, help-seeking, and recovery, impact on the course of psychological disorders. Additionally, wider cultural differences, such as views regarding power distribution, self-understanding, masculinity, religion, and acceptance of uncertainty, may also impact on the processes involved in the development, expression and maintenance of psychological disorders. In practice, however, this relation between ethnicity and mental disorders is not simple and may often be indirect and multifaceted. A better understanding of this relationship is of vital importance for at least two reasons. First, recent reports have highlighted the reality of health disparities and unequal treatment of different cultures and ethnic minorities. A recent study on psychiatric treatment, for instance, of primary care patients reported that only about half of the patients with anxiety disorders received mental health treatment at the time, and that members of ethnic minority groups were less likely to receive mental health treatment. Second, an individual's ethnicity and his or her cultural role/orientation seem to have a wide-ranging influence on the development and maintenance of psychological disorders, such as anxiety or depression. The present chapter will focus on both of these issues and explore the impact of ethnicity on mental disorders in detail. This is done using the example of posttraumatic stress disorder (PTSD), a common anxiety disorder following trauma with a particularly cultural influence. First, we aim to suggest ways in which theories of PTSD could be adapted in order to incorporate ethnicity and cultural roles. Second, we present preliminary data on the role of ethnicity in autobiographical memory, appraisals and posttrauma adjustment, demonstrating that there are important differences in the way Caucasian and Non-Caucasian trauma survivors perceive and appraise their trauma, and how they later make meaning of it. Towards the end of the chapter, implications for theory and clinical practice, i.e., treatment and prevention programs for PTSD and other disorders, are discussed.

Chapter 10 - This chapter describes recent empirical findings on maltreatment identification and impact in a diverse high-risk sample of adolescents involved in public sectors of care. A set of three related research questions is addressed. The first research question concerns the extent to which race matters in the institutional identification of maltreatment and need for protection. Secondly, the author address the question of whether race matters in whether youngsters view specific parenting behaviors as abusive. The final research question focuses on whether there are racial differences in the impact of maltreatment-related experiences. In each, the author center our focus on youngsters' own perceptions of their personal histories in the context of maltreatment identification. The findings reviewed suggest that matters of race in maltreatment identification are complex, as there appear to be racial differences in whether certain parent behaviors are labeled by adolescents as abusive, and in the institutional identification of maltreatment victimization. However, punitive parent behaviors, whether or not they are labeled as abusive, are strongly associated with psychological distress across racial groups. Thus, racial variability in the labeling and identification of maltreatment does not necessarily translate into differential impact of adverse family experiences on youth.

Chapter 11 - Racial and ethnic disparities in American health and healthcare are becoming increasingly apparent and are garnering a growing body of research attention. These disparities are particularly problematic regarding mental health service delivery to multicultural populations. The present study explores a variety of key parameters associated with the Multicultural Assessment Intervention Process (MAIP) model proposed by Dana (1993, 1998, 2000) and Dana, Aragon, and Kramer, (2002). This model provides a mental health agency and its practitioners with the necessary conceptual scaffolding and theoretical clarity to address service delivery disparities by positing that mental health consumers are best served when factors such as (1) consumer-provider ethnic/racial match, (2) consumer acculturation status and/or ethnic/racial identity, and (3) provider cultural competence are assessed and factored into the treatment process and clinical outcome. Toward this end, a sample of 123 university counseling center consumers was measured on the 4 previous independent variables (i.e., ethnic/racial match, acculturation status, ethnic identity, and staff cultural competence). Five clinical outcome dependent measures were assessed including Global Assessment of Function (GAF) pre and post treatment differences, and 4 subscales of the Brief Psychiatric Rating Scale (BPRS): Thinking Disturbance, Withdrawal/Retardation, Hostile-Suspicious, and Anxious-Depression, all of which served as dependent variables. A 2 x 2 x 2 x 2 factorial between-subjects multivariate analysis of covariance (MANCOVA) indicated a statistically significant multivariate interaction effect between Ethnic Match x

Client Acculturation x Client Ethnic Identity for the BPRS-thinking disturbance measure. Implications for the MAIP model with this college student population are discussed.

Chapter 12 – Background: The high incidence and increased prevalence of childhood obesity has led to multiple efforts for intervention specifically aimed at increasing levels of physical activity (PA). Preferences for physical activities and sedentary activities have been linked as potential mediators to objectively measured PA participation. However; little research has evaluated whether these preferences are related to Body Mass Index (BMI), particularly in African American children. The purpose of this study was to explore the relationships among BMI and preferences for physical activities and sedentary activities in urban African American youth, a population at increased risk for obesity related heatlh problems. Methods: Cross-sectional data were analyzed from 75 10- to 16-year-old African American children who were attending the local chapter of the National Youth Summer Program. Of the participants, 53.3% were male and 46.7% were female. The mean age of study participants was 12.29 ($\pm$ 1.86) years old. Participants mean grade level was 7.27 ($\pm$ 1.93). Eleven children and adolescents (14.6%) were at risk for becoming overweight and seventeen children and adolescents (21.2%) were overweight according to age-sex specific percentile BMI guidelines of the Centers for Disease Control (Kuczmarski et al., 2000). Due to age interaction, four separate multiple linear regression models were analyzed based on age category. Preadolescents were defined as 10-12 year olds and adolescents were defined as 13-16 year olds. The dependent variable was age- and gender-specific body mass index percentile. Independent variables were childrens' self-reported preferences for physical activities or sedentary activities with gender as a covariate. Preferences for physical activities and sedentary activities are represented via two scales with higher scores indicating higher preferences. Results: For preadolescents (n = 43) preference for physical activities significantly explained 16.4% of the variance in BMI (p = .028) after controlling for gender. A lower BMI was related to a higher preference for physical activities (β = -32.82, p = .01), mainly soccer and outdoor play. Also for preadolescents, preference for sedentary activities significantly explained 17.9% of the variance in BMI (p = .020) after controlling for gender. A lower BMI was related to a higher preference for sedentary activities (β = -31.25, p = .01). The major sedentary activities that were contributors were watching television, watching movies or videos on a VCR or DVD, playing video games, and listening to the radio, tapes or CDs. However, there were no significant relationships found among preferences and BMI for adolescent children (n =32). Conclusions: These results add to a growing body of literature explaining the potential influences of activity preference on BMI among African American youth; a high-risk, understudied population. More specifically, preadolescence might be an ideal time for obesity prevention in that the encouragement of activities could lead to increased activity levels for African Americans.

Chapter 13 - It is understood that diseases have been the biggest killers of people; they have also been decisive shapers of history. There is no doubt that Malaria, Yellow Fever, and related diseases had a direct impact on history and outcome of society's social and economic development. Yellow Fever could not be distinguished from Malaria, Dengue and other plagues that confronted sailors, soldiers, and colonists in tropical areas on both sides of the Atlantic. What is astonishing is how the mosquito played a significant role in determining the course of history.

Chapter 14 - The relative liberalism of American Jews is a phenomenon of enduring interest to specialists and laypeople alike. The ongoing American Jewish attachment to liberal politics and the Democratic Party defies rational-choice models and intuitive understandings of political orientation. Other groups with the same socioeconomic status as American Jews tend to be more conservative and/or Republican.

This essay begins (§I) with a description of the dimensions of American Jewish liberalism. It proceeds (§II) to a discussion of the more common theories that seek to explain the phenomenon, noting the deficiencies of each. It concludes (§III) that American Jewish liberalism is best viewed as an expression of "lived religion"; this expression functions to fulfill American Jews' self-definition and thereby to impede ethnic dissolution in an atomizing society.

Chapter 15 - Contemporary research on families and their adolescent offspring has been shaped by contextualism which underscores the importance of phenomena such as ethnicity, social class and family processes. Given current demographic trends, especially for Latinos, contextualism and the topic of ethnicity have gained impetus among researchers. Latinos currently comprise the largest group of immigrants in the United States, representing approximately 44 million people, with Mexicans alone representing 64% of this number. Latinos are not only the fastest growing ethnic group, they are also relatively young. In the two decades beginning in 1980 and ending in 1999, the proportion of Latino children in the United States increased from 9% to 16%. This represents the highest growth rate of any racial or ethnic group. In light of these trends and the importance of research on Latinos, this chapter explores the study of culture in family processes in Latino families with adolescent offspring. We are especially interested in within group Latino diversity and subgroup differences on familismo a phenomenon central to Latino family life. The importance of familismo is underscored by its protective mechanisms. For example it is believed to provide a buffering effect for high stress situations such as those that occur during acculturation and adjustment to a new country as well as stress related to developmental change typical during adolescence. Given the importance of familismo as a protective factor and ethnic signifier, this chapter explores Latino subgroup differences and changes in aspects of familismo which may occur as a function of acculturation and generational status.

Chapter 16 - Regional differences in clinical presentation of diabetic foot syndrome had been reported. The Eurodiale study, revealed considerable differences among diabetic foot ulcer (DFU) patients in different European centers. Although ethnicity sometimes becomes difficult to define but it can capture something that genes cannot. These include aspects of culture, behavior, environment, and social status. Objective: To study the presentation of diabetic foot syndrome in Egypt and point out the differences from what is reported from Western countries. Egypt is an African country but part of its territories lies in Asia. It could also be considered as a Mediterranean country. The author found that the majority of the studied diabetic patients (93.8%) didn't receive any prior education about proper foot care. Tinea pedis, dry skin and calluses were found in 43.6%, 44.6% and 5.7% of patients. Inappropriate footwear was used by 61.6% of patients. Most of diabetic foot ulcers were neuropathic (93.8%), while neuroischaemic and ischaemic ulcers were much less frequent (4.1% and 2.1% respectively). The majority of DFUs (80.7%) were of 3 months duration or longer (16.1 + 13.6 months). Most of ulcers (85.6%) were located on the plantar surface of the foot. The distribution of ulcer location was as follow; plantar forefoot (35.3%), plantar toes (34 %), inerdigital and dorsal toes (9.2%), plantar hindfoot (9.8 %), plantar midfoot (6.5%) and dorsal or lateral aspect of the foot (5.2%). Bacterial pathogens associated with infected diabetic foot ulcers were also to some extent different. S. aureus was the most common species (21.1%) isolated from infected DFU. However, it is much less prevalent than what is reported from Western countries. MRSA represented 42.8 % of the isolated Staphylococci.

It is concluded that, in Egypt, there are major differences in the presentation of diabetic foot syndrome than data reported from Western countries. These differences could lead to regional variation in the outcome and the management strategies. It could also help to elucidate the impact of social, cultural and environmental factors on the pathogenesis of the diabetic foot syndrome.

Chapter 17 - The face is one of the most important elements defining social interaction. Once the normal appearance of the face is altered, individuals encounter significant social problems. This is a situation that involves the facially disfigured but also those who interact with them. Due to medical advancements, patients who are facially disfigured because of cancer, related surgical procedures, and other treatments can now survive for an extended period of time. This survivorship is often accompanied with stigmatization as cancer survivors are viewed, and treated, differently because of their altered facial appearance. Despite its growing importance, the theme of the social consequences of cancer generated facial disfigurement has received limited scientific attention. Research tends to focus on patients' functional limitations and the manner in which they cope with their disfigurement. Less attention is placed on the social dimension of cancer generated facial disfigurement. In particular, limited research is available on the ways in which different social settings and groups affect the interaction of cancer patients who are facially disfigured. In this chapter, current research on these topics is reviewed underscoring findings in interaction patterns and outcomes. It is indicated that cultural and ethnic variations affect collective perceptions of, and responses to, cancer and disfigurement. The chapter concludes by stressing the importance of including cultural and ethnic components in the study of cancer generated facial disfigurement, the training of professionals, and development of pertinent protocols.

Chapter 18 - Race serves an important, yet controversial, role in many pharmacogenetic studies. The 2005 FDA approval of BiDil (isosorbide dinitrate/hydralazine), the first drug with a race-specific indication, fueled the debate regarding the risks and benefits of race-based studies. Proponents of BiDil contended that this drug's race-specific development and approval was appropriate and necessary. By focusing on African Americans, researchers were able to target a subgroup of patients who were more likely to respond to the drug, thereby increasing the likelihood of success and decreasing the time to market. They argued that race is a reasonable substitute for specific genetic information, yielding valuable information regarding relevant biological pathways. Critics, however, stated that race represents more than genetic information, often reflecting social and environmental factors. They argued that race-based studies perpetuate racism and lead to inferior care for populations that are considered inappropriate markets by the pharmaceutical industry. After considering these arguments, the author believe there is a role for race-based studies in pharmacogenetics. However, these studies must be designed and interpreted cautiously. Researchers must be aware of the social and ethical implications of their studies, and policy makers should prioritize research funding for studies involving financially disadvantaged populations.

Chapter 19 - There is little data concerning medical reports about the first Brazilian habitants, after the first Portuguese expeditions at the XVI Century. However, some historical records mention a variable expression of behavioral disturbances amongst some descendents from European Caucasians, Native Indians from the Brazilian coast and Africans brought to work as slaves. The mixing of these three groups during decades of miscegenation generated a wide spectrum of cultural, behavioral and genetic variants and to study this issue is crucial to understand how their biological and cultural idiosyncrasies might have influenced the present Brazilian neuroepidemiology. On the other hand, the current ethnical profile in Brazil presents an unusual and unique distribution across the country, with highly mixed groups living at the coast, contrasting with a scattered distribution of high inbreeding clusters found at the country side, were almost 30% of the population lives. The natural consequence is the often manifestation of recessive disorders in rural areas, several of them with major neuropsychiatric symptoms and other with important psychological consequences due to general life quality impairment. There are, in part, geographic reasons for this pattern, in cases of families living in isolated regions, but there are also intriguing cultural aspects. Some poor families own significant, but barren and desolated pieces of land, and some of them are recognized as wealthy, compared to their neighbors. Actually they avoid to "mix" themselves with other kindred, avoiding splitting their property with subjects other than their own siblings. Additional studies are crucial for the full understanding of the connection between the past Psychopathology of the first "Brazilians" and the nowadays neuropsychiatric profile at the general population.

In: Race and Ethnicity
Editor: Jonathan K. Crennan, pp. 1-59

ISBN: 978-1-60692-099-2
© 2010 Nova Science Publishers, Inc.

Chapter 1

UNDOING THE TOXIC DOINGS OF RACE AND RACISM IN A *'POST-RACE'* NORTH AMERICA

Ransford Danso

School of Community and Liberal Studies, Sheridan College Institute of Technology & Advanced Learning, 7899 McLaughlin Road, Brampton, Ontario, Canada L6Y 5H9

ABSTRACT

Race and racism are significant factors posing formidable challenges to racialized groups. Historically, race and racism have been implicated in the exclusion of 'people of colour' from full participation in North American society. Some scholars argue that North America has entered a *post-race* era when race does not matter as a factor in inter-group dynamics. Improvements have occurred in recent times for racialized groups in Canada and America. After centuries of racially motivated discrimination, stereotypes, and exclusionary policies, change came to America in November 2008, when the country elected its first racialized individual as president. Three years prior, in September 2005, Canada had appointed the first black person, remarkably, a woman, as the country's Governor General. Although epoch-making, the extent to which such events bespeak a post-race era in North American history is open to debate. The claim that North America has been ushered into a post-race Shangri-La is seriously challenged by the presence of 'refined' forms of racism, including the emergence of perhaps the newest strains – Islamophobia and Arabiphobia. Unfortunately, very little scholarly work exists on the status and articulations of contemporary racisms in the social work and ethnic relations literature. Almost nothing is known about how race and racism shape current processes such as the 'arabianization' of terrorism, 'islamization' of fundamentalism, 'muslimization' of extremism, or the 'asianization' of gang activity. For social workers, the lack of enhanced understanding of racialization processes impinges negatively on the provision of culturally sensitive social services to racialized clients. This chapter contributes to the social work and ethnic relations literature by presenting a critical analysis of the historical and contemporary statuses of race and racism and their role in shaping the lives and life chances of racialized groups in North American society. The chapter proposes an integrative counter-racism framework for addressing social problems engendered by the twin issues of race and racism. A number of recent events are drawn on to demonstrate that North America is far from being a monochromatic society. Race and racism remain resilient largely because North American society continues to function and individuals continue to behave in ways that suggest race will always matter in inter-group relations and public discourses. Given the complex and multiform nature of racism, an integrative counter-racism framework offers great promise, more so than single methodologies, for detoxifying the harmful doings of racism and other systems of social oppression.

INTRODUCTION

'Race' is an emotionally charged issue that continues to be the subject of contentious debates among academics, politicians, policymakers, community workers, human service providers, and laypeople alike. Especially in multiethnic societies, race and racism have often been major sources of tensions and social problems. The political histories of many countries are rife with stories of how these tensions have often degenerated into riots (*e.g.* the 'race riots' in the America, Australia, and France) and genocide, such as the notorious ethnic cleansing in the former Yugoslavia, and the near extirpation of the Jews by Nazi Germany during World War II. Race defines access to power, opportunities, and resources. It accords privilege and status to in-group ('we'/'us') members while disempowering out-group ('they'/'them') members. Historically, race and racism determined who belonged and who did not, as well as who got what when, how and where, or what people could expect from life (Tang, 2004; Foster, 2005; Hier an Bolaria, 2007; Wallis and Fleras 2009a, 2009b; Fleras, 2010). Without argument, significant improvements have occurred for many racialized groups in North America, including the appointment of the first black person, Michaëlle Jean, as the Governor General of Canada and the election of the first black person, Barack Obama, as President of the United States. Despite these historic breakthroughs, the 'race bubble' has still not burst in North American society, a situation that calls into question the claim that North America has been ushered into a post-race era (Foster, 2005) when race has lost all significance and potency.

Issues of culturally competent practice with ethnic minorities are fairly well documented in social work. However, a critical, reflective analysis of how contemporary articulations of race and racism mediate this practice has not received much attention in the social work literature. The lack of scholarly work on the salience of race and racism in social work education and training, research, and service delivery seriously limits practitioners' knowledge about the real struggles and oppressions within which racialized groups negotiate their lived experiences in North American society. Besides failing to emancipate racialized clients from oppressive social work practice (Boushel, 2000; Williams and Soydan, 2005), the lack of attention also creates barriers to developing ethnically responsive social services and programs. There is also very little comparative work on the status of race and racism in contemporary Canada and America in the ethnic relations literature. Using the example of blacks and Muslim and Arab North Americans, this chapter helps to fill these lacunae in the social work and ethnic relations literature by examining how the ideology of race and racism continues to entrench the oppression of people of colour in North America.

Focusing on racialized communities is warranted in that they share 'different but complementary experiences of racism' (Gilroy, 1990, p. 77). Besides implicating both race and racism in the social exclusion of racialized bodies from full membership and participation in North American society, the chapter also argues that the impacts of racism on the social functioning of racialized people are real although races themselves are nothing more than social and political constructions. The chapter further contends that, contrary to popular perceptions, there is hardly any evidence to support the claim that North America has been ushered into a 'colour-blind', 'post-race' era. If anything at all, race and racism have transformed themselves in such a way that they now occupy 'refined' statuses but their effects on racialiazed groups are no less debilitating than their historically crude forms.

The chapter begins with brief overviews of the academic debates on race and the origins of the *idea* of race. Although some commentators (*e.g.* Fanon, 1967) have suggested that we ignore the past and move on, it is important to recognize that the past impinges on the present in very profound ways. To understand why race is a social and political invention rather than a biological given, it is always important to approach it historically, taking due cognizance of the particular local context as well. After providing a critical analysis of the ways racism manifests itself in contemporary North America, the chapter discusses contemporary forms of racisms and the myths and discourses that underpin these 'new' racisms. Particular attention is paid to what may be considered the newest strains of racism in North America – *Islamophobia* and *Arabiphobia* – and how they impact North Americans of Muslim and Arab backgrounds. A critical analysis of the manifestations of the new race and racisms can provide helpful guidelines for developing efficacious strategies and methods of work for combating racism so that North America can become a truly egalitarian place for all groups of people. The chapter also examines the impacts of racial ideology and racism on the social functioning of blacks and racialized groups in Canada and America. An integrative counter-racism framework that combines different structural approaches is proposed as a promising model for achieving the objectives of the decolonization project.

Overview of the Race Debate

For the past six or so decades, theoretical and political debates have raged over the meaning and status of *race* as a social and analytical concept, especially in the social sciences. At issue are what constitutes race and why the notion of race is still widely used in popular, academic, and scientific discourses when it is generally accepted that races do not exit (Helms *et al.*, 2005; Sternberg *et al.*, 2005; Carey, 2006; Nayak, 2006; Satzewich and Liodakis, 2007; Wallis and Fleras, 2009b). Many scholars have suggested that the term race be placed between quotation marks every time it appears in social scientific discussion to denote its unnaturalness. However, some anti-racist scholars (*e.g.* Dei, 2009) argue that such use of race might lead to dismissing or disregarding the importance of the term in anti-racism discourse. The thought is that race is already on the table and that neither a figurative nor literal usage of race would make it vanish.[1]

---

[1] Stasiulis (2009) has also suggested that, although races are social constructions and that biologically there is only one (*i.e.* the human) race, within any given society and historical era, the process of racial categorization is social, political, and ideological, and profoundly affected by economic relations of domination and exploitation rather than simply found in nature. However, it remains that race, like gender, has biological referents and is most commonly associated with physiognomically based differences such as skin colour.

Scholars in the debates on race often align themselves with one of four camps. One group of writers (*e.g.* Hernstein and Murray, 1994; Rushton, 1995; Rowe, 2002) claim that race is a biological phenomenon that can be used to assign people into distinct racial groups. Opponents of this view contend that race is just a political construction that has been institutionalized and used to justify the domination and oppression of racialized groups (Boushel, 2000; Kim, 2004; Hall, 2005; Helms *et al.*, 2005; Smedley and Smedley, 2005; Nayak, 2006; Bell, 2007a; Colvin-Burque *et al.*, 2007). Proponents of the race-is-a-social-construction school of thought see race as the most deleterious of humanity's political inventions. According to these authors, race is a junk concept that must be cast into "the dustbin of analytically useless terms" (Miles, 1989, p. 72; see also Lentin, 2000; Hall, 2005). Although widely accepted as a human invention, can we just jettison race, given its resilience, pervasiveness, and chameleonic nature?

Other writers oscillate between the above two positions, asserting that while race has social meanings and reality that society attaches to it, it is also a 'biological' category for differentiation (see Omi and Winant, 1994). As Winant states, "race is not only real, but also illusory. Not only is it common sense; it is also common nonsense. Not only does it establish our identity; it also denies our identity. Not only does it allocate resources, power, and privilege; it also provides a means for challenging that allocation. Race not only naturalizes, but also socializes" (Winant, 1998a, p. 90; see also Bell, 2007a; Bell *et al.*, 2007). The emphasis of this school of thought is not that race is a genetic fact as such but that race has been so deeply etched upon social relations that it is now simply taken for granted. Scholars in the fourth camp eschew notions of essentialism and biological determinism but argue for a conceptualization of race that "integrates the biological and social, recognising that distinctions between the biological and the cultural are invariably socially constructed" (Kobayashi and Peake, 1994, p. 225). These writers claim that many have not adequately interrogated the biologically determinist or culturally reductionist view of race.

For social work educators, students, researchers, and practitioners improved understanding of the 'race question' is crucial to working effectively with racialized communities and providing them with culturally appropriate services (see Hall, 2005; Patni, 2006). Such knowledge is indispensable for the added reason that it will help social workers, who are committed to issues of access, equity, and social justice to avoid pitfalls associated with ethnocentric (Eurocentric and Anglo-American) biases and the oppressions created by the myth of 'colour-blindness' and 'racelessness' in North American society (Boushel, 2000; Williams and Soydan, 2005). As Hall (2005) points out, due to "Eurocentric hegemony race has been erroneously validated as the standard identity construct by social work education" (Hall, 2005. p. 102; see Boushel, 2000).

Social workers need to critically examine their social location and rid themselves of ethnocentric biases, prejudices, and stereotypes if they are to avoid reproducing oppression in their work with racialized clients (Colvin-Burque *et al.*, 2007; Danso, 2009a). As service providers and agents of social change, how social workers view race influences their perception and attitude towards racialized people and the type and quality of services made available to them. Consciously or otherwise, social workers bring their interpretations, conceptualizations, and experiences with race to social work education, research, and practice (Colvin-Burque *et al.*, 2007). Therefore, to prevent discrimination and oppressive service delivery, social work practitioners require a better understanding of race and racialization processes that create disadvantage, power imbalances, and inequities in society.

The Making and Becoming of Race

Notions of race are by no means of recent origin; in ancient and classical times, people did use the term in one sense or another (Solomos and Back, 1996). Perceptions of inter-group differentiation existed in ancient Greece, for instance, however, the Greeks, did not divide people according to phenotypic characteristics, but according to religion, status, class, and language. While notions of race have existed for a long time, many commentators suggest that the term race was first employed as a means of categorizing human bodies in the late seventeeth century (Nicholson, 1995). It was only then and in the following century, with the coming of such publications as *Natural System* (1759) by the Swedish botanist and natural historian, Carolus Linnaeus, that supposedly authoritative racial divisions of human beings were created.

The word race is said to have been used for the first time in the English language in 1508 in a poem by William Dunbar to refer to a line of kings (California Newsreel, 2003). Thus, the idea of race is in practice relatively recent, increasing in written records and becoming standardized and uniform in usage in the early eighteenth century (Smedley and Smedley, 2005; Wallis and Fleras, 2009b). Commonly regarded as the apogee of the Enlightenment, the eighteenth century was also the era when doctrines about race came to be articulated in a consistent manner. The so-called Enlightenment scholars classified humankind using morphological criteria as seen in many writings of the period, works that mirrored the 'exploration' of Africa and the 'discovery' of America (Delisle, 1993; Shah, 2009; Wallis and Fleras, 2009b). The Enlightenment was a major watershed in the philosophical thinking of the world. The intellectual environment of the eighteenth century converged with Enlightenment philosophies that perceived race with a particular lens. In creating a lens for looking distinctively at the world, the concept of race acquired a common-sense explanatory framework for explaining differences in civilization beyond simple reference to physical environmental factors or history (Smedley, 2007; Wallis and Fleras, 2009b).

The belief in the existence of races of humankind involved both the attribution of different origins to human groups, primarily based on geography, and cultural and social significance to racial boundaries. By the end of the eighteenth century, race had become more than just an idea; it now signified a new ideology about human differences and a new way of structuring society that had not existed before in human history (Delisle, 1993; Smedley and Smedley, 2005). The fabrication of a new type of taxonomy, based on deliberately misconstrued interpretation of the Bible, was needed to justify the enslavement of black Africans. From its inception, race was a culturally invented, folk idea about human differences. In North America, the ideology and the common-sense belief in the 'superiority' of whites, arose as a rationalization and justification for slavery, becoming prominent "at a time when Western European societies were embracing philosophies promoting individual and human rights, liberty, democracy, justice, brotherhood, and equality" (Smedley and Smedley, 2005, p. 22). Institutionalized within North American governments, laws, and society, racial practices became an important mechanism for justifying social inequalities as natural.

The development, proliferation, and entrenchment of 'scientific' and pseudo-scientific theories of race in the eighteenth century were to reach their zenith and solidify in the nineteenth century. From the nineteenth century, everything changes and race becomes a priority category and a concept widely accepted in European intellectual circles. Race now becomes the touchstone that explains universal history. All events huge and minute can now be understood by the existence of races and by their hereditary sociological and psychological characteristics. The past is now understandable even as the future is predictable. Henceforth, race becomes for some the basis of a new cosmogony (Delisle, 1993). By the late nineteenth century, western scientists had falsely enshrined the notion of race as a biological fact, arguing that all humans could be pigeonholed into one of a handful of distinct genetic groupings (races), that were hierarchically ordered in intelligence, civilization, beauty, and overall worth (Kim, 2004; Smedley and Smedley, 2005; Fleras, 2010).

Fixing species and thrusting human groups into taxonomic schemes became an insatiable obsession of nineteenth-century European science (Cresswell, 1996; Satzewich and Liodakis, 2007). The 'one drop of blood' idea, for instance, was concocted to support this taxonomic classification. The 'pure', 'chaste' white race must not be contaminated by 'inferior', 'defiled' races. Inter-racial marriages and relationships were therefore expressly tabooed; racialized (black) men caught in such relationships suffered lynching or death. Yet, white slave owners were clandestinely having affairs and making children with black (slave) mistresses. According to the one drop idea, every human being can belong in one and only one (mutually exclusive) racial category. The absurdity of such an idea, which also debunks the naturalness thesis of race, is attested to by the fact that individuals have multiple and interlocking identities and cultures. Therefore, it defies logic and commonsensical thinking to suggest that, for instance, a biracial individual of black and white parentage is always considered *black*, and can never be *white*. Race is such an amorphous, ideologically deceptive construct.

In the twentieth century, emphasis on notions of race shifted away from the extrapolation of racial inferiority and superiority on the basis of physical or phenotypical characteristics to a focus on genetics and the intelligence of members of different racial groups (Dei, 1996; Rowe, 2002; Helms *et al.*, 2005; Smedley and Smedley, 2005). The genetic conception of race that appeared in the mid-twentieth century remained as a definition and working hypothesis for many western scholars, politicians, and policymakers, as well as ordinary citizens. Thus, in the twentieth century, two conceptions of race existed: one that focused on human biogenetic variations exclusively and was the domain of science, and a popular one that dominated all thinking about human differences and fused together both physical features and behaviour (Smedley and Smedley, 2005). This popular conception was and still is the original meaning of race that western scholars in many fields focused their attention on in the latter part of the twentieth century and the early twenty-first century.

Race continues to matter in the twenty-first century, even when we should know better (Winant, 1998a; Smedley and Smedley, 2005; Wallis and Fleras, 2009b; Fleras, 2010). For "social work educators race is a critical part of identity formation" (Hall, 2005: 103). As a result, social work educators, students, researchers, and practitioners have historically promoted a static, unidirectional perspective of identity, and they bring their interpretations and experiences with race to social work education and eventually practice. How best, then, can social workers deliver de-racialized, liberating social services to racialized, oppressed bodies?

Old Wines in New Wineskins

No phenomenon stays the same forever; race and racism are subject to this 'natural' law. In North America, race and racism have undergone dramatic transformation such that they have become covert, subtle, and difficult to detect. The nuanced, muted expression of racial prejudice coincides with the emergence of societal norms in contemporary North America that promote the endorsement of egalitarian values and with personal motivations to avoid being prejudiced (see Hodson *et al.*, 2005; Henry and Tator, 2006). So, how do race and racism manifest themselves in North America today? What new forms of racisms now exist in Canada and America? What status do race and racism occupy in present-day Canada and America? How do contemporary race and racism differ from those of yore? What myths prop up these social enigmas?

North America has come quite some distance regarding the twin issues of race and racism. Improvements have occurred in how Canadians and Americans view race as well as in the way members of the dominant white culture interact with and relate to racialized bodies. Significant strides in achievement have also occurred in recent times for racialized groups in Canada and America. In Canada, multiculturalism policies exist to promote the coexistence of diverse ethno-cultural groups. Human rights principles, legislations, and laws now criminalize overtly racist acts and racially motivated hatred. After centuries of racially motivated discrimination, prejudices, and exclusionary policies and decision-making practices, change came to America on November 4, 2008, when the country elected its first racial minority individual, Barack Obama, an African American, as the 44th president. Just three years prior, on September 27, 2005, Canada had appointed the first black person, Michaëlle Jean, as the country's 27th Governor General. The remarkable thing about Michaëlle Jean's case is that she is also the first black woman appointed to the gubernatorial office.[2]

Developments such as these have led some writers and commentators to believe that North America has entered a post-race (race-neutral) era when race has lost all its significance, potency, and enduring power and as such does not matter anymore (see Foster, 2005; Doane, 2006, 2007; Ford and Delaney, 2008). Understandably, the wish of these commentators is for race to be eliminated from consideration in the mistaken hope of fostering a more egalitarian North America. All racialized groups and many members of the dominant, privileged (white) group wished raced would just vanish because of its punishing impact in shaping human destinies. It is in this regard that some writers (*e.g.* Ignatiev and Garvey, 1996) have provocatively called for the abolishing of the white race, that is, whiteness, by any means necessary.[3] Unfortunately, this hope or wish seems quite mistaken because race is so ingrained in people's thought processes that even perception *is* reality when it comes to race in North America (Fleras, 2010).

---

[2] Canada is a constitutional monarchy, with the Queen of England as the Head of State of Canada. The Governor General is the official representative of the Queen of England in Canada.

[3] Scholars like Ignatiev and Garvey (1996) are not calling for some grand genocidal conspiracy to execute every single white person. Rather, they argue for interrogation of the dominant status and privileges whiteness bestows on white people. According to Ignatiev and Garvey, the white race (*i.e.* whiteness), just like race itself, is nothing more than a product of historical and social processes. Therefore, once the 'reference point' (the 'norm' or 'standard' – whiteness as a social construction), against which everyone and everything else is measured is removed, the playing field would be level for all groups or people. Ignatiev and Garvey suggest that so long as the whiteness exists, all movements against racism are doomed to fail.

Although epoch-making, the extent to which events like the election of Barack Obama as President of America or the appointment of Michaëlle Jean as Governor General of Canada bespeak a post-race era in North American history is open to debate. Notwithstanding, the lived experiences of racialized groups, reflected in the examples discussed in this chapter, demonstrate that race and racism remain important factors in Canada and America (see Leach, 2005; Wallis and Fleras, 2009b; Fleras, 2010).

Race persists largely because it is constitutively embedded in settler societies. As some writers (*e.g.* Goldberg, 2002; Vickers, 2002; Thobani, 2007) note, race was not an error of perception or merely an exercise in rationalization, or even an accident of history. Rather, it was foundational to the nation-building project and statehood in North America, "resulting in a racial caste-like state well into the middle of the twentieth century, with whites occupying what virtually amounted to a racial dictatorship" (Fleras, 2010, p. 29; see also Wallis and Fleras, 2009c). As argued in this chapter, twenty-first century Canada or America is hardly colourless; both Canada and America are so profoundly racial and Eurocentric in their foundational principles, constitutional order, and governance that white interests and agendas are invariably secured, advanced, and normalized at the expense of racialized groups (see Omi and Winant, 1994; Goldberg, 2002; Doane, 2007; Fleras, 2010). This project operated as a system of apartheid to various degrees in different historical and geographical contexts, including America, Australia, Canada, and South Africa. Race has never been divorced from the functioning of the modern-state; neither do social relations have any real significance outside a non-raced context.

The claim that Canada and America have been transported to a post-race utopia raises more questions than it answers. Has race lost all its tenacity in social, political, and everyday interactions and conversations? At what point did North America cross the post-race threshold? What factors precipitated or catalyzed this transition into utopia? What characteristics define a post-race North America and differentiate it from a racist North America? Exactly how post-racial is a post-race North America? Is it humanly possible to attain a completely uncoloured society? On the other hand, if race and racism remain potent forces, how do they function and manifest themselves? What new forms of racism and racial ideologies now plague North American society? This chapter addresses these issues, contending that there is not enough convincing evidence to support the claim of a post-race Shangri-la in North America, certainly not in the contemporary period. Race and racism continue to retain their position and power in inter-group relations in North America, albeit in sophisticated ways than they did in the historical past.

Race and Racism as Moving Targets

Race and racism have a notoriously adaptive capacity than most social phenomena. They are, perhaps, the two most chameleonic social constructions in human history. Both are slippery targets ever shifting and metamorphosing into different forms in different historical and socio-spatial contexts; race and racism are a complex and contradictory dynamic (Banton, 2000). The chameleonic nature of race and racism makes them deceptively dangerous political inventions, and because they do not lend themselves to clear-cut definitions, they are able to escape identification. As Winant (1998b) and Fleas (2010) have noted, race and racism have developed a plethora of meanings such that their definition has become elusive. Race and racism are like a mirage; the closer you get to a precise definition, the more evasive they become. Fleras (2010) suggests that the lack of precision regarding what race and racism mean today seems helpful but it is often a source of confusion and provocation. What is clear though is that the 'crude', 'raw' status race and racism once occupied has been transformed in dramatic ways. Today, race and racism have repackaged themselves in ways that enable them to assume refined, camouflaged statuses in North American society.

Historically, racism existed in a raw, 'in-your-face' form in that it was socially acceptable and openly sanctioned by the dominant white culture in North America. In Canada as in America, state laws and legislations were enacted and policies instituted to define who got what where when. For instance, Jim Crow laws defined the social standing of blacks in America because of their alleged biological and moral inferiority (Bonilla-Silva, 2003). Canadian and American governments actively pursued a policy of 'cultural genocide' to extirpate aboriginal peoples' culture, which the 'civilized' European settlers perceived as 'barbaric'. The residential schools, for instance, were disguised 'cultural death camps' or 'cultural purgatories' whose sole purpose was to smother and strip native peoples of their cultural heritage. Both Canada and America also had blatantly racist immigration policies that, until a few decades ago, sought to create and maintain a 'white only' North American society. In Canada, these 'cultural gas chambers' existed as late as the 1990s.

Other policies and regulations gave official backing to racist practices in North America. In America, as in Canada, laws expressly sanctioned racial segregation in schools, theatres, buses, bars, and other areas of social life (Horton and Horton, 2004). For instance, in housing, a system of overt discrimination, in the form of zoning by-laws and 'race restrictive covenants' was created in the early 1900s, and even well into the twentieth century to deny 'undesirable' groups, typically Asians, blacks, and Jews access to housing in white neighbourhoods.[4] Zoning legislation was used as a barbed-wire social fencing around home values. Deed restrictions were primarily concerned with ensuring ethnic homogeneity. They excluded non-Caucasians from occupancy, except as domestic servants (Davis, 1992). Concentration of black families in residential areas with a predominant white population often resulted in the flight of white people from the area. NIMBY (Not-in-my-backyard) has a long history in North America; its tentacles reach into twenty-first century Canada and America.

Racism in its crude, unalloyed form was based on the notion of race as a biological construct or natural entity that not only differentiated humans into distinct, mutually exclusive racial taxonomies but also defined an individual's or a group's level of cultural advancement or intellectual capacity. Unalloyed racism argued that there was a 'natural' hierarchy of 'superior' and 'inferior' races (see Satzewich and Liodakis, 2007; Shah, 2009; Wallis and Fleras, 2009b). Propped by the indefensible one drop of blood thesis, this hierarchical arrangement precluded any form of racial mixing. As Wallis and Fleras (2009b, p. x) aptly put it, "the world's population was partitioned into bound and fixed categories of people whose distinctive assemblage of physical, mental, and moral attributes could be arranged in ascending/descending orders of superiority/inferiority. The application of this race logic proved disastrous to those negatively racialized." This view of race does not hold sway in

---

[4] Race restrictive covenants are contractual agreements among white real estate owners that prohibited the purchase, lease, or occupation of their premises by a particular group of people, typically blacks (see Danso and Grant, 2000).

present-day Canada or America, not because race fell off the face of the earth but because it has succeeded in transposing itself into a new racial key quite distinguishable from, yet identical to the historical.

Crude racism underpinned Western Europe's insatiable desire for empire across the globe. Crude racism was used to justify the enslavement of blacks, colonialism, mercantilism, and western imperialism (see Brattain, 2007; Cooper, 2009; Fleras, 2010) under the guise of the notorious voyages of discovery. The enslavement of blacks by whites is particularly noteworthy. Although other ethno-cultural groups, for instance, aboriginal peoples were once colonized and oppressed, historically, no racialized group was ever transported by the shipload across oceans and between continents to be enslaved as was done to blacks. That North American society was built off the backs of enslaved blacks is an undeniable historical fact. Many people believe that North American society, especially the United States, would not have been what it is today without institutionalized slave labour. Race and racism proved indispensable to the emergence of modern North America.

Quite interestingly, the United States Senate recently issued an official apology acknowledging the inhumane treatment and atrocities America committed against blacks through the institution of slavery (see Thompson, 2009). By accident or by design, the apology was rendered five months after Barack Obama became the first black president in America. Canada similarly apologized to the Japanese Canadian and Chinese Canadian communities and paid them compensation for putting Japanese Canadians in internment camps during World War II and for imposing a discriminatory 'head tax' on Chinese people via the Chinese Immigration Act of 1885. Not surprisingly, no one is talking about making restitution or reparations to blacks in North America.

Today, America and its allies, including Canada, are using refined forms of racism and racial ideologies, including the rhetoric of protecting the west's strategic interests, to advance the same imperialist project in the Middle East. Spearheaded by America, the west seeks to democratize the Arab world. Western imperialist military strategy invades and occupies the 'other' under the not-so-hidden cloak of a 'civilizing mission' of the Middle East (Dei, 2009). The raging war and carnage in Iraq began with America, under the George W. Bush administration, invading a sovereign nation on the pretext that Iraq under Saddam Hussein had stockpiled weapons of mass destruction (WMD) which, it was alleged, threatened world peace and security. However, history has not been kind to the architects of the Iraq invasion and their over-confidence because history has proven the case for the Iraq war to be completely unfounded; Iraq never had any WMD. History has an uncanny way of exposing the malicious schemes or conveniently optimistic pretensions of politicians and state leaders.

Times have changed, and so has North American society. Blatantly overt forms of individual and officially sanctioned racisms now seem to be the exception rather than the rule. There are hardly any laws today that expressly condone or promote racism. Just as historically laws and regulations gave legal support to racially motivated policies and practices, so too do laws and human rights legislations now criminalize many of the same forms of racism that were legal only a few decades ago. Unlike then, brazen racists and white supremacists are now routinely charged for disseminating hate propaganda (Anderson and Collins, 2007a; Fleras, 2010). Currently, in Canada, racism and discrimination based on race (or any markers of identity for that matter) are illegal and considered socially unacceptable. Blatant racism has resulted in class-action race-discrimination lawsuits against offending institutions (see Dei, 2007, cited in Fleras, 2010, p. 27 and Hussain, 2007, cited in Wallis and

Fleras, 2009b, p. x). On eight consecutive occasions, the United Nations has ranked Canada as the most liveable place on earth.

Despite this recognition or the existence of human rights legislation and individual freedoms, racism still persists in Canada as it does in America. In fact, the very existence of laws criminalizing racially motivated hatred or discrimination means that racism continues to exist in twenty-first century North America. In a supposedly post-race North America, racism has assumed a very subtle or 'polite' posture (Fleras, 2010) but still with devastating impact on racialized communities. Like Americans, Canadians now believe that in an enlightened twenty-first century, only hardcore racial bigots would commit racist acts. Many will beg to differ.

The refined status race occupies today often renders it very difficult to identify or prove. This chameleonic metamorphosis may have deluded or confused many into believing that North Americans have been transported to a post-race era. The reality remains: far from ushering us onto the threshold of a restored Garden of Eden, race and racism have only camouflaged or repackaged themselves; they continue to retain and unleash their oppressive power on racialized minorities. In the contemporary era, racism is expressed in racially neutral and euphemistic language to make them more politically acceptable in public discourses (see Satzewich and Liodakis, 2007). All the new formations and permutations of racisms in a so-called post-race North America are, in fact, old wines in new wineskins, and are articulated primarily through politically correct language (Henry *et al.*, 2009). The language of 'political correctness' enables racist elements to deny that they were being racist in their actions or intent.

Race remains a potent force primarily because contemporary North American society continues to function and individuals continue to employ the word (race) or behave in ways that suggest races do exist and will always matter. Social relations and everyday conversations remain racialized and they continue to invent the 'other' by inscribing difference. The mere mention of race commissions our understanding of a permanent difference and therefore a conception of 'otherness' (Cashmore, 1996). 'Othering/Otherizing' processes and racialized discourses construct difference as an aberration and therefore denounce it as a problem. Difference is then used as a tool by mainstream North Americans to oppress racialized bodies (Danso, 2009a). Difference – skin colour, ethnicity, gender, or physical disability – is not a deficiency because there is nothing innate to difference that makes it a social problem. Making difference a problem is *the* problem (Smith and Tudor, 2003). The othering process, by which racism labels the 'other' as 'social deviants', also provides the fodder for sustaining structural inequalities and oppression in society (Howarth, 2006). The daily life experiences of racialized minorities in North America are thus very much a function of their 'othered/otherized' status in this society.

If, as alleged, race and racism have decamped from North American society, it is largely due to the fact that both Canadians and Americans choose to mask their many forms of racism behind a mythology of racelessness and under a blanket of whiteness (Razack, 2002; Das Gupta *et al.*, 2007; Fleras, 2010). Mainstream North American society revels in a self-serving national mythology of a raceless Canada and a colour-blind America. Racism is endemic to North America, yet (almost) no one claims to be a racist (Bonilla-Silva, 2003). In Canada, the ideology and institutionalization of multiculturalism and human rights legislation have led to a complacent belief that racism is foreign to Canada.

Contrary to this gratifying myth, racism remains a powerfully divisive force in Canada, especially in its refined forms. Racialized individuals and groups continue to encounter significant barriers to access to employment, housing, and social services as well as political power. For instance, while multiculturalism and immigration and settlement policies encourage diversity and the exploitation of the human capital and economic worth of immigrants, these same policies neglect to encourage the participation and engagement of people of colour with the political process. Diversity and immigration policies continue to be eerily silent on access to political power for ethno-racialized groups. No wonder many racialized bodies are conspicuously absent from the corridors of power and policy decision making in Canada and America, perhaps more so in the former than the latter.

Compared to America, very few racialized individuals have been elected to public office in Canada. For instance, in the southern United States, a growing number of police chiefs, governors, and other elected officials are black (Foster, 2005). A significant number of mayors in urban America are also blacks. The situation is quite different in multicultural and 'equal-opportunity' Canada, which also claims to be less colour-conscious than America. The Canadian claim of innocence often finds expression in the constant juxtaposing of Canada with America when it comes to racial issues in Canadian contexts. Canadians just refuse to see and acknowledge the pervasiveness of racism (Dei, 2009). Canada prides itself on being the first country in the world to officially endorse and codify multiculturalism into public policy (Fleras, 2005, 2010) – with the passage of the Multiculturalism Act in 1988. Yet, Canada cannot boast of any significant number of *elected* people of colour in government or public service compared to America. Other than Michaëlle Jean, *appointed* the twenty-seventh Governor General – perhaps as a gesture of convenience more than a matter of principle or equality – no other black person or 'visible minority' has ever been *elected* Prime Minister in 'egalitarian' and 'colour-blind' Canada. As noted above, an elected racial minority individual currently holds the presidency in America. Even so, this history-making event occurred centuries after America became a sovereign state. This analysis underscores the fact that, contrary to prevailing beliefs, North American society is far from being a post-race society.

That North America is still a colour-conscious society is supported by many facts. Not only does race continue to be a key organizing principle in constructing Canadian and American society, it also remains deeply wired in people's psyche and behaviours and systematically reflected in social structures and institutions. Its tenacity means that race also remains a core component of minority identities and patterns of resistance (Young and Braziel, 2006; Agnew, 2007; Hier and Bolaria, 2007; Wallis and Fleras, 2009c). Omi and Winant (1993, cited in Dei, 2009, p. 231) underscore the role of race in defining identities. According to Omi and Winant, North American society is so thoroughly racialized that to be without a racial identity is to be in danger of having no identity at all. To be raceless is akin to being devoid of gender.

Goldberg and Solomos (2002) concede as much when they state that race is a social and political category around which individuals and groups construct identities or organize their resistance within the very context that denies or excludes them because of their identity. Racialized communities draw on race as identity construction, to challenge Eurocentric constructs, as grounds for recognition and equality as per equity and affirmative action programs, and as a basis for counter-racism politics (Goldberg and Solomos, 2002; Dei, 2009; Wallis and Fleras, 2009c). We are not experiencing a racism-free, colour-decoded utopia because race and racial ideologies continue to structure North American society in ways that value some lives more than others, and they continue to remain the foundations for systems of power and exclusion in Canada and America (Andersen and Collins, 2007a). As Wallis and Fleras (2009c) suggest, the common assumption of North America as a raceless society is simply a hegemonic lie peddled to perpetuate the domination and exploitation of people, as well as to reinforce a system of internal colonization based on race, class, gender, geography, or ancestry.

Case Illustrations

A host of examples can be cited to contest the claim of a post-race North America. Three recent events, all occurring in America suffice for purposes of this chapter: first, the financial package created by the Barack Obama administration to stimulate the American economy because of the current recession; second, the arrest of Henry Louis Gates Jr., a black professor at Harvard University, by the Cambridge, Massachusetts police; and third, events associated with Hurricane Katrina. Other examples, drawn from Canada combine with the American cases to demonstrate the salience and pervasiveness of race and racism in North American society. They also reinforce the fact that social relations and public discourses are still deeply constructed along racial lines.

In the heat of the debates surrounding the stimulus package, a subtly racist cartoon appeared in the *New York Post*. The cartoon, which implicitly compared the author of the stimulus bill, most likely President Obama, with a chimpanzee, depicted two white policemen shooting dead a big black chimpanzee (see Chan and Peters, 2009). The thought bubble in the cartoon read, "They'll have to find someone else to write the next stimulus bill." Different opinions have surfaced about the carton and the message it sought to convey. Some people have suggested that the cartoon was just a parody and that it referred to the United States Congress and not President Obama. However, the subtext of the cartoon is very troubling, and raises many questions.

If the cartoon referred to Congress, why did the cartoonist choose to use only one chimpanzee and not many? Why were the other 'apes', that is, white congressmen and congresswomen, also not shot dead? Why did the thought bubble say, "*They* will need *someone* else to write the next stimulus bill" (italics supplied) and not 'other people' but rather 'someone'? By the way, who are the 'they' in the thought bubble? Why was a chimpanzee used, instead of, say, a buffalo or an elephant? There are many types of apes with different hair colours; for instance, orangutans have reddish-brown furs. So, why did the cartoonist choose to use a black ape instead of a reddish-brown orangutan? Was the use of an ape innocently accidental, especially when considered against the backdrop of whites associating blacks with apes, savagery, or bestiality? In any case, are police officers not supposed to be agents of law enforcement, so what, if anything, do they have to do with economic policy decision making? In American politics, is it the President, Congress or the police that can 'kill' (veto) a bill?

The imagery depicted by the cartoon is a clear indication that racism is well and alive in American society, and that it functions in a subtly camouflaged way. Apparently, as a member of the dominant white culture, Mr. Sean Delonas, the cartoonist enjoys the privileges whiteness bequeaths to white people. Many people contend that Mr. Delonas is prejudiced against racialized groups and that he has tendencies to publish provocatively racist and inflammatory cartoons (see Chan and Peters, 2009). The cartoon also highlights the role of the media as agencies of socialization and as instruments for spreading and perpetuating stereotypes about racialized peoples (see Danso and McDonald, 2001; McDonald and Jacobs, 2005; Henry and Tator, 2006; Fleras, 2010). The media problematize visibility (people of colour) while normalizing invisibility (whiteness).

On July 16, 2009, a Cambridge, Massachusetts police officer, Sgt. James Crowley, arrested a black Harvard University professor, Henry Louis Gates Jr., in his own home allegedly for burglary. According to media reports, an anonymous eyewitness called the Cambridge police to report a probable break-in by two males (people of colour). The police responded to the call and found Henry Gates in his home. According to Gates' attorney, Gates had just returned from a trip to China and could not open the front door to his house because it was jammed shut. Gates, with the assistance of his driver, was trying to force the door open when the eyewitness, who later appeared on national television as a white woman, made the '911 call' to the police. Gates was later arrested and charged with disorderly conduct in his own home (see CNN, 2009). Following a public uproar, the prosecutor admitted it was a regrettable and unfortunate situation and dropped all charges against Gates five days after his arrest.

Many people were not at all surprised that a black individual would encounter racial profiling. Racial profiling is a common occurrence in the lives of black people, especially males, in American society. However, the Henry Gates episode, or *gateism*, is quite troubling in that Gates was arrested in his own home.[5] Not even confirmation by Harvard University police would convince the arresting officer that Henry Gates was, indeed, the individual he claimed to be. People from different backgrounds, including civil rights activists, believe that Henry Gates was *gatized* because he was black. This perception was largely crystallized for many by the comments one white police officer made in an email message he sent to a *Boston Globe* reporter.

The officer, Justin Barrett of the Boston Police Department, was so incensed by Professor Gates' conduct that he did not hesitate to call him a "banana-eating jungle monkey", and that had he been the arresting officer he would have pepper-sprayed the professor (Hanson, 2009). The 'banana-eating monkey' label sounds familiar; as discussed above with reference to the cartoon on the stimulus package, whites historically associated blacks with apes and animalism. Nothing could be more racially motivated and incendiary than such a reaction or comment, especially coming from someone who is supposed to work with and protect communities. Yet, Officer Barrett was very audacious to claim on national television that he is not a racist. The writing was on the wall; Barrett only wanted to save his job. Henry Gates is a 'banana-eating jungle monkey' but Justin Barrett is not a racist. Who is a racist then, and what constitutes racism or racially motivated stereotypes and prejudices in American society? At the time of writing this chapter, Officer Barrett had filed a lawsuit against the City of Boston and the Boston Police Department after he was put on administrative leave for his

---

[5] The term 'gateism', is coined in this chapter to describe the system or processes by which the dominant society and its state apparatus, including policing and law enforcement, abuse the rights and freedoms of members of racialized groups and criminalize their actions when there is no justification for such criminalization. Like other forms of contemporary racisms, gateism both disempowers and dehumanizes its victims – racialized bodies.

racial slurs. Barrett claimed in the lawsuit that the Mayor of Boston and the Boston Chief Police violated his civil and due process rights, which also inflicted emotional distress on him.

Hurricane Katrina, which struck the city of New Orleans in the summer of 2005 and is regarded as the most destructive and costly of storms in American history (Forgette *et al.*, 2008), presents yet another clear evidence of how race mediates people's thoughts, perceptions, and behaviours, as well as the actions or inactions of public authorities. Hurricane Katrina literally razed the city of New Orleans to the ground. A huge debate, framed along racial lines, surrounds the American government's response to Hurricane Katrina. Critics of the government's response to the disaster argue that the differential impact of Katrina was not a 'natural' disaster but the almost inevitable result of race-based policies that have worked against African Americans over centuries (De Parle, 2007; Stivers, 2007). In the midst of the disaster, the Mayor of New Orleans, Clarence Ray Nagin, an African American, could not contain his frustration and denounced slow moving federal officials responsible for delivering relief aid and services; he called for martial law (De Parle, 2007).

Polls taken in the aftermath of the hurricane suggest that the majority of African Americans believed race was a major factor in the slow government relief response (Stivers, 2007; Forgette *et al.*, 2008; Kaiser *et al.*, 2008). For instance, a survey conducted by The Pew Research Centre (2005, cited in Forgette *et al.*, 2008) found that 66 percent of blacks, compared to 17 percent of whites, felt that the government's response to the crisis would have been faster had the majority of the victims been white. Some commentators opined that the lack of planning and effective response in the post-hurricane period was largely due to the federal government's lack of interest in the suffering of black people in America. Given how the George Bush administration responded to Hurricane Katrina, one black hip-hop artist, Kanye West, voiced an opinion shared by many that George Bush did not care about black people (King, 2008).

Other commentators have also argued that blacks were hit harder by Hurricane Katrina than whites because, although New Orleans generally lies below sea level, the majority of blacks in New Orleans live in areas that are more prone to flooding; many whites live in much safer areas – on higher ground (De Parle, 2007). Apparently, geography conspired with race to deny the majority of African Americans access to evacuation and relief services. One of the areas the hurricane hit hardest was the Lower Ninth Ward, where the majority of the residents are African Americans (Curtis *et al.*, 2007). Media coverage accentuated the perception that race played a major role in aid and evacuation services during and after the hurricane. Media images frequently depicted blacks as looters, rapists, and victims while whites were mostly portrayed as gallant, civilized survivors (see Owens, 2008; Johnson *et al.*, 2009; Shah, 2009).

That race mediates the debates on how Hurricane Katrina affected the residents of New Orleans is borne out by one other fact. While the residents of New Orleans at the time the disaster struck came from different ethno-racial and cultural backgrounds, attention was disproportionately focused on the plight and conditions of white and black residents to the neglect of other ethnic groups. No one seemed to mind what happened to members of other ethnic groups or how the hurricane affected them (see King, 2008). Discourses on ethnic relations, have traditionally been based on a black/white dualist paradigm (Modood, 2007). Therefore, the majority of studies on racial prejudice and discrimination conducted in America have focused on anti-black prejudice (Meer and Noorani, 2008; Strabac and

Listhaug, 2008). This myopic, unbalanced focus has significant implications for the welfare of other racialized groups. It contributed to a neglect of the plight of groups like Native Americans during and after Hurricane Katrina. It also has implications for state policies and how other forms of prejudice or discrimination are addressed. For instance, while anti-Semitism tends to be seen by state authorities as paradigmatic of racism, anti-Muslim sentiment is often viewed as less evidently racial in orientation (Miles and Brown, 2003; Goldberg, 2006; Meer and Noorani, 2008).

The black/white dualist discourses that characterize ethnic relations studies have produced a system of *multidualism* (also *pludualism*). The concept of multidualism is introduced in this chapter to describe the system or institutional practice by which a deliberate, predetermined decision is made by the dominant cultural group to pick and privilege two preferred, supposedly superior, options from an array of equally important options as a matter of state policy and practice. Multidualism results in the hegemonic normalization and privileging of the selected options at the expense of the other options, which the dominant group considers inferior or unworthy. Throughout the history of humanity, multidualism always sought to promote and normalize only white cultural values and interests.

Canada's official policy of bilingualism within a multicultural framework provides one of the clearest illustrations of the concept of multidualism. Canada is a culturally diverse and cosmopolitan country, with over 200 ethno-linguistic groups. To manage this diversity, Canada became the first country in the world to proclaim a policy of multiculturalism in 1971, which was codified into law in 1988 as the Multiculturalism Act. Although Canada acknowledge the value of cultural diversity, the two 'founding' nations of Canada chose only two languages –English and French – as the official languages for the country. Enshrining bilingualism within a multicultural framework means that, while ethno-racialized groups, including First Nations peoples, are valued for their cultures and considered 'equal' to the dominant white culture in that respect, linguistically, they are perceived as inferior. Multidualism produces many contradictions, as demonstrated by the policy of bilingualism in Canada. In fact, Canada is full of contradictions. Canada has been described as an 'adventure' that resembles an "enigma wrapped around a mystery inside a riddle" (Fleras, 2010, p. 1).

Although specific to America, the three cases discussed above are by no means unique to the country. However, they epitomize the extent to which social relations and public attitudes are influenced by racial ideologies and how race and racism continue to impact the lived experiences of racialized people in North American society. With the possible exception of the Hurricane Katrina example (geographical location makes Canada much less prone to hurricane attacks than America), all the examples are reproduced in one form or another almost on a daily basis in Canada.

In Canada over the past few decades, various police forces, school boards (with their 'zero tolerance' policies – see Satzewich and Liodakis, 2007, pp. 166-168), employers, media groups, cultural productions, government policies, social service agencies, and private individuals, have also been labelled racist (Henry and Tator, 2006; Stazewich and Liodakis, 2007). For instance, a recent *Toronto Star* news article (Walkom, 2009) reported how the Canadian government arrested and jailed a Moroccan-born immigrant, Adil Charkaoui, living in Montreal for six years on suspicion of being an Al Qaeda sleeper agent. After six years, the Canadian government admitted it had no evidence whatsoever of that allegation or, indeed, anything else against Charkaoui that it was willing and ready to contest in court. Yet, the government still wanted to deport the 36-year landed immigrant – who, at the time of his release, was awaiting approval of his application for Canadian citizenship – to his native Morocco. As a face-saving tactic, the Canadian government claimed Charkaoui still 'meets the profile' of a sleeper agent – that is to say, he could be a potential terrorist or threat to Canadian national security.

In a similar incident, the Canadian government was implicated in the arrest and imprisonment of a Canadian citizen, Suaad Hagi Mohamud, by Kenyan authorities. Kenyan immigration officials arrested Mohamud, a Somali-born Canadian, as she was returning from a visit to her mother in Kenya in the summer of 2009. According to media accounts (*e.g.* Aulakh, 2009; Hume, 2009; Woods and Taylor, 2009), Kenya authorities and KLM airline officials claimed Mohamud's lips and eyeglasses did not match her four-year-old photo in her Canadian passport, and jailed her for twelve weeks. Apparently, the Canadian government and immigration officials did nothing to help Mohamud. Complicit, the Canadian government tried to stay away from Mohamud's case (Aulakh, 2009; Hume, 2009; Woods, 2009; Woods and Taylor, 2009) even as she languished in jail, fighting frantically to prove her identity by providing everything from a healthcare card, Shoppers Drug Mart Optimum card, Canadian Tire money to receipts from local dry cleaners, and, finally, DNA evidence. The Canadian government colluded with Kenyan officials to imprison Suaad Mohamud. Liliane Khadour, vice-consul and first secretary at the Canadian High Commission in Nairobi, Kenya, wrote to Kenyan authorities that Mohamud was an impostor (Hume, 2009; Woods and Taylor, 2009), a letter that further emboldened Kenya to send Mohamud to jail.

Although the Canadian government eventually helped to bring Mohamud back home (see Goddard, 2009) – but only after DNA evidence had established her identity beyond a shade of a doubt – race does seem to have played a major role in the ordeal Suaad Mohamud underwent, and Canadian officials have been accused of racism. As Hume states, "in Canada today, God help you if you're not white, because the federal government sure won't" (Hume, 2009, p. A6). As one might expect, Suaad Mohamud launched a $2.5 million lawsuit against the Canadian government (LeBlanc, 2009; Woods, 2009) so she could find out the cause of the bureaucratic neglect that left her agonizing in a Kenyan jail for three months.

A political storm nearly broke out between South Africa and Canada in late 2009. According to media accounts, the Immigration and Refugee Board (IRB), a politically appointed but allegedly arms-length body responsible for handling in-Canada refugee claims granted a white South African national refugee status in Canada. The applicant, Brandon Huntley, 31, alleged he was victimized in attacks by black South Africans because of his race. According to Casey (2009), IRB tribunal panel chair William Davis alleged Brandon Huntley provided clear and convincing proof of the indifference and inability or unwillingness of the South African government to protect white South Africans from persecution by black South Africans.

The ruling infuriated the governing African National Congress, which accused Canada of racism for granting a white individual refugee status (Corcoran, 2009). Some commentators saw the ruling as racist because there are many black African refugee claimants who have been in legal limbo for years regarding their application for refugee status in Canada (see Danso, 2009b). Others also pointed to the fact many refugee applications by members of racialized groups are routinely rejected. A *Globe and Mail* editorial comment cites the South African Police Chief, Bheki Cele, as saying that "criminals in South Africa look at what you have, rather than looking at your face."[6] According to the editorial, no credible human rights organization had found widespread racial discrimination against whites in South Africa, who after generations of apartheid rule still enjoy wealth out of proportion to their numbers. The editorial made a very important observation that there was a pool of readily identifiable people in South Africa who had been subjected to persecution – economic migrants from Mozambique, Somalia, and Zimbabwe targeted in 2008 in a wave of xenophobic violence that killed at least 62 people. Were their claims of persecution not equally justified, the editorial questioned?

As in America, the police, law enforcement, and security officials in Canadian cities disproportionately subject black and brown bodies to racial profiling (see Satzewich and Liodakis, 2007; Miller *et al.*, 2008; Tanovich, 2009; Fleras, 2010).[7] An institutional form of racism, racial profiling in turn spawns a number of racialized processes. For instance, while crime is often *africanized*, youth gangs are *asianized* and substance use *aboriginized*, and as discussed in detail below, terrorism is *muslimized* or *arabianized*. In that the police in Canada stop who they see instead of what they see, they invariably fuse crime, gang activity, substance use, or terrorism with race. Yet, police authorities vehemently deny racial profiling exists in policing and law enforcement (Fleras, 2010). As the police claim, criminal behaviour, not skin colour, is profiled. Therefore, the overrepresentation of certain minority groups in crime statistics or the prison system only reflects the fact that individuals from those groups engage in actions that are more likely to bring them into conflict with the law.

In North America, racial profiling raises the twin paradoxes of *under-policing* and *over-policing* of racialized communities. Under-policing occurs when the police do not take crimes seriously or do not conduct thorough investigations when minorities are the victims of crime (Satzewich and Liodakis, 2007). For instance, the Toronto police department has been accused of institutional racism because they allegedly trivialized the killings of black youth during the summer of 2005. A wave of youth gun violence swept through the City of Toronto in the summer of 2005, leading the media to label it the 'summer of the gun'. The overwhelming majority of the victims were black youth. It was alleged that had the victims being white, the police would have been more proactive in investigating the shootings and deaths. However, because the majority of the victims were members of racialized communities, they were regarded as disposable people not deserving of full police protection.

Over-policing refers to a situation where the police suspect members of racialized communities as the perpetrators of crime. In cases of over-policing, police resources and energies are targeted against groups based on the stereotype that they are over-involved in criminal activity (Satzewich and Liodakis, 2007). Since the police are alleged to find crime where they want or look for crime, they are more than likely to over-police targeted minority

---

[6] Editorial (2009). A broken system. *Globe and Mail*. Friday, September 4.

[7] Racial profiling is described as heightened scrutiny based solely or in part on race, ethnicity, aboriginality, place of origin, ancestry, or religion or on stereotypes associated with any of these factors rather than on objectively reasonable grounds to suspect that an individual is implicated in criminal activity (Tanovich, 2009, p. 157; see Fleras, 2010, pp. 61-65). The police also use other factors such as age, location, or time of day to racially-profile racialized people (Miller *et al.*, 2008). The Association of Black Law Enforcers defines racial profiling as an "investigative or enforcement activity initiated by an individual officer [or officers] based on his or her [their] stereotypical, prejudicial or racist perceptions of who is likely to be involved in wrong doing or criminal activity. This conduct is systematically facilitated when there is [*sic*] ineffective policy, training, monitoring and control mechanisms in the system" (Association of Black Law Enforcers, 2003, p. 2). Systematic or patterned denial of the existence of racial profiling in policing by police authorities contributes to the perpetuation of racial profiling in policing.

communities. This could involve over-patrolling particular neighbourhoods or communities. Therefore, a group's preponderance in the justice system, Satzewich and Liodakis (2007) suggest, may be as much a function of over-policing as it is a reflection of real group differences in criminal behaviour. The line between the two will always remain blurry.

Articulations of Contemporary Racisms

Using various examples, preceding sections discussed the notion that race and racism continue as intractable factors in North American society, although they have transformed themselves in striking ways to acquire refined statuses. Repackaging themselves has, however, not diminished the crippling impact of race and racism on racialized communities. This section discusses specific examples of contemporary racisms and the way they are articulated in Canada and America. The myths and discourses propping these racisms are also examined. Attention is focused specifically on 'cultural racism', 'nativism', 'aversive racism', 'perfunctory racism', 'symbolic racism', and 'democratic racism'. All these forms of contemporary racism are closely related to each other. As noted in a subsequent paragraph, the last form of racism – democratic racism – serves as the main vehicle for the articulation of the other racisms in North America.

In recent decades, *cultural racism* has replaced the traditional focus on skin colour racism (Dunn *et al.*, 2007). While not subscribing to the discredited notions of racial hierarchies or biological superiority/inferiority, that is, the universal discourse of dominance over racial inferiors (Fleras, 2010), cultural racism argues that foreign cultural practices pose a danger to national unity, identity, and citizenship (Fleras, 2004). Mainstream Canadian or American society is no longer defined as racially superior but as culturally normal and preferred, while subdominant groups are dismissed as a culturally dangerous threat to a secular and liberal society rather than innately inferior (Fleras, 2010). This form of repackaged racism claims that ethno-cultural diversity is the source of social problems, that is, social problems arise because of the coexistence of different cultural groups.

It is instructive to note that this view is very reflective of previous notions that 'race relations' problems, including race riots, were caused by biologically dissimilar racial groups coming into contact. Cultural problems are particularly accentuated if there is a wide 'cultural gap' between cultures. Cultures with close affinities or that are more similar to each other are less likely to have intercultural clashes than those that are significantly different. A good example of cultural racism is *Islamophobia*, which refers to fear or hatred towards Islam or people who practice the Islamic religion (see below). Islamophobia does not rely on perceptions of racial inferiority but rather racializes Islam as a threat to security and demonizes Islamic-based cultures and institutions as hindrances to integration (Dunn *et al.*, 2007; Gottschalk and Greenberg, 2008). To the extent that cultural differences are vilified as decadent, dangerous, irrelevant, or inferior, the racialization of ethno-cultural groups through claims of cultural superiority has proven as exclusionary as racial ideologies (Fleras, 2010).

Another new racism – *nativism,* which is similar to cultural racism – is also replacing older, biologically informed expressions of racism. Rodriguez (1999) defines 'nativism' as fear of 'foreignness', which has emerged in America largely as a reaction to immigration from Asia and Latin America. According to Rodriguez (1999), three main xenophobic sentiments are expressed towards non-white Americans. One sentiment relates to the allegation that American social and cultural values and the nation at large are in danger of being undermined, if not eroded altogether by the presence of many different non-English languages in American society. Another sentiment is the fear that racialized immigrants exploit multicultural ideology and affirmative action entitlements to maintain their distinct ethno-racial identities. The third sentiment is framed by a concern that immigrant minorities suck the social welfare system dry.

Aversive racism is a new form of democratic racism that has emerged in America (Henry *et al.*, 2009). Aversive racism is often displayed by well-meaning Americans who profess fairness and equality in terms of racism and public policy (Gaertner and Dovidio, 1986; Dovidio and Gaertner, 2004). Although well-intentioned people may genuinely profess egalitarianism and wish to improve conditions created by racial discrimination, they are largely characterized by a specific type of ambivalence: aversiveness (Dovidio and Gaertner, 2004). Unlike hard-core racial bigots and white supremacists who act on their attitudes and stereotypes, aversive racists would normally not put their beliefs and attitudes into action (Henry *et al.*, 2009). Aversive racists also believe in white supremacy but refuse to do anything about it. Although prejudiced and holding stereotypes against ethnic minorities, aversive racists tend not to act in discriminatory ways.

A characteristic feature of aversive racists is that despite their claims to being prejudice-free, they would avoid contact with the racialized group to which they are averse. Tokenism is a notable characteristic of aversive racists because, although, they may be inclined to advance egalitarian values or the concerns of minorities, or seek social justice, such efforts may, in reality be to reaffirm the averse racists' own lack of prejudice (see Henry *et al.*, 2009). Tokenism, according to Gaertner and Diovidio (1986), thus produces a condition where trivial gestures by aversive racists preclude the necessity for extensive, costly action.

In sum, aversive racism represents a particular type of ambivalence in which conflict is between feelings and beliefs associated with a sincerely egalitarian value system and unacknowledged negative feelings and beliefs about other racialized peoples (Dovidio and Gaertner, 2004; Henry and Tator, 2006). Aversive racism arises from processes that create opportunities for people to internalize values, norms, beliefs, and attitudes. In America, for instance, the denigration of black culture, black stereotypes, and the constant association of black people with poverty, crime, and deviance reinforces negative racial attitudes. A more current example of aversive racism in America is the strong opposition by many Americans to the healthcare reforms proposed by the current administration under President Barack Obama, which would make healthcare more accessible to millions of Americans, especially vulnerable and racialized populations.

Closely aligned with aversive racism is *perfunctory* or *polite racism*. People engaged in perfunctory racism consider themselves liberals and egalitarians. They often put up a façade of tolerant behaviour and act according to the demands and contingencies of a particular situation; they behave out of convenience rather than conviction (Fleras, 2010). Were the conditions that promoted the perfunctory behaviour or act removed, the perfunctory racist is more likely to engage in racist behaviour. Because of their previous behaviour, racially motivated perfunctory racists are less likely to be seen as racist. For the most part with a veneer of tolerance, perfunctory racism may express itself in a polite way, hence the name polite racism. Polite racism is couched in ways that allow members of in-groups to conceal their dislike of members of out-groups by way of coded language (Berry and Bonilla-Silva,

2007; Kobayashi and Johnson, 2007; Li, 2007; Moore, 2007). Polite racists assign significance to race in large part relying on euphemisms to express racial views without appearing racist.

As the name implies, polite racism tends to be unobtrusive rather than blatant, obliquely couched in the language of politeness and political correctness, and coded behind a deceptive front of colour-blindness to confuse or deflect. These make detection of polite racism very difficult (Coates, 2008). Very common in Canada, polite racism is particularly insidious because of the misleading smile it wears on its face, which leaves racialized peoples wondering whether it is a genuine, welcoming smile or a muted, contrived snarl. Polite racism involves a forced attempt to disguise a dislike of others through behaviour that outwardly is non-judgemental in appearance (Fleras, 2010). These politely aversive feelings are not demonstrated through outright hostility or hate, but through patterns of avoidance or rejection. Polite racism may consist of the look that 'otherizes' racialized populations as different, inferior, and out-of-place in North American society. This politeness is particularly manifest when racialized individuals are ignored or turned down for jobs, promotions, or accommodation. For instance, rather than expressly saying 'no blacks need apply', a polite racist may tell a prospective tenant that the unit is already rented out when, in fact, it is still available (see Danso, 2009b). Polite racism may appear to be a more refined form than its hate equivalent, yet, the effects on its victims is no less debilitating (Fleras, 2010).

Symbolic racism provides yet another vehicle for the expression of democratic racism. Symbolic racism is an attitude in which white North Americans make moral assertions about racialized groups' behaviour, concerning what they deserve, how they should act, whether or not they are treated fairly, and so on (Henry *et al.*, 2009). This type of racism is displayed in actions that are rationalized on a non-racial basis but in reality perpetuate the status quo because it continues the marginalization and exclusion of racialized bodies. Voting white rather than racialized candidates, opposing affirmative-action programs, and opposing healthcare reforms, as well as opposing desegregation in housing and education are examples of symbolic racist acts in America. Opposing employment equity as well as making inexorable demands for 'Canadian experience' from recent immigrants, when the only way they can acquire such experience is by being hired by a Canadian employer or working (in Canada) also constitutes symbolic racism in Canada. Symbolic racism is also manifested when the opinion or contributions of white students are applauded and validated while those of racialized students are trivialized or ignored.

Symbolic racism permits an individual to respect and uphold equal rights and opportunities for people of colour, yet, argue that minority groups are 'too pushy' because they make too many demands for equality and fairness too much, too quickly. Reflective of its name, symbolic racism operates through symbols rather than overt discrimination or 'redneck bigotry' (Henry *et al.*, 2009). Thus, there is strong or muted opposition to welfare, minority politicians, or fair housing laws because they symbolize the violation of cherished values and the making of unreasonable demands by racialized groups in North America.

In general, the new forms of racism occur at three main levels: individual, systemic, and cultural levels (see Fleras, 2005, 2010; Henry and Tator, 2006; Hamilton, 2007). Henry and Tator (2006) define *individual-level racism* as a form of racial discrimination that stems from conscious, personal prejudice. *Systemic-level racism* consists of social policies and practices entrenched in established institutions, which result in the exclusion or advancement of specific groups of people. It manifests itself in two ways: (1) institutional racism, which is racial discrimination that derives from individuals carrying out the dictates of others who are prejudiced or of a prejudiced society, and (2) structural racism which refers to inequities rooted in the system-wide operation of a society that exclude substantial numbers of members of particular groups from participation in major social institutions. *Cultural-level racism*, according to Henry and Tator (2006), is deeply embedded in the value system of North American society. It represents the tacit network of beliefs and values that encourages and justifies discriminatory actions, behaviours, and practices.

All these sophisticated forms of racism manifest themselves differently in different historical and spatial contexts. However, they all find expression primarily through the medium of democratic racism. According to Henry and colleagues, the main characteristic of democratic racism "is the justification of the inherent conflict between the egalitarian values of justice and fairness and the racist ideologies reflected in the collective mass-belief system as well as the racist attitudes, perceptions, and assumptions of individuals" (Henry *et al.*, 2009, p. 108). Democratic racism still permeates Canadian and American society and institutions, and it serves as an appropriate model for understanding how and why racism persists in North America. Democratic racism is related to all the racisms discussed above; it differs from them only in terms of the value conflict it posits.

Henry *et al.* (2009) define democratic racism as "an ideology in which two conflicting sets of values are made congruent to each other. Commitments to democratic principles such as justice, equality, and fairness conflict but coexist with attitudes and behaviours that include negative feelings about minority groups, differential treatment, and discrimination against them" (Henry *et al.*, 2009, p. 114). One outcome of the conflict is a lack of support for policies and practices that might improve the low status of racialized groups. Consider, for instance, the uproar and public outrage that many people have expressed against the proposed healthcare reform in America, with many people, including faith leaders publicly voicing disdain and hatred for Barack Obama. One church pastor preached his hatred for Obama, saying he wants Obama dead.

Myths and Discourses of Democratic Racism

Democratic racism articulates itself through the discourse of domination, which embodies collective myths, explanations, codes of meaning, and rationalizations that have the effect of establishing, sustaining, and enforcing democratic racism (Henry *et al.*, 2009). The existence of a plethora of myths and misconceptions about racism enables the dominant white culture in Canada and America to develop a pattern of denial that has led to a wholly inadequate response to racism. The rest of this section summarizes some of the prevailing myths that underpin democratic racism (see Henry and Tator, 2006, pp. 24-29).

The *discourse of denial* maintains that racism cannot possibly exist in a democratic society because it upholds liberal principles. Acts of racism are dismissed as isolated incidents relating to a few prejudiced individuals, economic instability, or the consequence of 'undemocratic' traditions that are disappearing from North American society (Henry and Tator, 2006; Doane, 2007; Wallis and Fleras, 2009c). Refusing to acknowledge the reality of racial profiling in policing as police authorities in Toronto are wont to do (see Tanovich, 2009; Fleras, 2010) is an example of such a discourse. This discourse chooses to ignore the devastating impact of discrimination, prejudice, and racial ideology on the lives of racialized persons. It resists the notion that the structures and institutions making up North American society and the cultural values embedded in these institutions are inherently racist. No amount of denial of the existence of racism can dislodge an entrenched whiteness in North America (Wallis and Fleras, 2009c).

Another discourse propping democratic racism is the *myth of colour-blindness*. Through this myth, white people insist they do not notice the skin colour of racialized bodies. That is fascinating! How possible is it to observe anyone without being conscious of his/her skin colour? Is skin colour not the most conspicuous component of any person's identity, and is skin pigmentation not the first marker of identity any person would most likely evoke to identify or describe an individual? Gotanda (1991, cited in Henry and Tator, 2006, p. 25) describes this strategy of observing but not noticing as a 'technical fiction'. Recent developments in Canada and America, including, for instance, the perception that Barack Obama is not an American-born citizen and therefore cannot be a president of America, belie the notion of a colour-blind Canada or America. How can white people consciously label racialized bodies 'people of colour' but at the same time be 'blind' to the same (skin) colour they use to identify *visible minorities*? Why do government statisticians, demographers, and census officials, as well social researchers, and school boards continue to collect race-based statistics for policy decision-making, program planning, and service delivery purposes (see Wallis and Fleras, 2009c, p. 260)? At what point in the history of North America did social relations, access to social power, resources, and opportunities cease to be defined along colour lines such that North America is now a monochromatic or colourless society?

The *discourse of equal opportunity* argues that treating everyone the same guarantees fairness to all people. The assumption underlying this discourse is the notion that societal resources and opportunities are evenly distributed and that racialized people have access to them as equally as white North Americans. History, however, teaches us that the playing field has never been level for all groups in society. Besides, the discourse ignores the social construction of race, in which power and privilege belong to those who are white. According to Crenshaw (1997), equal opportunity represents a passive approach and does not require the dismantling of white institutional power or the redistribution of social power.

Democratic racism also hinges on a discourse that *blames the victim* (racialized people) for their problems. The discourse of blaming the victim maligns ethnicized cultures, arguing that 'deficiencies' in ethnic minority cultures prevent them from being able to participate fully in North American society. This discourse alleges that if racialized people are disadvantaged it is because their recalcitrant members refuse to adapt their 'different', 'traditional' cultural values and norms to fit into mainstream society while at the same time making unreasonable demands on society (Henry and Tator, 2006). Culture supremacists claim that the failure of certain ethno-cultural groups to succeed and integrate into the dominant society is largely due to the wide 'ethno-racial gap' between white cultures and ethnic minority cultures.

With the *discourse of reverse racism*, members of the dominant white culture claim they are now the victims of a new form of oppression and exclusion. Initiatives and programs such as anti-racism and equity policies are maligned in strong, emotive language that they constitute 'apartheid in reverse', a 'new inquisition' against white North Americans (Henry and Tator, 2006, p. 26). People concerned with social justice and inequalities are often accused of belonging to radical, extremist groups. The argument is that the issue of race is being used as a cover for promoting conflict in pursuit of other questionable political ends. Those concerned with racial oppressions have been labelled as radicals who are using an anti-racism platform to subvert mainstream fundamental institutions, values, and traditions.

The *discourse of multiculturalism* articulates the idea that accommodating ethno-cultural diversity into society in general and social organizations and institutions in particular will guarantee the achievement of ethno-racial tolerance and harmony (Henry and Tator, 2006; see Satzewich and Liodakis, 2007). This discourse, which appears to be more commonly articulated in Canada than in America, suggests that the dominant group's way of doing things remains superior even though one must accept the idiosyncrasies of ethnic minorities – the 'others'. This minimal form of recognition of the value of difference is at the heart of multiculturalism policy and practice in Canada (Henry and Tator, 2006). It is a limited form of recognition of cultural diversity in that it enables the dominant group to create a ceiling on tolerance by specifying what differences are tolerable.

In creating such a ceiling, multiculturalism adopts a top-down approach that works with acts of tolerance in place of acts of appreciating and valuing difference (Dei, 2009). This ceiling is reflected in negative reactions to multiculturalism in opinion polls and surveys, which report many members of the dominant white group maintaining that 'we' cannot tolerate too much difference because it stokes dissent, disruption, and conflict. According to this view, paying unnecessary attention to cultural differences leads to disorder, disharmony, and 'ethno-cultural balkanization'. Where possible, the dominant culture tries to make room for *their* idiosyncratic cultural differences. Henry *et al.* (2009, p. 117) consider this discourse an articulation of democratic racism because it involves processes in which declarations of the need for tolerance and harmony usually conceal the messy business of structural and systemic inequality and the unequal relations of power that continue to function in a liberal democratic society.

The hallmark of the *discourse of national identity* is that it negates, silences, erases, or omits the contributions of ethno-racial communities. Racialized groups are relegated to a position outside of the 'national project' because their cultures are discredited as not being progressive, or having anything worthwhile to contribute to 'civilization'. The notion of 'hyphenated' Canadians or Americans has been an integral part of the discourse on national identity, but, in Canada, this has always been limited to two identities or cultural solitudes: English Canada and French Canada (Henry and Tator, 2006) – another classic example of multidualism in Canada. Not only does the dominant culture conveniently fail to acknowledge the existence of a third founding nation (First Nations peoples), it also ignores the cultural plurality that existed within aboriginal communities when European colonizers settled in North America. Invariably, the contributions of First Nations peoples and racialized groups to nation building in North America have been ignored or rendered a nonentity in the process. Multidualism is indispensable to the functioning and entrenchment of the white culture in North America.

Islamophobia and Arabiphobia

The notion that North America has transitioned into a post-race state is seriously challenged by the emergence of newer strains of racisms – Islamophobia and Arabiphobia.

The term 'Islamophobia' has become quite prominent in media commentaries and public discourses especially since the September 11, 2001 (popularly known as 9/11) attacks on the World Trade Center and the Pentagon in America. However, because of its relative recency, compared to other forms of social oppression, Islamophobia has not received much attention in the social work and ethnic relations literature.

Islamophobia refers to the hatred or fear of Islam as well as followers of the Islamic religion, that is, Muslims. At its core, Islamophobia reflects deep-seated and largely unexamined anxieties, fears, and distrust of the Islamic religion and Muslim cultural practices (Soldatova, 2007; Gottschalk and Greenberg, 2008). Islamophobia serves to inappropriately identify Muslim individuals by their religion when, in fact, the issues in question often have more to do with politics, economics, or public policy than religion (Henry and Tator, 2006). Some writers (*e.g.* Miles and Brown, 2003) have suggested that because the 'othering' of Muslims tends to be constructed in religious rather than biological or physical terms, Islamophobia cannot possibly be considered racism, a position this author deems untenable. Religion and ethnicity are integral and overlapping components of group culture and personal identity such that it is difficult to disparage a group's religion while at the same time appreciating its ethnic heritage. Such a distinction is hard to sustain. Therefore, contrary to official rhetoric, many Muslims believe that the so-called 'war on terror' is, in fact, a camouflaged crusade by the Christian west to exterminate both Islam and the Arab culture. In line with other writers (*e.g.* Satzewich and Liodakis, 2007; Soldatova, 2007; Meer and Noorani, 2008), this chapter articulates the position that Islamophobia manifests itself as a form of both religious and racial hatred especially toward anyone perceived as 'Arabian' or 'Middle Eastern'.

Confusion surrounds the genesis of the term Islamophobia. One source (see Strabac and Listhaug, 2008) places the origin of the term Islamophobia in the late 1980s. However, according to Cesari (2006, cited in Lee *et al.*, 2009), the construct Islamophobia was first coined in 1922 by Etienne Dinet and later popularized by the Runnymede Trust, a British think tank, in the 1990s as unfounded hostility and antagonism towards Islam or dislike of Muslims. Regardless of its historical roots, a succession of recent international events has led to a dramatic increase in attention to Islam and Muslims and, indeed, people of Arab ethnic background in ordinary conversations and public discourses as well as media portrayals in the west (Kulwicki *et al.*, 2008; Strabac and Listhaug, 2008; Lee *et al.*, 2009).

The Runnymede Trust has outlined a number of propositions to determine when Islamophobia is manifested. According to the Runnymede Trust, Islamophobia is present when:

- Islam is perceived as a single monolithic bloc, static and impervious to change or modern realities.
- Islam is the 'other' which lacks aims or values in common with other (western) cultures.
- Islam is irrational, barbaric, and engaged in a 'clash of civilizations' with the west.
- Islam is violent and aggressive and supports terrorism, which poses a threat to world peace and security.
- Islam is seen as a political ideology, used for political or military advantage.

- Criticisms made by Islam of the west are rejected out of hand, because it is considered an inferior religion.
- Hostility and discriminatory practices toward Muslims and exclusion of Muslims from mainstream society are justified as natural and normal.
- Islam is incompatible with tolerance and pluralism (Runnymede Trust, 2000, cited in Fleras, 2010, pp. 329-330).

Although many westerners display a long history of animosity and anti-foreigner sentiments towards Islam and Muslims, the 9/11 attacks and subsequent portrayals of the attacks have been a major contributor in intensifying negative, hateful, and fearful perceptions of Muslims and Arabs (Scheufele *et al.*, 2005; Henry and Tator, 2006). Since 9/11, Muslim and Arab communities across North America have experienced a significant increase in harassment, hate crimes, and racial bias and discrimination in their neighbourhoods, workplaces, and schools (Swahn *et al.*, 2003; Cainkar, 2004, 2006; Sheridan, 2006; Kulwicki *et al.*, 2008; Strabac and Listhaug, 2008; Lee *et al.*, 2009). They have also witnessed a surge in the destruction of their properties, while being subjected to defamatory commentaries and discourses of the media, politicians, and public authorities that have served to reinforce and crystallize the message of their 'otherness' (Henry and Tator, 2006). According to the Canadian Islamic Congress, anti-Islam/Muslim hate crimes, harassment, intimidation, and violence increased 1600 percent in Canada in the days immediately following 9/11 (Henry and Tator, 2006; Satzewich and Liodakis, 2007).

Similar developments occurred in America. Swahn *et al.* (2003) analyzed newspaper reports to identify incidents of Islamophobia immediately after the 9/11 attacks. The study reported 100 incidents in the period from September 1, 2001 to October 11, 2001. It was found that only one of the reports was made prior to September 11, 2009. According to Swahn and colleagues (2003), the remaining 99 incidents involved 128 victims and 171 perpetrators, with the most violent crimes occurring within ten days after September 11.

Islamophobia is conflated with xenophobic attitudes and practices to create an oppressive system of *Arabiphobia*, a term used in this chapter to encompass individual, socio-political, and hegemonic processes, behaviours, perceptions, and inclinations that satanize people of Arab ancestry while vilifying Arabic culture as barbaric, violent, and decadent. Essentially, while Islamophobia denigrates the Islamic religion specifically, Arabiphobia encompasses the vilification of both Islam and Arab culture. In that it demonizes Arabian cultures, Arabiphobia de-legitimates the invaluable, path-breaking contributions the Arab world made to civilization – in the arts, science, government, mathematics, algebra, and astronomy. Both Arabiphobia and Islamophobia seek to denigrate and brand Arabian cultures and institutions as a threat to the security of the so-called 'civilized' world. Arabiphobia thus serves as a medium by which Arabic culture and institutions are demonized as barriers to peace, progress, and integration. Arabiphobia creates the conditions for the expression of other anti-Arab processes.

Racializing processes engendered by Arabiphobia include the *arabianization* of terrorism, *islamization* of (religious) fundamentalism, and the *muslimization* of extremism. In tandem, these processes enable the isolated events of a small number of extremists to be overblown in the media, thereby reinforcing people's worst expectations and darkest concerns; providing proof that perpetuates prejudicial stereotyping of Muslim men as violent tyrants or terrorists, and Muslim women as helplessly oppressed, burqa-bearing submissives at odds with modernity. Arabiphobia then convinces many in the west of the irreconcilable differences between the west and Arabian 'otherness' (Fleras, 2010). In short, Arabiphobia condemns Islam and the Arab world in their entirety as 'violent', 'radical, and 'extremist' while conveniently ignoring the existence of a moderate Arab majority (see Mazarr, 2007; Lee *et al.*, 2009). The majority of Muslims and Arab North Americans are law-abiding citizens who stand up against violence, terrorism, and extremism (see Ross, 2009). Unfortunately, they do not attract the attention or respect of Islamophobes (Alliance of Civilizations, 2006). Of course, racial ideologies do not distinguish between or among colour-coded bodies and/or their actions; the actions of a 'few misguided, bad apples' are automatically extrapolated to the whole (racialized) group. Ironically, when white North Americans deny that racism still exists in this society, they are quick to identify whites' acts of racism as isolated phenomena, perpetrated by a 'few misguided, bad apples'. Racial ideology never ceases to amaze.

In the post-9/11 period, North American governments have actively pursued more punitive and hard-line anti-terrorism legislations and policies that adversely affect 'Arab-looking' individuals and Muslim communities (Frost, 2008). Arat-Koç (2010) argues that Islamophobia informs a great deal of the new security agenda in North America. Public policies such as the Anti-Terrorism Act (in Canada) are a demonstration of a new tension that has emerged in North America since 9/11 that challenges democratic liberal values. Since the Anti-Terrorism Act was passed, Canadian security forces, including the Royal Canadian Mounted Police (RCMP) and Canadian Security Intelligence Service (CSIS) have questioned, or arrested hundreds of Muslim Canadians about their travel patterns, prayer habits, associations, and other seemingly innocuous matters (Henry and Tator, 2006). As a result, Muslim and Arab North Americans are increasingly worried about how their travel patterns, their charitable donations, and their remittances to friends and family members overseas will be interpreted by other North Americans and by police and security forces (see Satzewich and Liodakis, 2007). The debate over post-9/11 legislations and policies are indicative of a conflict between preserving public rights to security and securing the basic rights and freedoms of all North Americans.

Besides specific national security and anti-terrorism laws, North American governments have also instituted restrictive immigration practices; international and 'ethnic' students are increasingly under surveillance; civil liberties have been restricted or curtailed in the interest of national security (Andersen and Collins, 2007b). In Canada, the RCMP warned all security officials that any young, educated, well-dressed Arab or Muslim male living in Canada is a potential terrorist and therefore must be investigated (Tanovich, 2009). The much-publicized story of Maher Arar, a Syrian-born Canadian demonstrates how Arabiphobia manifests itself in North America. With the complicity of Canada, American authorities arrested Arar in 2002 as he was returning home to Montreal from a visit abroad. The United States claimed Arar had links to the terrorist group Al Qaeda. Arar was sent to Jordan and later to Syria where he was imprisoned and tortured for one year; he was released in 2003 when no evidence of links to Al Qaeda was found against him. The Canadian government ended up paying a very hefty compensation of $11.5 million to Arar (including $1.5 million to cover his legal costs) for its role in abusing Arar's human rights, freedom, and civil liberties.

Canadian and American state surveillance apparatus has been trained on Muslims and Arabs in an attempt to catch the 'adversary'. Muslims and Arab North Americans feel besieged (see Henry and Tator, 2006); they have been eyed with suspicion and scepticism, rather than being invited to the table to offer assistance or advice on improving national and regional security for North America. One study done in the United States (Ibish and Stewart, 2003) reported how an Arab American student who applied for a position at a Dallas bank was asked during an interview if he was not going to blow up the building if hired. Although he was hired, he was treated with suspicion and questioned after using the telephone. He was also harassed over sick days, and noticed that someone was tampering with his work to create errors after he had submitted it. Increased surveillance of Muslim and Arab communities has resulted in concerns about increased deprivations and abuses of liberty, loss of privacy, further questions, or worse (Henry and Tator, 2006).

'Othering' and targeting the Muslim/Arab community in North America has also had devastating psychological repercussions especially among the youth. Not only has many a Muslim youth felt a loss of self-esteem or feelings of inferiority and worthlessness, they have also been subjected to suicidal ideation and behaviours (Bullock and Jafri, 2001). The cumulative result of the rising tide of Arabiphobia and Islamophobia is a rabid mistrust that reinforces the status of North Americans of Arab origin as the 'enemy within' or those whose only stock in trade is 'home-grown terrorism'. One would be hard-pressed to find evidence of how any one religion, besides Islam, has been so vilified and satanized by the west. Nowhere is this vilification more pronounced than in media coverage and portrayal of Muslims and Arabs.

The use of defamatory language, especially in the media and by government officials (Danso, 2009b), adds another layer to the complexities involved in Arabiphobia. The individuals who attacked the World Trade Center are depicted as (Islamic) 'terrorists'. It has become an unquestioned practice to brand any Muslim or Arab North American, who engages in any kind of deviant or anti-social behaviour, a terrorist. At the same time, white North Americans who engage in or commit similar acts of terror are less likely to be labelled terrorists. For instance, although he was executed, Timothy McVeigh who bombed the Murrah Federal building in Oklahoma City on April 19, 1995 (Wright, 2007) was rarely, if ever, labelled a terrorist. Thus, there is a biased, self-fulfilling perception among many Canadians and Americans that only people of Middle Eastern or Arabian heritage engage in terrorist acts and that Islam breeds violence and radicalism.

Arabiphobia highlights other realities that now characterize the lives of Muslim Canadians and Americans. Muslims and Arabs in North America face a double agony related to their status (1) as immigrants and (2) as followers of the Islamic religion (Strabac and Listhaug, 2008). Just being immigrants of Arab origin is a sufficient-enough reason or a source of ethno-racial prejudice and discrimination against Arab North Americans. Such ethno-racial prejudice is part of the 'generic anti-immigrant' sentiments (Henry and Tator, 2006; Strabac and Listhaug, 2008) displayed by mainstream North Americans towards racialized communities. 'Specific anti-Muslim' prejudice is based on the Islamic religion. This aspect of Arabiphobia has developed largely because of stereotype-inducing processes in the last few decades in North America and elsewhere in the west (Swahn et al., 2003; Cainkar, 2004; Sheridan, 2006; Frost, 2008; Kulwicki et al., 2008; Meer and Noorani, 2008).

Arabiphobia may be exacerbated by the visibility of people of Arab background because of the way they dress (Al-Krenawi and Graham, 2003; Kulwicki et al., 2008). Arab women who wear the *hijab* (a headscarf) or the *niqab* (a veil worn over the head and shows only the eyes) are particularly at risk of Arabiphobia because of their high level of visibility. The hijab is a conspicuous and defining piece of religious dress in Canada and America (Cainkar, 2004; Sheridan, 2006; Kulwicki *et al.*, 2008). Recently, in Canada, there have been arguments as to whether Muslim women can wear the niqab to vote. The niqab has been criticized as being a 'mark of separation' and that it can also hide one's physical identity (see Satzewich and Liodakis, 2007). For Arab women, the hijab is often a source of ridicule, contempt, and negative comments by non-Muslims (Naber, 2000; Cainkar, 2004; Sheridan, 2006). Arab or Muslim women who wear the niqab are often treated with suspicion as potential female suicide bombers.

Impact of Race and Racism in Social Functioning

Race affects human relations and social functioning in very profound ways. Race is the prism through which interpretation of human experiences and people's relationships to social institutions are understood or articulated (Hamilton, 2007). Appleby (2007a) defines social functioning as a person's overall performance in his/her social roles within a given social context. In much broader terms, social functioning refers to the ability of people to perform their social roles as well as the extent to which society enables individuals and groups to interact in normal ways and carry out their roles in society (Chappell, 2006). How effectively individuals perform their social roles is largely conditioned by, constrained by, and dependent upon the colour of their skin. The tentacles of race and racism are now so long and have such a stranglehold on society that it is difficult to disentangle them from the normal social, economic, and political circumstances in North American society.

Race may be considered perhaps the most oxymoronic terms in the social science literature in that it is, simultaneously, the nothing-but-everything dynamic that structures inclusion and exclusion. Race may be an illusive concept, but the social consequences of racism are real. Although many people reject the reality of race, countless others perceive it to be real and act accordingly thereby reaffirming W. I. Thomas's notion that things do not have to be real to be real in their consequences and effects (Fleras, 2010, p. 28). This reality deeply influences how mainstream North America constructs and relates to racialized people (Hall, 2005; Colvin-Burque *et al.*, 2007). Omi argues that "the idea of race and its persistence as a social category, is only given meaning in a social order structured by forms of inequality that are organized, to a significant degree, by race" (Omi, 2001, p. 254).

The all-powerful marker and central organization principle, race is also the means for creating, maintaining, and enforcing social order; it is the lens through which differential opportunity and inequality are structured, often supported by social policy (Murji and Solomos, 2005; Smedley and Smedley, 2005; Henry and Tator, 2006; Hamilton, 2007). For centuries, morphology and ancestry have influenced "where people live, where they work, and what they can expect from life" (Wallis and Fleras, 2009c, p. 251). Numerous research studies have documented the entrenchment of racism in Canada and the United States. Persistent patterns of oppression and denial of access have been recorded in housing, employment, education, politics, healthcare, police treatment, business, and social services (Leach, 2005; Henry and Tator, 2006). Hallmarks of all racist societies, these systems of dominance and inequality are communicated and reproduced through processes and agencies of socialization and cultural transmission: the family, mass media, schools and universities, law enforcement, and the justice system, as well as symbols and images, art, music, entertainment, and literature.

Racial discrimination, defined as the differential or unfair treatment of people based on their race or ethnic origin, reduces people of colour to second-class citizens. Racial discrimination involves reifying and putting prejudicial thoughts and beliefs into action, and ensuring that members of racialized groups are excluded for reasons unrelated to their capabilities, industry, or general merit: they are judged solely on their membership of a targeted (racialized) group. Racial discrimination may also involve the use of coded or euphemistic language (Moore, 2007; Lee *et al.*, 2009), derogatory labels (*e.g.* 'nigger', 'extremists', 'fundamentalists'), and telling racial jokes. By denigrating targeted groups, the dominant (white) group creates conditions under which racialized groups can often do no more than confirm the stereotypes that inspired the original racist belief.

Racist ideologies and practices have grave material consequences, severely affecting racialized people's lives and threatening their present and future wellbeing in North American society. For example, the negative images ascribed to blacks by white North Americans have so haunted the black psyche that an abiding self-hatred, self-denunciation, and despondency have developed in some black people, particularly the youth (Ruggles and Rovinescu, 1996). As victims of benign or polite racism – the kind of contemporary racism that wears a deceitful smile on its face (Foster, 1996; Henry and Tator, 2006; Fleras, 2010) – many black people have also come to abhor the stereotypes ascribed to them that they are understandably at pains to avoid an identification with such an image.

Studies comparing self-esteem among blacks and whites in America found that blacks tend to report higher self-esteem than whites (Zeigler-Hill, 2007). However, the combination of centuries of slavery, racial segregation, discrimination, and oppression has had a pernicious impact on blacks that significantly weakens or offsets any positive effects the alleged positive self-esteem may have produced. A recent study (Harper *et al.*, 2007) also found that the life expectancy gap is narrowing between blacks and whites in America. However, other research has also reported that blacks' continuing experiences with discrimination and denial of access to economic and political power largely account for the many well-documented health disparities that affect blacks (Mays *et al.*, 2007). Mays *et al.* (2007) have suggested that the legacy of poor health among African Americans, despite the overall improved conditions of their lives, is one compelling reason for healthcare providers and social workers to take a harder look at the role race and racism play in service delivery.

For black people be they in Canada or America, the history of their settlement as well as their present-day life experiences are one of xenophobia, racism, and 'footnote' existence. Now, as historically, racism has forced blacks to the lower rungs of society. In a study of occupational achievement by blacks and whites in Toronto, Darden found that race was "the most significant variable that negatively affects the chances of blacks achieving equal occupational status with whites" (Darden, 2005, p. 48). Darden's study also found that, compared to whites, blacks tended to be overrepresented in menial jobs but underrepresented in professional and managerial positions, even when they had identical socio-demographic characteristics as whites.

The volumes of studies done in the United States always come to similar conclusions; white racism and discrimination are always cited as the reason for the existence and perpetuation of these barriers (Cohen and Huffman, 2007). Roscigno *et al.* (2007) report similar findings in their study of race- and gender-based discrimination in employment.

According to Roscigno and colleagues (2007), racial discrimination produces multiple outcomes, including social exclusion, inequalities in material rewards, or potential blocks to mobility for blacks. Whether in Canada or America, blacks tend to live in poor, 'ghettoized' neighbourhoods although some writers (*e.g.* Walks and Bourne, 2006) claim that ghettos are an American problem rather than a Canadian malaise. Blacks experience profound disadvantages in the North American housing market, including low levels of homeownership (Myles and Hou, 2004; Wilson, 2007). The 'black experience' in North America could best be summarized as one of daily struggle for survival, and of despondency that continues to exist in an atmosphere of xenophobia, intolerance, racism, and exclusion. Whether forcibly transported across oceans and between continents as slaves or admitted as immigrants or refugees, blacks in North America have never escaped overt prejudice, stereotypes, racism, and xenophobia.

The institutionalization and entrenchment of racial discrimination in North American social institutions and value systems has excluded blacks from politics and the political process, too. For instance, in a study of ethnic minority groups and Canadian elections Toasts and Najem (2002, cited in Black and Erickson, 2006) found that racism and discrimination were major factors that inhibited the political success of blacks and racialized candidates. As previously noted, multiculturalism and immigration and settlement policies and programs do not encourage access to political power and effective participation of immigrants of colour in the political process in Canada. Immigrants of colour are exploited for their economic worth while being denied a political voice in matters and decision-making processes that affect their daily lives. Until they become Canadian citizens, immigrants cannot vote in elections.

As an oppressed group, blacks may try repeatedly to be accepted into the wider North American society but often their efforts are thwarted by racial prejudice and discrimination. Frustration, failure, and psychosocial stress then become their lot because they are barred admittance into mainstream life. On the individual scale, prejudice and discrimination commonly result in personality disorganization. Subjected to constant prejudicial and racist treatment, many a black person in North America is not able to function effectively and may cave in or 'break down' under pressure from a social system that is consistently designed to frustrate or exclude him/her. At the group level, many black communities have succumbed to social disorganization, a situation usually indexed by anti-social behaviour, drug use, broken homes and single-parenthood, unemployment, poverty, mental ill health, and short life span.

Deviance is said to have a body and a face in North America – and they are black – although not in reality but in the public imagination (Lubiano, 1998). For instance, in American public debates, dependence on social welfare, inner-city violence, urban decay, and heavy drug use have a colour-coded face – black (White, 2007; Fleras, 2010). It is not the case that blacks are genetically programmed or predisposed to engage in deviant behaviour, because ethnicity is not a biological determinant of deviance (Fleras, 2005). Rather, blacks have been socially constructed and depicted as having an 'innate' propensity to commit crime – a portrayal that abides in, and feeds on the public's fantasy and imagination in a self-serving way. The 'black condition' in North America is a direct outcome of the enslavement blacks have endured in this society for centuries. Historically, no racialized bodies were ever hauled as freight between continents to be permanently enslaved except blacks. The dehumanizing experience of slavery alone makes the racism blacks face unique from that of any other racialized groups in North American society.

Racism may also affect people (whites) on the other side of the divide though (Jordan and Weedon, 1995, Spanierman *et al.*, 2006). White people with different social locations, that is, membership in different social divisions, may be oppressed in relation to the dominant white, middle-class heterosexual male subject. However, whites hold an advantage – what McIntosh (2007) has described as the *invisible knapsack* and Johal has labelled a *pigmentary passport* "of privilege that allows sanctity as a result of the racial polity of whiteness" (Johal, 2005, p. 273). While insulating them from privilege, skin colour mitigates the impact of oppression for many white people. Whiteness is a luxury racialized bodies do not enjoy (Dei, 2009). The same set of processes that advantage and insulate whites from privilege disadvantage African Americans (Shapiro, 2004). Yet, most white North Americans will deny being racist.

In Canada, there is a prevailing self-serving myth that, unlike 'our neighbours to the south' (Americans), Canadians are not racist because racism is foreign to Canada (Henry and Tator, 2006; Aylward, 2009; Dei, 2009; Fleras, 2010). As previously noted, state policies of multiculturalism have presented Canada as a welcoming and egalitarian society for immigrants and refugees, while in reality these policies work to create structures that keep African Canadians and other people of colour in a marginal social, political, economic, and cultural relationship to Canada. Such collective mythologies are dangerously insidious in that they serve to erase the history of colonization, slavery, and racist immigration policies and practices (Dua *et al.*, 2005; Aylward, 2009), and their detrimental impact on the social functioning of blacks and other racialized bodies.

The same Europeans who immigrated to America were the ones who also crossed the same Atlantic Ocean to settle in Canada. Why then would the latter be less racist than the former? Is there anything so magical about the '49th parallel' that makes whites north of the parallel immune to racism or racial prejudice? Is it because Canada is multicultural, and a multicultural society just *cannot* be racist? The question that arises then is why does study after study (*e.g.* Galabuzi, 2006; Ornstein, 2006; Picot *et al.*, 2007; Wallis and Kwok, 2008) keep finding that, in Canada, racialized groups continue to live in poverty and have disturbingly high levels of unemployment and economic deprivation? Poverty is deeply racialized and feminized in Canada (Wallis and Kwok, 2008). Why is it that skilled immigrants are denied access to hiring and job opportunities when there is a shortage of skilled professionals in Canada (Danso, 2009a)? According to The Colour of Poverty Campaign (2009), between 1980 and 2000, while the poverty rate for non-racialized (*i.e.* European heritage) populations fell by 28 per cent, poverty among racialized families rose by 361 percent. Canada "is characterized in national mythology as a nation of innocent racism" (Dua *et al.*, 2005, p. 1). The debilitating result of the persistent myth of a raceless Canadian society has been the frustratingly slow and patchwork response of Canadian governments, institutions, and other organizations to racist laws, policies, and practices (see Aylward, 2009).

The experiences of blacks in North America provide concrete evidence that not only substantiates the social construction thesis of race, but also point social workers and people concerned with social justice and social change to the need to critically interrogate the *theory* and practice of race. Social workers' attempts to debunk the 'naturalness' of race will go a long way to diffuse racial tensions and remove barriers to social inclusion as well as access to culturally competent social work practice and service delivery. If only the conditions that racism creates would be eliminated, for instance, through bold, effective social policies, public education, and advocacy, it would go a long way to reduce the number of social problems blacks, Arabs, Muslims, native Canadians and Americans, and other racialized bodies encounter in their daily life in North American society. It is only by critically interrogating race and racism that the 'social pathologies' confronting racialized groups in North America can be eliminated. With a deep concern for attending to issues of social exclusion and discrimination against marginalized populations in society and the commitment to social justice as an important aspect of its mission and guide for practice (Graham, 2009), social work has the tools to tackle systemic and institutional racisms to emancipate oppressed and vulnerable groups in North American society.

Reversing Race and Racisms

Structural-Oriented Approaches to Social Change : An Overview

Social work seeks to address racism, discrimination, inequalities, and other forms of social injustices by incorporating structural frameworks and principles into social work education and practice (Graham, 2009). The range of structural frameworks traditionally used in social work include radical, anti-oppressive, anti-racist, anti-discrimination, and empowerment approaches. Others are feminist, postmodernism, and poststructuralist perspectives. While most of these frameworks emerged from or as part of the radical and critical social work (re)awakening of the 1980s, especially in the United Kingdom (see Healy, 2005; Payne, 2005; Mullaly, 2007), many of them draw on other social science theories, particularly Marxism (Healy, 2005; Mullaly, 2007; Rogowski, 2008). Structural social work, for instance, is based on critical social science paradigm.

Structural social work sees social structures and institutions as the source of social problems. According to structural social workers, social institutions function in such a way that they oppress and discriminate against people along many dimensions of identity: race, class, gender, ethnicity, age, disability, religion, and so on (Healy, 2005; Mullaly, 2007). Because social structures and institutions are interdependent, they reinforce and feed into each other. Therefore, approaches for creating social change must focus on all levels of social institutions simultaneously and holistically; piecemeal, one-level-at-a-time strategies would not be effective. This underscores the need for a comprehensive approach to social change, such as the integrative counter-racism framework proposed in this chapter. The next few paragraphs provide an overview of three structural approaches commonly used to address social problems: anti-oppressive practice, anti-racist, and anti-discrimination social work. Following the review is an in-depth discussion of the conceptual basis and practice implications of the integrative counter-racism model.

Anti-Oppressive Practice

Emerging in the 1980s, anti-oppressive practice (AOP) has developed as a dominant theory in critical social work practice (see Dominelli, 2002a, 2002b; Healy, 2005; Thompson, 2006; Danso, 2009a). According to Dominelli, AOP is a

> ... form of social work practice, which addresses social divisions and structural inequalities in the work that is done with 'clients' (users) or workers. Anti-oppressive practice aims to provide more appropriate and sensitive services by responding to people's needs

regardless of their social status. Anti-oppressive practice embodies a person-centered philosophy, an egalitarian value system concerned with reducing the deleterious effects of structural inequalities upon people's lives; a methodology focusing on process and outcome; and a way of structural social relationships between individuals that aims to empower service users by reducing the negative effects of hierarchy in their immediate interaction and the work they do' (Dominelli, 2002a, p. 6).

Strengths of the AOP perspective include the fact that AOP has helped to analyze and respond to social issues and challenges posed by globalization and international migration (Valtonen, 2002, Nash *et al.*, 2006). AOP has helped social workers to put into action new knowledge about various ethnic minority groups, women, disabled, and older people in social relations. Unlike micro-social work perspectives, AOP places the value of social justice centre stage in all dimensions of social work practice by offering a clear linkage between social work and social justice (George, 2000). The strengths of AOP are punctuated by certain limitations.

One limitation of the AOP approach is that it tends to focus attention more on structural issues to the neglect of micro or individual-level issues. According to Payne (2005), a strong critique of *'psy'* discourse underpins AOP, accompanied by the prioritization of structural analysis of clients' experiences. The lopsided focus could lead social workers to neglect individual psychological and personal factors that may contribute substantially to elevated risk in some contexts, such as child protection, mental health, and work in corrections. Although AOP offers many examples of societal and organizational changes and strategies (see Barnoff and Moffatt, 2007), it is not as clear how social workers who work directly with individuals and families could utilize AOP in their practice (Sakamoto and Pitner, 2005). Some writers have therefore concluded that AOP does not offer enough·prescriptions to 'immediate' problems of individuals and families (Payne, 2005; Sakamoto and Pitner, 2005). With its largely Eurocentric worldview and biases, AOP may even be more oppressive to ethno-racial minority clients. The proposed integrative counter-racism approach overcomes this limitation, for instance, by de-emphasizing recourse to ethnocentric and monolithic approaches to social change, and emphasizing, instead, critical self-reflection and the need to integrate private (personal) with public (systemic/structural) resources to resolve structural issues as the two spheres exist in a mutually reinforcing relationship.

Anti-Racist Approaches

Anti-racist social work seeks to isolate and challenge racism through direct action at personal and institutional levels (Fleras, 2005; 2010). Anti-racism entails active personal involvement for dislodging those cultural values, personal prejudices, discriminatory behaviours, and institutional structures of society that perpetuate racism. Anti-racism measures include confronting hate groups, direct action through protest or civil disobedience, boycotts, litigation, or laws and regulations, as well as learning/unlearning through education and interaction. Institutional anti-racism strategies comprise measures and mechanisms for dismantling the structural basis of organizational or systemic racism. A key criticism of anti-racist approaches, as Graham (2009) points out, is that they have not been adequate to account for a wide range of social divisions in society. Therefore, race, gender, and other markers of social identity have "required more study in their own right" (Graham, 2009, p.

272). Another criticism is that anti-racist frameworks sometimes subsume race under class, an approach Dei (2009) describes as very dangerous.

Anti-Discrimination Frameworks

Anti-discriminatory approaches seek to deal with differential treatment on the bases of social divisions such as race, age, gender, disability, or religion. Taking a primarily socialist-collectivist view (Payne, 2005), anti-discriminatory practice emerged from concerns within radical social work thought for vulnerable and oppressed populations. An important aspect of much of anti-discriminatory theory is the analysis of the origins of discrimination (Payne, 2005).

Thompson's (2003) work is considered one of the major contributions to anti-discrimination social work scholarship (see also Dalrymple and Burke, 1995). Thompson's (2003) anti-discriminatory theory links the personal (psychological), cultural, and social (structural) levels of analysis of social issues. According to Thompson, the personal level relates to interpersonal relations, and personal or psychological feelings, dispositions, and behaviours and actions between people, including social work practice, which is done at this level (Payne, 2005). The interpersonal relationships occur within a cultural context, which influences and forms individual thoughts and actions, that is, the shared ways of thinking, feeling, and acting. This is about within-group conventions and commonalities, an assumed consensus about what a group considers 'normal' as well as the perception that people identify with social norms created within particular groups or cultures. People internalize these group/cultural norms. The personal and cultural levels are in turn embedded in a structural level, which constitutes an established order and a set of accepted social divisions. As Payne (2005) notes, the established social order and its structures, and the cultural norms and assumptions and personal behaviours that result derive from the collective acceptance of the social order and its divisions. Practitioners' influence over matters tends to diminish progressively from the personal level to the structural level.

Anti-discriminatory approaches have been criticized on a number of grounds. For instance, although anti-discriminatory approaches emphasize the importance of responding to discrimination and oppression, especially on grounds of race, and ethnicity, and represent values that should permeate social work, *"it is not clear that they can form the basis for a distinctive approach in themselves"* (Payne, 2005, p. 293, emphasis supplied); other approaches will usually also be required, Payne (2005) concludes. In addition, anti-discrimination strategies have often focused only on racism and ignored important cultural aspects of discrimination, such as religion. Thus, it is not clear how effectively anti-discriminatory perspectives can address social issues raised by Islamophobia and Arabiphobia as new forms of contemporary racism. Similarly, anti-discriminatory approaches are blamed for their focus on black/white binaries or distinctions, as if other forms of racialized relations did not matter.

That structural social work approaches have made significant contributions towards addressing social problems and creating a more socially just and egalitarian society is beyond question. However, because they have traditionally been used in a stand-alone fashion, on the assumption that each approach was powerful enough to address systems of oppression all by itself, many of the frameworks have not been effective in their purpose. In the case of radical social work, for instance, because it was used alone, it ignored both patriarchy and racism as sources of oppression (Dominelli, 1997). Black social workers criticized the early radical social work school for largely ignoring anti-racist social work practice (see Stasiulis, 2009). Regarding feminist social work, although it emphasizes transformational politics and the decoding of patriarchy and sexism, and stresses "the links between the personal and the political better than any other theory" (Mullaly, 2007, p. 242), some feminist theorists and practitioners limit this transformation to a constituency of women only. Therefore, black women, for instance, criticized the early feminist movement for overlooking the particular, complex situation of women of colour (see Dominelli, 1997; Healy, 2005; Payne, 2005; Mullaly, 2007; Stasiulis, 2009). The variety of feminist analyses that exist with respect to the fundamental sources of oppression in society thus suggests that there are differences in opinions and strategies regarding how to deal with gender-based inequality (Mullaly, 2007).

The limitations characterizing existing structural frameworks underscore the fact that more creative and effective methodological approaches are needed to address contemporary systems of racism and oppression. With this in view, this chapter reframes the approach to combating racism by proposing an integrative counter-racism model that combines different perspectives and strategies, including anti-racist, empowerment, anti-oppressive, anti-discriminatory, and feminist perspectives, for creating social change.

CONCEPTUALIZING THE INTEGRATIVE COUNTER-RACISM FRAMEWORK

Racisms are structural phenomena that function as a complex dynamic; therefore, approaches to addressing these social cancers must be comprehensive and integrative in nature. Interlocking problems demand integrative solutions and methods of work. Because social phenomena are so dynamic and intertwined, the transformative power of traditional frameworks for resolving social problems is often diminished. An eclectic, integrative strategy will be more efficacious than single methodologies in effecting social change.

The integrative counter-racism (ICR) framework is an umbrella structural-oriented approach to social transformation. It brings under its ambit a variety of domains that have traditionally been separated or used in isolation by structural social workers. The ICR model takes as its point of departure the notion that any relations, structures, institutions, or systems imbued with human imprint are (potential) sources of social oppression. The model further posits that all sites or axes of domination constitute both targets and vehicles or tools for social transformation. In other words, the cause must also be the solution. Furthermore, all social relations are power relations; social relations either empower (privilege) or disempower (marginalize) some groups at the expense of others. These unequal power relations are historically contingent and they occur within particular spatial contexts, including the local and the global contexts.

Unlike some social change approaches (*e.g.* AOP perspectives), which tend to focus more on structural issues to the neglect of individual-level issues, the ICR framework argues that the 'personal is societal' and the 'local global'. This means that there is a mutually reinforcing, bidirectional relationship between events at the personal or local level and those occurring within the global arena, even if the relationship is tenuous or indirect. Individuals are enmeshed within a family, which, in turn is located within a local community and the community is linked to a regional context; the regional connects to the national and the national to the global, creating a dynamic 'chain of contexts'. For instance, the 9/11 attacks on America, and the resulting 'war on terror', have had many and varied repercussions not only for nations but also private individuals. The coercive, hostile, and undemocratic measures instituted to justify the notorious war on terror serve to deepen racial divides and infringe on human rights and social justice (Wallis and Fleras, 2009c). They have led to a strong global backlash of Islamophobia and Arabiphobia against individuals of Muslim or Arab background.

Conceptually, the ICR framework consists of four components or dimensions: constituent frameworks; sources and/or targets; intervention strategies; and change outcomes (see diagram). The chain of contexts posited within the ICR model creates a 'looping effect' (also 'feedback effect') between and among the four components. Whatever happens in any one component directly/indirectly affects and is affected by changes in the other components. The first dimension of the ICR model represents the various frameworks used for resolving structural or systemic issues. These frameworks constitute the operating units of the ICR model and they can be used with various client systems. The client systems can range from the individual or families through communities to supranational bodies, such as the United Nations Human Rights Council or the International Court of Justice. The constituent frameworks dimension of the ICR formulation demonstrates that there is opportunity for the simultaneous application of different frameworks to address a given social problem and achieve the goal of creating social change and a better society.

The second component of the model is the source and/or target component. This component reflects the fact that, although client systems are supposed to be the targets or focus of change, they can also be the source of personal or social problems because of the way they function or interact with other client systems or contexts. This dimension of the ICR model thus acknowledges as source and solution the interplay of social forces and individual experiences (see Fleras, 2010). To this end, integrative counter-racism approaches reject an either/or approach in favour of a both/and perspective, which embraces contextuality, connectedness, and simultaneity of unequal relations. The both/and strategies enable an ICR model to acknowledge the interplay of structure with agency (Dei, 2005).

Both/and strategies highlight the fact that all human relations are sites of personal or social problems. For instance, because individuals have multiple identities, due to their membership in various social divisions, they can be targets of oppression at one time and perpetrators of oppression under a different circumstance. A white woman may experience sexism for being female. However, her whiteness accords her privileges that a middle-class Chinese woman does not enjoy. Thus, whiteness insulates the white woman from privilege while the Chinese woman may bear 'the full brunt' of discrimination based on race. To address the problem of sexism or racism facing these two similar yet different individuals requires in-depth, holistic analyses of the privileges and power whiteness bequeaths to the white woman as well as the power and privilege a middle-class status gives to the Chinese woman, that is, in comparison to a poor, low-income Chinese woman.

Under the ICR formulation, accomplishing the ultimate goal of social change requires application of specific strategies, interventions, and methods of social transformation (third component of the ICR model). The type of strategies and techniques used will largely depend on the nature of the problem being addressed. However, because social problems overlap, no one method of work or intervention technique will ever be adequate to address the problem all by itself. Some combination of strategies will always be required to address a particular social problem regardless of the historical or spatial context. The final component of the ICR model – change outcomes – relates to the desired goal or outcome of the change process. Outcomes could be improvement in an individual's personal circumstances, de-racialized inter-group relations, changes in discriminatory social policies, unconstrained access to resources and opportunities, or improved bilateral or multilateral relations between and among nations.

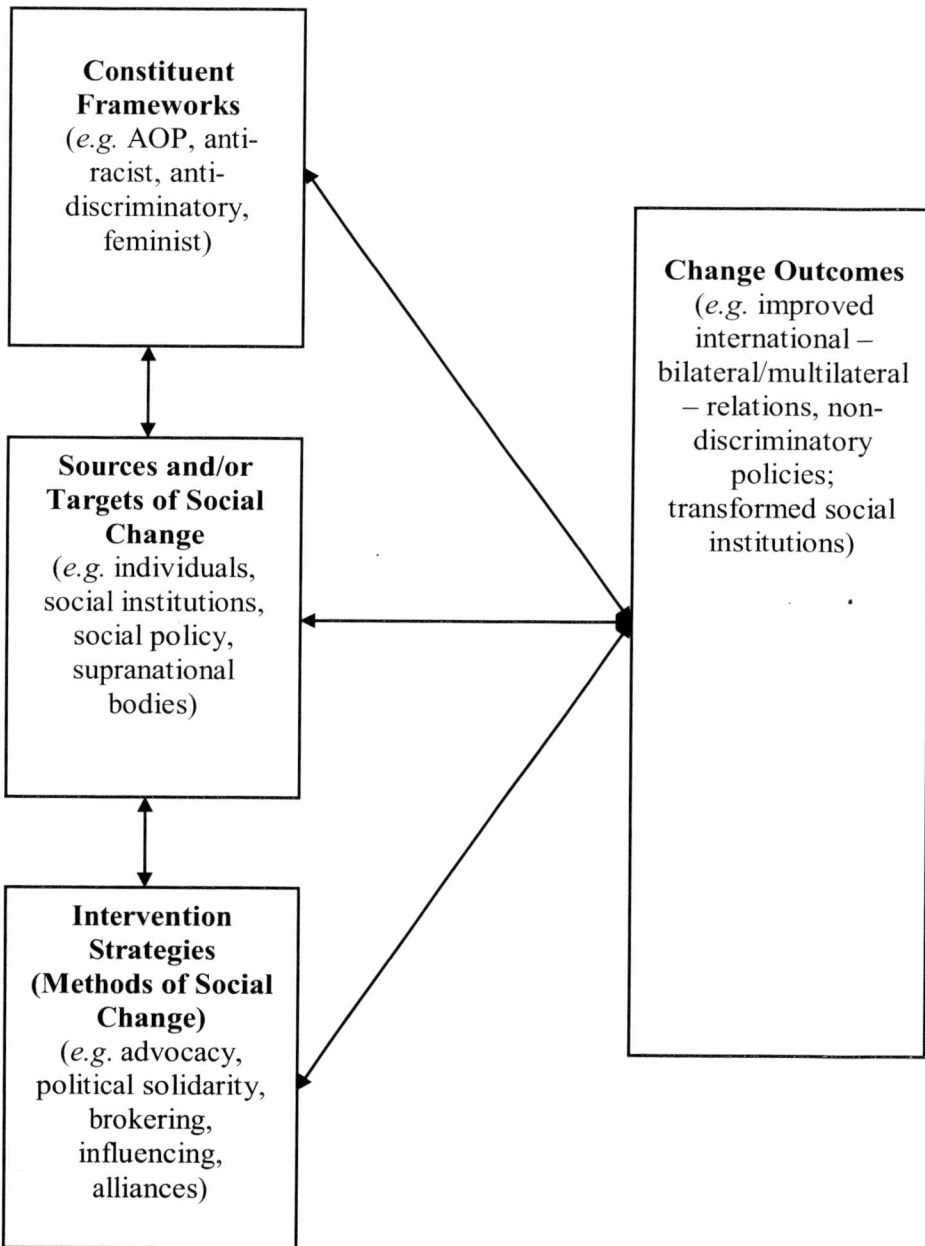

Constituent Frameworks
(*e.g.* AOP, anti-racist, anti-discriminatory, feminist)

Sources and/or Targets of Social Change
(*e.g.* individuals, social institutions, social policy, supranational bodies)

Intervention Strategies (Methods of Social Change)
(*e.g.* advocacy, political solidarity, brokering, influencing, alliances)

Change Outcomes
(*e.g.* improved international – bilateral/multilateral – relations, non-discriminatory policies; transformed social institutions)

Model of Integrative Counter-Racism Framework.

UTILITY AND PRACTICE IMPLICATIONS OF THE ICR MODEL

The ICR framework is a dynamic, utilitarian tool with many practical implications for both social activism and social work practice and education. The eclectic nature of the model affords both flexibility and opportunity to address complex social problems by combining different strategies and techniques in such a way that the strengths of the various approaches are accentuated while the limitations of any one approach are neutralized or offset by the strengths of the other approaches. Consider the following case scenario and how the ICR model can be applied to address the issues involved.

Abisiri (pseudonym) is an Iranian-born, single parent, Muslim woman living in New York City. She has worked at a private investment company as a financial advisor for ten years. She is always bypassed for promotion at her workplace. She does not know why she is not promoted and her supervisor has not given her any explanation. Given social location, Abisiri faces at least five intersecting forms of oppression at the same time – as an Arab (racism/Arabiphobia), woman (sexism), immigrant (xenophobia), Muslim (Islamophobia), and single parent (classism). Each of the markers of her identity makes her a minority and therefore a likely target for differential treatment and thus oppression. Strategies for addressing Abisiri's needs or problems that relied solely on one perspective (*e.g.* feminist, anti-sexist, or anti-classist approaches), will not be effective enough. To improve Abisiri's situation requires a social change approach that combined anti-oppression, anti-racist, feminist, anti-sexist, and anti-Islamophobia perspectives with empowerment and other frameworks. Such an approach should also be capable of conducting detailed micro-level analyses of personal problems. In sum, eclecticism is germane to efficacious utilization of the ICR framework.

Applying the ICR model to Abisiri's case would enable social workers to pull apart for detailed examination the factors that led to Abisiri's single-parent status, the causes or reasons for immigrating to America, and why she is bypassed for promotion. It would also assist practitioners in examining the connections between the various forms and the salience of each type of oppression she faces, and what needs to be done about each and all of the oppressions. Applying the ICR model may reveal that Abisiri is denied promotion because she does not demonstrate professional competence or a commendable work ethic as expected. In other words, her inability or failure to receive promotion may not be related to her minority status at all, or any marker of her identity for that matter. At the same time, however, the model can point out that she is not promoted because of her race, gender, or religion. Thus, the ICR framework can facilitate multifactor analyses of complex, interlocking social problems many of which are caused by racial prejudice or discrimination. Elsewhere (Danso, 2009a, 2009b), I have called for approaches to social change that address the intersection of racism, sexism, immigration status, and other sources of oppression holistically to ensure effective integration of racialized minorities.

In short, the above case scenario demonstrates that, within the ICR model, the salience of the factors that cause personal or structural problems can be assessed to ascertain the relative weight each factor contributes to a given personal or structural problem. Unlike many existing approaches some of which tend to subsume some factors (of identity) under others, the ICR model has the potential to enable multifactor analysis. To use a 'global' example, the model would enable analyses of how global events since September 11, 2001 have led to the development of anti-terrorist laws and stricter immigration policies and how they impact particular groups of people, especially Muslims and Arabs.

Existing structural frameworks often confine themselves to local or national-level analyses. As this chapter has demonstrated, racism and racial ideologies developed historically as integral parts of the systems of colonization, imperialism, capitalist expansion, and the insatiable desire by western European nations to forge empire by dominating the world, especially 'black Africa' and 'yellow Asia' (see Wallis and Fleras, 2009b). That worldwide system exists today, albeit in transformed, even sophisticated forms. The ICR model permits comparative analyses of historical and contemporary forms of race and racism and by so doing offers concrete guidelines for dealing with global and systemic-level problems.

Another practical advantage of the ICR model is that it does not focus only on working with or changing social structures and institutions. Instead, it is 'a generalist' model of practice that requires knowledge and skills for working with various client systems (*i.e.* individuals, families, groups, communities) and at different levels, including regional, national, and international contexts, and it always make the connection between the personal/local and the global. Thus, the ICR model builds on the feminist notion that personal experiences have their origins in political structures and that personal behaviour reflects and reinforces broader political processes (Dominelli, 2002c; Healy, 2005). The ICR model conceives the personal as the social and the local the global.

Although many structural problems are directly related to or caused by events in the international arena and affect nations and private citizens in much the same way, traditional frameworks do not always factor the global context into their analyses or examination of structural problems. One way of addressing 'international problems' (*e.g.* racism or terrorism), that is, factoring the global variable into the problem solving equation, is building political solidarity, coalitions, and alliances alongside the mobilization of international resources, both human and material. The international conference the United Nations organizes to fight racism, xenophobia, and intolerance serves as a good illustration. Two such conferences – the World Conference Against Racism, Racial Discrimination, Xenophobia and Related Intolerance and the Durban Review Conference (also known as Durban II) were held in Durban, South Africa (2001) and Geneva, Switzerland (2009) respectively. Such forums create opportunities for cooperation, dialogue, and negotiation, as well as sharing of ideas and strategies for solving global and national problems. The international tribunal set up to prosecute people who commit genocide or human rights violations provides another example.

In general, the ICR formulation does not just seek to change racist practices or racialized relations; more importantly, it strives to 'create a new society based on living together with our differences in ways that enhance diversity without sacrificing equality' (Fleras, 2005, p. 99). A key assumption of the ICR perspective is that race, class, gender and other markers of identity or social group membership are intertwined strands of a wider, more complex, and self-perpetuating system of privilege and power. This interdependence makes one fact very clear: if we really are serious about creating a new, inclusive, and egalitarian society based on the principle of treating people equally yet as equals, then reversing or detoxifying the toxic doings of race and racism must be confronted in a comprehensive and integrative manner (Fleras, 2010, p. 86).[8] An ICR approach offers such opportunities and possibilities.

---

[8] The term 'equality' is used in this chapter not in the liberal sense of everyone being equal in the same way – since that would not ensure fairness, and will end up being oppressive – but in the sense of changing social

APPLICATION OF THE ICR MODEL: GENERAL CONSIDERATIONS

The ICR framework is an action-oriented, advocacy tool for combating both historical and contemporary racisms. The framework seeks to connect broader questions about systemic racism to the (re)production of social oppression, domination, and the marginalization of vulnerable groups in North American society. Because racial ideologies often lie at the root of many social problems, changing oppressive social structures, policies, and relationships becomes a fundamental goal of integrative counter-racism social justice education and practice. Confronting contemporary racisms to undo their toxic doings must be a major goal of transformative (integrative) counter-racism social work practice. Race is one of the social paradoxes of the twenty-first century (Pascale, 2007). In both Canada and the United States, race is both central and submerged, both unimportant and all consuming, a social fabrication and a material reality. Therefore, if social workers/activists do not speak of race as a central entry point to integrative counter-racism social work practice, we cannot solve the problem of contemporary racisms (Dei, 2009). Naming race and asserting the rights of racialized groups should form an integral part of ICR-oriented strategies.

With its concern for social justice and commitment to working with people who have been oppressed by structural inequalities and assisting them to reverse the situation into which they have been forced (Dominelli, 2002a), the ICR perspective affords opportunities to develop effective methods of work to create a more inclusive and egalitarian North American soceity. The examples discussed in this chapter demonstrate that multiple forms of oppression frame racialized people's lives; therefore, combating racial oppression is better served by adopting a combined model or framework (see McDonald and Coleman, 1999; Keating, 2000; Dei, 2009). Samuel (2006) has suggested that only an integrative approach, such as the proposed ICR framework, has the capacity to deliver the good of changing both individual-level and institutional-level racisms with any hope of success.

Contesting systems of racism calls for a clear understanding that defective social systems and racialized relations are the source of social problems. Operating from the premise that society in generally oppressive (Healy, 2005; Mullaly, 2007), decolonizing projects utilizing the ICR framework should include transforming unequal social and power relations shaping social interactions between minorities and mainstream North American society into an egalitarian one (Dalrymple and Burke, 1995; Keating, 2000; Van wormer, 2004; Henry and Tator, 2006; Mullaly, 2007; Fleras, 2010). This transformation should demand a critical examination of the social conditions under which ethnic minorities are forced to live and an understanding of institutionalized and internalized operation (Moane, 2003).

Practitioners must recognize that control of, and access to social power determines access to resources and opportunities. It is the unequal distribution or control of power that are at the root of all social problems and injustices (Fleras, 2005), whether these are based on race, gender, class, ethnicity or some other characteristic of social group membership. Therefore, in resisting systems of racism and oppression, we need to go beyond merely acknowledging the material conditions that structure social inequalities to interrogate white power and privilege and its rationale for dominance and supremacy (Dei, 1996, 2009; McIntosh, 2007). Of course, feathers are ruffled and rights run thin when power and privilege are threatened (Dei, 2009).

---

structures, institutions, and systems as well as social relations that foster power sharing and redistribution (Dei, 1996).

However, the decolonization project will be successful only as it is able to address power imbalances and the differential access to social power in North American society (see Grabb, 2007). The ICR framework is an educational and political action-oriented strategy that requires political engagement rather than mere intellectual or academic philosophizing, or uncritical interrogation of processes that reproduce and sustain white dominance, power, and privilege (Dei, 1996, 2009; Graham, 2009). Unpacking the privileges whiteness accords white people is non-negotiable in the counter-racism project.

The understanding must be clear for practitioners and agents of social change: that social structures and institutions have been developed by the dominant culture to serve its interests, to meet its needs, and to maintain its power (Appleby, 2007b; Mullaly, 2007). For instance, politicians convince their constituencies to elect them to government, that is, transfer their decision-making power to them. Yet, after securing this power (mandate), many politicians betray the trust reposed in them. They play a major role in creating and implementing policies and legislations that disadvantage already vulnerable populations. Marginalized groups become further oppressed because they are deprived of a voice in policy decision-making mechanisms that affect their daily lives. Real authority and power must reside with the people to make their own decisions and determine their own destinies. The work for integrative counter-racism social workers, therefore, is to work towards preventing the conditions or processes that result in such oppressions. The goal and focus of this aspect of the change process is to empower disempowered groups so they can take control of their own lives (Danso, 2009a). This "act of empowerment is located in resistance to the consequences of marginalization" (Graham, 2004, p. 45) – silencing of voices, constrained access to social and political power, poverty, unemployment, substandard housing, poor health, psychological stress, and so on, which are the lived realities of racialized populations.

The rising significance of religion in contemporary public discourses, policy decision-making, economics, and geopolitics requires ICR activists to be capable of addressing religious-based discrimination, including anti-Semitism and Islamophobia and related oppressions such as the arabianization of terrorism, islamization of fundamentalism, and the muslimization of extremism. Social justice educators, students, researchers, and practitioners alike should lobby and advocate for social work interventions and practice principles that recognize the rights and freedoms of religious minorities, as enshrined in human rights codes and regulations. Such lobbying must critically examine the intersections of race, class, gender, ethnicity, and religious issues to provide an integrative understanding of oppression as well as individual and collective resistances (Calliste, 1996). Counter-racism activists should lobby and pressure national and supranational governments, authorities, policymakers, and human rights commissions to fully investigate complaints of Arabiphobia or anti-Semitism as systemic complaints and demand inquiry into racism in access to and delivery of culturally appropriate social services.

Rather than waiting to be prodded into action, social change agents must proactively interrogate the underlying causes of all forms of social oppression, including questioning the devaluing of the knowledge, credentials, and professional experience of immigrants, especially immigrants of colour and the silencing of certain voices in the workplace and in society (Danso, 2009a). In Canada, perhaps more so than in America, a new, systemic form of (occupational) racism is being perpetrated against immigrants of colour. This racism, ubiquitous across Canada, manifests itself in employers' uncompromising demand for Canadian experience. The unbending demand for Canadian experience is seen as discriminatory and unjust, especially if it is unrelated to an individual's industry or abilities. Is it ever possible for any newcomer to acquire Canadian experience without being hired by a Canadian employer? The demand for Canadian experience puts newcomers in a catch-22 quandary: without a job, newcomers cannot acquire Canadian experience, and without that experience, they are denied access to hiring and employment opportunities (Danso, 2009a). Using integrative strategies, we must question the role the state, private entities, and institutionalized practices play in normalizing such systemic, made-in-Canada racisms and discriminations.

Use of the ICR model to combat social injustices also necessitates the formation of broad-based, inter-ethnic alliances of community-led activists, lobbyists, and advocates (see Bishop, 2002; Kivel, 2007). Coalitions and alliances with different groups should use the stories and lived experiences of disadvantaged groups as entry points to analyze policies and practices that prop systems of oppression and generate alternatives to the status quo. Coalitions and partnerships with different groups can then develop these strategies further by drawing on the energies, differential insights, and diverse avenues to empower coalition members (Bell, 2007b; Danso, 2010). Alliances, with both oppressed and oppressor groups, should go beyond the oft-confused subject of identity politics to reframe the resistance effort as a "political project that engages directly with the structures into which [racism] is built to avoid a racist discourse that stresses identity, community, culture and tradition and neglects intersectionality, and most importantly, politics" (Lentin, 2000, pp. 104-5). The Civil Rights movement illustrates the power and potential of alliances and coalitions in bringing about social transformation.

As noted, alliances should not be limited to the domestic sphere only; they should extend to include the global context because global events have often been part of the 'axes of exploitation'. That the global is complicit in the oppression minorities and racialized people experience suggests that it should be both a target and source of social change. A case in point is the domination of western cultural values and the ever-growing power of transnational capital – even in areas such as China and eastern Europe, that have long been avowedly anti-capitalist (Stasiulis, 2009). Global capital has been implicated in the exploitation of local labour in the developing south.

A basis for forming global alliances could be the creation of a 'contact list' of global social activists. For instance, the growing international contact among feminists, and growing exposure to analyses by and about women in the developing world (Stasiulis, 2009), should provide an impetus for building international political solidarity and coalitions for feminists. One effect of such exposure, Stasiulis (2009) points out, has been to unmask the Eurocentric and anglicized assumptions about women's role in much North American and European feminist writing. According to Stasiulis (2009, p. 105), it is only by keeping in view the larger context of global and national economic, political, and social realities that any movement seeking to understand the complex intersections between gender, race, ethnicity, class, and religion can avoid becoming inward-looking and blandly pluralistic. Stasiulis emphasizes that a focus on the global can result in the development of a politics of social transformation that truly moves beyond the fragments.

Alliance building guided by bottom-up, grassroots philosophies as well as social movement strategies, and situated within a context of political organizing, mobilizing, and advocacy is indispensable because the decolonization project is by definition a political enterprise (Calliste, 1996; Haynes and Mickelson, 2006). Top-down approaches to social change are totalizing. Statsiulis sums it up when she states that totalizing politics are unrealistic and less effective than alliances based upon grassroots activism, whose social configuration is determined by the specific issue (Stasiulis, 2009, p. 105). Non-totalizing strategies should include creating groups and organizations to forge communities and cultures of resistance to oppose racialized hostility (Graham, 2004). By creating groups and organizations, social workers and activists can make a big difference by helping to use local approaches, including social action to problem solving.

Consensus becomes a major issue in alliance building and political organizing. Oftentimes, consensus is needed for change to happen. While consensus is important, it is not always a sufficient condition for building political solidarity. As agents of social transformation, we cannot always have unanimous decisions on every single issue to initiate change. Numbers matter but we can and must initiate change whenever the need arises, with or without consensus. In other words, social activists can play two interrelated roles in bringing about social transformation – as *initiators*, who originate the change process and as *catalysts*, who accelerate the process.[9]

Even as social workers fight to eradicate racisms and systems of oppression, they need to ensure that in their own work with client groups, their services are provided in an ethnically sensitive and non-oppressive manner. Practitioners using ICR approaches to undo the crippling effects of race and racism ought to be aware that culture is dynamic and that people are embedded in a complex web of cultures and identities, which intersect with and are affected by an equally complex array of factors. Ethnocentric inclinations and monolithic approaches to social change will be counterproductive. Therefore, conceptualizations of culturally competent practice that pathologize and focus only on 'ethnic clients' without factoring the dominant (white) society into the equation, and which also assume the 'expert', Anglo-Americanized identity of the worker and the 'pathologized ethnic' client (Williams and Soydan, 2005; Williams, 2006), are myopic in focus. Such conceptualizations often have a Eurocentric bias and perceive ethno-racialized clients as 'the problem' such that merely knowing about minorities' cultures would enable the (white) social worker or activist to develop effective assessment tools and intervention plans for positive outcomes in the work with racialized clients. This is dangerous and would seriously limit the effectiveness of the resistance effort.

The social work role is an intensely political one in which practitioners occupy a privileged status, at least in contrast to clients (Rossiter, 2001; Healy, 2005; Heron, 2005). In fact, all social work is political (Haynes and Mickelson, 2006). As such, practitioners seeking to transform oppressive social structures and relations and undermine supremacist beliefs and practices should be careful not to counteract or neutralize their own work. Oppression is oppression no matter who the oppressor is or the source of the oppression. Counter-racism activists must adopt an ongoing reflective stance on their position within social structures to minimize the disempowering effects and consequences of their social divisions and to avoid reproducing oppressive social relations in program planning and service delivery (Colvin-

---

[9] The term 'catalyst' is not used here in the chemistry sense of a substance or agent that precipitates an action without undergoing change itself. Rather, I employ the term to denote the transformative role people can play in the social change process. I argue that the change process is very dynamic and powerful and that agents of social transformation affect (change) and are affected (changed) by any change process. Otherwise, they contribute to entrenching the oppressive status quo; they become oppressors themselves, contrary to their stated goals or aspirations.

Burque *et al.*, 2007). Critical consciousness can energize and empower individuals and groups to speak boldly about social injustices and draw the public into the fight against the new (democratic) racisms (Diemer *et al.*, 2006). Challenging one's socio-political location as well as that of dominant institutions, practices, and ideologies has become an important tool for real social change (Green and Sonn, 2006). In short, ICR practitioners must be prepared to be affected or changed by the very change process they are employing to create a more just and egalitarian society.

Structured and targeted intervention programs can also provide support for challenging contemporary racisms (Diemer *et al.*, 2006). Race and racism are unsettling issues for many people, especially white people (Dei, 1999, 2009; Samuel and Wane, 2005). Many white people try to avoid these subjects by being perfunctory or politically correct. Social workers would be perpetuating the racialized/racist status quo if they too tried to be defensive, acquiescent, or 'toed the line'. If social workers do their work well, the anger and "poison that [sit] inside people in regards to race, class, gender, etc. will come to the surface" (Vazquez, 2006, p. 186, see James, 2007). Political correctness will go away as a result and honest, authentic engagement and dialogue will occur. Genuine social transformation and a true post-race Garden of Eden will have become a reality in North America. We must not postpone the fight to detoxify the pernicious doings of either historical or contemporary racisms; the time for meaningful action is now.

CONCLUSION

Race is one of the paradoxes of human history. Race is as chameleonic as it is oxymoronic; it is the ever-changing constant in North America. Race is what it is not. Race mattered historically; it matters now. Race enables and disables; it defines a person's position in society and puts him/her there. Almost no one believes in race; still race continues to be central yet submerged, unimportant, yet, all-consuming, a social fabrication, yet, a material reality. Although race is a familiar part of the social landscape, it remains conflicted in meanings and unrestrained by the demands of logic, proof, or coherence (Pascale, 2007; Wallis and Fleras, 2009b; Fleras, 2010). In North America, as in all racist societies, social rewards are allocated on the basis of membership in a racial group, such that race remains a key organizing principle and predictor in defining who gets what where when (Hier and Bolaria, 2007; Wallis and Fleras, 2009b). Race has grave material consequences for racialized groups. Racialized bodies bear the brunt of negative treatment, ranging from snubs, to half-hearted, ethnically-insensitive service delivery, to blatant racisms resulting in class-action race-based discrimination lawsuits (Dei, 2007, cited in Fleras, 2010; Hussain, 2007, cited in Wallis and Fleras, 2009b). Almost everything with a human imprint or touch to it is raced or racialized, a system so constructed to privilege and empower members of the white culture.

Historically, race and racism existed in a crude, unalloyed state, socially endorsed and legally sustained by a system of state policies and regulations. This institutionalized system sanctioned segregation in housing, schools, theatres, bars, buses, and many other areas of social life in North America. While the invention of race proved beneficial to the dominant white culture, bestowing unearned privileges and power on whiteness, racial ideologies and racialized relations proved devastating for racialized populations. While immigration policies sought to create a 'white North America', and the one-drop of blood ideology tabooed racial mixing (*i.e.* interracial marriages), other policies denigrated racialized bodies, treating them, especially blacks, as non-humans. Historically, whites associated blacks with animalism, savagery, and bestiality.

Today, as Canadian and American societies have progressed, so, too, have race and racism transformed themselves by acquiring a refined status that makes them more subtle, covert, and difficult to identify. Contemporary racisms articulate themselves primarily through the medium of democratic racism, which is propped by a host of myths and discourses, including the discourse of denial, the discourse of equal opportunity, and the discourse of blaming the victim. Others include the discourse of reverse racism, the discourse of multiculturalism, and the discourse of national identity.

Two virulent strains of racism have recently emerged in North America and the west – Islamophobia and Arabiphobia – especially since the events of September 11, 2001. Both forms of racism are directed at Islam and people who practice the Islamic religion (Muslims) as well as people from Arab backgrounds. Islamophobia denigrates Islam as a religion that breeds violence and fundamentalism, while branding Muslims as extremists, and Arabs as terrorists. Arabiphobia denotes racializing processes, attitudes, perceptions, and tendencies that demonize Islam and Arab cultures in general. In doing so, Arabiphobia conveniently ignores the pioneering role and contributions of the Arab world to the advancement of human society – in science, mathematics, algebra, and astronomy. That Arabiphobia has created a strong backlash against Arabs and Muslims, especially in the west, needs no reiteration. Suffice it to say that Arabiphobia has put Arabs and Muslims under a global scrutiny that has excluded them from full membership and participation in North American society and elsewhere in the west.

These degrading experiences are not unique to Arabs or Muslims alone; other racialized minorities, especially blacks, encounter them to various degrees in North America. For blacks, the long history of the slavery they endured differentiates their experiences with race-discrimination from those of other ethnic minorities. For blacks in North America, their marginalization and oppression are largely the result of their being 'othered' by the dominant white group. Now, as historically, entrenched institutional, systemic, and individual racist ideologies and racialization practices have entrenched and 'normalized' processes that exclude blacks, relegating them to a 'footnote' status in North American society. Far from belittling the oppressions other racialized groups have faced, the fact remains that, in the history of the world, no other racialized bodies were ever forcibly transported by the shipload across oceans and between continents to be permanently enslaved as was done to blacks in North America. The vestiges of this dehumanizing treatment still abide in and haunt the black psyche despite improvements in their situation in North American society. Race and racism remain significant factors that pose formidable challenges to racialized peoples in Canada and America, yet many Canadians revel in a self-gratifying perception that Canada is a raceless society, while Americans relish a belief that America is a merit-based rather than a colour-conscious country. Some writers and commentators have been deluded by a false optimism into believing that North America has ushered itself into a post-race utopia where race has lost all its salience, potency, and tenacity. Many beg to differ because there is no evidence to suggest that North America now enjoys a restored Garden of Eden.

Unquestionably, improvements have occurred in recent times for racialized groups in North America. After centuries of racially motivated discrimination, stereotypes, and exclusionary policies, change came to America in November 2008, when the country elected its first racialized individual, Barack Obama, an African American, as president. Three years prior, in September 2005, Canada had appointed the first black person, Michaëlle Jean, as the country's Governor General. The remarkable thing about Jean's case is that she is also the first black woman ever appointed to the gubernatorial office.

Although significant and historic, the extent to which such events bespeak a post-race Shangri-La in North American history is open to debate. Drawing on many recent developments and examples, this chapter has demonstrated that North America is far from being a monochromatic society. The existence of laws criminalizing racially motivated discrimination and hate crimes is proof that race and racism are alive and well in North America, albeit in muted and covert forms. Race and racism remain resilient largely because North American society continues to function and individuals continue to behave in ways that suggest race will always matter in inter-group relations and public discourses. According to Wallis and Fleras (2009b), a race-neutral North America will continue to remain a mirage until both whites and racialized minorities acknowledge the hegemonic system in which they operate, the degree to which whiteness permeates every issue and institution in society, and how white privilege defines the distribution of resources and opportunities as well as access to the rewards of society.

From the earliest times imaginable, and especially following the invention of race, much of the adventure called the human expereince has been nothing but suffering, heartaches, hatred, and injustices. For much of the time humans have inhabited planet earth, it has been one group dominating, exploiting, or oppressing another. However, the invention of race culminated in the establishment of a social and political system by which the world's populations were randomly pigeonholed and thrust into a hierarchical arrangement of races in which the 'pure', 'civilized' white race always occupied the top rung and dominated the rest of humanity. Obviously, it still has not dawned on humanity to try to live without oppression for even the minutest fraction of the time life has existed on earth to see what difference peace, harmony, respect, and unity can make. So, how about de-racing race, recalibrating the vitriolic vilification of difference as a devil and embracing its worth, and above all letting fairness roll on like a river and social justice as a never-failing stream? Why is it so difficult for us – so-called rational thinking beings, as opposed to lower forms of life – to accept the stark reality that we are differently similar to each other, and that the beauty of life itself resides in the diversity that characterizes and defines human society, that is, human existence?

Because racism is a complex, multiform system, traditional approaches, often used in a stand-alone fashion, have not been effective enough in dismantling this crippling system. Single methodologies are not effective in addressing overlapping systems of oppression; structurally interlocking problems require structurally integrative solutions. Therefore, our best hope of creating a better and more inclusive society lies in integrative methodologies, such as the integrative counter-racism (ICR) framework introduced in this chapter. Integrative counter-racism frameworks have great promise to transform North America into a truly egalitarian society. Only then can we realistically speak of a post-race era in the history of this vast continent with its array of cultures, ethnicities, geographies, and histories.

In undertaking the emancipating project, the need to integrate counter-racist resistance and scholarship with democratic and social justice traditions becomes supreme, given the refined and ubiquitous forms of contemporary racisms (Wallis and Fleras, 2009c). Such a strategy, Paul Gilroy states, will "make a different inventory of political tasks around 'race' and to undertake them in a new spirit" (Gilroy, 2000, p. 335). The new national and global racial hegemony of the twenty-first century presents many significant challenges to the resistance effort yet must we soldier on until the world becomes a better place to live. Together, as counter-racist activists, practitioners, and scholars, we can challenge the contradictions and hypocrisies of liberal societies, including North American society, while maintaining our focus on the exploited, the devalued, the sidelined, and the oppressed (Wallis and Fleras, 2009c). We must reinvent resistance to racial inequality, and all forms of social injustice and oppression and to build and sustain the hope for a just and egalitarian world. The time when we must intensify the resistance project and detoxify the toxic systems of racism and oppression is now! Integrative counter-racism strategies offer the best hope of a solution.

REFERENCES

Agnew, V. (2007). Introduction. In: Agnew, V. (Ed.), *Interrogating Race and Racism* (3-136). Toronto: University of Toronto Press.

Al-Krenawi, A. & Graham, J. R. (2003). Social work practice with Canadians of Arab background: Insight into direct practice. In: A. Al-Krenawi, & J. R. Graham, (Eds.), *Multicultural Social Work in Canada: Working with Diverse Ethno-racial Communities* (174-201). Don Mills, ON: Oxford University Press.

Alliance of Civilizations (2006). *Research Base for the High-Level Group Report: Analysis on Media.* New York: United Nations.

Andersen, M. L. & Collins, P. H. (2007a). Why race, class, and gender still matter. In: M. L. Andersen, & P. H. Collins, (Eds.), *Race, Class, & Gender: An Anthology* (6th ed., 1-16). Belmont, CA: Thomson Wadsworth.

Andersen, M. L. & Collins, P. H. (2007b). Systems of power and inequality. In: M. L. Andersen, & P. H. Collins, (Eds.), *Race, Class, & Gender: An Anthology* (6th ed., 61-90). Belmont, CA: Thomson Wadsworth.

Appleby, G. A. (2007a). Framework for practice with diverse and oppressed clients. In: G. A., Appleby, E. Colon, & J. Hamilton, (Eds.), *Diversity, Oppression, and Social Functioning: Person-in-Environment Assessment and Intervention* (2nd ed., 1-15). Boston: Pearson Education, Inc.

Appleby, G. A. (2007b). Dynamics of oppression and discrimination. In: G. A., Appleby, E. Colon, & J. Hamilton, (Eds.), *Diversity, Oppression, and Social Functioning: Person-in-Environment Assessment and Intervention* (2nd ed., 52-67). Boston: Pearson Education, Inc.

Arat-Koç, S. (2010). Whose transnationalism? Canada: "Clash of civilizations" discourse, and Arab and Muslim Canadians. In: M. A., Wallis, L. Sunseri, & G. E. Galabuzi, (Eds.), *Colonialism and Racism in Canada: Historical Traces and Contemporary Issues,* (266-283). Toronto: Nelson Education Ltd.

Association of Black Law Enforcers (2003). *Official Position on 'Racial Profiling' in Canada.* Toronto: Association of Black Law Enforcers.

Aulakh, R. (2009). Woman hopes DNA unlocks Kenya trap. *Toronto Star*, Wednesday, July 22, A1 and A15.

Aylward, C. (2009). Canadian critical race litigation: Wedding theory and practice. In: M. Wallis, & A. Fleras, (Eds.), *The Politics of Race in Canada: Readings in Historical Perspectives, Contemporary Realities, and Future Possibilities* (209-216). Don Mills, ON: Oxford University Press.

Banton, M. (2000). Racism today. *Ethnic and Racial Studies, 22(92)*, 606-615.

Barnoff, L. & Moffatt, K. (2007). Contradictory tensions in anti-oppression practice in feminist social services. *Affilia: Journal of Women and Social Work, 22(1)*, 56-70.

Bell, L. A. (2007a). Overview: Twenty-first century racism. In: M., Adams, L. A. Bell, & P. Griffin, (Eds.), *Teaching for Diversity and Social Justice* (2nd ed., 118-122). New York: Routledge.

Bell, L. A. (2007b). Theoretical foundations for social justice education. In: M., Adams, L. A. Bell, & P. Griffin, (Eds.), *Teaching for Diversity and Social Justice* (2nd ed., 1-14). New York: Routledge Taylor & Francis Group.

Bell, L. A., Love, B. J. & Roberts, R. A. (2007). Racism and white privilege curriculum design. In: M., Adams, L. A. Bell, & P. Griffin, (Eds.), *Teaching for Diversity and Social Justice* (2nd ed., 123-144). New York: Routledge.

Berry, B. & Bonilla-Silva, E. (2007). 'They should hire the one with the best score': White sensitivity to qualification differences in affirmative action hiring decisions. *Ethnic and Racial Studies, 31(2)*, 215-242.

Bishop, A. (2002). *Becoming an Ally: Breaking the Cycle of oppression in People* (2nd ed.). Halifax: Fernwood Publishing.

Black, J. H. & Erickson, L. (2006). Ethno-racial origins of candidates and electoral performance: Evidence from Canada. *Party Politics, 12(4)*, 541-561.

Bonilla-Silva, E. (2003). Racism Without Racists: Color-Blind Racism and the Persistence of Racial Inequality in the United States. Lanham, MD: Rowman and Littlefield Publishers.

Boushel, M. (2000). What kind of people are we? 'Race', anti-racism and social welfare research. *British Journal of Social Work, 30(1)*, 71-89.

Brattain, M. (2007). Race, racism, and antiracism: UNESCO and the politics of presenting science to the postwar public. *American Historical Review, 112(5)*, 1-53.

Bullock, K. & Jafri, G. (2001). Media (mis)representations: Muslim women in the Canadian nation. *Canadian Woman Studies, 20(2)*, 35-40.

Cainkar, L. (2004). The impact of 9/11 on Muslims and Arabs in the United States. In: Tirman, J. (Ed.), *The Maze of Fear: Security & Migration after September 11* (215-239): New York: The New Press

Cainkar, L. (2006). Space and place in the metropolis: Arabs and Muslims seeking safety. *City and Society, 17(2)*, 181-209.

California Newsreel (2003). *Race–The Power of an Illusion.* Available online at http://www.pbs.org/race

Calliste, A. (1996). Antiracism organizing and resistance in nursing: African-Canadian women. *The Canadian Review of Sociology and Anthropology, 33(3)*, 361-390.

Carey, G. (2006). Race – social, biological, or lemonade? *American Psychologist, 61(2)*, 176.

Casey, D. (2009). White South African granted refugee status. Available online at http://www.ottawasun.com/news/ottawa/2009/08/28/10659546.html.Retrieved September 6, 2009.

Cashmore, E. (Ed.) (1996). *Dictionary of Race and Ethnic Relations* (4th ed.). London and New York: Routledge.

Chan, S. & Peters, J. W. (2009). Chimp-stimulus cartoon raises racism concerns. *The New York Times*, February 18. Available online at http://cityroom.blogs.nytimes. com/2009/ 02/18/chimp-stimulus-cartoon-raises-racism-concerns/. Retrieved August 19, 2009.

Chappell, R. (2006). *Social Welfare in Canadian Society* (3rd ed.). Toronto: Thomson Nelson.

CNN (Cable News Network) (2009). Charge against Harvard professor dropped. June 21. Available online at http://www.cnn.com/2009/CRIME/07/21/massachusetts.harvard. professor.arrested/. Retrieved August 10, 2009.

Coates, R. D. (2008). Covert racism in the USA and globally. *Sociology Compass, 2(1)*, 208-231.

Cohen, P. N. & Huffman, M. L. (2007). Black under-representation in management across U.S. labor markets. *The Annals of the American Academy of Political and Social Sciences, 609(1)*, 181-199.

Colvin-Burque, A. Zugazaga, C. B. & Davis-Maye, D. (2007). Can cultural competence be taught? Evaluating the impact of the soap model, *Journal of Social Work Education, 43(2)*, 223-241.

Cooper, A. (2009). Acts of resistance: Black men and women engage slavery in Upper Canada, 1793-1803. In: Wallis, M. & Fleras, A. (Eds.), *The Politics of Race in Canada: Readings in Historical Perspectives, Contemporary Realities, and Future Possibilities* (239-249). Don Mills, ON: Oxford University Press.

Corcoran, B. (2009). *Refugee status of white South African in Canada condemned*, September 2. Available online at http://www.irishtimes.com/newspaper/world/2009/ 0902/1224253 665847.html. Retrieved September 9, 2009.

Crenshaw, K. (1997). Color-blind dreams and racial nightmares: Reconfiguring racism in the post-civil rights era. In: Morrison, T. & Lacour, C. B. (Eds.), *Birth of Nation'Hood: Gaze, Script, and Spectacle in the O. J. Simpson Case* (97-168). New York: Pantheon Books.

Cresswell, T. (1996). *In Place/Out of Place: Geography, Ideology, and Transgression*. Minneapolis: University of Minnesota Press.

Curtis, A., Mills, J. W., Kennedy, B., Fotheringham, S. & McCarthy, T. (2007). Understanding the geography of post-traumatic stress: An academic justification for using a spatial video acquisition system in the response to Hurricane Katrina. *Journal of Contingencies and Crisis Management, 15(4)*, 208-219.

Dalrymple, J. & Burke, B. (1995). *Anti-oppressive Practice: Social Care and the Law*. Buckingham: Open University Press.

Danso, R. (2009a). Emancipating and empowering de-valued skilled immigrants: What hope does anti-oppressive social work practice offer? *British Journal of Social Work, 39(3)*, 539-555.

Danso, R. (2009b). *Restoring Human Functioning: Impact of Social Policy and Social Networks in the Resettlement and Integration of Refugees in Western Societies*. Köln, Germany: Lambert Academic Publishing.

Danso, R. (2010, forthcoming). Diversity in the field. In: Drolet, J., Clark, N. & Allen, H. (Eds.), *Canadian Field Experiences and Practices*. Don Mills, ON: Pearson Education Canada.

Danso, R. & Grant, M. (2000). Access to housing as an adaptive strategy for immigrant groups: Africans in Calgary. *Canadian Ethnic Studies, 32(3)*, 19-43.

Danso, R. & McDonald, D. A. (2001). Writing xenophobia: Immigration and the print media in post-apartheid South Africa. *Africa Today, 48(3)*, 114-137.

Darden, J. (2005). Black occupational achievement in the Toronto Census Metropolitan Area: Does race matter? *The Review of Black Political Economy, 33(2)*, 31-54.

Das, Gupta, T., James, C. E., Maaka, R., Galabuzi, G. E. & Andersen, C. (Eds.) (2007). *Race and Racialization: Essential Readings*. Toronto: Canadian Scholars' Press.

Davis, M. (1992). *City of Quartz: Excavating the Future in Los Angeles*. New York: Vintage Books.

De Parle, J. (2007). Broken levees, unbroken barriers. In: Andersen, M. L. & Collins, P. H. (Eds.), *Race, Class, & Gender: An Anthology* (6th ed., 143-146). Belmont, CA: Thomson Wadsworth.

Dei, G. J. S. (1996). *Anti-racism Education: Theory and Practice*. Halifax: Fernwood Publishing.

Dei, G. J. S. (1999). The denial of difference: Reframing anti-racist praxis. *Race, Education and Ethnicity, 2(1)*, 17-37.

Dei, G. J. S. (2005). Anti-racist education-Moving yet standing still. Editorial commentary. *Directions, 3(1)*, 6-9.

Dei, G. J. S. (2009). Speaking race: Silence, salience, and the politics of anti-racist scholarship. In: Wallis, M. & Fleras, A. (Eds.), *The Politics of Race in Canada: Readings in Historical Perspectives, Contemporary Realities, and Future Possibilities* (230-238). Don Mills, ON: Oxford University Press.

Delisle, E. (1993). *The Traitor and the Jew: Anti-Semitism and Extremist Right-wing Nationalism in French Canada from 1929 to 1939*. Montreal: Robert Davies Publishing.

Diemer, M. A., Kauffman, A., Koenig, N., Trahan, E. & Hsieh, C. A. (2006). Challenging racism, sexism, and social injustice: Support for urban adolescents' critical consciousness development. *Cultural Diversity and Ethnic Minority Psychology, 12(3)*, 444-460.

Doane, A. (2006). What is racism? *Racial Discourse and Racial Politics, 32* (2-3), 255-275.

Doane, A. (2007). The changing politics of colour-blind racism. In: Coates, R. D. & Dennis, R. M. (Eds.), *The New Black: Alternative Paradigms and Strategies for the 21st Century* (Research in Race and Ethnic Relations, *14*, 159-174). Oxford, UK: JAI Press, Inc.

Dominelli, L. (1997). *Anti-Racist Social Work* (2nd ed.). London: Macmillan.

Dominelli, L. (2002a). Anti-oppressive practice in context. In: R., Adams, L. Dominelli, & M. Payne, (Eds.), *Social Work: Themes, Issues and Critical Debates* (2nd ed., 3-19). Basingstoke: Palgrave Macmillan.

Dominelli, L. (2002b). *Anti-Oppressive Social Work Theory and Practice*. Basingstoke: Palgrave Macmillan.

Dominelli, L. (2002c). *Feminist Social Work: Theory and Practice*. (Basingstoke: Palgrave Macmillan.

Dovidio, J. F. & Gaertner, S. L. (2004). Aversive racism. In: Zanna, M. P. (Ed.), *Advances in Experimental Social Psychology* (vol. 36, 1-52). San Diego, CA: Academic Press.

Dua, E., Razack, N. & Warner, J. N. (2005). Race, racism, and empire: Reflections on Canada. *Social Justice, 32(4)*, 1-10.

Dunn, K. M., Klockerm, N. & Salabay, T. (2007). Contemporary racism and Islamophobia in Australia. *Ethnicities, 7(4)*, 564-589.

Fanon, F. (1967) [1952]. *Black Skin, White Masks* (English translation by Charles Lam Markmann). New York: Grove Press.

Fleras, A. (2004). Racializing culture/culturalizing race: Multicultural racism in a multicultural Canada. In: Nelson, C. A. & Nelson, C. A. (Eds.), *Racism, Eh? A Critical Interdisciplinary Anthology of Race and Racism in Canada* (429-443). Concord, ON: Captus Press.

Fleras, A. (2005). *Social Problems in Canada: Conditions, Constructions, and Challenges* (4th ed.). Toronto: Pearson Education Canada, Inc.

Fleras, A. (2010). *Unequal Relations: An Introduction to Race, Ethnic, and Aboriginal Dynamics in Canada* (6th ed.). Toronto: Pearson Education Canada.

Ford, C. & Delaney, J. (2008). Is official multiculturalism failing in its own heartland? *Epoch Times* January 3. Available online at http://en.epochtimes.com/news/8-1-3/63557.html. Retrieved August 10, 2009.

Forgette, R., King, M. & Dettrey, B. (2009). Race, Hurricane Katrina, and government satisfaction: Examining the role of race in assessing blame. *Publius, 38(4)*, 671-691.

Foster, C. (1996). *The Meaning of Being Black in Canada*. Toronto: Harper Collins Publishers Ltd.

Foster, C. (2005). *Where Race Does Not Matter: The New Spirit of Modernity*. Toronto: Penguin.

Frost, D. (2008). Islamophobia: Examining causal links between the state and 'race hate' from 'below'. *International Journal of Sociology and Social Policy, 28 (11/12)*, 546-563.

Gaertner, S. L. & Dovidio, J. F. (1986). The aversive forms of racism. In: S. L. Gaertner, & J. F. Dovidio, (Eds.), *Prejudice, Discrimination and Racism* (61-89). New York: Academic Press.

Galabuzi, G. E. (2006). *Canada's Economic Apartheid: The Social Exclusion of Racialized Groups in the New Century*. Toronto: Canadian Scholars' Press.

George, U. (2000). Toward anti-racism in social work in the Canadian context. In: Calliste, A. & Dei, G. J. S. (Eds.), *Anti-Racist Feminism: Critical Race and Gender Studies* (111-122). Halifax: Fernwood Publishing.

Gilroy, P. (1990). The end of anti-racism. *New Community, 17(1)*, 71-83.

Gilroy, P. (2000). *Against Race: Imagining Political Culture Beyond the Colour Line*. Cambridge, MA: Harvard University Press.

Goddard, H. (2009). 'This nightmare will be over'. *Toronto Star*, Wednesday, August 12, p. A6. Goldberg, D. T. (2002). Racial states. In: D. T. Goldberg, & J. Solomos, (Eds.), *A Companion to Racial and Ethnic Studies* (233-258). Malden, MA: Blackwell.

Goldberg, D. T. (2006). Racial Europeanization. *Ethnic and Racial Studies, 29(2)*, 331-364.

Goldberg, D. T. & Solomos, J. (Eds.) (2002). *A Companion to Racial and Ethnic Studies*. Malden, MA: Blackwell.

Gottschalk, P. & Greenberg, G. (2008). *Islamophobia: Making Muslims the Enemy*. Toronto: Rowman and Littlefield Publishers.

Grabb, Edward G. (2007). *Theories of Social Inequality* (5th ed.). Toronto: Nelson.

Graham, M. (2004). Empowerment revisited – Social work, resistance and agency in black communities. *European Journal of Social Work, 7(1)*, 43-56.

Graham, M. (2009). Reframing black perspectives in social work: New directions? *Social Work Education, 28(3)*, 268-280.

Green, M. J. & Sonn, C. C. (2006). Problematising the discourses of the dominant: Whiteness and reconciliation. *Journal of Community and Applied Social Psychology, 16(5)*, 379-395.

Hall, R. E. (2005). Eurocentrism in social work: From race to identity across the lifespan as biracial alternative. *Journal of Social Work, 5(1)*, 101-114.

Hamilton, J. (2007). Racism: African Americans and Caribbean islanders. In: G. A., Appleby, E. Colon, & J. Hamilton, (Eds.), *Diversity, Oppression, and Social Functioning: Person-in-Environment Assessment and Intervention* (2nd ed., 68-92). Boston: Pearson Education, Inc.

Hanson, J. (2009). He's a banana-eating monkey, but I'm not a racist. *The Situationist*, August 3. Available online at http://thesituationist.wordpress.com/2009/08/03/hes-a-banana-eating- monkey-but-im-not-a-racist/. Retrieved August 10, 2009.

Harper, S., Lynch, J., Burris, S. & Smith, G. D. (2007). Trends in the black-white life expectancy in the United States, 1983-2003. *Journal of the American Medical Association, 297(11)*, 1224-1232.

Haynes, K. S. & Mickelson, J. S. (2006). *Affecting Change: Social Workers in the Political Arena* (6th ed.). Boston: Pearson Education, Inc.

Healy, K. (2005). *Social Work Theories in Context: Creating Frameworks for Practice*. Basingstoke: Palgrave Macmillan.

Helms, J. E., Jernigan, M. & Mascher, J. (2005). The meaning of race in psychology and how to change it. A methodological imperative. *American Psychologist, 60(1)*, 27-36.

Henry, F. & Tator, C. (2006). *The Colour of Democracy: Racism in Canadian Society* (3rd ed.). Toronto: Nelson Thompson.

Henry, F., Tator, C., Mattis, W. & Rees, T. (2009). The ideology of racism. In: M. Wallis, & A. Fleras, (Eds.), *The Politics of Race in Canada: Readings in Historical Perspectives, Contemporary Realities, and Future Possibilities* (108-118). Don Mills, ON: Oxford University Press.

Heron, B. (2005). Self-reflection in critical social work practice: Subjectivity and the possibilities of resistance. *Reflective Practice, 6(3)*, 341-351.

Hernstein, R. J. & Murray, C. (1994). *The Bell Curve: Intelligence and Class Structure in American Society*. New York: Free Press.

Hier, P. S. & Bolaria, B. S. (Eds.) (2007). *Race and Racism in 21st Century Canada: Continuity, Complexity, and Change*. Peterborough, ON: Broadview Press.

Hodson, G., Hooper, H., Dovidio, J. F. & Gaetner, S. L. (2005). Aversive racism in Britain: The use of inadmissible evidence in legal decisions. *European Journal of Social Psychology, 35(4)*, 437-448.

Horton, J. O. & Horton, L. E. (2004). *Slavery and the Making of America*. New York: Oxford University Press.

Howarth, C. (2006). Race as stigma: Positioning the stigmatized as agents, not objects. *Journal of Community and Applied Social Psychology, 16(6)*, 442-451.

Hume, C. (2009). Is citizenship now defined by the colour of your skin? *Toronto Star*, Wednesday, August 12, A6.

Ibish, H. & Stewart, A. (2003). *Report on Hate Crimes and Discrimination Against Arab Americans: The Post-September 11 Backlash,* September 11, 2001-October 11, 2001. Washington, DC: American-Arab Anti-Discrimination Committee.

Ignatiev, N. & Garvey, J. (1996). Editorial. Abolish the white race by any means possible. In: Ignatiev, N. & Garvey, J. (Eds.), *Race Traitor* (9-11). Routledge, New York and London.

James, R. (2007). Trip leaves group changed forever: Descendants deal with emotional fallout of slave dungeon. *The Toronto Star*, March 19. Available online at http://www.thestar.com/article/193489. Retrieved June 29, 2009.

Johal, G. (2005). Order in KOS: On race, rage, and method. In: G. Dei, & G. Johal, (Eds.), *Critical Issues in Anti-racist Research Methodology* (269-293). New York: Peter Lang.

Johnson, J. D., Olivo, N., Nathan, G., William, R. & Leslie, A. N. (2009). Priming media stereotypes reduces support for social welfare policies: The mediating role of empathy. *Personality and Social Psychology Bulletin, 35(4)*, 463-476.

Jordan, G. & Weedon, C. (1995). *Cultural Politics: Class, Gender, Race and the Postmodern World.* Oxford: Blackwell.

Kaiser, C. R., Eccleston, C. P. & Hagiwara, N. (2008). Post-Hurricane Katrina racialized explanations as a system threat: Implications for whites' and blacks' racial attitudes. *Social Justice Research, 21(2)*, 192-203.

Keating, F. (2000). Anti-racist Perspectives: What are the gains for social work? *Social Work Education, 19(1)*, 77-87.

Kim, C. J. (2004). Unyielding positions: A critique of the 'race' debate. *Ethnicities, 4(3)*, 337-355.

King, C. R. (2008). George Bush may not like black people, but no one gives a dam about indigenous peoples: Visibility and Indianness after the hurricanes. *American Indian Culture and Research Journal, 32(2)*, 35-42.

Kivel, P. (2007). What does an ally do? In: M. L. Andersen, & P. C. Collins, (Eds.), *Race, Class, & Gender: An Anthology* (6th ed., 550-557). Belmont, CA: Thomson Wadsworth.

Kobayashi, A. & Johnson, G. F. (2007). Introduction. In: Johnson, G. F. & Enomoto, R. (Eds.), *Race, Racialization, and Anti-Racism in Canada and Beyond* (3-16). Toronto: University of Toronto Press.

Kobayashi, A. & Peake, L. (1994). Unnatural discourse: 'Race' and gender in geography. *Gender, Place and Culture, 1(2)*, 225-243.

Kulwicki, A., Khalifa, R. & Moore, G. (2008). The effects of September 11 on Arab American nurses in Metropolitan Detroit. *Journal of Transcultural Nursing, 19(2)*, 134-139.

Leach, C. W. (2005). Against the notion of a 'new racism'. *Journal of Community & Applied Social Psychology, 15(6)*, 432-445.

Leblanc, D. (2009). Tearful Canadian describes Kenyan ordeal. *The Globe and Mail.* Available online at http://www.theglobeandmail.com/news/national/tearful-canadian-describes-kenyan-ordeal/article1266247/. Retrieved August 27, 2009.

Lee, S. A., Gibbons, J. A., Thompson, J. H. & Timani, H. S. (2009). The Islamophobia scale: Instrument development and initial validation. *International Journal for the Psychology of Religion, 19(2)*, 92-105.

Lentin, A. (2000). 'Race', racism and anti-racism: Challenging contemporary classifications. *Social Identities, 6(1)*, 91-106.

Li, P. S. (2007). Contradictions of 'racial' discourse. In: V. Agnew, (Eds.), *Interrogating Race and Racism* (37-54). Toronto: University of Toronto Press.

Lubiano, W. H. (Eds.) (1998). *The House That Race Built.* New York: Vintage Books.

Mays, V. M., Cochran, S. D. & Barnes, N. W. (2007). Race, race-based discrimination, and health outcomes among African Americans. *Annual Review of Psychology, 58*, 201-225.

Mazarr, M. J. (2007). *Unmodern Men in the Modern World: Radical Islam, Terrorism, and the War on Modernity.* New York: Cambridge University.

McDonald, D. A. & Jacobs, S. (2005). (Re)writing xenophobia: Understanding press coverage of cross-border migration in South Africa. *Journal of Contemporary African Studies, 23(3),* 295-325.

McDonald, P. & Coleman, M. (1999). Deconstructing hierarchies of oppression and adopting a 'Multiple Model' approach to anti-oppressive practice. *Social Work Education, 18(1),* 19-33.

McIntosh, P. (2007). White privilege: Unpacking the invisible knapsack. In: M. L. Andersen, & P. H. Collins, (Eds.), *Race, Class, & Gender: An Anthology* (6th ed., 98-102). Belmont, CA: Thomson Wadsworth.

Meer, N. & Noorani, T. (2008). A sociological comparison of anti-Semitism and anti-Muslim sentiment in Britain. *The Sociological Review, 56(2),* 195-219.

Miles, R. (1989). *Racism.* London: Routledge.

Miles, R. & Brown, M. B. (2003). *Racism* (2nd ed.). London: Routledge.

Miller, J., Gounev, P., Pap, A. L., Wagman, D., Balogi, A., Bezlov, T., Simonovits, B. & Vargha, L. (2008). Racism and police stops: Adapting US and British debates to Continental Europe. *European Journal of Criminology, 5(2),* 161-191.

Moane, G. (2003). Bridging the personal and the political: Practices for a liberation psychology. *American Journal of Community Psychology, 31*(1/2), 91-101.

Modood, T. (2007). *Multiculturalism: A Civic Idea.* London: Polity.

Moore, R. B. (2007). Racist stereotyping in the English language. In: M. L. Andersen, & P. H. Collins, (Eds.), *Race, Class, & Gender: An Anthology* (6th ed., 365-376). Belmont, CA: Thomson Wadsworth.

Mullaly, B. (2007). *The New Structural Social Work* (3rd ed.). Don Mills, ON: Oxford University Press.

Murji, K. & Solomos, J. (Eds.),. (2005). *Racialization: Studies in Theory and Practice.* Oxford: Oxford University Press.

Myles, J. & Hou, F. (2004). Changing colours: Spatial assimilation and new racial minority immigrants. *Canadian Journal of Sociology, 29(1),* 29-58.

Naber, N. (2000). Ambiguous insiders: An investigation of Arab American invisibility. *Ethnic and Racial Studies, 23(1),* 37-61.

Nash, M., Wong, J. & Trlin, A. (2006). Civic and social integration: A new field of social work practice with immigrants, refugees and asylum seekers. *International Social Work, 49(3),* 345-63.

Nayak, A. (2006). After race: Ethnography, race and post-race theory. *Ethnic and Racial Studies, 29(3),* 411-430.

Nicholson, L. (1995). Interpreting gender. In: Nicholson, L. & Seidman, S. (Eds.), *Social Postmodernism: Beyond Identity Politics* (39-67). Cambridge: Cambridge University Press.

Omi, M. A. (2001). The changing meaning of race. In: N. J., Smelser, W. J. Wilson, & F. Mitchell, (Eds.), *America Becoming: Racial Trends and Their Consequences* (volume 1, 243-263). Washington, D.C: National Academies Press.

Omi, M. A. & Winant, H. (1994). *Racial Formation in the United States: From the 1960s to the 1990s* (2nd ed.) New York: Routledge.

Ornstein, M. (2006). *Ethno-racial Groups in Toronto, 1971-2001: A Demographic and Socio-Economic Profile*. Toronto: Institute for Social Research, York University.

Owens, L. C. (2008). Network news: The role of race in source selection and story topic. *Howard Journal of Communications, 19(4)*, 355-370.

Pascale, C. M. (2007). *Making Sense of Race, Class, and Gender: Common-Sense, Power, and Privilege in the United States*. New York: Routledge.

Patni, R. (2006). Race-specific vs. culturally competent social workers: The debates and dilemmas around pursuing essentialist or multicultural social work practice. *Journal of Social Work Practice, 20(2)*, 163-174.

Payne, M. (2005). *Modern Social Work Theory* (3rd ed.). Chicago: Lyceum Books.

Picot, G., Hou, F. & Coulombe, S. (2007). *Chronic Low Income and Low-Income Dynamics Among Recent Immigrants*. Analytical Studies Branch Research Paper Series. Ottawa: Statistics Canada.

Razack, S. (Ed.) (2002). *Race, Space, and the Law: Unmapping a White Settler Society*. Toronto: Between the Lines.

Rodriguez, N. (1999). U.S. immigration and changing relations between African Americans and Latinos. In: C., Hirschman, P. Kasinitz, & J. DeWind, (Eds.), *The Handbook of International Migration: The American Experience* (423-432). New York: Russell Sage Foundation.

Rogowski, S. (2008). Social work with children and families: Towards a radical/critical practice. *Practice, 20(1)*, 17-28.

Roscigno, V. J., Garcia, L. M. & Bobbitt-Zeher, D. (2007). Social closure and processes of race/sex employment discrimination. *The Annals of the American Academy of Political and Social Sciences, 609(1)*, 16-48.

Ross, O. (2009). 'Ideas are the best' weapons. *Toronto Star*, Wednesday, August, 12, A8.

Rossiter, A. (2001). Innocence lost and suspicion found? Do we educate for or against social work? *Critical Social Work, 2(1)*, 1-8. Available online at www.criticalsocialwork.com. Retrieved June 29, 2009.

Rowe, D. C. (2002). IQ, birth weight and number of sexual partners in white, African American, and mixed-race adolescents. *Population and Environment, 23(5)*, 513-524.

Ruggles, C. & Rovinescu, O. (1996). *Outsider Blues: A Voice from the Shadows*. Halifax: Fernwood Publishing.

Rushton, J. P. (1995). *Race, Evolution, and Behaviour: A Life History Perspective*. New Brunswick, NJ: Transaction Publishers.

Sakamoto, I. & Pitner, R. O. (2005). Use of critical consciousness in anti-oppressive social work practice: Disentangling power dynamics at personal and structural levels. *British Journal of Social Work, 35(4)*, 435-452.

Samuel, E. (2006). *Integrative Antiracism: South Asians in Canadian Academe*. Toronto: University of Toronto Press.

Samuel, E. & Wane, N. (2005). Unsettling relations: Racism and sexism experienced by faculty of color in a predominantly white Canadian university. *The Journal of Negro Education, 74(1)*, 76-87.

Satzewich, V. & Liodakis, N. (2007). *'Race' and ethnicity in Canada: An introduction*. Don Mills, ON: Oxford University Press.

Scheufele, D. A., Nisbet, M. C. & Ostman, R. E. (2005). September 11th news coverage, public opinion, and support for civil liberties. *Mass Communication & Society, 8(3)*, 197-218.

Shah, H. (2009). Legitimizing neglect: Race and rationality in conservative news commentary about Hurricane Katrina. *Howard Journal of Communications, 20(1)*, 1-17.

Shapiro, T. M. (2004). *The Hidden Cost of Being African American: How Wealth Perpetuates Inequality*. New York: Oxford University Press.

Sheridan, L. P. (2006). Islamophobia pre- and post-September 11, 2001. *Journal of Interpersonal Violence, 21(3)*, 317-336.

Smedley, A. (2007). *Race in North America: Origin and Evolution of a World View* (3rd ed.). Boulder, CO: Westview Press.

Smedley, A. & Smedley, B. D. (2005). Race as biology is fiction, racism as a social problem is real: Anthropological and historical perspectives on the social construction of race. *American Psychologist, 60(1)*, 16-26.

Smith, B. & Tudor, K. (2003). Oppression and pedagogy: Anti-oppressive practice in the education of therapists. In: C. Lago, & B. Smith, (Eds.), *Anti-discriminatory Counselling Practice* (135-150). London: Sage Publications Inc.

Soldatova, G. (2007). Psychological mechanisms of xenophobia. *Social Sciences, 38(2)*, 104-120.

Solomos, J. & Back, L. (1996). *Racism and Society*. Basingstoke: Macmillan Press Ltd.

Spanierman, L. B., Armstrong, P. I., Poteat, V. P. & Beer, A. M. (2006). Psychosocial cost of racism to whites: Exploring patterns through cluster analysis. *Journal of Counseling Psychology*, 53 *(4)*, 434-441.

Stasiulis, D. K. (2009). Theorizing connections: Gender, race, ethnicity, and class. In: Wallis, M. & Fleras, A. (Eds.), *The Politics of Race in Canada: Readings in Historical Perspectives, Contemporary Realities, and Future Possibilities* (95-107). Don Mills, ON: Oxford University Press.

Sternberg, R. L., Grigorenko, E. L. & Kidd, K. K. (2005). Intelligence, race, and genetics. *American Psychologist, 60 (1)*, 46-59.

Stivers, C. (2007). 'So poor, so black': Hurricane Katrina, public administration, and the issue of race. *Public Administration Review* (Special Issue), *67 (1)*, 48-56.

Strabac, Z. & Listhaug, O. (2008). Anti-Muslim prejudice in Europe: A multilevel analysis of survey data from 30 countries. *Social Science Research, 37 (1)*, 268-286.

Swahn, M. H., Mahendra, R. R., Paulozzi, L. J., Winston, R. L., Shelley, G. A., Taliano, J., Frazer, L. & Saul, J. R. (2003). Violent attacks on Middle Easterners in the United States during the month following the September 11, 2001 terrorist attacks. *Injury Prevention, 9 (2)*, 187-190.

Tang, K-L. (2004). Internationalizing anti-racism efforts: What social workers can do. *Journal of Ethnic and Cultural Diversity in Social Work, 12 (3)*, 55-71.

Tanovich, D. M. (2009). What is it? In: Wallis, M. & Fleras, A. (Eds.) (2009), *The Politics of Race in Canada: Readings in Historical Perspectives, Contemporary Realities, and Future Possibilities* (155-165). Don Mills, ON: Oxford University Press.

The Colour of Poverty Campaign (2009). Understanding the racialization of poverty in Ontario: An introduction in 20017. In: M. Wallis, & A. Fleras, (Eds.), *The Politics of Race in Canada: Readings in Historical Perspectives, Contemporary Realities, and Future Possibilities* (196-197). Don Mills, ON: Oxford University Press.

Thobani, S. (2007). *Exalted Subjects: Studies in the Making of Race and Nation in Canada.* Toronto: University of Toronto Press.

Thompson, K. (2009). Senate backs apology for slavery. *Washington Post*, June 19. Available online at http://www.washingtonpost.com/wp-dyn/content/article/2009/06/18/ AR200-9061803877.html. Retrieved August 10, 2009).

Thompson, N. (2003). *Anti-Discriminatory Practice* (3rd ed.). Basingstoke: Palgrave Macmillan.

Thompson, N. (2006). *Anti-discriminatory Practice* (4th ed.). Basingstoke: Palgrave Macmillan.

Valtonen, K. (2002). Social work practice with immigrants and refugees: Developing a participation-based framework for anti-oppressive practice part 2. *British Journal ofSocial Work, 32(1)*, 113-20.

Van Wormer. K. (2004). *Confronting Oppression, Restoring Justice: From Policy Analysis to Social Action.* Alexandria, VA: Council on Social Work Education.

Vasquez, H. (2006). Article for 'diversity stories in community research and action'. Facing resistance in waking up to privilege. *American Journal of Community Psychology, 37* (3-4), 183-189.

Vickers, J. (2002). *The Politics of 'Race': Canada, Australia, and the United States.* Ottawa: Golden Dog Press.

Walkom, T. (2009). Six years in legal labyrinth. *Toronto Star*, August 26. Available online at http://www.thestar.com/article/686404. Retrieved August 26.

Walks, R. A. & Bourne, L. S. (2006). Ghettos in Canada's cities? Racial segregation, ethnic enclaves and poverty concentration in Canadian urban areas. *The Canadian Geographer, 50(3)*, 273-296.

Wallis, M. & Fleras, A. (Eds.) (2009a). *The Politics of Race in Canada: Readings in Historical Perspectives, Contemporary Realities, and Future Possibilities.* Don Mills, ON: Oxford University Press.

Wallis, M. & Fleras, A. (2009b). Conceptualizing the politics of race: Taking race seriously. In: M. Wallis, & A. Fleras, (Eds.), *The Politics of Race in Canada: Readings in Historical Perspectives, Contemporary Realities, and Future Possibilities* (x-xxiv). Don Mills, ON: Oxford University Press.

Wallis, M. & Fleras, A. (2009c). Theorizing race in Canada: Future possibilities. In: M. Wallis, & A. Fleras, (Eds.), *The Politics of Race in Canada: Readings in Historical Perspectives, Contemporary Realities, and Future Possibilities* (251-261). Don Mills, ON: Oxford University Press.

Wallis, M. A. & Kwok, S. (Eds.) (2008). *Daily Struggles: The Deeping Racialization and Feminization of Poverty in Canada.* Toronto: Canadian Scholars' Press.

White, I. K. (2007). When race matters and when it doesn't: Racial group differences in response to racial cues. *American Political Science Review, 101(2)*, 339-350.

Williams, C. & Soydan, H. (2005). When and how does ethnicity matter? A cross-national study of social work responses to ethnicity in child protection cases. *British Journal of Social Work, 35(6)*, 901-920.

Williams, C. C. (2006). The epistemology of cultural competence. *Families in Society, 87(2)*, 209-220.

Wilson, G. (2007). Racialized life-chance opportunities across the class structure: The case of African Americans. *The Annals of the American Academy of Political and SocialSciences, 609(1)*, 215-232.

Winant, H. (1998a). Racial dualism at century's end. In: Lubiano, W. H. (Ed.), *The House That Race Built* (87-115). New York: Vintage Books.

Winant, H. (1998b). Racism today: Continuity and change in the post-civil rights era. *Ethnic and Racial Studies, 21(4)*, 89-97.

Woods, A. (2009). Ottawa in Kenya case. Available online at http://www.thestar.com/article/ 687145. Retrieved August 27, 2009.

Woods, A. & Taylor, L. C. (2009). Whose fault? *Toronto Star*, Wednesday, August 12, A1 and A6.

Wright, S. A. (2007). *Patriots, Politics, and the Oklahoma City Bombing*. New York: Cambridge University Press.

Young, J. & Braziel, J. E. (Eds.) (2006). *Race and the Foundation of Knowledge: Cultural Amnesia in the Academy*. Champaign, IL: University of Illinois Press.

Zeigler-Hill, V. (2007). Contingent self-esteem and race: Implications for the black self-esteem advantage. *Journal of Black Psychology, 33(1)*, 51-74.

In: Race and Ethnicity
Editor: Jonathan K. Crennan, pp. 61-112

ISBN: 978-1-60692-099-2
© 2010 Nova Science Publishers, Inc.

Chapter 2

CULTURAL UNDERSTANDING IN EFL READING IN ARGENTINA: A THRESHOLD OF CULTURAL AWARENESS OF OTHERNESS

Melina Porto[*]

National University of La Plata and CONICET, Argentina

ABSTRACT

This study approaches a topic which is highly germane to the enhancement of foreign/second (L2) language education: the manner in which learners glean cultural perspectives during reading, in this specific case EFL reading (English as a Foreing Language) in Argentina. The importance of cultural perspectives for enhancing the comprehension of L2 texts has been widely acknowledged by theorists and researchers in the field. The chapter reports part of the results of a broader study carried out in 2005, whose specific aim was to describe the comprehension of the cultural content of a literary narrative text through response writing tasks and visual reformulations. About 200 Argentine college students (prospective teachers and translators of English) voluntarily participated in the study. They were Caucasian, mostly female, middle class, Spanish-speaking, between 19-21 years of age, and were enrolled in the course English Language II at the National University of La Plata in Argentina. This is a prestigious, public, access for all university in a developing country. The results corresponding to a culturally loaded text, written in English (a foreign language), are reported here. The selection, a fragment from *Desert Wife* (Faunce, 1961: 173-181), describes one Christmas celebration in a Native American context with an outsider perspective, i.e., with a narrator who participates in the celebration described but is not a member of the culture represented in the text. In reaction to this text the participants produced a response writing task in Spanish, a response writing task in English, and a visual reformulation (among other tasks), whose analysis serves as the foundation of this chapter. Data were analyzed in terms of culturally distinctive idea units and textual modifications (reader behaviors). Both measures of analysis (*amount* of free recall in the form of cultural idea units and the *kind* of information recalled in the form of reader behaviors) are consistent with Carrell

---

[*] Corresponding author: melinaporto@speedy.com.ar

(1984c), Steffensen, Joag-Dev and Anderson (1979), and Sharifian, Rochecouste and Malcolm (2004), among others. Results showed different levels of apprehension of cultural aspects during reading, i.e. different degrees of depth, complexity and details with respect to the cultural reality of the Navajos. In general, the approach to Otherness was limited to the perception of what was exotic or exciting about the Navajo culture, without a genuine effort to become familiar with what was strange. The difficulty this population revealed in approaching Otherness manifested itself in the abundance of stereotyped perspectives about the Native Americans in the written tasks produced.

INTRODUCTION

In the framework of globalization, and from a theoretical perspective, the notion of culture is nowadays embraced as pedagogically and educationally relevant within foreign language (L2) education in this country. It is accepted that education in general and L2 education in particular are framed within specific socio-cultural contexts (Luke, 2003). This means that all learners, as individuals with idiosyncratic identities involving multiple and varied dimensions (language, ethnicity, gender, socio-economic status, educational background, physical appearance, special capacities, and others) (McCarthey and Moje, 2002; Peyton Young, 2001) will appropriate English, each one in their own ways, to face and negotiate the world, decoding its multiple systems of symbolic, social, and cultural meanings (Cots, 2006). In the particular context in which this study was carried out, i.e. a public, access for all university in a developing country with an unstable economy, constant poverty and unemployment in disadvantaged areas, and an emerging democracy, the significance of English as an international language or lingua franca in a globalized world is being increasingly understood. In our setting, English becomes a form of cultural capital (Luke, 2003), which learners will use together with other forms of social and economic capital, to open up to the world and have access to knowledge and information, to health, education, work, economic growth, etc. - through different resources and means. For these learners, English becomes a resource, a tool, that they will use within the school, but also outside it (possibly in the home, the community, and the society at large), to enrich their lives in different facets (linguistic, social, cultural, academic, moral) and fight the inequalities to which they may be consciously or unconsciously subjected in the course of their lives (Chen, 2005).

This idea of empowering my learners to face the world as independent, responsible, and critical citizens (who happen to live in a disfavored country) motivated this study. Crucial to this aim is the development of their ability to become critical readers in English, a foreign language in their home country. This ability involves the necessary knowledge, skills, and attitudes (Sercu, 2006) to "read" the world, to generate their own access to knowledge through multiple and varied ways of knowing, and to resist the identities often cast upon them as Third World citizens (Berg, 2003; Chien-Hui Kuo, 2003).

It was therefore particularly important to acknowledge, at the beginning of this study, that culture pervaded these learners' lives, shaped what learning was for them, what reading both in Spanish and in English involved, and who counted as a good learner and reader (in both languages) in our setting (Alvermann 2001; Ruano, 2005; Shah, 2004). Who the learners were, what they believed in, how they lived, and what family, community, and school environments they were immersed in made a difference in how they learned, how they engaged in reading, and what role language learning in general and L2 reading in particular played in their lives (Burgess, Hecht and Lonigan 2002; Gee 2001).

However, foreign language education in our setting misses this cultural dimension in its daily pedagogic reality – though as said earlier, the necessary integration of language and culture in the L2 classroom is well recognized. In practical terms, this means that reading is in general taught as a decontextualized skill, and the comprehension questions which teachers usually pose after a reading text lead students to assume that its "meaning" is self-contained and can be derived by simply inspecting the language in the text with sufficient detail. The motivation for this study, therefore, stemmed from the need that educators in this country acknowledge that as culturally responsive educators, they must make connections with their learners as individuals while at the same time understanding the socio-cultural and historical contexts that influence their engagement with literacy, in particular their interactions with L2 reading (Edwards and Pleasants, 1998; Klingner and Edwards, 2006). In this sense, culturally responsive educators in this country need to find out how their learners approach L2 reading, looking across the multiple layers of the home, the community, the school, and the society at large.

Being literate in a foreign or second language in the 21st century involves the capacity to participate in a multiplicity of ways of reading in a plurality of Discourses in the framework of socially and culturally diverse contexts (Fitzgerald, 2003; Jiménez, 2003; Klingner and Edwards, 2006). This capacity involves the ability to perceive, interpret, and examine the cultural perspectives explicitly or implicitly embedded in L2 reading materials – the focus of this study, and a dimension many times forgotten in this setting. One tenet of this study in this respect was that for congruence to exist between how L2 reading is taught and the students' opportunities of becoming critical, independent and responsible readers, educators need to make attempts to understand the underlying social, cultural, and language networks of their learners.

More specifically, this article approaches a topic which is highly germane to the enhancement of foreign language education: the manner in which learners glean cultural perspectives from their reading of literary narrative texts, and the process of interpretation within this cultural dimension. Although the importance of cultural perspectives for enhancing the comprehension of L2 texts as well as for enhancing L2 education in general has been widely acknowledged by theorists and researchers in the field, educators in this area of the world need to become more fully engaged with culturally responsive literacy practices. This study constitutes one move towards awareness in this direction in this country.

Background of the Study

About 200 prospective teachers and translators of English enrolled in English Language II for the 2005 course at the National University of La Plata in Argentina participated in this study in partial fulfillment of their course requirements[1]. The syllabus in this subject is

---

[1] The number of participants in this study is a distinguishing characteristic of this research project. Comparatively, other studies involve significantly fewer subjects. A review of the literature to observe this aspect revealed the following information: Lipson (1983) works with 32 students; Carrell (1984c): 80, in 4 groups of 20; Kimmel

literature-based, with an exclusive focus on narratives. Although narrative instruction with a strong linguistic focus is a core element in this course, learners are provided guidance in treating literary texts as illustrative of cultural issues. This cultural dimension is explicitly addressed in our classroom. Participants were college students, Caucasian, mostly female, middle class, Spanish-speaking, between 19-21 years of age. The medium of instruction was English (a foreign language) and students were required to have CAE (Cambridge Certificate in Advanced English) level at this stage. This chapter reports part of the results of a broader study, specifically the results corresponding to a fragment from *Desert Wife* (Faunce, 1961: 173-181). The larger study aimed at describing the comprehension of the cultural content of three literary narrative texts through response writing tasks and visual reformulations (Porto, 2003). These literary texts described different Christmas celebrations with different cultural loads presented through different perspectives. One text offered a relatively close cultural reality to the learners, in a Brazilian context, and was written in Spanish (selection from *Mi planta de naranja-lima*, de Vasconcelos, 1971:39-43). Another text, written in English, portrayed a different cultural reality to the participants, set in a Canadian-American context (fragment from *Cat's Eye*, Atwood, 1998: 137-140). The third text, which is the focus of this chapter, offered a totally remote cultural reality. In response to this fragment from *Desert Wife,* written in English, the learners produced a response writing task in Spanish, a response writing task in English, and a visual reformulation (among other tasks), whose analysis serves as the foundation of this chapter.

Rationale

The research reported in this chapter is grounded in a socio-cultural conception of reading in general and cultural perspectives in L2 reading in particular.. The main tenets underlying this study as well as their significance for usual practices in Argentina are described below.

Conceptions of reading in this study

Reading is a multidimensional and multivalent processes (Bernhardt, 2003; Paris and Paris, 2003). The possibility of diversity in reader response to textual content is related not only to the fact that the questions to be answered during reading vary from reader to reader but also to contextual factors both at a mental level (schemata) and a situational level (specific limitations of the context in which a text is read). This context includes social, cultural, political, geographical, and historical aspects – among others (Berg, 2003; Burgess, Hecht and Lonigan, 2002; Gee, 2001; Fitzgerald, 2003; Labbo, 2000; Jiménez, 2003; McCallister, 2002; Moje, 2000; Peyton Young, 2001). It also includes assumptions about the preceding text, the immediate context, cultural knowledge, common sense knowledge, etc.

---

and Magginitie (1984): 225, though later 2 groups of 16 are compared; Schraw et al. (1993): Experiment 1 (51, in 3 groups), Experiment 2 (65, in 2 groups), Experiment 3 (88 in 4 groups of 20); Gradwohl Nash et al. (1993): 84 in groups of 20; Wright and Rosenberg (1993): 58 (one group of 28, another of 30); Steffensen et al. (1979): 39; Mannes (1994): Experiment 1 (45, in 3 groups), Experiment 2 (20, in 2 groups); Robins and Mayer (1993): Experiment 1 (93), Experiment 2 (97), Experiment 3 (86), (each experiment in 4 groups); Steffensen (1988): 20; Alderson and Urquhart (1988): 37; Hudson (1982): 80 in groups; Rigg (1988): 48; Sharifian, Rochecouste and Malcolm (2004): 10.

(Bernhardt, 2003). The implication is that we cannot remove reading, and literacy in general, from their complex social, cultural, and economic contexts (Luke, 2003). This conclusion notwithstanding, there is a tendency in this country to narrow the issue to one aspect (e.g. in reading the narrowing focuses on cognitive processing, phonological decoding, word recognition, or text comprehension). This narrowing misses the point of reading as genuine social and communicative practice (Berg, 2003). Splitting literacy into de-contextualized skills, a frequent practice in Argentina, takes reading out of its socio-cultural and communicative contexts (Berg, 2003). This study constitutes one move away from this tendency.

This socio-cultural dimension of reading comprises the economic and historical events which influence how students see themselves and others, because these understandings translate into the ways that they appropriate or reject specific forms of reading (and literacy) (Jiménez, 2003). Just as readers can come to understand themselves in particular ways as a result of a reading experience, each reading experience plays a role in their identifications and positionings (McCarthey and Moje, 2002). Who students are as individuals in terms of race, gender, social class, educational, historical, and cultural backgrounds, religion, sexual orientation, physical appearance, special capacities, and many other factors simultaneously influences and contributes to how they conceive of reading (Chen, 2005; Chien-Hui Kuo, 2003; Gallas and Smagorinsky, 2002). Concomitantly, their multiple identities may shift as a result of reading new material within a particular context, especially material that challenges some of their beliefs based on their social and cultural background (McCarthey and Moje, 2002).

Cultural perspectives in L2 reading

This investigation attributes an important role to cultural factors in the process of L2 reading and in literacy education in general (Berg, 2003; Byram and Grundy, 2003; Byram, Nichols, and Stevens, 2001; Klingner and Edwards, 2006; Kramsch, 1993, 1998; Labov, 2003; Moje, 2000). Defining the term culture is problematic, because definitions come from the humanities and the social sciences and involve disciples such as history, ethnography, sociology, anthropology, sociolinguistics, literature, and cultural studies, among others (Kramsch, 1995). Both descriptively and methodologically, the concept is too wide and vague (Byram and Grundy, 2002; Deveney, 2007) and there exist no solid models to aid in its description (Archer, 1997). In this chapter, culture C1 (the participants') and culture C2 (other) are not seen as objective, monolithic entities but rather the conception of culture embraced here is one of social construction, i.e. the result of the perceptions of oneself and others in the context of a multifaceted reality representative of different subcultures such as social class, race, gender, age, religion, sexual orientation, and education, among others (Blanco, 2000; Geertz, 1974; Hugo, 2002; Labbo, 2000, Mahar, 2001; Shah, 2004; Sloane, 2005; Warley, 2003). "One of the major ways in which culture manifests itself is through language. Material culture is constantly *mediated, interpreted and recorded – among other things – through language.* It is because of that mediatory role of language that culture becomes the concern of the language teacher. Culture in the final analysis is always *linguistically mediated membership into a discourse community, that is both real and imagined."* (Kramsch, 1995: 85).

In order to capture the cultural aspects in a text, it is essential to have attitudes of curiosity, openness, and willingness to suspend disbelief and value judgments with regard to other people's beliefs and behaviors (Byram and Morgan, 1994; Mountford and Wadham-Smith, 2000; O'Byrne, 2003). There must also exist willingness to approach the unfamiliar, recognizing the importance of understanding the manifestations of a different culture in the context in which they are framed (Shah, 2004). As language learning offers a new window on experience, L2 reading offers learners the possibility of perceiving things in new ways (Dlaska, 2003). From this perspective, a definition of culture should involve an imaginative dimension. As Kramsch (1995: 85) puts it, "Culture, then, constitutes itself along three axes: the diachronic axis of time, the synchronic axis of space, and the metaphoric axes of the imagination." Emotions are a key aspect in this imaginative dimension of culture (Byram, Gribkova, and Starkey, 2002).

The cultural dimension of reading is therefore a complex one, as readers constantly adapt their reading habits, behaviors, motivations and performance as well as their multiple and varied identities to their textual, social, cultural, and physical surroundings (Sarroub, 2002). This unconscious and pervasive adaptation has been referred to in the literature as in-betweenness (Sarroub, 2002), which signifies that we live and participate in multiple worlds and as we do, we occupy the in-between spaces of two (or more) cultures. To make sense of the world and to make sense of texts, individuals in a given culture draw on multiple resources, experiences, knowledge, etc. (Moje et al., 2004). Being "in-between" different resources, funds of knowledge, or Discourses affects one's literate, social, and cultural practices, including one's encounters with reading.

Terminology is laxly used in the literature within this cultural dimension of language education. There is a significant difficulty in the available terminology to capture the complexity of the issues involved in this cultural dimension of L2 education in general, and EFL reading in particular as described above. This difficulty reveals itself in the variety and multiplicity of currently available terms. The following ones, used loosely and interchangeably (when appropriate) abound: native and foreign text and culture (Steffensen, Joag-Dev and Anderson, 1979: 10), culture in the singular (despite the impossibility of singling out any one culture as a homogenous construct as the authors themselves acknowledge; Byram, 2001: 98; Byram, Gribkova and Starkey, 2002: 9; Byram and Grundy, 2002: 193; Byrnes, 2008: 108; Erez and Gati, 2004: 585; Kramsch, 1995: 85; Kramsch et al, 1996: 100; Garner, 2008: 117; Steffensen, Joag-Dev and Anderson, 1979: 17), cultural representations (now in the plural; Kramsch et al, 1996: 106), cultural content (Abu-Rabia, 1998: 203; Smith-Maddox, 1998: 312); cultural meaning (Byrnes, 2008: 108), cultural significance (Steffensen, Joag-Dev and Anderson, 1979: 12); cultural difference (Deveney, 2007: 311; Kramsch, 1996: 100; Rollin, 2006: 58), cultural types (Deveney, 2007: 313), cultural discontinuity (Deveney, 2007: 311), cultural presuppositions (Kramsch et al, 1996: 106), cultural contexts (Kramsch, 1995: 90), elements or features of a cultural schema (Sharifian, Rochecouste and Malcolm, 2004: 206), cultural understanding (Byram, 2001: 100; Byram, Gribkova and Starkey, 2002: 27; Kramsch, 1995: 88; Sharifian, Rochecouste and Malcolm, 2004: 222;), understand Otherness/diversity (Alred and Byram, 2002: 348; Garner, 2008: 118; Rollin, 2006: 58); comprehend (Lipson, 1983: 448; Sharifian, Rochecouste and Malcolm, 2004: 204; Steffensen, Joag-Dev and Anderson, 1979: 19). Overall, the foregoing reveals the lack of unifying terminology in the literature and the difficulty of capturing the complexity of the topic through specific terms when writing about it.

Indeterminacy of Interpretation

The conception of the interpretation process as indeterminate (Moreiras, 1991) is at the heart of this research. A reader may obtain different meanings from the same text if this is read at different times and with varied intentions because as participant-observer, a reader has different perspectives, different foci of attention, and different affiliations with the characters and the events in a story – which he/she can exploit in each reading (Byram and Grundy, 2002; Kramsch, 2003). From this perspective, any reading is necessarily idiosyncratic. The perspective that a reader adopts when reading affects his/er assessment of the importance of the textual content and has an impact on interpretation. As mentioned elsewhere, this possibility of diversity in reader response to textual content is related to contextual factors ranging from situational to social, cultural, political, geographical, and historical – among others (Berg, 2003; Burgess, Hecht and Lonigan, 2002; Gee, 2001; Fitzgerald, 2003; Jiménez, 2003; McCallister, 2002; Peyton Young, 2001). Although this concept of textual freedom means that any interpretation is provisional, the reader's task is to find the interpretative boundary for a text or, in other words, to reach an interpretation which is anchored in textual information.

Insider and outsider perspectives in L2 reading

Within the cultural dimension of L2 education, the perspective with which the cultural background is presented in a text is important in the process of L2 reading. Texts may present cultural content with an insider perspective, i.e., with a narrator who participates in the events described and is a member of the culture represented in the text, or with an outsider perspective, i.e., with a narrator who participates in the events described but is not a member of the culture represented in the text (see section on Materials). This difference is crucial as the insider/outsider perspectives, through their difference in voice, may determine how readers will perceive the culture in question (Yakota, 1998). Another aspect in relation to this topic is the perspective (insider versus outsider) through which a reader accesses a text, especially its cultural content. The readers' insider / outsider perspectives in their approach of this cultural dimension of L2 reading content constitute a key element in the Model of Cultural Apprehension offered in this chapter (see below).

Distinguishing Features of This Study

This study has several features which distinguish it from others available in the field.

As mentioned before, this study focuses on a literary narrative texts, while expository texts are more frequently explored in the literature. The text is also unmodified and authentic (cf. the usual artificially contrived, or experimentally modified texts).

The impact of the perspective (insider/outsider) with which the cultural background is presented in a text in the process of L2 reading is also a significant feature, only explored in Mannes (1994). Sharifian et al (2004) discuss this distinction in theoretical terms but they make no mention of perspective in the fragments used, for instance. Although this perspective aspect is implicit in many studies which explore the culture dimension of reading, in this case the focus is explicit, not only in the perspective of the prompt text, but also in the Model of Cultural Apprehension.

In addition, most studies use immediate recall protocols or summaries as their main instrument of data collection. This study uses response writing tasks, a variation of immediate recall that allows participants to project their own interpretations of the prompt text (cf. summaries). The response writing tasks, as explained in the data analysis section, necessarily involve some summarizing to some extent.

In alignment with the literature, this study incorporates, as a measure of analysis, the textual modifications produced by the participants in their response to the fragment. However, the modifications investigated in this study include 16 reader behaviors (listed and defined in the Appendix), while most studies focus on only 2 to 5 behaviors.

Focusing on *culturally significant* idea units in data analysis is new. Previous studies quantify *all* the idea units in the texts.

This study is singular in that it combines prompt texts in the L1 and the L2, and response writing tasks also in the L1 and the L2. The inclusion of a visual task in addition to these writing tasks is also unique to my knowledge. Therefore, the modes of response seem to be new as well as the rationale that this last instrument (visual reformulation) collects affective data or data indicating response to literary texts.

Consistent with Sharifian, Rochecouste and Malcolm's (2004) concept of a continuum in varying degrees of familiarity with cultural schemas, the broader study (of which this chapter is a part) used three prompt texts with varying degrees of culturally accessibly.

METHODOLOGY

Research Question

How do learners approach the cultural content of literary narrative texts during EFL reading in this setting?

Materials

Several reasons motivated the use of literary narrative texts in this study. First, the syllabus in this subject is literature-based, with an exclusive focus on narratives. Also, the writing of anecdotes is a course requirement. Second, the belief, both popular and academic, about the preference of students for the narrative as well as about the motivating power of stories seems convincing, at least intuitively (Kamberelis and Bovino, 1999). Third, many L2 learners already possess the relevant pre-requisites for the narrative task, i.e., they possess the rhetorical schema of the short story as well as the capacity to use it (Paris and Paris, 2003; Singer and Donlan, 1994; Strömqvist and Day, 1993). In particular, adults have the pre-requisites for the production of short stories and only need to acquire a small portion of the foreign language to be able to apply the strategies that they already have. Fourth, considering that the narrative socialization through the oral discourse of our daily lives is significant (Paris and Paris, 2003), many researchers have suggested that narrative genres are easier to learn and more natural than the informative genres (Kamberelis and Bovino, 1999) and that they are fundamental to beginning reading (Paris and Paris, 2003). Besides, in general, formal education privileges the narrative genre, contributing to its accessibility (Byrnes, 2008; Duke, 2000; Kamberelis and Bovino, 1999). Fifth, fiction allows us to bring to the surface the feelings and thoughts that guide the values and beliefs of our life styles and encourages awareness of them (Ooka Pang, Colvin, Tran, and Barba, 1998). Stories cultivate personal and interpersonal understanding (what motivates characters, how different characters interact, how their objectives and ways of reaching them conflict, etc.; Kamberelis and Bovino, 1999). Narrative genres model their messages so as to express inferences about human beliefs, attitudes, values, motivations, and objectives through the inclusion of structural elements and their organization (Kamberelis and Bovino, 1999). Finally, narratives are powerful because they help learners define themselves and build bridges toward others by offering contrasts with different perspectives (Boyle and Peregoy, 1998). Cultural information is present in almost all the narrative elements, which facilitates the accurate portrayal of certain cultural aspects through the presence of information rich in details (Yakota, 1998). Cultural details give life to a short story and offer readers a window on the life of the culture they are reading about (Yakota, 1998). Literature provides "this imaginative leap that will enable learners to imagine cultures different from their own" (Kramsch, 1995: 85).

Choosing the theme of the story was a problem. Although the theme is a crucial aspect related with comprehension, it is more dependent on the learners' prior knowledge and their reasoning capacity (Singer and Donlan, 1994) and more likely to be affected by their individual experience and cultural baggage (Oller, 1995) than any other aspect of the narrative structure. The area of celebrations and rituals was chosen because, being cultural events in themselves, they guaranteed the presence of both implicit and explicit cultural elements.

The culturally marked text on which this chapter rests is written in English, is a selection of *Desert Wife* (Faunce, 1961: 173-181), and describes a Christmas celebration by the Navajo in the US with an outsider perspective, i.e. with a narrator who participates in the celebration described but is not a member of the culture represented in the text (fragment appears in Appendix). Considering that a well-organized narrative structure (with patterns such as problem-solution, cause-effect, etc.) facilitates recall (Bower, Black, and Turner, 1994; Oller, 1995), the key element in the selection of the story was the quality of its structure (the presence of clearly delineated characters, a definite context, a clear theme, clear narrative episodes, resolution, etc.). Another equally important characteristic was the presence of elements that make a text less abstract and stimulate cognitive interest (such as active constructions, examples, images, descriptions, analogies, comparisons, humor, emotion, metaphors, vivid vocabulary, contextual information, etc.). These considerations notwithstanding, this fragment was one of three used in a broader study, and intended to reflect a totally remote cultural reality to the learners. In this sense, this fragment was distant in terms of cultural content (a different country and ethnic group) as well as in terms of the learners' experiences and background (setting, era, age of protagonists). In other words, of the three texts used in the larger study (not reported here), this one was the most challenging to the participants' capacity to approach Otherness in this particular cultural context.

Because of the unfamiliar cultural reality portrayed in this fragment, I considered the possibility that too many different or strange cultural aspects would result in problems of overload. Added to this, Christmas is a Christian festival introduced to the Native Americans by the American narrator, Hilda, and her husband. In this sense, the fragment is culturally rich and complex, as several layers are intertwined: Hilda's mainstream American culture; the Navajo's culture; the lack of cultural significance that a Christian celebration has for the Navajo; and the portrayal of the Native American culture through Hilda's eyes, which brings about issues of stereotyping, unconscious racism, and implicit and explicit derogatory perspectives on occasions. At the same time, however, a text without difficulties, i.e., with total stability and high predictability, was not desirable or possible, as no text can explicitly mention all connections. On the basis of these considerations, the selected text included information that the learners would be able to relate or contrast with their own experiences such as the dances, food, sleeping habits, and cooking customs. These aspects, among others, would allow them to make connections with their prior knowledge of and/or imagination about a Christmas celebration by a pagan group like the Native Americans, helping make the text interesting and comprehensible. In addition, some parts of the text presented a lot of factual and culturally novel and rich information (dances, cooking) through the eyes of an observer (not a Navajo), which in general contributed to its clarity. The narrator (an outsider) meticulously describes different elements such as the context, the characters, the life habits of the Navajo, characteristics about their physical appearance and personality, and their customs and rituals (described in great detail). She also includes colorful and vivid portrayals of such customs, and offers explanations and interpretations for the cultural information mentioned. Other times, of course, Hilda fails to describe or interpret what she observes from the point of view of the Navajos. In this sense, her outsider portrayal of the Navajo permeates, at times, a condescending view of the Native Americans. However, these learners were well trained in the use of a critical discourse analysis approach in their reading of literary texts in this course. I hypothesized that this fact would soften the impact of the significant cultural load of this text.

I also anticipated that the outsider perspective in *Desert Wife* would facilitate the learners' access to the cultural content of the fragment for several reasons. First, this perspective offered the values that the narrator associated with some behaviors of the Native Americans, which would help learners explain those behaviors to a certain extent by contrasting them with their own. Second, this perspective offered abundant cultural information, new and factual, through the eyes of an observer, which would contribute to its accessibility. As said before, these learners were trained in a critical discourse approach to reading, and I assumed that they would be able to identify the narrator's biases and prejudiced views on occasions, and to access the cultural information about the Navajo that they needed in order to do the written tasks. Finally, this perspective went beyond the mere description of cultural information towards explanation and interpretation. At some points in the text, the narrator Hilda attempts to explain and interpret the observable behaviors of the Navajo. Because of these reasons, this text is necessarily long as the outsider perspective involves the inclusion of descriptions, explanations, and interpretations which are not explicit in texts with an insider perspective (as insiders do not need to make explicit the implicit values associated with their behaviors).

I pilot tested the text with a sample of other second-year students at this university. A copy of the fragment is included in the Appendix. I also include in the Appendix a brief commentary about the use of terminology in relation to the Native Americans.

Data Collection and Instrumentation

Primary data sources

The primary data sources were the following: a) a reading response task in Spanish; b) a reading response task in English; c) a visual reformulation.

The participants received general information about the research project and signed a consent form. They received written instructions for each task they were required to do, and completed all tasks individually. At the end of data collection, they were debriefed and had the possibility of elaborating on their understanding of the story.

The learners read the text and wrote a response writing task in Spanish, a response writing task in English, and a visual reformulation. There was no time limit to read the text and learners were allowed to take notes. They completed each task in the order they preferred and were free to choose the length for each task as well as the language to be used in the visual reformulation (L1 or L2). The immediate free recall involved in these tasks is a standard procedure in similar studies (Carrell, 1984c; Lipson, 1983; Steffensen, Joag-Dev and Anderson, 1979; Steffensen, 1984; Sharifian, Rochecouste and Malcolm, 2004).

The main reason for the inclusion of the response writing task as a task (instead of a proper summary, for instance) was to allow readers to respond to the fragment in their own ways (instead of having to retell the text accurately). I anticipated, however, that this response task would necessarily include, in some way or another, a sort of self-directed summary of portions of the prompt text. The response writing task in Spanish offered the possibility of observing the interaction between the L1 and the L2, especially considering that L2 readers and writers use their L1 discourse knowledge during reading and writing (Bernhardt and Kamil, 1995; Bernhardt, 2003; Droop and Verhoeven, 2003; Fitzgerald, 2003; Koda, 1994). Added to this, even though learners had CAE level as mentioned elsewhere, there was the possibility that potential difficulties in the participants' use of their L2 would inhibit their knowledge of some of the requirements of the narrative task, fundamental for the production of a response writing task in the L2.[2]

One of the reasons for the inclusion of the visual reformulation among the written tasks was its simplicity and power of representation (Derrida, 1994) as well as its usefulness to justify emotional responses in reading (Sadoski and Paivio, 1994). To put oneself in someone else's shoes requires imagination (Byram and Grundy, 2002; Kramsch, 1995), and the visual reformulation aimed to offer a forum for its manifestation (Burnett and Gardner, 2006). The idea was that students reacted visually with the purpose of accessing their non-verbal, imaginative systems (Arizpe, 2001; Pope Edwards and Mayo Willis, 2000; Sadoski and Paivio, 1994). Another reason resided in the power of images as a strategy to recall textual information (Sadoski and Paivio, 1994). The integration of textual information in visual format is related with the comprehension, integration, and appreciation of reading material (Pope Edwards and Mayo Willis, 2000; Sadoski and Paivio, 1994). Finally, the visual reformulation aimed at stimulating the cognitive through the affective in order to satisfy the

---

[2] The response writing tasks in the L1 and the L2, as well as the use of a prompt text in Spanish (L1) in the broader study, address another critical aspect of the larger study (which I do not discuss here) that aimed at answering the following questions, among others: Does the language difference (in the prompt texts, and the response writing tasks) matter in the cultural dimension of L2 reading? What happens when readers experience culturally unique content in L1 reading? What role does translation across languages play in this cultural dimension of reading?

perceived need to unify the cognitive sphere and the affective domain (Burnett and Gardner, 2006; Byram and Grundy, 2002; Kramsch, 1995, 2003; Millard and Marsh, 2001; Sanders Bustle, 2004; Tierney, 1994), specially acute in countries like Argentina where many times the educational environment limits the development of this imaginative dimension.

Even though the participants were advanced learners of English (CAE level), their productive capacity was crucial to the creation of a visual reformulation because this task required the inclusion of a strong narrative component – given the narrative nature of the selected fragment itself. The narrative element in this task required the integration of different kinds of knowledge, including linguistic, cognitive, social, and pragmatic capacities (Allen et al., 1994). At a linguistic level, participants needed control over the logical and temporal organization. At a cognitive level, they had to be able to use the typical elements in short stories such as events, aims, and consequences and to know how these elements interrelate. At the level of social knowledge, learners needed to be able to explain the motivations and the behaviors of the characters and to include information about their mental states. At a pragmatic level, they had to know how to create the frame or context for a story, to be able to distinguish the different voices present in a story (e.g. narrator and characters), to be able to distinguish the main and secondary characters and refer to them, and to have the skill not to confuse their roles and activities. In sum, the visual reformulation required a high productive capacity (Allen et al., 1994).

Learners were well trained to produce the response writing tasks and the visual reformulation. They had produced these tasks on several occasions in response to other literary texts used in this course during the year, and prior to implementing this study. I therefore anticipated that the tasks would not pose problems. Specifically for the visual reformulations, learners knew that a visual reformulation is defined as the visual representation of textual content including the combination of words, phrases, and/or sentences with visual information in different formats of varying complexity such as charts, tables, graphs, grids, mind maps, flowcharts, diagrams, drawings, and the like. Considering that there were likely to be individual differences in the participants' capacity to produce a visual reformulation as well as in their preference for some of these options, they were free to choose any format. I discouraged the production of a pure visual reformulation (e.g. only drawings without words, phrases or sentences) because it would have resulted in highly idiosyncratic productions, making their analysis and interpretation difficult. There was no time limit to accomplish the tasks or a word limit.

Overall, then, and in consonance with the theoretical framework on identity on which this study rests, the response writing tasks and the visual reformulation allowed for the emergence of idiosyncratic responses to this fragment, shaped by the learners' multiple cultural identities, by encouraging their imaginative and personal reactions. Complementary to this, in alignment with socio-cultural perspectives on reading, the learners' responses are also idiosyncratic precisely because they are framed within this specific socio-cultural context. As mentioned elsewhere, even though these tasks necessarily involved some summary writing, they went beyond that by encouraging imaginative and personal responses as well. A skilled reader can, with the appropriate knowledge of text structure, summarize a text but have little understanding of the cultural dimension behind it. However, to produce the response writing tasks and the visual reformulation, summarizing alone was not enough. The participants had to make sense of the cultural cues as well as the culturally situated information in the fragment, relate them to their own cultural parameters, and in so doing bring in their experiences, knowledge and background to their interpretation. Added to this, participants were free to respond to particular aspects of the fragment which called their attention, without being committed to reflecting Hilda's view of the Navajos, i.e. the view of the cultural outsider and narrator of the text. I anticipated that this freedom would generate varied responses, which I would be able to place in the different stages within the Model of Cultural Apprehension described in the data analysis section.

Secondary data sources

The secondary data sources were the following: a) questionnaire about reading in Spanish; b) questionnaire about reading in English; c) biographical information; d) individual interviews at the beginning, middle, and end of the academic year; d) questions to elicit the learners' prior knowledge about the text topics; e) text underlined by the learners with the parts they perceived as problematic or difficult for any reason; f) open questions eliciting the participants' emotional reactions awoken by the text.

The learners answered two questionnaires (in Spanish) about reading, one about reading in English and the other about reading in Spanish. These questionnaires aimed at gathering information about different aspects such as their interest in reading, their reading habits (as well as those of family members), their favorite authors and titles, the time spent on reading outside formal education, their knowledge about the reading process, difficulties experienced during reading, attitudes towards reading, availability of reading material at home, and the time spent at libraries, among others. The participants' visions of and attitudes toward reading were important because they delineated how subjects conceived of reading and what values and assumptions they associated with it (Artelt, 2005; Burgess, Hecht, and Lonigan, 2002; Gee, 2001; Worthy, Moorman, and Turner, 1999). Some relevant questions from the questionnaires, which I pilot tested with a sample of other second-year students at this university, are included in the Appendix.

Learners also answered some questions designed to elicit their prior knowledge in relation to the topic of the text. These questions were open, of the kind *Write everything you know about ... If you are not sure, write what you think you know,* and aimed at identifying the learners' prior knowledge about the Navajo as well as their imagination of a Christmas celebration in a Native American context and their attitudes toward it – fundamental as they constitute the point of entrance to the text. The learners answered these questions before reading the text. Although the participants lacked specific knowledge about the Navajo, I anticipated that they would be able to use their knowledge of tribal communities (of the US) and tribal rituals and customs in general as acquired throughout their school lives in order to access the text. I also thought it would be easy for these learners to relate this general knowledge gained at school with their personal experience of Christmas in their cultural context, and on this basis anticipate similarities and contrasts. For instance, I hypothesized that learners would be familiar with the following cultural details: that a Navajo celebration would be a *community* celebration (as opposed to a *family* celebration), that it would be a celebration in the *open air* (not in a *home*); that it would be an *active* festivity with the presence of dances, fires, and music (in contrast with a family dinner around a Christmas table), that there would be rituals of some kind (as there exist in their own Christmas traditions), and that the Navajos would wear idiosyncratic outfits for the occasion (just as they themselves do), among others. I therefore estimated that there would be no need to use some pre-reading adjunct (e.g. advanced organizer, thematic organizer, preview, etc.) to alert readers to key concepts as the text offered rich and varied indices to trigger the activation of their prior knowledge of and/or world experience related to the text topic. These indices were specific lexical items, diagnostic words which activate the Christmas celebration schema, a title, images (vivid descriptions of places, characters, and events), signaling vocabulary for each element in the narrative structure, etc..

In addition, learners completed a questionnaire with their personal details (with pseudonyms). This information was general and included aspects such as age, gender, nationality, date and place of birth, place of residence, marital status, number of children (if any), type of housing (family, rented, dorm, etc.), people they lived with, education of parents, and year of entrance to university. This information aimed at discovering the characteristics of the wider socio-cultural context (home, cultural, ethnic community) within which these learners read and wrote (Luke and Elkins, 2002; Rogers, 2002).

I complemented the investigation of these aspects about the participants (i.e. reading habits in L1 and L2, prior knowledge about the Navajos, and personal information) with multiple interviews conducted at the beginning, middle, and end of the academic year (as in Alred and Byram, 2002). The assumption behind this data collection procedure was that the multiple observations of the participants over time was likely to account for all the ways they might identify (or not) with aspects of the text at hand. The procedure is consonant with the prominent role of the different aspects of the learners' individualities in a socio-cultural conception of L2 reading as described in the theoretical framework (Alred and Byram, 2002).

As in Cohen et al (1984), I told learners to underline in the text the portions they found to be problematic or confusing for any reason (reasons related with the language, the plot, the cultural content, or any other) as they read the text. The aim here was to observe which portions of the fragment the learners *perceived* as problematic.

Finally, I thought it would be interesting to observe the kinds of feelings aroused by the text. Learners answered three open-ended questions: How does the text make you feel and why?; Do you identify with the celebration described? Why or why not?; and Would you feel at ease in a celebration of this kind? Why or why not? As with the visual reformulation, the aim of this data source was to take into account the affective domain involved in L2 reading.

Data Analysis

The data analysis described below needs to be framed within an understanding of the complexity of reader response and its social situated-ness, the elusiveness of the notion of culture as well as the difficulty to define it, and the complexity of interpreting literary narrative texts due to the overlapping socio-cultural factors involved in any interpretation - as acknowledged in the theoretical framework.

I present below the overall data analysis plan, which involved the following aspects: L1-L2 relationship; global coherence; a Model of Cultural Apprehension; specific reader behaviors in the approach of cultural content; and additional elements related with the visual reformulation. A detailed description of the measures and procedures involved in this data analysis phase is included in the Appendix.

L1-L2 relationship

Although the focus of this study as revealed in the research question was to inspect how learners approached the cultural content of literary narrative texts during EFL reading in this setting, I needed to take into account a number of issues. First, these were EFL learners, so it was important to consider the role that reading in the L1 and the L2 played. To observe this relationship, I used the information in the questionnaires about reading in both languages as well as in the interviews I conducted during the year in order to gain a global picture. In addition, I required the production of *two* response writing tasks, one in English and one in Spanish. Also, the larger study used another fragment, written in Spanish, about a Christmas celebration in another socio-cultural context specially included to observe this interaction.

Global coherence

Second, I needed to have a measure showing a holistic evaluation of each task, or in other words, its overall impression, or global coherence. I thought that determining the coherence of the written tasks would help me differentiate between problems related with language issues in the L1 and the L2 (language ability, writing skill, reading skill, etc.), and those related with the perception/ apprehension of the cultural aspects in the text. I could perfectly well foresee student productions which would be fully coherent as pieces of writing (meaning that the writers had a good command of the language/s), but which would show no grasp of the cultural significance of the events, situations, background, characters, and other elements in the text. The converse was also possible, i.e. participants with different degrees of cultural awareness and sensitivity, but poor linguistic skills (poor knowledge of the language/s, and poor reading and/or writing skills, either in Spanish or English). This measure would also help me explore the interaction between the L1 and the L2 further: if I assigned the same global coherence to a participant's response task in Spanish and in English, I would be able to fully rule out the language factor. This was something that would leave me ample room for maneuver within the cultural dimension of the study.

To determine the holistic evaluation, overall impression or global coherence of each task, I chose a scale 1 – 5, which I adapted from Penningroth and Rosenberg (1995). In this scale, 1 amounts to an inadequate text in which it was hard to decipher what the writer is trying to say, with little or no coherence at all, and 5 refers to a completely coherent piece of writing.

> *Holistic evaluation, overall impression or global coherence of the participants' productions*
>
> - Level 1: *inadequate.*
> - Level 2: *partially adequate.*
> - Level 3: *adequate.*
> - Level 4: *good.*
> - Level 5: *very good.*

Cultural apprehension: A general model

Finally, within this cultural dimension, which is the focus of this chapter, the ultimate aim was to discover how these EFL readers approached or apprehended the cultural content of this fragment. I designed a Model of Cultural Apprehension during L2 reading, which I adapted from Alred, Byram, and Fleming (2006), Byram and Morgan (1994), Byram and Fleming (2001), Kramsch (1993, 1998), and Neuner and Byram (2003). Consistent with Sharifian, Rochecouste and Malcolm (2004), I propose here that the apprehension, comprehension or understanding[3] of the cultural aspects of (literary narrative) texts during L2 reading is not an all or nothing affair, but rather a question of degrees as well as increasing levels of complexity, accuracy, and details. More specifically, this is a six-stage model which attempts to describe the different ways in which learners may approach cultural issues during EFL reading.

I needed a measure of cultural apprehension which was congruent with the theoretical perspectives that framed this study. In this sense, it is important to observe that this model acknowledges the multiple and varied factors (al the level of the individual, the context in which reading occurs, the socio-cultural context, and the historical and global context) which influence reading in a given culture, in particular the aspects identified as central in this theoretical framework: the perspective (insider versus outsider) through which cultural aspects are portrayed in a text and through which a reader accesses a text; the crucial influence of a reader's native culture on reading (in its multiple dimensions such as socio-economic status, race, gender, age, religion, sexual orientation, educational background, physical appearance, special capacities, and others); and the flexibility of reader responses given this interplay of factors. On this basis, I suggest here that this model offers a solid framework for the exploration of the cultural dimension of reading in a foreign language, especially the stages through which the cultural aspects of a given text may be approached during EFL reading. I develop this model fully in the Appendix.

I assigned one level of cultural apprehension (0,1,2,3,4,5) to each written task using this model. Levels 0 and 1 are critical, because they involve the perception, or lack of perception, of cultural elements (cultural details, similarities, differences, always on the basis of the reader's own culture). The perception of the different, exciting, and attractive elements of a given culture is possible through the identification of key vocabulary, and works as a bridge for stages 2, 3, 4, and 5 in the Model.

Model of Cultural Apprehension during foreign/second language reading

Level 0.   Omission, total rejection, or total acceptance of cultural aspects.

Level 1.   Perception/identification of cultural differences. Access to levels 2, 3, 4, and 5.

Level 2.   Identification of own values and ideas. Identification of the cultural assumptions behind one's own culture (insider perspective).

Level 3.   Perception of culture C2 from one's own frame of reference (outsider perspective).

Level 4.   Perception of culture C2 from the frame of reference of members of culture C2 (insider perspective).

Level 5.   Perception of culture C1 from the perspective of culture C2 (outsider perspective).

Cultural idea units

How to assign level 1 to the participants' productions turned out to be problematic. I realized that I needed to identify some a priori elements for coding, simply to organize the wealth of data I was confronted with. I identified the culturally distinctive idea units

---

[3] See issue about terminology (pp.6-7).

mentioned in the fragment with the help of a US native speaker, or in other words, the idea units related with the Native American culture, not those related with Hilda's American cultural background. Within this cultural dimension, the first thing I did was to observe these idea units as recalled by the participants in the written tasks. This measure of amount of free recall in the form of idea units is consistent with Carrell (1984c), Steffensen, Joag-Dev and Anderson (1979), and Sharifian, Rochecouste and Malcolm (2004), all of whom consider these idea units as the "important propositions" in the text (Steffensen, Joag-Dev and Anderson, 1979: 12). Those learners who were able to recall (i.e. identify or perceive) these idea units in the tasks reached level 1 in the Model of Cultural Apprehension. The omission of idea units was as significant as their inclusion. A caveat here is that these idea units are only *indicative* of a first step toward cultural apprehension, i.e., level 1 in the Model of Cultural Apprehension. The recall of particular idea units, atomistic as it may appear at first glance, presupposes the reader's *perception* of such ideas, with the concomitant awareness of the Otherness behind them – something that constitutes the point of entrance to higher levels of cultural understanding. A preliminary analysis of the idea units identified and codified at this stage led me to add, drop, and/or collapse elements to reflect the key cultural aspects in this text as accurately as possible[4].

Cultural apprehension: Specific reader behaviors

Apprehending the cultural content of reading material required, as mentioned before, the openness of mind to discover new horizons of ideas, something many learners had difficulty in doing. The process of cultural understanding, as portrayed in the model above, necessarily involved learners elaborating, distorting, inferencing, generalizing, and simplifying (among other behaviors) the cultural content of what they had read, depending on the level of cultural apprehension they had reached. I therefore decided to observe what learners did in the written tasks, i.e. how they modified the content of the text in writing the reading response and visual reformulation tasks.

This procedure of observing the *kind* of information recalled is a standard measure in studies of this kind (Steffensen, Joag-Dev and Anderson, 1979; Sharifian, Rochecouste and Malcolm (2004). However, in all cases the measures of analysis are more general than the ones designed for this study. For instance, Steffensen, Joag-Dev and Anderson (1979: 15) focus on two broad changes that people make when recalling passages, namely elaborations or "culturally appropriate extensions of the text" and distortions or "culturally inappropriate modifications of the text". Sharifian, Rochecouste and Malcolm (2004: 211) include five elements in their classification index for recalled idea units, namely "correct recall, partial recall, distortion/reinterpretation, addition, omission". In this study, the text modifications considered are more varied and specific. A list appears below (I define each element in the Appendix):

---

[4] The idea units I identified in the fragment (with the help of a US native-speaker) took the form of short phrases/propositions. I then codified them in the participants' written tasks. The idea units were the following (Table 2): *desert landscape; Navajo dressed in their best clothes; a community celebration; fires; dances and music; handmade musical instruments; wrestling and racing; families eat together; eating and eating; bread making; Native Americans stroll with raw beefsteaks; stew preparation; coffee preparation; happiness and fun;* and *food in general* –among others.

Cultural apprehension: specific reader behaviors

Elaborating cultural information
Distorting culture C2
Intruding cultural details from own culture
Making evident errors
Inferencing appropriately from the texts
Inferencing inappropriately (inferences not motivated or justified by textual content)
Including irrelevant information
Rationalizing
Simplifying
Generalizing
Making evaluative comments
Including an adequate morale
Including an inadequate or wrong morale
Explicitly including the feelings and motivations of the characters, appropriately inferred from the text
Explicitly including the feelings and motivations of the characters, wrongly inferred from the text or not motivated or justified by its textual content
Including culturally adequate details

Visual reformulations: additional elements[5]

Finally, given the visual nature of the visual reformulations, for this task in particular I observed and codified the presence of the following additional elements:

(a) images both at the level of the paragraph and the whole text;
(d) visual portrayal of stereotypes from the learners' native culture;
(e) visual portrayal of stereotypes from the Native American culture.

The main measurement I used to answer the research question was the Model of Cultural Apprehension. I integrated each piece of data, from the response tasks to the measure of prior knowledge to the information about personal background to the questionnaires about reading habits (in fact, all the collected data) in my decision-making regarding the assignment of a level in this model to each written task produced by the students (response writing task in Spanish, response writing task in English, and visual reformulation). For instance, if I thought that a task should be assigned level 4, which reveals a fairly sophisticated approach of cultural content, I checked that the information regarding the literacy environment in the home and the student's reading habits and preferences in both languages (to name some aspects in the data sources) aligned with the demands in this level (see Appendix). If I found any incongruent information, or any information which did not allow me to confirm the appropriateness of such level on the basis of all the available data sources and measures of analysis, I started afresh (e.g. the overall coherence of the task, the student's own perception

---

[5] Something to take into account in the analysis of the visual reformulations is the little guidance that exists for the interpretation of these data, as Burnett and Gardner (2006) point out.

of his/her prior knowledge regarding the Navajo, etc.). I also explicitly compared the response writing tasks in both languages.

Data were triangulated with the help of two research assistants, who worked as external readers/ coders/analysts of all data sources. A consistency rate (agreement) of 95% or more among researcher and research assistants in the different stages of coding and analysis was reached, representing acceptable inter-rater reliability. In addition, the existence of multiple and varied data sources also contributed to triangulating results. When I could not confirm a category of analysis through evidence from two or more data sources, I re-thought, re-named, collapsed with other categories, or simply refuted the category. Triangulation is crucial in studies of cultural understanding basically for two reasons: first, any portrayal (here textual representation) of a given culture is always open to objection as any representation will reveal certain cultural aspects and hide others; second, all the participants involved in a study of this kind (learners, teacher, researcher, external coders) go through the stages of cultural apprehension described in the model above in relation to another culture, adding a layer of complexity to the analysis.

RESULTS

I will first report the results corresponding to the primary data sources (response writing task in Spanish, in English, and visual reformulation) in order to move afterwards to the secondary data sources, which will work as a frame for the overall picture. I will conclude the section with an analysis of two students' work with the intention of giving a flavor of the type of responses that were recorded.

Results about the Primary Data Sources: Response Writing Tasks and the Visual Reformulations

I will start with the results related to the Cultural Apprehension Model, move on to the coherence results, and then focus on the reader behavior results. In so doing, my aim is to offer an integrated view of how I tried to answer the research question, i.e. How do EFL learners approach the cultural content of literary narrative texts during reading in this setting?

Cultural apprehension

Regarding the levels of cultural apprehension in the model, the most interesting result to note is that the majority of the learners perceived cultural aspects (between 69% and 73% in the response writing tasks and 83% in the reformulations; level 1). This pervasive perception of the different, exotic, and attractive features in the cultural content of the text (such as the fires, dances, food preparation, clothing and many others) helped these learners focus their attention on the differences between themselves and others. Together with the fact that the omission of cultural aspects (level 0) varied between 15,28% and 26,39% depending on the task, both results reveal the openness of these learners to investigate new horizons of ideas, despite their difficulty at times to do so. This difficulty was revealed here in the form of a superficial and stereotypical approach of the textual content, represented by level 3 in this model. Level 3 was high - between 63,89% and 69,4% in the response writing tasks, and 47,22% in the reformulations. Although the majority of the learners were interested in discovering alternative perspectives in the interpretation of familiar and unfamiliar phenomena within the cultural practices of the Navajo (as revealed by the results related to levels 0 and 1 in the model), their own frames of reference tended to mediate this interpretation (level 3). Put differently, these learners did distance themselves from their own perspectives in a way, but had difficulty in relativizing their views and favoring those of others, which led them to judge Otherness on the basis of their own cultural parameters, resulting in distorted perspectives. This is the underlying process represented by level 3. In brief, the recognition of diversity within a culture/subculture implies going beyond the initial and incidental comparison and confrontation, represented in this model by level 1, to be able to have access to the perspective of others, to alternative interpretations of the world (Byram, 2000), examining stereotyped visions (Byram and Fleming, 2001; Kramsch, 1993, 1998; Neuner and Byram, 2003), which were usually associated with level 3 in this model

Another important result is that only 11% of the learners reached level 4, a level that required the perception of culture C2 from the frame of reference of members of this culture, i.e., from an insider perspective. In this sense, the experience with this text shows that it is difficult to get from a text more than what one is *willing* or *ready* to know about another culture, because a lot tends to be lost in the interpretive process in this respect (Moreiras, 1991). The low percentage in this level also supports the existence of a threshold of cultural awareness of others, beyond which what was different or novel remained inaccessible. The existence of this threshold can be understood if one considers that in order to capture the cultural aspects in a text, one needs to have attitudes of curiosity, openness, and willingness to suspend disbelief and value judgments with regard to other people's beliefs and behaviors (Byram and Morgan, 1994; Mountford and Wadham-Smith, 2000; O'Byrne, 2003). There must also exist willingness to approach what is not familiar, recognizing the importance of understanding the manifestations of another culture in the context in which they are framed - precisely what level 4 involves. However, this approach to Otherness is not limited to the perception of what is exotic or exciting about a culture or subculture, i.e. level 1, but goes beyond and is hard to achieve. Few students made a genuine effort to get familiar with the weird, to enter the Navajos' minds and hear their inner voice, judging and evaluating the actions and beliefs present in the text from the perspective and the world of the Navajos themselves (Byram and Morgan, 1994; (Byram, Gribkova, and Starkey, 2002; Mountford and Wadham-Smith, 2000; O'Byrne, 2003). To reach level 4, learners should have attempted to do all of this – something that was infrequent. In fact, as mentioned before, the prevalent approach to the cultural content of the text was of a superficial and stereotypical kind, congruent with level 3 in the model.

The low percentage obtained for level 4 in the tasks (11%) shows that the opaque portions in this text required extreme perception to be accessed, and may not have allowed for the activation of the learners' prior horizon of ideas. The difficulty of many learners to capture Otherness may have originated in the role of personal prejudices, bias, partial information, and suppositions regarding intentions (all of these, characteristic of level 3) in the process of appreciation and evaluation of textual content. The use of prejudiced, denigrating or negative adjectives abounded in the written tasks, in general associated with contrasts between the Navajo and the narrator (Hilda) and her culture, and expressed through dichotomies such as Indian reservation / civilization; wild life reservation / people from the town; aboriginal reservation / society, white people, white race. Most of the stereotyped references observed in the tasks were about the Navajo themselves. Learners visualized them as dark Indians with feathers, hair bands, dressed in tiny cloths, with their chests uncovered, living in huts, in a deserted landscape with cactuses and some hills, and yelling like pirates (sometimes in their horses).

Nobody reached levels 2 or 5 in any of the tasks. This is not surprising, because the study was not especially designed to access the learners' own values and ideas and the cultural assumptions behind their culture (level 2, insider perspective). The perception of the learners' culture from the perspective of the Navajos or the Americans was not a focus either (level 5, outsider perspective).

More specifically about level 1, the most frequently mentioned element in the tasks was the reference to the dances and the music for entertainment (65,2% in both response writing tasks and 83,3% in the visual reformulation). The learners considered it essential to the celebration and completely accessible.[6] The other aspects judged to be essential and accessible by between 60% and 100% of the learners were included in the tasks in significantly lower percentages such as the community celebration (23,6%), the Navajo dressed in their best clothes (16,6%), 200 Navajos present in the celebration (scarce mention), family meeting to eat (15, 2%), specific activities such as wrestling and racing (12%), the habit of rising early (11% in both response writing tasks, and only 1,3% in the visual reformulations), and wood supply (3,1%) (Table 2).

Learners did not significantly include in the tasks the aspects they considered to be auxiliary. Such was the case of the washing of the dishes (10,1%), the stew preparation (8,3%), strolling with raw beefsteaks in their hands (4,1%), and the preparation of coffee (1,8%) (the last three were perceived to be completely accessible). The exceptions were the fires which were considered auxiliary by 79% of the learners but were mentioned by between 43% and 63% depending on the task (Table 2).

Reader behaviors

Now with regard to reader behaviors in the learners' approach of the cultural content of this text, in general these learners had difficulty relativizing a given phenomenon, i.e., perceive it as specific of a certain time and place instead of the norm. Consider that this text is one of three in a broader study, especially selected because of its remoteness in several parameters. The students' lack of understanding regarding the importance of some phenomena did not contribute to the achievement of a genuine understanding of the Navajos. Although some learners became aware of the complexity and the diversity of the values in this native culture and were conscious of the ambiguity of their own perspective in view of that of the Native Americans, revealed by level 4 in the Model of Cultural Apprehension, many times they did not adequately frame the interpretations they made and presented a monolithic and homogeneous view of this culture. This approach, as mentioned before, was revealed in this study as prominent levels 1 and 3, and a low level 4. I observed some recurrent reader behaviors congruent with this approach, namely high percentages of distortions, intrusions, errors, rationalizations, simplifications, and inadequate interpretations,

---

[6] Another data source not described in this chapter was a questionnaire in which students ranked each identified and coded culturally significant idea unit as essential or auxiliary to the celebration in this cultural context. They also had to rank each element in relation to its perceived accessibility or inaccessibility (see table 2).

and relatively low percentages of elaborations and adequate interpretations. I offer more details about these reader behaviors below.

About 49.9% of the learners intruded cultural information from their own culture and 59,2% distorted the cultural information presented by the text. By contrast, elaborations were relatively low (25,4%). This finding does not surprise, considering the superficial and stereotyped knowledge about the Navajo culture that learners had. The significant intrusions from the learners' own culture can be explained taking into account that it is possible that the visual memory of a personal event related with certain narrative episodes in the text had provoked the filtering of contextual information and the generation of intrusions (Allen et. al., 1994). Consistent with Singer and Donlan (1994), it is possible that the perceived difficulty of some portions of the text had inclined learners to direct their attention to anything familiar in the textual content, in an attempt to arrive at a reconstructive memory of the story (Table 1).

About half the learners made adequate inferences in the response writing tasks (43% in Spanish, 48% in English), decreasing to 19,44% in the visual reformulations. In agreement with Bower, Black and Turner (1994), these learners included in the tasks the implicit actions belonging to the Christmas schema in a Native American community which were not present in the fragment they had read. Many times the learners made inferences, expressed relations, or reached conclusions not present in the text neither motivated by it. The response writing tasks generated about 40% of wrong inferences of this kind, falling to 16.6% in the reformulations. Learners also included inferred feelings in the tasks (an average of 21% in all tasks), which may be seen as an attempt to comprehend the actions and behaviors of the members of the other culture. The inclusion of wrong inferred feelings fluctuated between 37,5% and 52,7% depending on the task (Table 1).

A surprising finding is related to the fact that the presence of irrelevant information in the tasks was scarce (not over 9%, only 4% in the visual reformulations). I had anticipated that learners would include a lot of irrelevant information for two reasons: first, they lacked solid cultural knowledge to evaluate the relevance of textual content; second, the text included abundant culturally detailed content as well as attractive information which was significant at the level of each narrative episode - though not necessarily at a global level. This result means that learners responded to indices in the text which revealed which parts were likely to be important (Table 1).

Only between 16% and 18% of the learners made personal and adequate interpretations of textual content, mentioning possible messages or a morale they thought the text was supposed to give. Concomitantly, about 69% of inadequate interpretations were found in the response writing tasks, and 31,9% in the visual reformulations. Both adequate and inadequate interpretations were lower for the visual reformulations, maybe because of the visual nature of the task itself. These interpretations were accompanied by evaluative language, which revealed the learners' attitudes toward the propositions mentioned in the text (Table 1).

Faced with a cultural difference or a contradiction of their own cultural expectations, learners adopted one of the following strategies (adapted from Archer, 1997): a) they corrected one aspect of culture C2 so as to make it consistent with C1; b) they modified aspects of both cultures; and c) they corrected one aspect of culture C1 to match culture C2. This process of rationalizations involved relating aspects of both cultures which should not have been related, reaching between 41,67% and 70,83% in the response writing tasks in Spanish and English respectively.

Table 1. Analysis of the response writing tasks (RWT) and the visual reformulations

	Desert Wife		
	RWT *Spanish*	*RWT* *English*	*Visual* *Reformulation*
Frame - no theme	0,00	1,39	8,33
Frame - adequate theme	33,33	33,33	43,06
Frame - partially adequate theme	50,00	45,83	30,56
Frame - inadequate theme	9,72	11,11	1,39
Without frame or theme	2,78	2,78	11,11
Without frame - adequate theme	2,78	2,78	6,94
Without frame - inadequate theme	1,39	1,39	0,00
Elaborations	23,61	29,17	23,61
Distortions	61,11	61,11	55,56
Intrusions	55,56	43,06	51,39
Inferences	43,06	48,61	19,44
Wrong inferences	38,89	41,67	16,67
Irrelevant information	9,72	9,72	4,17
Inferred feelings	20,83	22,22	22,22
Wrong inferred feelings	52,78	44,44	37,50
Evaluative language	26,39	37,50	9,72
Adequate morale/interpretation of learners	18,06	16,67	16,67
Inadequate morale/interpretation of learners	69,44	68,06	31,94
Rationalization: two textual elements	41,67	44,44	5,56
Rationalization: one textual element; one inv	70,83	63,89	11,11
Explicit errors	87,50	87,50	58,33
Simplifications	65,28	61,11	56,94
Generalizations	33,33	31,94	27,78
Cultural details	38,89	44,44	48,61

This means that learners used the resources at their disposal to approach Otherness (in general from an ethnocentric position), i.e. they accommodated different cultural features in order to fit in with their own reality. In other words, they had difficulty recognizing the importance of Native American cultural aspects within their cultural context (Alred, Byram, and Fleming, 2006; Byram and Grundy, 2003; Byram, Nichols, and Stevens, 2001). In this process of rationalizations, and congruent with Archer (1997), many students resisted alternative perspectives and rejected them through devaluation and stigmatization of those ideas as ridiculous using denigrating techniques.

Added to this, there was an overwhelming presence of explicit errors in the tasks (87,50% in both response writing tasks and 58,33% in the reformulations) as well as simplifications of textual content (between 61% and 65% in the response writing tasks and 56% in the reformulations). The inclusion of generalizations reached an average of 30% in all cases.

Table 2. Perceived accessibility of cultural aspects in idea units, assessment of their importance, and their inclusion in the tasks

	Accessibility of idea units						Importance		Inclusion in the tasks		
	1	2	3	4	5	6	Essential	Auxiliary	RWT	RWT	VR
	Completely Accessible	Moderately Accessible	Perceived as obstacle	Perceived as serious obstacle	Not Accessible	I do not remember			Response task Spanish	Response task English	Visual Reformulation
Desert landscape	37,50	18,06	9,72	0,00	6,94	26,39	56,94	43,06	0,00	0,00	1,39
Dressed in best clothes	87,50	8,33	2,78	0,00	0,00	1,39	61,11	38,89	19,44	13,89	16,67
200 Navajos present	76,39	8,33	8,33	0,00	1,39	2,78	62,50	37,50	2,78	8,33	2,78
Community celebration	70,83	13,89	4,17	2,78	2,78	5,56	90,28	9,72	23,61	23,61	23,61
Fires	44,44	25,00	19,44	8,33	1,39	1,39	19,44	79,17	43,06	44,44	63,89
Stroll with raw beefsteaks	40,28	12,50	16,67	8,33	2,78	18,06	33,33	63,89	5,56	4,17	2,78
Wood supply	52,78	19,44	9,72	5,56	4,17	8,33	79,17	20,83	5,56	2,78	1,39
Dances and music	87,50	8,33	1,39	0,00	0,00	2,78	76,39	23,61	63,89	66,67	83,33
Musical instruments	68,06	8,33	5,56	1,39	1,39	16,67	34,72	65,28	4,17	4,17	6,94
Wrestling and racing	44,44	33,33	9,72	2,78	0,00	9,72	65,28	33,33	15,28	9,72	11,11
Efficiency and inteligence	26,39	15,28	8,33	6,94	2,78	40,28	45,83	50,00	2,78	2,78	2,78
Families eat together	80,56	11,11	0,00	1,39	2,78	2,78	81,94	18,06	13,89	18,06	13,89
Eating and eating	70,83	13,89	5,56	2,78	0,00	6,94	44,44	55,56	6,94	6,94	0,00
Washing the dishes	65,28	12,50	6,94	5,56	0,00	9,72	40,28	58,33	9,72	9,72	11,11
Bread making	76,39	13,89	6,94	1,39	0,00	1,39	45,83	52,78	29,17	23,61	36,11
Stew preparation	36,11	22,22	23,61	5,56	2,78	9,72	33,33	66,67	8,33	9,72	6,94
Preparing coffee	34,72	18,06	13,89	5,56	4,17	22,22	16,67	81,94	0,00	1,39	4,17
Meet - food									75,00	63,89	73,61
Happiness and fun									41,67	38,89	38,89

(percentages)

A simple reason for this result may be tied to the fact that the memory of specific episodes decreased with the time that evolved between the actual reading of the text and the writing of the tasks.

Finally, learners included cultural details in the tasks (between 38% and 48%), something I failed to anticipate because this was a remote culture. Here it is possible that the rich cultural details in the text called the learners' attention because of their sensational·tenor, therefore facilitating their recall (Maccabe and Peterson, 1990) (see Table 1).

Results about the Secondary Data Sources

Through multiple interviews and a questionnaire, I gathered information regarding these learners' conceptions of reading as well as their reading habits and preferences both in English and in Spanish. Their analysis revealed learners with strong internal motivations, who liked to read in both languages, who thought that reading was important in their lives, who appreciated books as presents, who talked with family members and friends about their readings, who had access to varied reading material, and who had grown in homes that encouraged reading. The students' visions of and attitudes toward reading were important because they delineated how these learners conceived reading and what values and assumptions they associated with it. The attitudes and beliefs revealed by the interviews and questionnaire showed students who were motivated and who were immersed in contexts that valued and encouraged reading. All of the foregoing allowed me to foreground, in this study, the impact of the socio-cultural contexts associated with L1 and L2 reading for these learners. At the same time, it guaranteed a good reading performance and discarded difficulties related with their reading abilities. These facts, together with their attested CAE level of English attainment, which ruled out significant linguistic deficits, allowed me to frame the reading difficulties observed in the tasks within the cultural dimension of L2 reading.

The questions designed to elicit the learners' prior knowledge about the text topic were revealing. Learners included multiple and varied elements related with a Christian celebration by a pagan group, as they imagined it, such as: the dances (50%), the typical food (37.5%), the festive spirit (22%), religious rituals (34,7%), pagan rituals (25%), references to polytheism and sacrifices (9,7%), the fires (26,4%), the songs (23,6%), the special outfits for the occasion (18%), and the idea that each tribe celebrated on its own (individual celebration; 19,4%), among others. Learners referred to a considerable number of additional characteristics, none above 11%, such as the following: community celebration, poor celebration, the duration (from one week to one month), the activities of the women (cooking) and the men (hunting), the painted faces of the Navajo, the drinking, etc. They also mentioned elements associated with their own culture that they thought were not present in a celebration of this kind such as the Christmas tree, the Christmas presents, Santa Claus, and the fireworks. These responses revealed learners who were quite knowledgeable about a Christian celebration in a Native American context.

As in Cohen et al (1984), I told learners to underline in the text the portions they found to be problematic or confusing for any reason (reasons related with the language, the plot, the cultural content, or any other) as they read the text. About 87% of the learners underlined isolated words or short phrases, clearly difficulties related with vocabulary. Another 12% marked the names of the characters. With very low percentages, they also underlined longer fragments such as the reference to the episode of Lady Betty (8,3%), the preparation of coffee, the dances (both with 4%), and the preparation of the stew (only 1,3%), among others. Consistently, between 35% and 88% of the learners ranked all these aspects as completely accessible. In this sense, this underlining reveals that as far as the learners' *perceptions* of the textual content are concerned, no major problematic aspects were identified. However, as mentioned in the results section based on the primary data sources, many difficulties were in fact observed.

The text arose a variety of feelings, both positive and negative, though none above 29%. Learners mentioned the following emotional reactions generated by the fragment, among many others: happiness, melancholy, curiosity, tenderness, solidarity, pity, fear, and loneliness. In addition, the text did not bring to the surface significant personal memories, because of its remote cultural content. About 60% of the learners said they did not identify themselves with the textual content, the reasons being not having gone through a similar experience and the different culture. Surprisingly, 60,9% said they would feel at ease in a celebration of this kind precisely because of the cultural differences, in particular the fact that it was a community celebration (63,4%). This reveals the openness of the participants to get in touch with other cultures. Learners were attracted to this culture, and explicitly mentioned feeling curious and interested (36%).

TWO EXAMPLES

Two sets of three tasks belonging to two students will be described here. The first set belongs to Ciro (pseudonym). The response writing task in Spanish, written first, is quite detailed and includes a frame or setting for the story as well as an adequate theme. The specific name of the Native American reservation, Covered Water, is mentioned. There is an attempt to list the cultural differences between a Christmas celebration for Hilda and her husband and for the Navajo, but this attempt is filtered with an intrusion from this learner's culture ("a specific meal") and his/her evaluation regarding the meaning of the celebration for the Navajo. Notice the possibly derogative diminutive in "little warm fires". Considerable space is devoted to the lack of religious connotation attached to Christmas in a Native American context, with an emphasis on its festive spirit and the ultimate aim of entertainment. There is an intrusion in the reference to the "building" ("edificio") where Hilda and Ken live, which is then referred to as a "store" ("puesto"). The point here is not whether Ciro remembers where the couple lived exactly (a farm, a reservation, a store) but rather that Ciro intrudes a common place to live in from his/her cultural reality nowadays, i.e. a "building" (Spanish "edificio"). In addition, Ciro assumes that because Hilda and Ken are referred to as a couple in the text, they must be married, and therefore uses terms like "husband" for Ken and "Mrs" for San Chee. The response writing task mentions a lot of the episodes described in the text, such as the Navajo dancing, playing their hand-made musical instruments, horse-riding for the men, cooking for the women (cakes and bread-making), with culturally adequate information. This learner mentions varied inferred feelings in reference to the situation in general and the narrator (nostalgia, sadness, anguish). Halfway through the response writing task, Ciro supplies his or her own elaboration, in general supported by the text, by mentioning that Hilda aimed at "adjusting" to the wild life habits of the Navajo. Added to this, he/she inserts an idiosyncratic interpretation, globally motivated by textual content, namely that Hilda is trying to "educate these people". This interpretation enacts a recurrent contrast in most response writing tasks, namely the opposition between the "civilization of the white race" and the "wild life" of the Navajo, or in other words, the dichotomy between civilized and savage. The Navajo are referred to as *aborigines (aborigen)* while the narrator and her husband are referred to as *men of the white race (los hombres de raza blanca)*. The response writing task closes with the reference to Hilda and Ken, in particular her feelings towards their situation in the reservation, away from the Navajo now – following the pattern in the prompt fragment.

La historia transcurre en una reservación natural llamada Covered Water donde una pareja (la narradora y su esposo) están establecidos hace más de un año. En esta ocasión es Navidad y los habitantes de la reservación (indios Navajos) están preparándose para los festejos. Para la narradora y su grupo de gente la Navidad significa fueguitos cálidos, una comida en particular, y regalos envueltos en papel tissue. Mientras que para los Navajos sólo significaba fueguitos cálidos. Todas las familias se acercan al edificio donde vive la narradora y su esposo Ken y se disponen a hacer los preparativos para el festejo. Los indios están vestidos con sus mejores ropas y se agrupan junto a sus familias. Mientras las mujeres cocinan tortas y pan, los hombres entrenan sus caballos. Una vez preparada la cena todos disfrutan alrededor de las fogatas ubicadas en varios lugares de la reservación. Mientras transcurre el día realizan danzas y cantos al son de una música típicamente aborigen y producida, también, por instrumentos caseros. Sin embargo, no hay en ellos ni en sus danzas más que el mero propósito de divertirse, reir, y pasar un momento agradable. Se ve claramente que la Navidad no tiene para ellos el mismo sentido que tiene para los hombres de raza blanca. Ven la Navidad como una fiesta, un momento de felicidad, pero sin ningún sentido religioso. Durante el transcurso de la historia se ve cómo la narradora (que ha pertenecido a la civilización) trata de amoldarse a la vida salvaje así como también a los hábitos y costumbres de los Navajos. Al mismo tiempo, se ve cómo ella trata, en cierto modo, de "educar" a esta gente. Mrs Chee (narradora) parece dispuesta a adaptarse a dicha vida pero en cierto momento algo ocurre que le trae recuerdos de su vida antes de instalarse allí. Cuando los festejos finalizan y los Navajos se alejan del puesto donde festejan, uno de los personajes llamado Robert se acerca a Mrs Chee y la saluda en Inglés, deseándole una Feliz Navidad. El hecho que hablaba Inglés trae a Mrs Chee un sentimiento de nostalgia hacia la civilización, un deseo de volver a ella y dejar atrás todo lo relacionado con la Reservación. Aunque cuando entra al puesto Mrs Chee trata de esconder su tristeza y de evitar que Ken vea sus lágrimas, éste se da cuenta. Mrs Chee desea expresarle sus deseos y sus angustias pero se da cuenta que en la realidad no le importa el lugar siempre y cuando esté trabajando junto a él.

Using Penningroth and Rosenberg's (1995) five-point scale (see section on data analysis), this response writing task's holistic evaluation (i.e. the overall coherence of the task) was ranked with a 4. Recall that in this scale 1 amounts to an inadequate text in which it is hard to decipher what the writer is trying to say, with little or no coherence at all, and 5 refers to an excellent and completely coherent piece of writing. The overall impression of this response writing task is good, despite the perhaps excessive space devoted to the elaboration around the festive spirit of this celebration, with the author's opinions, evaluative comments and personal interpretations. With respect to the Model of Cultural Apprehension during foreign/second language reading (see Appendix), this task was judged as reaching level 3, which involves the perception of another culture from this learner's frame of reference, or in other words, approaching another culture from an outsider perspective as an observer. This approach helps comprehend another culture only superficially, analyzing and explaining from outside. Even though Ciro's account of some of the Navajo habits and customs is quite detailed and culturally appropriate, his/her attempt at interpreting the Navajo ways of life through their eyes, i.e. level 4 in this model, is modest. Ciro does not try to find the motivations (values and beliefs, for instance) behind the Navajos' observable behaviors, which is a characteristic of level 4. Another element which refrained us (researcher and research assistants) from assigning a higher level in this model was Ciro's own derogative address to the Navajo: the word *Indians* (*indios*) appears in the response writing task as well as expressions such as *these people* (*esta gente*). While the term *Indian* is not considered a derogatory term in the US context (see Appendix, pp.46-47) , it is indeed a pejorative term in these learners' setting.

Ciro's response writing task in English, written second, is a reflection of its counterpart in Spanish. In this version, Ciro makes some vocabulary modifications: the diminutive for the fires is lost (just "warm fires"); the Navajo "dressed in their best clothes" are now "very well" dressed; the "building" is now a "store"; the "reservation" is also referred to as a "farm" – an interference from the reference to Hilda and Ken's farm in the text. The overall tenor of this response writing task is the same as the previous one, though this version in English misses many of the details found in the response writing task in Spanish such as the reference to the baking of the cakes and the bread, the horse-riding, the hand-made musical instruments, etc. The only culturally adequate detail this response writing task adds is the fact that the dances were performed by the older men. Another interesting aspect in this text is the way Ciro uses modality to convey his/her attitude towards the propositions included in his/her writing, in particular to distance himself/herself from the textual content (notice the use of modal lexical items such as the adverb "apparently", the expression "*sort of* melancholy", and the adjective in "*strange* feelings of..."). Also, the regurgitation around the dichotomy "civilization – wild life" is lost in this version, which is shorter. On this basis, the holistic evaluation of this task was higher (5), though the same level 3 was assigned in the Model of Cultural Apprehension, for the same reasons.

> The story takes place in a Wild Reservation where a couple have lived for almost a year. The couple, the woman called Mrs Chee and her husband Ken live in a kind of store placed in the reservation. On this particular occasion all the inhabitants of the reservation (all the Navajos) have come near the store to celebrate Christmas with them. Christmas for the narrator and her friends meant warm fires, berries and presents wrapped in tissue chapters but for the Navajos it just meant warm fires. They arrive at the farm very well dressed, and start dancing and singing. This celebration consists of the dinner prepared by the women and afterwards a sort of dancing performed by the older men. However, their songs and dances aren't done with a ceremonial purpose. In fact the men dance not because it is part of a ritual but rather, to the Navajo and the couple's amusement. The festival occurs in a warm atmosphere, each family around the fire they have built up and everybody seems to be happy and enjoying themselves. After the celebration is over, all the Navajos leave the place and get ready to go back to the heart of the reservation. At that moment something occurs and it's going to bring strange feelings of melancholy and sadness in Mrs Chee. One of the men named Robert and who, apparently, is the only one that speaks English except for Ken and Mrs Chee, wishes Mrs Chee Happy Christmas. Mrs Chee feels a sort of melancholy and longing for her home in the civilization. She tries to hide her feelings and not let Ken see her sadness. In the end, she realizes that the place where she lives is not of crucial importance, as long as she is accompanied by Ken and they are working together.

The visual reformulation, written last, is richer in details compared to the response writing tasks. In addition to the fires, the music, the singing, the dances, and the cooking (which constitute culturally adequate details), Ciro mentions additional details such as the fruitcake, the cutting up of the meat, giving meat to the Navajo families, and the candies, among others. An interesting distortion appears in the reference to the Navajo men yelling like "Comanches" instead of "pirates". Confusion and errors are revealed here, once again, with respect to the setting ("Wild life reservation", "the camp"). The visual reformulation misses a lot of the over-elaboration regarding the festive spirit of the celebration found in the response writing tasks as well as the interpretation around the notion of "educating" the Native Americans which we saw in the first response writing task. Perhaps the visual nature of this task, which Ciro chose to reflect in the form of a chart, contributed to retaining the culturally adequate details while at the same time distancing from the over-elaboration of personally relevant interpretations and the attribution of wrong inferred feelings. Taking into account the foregoing, this task's holistic evaluation was judged to be 5 and the level of cultural apprehension, 4 - higher than the response writing tasks. Level 4 in this model involves the comprehension of another culture from an insider perspective, something that Ciro attempts to do here.

Moving now to the second example, Amadeus's (pseudonym) response writing task in Spanish, written in the first place, reflects his/her idiosyncratic attempt to make sense of the text. This attempt contrasts with Ciro's in a radical way, in the sense that it amounts almost exclusively to Amadeus' analysis and personal interpretations of textual content. Although Amadeus frames his/her view of the fragment in overall congruence with its content, there is no specific description of the actions and behaviors of the Navajo, which abounded in the prompt text. Nor is there an attempt to reflect the Navajos' values and beliefs, which might account for their actions and behaviors in this context. Amadeus presents his/her own view of the text, worded in a personal way, as an outsider to the Navajos' world and their perspective as guests in this Christmas celebration.

> Una pareja de blancos invita a una tribu de indios Navajos a celebrar la Navidad con ellos. La motivación de esta invitación es un deseo de "observar" la forma en que los indios festejan algo totalmente ajeno a su cultura como es la Navidad.
>
> La historia está narrada por San Chee – la chica en la pareja de blancos - y con su manera de relatar deja entrever sus sentimientos, temores y certeza de "no pertenencia" en relación a los eventos incluidos en el cuento.
>
> Creo que el foco de atención del lector debe ser puesto en la total falta de *ingenuidad* de los comentarios de San Chee.
>
> Hay un deseo muy marcado de resaltar la extrañeza de las costumbres aborígenes, testificadas y consignadas como si se tratara de hábitos de la vida silvestre.
>
> A pesar de que a lo largo prevalece un clima de "alegría", San Chee, una vez acabada la fiesta, siente tristeza y añoranza de las Navidades Occidentales. Finalmente, teme que su pareja decida mudarse con los indios.

Amadeus' whole response writing task revolves around the dichotomy between the two cultures, with the focus on the "strangeness" and the "wild" aspect of the Navajo's habits and customs. The multi-episodic nature of the original text is lost here, as Amadeus only refers to the "events included in the text" in general without really mentioning or describing any in detail. Amadeus' task, in this sense, reflects the top-down processing that Sharifian, Rochecouste and Malcolm (2004) observed in their study too. In addition, this learner provides his/her own rationalizations for the textual content, relating elements in the text which could in fact be related but without explaining why, or how (e.g. the general happiness in the celebration and San Chee's sadness in the end). Amadeus also relates one element present in the text with another one of his/her creation. For instance, he/she attributes an invented motivation for the celebration in the beginning of the response writing task, namely that the white couple invite the Navajo with the specific purpose to "observe" them. Inferred feelings abound, such as the following: the feeling of happiness after the celebration; the feeling of "not belonging" experienced by San Chee; her "fear" that Ken wants to move with the Navajo; San Chee misses "Occidental Christmas celebrations". The adjective "Occidental" here is interesting, and one could wonder whether Amadeus wanted to suggest a contrast with "Oriental". He/she does not explore the dichotomy further, however. Added to this, his/her personal interpretations, in general supported by the text, include at times specific and sophisticated vocabulary. For instance, the white couple "wish to observe" the Navajo in this celebration; San Chee's comments lack "ingenuity" (without mentioning which comments in particular); and the "wish to stress the strangeness of the aboriginal customs, testified as if they were wild life habits". Notice the error in the reference to San Chee as a "girl". On the basis of the considerations above, this response writing task was holistically evaluated as partially adequate (level 2), i.e. a text with an adequate main idea but without detailed events or episodes. In relation to the Model of Cultural Apprehension, the fact that no specific episodes, habits, customs, details or the like are included here led us to assign level 0 to this task, as Amadeus failed to perceive the culturally specific events in the prompt text, which led to their omission, or he/she perceived them erratically. Concomitantly, this response writing task was also coded as reaching level 3 in this model, with this learner interpreting Otherness from his/her ethnocentric position, interpreting and re-interpreting the other culture as an outside observer. This resulted in a globally adequate response writing task (congruent with the overall tenor of the prompt text), but framed within the author's idiosyncratic interpretation. Amadeus reacted so strongly to the text that he/she included abundant evaluative comments and inferred morals about the message the text was supposed to convey in his/her view.

Amadeus' response writing task in English, written in the second place, mirrors the previous one. In both response writing tasks, the Navajo are referred to as *Indians*. Considering the fragment itself was written in English, I had anticipated that learners might be tempted to easily pick details from it to include in this task. However, both response writing tasks are of the same tenor, with the exception of the inclusion of two details not mentioned in the response writing task in Spanish: the references to Betty and to the danger that the Navajo's fires caused. The wish of the couple to "observe" the way the Native Americans participate in a Christmas celebration is replaced by a wish to "find out" about it in this version.

> San Chee and Ken – a couple living in a farm near a reservation of Navajo Indians – invite a group of these Indians to celebrate Christmas with them.
> The couple wants to find out something about the way in which Navajos celebrate Cristmas, which seems to be quite a new thing to the tribe.
> The story is narrated by San Chee, who lets the reader share her own feelings about the series of episodes she is telling.
> Everyone seems to be very happy about the celebration. However, San Chee (and someone called Betty who might be a member of western civilization as web as San) feels a bit frightened about certain behavior of the Indians – for example, about the damage which could be caused by the fires the tribe lights.
> As a conclusion, I daresay that the story is trying to highlight the differences between "civilized customs" and "wild customs." Everything related to the "wild" way of life is witnessed by white peple as animals are observed in their cages in a zoo.

This response writing task also presents a personal view of the text. Although the dichotomy between civilized and savage is globally warranted by the text and is present here in particular in the last paragraph, Amadeus closes this writing response task with an idiosyncratic comparison of the Indians with "animals observed in their cages in a zoo". Again, even though this view could be a plausible interpretation of textual context, it is not described, explained, or justified by this learner. The elements mentioned for the previous response task before also appear here. There is an error in the reference to "Betty" as a "member of western civilization". On the basis of the comments made for the previous response writing task, this task's holistic evaluation and level of cultural apprehension are the same as in the response writing task in Spanish.

Finally, in the visual reformulation, written last, stereotypes refer to the Navajo themselves while only a small portion make reference to the learners' national culture (e.g. Christmas tree, with ornaments and a star on its top). For instance, the Navajo are portrayed as dark Indians with feathers and hair bands, and living in huts. There is an evident error in the fact that the narrator is described as male despite the recurrent reference to her in the text as a woman. Notice the reference to Hilda and Ken as a family, while in the text they are described as a couple. In a bubble, Amadeus re-states what for him/her is the main focus of the text, i.e. the clash between two cultures. Because of the visual nature of this task, Amadeus misses a lot of his/her personal views about textual content, which we observed in both of his/her response writing tasks. This makes the visual reformulation appear more solid, free of idiosyncratic perspectives. We observe what Sharifian, Rochecouste and Malcolm (2004: 212) call "minimal discourse", i.e. the use of single words and elliptical utterances which capture complete propositions and events in the prompt text. As mentioned before, even though these views in the response writing tasks are well-framed within the text's overall meaning, they are worded in Amadeus' particular style, which reveals his/her alignment with a condescending and racist view of the Navajo. On this basis, this task's holistic evaluation was adequate (level 3) and the level of cultural apprehension was 3 again, the reason being that there is no attempt to approach the Otherness in the Navajo's ways from an insider perspective.

Discussion

As mentioned in the beginning, these learners were trained in a critical discourse perspective in EFL reading at this university. This means that they made an effort, with more or less success, to search for significant cultural patterns behind what was visible, and to reflect on the adequacy with which the perspective of the native American culture offered by the text genuinely represented its perspective and voice. This is what we see Amadeus doing in the tasks described above.

Another comment warranted by this study is that whatever was different, or unfamiliar in this text in relation to the Native American culture revealed itself as problematic. The difficulty the learners experienced to apprehend alternative visions of the world may have stemmed from the way in which life generally promotes uniformity and continuity through collective patterns of behavior (Parsons, 1951). Although the text offered a plurality of options and perspectives to the students, the predominance of level 1 in the written tasks as revealed by the Model of Cultural Apprehension means that these learners focused almost exclusively on the identification of some superficial cultural differences.

The response writing tasks and the visual reformulations revealed varied affective reactions towards the culture of the Navajo. The initial confrontation with what was different produced feelings of disorientation, rejection, disbelief and surprise, excitement and euphoria before the different and the unknown, and shock in the face of cultural differences. This kind of reaction is natural and important because it constitutes the first step towards the appreciation of the unknown. Under some circumstances, when certain textual information did not match the learners' available schemata or was too divergent, it was ignored or rejected. For example, in some cases, learners omitted some episodes altogether while in others, they elaborated on the textual content and produced inadequate interpretations which resulted in highly idiosyncratic response writing tasks and visual reformulations. On other occasions, learners recalled best the information that was different and surprising and they included it in their productions, even when this information contradicted or conflicted with their prior knowledge (as revealed in the questions designed to elicit this knowledge) as long as it was perceived as convincing and possible. These results are consistent with the theory of schematic knowledge about cognitive interest (Yarlas and Gelman, 1998) that posits that to be of interest, new information must be assimilated to an existing schema (resulting in the elaboration of the schema through the inclusion of explicative information) or accommodated by means of restructuring (producing the modification of the schema, i.e. the new information makes individuals change their ideas).

The foregoing is related to the fact that student interest in reading material depends on its degree of surprise or novelty. Wade et al. (1999) argue that learners will be interested in reading material that they consider novel or abnormal. From this perspective, a completely familiar and predictable text will not be interesting. The fact that this text offered a different view of a Christmas celebration, including elements which were totally incongruous with a typical celebration in Argentina, could have been crucial to generate student attraction. The authors also suggest that an extremely weird or unpredictable situation will not generate much interest. In this sense, it was possible that the celebration described in *Desert Wife* was perceived as totally atypical or abnormal, required excessive effort to be apprehended, appeared uninteresting, and became inaccessible. This study seems to contradict this conclusion as the text generated interest and curiosity – reflected not only in the content of the learners' productions as described elsewhere here, but also on their length: the student excerpts reproduced here are some of the shortest, with the maximum recorded length in this study being one page. The fact that the text portrayed a vivid and unusual world, materialized in the different episodes described (dancing, wrestling, racing, cooking, etc.) may have neutralized the possible negative effects of the surprise and strangeness generated by its content. Besides, although attractive details are not necessary to generate interest, readers tend to judge the information with a sensational touch as important and interesting (Maccabe and Peterson, 1990). This type of information abounded in this text.

The alternative visions of the world which were related with certain concepts (e.g. community celebration) generated emotional reactions. An extreme discrepancy did not necessarily produce an extreme emotion because the awoken emotions depended on the importance of activated beliefs within the learners' value systems. The emotional commitment with the text topics had a crucial role in interpretation as learners tended to remember information selectively (particularly that information which was congruent with activated beliefs) and to distort incongruent information. Those topics which turned out to be central to the learners' value systems generated more emotional commitment than others (for example, hospitality, the meaning of Christmas beyond the festive aspect, loneliness, solidarity, love, sharing, and nostalgia). When learners held a deep belief, and it was confronted (attacked, threatened or rejected) by textual information (e.g. the lack of religious connotation in this celebration for the Native Americans), their perspectives of the world were altered and they had difficulty handling the confrontation.

Finally, the analysis of the response writing tasks and the visual reformulations revealed different levels of apprehension of cultural aspects during reading, i.e. different degrees of depth, complexity and details with respect to the cultural reality of the Navajos. In general, the approach to Otherness was limited to the perception of what was exotic or exciting about the Navajo culture (level 1 in the Model of Cultural Apprehension), without a genuine effort to become familiar with what was strange – as revealed by the low percentages associated with level 4. The learners' stereotyped approach to this Otherness, represented by level 3, was characterized by a high presence of distortions, intrusions, errors, rationalizations, simplifications, and inadequate interpretations, and relatively low percentages of elaborations and adequate interpretations.

Note of Caution

Successful reading comprehension is not a mere indicator of reading capacity per se but reveals the success individuals have experimented in their learning of how to use language appropriately in educational contexts and how well they have learned to behave in the school system (college in this case) (Berg, 2003; Bernhardt, 2003). Besides, many factors affect reading, which generates individual differences (Paris, 2005). In general, readers with a rich knowledge base and flexible access to this knowledge may reach a coherent representation of a text more efficiently than other readers. Variables such as text difficulty, task difficulty, distribution of attention resources during reading, and personal characteristics (impulsivity, reflexivity, etc.) affect reading behavior. From the foregoing, reading performance with a limited number of texts may inaccurately reflect reading capacity (in this study three texts were used; the results corresponding to only one text are reported here). This fact notwithstanding, the available data have significant variability with several dimensions or layers. For the text reported in this chapter, there were 600 sources of variability (200 participants doing three tasks based on the text), which permitted to check the global consistency of all data sources.

Discussions about culture tend to be simple, with utopian appeals to the tolerance of ideas different from our own and the avoidance of prejudices. As far as the learners are concerned, the appreciation of the significance and importance of certain cultural aspects presupposes the capacity for abstraction and analysis (Alred, Byram, and Fleming, 2003; Byram and Fleming, 2001; Byram and Grundy, 2003; Neuner and Byram, 2003) – which only those learners with a high cognitive and moral development may reach. In relation to teachers, many find the area of culture unfamiliar (Kramsch et al, 1996; Sercu, 2006). There exists a gap in the knowledge of teachers (and researchers) about other cultures. This knowledge is in general intuitive and fails to be systematic (Byram, 2000, 2001). Considering that teachers (and researchers) go through the same process as the learners themselves in the apprehension of a different culture, they also have an inadequate basis for comprehension. The risk of inappropriately assigning meanings to the behaviors of members of other cultures on the part of teachers, learners, and researchers is always latent.

Research Significance

The results described here have immediate relevance in the field of language education. The description of the approach of the cultural aspects of the reading materials to be used in the classroom, together with the systematization of this description in specific stages or levels as portrayed in the Model of Cultural Apprehension, may have immediate applications in different second/foreign language education contexts worldwide as well as in the education of English language learners (ELLs) in the US context and other English-speaking countries with similar characteristics.

Specifically in the teaching of foreign/second languages, considering that the reading materials generally used tend to present cultural realities alien to the learners, it is possible that many learners experience negative encounters with L2 reading owing to extra-linguistic factors of this kind rather than linguistic deficits as it is usually assumed in Argentina. The inadequate selection of reading materials, from the point of view of their cultural load, may generate frustrating reading experiences. The description of the different kinds of approach of the cultural content of the texts used in this study, materialized in clear and specific levels or stages in the Model, will contribute to guaranteeing an adequate selection of reading materials on the part of classroom teachers. In addition, it is important to assess the cultural accessibility of reading materials according to factors such as age, gender, interest, motivation, socioeconomic status, prior educational background, and learner values and beliefs, among others. These factors affect the level of cultural accessibility or inaccessibility of different reading texts for different classrooms.

Both in foreign and second language learning contexts, children and adults appreciate interesting and personally significant reading material, i.e. familiar rather than unfamiliar texts. The affective response of readers to reading material from their own culture encourages them to look for texts that affirm their most valuable concepts and values, and reject or avoid texts that do the contrary (Mathewson, 1994; Rasinski and Padak, 1998a; Rasinski and Padak, 1998b). Material of this kind creates multiple opportunities to relate their prior knowledge with the ideas present in a text, understanding and apprehending the new in relation to what they already know (Harste, 1994; Pearson and Stephens, 1994). In addition, it is assumed that memory and comprehension increase and that more pleasure is generated by the reading of familiar texts rather than unfamiliar ones, i.e. personally relevant texts. Considering that human knowledge is oriented toward the relevant, readers may be reticent to collaborate if they are not interested. This has motivated teachers to offer reading material with significant experiences with which learners may identify (Oller, 1995). Interest is supposed to constitute the foundation to guarantee independent learning and the concept of *disposition for learning* is used to refer to the idea that learners learn more enthusiastically when they experience the need and interest to read. From this perspective, those learners who have not been exposed to interesting, motivating, and familiar reading material have fewer opportunities to understand what it means to be a successful reader (Jiménez, 1997).

Finally, the tendency towards the multilingual, multiethnic, and multicultural classroom in many contexts worldwide points to the importance of cultural factors in EFL/ESL education as well as in education in general (Farfan-Cobb and Lassiter, 2003; Labov, 2003; Ruano, 2005; Shah, 2004). From this perspective, this study may also be relevant in the context of English language learners (ELLs) in native language education in multilingual, multiethnic, and multicultural classrooms in English-speaking countries internationally.

CONCLUSION

The research reported in this chapter investigated the ways in which cultural content is conveyed in literary narrative texts, and the ways in which – and the extents to which – learners from one culture apprehend or understand the cultural references in the literature of another language and culture. The major contribution of this study in EFL and ESL contexts worldwide and in the education of ELLs in the US (and other English-speaking countries with similar characteristics) resides in the Model of Cultural Apprehension described here. The description of the approach of the cultural content of (narrative) texts, through the in-depth exploration of the stages or levels in this Model, has an impact on the following areas: a) the selection of reading material in L1 (mother tongue) and L2 contexts (considering cultural load, and insider/outsider perspectives in the presentation of cultural information); b) instructional techniques in working with L2 readers and English language learners (ELLs) (e.g. awareness-raising strategies about the cultural aspects in a text; techniques/strategies contributing to the perception, apprehension, interpretation, etc. of cultural information; etc.); and c) multicultural education in the framework of globalization and increasingly multilingual, multiethnic, and multicultural educational contexts around the world.

REFERENCES

Abu-Rabia, S. (1998). Social and cognitive factors influencing the reading comprehension of Arab students learning Hebrew as a second language in Israel. *Journal of research in Reading, 21/3*, 201-212.

Alderson, J. C. & Urquhart, A. H. (1988). This test is unfair: I'm not an economist. In: P. Carrell, (Eds.). *Interactive Approaches to Second Language Reading*. Cambridge: Cambridge University Press, 168-182.

Allen, M. et al. (1994). Children's narrative productions: A comparison of personal event and fictional stories. *Applied Psycholinguistics, 15*, 149-176.

Alred, G. & Byram, M. (2002). Becoming an intercultural mediator: a longitudinal study of residence abroad. *Journal of multilingual and multicultural development, 23*, 339-352.

Alred, G., Byram, M. & Fleming, M. (2003). *Intercultural experience and education*. Clevedon: Multilingual Matters.

Alred, G., Byram, M. & Fleming, M. (2006). *Education for intercultural citizenship: concepts and comparisons*. Clevedon: Multilingual Matters.

Archer, M. (1997). *Cultura y teoría social*. Buenos Aires: Nueva Visión.

Arizpe, E. (2001). 'Letting the story out': Visual encounters with Anthony Browne's *The Tunnel. READING literacy and language*, 115-119.

Artelt, C. (2005). Cross-Cultural Approaches to measuring Motivation. *Educational Assessment, 10*, 231-255.

Bell, C. & Perfetti, C. (1994). Reading Skill: Some Adult Comparisons. *Journal of Educational Psychology, 86*, 244-255.

Blanco, O. (2000). *Cultura popular y cultura de masas: Conceptos, recorridos, polémicas*. 1a. ed. Buenos Aires: Paidós.

Berg, C. (2003). The role of grounded theory and collaborative research. *Reading Research Quarterly, 38*, 105-111.

Bernhardt, E. (2003). Challenges to reading research from a multilingual world. *Reading Research Quarterly, 38*, 112-117.

Bernhardt, E. & Kamil, M. (1995). Interpreting relationships between L1 and L2 reading: Consolidating the linguistic threshold and the linguistic interdependence hypotheses. *Applied Linguistics, 16*, 15-34.

Boyle, O. & Peregoy, S. (1998). Literacy Scaffolds: Strategies for First- and Second-Language Readers and Writers. In: M. Opitz, (Eds.), *Literacy Instruction for Culturally and Linguistically Diverse Students. A Collection of Articles and Commentaries* (150-157). Newark, Delaware: International Reading Association Inc.

Bower, G., Black, J. & Turner, T. (1994). Scripts in Memory for Text. In: R., Ruddell, M. Ruddell, & H. Singer, (Eds.), *Theoretical Models and Processes of Reading*, 4th ed. (538-581). Newark, Delaware: International Reading Association Inc.

Briggs, P., Austin, S. & Underwood, G. (1984). The effects of sentence context in good and poor readers: A test of Stanovich's interactive-compensatory model. *Reading Research Quarterly, XX*, 54-61.

Burgess, S., Hecht, S. & Lonigan, C. (2002). Relations of Home Literacy Environment (HLE) to the development of reading-related abilities: A one-year longitudinal study. *Reading Research Quarterly, 37*, 408-426.

Burnett, C. & Gardner, J. (2006). The One Less Travelled By...: The experience of Chinese Students in a UK University. In: M. Byram, & A. Feng, (Eds). *Living and Studying Abroad. Research and Practice* (64-91). Clevedon: Multilingual Matters.

Byram, M. (2000). Intercultural Communicative Competence: the Challenge for Language Teacher Training. In: A. Mountford, & Wadham-Smith, N. (Eds), *British Studies*: *Intercultural Perspective* (95-102). London: Longman in association with The British Council.

Byram, M. (2001). Language teaching as political action. In Bax, M. & Zwart, J. (Eds), *Reflections on Language and Language Learning. In honour of Arthur van Essen* (91-104). John Benjamins Publishing Company.,

Byram, M. & Morgan, C. (1994). *Teaching-and-Learning Language-and-Culture*. Clevedon: Multilingual Matters.

Byram, M. & Fleming, M. (2001). *Perspectivas interculturales en el aprendizaje de idiomas: enfoques a través del teatro y la etnografía*. Cambridge: Cambridge University Press.

Byram, M. & Grundy, P. (2002). Introduction: Context and culture in language teaching and learning. *Language, Culture, and Curriculum, 15*, 193-195.

Byram, M. & Grundy, P. (2003). *Context and culture in language teaching and learning*. Clevedon: Multilingual Matters.

Byram, M., Nichols, A. & Stevens, D. (2001). *Developing intercultural competence in practice*. Clevedon: Multilingual Matters.

Byram, M., Gribkova, B. & Starkey, H. (2002). *Developing the intercultural dimension in language teaching*. Council of Europe, Language Policy Division.

Byrnes, H. (2008). Articulating a foreign language sequence through content: A look at the culture standards. *Language Teaching, 41*, 103-118.

Carrell, P. (1983a). Three components of background knowledge in reading comprehension. *Language Learning, 33*, 183-207.

Carrell, P. (1983b). Background knowledge in second language comprehension. *Language Learning and Communication, 2*, 25-34.

Carrell, P. (1984a). Schema theory and ESL reading: classroom implications and applications. *Modern Language Journal, 68*, 332-343.

Carrell, P. (1984b). Evidence of a formal schema in second language comprehension. *Language Learning, 34*, 87-112.

Carrell, P. (1984c). The Effects of Rhetorical Organization on ESL Readers. *TESOL Quarterly, 18*, 441-469.

Cohen, A. et al (1988). Reading English for specialized purposes: discourse analysis and the use of student informants. In Carrell et al (eds). *Interactive Approaches to Second Language Reading* (152-167). Cambridge: Cambridge University Press.

Derrida, J. (1994). *Márgenes de la Filosofía.* Segunda edición. Traducción de Carmen González Marín. Madrid: Ediciones Cátedra.

Deveney, B. (2007). How well-prepared do international school teachers believe themselves to be for teaching in culturally diverse classrooms. *Journal of Research in International Education, 6,* 309-332.

Droop, M. & Verhoeven, L. (2003). Language proficiency and reading ability in first- and second-language learners. *Reading Research Quarterly, 38,* 78-103.

Duke, N. (2000). 3.6 minutes per day: The scarcity of informational texts in first grade. *Reading Research Quarterly, 35/2,* 202-224.

Erez, M. & Gati, E. (2004). A Dynamic, Multi-Level Model of Culture: From the Micro Level of the Individual to the Macro Level of Global Culture. *Applied Psychology: An International Review, 53/4,* 583-598.

Farfan-Cobb, I. & Lassiter, L. (2003). How National Foreign Language Week Promotes Cultural Awareness at a Historically Black University. *Foreign Language Annals, 36,* 397-402.

Faunce, H. (1961). *Desert Wife.* Lincoln: University of Nebraska Press.

Fitzgerald, J. (2003). Multilingual reading theory. *Reading Research Quarterly, 38,* 118-122.

Gallas, K. & Smagorinsky, P. (2002). Approaching texts in school. *The Reading Teacher, 56,* 54-61.

Garner, P. (2008). The challenge of teaching for diversity in the college classroom when the professor is the 'other'. *Teaching in Higher Education, 13,* 117-120.

Gee, J. (2001). Reading as situated language: A sociocognitive perspective. *Journal of Adolescent & Adult Literacy, 44,* 714-725.

Geertz, C. (1974). *The Interpretation of Cultures.* New York: Basic Books.

Gradwohl Nash, J. et al. (1993). Writing From Sources: A Structure-Mapping Model. *Journal of Educational Psychology, 85,* 159-170.

Harste, J. (1994). Literacy as Curricular Conversations about Knowledge, Inquiry, and Morality. In: R., Ruddell, M. Ruddell, & H. Singer, (Eds.), *Theoretical Models and Processes of Reading,* 4th ed. (1220-1242). Newark, Delaware: International Reading Association Inc.

Hemphill, L., Picardi, N. & Tager-Flusberg, H. (1991). Narrative as an index of communicative competence in mildly mentally retarded children. *Applied Psycholinguistics, 12,* 263-279.

Hudson, T. (1982). The effects of induced schemata on the "short circuit" in L2 reading: Non-decoding factors in L2 reading performance. *Language Learning, 32,* 1-31.

Hugo, J. (2002). Learning Community History. *New Directions for Adult and Continuing Education, 95,* 5-25.

Jiménez, R. (1997). The strategic reading abilities and potential of five low-literacy Latina/o readers in middle school. *Reading Research Quarterly, 32,* 3, 224-243.

Jiménez, R. (2003). Literacy and Latino students in the United States: Some considerations, questions, and new directions. *Reading Research Quarterly, 38,* 122-128.

Kamberelis, G. & Bovino, T. (1999). Cultural artifacts as scaffolds for genre development. *Reading Research Quarterly, 34,* 2, 138-170.

Kimmel, S. & Magginitie, W. (1984). Identifying children who use a perseverative text processing strategy. *Reading Research Quarterly, XIX,* 162-172.

Klingner, J. & Edwards, P. (2006). Cultural considerations with Response to Intervention Models. *Reading Research Quarterly, 41/1,* 108-117.

Koda, K. (1994). Second language reading research: problems and possibilities. *Applied Psycholinguistics, 15*, 1-28.

Kramsch, C. (1993). *Context and Culture in Language Teaching.* Oxford: Oxford University Press.

Kramsch, C. (1995). The cultural component of language teaching. *Language, Culture, and Curriculum, 8*, 83-92.

Kramsch, C. (1998). *Language and Culture.* Oxford: Oxford University Press.

Kramsch, C. (2003). The Privilege of the Nonnative Speaker. In *The Sociolinguistics of Foreign-Language Classrooms: Contributions of the Native, the Near-Native, and the Non-Native Speaker. Issues in Language Program Direction*, A Series of Annual Volumes, 251-262. ERIC Document ED481796.

Kramsch, C. et al. (1996). Why Should Language Teachers Teach Culture? *Language, Culture, and Curriculum, 9*, 99-107.

Labbo, L. (2000). RRQ Snippet: What will classrooms and schools look like in the new millennium? *Reading Research Quarterly, 35*, 130-131.

Labov, W. (2003). When ordinary children fail to read. *Reading Research Quarterly, 38*, 128-131.

Lipson, M. (1983). The influence of religious affiliation on children's memory for text information. *Reading Research Quarterly, XVIII*, 448-457.

Luke, A. & Elkins, J. (2002). Towards a critical, worldly literacy. *Journal of Adolescent & Adult Literacy, 45*, 668-673.

Maccabe, A. & Peterson, C. (1990). What makes a narrative memorable? *Applied Psycholinguistics, 11*, 73-82.

Mahar, D. (2001). Positioning in a middle school culture: Gender, race, social class, and power. *Journal of Adolescent & Adult Literacy, 45*, 200-209.

Mannes, S. (1994). Strategic Processing of Text. *Journal of Educational Psychology, 86*, 577-588.

McCallister, C. (2002). The power of place and time in literacy teaching. *Journal of Adolescent & Adult Literacy, 46*, 6-13.

Mathewson, G. (1994). Model of Attitude Influence upon Reading and Learning to Read. In Ruddell, R., Ruddell, M. & Singer, H. (Eds.), *Theoretical Models and Processes of Reading*, 4th ed. (1131-1161). Newark, Delaware: International Reading Association Inc.

Millard, E. & Marsh, J. (2001). Words with pictures: The role of visual literacy in writing and its implication for schooling. *READING literacy and language*, 54-61.

Moje, E. (2000). RRQ Snippet: What will classrooms and schools look like in the new millennium? *Reading Research Quarterly, 35*, 128-129.

Moje, E., McIntosh Ciechanowski, K., Kramer, K., Ellis, L., Carrillo, R. & Collazo, T. (2004). Working toward third space in content area literacy: An examination of everyday funds of knowledge and Discourse. *Reading Research Quarterly, 39*, 38-70.

Moreiras, A. (1991). *Interpretación y diferencia.* Madrid: Visor.

Mountford, A. & Wadham-Smith, N. (Eds). (2000). *British Studies: Intercultural Perspectives.* London: Longman in association with The British Council.

Neuner, G. & Byram, M. (2003). *Intercultural competence.* Strasbourg: Council of Europe, Language Policy Division.

O'Byrne, B. (2003). The paradox of cross-age, multicultural collaboration. *Journal of Adolescent & Adult Literacy, 47*, 50-6.

Oller, J. W. (1995). Adding abstract to formal and content schemata: Results of recent work in Peircean semiotics. *Applied Linguistics, 16*, 273-306.

Ooka Pang, V. et al. (1998). Beyond Chopsticks and Dragons: Selecting Asian American Literature for Children. In: M. Opitz, (Eds.), *Literacy Instruction for Culturally and Linguistically Diverse Students. A Collection of Articles and Commentaries* (204-212). Newark, Delaware: International Reading Association Inc.

Paris, S. (2005). Reinterpreting the development of reading skills. *Reading Research Quarterly, 40*, 184-202.

Paris, A. & Paris, S. (2003). Assessing narrative comprehension in young children. *Reading Research Quarterly, 38*, 36-76.

Parsons, T. (1951). *The Social System*. London: Routledge & Kegan-Paul Ltd.

Pearson, D. & Stephens, D. (1994). Learning about Literacy: A 30-Year Journey. In: R., Ruddell, M. Ruddell, & H. Singer, (Eds.), *Theoretical Models and Processes of Reading*, 4th ed. (22-42). Newark, Delaware: International Reading Association Inc.

Penningroth, S. & Rosenberg, S. (1995). Effects of a high information-processing load on the writing process and the story written. *Applied Psycholinguistics, 16*, 189-210.

Peyton Young, J. (2001). Displaying practices of masculinity: Critical literacy and social contexts. *Journal of Adolescent & Adult Literacy, 45/1*, 4-14.

Pope Edwards, C. & Mayo Willis, L. (2000). Integrating Visual and Verbal Literacies in the Early Childhood Classroom. *Early Childhood Education Journal, 27*, 259-265.

Rasinski, T. & Padak, N. (1998a). Selecting and using Multicultural Literacy. In: M. Opitz (Eds.), *Literacy Instruction for Culturally and Linguistically Diverse Students. A Collection of Articles and Commentaries* (180-183). Newark, Delaware: International Reading Association Inc.

Rasinski, T. & Padak, N. (1998b). Multicultural learning Through Children's Literature. In: M. Opitz (Eds.), *Literacy Instruction for Culturally and Linguistically Diverse Students. A Collection of Articles and Commentaries* (pp. 198-203). Newark, Delaware: International Reading Association Inc.

Rigg, P. (1988). The Miscue-ESL Project. In Carrell, P. et al. (Eds.). *Interactive Approaches to Second Language Reading* (206-219). Cambridge: Cambridge University Press..

Robins, S. & Mayer, R. (1993). Schema Training in Analogical Reasoning. *Journal of Educational Psychology, 85*, 529-538.

Rogers, R. (2002). "That's what you're here for, you're suppose to tell us": Teaching and learning critical literacy. *Journal of Adolescent & Adult Literacy, 45*, 772-787.

Rollin, H. (2006). Intercultural Competence for Students of Spanish: Can we teach it? Can we afford not to teach it? *Language Learning Journal, 34*, 55-61.

Ruano, C. (2005). Understanding the cultural construction of wealth and power differentials through ethnographic narrative analysis in Colombia. *Teaching in Higher Education, 10*, 519-526.

Ruddell, R. & Unrau, N. (1994). Reading as a Meaning-Construction Process: The Reader, the Text, and the Teacher. In: R., Ruddell, M. Ruddell, & H. Singer, (Eds.), *Theoretical Models and Processes of Reading*, 4th ed. (996-1056). Newark, Delaware: International Reading Association Inc.

Sadoski, M. & Paivio, A. (1994). A Dual Coding View of Imagery and Verbal Processes in Reading Comprehension. In: R., Ruddell, M. Ruddell, & H. Singer, (Eds.), *Theoretical*

Models and Processes of Reading, 4th ed. (582-601). Newark, Delaware: International Reading Association Inc.

Shah, S. (2004). The researcher/interviewer in intercultural context: a social intruder! *British Educational Research Journal, 30*, 549-575.

Sharifian, F., Rochecouste, J. & Malcolm, I. (2004). 'But it was all a Bit Confusing...': Comprehending Aboriginal English texts. *Language, Culture and Curriculum, 17*, 203-228.

Sanders Bustle, L. (2004). The role of visual representation in the assessment of learning. *Journal of Adolescent & Adult Literacy, 47/5*, 416-423.

Sarroub, L. (2002). In-betweenness: Religion and conflicting visions of literacy. *Reading Research Quarterly, 37*, 130-148.

Sercu, L. (2006). The foreign language and intercultural competence teacher: the acquisition of a new professional identity. *Intercultural Education, 17*, 55-72.

Singer, H. & Donlan, D. (1994). Problem-Solving Schema with Question Generation for Comprehension of Complex Short Stories. In: R., Ruddell, M. Ruddell, & H. Singer, (Eds.), *Theoretical Models and Processes of Reading*, 4th ed. (520-537). Newark, Delaware: International Reading Association Inc.

Sloane, F. (2005). The scaling of reading interventions: Building multilevel insight. *Reading Research Quarterly, 40*, 361-366.

Smith-Maddox, R. (1998). Defining culture as a dimension of academic achievement: Implications for culturally responsive curriculum, instruction, and assessment. *The Journal of Negro Education, 67/3*, 302-317.

Stanovich, K. (1980). Toward an interactive-compensatory model of individual differences in the development of reading fluency. *Reading Research Quarterly*, XVI, 32-71.

Steffensen, M., Joag-Dev, C. & Anderson, R. (1979). A cross-cultural perspective on reading comprehension. *Reading Research Quarterly*, XV, 10-29.

Steffensen, M. (1988). Changes in cohesion in the recall of native and foreign texts. In: P. Carrell, et al. (Eds.). *Interactive Approaches to Second Language Reading* (140-151). Cambridge: Cambridge University Press.,.

Strömqvist, S. & Day, D. (1993). On the development of narrative structure in child L1 and adult L2 acquisition. *Applied Psycholinguistics, 14*, 135-158.

Schraw, G. et al. (1993). Interactive Effects of Text- Based and Task- Based Importance on Learning from Text. *Journal of Educational Psychology, 85*, 652-661.

Tager-Flusberg, H. & Sullivan, K. (1995). Attributing mental states to story characters: A comparison of narratives produced by autistic and mentally retarded individuals. *Applied Psycholinguistics, 16*, 241-256.

Tierney, R. (1994). Dissension, Tensions, and the Models of Literacy. In: R., Ruddell, M. Ruddell, & Singer, H. (Eds.), *Theoretical Models and Processes of Reading*, 4th ed. (1162-1182). Newark, Delaware: International Reading Association Inc.

Wade, S. et al. (1999). Using think-alouds to examine reader-text interest. *Reading Research Quarterly, 34*, 194-216.

Warley, J. (2003). *La cultura : Versiones y definiciones*. Buenos Aires: Biblos.

Worthy, J., Moorman, M. & Turner, M. (1999). What Johnny likes to read is hard to find in school. *Reading Research Quarterly, 34/1*, 12-27.

Wright, R. & Rosenberg, S. (1993). Knowledge of Text Coherence and Expository Writing: A Developmental Study. *Journal of Educational Psychology, 85*, 152-158.

Yokota, J. (1998). Issues in Selecting Multicultural Children's Literature. In: M., Opitz (Ed.), *Literacy Instruction for Culturally and Linguistically Diverse Students. A Collection of Articles and Commentaries* (184-197). Newark, Delaware: International Reading Association Inc.

APPENDIX

Sample of Multiple-Choice Questionnaires about Reading in Spanish and in English

The questionnaires aimed at gathering information about the participants' conceptions of reading as well as their reading habits and preferences in both languages. These multiple choice questionnaires (one about reading in Spanish; another one about reading in English) were written and answered in Spanish and focused on the following aspects: motivations for reading, time devoted to reading, self-concept as readers, available reading material at home and in the community, the place of reading at home and in the community, interest in reading, difficulties experienced during reading, strategies to become better readers, etc. A sample of questions is included below (for reasons of space, the response options are not included here). The investigation of these issues was complemented with multiple interviews conducted at the beginning, middle, and end of the academic year.

1. What kind of material do you read in Spanish (English)? Choose up to 10 options and arrange them from 1 to 10 (1= most important; 10= least important).
2. Why do you read in Spanish (English)? Choose up to 3 reasons and arrange them from 1 to 3 according to the frequency you read for these reasons (1=most frequent; 3 =least frequent).
3. How would you rate yourself as a reader in Spanish (English)?
4. Do you like to read in Spanish (English)? Why? Why not?
5. Do you have a favorite author in Spanish (English)?
6. Do you have a favorite title in Spanish (English)?
7. How much time a day do you spend reading in Spanish (English)?
8. What difficulties do you have when you read in Spanish (English)? Choose the two most problematic options.
9. What would you do to become a better reader in Spanish (English)? Choose the three most important options in your opinion.
10. Do you receive books in Spanish (English) as presents? How many a year? Who gives you these books?
11. Do you go to the library? How much time a week do you spend there?
12. Do your family/ friends/ classmates read in Spanish (English)?
13. Do you talk with somebody about what you read in Spanish (English)? With whom?

Fragment from *Desert Wife* (Faunce, 1961: 173-181)

Kismas

Before the birth of Mrs. White Hat's baby, more frequently while the wind blew in October and without ceasing, after that dance Polly and I attended, the heathen asked, "How long 'till Kismas?"

Christmas to us meant warm fires, red berries, gifts in tissue chapter. We found that the Navajo "Kismas" included the warm fires, but everything else was novel enough to make history.

We planned to watch the benighted Navajo cook dinner; we had even declared we would eat with them; we would spend the day watching their games. For our treat we prepared a hundred small bags each containing candy, cookies and a red apple.

Christmas Eve the heathen began to arrive over these hills. There were wagonloads of women and children and scores of men and young people on horses. Everybody was dressed in his hest: beads, bracelets and silver belts glistened against the bright-colored velvet shirts and glossy sateen skirts, with miles and miles of flounces. I had made several of the skirts and I knew how many miles long a flounce was.

By dark some two hundred Navajos were present. The Utcitys were there: the head of the house in all his dignity, the Little Bidoni and his three wives, soft-spoken and sweet, and all the other sons and daughters and husbands and wives; the Little Cranks, living up to their name; the Old Lady and Old Man, with their children and grandchildren; Robert, greeting old friends, and White Hat and Mrs. White Hat and the children; Japon and his wife and their progeny, Mrs. Japon and the Old Lady giving each other a wide berth. Cla was present with his brothers and the Old Buzzard. Everybody's friends were present and all their relatives.

Apparently they expected "Kismas" to begin at once. Expecting to supply meat for the Christmas dinner, Ken had killed a beef, but now he took down a hind quarter and cut steaks and more steaks until there was enough to go around. The adults came and took what they needed for their families for supper and for breakfast on Christmas morning. What they did not eat at once they were afraid to put down because some one would steal it, so all the evening they strolled about with great raw beefsteaks in their hands. Mrs. Japon and the Old Buzzard each had two.

We had provided several loads of wood so they could help themselves; and the Christmas fires, big and little, were all over the place. They were so all over the place, we were uneasy. One family settled down and built their fire within two feet of the walls of that frame shack of a store building. Ken had to go out and insist that they move elsewhere. They were indignant and thought it quite fussy in me to go out and shovel dirt over the bed of live coals they left.

Big fires were built on the level space, where the dancing was to be, and these, added to the light of a full moon, made the night so bright we could see the whole landscape around. The dancing was just for the Indians' amusement and ours and was in no sense ceremonial.

Now and then some of them danced a figure from a ceremonial dance but without the costumes and other accessories. The music was made on a clay water jar with water in it and a rawhide stretched over the top. One fellow played this, or beat it, and others shook rattles made of paper bags with beans in them.

The best dance of the lot was one performed by some of the older men. They had to dance and sing because the younger men knew neither the proper songs nor the dance; and

Utcity, the Singer, and the other six who made up the figures sang, laughed and kept up the most violent sort of exercises until they dropped panting to the ground. They all assured us that when they were young men they could keep it up all night, but now they were old and full of meat besides, and they couldn't do what they used to do.

With that dance and others, and wrestling and racing about the fires, there was plenty of activity. There was nothing cold or solemn about the gathering; every one was laughing and happy. They were a most fun-loving people and laughed at the same things we thought funny.

All the evening I was trying to bake two loaves of fruit cake. It was done when we finally went to bed at midnight -done with a thick crust an inch deep all over it and a core of good cake in the middle. Keeping an oven fire of pitch wood and watching the dancing outside had been too much for the success of the cake. The wood-burning stove was temperamental at its best.

All night we smelled the piñon smoke from the camp fires, and when a different smoke drifted into our window, we got up and followed it to find that some one had put box boards on his fire. Lady Betty was nervous and growled every time we or any one else moved. When we got back in bed, after tracing the source of non-piñon smoke, she came to the side of the bed and put her cold nose in my hand. After a little she lay down with a loud sigh, but got up at once if she could not feel my hand. My arm was numb from keeping the hand where she could reach it. Poor Betty! She didn't get much sleep that night and a hard day she had ahead of her, too. Wild reservation life was no joy to a blooded bulldog like Betty.

What with our uneasiness about the Indian fires and their early rising habits, we were up early Christmas morning. While the men and boys went out to the flat mesa to race their horses, we women folk thought about dinner for the crowd. By eleven o'clock Mrs. White Hat and Mrs. Japon began making bread and the efficient way they went about it was a lesson to me.

A twenty-five-pound sack of flour, a frying pan or Dutch oven, a can of baking powder and a bucket of well water was the total of their equipment. They rolled back the top of the sack, put in a pinch of baking powder and mixed in enough water with their hands to make a dough stiff enough to handle easily. This was pulled and patted into a cake that covered the bottom of the cooking pan and fried in an inch or two of fat. The finished cakes were stacked in piles. It was an interesting performance; but after I had watched for a time, I realized they could not bake enough bread for the crowd that way, so I started to make biscuits in the oven. That was a full-time job. I learned then that one sack of flour just fills a washtub with biscuits.

While we women were preparing the bread, Ken had cut up the meat. Some women built up stones about the cooking fires to set tubs on, and soon we had three tubs of the meat simmering, each with an attendant stirring it with a long splinter of wood from the woodpile. The wash boiler did duty as a coffee pot. There was a forked cedar in it to hold the bag of coffee down. I was sure the whole dinner would be flavored with cedar, but it wasn't.

Other women I set to peeling onions and potatoes, and very handy they were at it too. These we added to the meat tubs. When everything was all well cooked, I mixed a pail of flour and water for thickening and added that, with salt, pepper and chili. The cooks tasted it often and said it was very good.

One of the children was sent out to the mesa edge to call the men; and in a few minutes they charged in, the ponies running pell-mell between the camp fires and jumping over the clutter of camp stuff, the Indians yelling like pirates and quirting on both sides. I never had heard a pirate yell, but I was sure a Navajo must be as good a yeller as a Comanche, and nothing else *could* make so much noise, unless it was a pirate.

The dripping ponies were left at one side and the Indians came to the fires. I dipped the stew into pans, all we had in the store; and then we passed tin cups of coffee and spoons for the stew. The family groups sat together and everybody ate and ate. Some of the heathen, I know, had not had a square meal for a month.

After the meal was over, the women cleaned the soot from the tubs and boiler with sand, while I scalded the spoons and pans. They were willing enough to do it, though they would have gone away and left everything dirty, if I had not suggested the dishwashing. I thought it best they do some little thing for their meal.

When that was done, the children lined up to get the bags of candy. I passed them out and soon became suspicious about the length of the line. Investigation revealed Mrs. Little Crank and a score of other mothers standing around the corner of the store, putting bags of candy into their blankets and sending the children back to stand in line for another. There was a sort of appreciation in the Navajo, but it was the sort that wanted all they could get from any one who wasn't looking.

By the middle of the afternoon they were all gone and we were allowed to eat something ourselves. Tired! But we agreed we had never seen such a Christmas and would not see another in a lifetime.

Among the last to go was Robert, who came to me and spoke in English, a thing he did not often do, as I had learned Navajo. "I wish you a Merry Christmas, San Chee (my name)," he said.

All day I had been too busy and excited to think, but that little attention made me homesick for something not Indian; and I stumbled into the store and hurried through to the living room, so Ken would not see the tears in my eyes.

He locked the store, polished the lamp chimney which I had not had time to touch and followed me. He set the lamp on the table and handed me an envelope.

'Merry Christmas," he said. He turned at once to undress and I knew he knew I did not want him to see me cry.

In the envelope was the receipt for the second payment on the farm.

"Ken," I gasped.

"Better get to bed. It's been a long day," he answered sleepily.

Half undressed, I sat on the edge of the bed. Outside a cold moon climbed to where I could see it through the window. We had been at Covered Water more than a year. Did Ken want to own a farm or would he rather stay on the reservation?

The moon climbed higher, and the shell of a house snapped and cracked in the cold. The air was freezing; I could see my breath in the moonlight, but still I sat.

I thought Ken asleep but suddenly he rolled over and spoke to me. When I faced him, he grinned at me in the moonlight.

With a gesture, I finished undressing and pulled the warm covers over me. My teeth were chattering and I blew out my breath sharply, to see the wraith of it in the moonlight. What difference whether we worked here or there, so we worked together?

Terminology Discussion around the Native Americans

Below is the response I obtained when I contacted the NIN (Native Information Network) in the US asking about the use of the term "Indian" and "Native American" and their possible derogatory and discriminatory connotations. The information was supplied by Mary Ahenakew, Resource Center, NIN (Native Information Network), at nin@si.edu, and is reproduced here with her permission.

"The term "Indian" is not considered a stereotype or derogatory term. The terms Native American and American Indian are both accepted terms in the U.S. We have received many inquiries about the name of the museum- why it isn't called the National Museum of the Native American instead of American Indian? The term "heathen" is a derogatory word. The Europeans called the Native people "heathens" because in their minds any one who was not Christian and specifically not Catholic were considered "without religion" or "not knowing God" which is what the term "heathen" means.

Our museum, the Smithsonian's National Museum of the American Indian was created by an Act of Congress signed by the first President Bush on November 28, 1989.

As a result of Columbus' geographical error, the term "Indian" has been used for over 450 years and the term "American Indian" since World War II. The term "Native American" is relatively new in comparison. It dates from the last 20 or so years and is problematic as people have argued that any person born in America is a Native American. In Canada, native people prefer the term "First Nations" or "First Nations people." People have various individual preferences; whenever possible native people like to be referred to by their tribal names rather than by a general term and since you are writing an article about a person form the Blackfoot Nation you can use their name when referring to him.

When we joined the Smithsonian museums, we added National to the existing name, Museum of the American Indian. We wanted to avoid changing the name so completely that people would not be aware that this was the same museum. Also, we wanted a name that people all over the world would understand. People in Asia, Europe, etc. know what American Indian means, but many are unfamiliar with the term Native American, and would not have known what our museum was about.

Also, the U.S. government uses the term American Indian or Indian. That's evident by the names of all the federal institutions: U.S. Department of the Interior, Bureau of Indian Affairs; Indian Health Service; National Congress of the American Indian; Indian Arts & Crafts Board; U.S. Senate Committee on Indian Affairs; U.S. Department of Education, Office of Indian Affairs The book *Desert Wife* by Hilda Faunce is not in the Oyate books to avoid list. Oyate is a Native organization working to see that Native American lives and histories are portrayed honestly in books for children (http://www.oyate.org).

WILD LIFE RESERVATION

Navajos

Christmas Eve

Americans → [San Chee and Ken]

Navajo Families

makes fruitcake

gives meat to each of the Navajo families

↓

finished by bedtime

they are very tired.

they gather and make fires all over the camp.

↓ there is ⎰ singing / dancing / laughing.

they have fun.

Christmas Morning

[San Chee]

↓

makes bread, cakes and biscuits → helped by the Navajo Women

→ she is surprised at how these women make their way around the kitchen.

Ken → cuts up meat and prepares the fire.

The meal

They eat and some Navajo men yell like Comanches.

After the meal → San Chee gives candies to the children.

↓

Robert (one of the indians) says "Merry Christmas" to San Chee in English.

⎰ - this makes her feel a bit homesick. / - she cries → doesn't want Ken to see her.

they go to sleep

↓

San Chee thinks that it doesn't matter where they have to work as long as they are together.

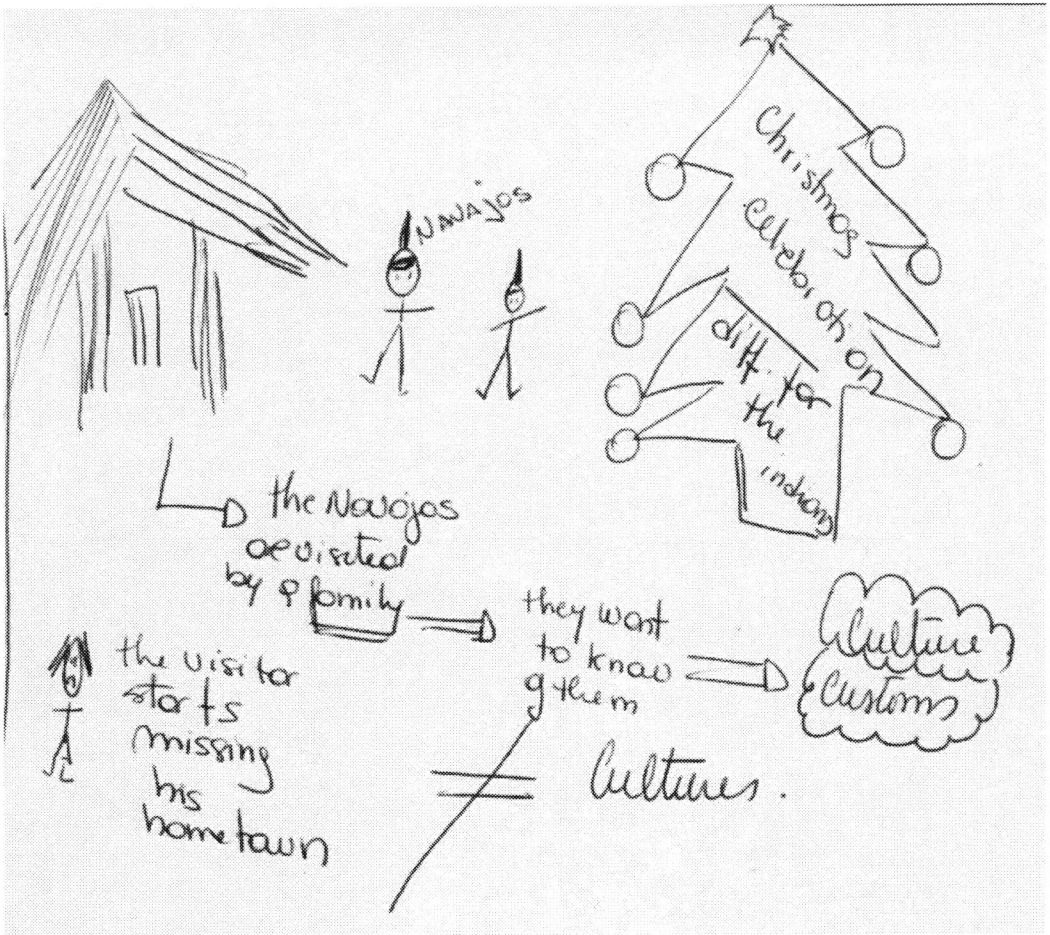

APPENDIX. DATA ANALYSIS

This Appendix includes detailed information regarding the data analysis measures and procedures.

1. Holistic Evaluation, Overall Impression or Global Coherence of the Participants' Productions

I refined the original 1-5 scale by Penningroth and Rosenberg (1995) depending on the presence, in each task, of one or several of the aspects mentioned below.

Holistic evaluation, overall impression or global coherence of the participants' productions

- Level 1: *inadequate.*
  (a) a text plagued by errors; or
  (b) a text without many errors but only the learner's interpretation, not motivated or justified by textual content; or
  (c) a text with obstacles, i.e. a facilitating condition of an imminent action is missing; or
  (d) a text with distractions, i.e. with unexpected actions or events which create new aims for the reader, carrying him/her temporarily or permanently outside the Christmas schema in this cultural context; or
  (e) a dysfunctional text, with the gathering of isolated and/or erratic events from the story without a conceptual framework behind their recovery, with problems in the order of information, and/or more or less adequate details but which reflect the absence of the schema.

- Level 2: partially adequate.
  (a) an adequate main idea but without detailed events or episodes; or
  (b) adequate (cultural) details but with a main idea with errors.

- Level 3: *adequate.*
  An adequate main idea with a general description of events and episodes.

- Level 4: *good.*
  An adequate main idea with a specific description of events and episodes.

- Level 5: *very good.*
  An adequate main idea with a specific description of events and episodes, with rich cultural details and/or culturally authentic dialogues and/or vivid and powerful vocabulary; and/or the use of narrative resources.

More specifically, variations in my assignment of this global coherence depended on the presence (or absence) of the following aspects:

(a) an easily identifiable plot (one can confidently say what is happening) by means of a clear sequence of events (temporal and events sequences);

(b) a clear story development (plot and relevant details) where the writer remains on task/topic/focus, without digressions (each linguistic and non-linguistic element present in the tasks contributes to the story development), with a good organization;

(c) a context of situation by means of which the writer orients the reader;

(d) vivid and powerful vocabulary;

(e) cultural details; and

(f) details (cultural and others) organized following a discernible plan.

I considered the impact of mechanical errors (punctuation, grammar, lexis, etc.) on the coherence of the written productions only when they interfered with communication.

2. Model of Cultural Apprehension

I include below a description of this Model.

Model of Cultural Apprehension during foreign/second language reading

Level 0.   Omission, total rejection, or total acceptance of cultural aspects.

Level 1.   Perception/identification of cultural differences. Access to levels 2, 3, 4, and 5.

Level 2.   Identification of own values and ideas. Identification of the cultural assumptions behind one's own culture (insider perspective).

Level 3.   Perception of culture C2 from one's own frame of reference (outsider perspective).

Level 4.   Perception of culture C2 from the frame of reference of members of culture C2 (insider perspective).

Level 5.   Perception of culture C1 from the perspective of culture C2 (outsider perspective).

Level 0. Omission, total rejection, or total acceptance of cultural aspects

Here learners may fail to perceive cultural aspects, which leads to their omission; or they may perceive them erratically, either accepting or rejecting them.

Level 1. Perception/identification of cultural differences

This level involves the perception of cultural differences, with the identification of the different, exciting, attractive, etc. elements of a given culture. This level is accessed through the identification of key vocabulary. The perception of cultural differences through comparison, confrontation, and contrast works as a bridge for stages 2, 3, 4, and 5 below.

Level 2. Identification of own values and ideas. Identification of the cultural assumptions behind one's own culture

Comprehending culture C1 from an insider perspective means visualizing one's behavior, values, ideas, etc. in light of one's cultural parameters. Given its excessive familiarity, observing one's cultural reality is not easy. The access to this level requires guidance (e.g. the teacher's) as in general, access is accompanied by the lack of cultural sensibility and ethnocentric positions.

There is interest in the discovery of alternative perspectives in the interpretation of familiar and unfamiliar phenomena within one's cultural practices as well as disposition to question the values and assumptions within those practices. Reflecting on one's culture reveals one's attitudes toward it. In this process, one distances him/herself from the familiar, and this distance makes the familiar look different, strange, unfamiliar. In this process, the identification of the stereotypes about one's culture leads to awareness of oneself and one's cultural reality.

Level 3. Perception of culture C2 from one's own frame of reference

This level involves comprehending culture C2 from an outsider perspective and requires awareness of how the behavior, values, and ideas of others are interpreted from the perspective of one's cultural frame of reference, i.e. as an observer.

Although there exists factual knowledge about culture C2 (social, historical, geographical, political, etc.) as well as about its norms of social interaction, the comprehension of culture C2 from an outsider perspective tends to be stereotyped. The identification of stereotypes constitutes one way of classifying culture C2 in manageable categories (Widdowson, 1995), is the first step toward the appreciation of the unknown, and makes access to levels 4 and 5 possible. However, the mere accumulation of stereotypes helps comprehend another culture only superficially, analyzing and explaining from the outside, i.e. as an observer.

Level 4. Perception of culture C2 from the frame of reference of members of culture C2

This stage involves the comprehension of culture C2 from an insider perspective. How members of another culture behave is interpreted in light of their own cultural norms.

Awareness about how others behave according to their own cultural norms is partly gained through information about the private world of the other. The perceptions that the members of another culture have of themselves make the access to their cultural codes possible, even though they influence the selection of content and the perspective adopted by outsiders.

Different areas can be analyzed, in particular those directly related with the experiences of the members of a given culture (e.g. home, work, community, food, dress, celebrations and festivities, traditions, etc.). There exists the capacity to describe the phenomena of contemporary life in this culture and explain the connotations and semantic fields of key words revealing cultural schemata - always from an insider perspective. However, this level amounts to more than information in these areas, adding layers of description and interpretation with the aim of leading to the identification of the value systems, social norms, and expectations of the members of culture C2.

Level 5. Perception of culture C1 from the perspective of culture C2

This means apprehending culture C1 from an outsider perspective. This level involves awareness of how one's own behavior is seen through the eyes of the members of other cultures.

The capacity to recognize and articulate the difficulties found in the process of perceiving a culture from inside (level 4) is present here. Also, there is the capacity to accept that one's cultural perspective and one's values and expectations influence one's visions. The decentralization in relation to one's cultural parameters allows for awareness about their cultural relativity. One is able to explore one's reactions to one's behavior as well as the behavior of others. It is possible to place oneself in the shoes of the other through imagination. This level matches Kramsch's "third perspective" (Kramsch 1993: 210), which permits the adoption of both insider and outsider perspectives in the apprehension of C1 and C2.

A critical and reflexive attitude is present. Facts are not accepted without critical analysis about their validity. One is able to go beyond description, appreciating diversity and exploring different alternative interpretations in the representation of another culture.

What is specific about one's culture is used to explain aspects of the other culture. One can critically observe one's culture and one's society, evaluating them from the perspective of culture C2, which guarantees the critical distancing and the decentralization of one's beliefs. Seeing one's cultural norms through the eyes of an outsider facilitates the understanding of how an outsider might react to these norms. This level is crucial since there cannot possibly be negotiation of shared meanings or understanding of the other's world if the relationship between one's views and those of others is not captured. The validity of culture C2 is acknowledged and appreciated in its own terms.

3. Cultural Apprehension: Specific Reader Behaviors

I define below the textual modifications produced by the participants in this study, which I observed and codified in the written tasks.

Elaborations: information from an appropriate schema; culturally appropriate extensions from the text (with more or less precision).

Distortions of the target culture or C2: culturally inappropriate information; culturally inappropriate textual modifications.

Evident errors: an action leads to an unexpected or inappropriate result; explicit errors without an identifiable cultural base; strange details, not motivated or justified by textual content or the Christmas schema.

Intrusions from the native culture or C1: from the learners' own ideas and culture.

Inferences from the text: inferences motivated or justified by textual content.

Wrong inferences: inferences not motivated or justified by textual content.

Irrelevant information: information (about events, places, characters, thoughts and feelings of certain characters, etc.), not necessarily referring to cultural aspects, which have no place in the flow of the key events in the story; the result of a local reading and of assigning the same value or importance to all the text, with the focus on information which was not intended to be focal.

Rationalizations: link among details and presentation of such details as apparently coherent. Of two types, depending on whether one text detail is linked to another not present in the text itself (inventions) or whether two text details are related (with the use of cohesion to relate elements which should not have been connected).

Reductions/simplifications: reduction/simplification of textual information, with fewer words and details than the original text; use of general vocabulary; presence of general propositions, i.e. with terms which summarize the most basic actions of the Christmas schema in the text.

Generalizations: a more significant reduction in which general words replace specific nouns; presence of general propositions, of a more topical nature than reductions.

Evaluative comments from the learners: inclusion of an opinion or attitude from the learners about an idea in the text (not the mere copying of the opinions of the characters or the opinions of the writer of the text).

Adequate morale/ interpretation from the learners: based on textual information.

Inadequate or wrong morale/ interpretation from the learners: not motivated or justified by textual content or the Christmas schema.

Explicit inclusion of the feelings and motivations of the characters: inferred from the text.

Explicit inclusion of the feelings and motivations of the characters: wrongly inferred from the text or not motivated or justified by its textual content.

Culturally adequate details.

In: Race and Ethnicity
Editor: Jonathan K. Crennan, pp. 113-135
ISBN: 978-1-60692-099-2

Chapter 3

THE POSSIBLE SELVES OF DIVERSE ADOLESCENTS: CONTENT AND FUNCTION ACROSS GENDER, RACE AND NATIONAL ORIGIN

Daphna Oyserman[1] and Stephanie Fryberg[2]

[1]Univeristy of Michigan; MI, USA
[2]The University of Arizona, AZ, USA

ABSTRACT

This chapter provides an overview of what is known about content of possible selves and implications of possible selves for outcomes for male and female teens differing in race/ethnicity (African American, Asian American, Latino, Native American, and white teens). Although findings are somewhat ambiguated by heterogeneity in time focus (e.g. 'next year', 'when you are an adult', 'in five years'), it appears that expected possible selves for the near future most commonly focus on academic and interpersonal domains, while fears are more diverse. There is some evidence that number of academic possible selves declines across the transition to middle school and from middle to high school. Low income, rural and Hispanic youth are at risk of having few academic or occupational possible selves, or having such general possible selves in these domains that they are unlikely to promote self-regulation. For a number of reasons, possible selves of girls may function more effectively as self-regulators. Moreover, there is at least some evidence that content of possible selves and especially the existence of strategies to attain these selves is predictive of academic attainment and delinquent involvement.

Self-concepts are what we think about when we think about ourselves. They are semantic, but also visual and affective representations of who we were, who we are, and who we can become. Although children develop some sense of self in the early years of life, with increased abstract reasoning ability in adolescence, youth begin to establish a sense of the selves they can become in addition to already developed sense of self based on current appearance, skill and competencies (e.g., Harter, 1982; Marsh, 1989; Oyserman, 2001). In adolescence these possible or imagined future selves become increasingly central to self-regulation and well-being (for similar perspectives see Cantor and Kihlstrom, 1987; Csikszentmihalyi and Larson, 1984).

The idea that the self is temporal and that the future-oriented components of the self are critical to understanding well being can be traced to William James (1890/1950). According to James, individuals narrow down various possibilities for the selves they might become only as needed, having a natural tendency to incorporate as much as possible into the self. Thus developing a sense of the self one might become involves choices- some voluntary, others forced. While individuals might *wish* to be all things simultaneously, they cannot *strive* be all things – because the activities involved in different selves conflict. The 'bon vivant' self and the 'quiet scholar' self would not be able to agree on how to spend the evening. The popular girl would want to hang out while the 'A' student would want to be home studying. Choice or at least compromise is necessary between these competing visions of the self one could be – both cannot be the most important self-goal at the same time. While painful, these are voluntary choices between selves one may equally likely attain.

Choices may also be less voluntary when individuals find themselves unable to attain a possible self. Striving and persistently failing to become like a desired self is painful, and so, James suggests, we eventually drop desired selves we had once striven to attain when it becomes clear that they will never be attained. Childhood wishes to become an Olympic gymnast or professional ballerina fade and practicing the cello falls to the wayside in part because it is much less painful *not* to become something one is uninterested in than to not become something one wishes to be. Thus, according to James (1890) we all have to give up on some aspirations and stake a claim on the person we will become. Over time, and with accumulating failure feedback, we eventually give up on becoming those aspects of our desired selves that are too painful to keep striving for in the face of repeated failures. We do this because our sense of worth or self-esteem is a dynamic proportion, the ratio of our aspirations (the selves we wish to attain) divided by actual attainments (the selves we are); self-esteem is battered unless aspirations are periodically pruned to come into line with attainments. Thus, following from James' perspective, the selves we strive to become focus motivational attention, guide behavior and are an important sources of positive self-regard.

Despite the assumed importance of present, past, and future selves on understandings of the self-concept, future selves were not the focus of research until the mid-1980s when Markus and Nurius (1986) refocused attention on future or possible selves. At the same time, other social and personality psychologists interested in personal strivings and personal projects and life tasks (e.g. Cantor 1990; Kennon and Emmons, 1995), gave new life to the future-oriented elements of the self-concept and to the modern perspective that these future selves are critical to motivation. Since then, a body of empirical evidence has accumulated on the content and the consequences of possible selves in adolescence, the linkage between possible selves and self-esteem, and the influence of possible selves on the self-regulation of behavior.

Although much of the research evidence is based on single studies, is correlational and involves small scale samples and qualitative methods, not all of it is and across studies there is evidence both for the postulated link between self-est
m and possible selves and for the postulated link between possible selves and behavior. Thus, adolescents who believe that *positive* possible selves *are likely* to be attained have higher self-esteem than those who do not (Knox et al, 1998); adolescents with both academically oriented possible selves and strategies are significantly more likely to attain improved grades than

those without these possible selves (Oyserman, Bybee, Terry, and Hart-Johnson, 2004). Moreover, experimental evidence indicates that shifts in possible selves can lead to shifts in academic behavior (e.g. Oyserman, Terry, and Bybee, 2002).

Following James, in the current chapter, we assume that possible selves play a motivational and self-regulatory role in shaping future behavior. This chapter begins with a definition of possible selves and a brief overview of how possible selves are measured. We then fit possible selves into a developmental context as an aspect of self-concept susceptible to contextual influences and outline why it is important to study possible selves of minority youth. Using this as our structure, we review the literature on content of possible selves and implications of possible selves for outcomes for male and female teens differing in race/ethnicity (African American, Asian American, Latino, Native American, and white teens).

We used the on-line Psychlit and the key words: Possible selves and each of the following adolescence, African American, Black, Hispanic, Latino, Mexican American, Asian American, Asian, American Indian, and Native American to search for literature as well as adding any additional research we were aware of. The literature on possible selves is limited by use of somewhat different measures of possible selves, differing reference periods for possible selves, correlational or qualitative designs and use of either mono-racial ethnic samples or small samples. However, enough literature has accumulated to make a summary valuable and to allow for some tentative conclusions. To foreshadow our conclusions, although somewhat ambiguated by heterogeneity in reference period for possible selves (e.g. 'next year', 'when you are an adult', 'in five years,' 'in the future'), our review suggests that expected possible selves most commonly focus on academic and interpersonal domains, while fears are more diverse. There is at least some evidence that content of possible selves and especially the existence of strategies to attain these selves is predictive of academic attainment and delinquent involvement.

WHAT ARE POSSIBLE SELVES?

Possible Selves are the Future-Oriented Component of a Multifaceted Self-Concept

Possible selves are the selves we imagine ourselves becoming in the future, the selves we hope to become, the selves we are afraid we may become, and the selves we fully expect we will become. Possible selves can be distally imagined – 'the self I will become as an adult', or more short term – 'the self I will become next year'. The source of these selves is varied. Possible selves can be rooted in one's own experience and past behavior or accomplishments. Thus, high performing students may have an easier time imagining positive academic possible selves than low performing students (e.g. Leondari, Syngollitou, and Kiosseoglou, 1998). Possible selves can be rooted in what important others believe one should become. They can also be rooted in one's own values, ideals and aspirations. Thus, low performing students who come to believe that they can succeed in spite of obstacles or that they are obligated to improve their performance given family expectations may be able to create and sustain academic possible selves in spite of lack of previous academic successes. In many ways, it is this latter group, the low performers, that are the more interesting cases in which to study possible selves since it is in this case that possible selves have to be created from something other than simple repetition of current and past outcomes.

Positive, expected selves, and feared or to be avoided selves are often studied separately, either as summaries or counts of the number of positive and negative possible selves over all, or in terms of content (e.g. academic, interpersonal). Expected and feared possible selves can also be studied in conjunction. *Balance* refers to the construal of both positive expectations and fears in the same domain (e.g., I expect to be popular and have lots of friends and I am afraid that I'll be alone, that other kids' parents won't let them hang out with me). Youths with balanced possible selves have both a positive self-identifying goal to strive for and are aware of the personally relevant consequences of not meeting that goal. This balance may preserve motivation to attain the positive possible self and therefore avoid the negative self, leading these youths to make more attempts to attain expected selves and avoid feared ones. Balance may also decrease the range of strategies deemed acceptable in attempting to attain positive possible selves. Strategies that may both increase the possibility of attaining a positive self and reduce the possibility of avoiding the negative self with which it is balanced will be discarded. Only strategies that simultaneously increase the possibility of attaining the positive self and avoiding the negative self will be attempted (Oyserman and Markus, 1990b).

Lack of balance in possible selves may mean that youths are more likely to act without taking into account possible negative consequences for a possible self. This oversight is likely to result in surprise and bewilderment when attempts to attain a positive possible self result in unforeseen negative consequences for the self. Thus, a youth with expectations of becoming accepted by his peers at school who is lacking feared possible selves focused on rejection may think that breaking into school after hours and marking his initials on the walls will help him attain this possible self without taking into account that this behavior is illegal and that youth involved in delinquency may not be socially accepted. By writing his initials on the walls he imagined promoting social possible self without taking into account that he is also providing officials with clues as to who to prosecute. Being expelled and getting into trouble may not be an intended consequence, particularly if the result is that he becomes less accepted.

In addition to measuring balance, possible selves can differ in whether they are linked with behavioral strategies. Possible selves linked with strategies should be better able to promote behavior change. Thus the difference between a youth whose possible self is to pass the eighth grade and one whose possible self is to pass the eighth grade by coming to school on time each day and not cutting class with friends is that one has a possible self linked to action sequences while the other does not. For one youth, evoking the goal automatically evokes strategies, actions to be taken and avoided. For the other youth, evoking the goal may simply evoke an image of the self at the end state, necessary but perhaps not sufficient, for movement toward the goal to occur (Oyserman, Bybee, Terry, and Hart-Johnson, 2004).

Possible Selves Are Social Constructions

Possible selves are always importantly social. When possible selves are based on one's own past successes and failures, they are social, because these successes and failures are frequently successes and failures *relative* to the attainments of comparable others. Grades are relative to the extent that teachers standardize grading to fit actual accomplishments of students. Similarly, when possible selves are based on one's own values, ideals and aspirations, they are social, because these values, ideals and aspirations are also importantly shaped by social contexts (Oyserman, 2002). For example, aspirations are importantly shaped by consensual stereotypes about what people like me (a girl, a rural kid, an American Indian) can become. As social contexts shift, so too may possible selves. The same rural kid can develop a 'college bound' possible self with appropriate feedback and role models. Further, although possible selves are based on past successes and failures, they are not limited to them. For example, although in general, academically successful high school students will find it easier to sustain possible selves focused on school success than academically failing high school students, not all students will translate proximal academic possible selves into adult career-related possible selves. Thus, in a relatively large scale study of adult possible selves of highly academically successful adolescent boys and girls in Northern Ireland, Curry and colleagues (1994) found that highly academically successful girls were significantly less likely to form career-oriented possible selves than boys. Instead, girls were more likely to imagine a future either at home raising children, or a career based not on ability but on balancing home and some sort of job. Simply knowing academic track and past attainment was not sufficient; gender also influenced content of possible selves.

Both specific others and social contexts more generally play an important role in the creation and maintenance of possible selves. Significant others (e.g. parents), role models, and media images are examples of the models used to instantiate possible selves, but so too are important socio-cultural identities. That is, we can become the kind of person that people of our group can become; we fear disappointing important groups by failing to attain group norms and standards. In our own research with African American youth in Detroit, this can be seen clearly in possible selves such as "Become a proud Black woman" in which adherence to group values *is* the possible self. In this way, possible selves are tightly connected to racial, ethnic, gender and cultural identities, and perceived in-group norms. Individuals learn not only who people like them can become, but also who people not like them can become, creating both a series of possible 'me's' and a series of 'not me's', selves one does not strive for or actively tries to avoid. For example, in a series of interviews urban high school students reported common stereotypes of Asians and Latinos, with Latinos linked to manual labor and Asians linked to doing well in school (Kao, 2002). It is reasonable to assume that teens surrounded by pro or anti academic expectations for their group are likely to find development of academic possible selves facilitated in the former and impeded in the latter case since for former but not the latter teens, others will help sustain and maintain the possible self. Because local norms can be changed or shifted, possible selves are also open to change when norms are perceived to change.

Possible Selves Are Shaped by Social Context

Adolescents learn about what is possible and what is valued through engagement with their social context (Oyserman and Markus, 1993). When social contexts lack images of possible selves for 'people like us' in a particular domain, possible selves in this domain are likely to be missing entirely or will be so global as to be useless as a self-regulatory mechanism. Feedback can be reinforcing or restrictive and undermining. In studying minority youths, low socio-economic status youths, and girls, the issue of social contextual undermining and restricting is of particular interest. For example, youth in rural or urban inner-city settings may experience a restriction of possibilities both because specific role models for a range of academic and occupational outcomes are missing and because important social identities may be felt to conflict with certain possible selves. In rural settings, given lack of occupational opportunities, a youth might lack role models of choosing a career rather than simply settling for a job. Thus, in a qualitative interview study (Shepard, 2001), the adult hoped for and feared possible selves generated by rural 17-19 year old adolescent girls in British Columbia did not focus on education and fewer than 10% mentioned occupations, with even these few mentions being vague and general (e.g., "I want a job."). Instead, possible selves focused on personal attributes ("Someone people can like and trust"), relationships ("develop closer relationships with my brother and sister"), and possessions ("I want a jeep"). Similarly, in inner city contexts with high unemployment rates, it may be hard to instantiate specific and detailed occupational possible selves and media images of occupational possible selves for one's racial group may be equally limiting, leaving the implied message that one cannot be both a member of one's racial group and also a member of various professions.

Social contexts also provide important feedback to adolescents and young adults about whether a possible self is positively or negatively valued. Thus, the same possible self can be a positive expected possible self or a dreaded and to-be avoided feared possible self, depending on social contextual feedback. Graduating medical students in primary care specialties were more likely to view becoming a primary care physician as a positive possible self if they had a mentor whose professional and personal life refuted negative stereotypes about people in their specialty (Burack, Irby, Carline, Ambrozy, Ellsbury, and Stritter, 1997).

Similarly, social contexts can shift the perceived likelihood that an expected or feared possible self is likely. Teens whose parents divorced are more likely to have feared possible selves focused on problems in marriage (Carson, Madison, and Santrock, 1987). Similarly, teens are more likely to generate feared possible selves focused on developing mental health problems when they have experienced maternal separations due to maternal mental health problems (Oyserman, Bybee, and Mowbray, 2005). These effects of situations are also found in experimental manipulations of likelihood of attaining a possible self: College undergraduates rated career as compared to marital, and parental possible selves as more (or less) likely to be attained when they received false feedback that their personality matched (did not match) the personality of people who attained career success (or were successful parents) (Kerpelman and Pittman, 2001). The link between possible selves and congruent behavior has also been shown experimentally: College undergraduates primed to think of 'success after hard effort' possible selves were more persistent as compared to undergraduates primed to think of 'success due to stroke of luck' possible selves (Ruvolo and Markus, 1992).

Because it is a context central to attainment of both academic and social possible selves and because youths spend a large portion of their day at school, school as a social context has been a particular focus of possible self research. Although school transitions have not been the explicit focus of possible self research, content of academic or school-focused possible selves are likely to shift focus across school transitions because these transitions result in changing social contexts (from more personalized to more regimented, from learning to outcome focused). As contexts shift, the meaning of academic success shifts from trying and improving to attaining successful outcomes. Thus, from early adolescence on, becoming a successful student should increasingly focus on grades, performance, and comparisons with others rather than personal mastery or involvement. For these reasons, we assume that adolescents' academic possible selves are less likely to focus on learning (e.g. "I expect to learn new things in school", "I want to avoid being bored in class") and more likely to focus on outcomes (e.g. "I expect to get good grades," "I want to avoid failing."). Indeed, in our own lab, when we ask Detroit middle school students to generate possible selves, they commonly mention passing, getting good grades, avoiding failing or getting good grades, but rarely mention expecting to learn new things, or wanting to avoid not learning.

There is also some evidence that school and academic success may become less salient possible selves as youth move from elementary to middle and high school. Anderman and colleagues report that in elementary school, boys' possible selves were more likely to focus on being a good student than in middle school, with likelihood of 'good student' possible selves declining across the middle school years (Anderman, Hicks, and Maehr, 1994 as described in Anderman, Anderman and Griesinger, 1999; Anderman et al., 1999). In our own lab, our longitudinal research on the middle to high school transition in Detroit also shows an overall decline in the number of academic possible selves. However, the data do not appear linear, each fall students generate more academic possible selves than they do by the end of the academic year.

Yet if students are actively engaged, positive academic possible selves can also be increased across these years. This is shown in a small group based brief universal intervention with urban African American middle school youth. The intervention increased academic possible selves and balanced possible selves in the year after the intervention (in comparison with intervention and control youth and controlling for previous year's GPA) (Oyserman, Terry, and Bybee, 2002). This effect was replicated in a larger experimental trial that also documented that change in possible selves mediated significant change in school behavior, grades, and depression (Oyserman, Bybee, and Terry, 2005). Effects may not be easy to attain – another intervention did not find effects on possible selves when African American elementary and middle school youth received mentoring for various lengths of time (Lee and Cramond, 1999).

WHY STUDY POSSIBLE SELVES OF MINORITY YOUTH?

There are two key reasons why a focus on possible selves of minority youths is needed. First, because possible selves mediate between values and actual behavior, understanding possible selves is critical to narrowing the gap between Mexican American, African American, American Indian and white youth. Possible selves are critical to understanding the gap when it is in the opposite direction as well – such as the case with Asian Americans. That is, higher achieving and lower achieving groups may differ systematically in the nature of their possible selves. Because possible selves are socially constituted and maintained, it is likely that racial/ethnic groups differ systematically in their possible selves so that a second reason to study possible selves of racial/ethnic minority youth is to gain better understanding of the interface between possible selves and content of racial/ethnic identity. Such understanding would allow for development of effective interventions to reduce the achievement gap and decrease risk of other negative outcomes contained in stereotypes. Stereotypes about minorities are focused on the important domains of adolescence – academic achievement, interpersonal and relational style, and engagement with risky activities. When minority youths imagine what is possible for them, preformed images in these domains are likely to be highly accessible. Thus, for example, part of the answer to the question 'am I likely to do well in school?' comes from group images. Are 'we' stereotyped as a model minority or as dumb and lazy?

For minority youth, shared ideas about who one is, where one belongs, what is possible for the self and what is not, are reflected in culturally significant metaphors, images, stories, proverbs, icons, and symbols (Oyserman and Harrison, 1998). These shared ideas or images are shaped by contact and interface with American society (Oyserman, Kemmelmeier, Fryberg, Brosh, and Hart-Johnson, 2004) and carry with them socially contrived messages about what targets of those messages can and cannot do. Hence, what it means to be American Indian, African American, Asian American or Mexican American is particularized by culture of origin, and its interface with both mainstream American culture, and mainstream America's views of one's group. Studying the possible selves of minority youth provides a window into the motivational world of these youths.

WHY FOCUS ON ADOLESCENCE?

Following Erikson's (1968) model of psychosocial development, adolescence is the life phase focused on identity development. Adolescence is a *psychosocial moratorium*, during which time youth are free to try on possible selves without suffering sanctions from misbehavior related to their conception of how a person with such a self would act. Erikson defines active identity seeking as a moratorium phase in which youth try out, without commitment, various roles. Once roles have been tried, young adults *achieve* a sense of identity, picking a smaller set of possible selves to commit to becoming. Erikson recognized that not all youth went through a phase of trying on or actively seeking an identity, either because they decided on adult identities to strive to become early in adolescence without much seeking (what Erikson termed *foreclosure*) or because they are neither searching for adult selves nor settled on future selves, but were simply unsure (what he termed *identity diffusion*). While the possible self model does not require that Erikson be correct, it is compatible with his model of phases of identity development. Specifically, during moratorium youth should have more and more varied possible selves, though not necessarily strategies to attain them. During achievement and foreclosure phases, youth should rate their possible selves as more certain to be attained and should have few possible selves that are vague or lack strategies. The difference in possible selves of achievement and foreclosure youth should be in their content not their number or their perceived certainty of occurring. Given that foreclose and achievement phases differ in how much youth engaged in active seeking prior to choosing, with foreclosure youth seeking less, the possible selves of achievement youth should be more diverse and less likely to simply mirror the content of in-group stereotypes than the possible selves of foreclosure phase youth.

We did not find many empirical tests of the connection between possible selves and identity development phase. Those we found focused on Marcia's (1980) operationalization of Erikson's phases of identity formation – with the assumption that as youth pass through the moratorium phase on the way to identity resolution of some type, they should be actively imagining more possible selves than prior (e.g. identity diffusion) or later identity phases (e.g. identity achievement), and that those who do not seek an adult identity at one time point (e.g. identity foreclosure), may do so at another. Dunkel (2001) tested whether possible self construction is indeed related to adolescent identity development phase using the EOM-EIS2 operationalization of identity status (Marcia, 1980) with 17-25 mostly white psychology undergraduates. Students who scored in the 'Moratorium' phase and 'low profile' respondents (who did not score high in any of the identity phase subscales) reported more positive possible selves than students who scored in the 'Foreclosure' or 'Diffusion' identity phase. Not only did 'Moratorium' phase students have more positive possible selves, they also endorsed more neutral and more negative possible selves than did individuals in the other four groups. In addition, students who had either completed an identity seeking phase (coded as Identity Achieved) or had never sought an identity (coded as Identity Foreclosed) rated their positive and neutral possible selves as more certain and likely to be achieved than did students who scored in the Moratorium, Diffusion or low profile groups. These findings, though focused on somewhat older adolescents and young adults, lend support to the relevance of developmental phases of identity development to the construct of possible selves.

HOW ARE POSSIBLE SELVES MEASURED?

Three general formats appear in the published literature, a close-ended format yielding sum scores of positive and negative possible selves across domains, an open format content coded for domain, a closed-format focusing on a specific type of possible self (typically academic possible selves). Markus and Nurius (1986) [1] introduced a close-ended measure to assess the number of positive and negative possible selves in their research with college students, subsequent use of this measure also typically involves college students (e.g. Dunkle, 2001; Leondari, Syngollitou, and Kiosseoglou, 1998). Open-ended measures suitable for use with children and adolescents are reported for children as young as 10 or 11 (Lobenstine et al., 2001; Shepard and Marshall, 1999). We also found a number of close-ended measures [2]

---

[1] Markus (1987) provides one week stability and reliability information for this measure, describing positive, negative and neutral selves.

[2] Anderman, Anderman & Griesinger (1999) studied academic and social possible selves in white Midwestern 7th graders and a separate sample of African American and European American Southeastern high school students. Using a five year time horizon, students rated the likelihood that they would attain Academic Positive Possible Selves (rating the likelihood of being a good student, being smartest in class, doing better than other students, being on the honor roll, and get rewarded for doing well), Social Positive Possible Selves (rating the likelihood of being popular, chosen first for teams and groups, having lots of friends and being competitive), and of Academic Negative Possible Selves (rating the likelihood of doing as little school work as possible, being interested in school work (reversed), wanting to quit school, getting good grades (reversed), and being a poor student). Academic positive possible selves were reliable in both samples, Chronbach's α = .73 (white sample), .62 (mixed sample), social possible selves were reliable only in the white sample, Chronbach's α = .69, and negative academic possible selves were reliable only in the mixed race sample, α =.71 (other than stating unreliable, no further α information available for the other sample for social or

for teens and college students focused specifically on academic (Anderman, Anderman and Griesinger, 1999, Kemmelmeier and Oyserman, 2001b; Kemmelmeier, Oyserman, and Brosh, 2003) and social (Anderman, Anderman and Griesinger, 1999) possible selves.

A detailed description of an open-ended possible selves measure and coding schema for Black and White adolescents is provided by Oyserman and Markus (1990), the measure they developed in their study with low-income high school and institutionalized youth is also used by others focused on risky behaviors in the middle and high school years (e.g. Aloise-Young, Hennigan, and Leong, 2001). This initial format was later modified to include questions about strategies to attain possible selves in subsequent research with African American, Hispanic and low-income white middle and high school students (Oyserman and Saltz, 1993; Oyserman, Gant and Ager, 1995, Study 1; Oyserman, Bybee, Terry, and Hart-Johnson, 2004). An alternative open-ended format focuses on hoped for and feared possible selves, elicits ratings of likelihood of attaining each possible self and ratings of how much each possible self is hoped for or feared (Cross and Markus, 1991), although initially used in research with middle to older aged adults, this format is also used in research with white middle class high school students (Knox, Funk, Elliott, and Bush, 2000).

Across research, possible self measures also differ in their reference point. Some measures refer to "the future" with no further specification; other measures specify a reference point in terms of chronological ("next year") or developmental ("as an adult") time. Clearly measure and reference point influence findings, though we only found one study (Oyserman and Markus, 1990) that explicitly compared results from one reference point to another. These authors found that use of the "adult" reference point resulted in results that were more similar across youth and did not distinguish among youth differing in delinquent involvement while use of a "next year" reference point result in more heterogeneous responses that were significantly related to delinquent involvement.

WHAT DO WE KNOW ABOUT THE RELATIONSHIP BETWEEN POSSIBLE SELVES AND IMPORTANT OUTCOMES IN ADOLESCENCE?

Possible Selves and Academic Outcomes

Possible selves have been linked to academic attainments. At the middle school level, Midwestern mostly white seventh graders with positive academic possible selves had

---

negative academic selves). Briefer scales of academic possible selves were developed in the work of Oyserman and her colleague, Markus Kemmelmeier. In a study with primarily white college students they asked "How do you think you will do in school next year, overall what are your chances of being successful in the future, how easy or hard will it be for you to find a really good job when you finish school, how confident are you that you will succeed in the future" Cronbach's α = .78 (Kemmelmeier & Oyserman, 2001b), with the Chronbach α reliable (.71) in a subsequent study with Arab Israeli and German high school students (Kemmelmeier, Oyserman, & Brosh, 2005). Similarly, in a study with mostly white college students, they asked students to rate the likelihood of the following academic possible selves: do well in school, get good grades, understand the material in my classes (Cronbach's α = .88), and strategies to attain these possible selves: using my time wisely, handling problems that come my way successfully, coping well with distractions, and striving persistently toward my goals (Cronbach's α = .80), moreover, since the two scales correlated at r = .45, they were averaged as a single score for subsequent analyses (Kemmelmeier & Oyserman, 2001b).

improved GPA from 6th to 7th grade, especially when their academic possible selves were more positive than their current academic self-concept (Anderman, Anderman and Griesinger, 1999). In a mixed raced sample of 6th-8th graders, positive academic possible selves predicted higher endorsement of performance goals - wanting to do schoolwork in order to prove one's competence or to appear more able or competent than other students (Anderman et al, 1999). Even in samples at high risk of academic problems due to high poverty concentration, when youth had more academically focused possible selves and strategies to attain them, they had significantly improved grades (controlling for previous year GPA) compared with youth lacking these possible selves (Oyserman, et al., 2004).

With regard to college, students (male and female) who were math/science schematic took and planned to take more math and science courses than their peers (Lipps, 1995, Study 2). Female college students with a positive math/science self-schema performed better on a math test than those who were either aschematic or had negative math/science self-schemas (Lips, 1995, Study 1).

Possible Selves and Delinquent Involvement

Possible selves have also been linked with delinquent involvement. Youth may initially view a delinquent lifestyle as a means to create possible selves such as "independent," "daring," "competent," or "fun-loving and adventurous." The negative self-definitional consequences of delinquency may not be taken into account, especially by youths who lack balanced possible selves (Oyserman and Markus, 1990a; 1990b). In a study of four subgroups of primarily African American adolescent males who varied in level of official delinquent involvement from the state maximum security lockup facility for juveniles to high school students attending the schools most commonly cited as the last school attended by these youth, with midrange levels of delinquent involvement including youth in living in group homes after delinquent adjudication and youth attending schools of attention after more minor involvement with police or school infractions, Oyserman and Markus (1990a; 1990b) find differences in content of next year expected possible selves, next year feared possible selves and extent that expected and feared selves are 'balanced' or represent what the youth wants to attain and avoid in a specific domain. For public school and community placement youth, the most common expected possible self generated focused on doing well in school and accounted for nearly a third of responses. For the two most delinquent groups, however, "getting along in school" is only the third or fourth most frequent response, accounting for only 13.9% of the responses given by the training school youth. Similarly, the achievement-related response of "having a job," which is the third or fourth most frequently generated possible self for the public school and community placement youth does not appear at all for the two most delinquent groups. Instead, what appears in these positions is a variety of *negatively* valued possible selves: "junkie," "depressed," "alone," "flunking out of school," "pusher," "criminal." Note that these negative selves are generated not in response to the query about feared selves, but in response to expected possible selves. The amount of official delinquency predicted greater likelihood of generating these kinds of negative selves as expected next year possible selves. Lower likelihood of generating next year expected selves focused on doing well or getting along in school, and higher likelihood of materially focused next year expected possible selves (e.g. expecting to have a car or nice clothes).

With respect to the possible selves that are hoped for in the next year, there is more homogeneity among the four groups, all groups indicate with about equal frequency the hope to "have friends" and, indeed, this is the most frequently generated hoped-for possible self of the two most delinquent groups. In contrast with the expected selves, "having a job" is a commonly hoped-for possible self for all the groups including the two most delinquent groups. "Getting along in school" is a frequently generated hoped-for self by all but the training school youth, where it is replaced by the material hoped for selves (e.g. having certain types of clothes or cars). Feared possible selves show striking differences across the four groups. By far the most frequently generated feared possible self of the public school youth is that of "not getting along in school." It accounts for nearly a quarter of all responses to this question. For the other three groups, however, the most frequently generated response is the fear of being criminal–a "thief," a "murderer." For the two most delinquent groups this fear explains a third of all their responses. In contrast, the fear of being criminal does not appear at all among the five most frequent responses of the public school youth and only 8% mentioned this self at all. The amount of official delinquency predicted fearing criminal selves and fearing school failure. Generally, the percentage of youth generating school failure selves decreased, whereas the percentage of youth generating criminal selves increased across groups from public school to training school youth.

When the balance between the expectations and fears of the four groups of youth was examined, the officially nondelinquent youth showed significantly more balance between their expectations and fears than did the most officially delinquent youth. More tÒôn 81% of nondelinquents had at least one match between their expected and feared selves, whereas this was true for only 37% of the most delinquent groups. Of the most officially delinquent youth in this sample, 33% to 37% feared becoming criminal. Yet, these feared selves were not balanced by expectations that focused on avoiding crime and attaining conventional achievement. The two most delinquent groups do not expect to "have a job" and only 14% to 19% of them expect to "get along in school." Although these delinquent youth have the type of feared selves that might be associated with the avoidance of delinquent activity, many of them seem to be missing the expected possible selves that could provide the organizing and energizing vision of how they might avoid criminal activity, and what they might expect if they do.

Self-reported delinquency data (collected 2-3 months after the self-concept measures) were available for the least officially delinquent youth – the public school and community placement youth. Controlling for sex, race, and sample source, balance significantly predicted self-reported delinquency among these youth. This effect remained even when controlling for the impact of expecting negative selves. The relationship between self-esteem and delinquent involvement was non-linear and not significant, (Oyserman and Markus, 1990a; 1990b).

These findings were substantively replicated in a subsequent study with another African American sample showing that controlling for other factors, youth who were in public school (officially nondelinquent youth) were more likely to have balanced possible selves, to believe that they were attempting to attain expected selves and avoid feared selves, and to view individuated and achievement-oriented selves as important than youth in detention after felony arrest, these differences were replicated when the public school sample only was used and youth were compared in their level of self-reported delinquent involvement (Oyserman and Saltz, 1993). Using a somewhat different approach, Newberry and Duncan counted number of positive and negative possible selves among high school students and found that having fewer positive and more negative possible selves correlated with self-report delinquent involvement (Newberry and Duncan, 2001).

Possible Selves and Health Risk Behaviors

Balance in possible selves is also related to substance use in junior high school aged youth. Aloise-Young, Hennigan, and Leong (2001) looked at the relationship between possible selves, cigarette and alcohol consumption among 6th-9th grader in a large sample (n=1606) of Los Angeles youth, about 45% Anglo, with most of the other students being Hispanic. Youth who smoked and drank more had significantly fewer balanced possible selves, no gender or ethnicity interaction effects were found. The relationship between balance and substance use was stronger after 6th grade because in 6th grade relatively few of these behaviors were reported. By the 9th grade, a quarter of youth without any positive expected selves reported heavy substance use, as compared with only 1% of those with three positive expected selves. These results substantively replicate an earlier study examining self-schemas, possible selves, and risky behavior (alcohol use/misuse, tobacco use, and sexual activity) in 8th graders and then a year later after they had transitioned to high school (9th grade) (Stein and Markus, 1998). A bi-directional relationship indicated that 8th grade popularity self-schema scores were predictive of 9th grade risky behaviors and that engagement in risky behaviors in 8th grade contributed to the conceptualization of the self as currently deviant and positively predicted the deviant self-schema scores in the 9th grade. Involvement in risky behaviors increases subsequent negative possible selves and the reverse, negative possible selves predict subsequent risky behaviors. Thus possible selves have been implicated in both promoting positive outcomes – academics and in increasing risk of negative outcomes – delinquency, alcohol and tobacco use, and early sexual activity. The next sections use the framework laid out to focus on gender, race and ethnicity.

GENDER DIFFERENCES IN POSSIBLE SELVES

In adolescence, girls and boys differ in self-esteem, in the extent that self-concept contains others and relationships to them, and in their cognitive and emotional maturity. All of these gender differences may relate to differences in possible selves. With regard to self-esteem, on average, girls have lower self-esteem than boys. Indeed, higher self-esteem is associated with greater confidence that positive possible selves will be attained (Knox et al., 1998). Thus on average, girls should be less sure that they will attain their possible selves and more certain that negative possible selves may occur – taken together, these perceptions may reduce their commitment to any particular positive possible self while focusing energies on avoiding negative possible selves. Those with lower self-esteem may be more prone to give up on possible selves, following James' (1890) notion that low self-esteem stimulates pruning of possible selves that are deemed unattainable. Second, with regard to social or relational content of self-concept, those with more social content may be more open to contextual influence, both because obligations to important others may be perceived as more central to self-concept and because others' successes and failures are more likely to be incorporated into self-concept. This means that girls may be more susceptible to contextual influences – taking on as their own both successes and failures of related others. Third, with regard to gender differences in cognitive development, the self may have more influence on the behavior of girls than of boys to the extent that girls are better able to develop 'if-then' consequential strategies related to their possible selves. While remaining confident that one's possible selves can be attained and being less influenced by context may seem positive, to the extent that the self is not engaged or turned on in everyday behavioral situations, this confidence may have little effect on actual behavior. In our own research, we found boys' possible selves less influenced by social contextual information about likelihood of academic failure while also being at higher risk of academic failure themselves, it was as if girls took information about other's failure as a cautionary tale to increase vigilance, boys did not (Oyserman, Gant, and Ager, 1995, Study 3). In this section, we review evidence of gender differences in these three areas as they relate to possible selves.

SELF-ESTEEM

With regard to self-esteem and content of possible selves, we found little evidence to explain why gender differences occur. Male and female college students do not differ in the number of balanced possible selves they generate (Oyserman, Gant and Ager, Study 1). Boys and girls do not differ in the number of positive possible selves they have. No gender differences in number of expected possible selves were found in a 6th-9th grade sample, with 2.4-2.6 expected possible selves generated across each grade and gender (Aloise-Young et al., 2001). No gender differences were found in positive possible selves in a sample of 14-15 year old high school students although girls had significantly lower self-esteem than boys (Leondari, Syngollitou, and Kiosseoglou, 1998).For girls, the likelihood of attaining negative possible selves is also negatively associated with higher self-esteem (Knox et al, 1998). However in a large scale study with predominantly white Ohio high school students, gender differences in feared possible self content and likelihood were found (Knox, Funk, Elliott, and Bush, 2000). Specifically, high school girls rated feared possible selves as more likely than boys (overall $M = 5.4$, range = 1-19) and described more feared relational possible selves whereas boys generated more feared possible selves related to occupation, general failure, and inferiority (Knox et al., 200). No gender differences in likelihood or content of hoped-for possible selves were found ($M = 8$ range = 1-19), though girls rated hoped for selves on average as more hoped for than boys. The three most frequently mentioned hoped for possible selves for boys and girls (in descending order of frequency) were occupation, relationship, and education. Physical illness, general failure, relationships were the most frequent feared possible selves for boys, for girls, relationships, illness, failure were the order. Boys were more likely to have occupation and general failure fears while girls were more likely to have relationship fears.

SENSITIVITY TO SOCIAL CONTEXT

Another possibility is that girls' possible selves are more sensitive to social contextual feedback – incorporating both negative and positive possible selves more easily into self-concept. We already noted Curry et al.'s (1994) finding that girls took into account their likely need to take on parenting roles in imagining possible selves related to careers, however, this research did not directly address sensitivity to contextual feedback, since both boys and girls in this research could be seen to be responding to social norms about appropriate gender roles in adulthood. In our lab, we addressed these issues more directly by assessing the response of teenaged girls and boys to social comparison information, finding that girls were more likely to shift up their academic possible selves when they thought of someone their same gender who was succeeding in school, and more likely to shift down these possible selves when they thought of someone they knew who was failing in school (Kemmelmeier and Oyserman, 2001a; 2001b, Kemmelmeier, Oyserman, and Brosh, 2005).

In these studies with Arab Israeli high school students, German high school students and mostly European American university students– girls were more likely to assimilate outcomes of significant others to their own academic possible selves, whether the other that was brought to mind is successful or a failure. We speculated that this effect was at least partially mediated by differences between boys and girls in how the self-concept is organized. That is, is self-concept a way of clarifying how one is unique, agentic, different and separate from others (an 'independent self-focus'), or a way of clarifying how one is connected and related to others, embedded in relationships, and responsible for others (an 'interdependent' self-focus) (Markus and Oyserman, 1989). Indeed, girls' assimilation of others outcomes into their own possible selves was due in part to interdependence, as shown in a set of mediation analyses (Kemmelmeier et al., 2005).

COGNITIVE DEVELOPMENT

In addition to self-concept differences in possible self content, certainty, and susceptibility to social influence, gender differences may occur due to differences in cognitive and social development. In adolescence, girls are faster to develop self-awareness, self-reflection and abstract reasoning; their self-concepts contain more relational content, and by mid-adolescence, are they are more likely to begin thinking about the integration of future work and family roles. Curry, Trew, Turner and Hunter (1994) provide a useful review of gender differences in adolescence. They note that adolescent girls attain ego-development milestones earlier than boys and so may be both more concerned about future selves and concerned at earlier ages than boys. In terms of possible selves, these differences imply first, that possible selves will have less self-regulatory power for boys than for girls and second, that girls are less likely to develop strictly task-focused possible selves and will attempt to juggle more numerous possible selves connecting the self to others. For example, rather than choose between school and family focused possible selves, girls may remain torn between their personal desire to do well in school, and their belief that they are expected to also be a good family member. Following James' model, girls may have lower self-esteem because they are unable to give up or prune low likelihood possible selves, resulting in relatively modest ratios of current successes compared with domains of aspiration.

CONTENT OF POSSIBLE SELVES AMONG ETHNIC/RACIAL MINORITIES

In our review of the literature, we found studies describing content of possible selves among African American, American Indian, Asian American, and Hispanic youth, with little information on possible selves of other ethnic, racial or national minorities. In this section we review what is known about content of possible selves in these groups.

African American Adolescents

Academic or school-related possible selves predict positive change in grades (controlling for previous grades) even among low income African American middle school students when the possible selves are linked with strategies (Oyserman et al., 2004). There is evidence that academic and occupational possible selves are common among African American youth, although between race differences have not been fully explored, whites and blacks may differ in the cultural values associated with academic or school-related possible selves and in whether emphasis is on attaining positive academic possible selves or avoiding negative academic possible selves. Oyserman and Markus (1990) find African American public high school students are more likely to generate doing well in school as a hoped for self than white students; in a middle school sample Anderman and colleagues report African American 6th - 8th graders are less likely to report positive academic possible selves than other (primarily white) youth (Anderman et al, 1999). In a college sample (Oyserman et al., 1995, Study 1) no between race difference was found in total number of balanced possible selves, but Black and White undergraduates differed significantly in the number of balanced possible selves that were in the academic domain of school and/or work, with Black students having fewer such balanced school-related pairs of possible selves. Although they had fewer balanced possible selves focused on the academic or occupational domain, Black students described significantly more strategies they were currently using to *attain* their school-related possible selves (no race differences were found in the number of currently used strategies generated to avoid feared achievement-related possible selves).

Moreover, whereas for white students balance in academic possible selves positively correlated with generating strategies to approach positive possible selves, balance was correlated with generating strategies to avoid negative possible selves for Black students. Among White students, Individualism and the Protestant Work Ethic were positively correlated with generating strategies to approach academic possible selves. The relationship between cultural values and strategies was sharply different for African American students. For Black students, the Protestant Work Ethic did not relate to possible selves, instead, those who were lower in Individualism, higher in Collectivism, and higher in endorsement of a positive Racial Identity generated more strategies to approach academic possible selves (see also Oyserman and Harrison, 1998). This positive relationship between Collectivism and academic possible selves was also found in a study with male African American high school students, those who valued interconnection generated more balanced academic possible selves (Oyserman and Saltz, 1993 high school subsample). These studies are important because they link academic possible selves with racial/ethnic identity of minority youth.

Given the importance of academic possible selves, we looked for evidence of that malleability among African American students and found that academic possible selves are amenable to change, as documented in a brief small group based after school program for low-income, urban African American eighth graders. Controlling for previous grades, gender, and levels of possible selves, youth in the 6-week after-school intervention group had significantly more balanced academic possible selves and significantly more concrete strategies to attain these academic possible selves by the end of the academic year than control group youth (Oyserman, Terry, and Bybee, 2002). We have now replicated this effect showing improved academic outcomes two full years after the possible selves focused intervention. There is also evidence that academically oriented possible selves may not always be the most central or important possible selves for African American youth. In an open-ended interview with a small sample of rural African American mother-daughter pairs about teen's desired selves, academic and occupational possible selves were the most frequently mentioned, but not necessarily described as one's most central possible self – for some teens attainment of personality attributes rather than attainment of occupational and academic possible selves was the most central self (Kerpelman, Shoffner, Ross-Griffin (2002).

American Indian Adolescents

Although school and relationship possible selves are most common among American Indian students, possible selves about poverty and material things were also quite common. Fryberg and Markus (2005) examined the content of possible selves in three samples of American Indian students -- American Indian high school students who live on a reservation, but attend school off the reservation, American Indian university students at a mainstream university, and American Indian university students attending an American Indian university (half who grew up on Indian reservations and half who did not). When asked to think about their possible selves in the coming year the most common hoped for possible self across samples was to be successful in school and to get good grades, the most common feared possible self focused on school failure. All three samples mentioned having relationships and material things and feared not having relationships and living in poverty as the next most common possible selves. However, American Indian high school students and the American Indian university students from the reservation were less likely to mention relationships and were more likely to mention poverty than were the other American Indian samples. A second study (Fryberg and Markus, 2005) compared American Indian junior high, high school, and college students and found that junior high and high school students generated more expected possible selves about success in school and more feared selves about poverty and deviance than did American Indian college students. These descriptive studies provide evidence that academic possible selves are common among high risk American Indian youth in junior high and high school. A final experimental study focused on consequences of social contexts on academic possible selves. Compared to no prime control, students asked to rate American Indian-themed mascots later generated fewer academic possible selves (Fryberg, Markus, Oyserman, and Stone, 2005). Making salient thoughts about Indian mascots reduced salience of academic future selves. This study is important because it focuses directly on the impact of stereotyped images in the social context of minority youths on their possible selves.

Asian American Adolescents

Compared with African American and American Indian youth, considerably less research attention has focused on the possible selves of Asian American youth. One small scale qualitative study suggests that academic possible selves are likely to be common among Asian Americans (Kao, 2000). Using focus groups and interviews with African American, Hispanic, Asian American, and white youth at an urban high school, Kao (2000) found that all students (including Asian Americans) associate Asian American students with doing well in school, in particular high achievement in math and sciences. The author uses qualitative, content analyses to contend that the expectation by others and one's own group to do well in school help to facilitate the development of academic possible selves for Asian Americans.

No other research on Asian American adolescents was available; however, one study (Fryberg and Markus, 2005) using college students provides some empirical evidence for the prevalence of achievement related possible selves in this racial/ethnic group. In terms of content of possible selves, the majority of Asian American college students sampled reported at least one expected or hoped for self related to success in school (88.5%). The second most common responses included having relationships (70%) and positive psychological attributes (57.7%). Asian Americans did not differ from European American college students in the frequencies of these responses (although sample sizes were relatively small). In terms of feared selves psychological attributes were the most common feared possible self of Asian American and European American students (84.6% and 81.1% respectively), with failing in school (61.5% and 75.7%) and lacking relationships (65.4% and 67.6) the second and third most common possible selves respectively.

Hispanic American/Latino Adolescents

We found six studies that explicitly focused on possible selves among Latino youth. Controlling for previous grades, academic possible selves and strategies to attain them predict improved academic outcomes even in high poverty Latino youth (Oyserman et al., 2004). A number of studies suggest that having such academic possible selves may not be common among Latino youth. In a descriptive study of ninth graders, feared, not hoped for educational and occupational possible selves related to risk status for student dropout (Yowell, 2002). A third study with a smaller sample of 13-14 year old Latino youth, found boys more likely to report occupational possible selves as central than girls and girls more likely to report constrained possible selves. Both genders showed high but vague educational and occupational hoped for possible selves and global feared selves that focused more on about well-being than either academics or occupation (Yowell, 2000). Potentially the lack of specificity has to do with negative stereotypes about the likely attainments of Latiê«s. Among urban African American, Asian, Hispanic and white 9th -12th grade high school students, stereotypes about Hispanics focused less on their current academic performance and more on their future likely occupational concentration in manual labor, influencing the nature of their possible selves (Kao, 2000). The notion that academics may not be central to Latinos possible selves was underscored in the findings from a small qualitative study (Lobenstine, et al., 2001) that focused on adult hoped for and feared possible selves among teenaged mostly Puerto Rican (raised in the U.S.) girls recruited from youth agencies. While career and education were central hoped for selves, failing to attain career and educational goals were not common fears. The three most common hoped for selves (with at least 60% of respondents generated these) were family, career and education, with feared possible selves, the four most common (at least 60% of respondents generated these) feared selves were be a victim of violence, drug/alcohol abuse, be lonely/broken hearted, be poor/homeless, in addition, almost half of teens for feared dying young. The only feared self focused on occupation/education was high school dropout with 20% of teens generating this (Lobenstine et al., 2001). Day, Borkowksi, Punzo, and Howsepian (1994), utilizing a sample of 83 3rd-5th graders, showed that a brief intervention focusing on the vividness and salience of both proximal and distal possible selves could increase links between current academic performance and future occupational as well as academic possible selves. Comparing three intervention conditions (child-only, parent and child, or no instruction), they found that participants in the child-only intervention group hoped for more prestigious jobs than children in the no-instruction control group and that children in both instructional groups expressed increased expectation that they could become doctors, lawyers, or pilots after having been exposed to more specific information about these occupations. In our own lab, we find that a brief intervention focused on increasing salience and specificity of next year academic possible selves (and strategies to attain them) increases academic outcomes, especial school attendance, for Hispanic youth and that the effects are maintained two years post intervention, through the transition to high school.

CONCLUDING COMMENTS

In the current chapter, we reviewed what is known about the relationship between possible selves and attainment of important life tasks (e.g. school success) or avoidance of risky behavior (e.g. delinquency, early initiation of sexual activity, smoking, alcohol or drug use during adolescence, showing that academic possible selves, balanced academic possible selves, and strategies to attain these possible selves have positive influence on academic outcomes and are related to reduced risk of negative outcomes in adolescence. We reviewed the literature on content of possible selves for diverse youth during this life phase and explored whether gender, racial/ethnic differences were found. Gender differences were found, girls' possible selves are more susceptible to social context and girls feel more certain that negative possible selves may indeed occur, susceptibility to social context is at least in part mediated by girls' higher interdependence. Given the literature showing between ethnic group differences in interdependence among racial and ethnic groups within the U.S. (Oyserman, Coon, and Kemmelmeier, 2002), this means that possible selves of Hispanic and

Asian American youth may also be more susceptible to social context – although to date no research has been carried out on this issue. The literature on race/ethnicity is composed mostly of single group studies so that direct comparisons between groups are not possible. However, the available evidence points to similarities across quite different youth – arguing that possible selves can be viewed as the personalized expression of the life tasks of adolescence – because all teens must figure out who they can become in the important social domains of adolescence – school/work, family, and friends, these possible selves dominate content of future oriented self-images. Moreover, teens must also articulate for themselves how to handle risks – of school failure, involvement with drugs or other substances, loneliness, and where relevant, poverty or mental health problems, and these are articulated in feared possible selves. African American and American Indian youth appear similar to white youth in envisioning possible selves that include academic or school-related outcomes; while less research is available for Asian Americans, this appears to be the case for this group as well. With regard to Hispanic youth, academic possible selves may be less common, though when they are part of the self, they have the same beneficial effects. Evidence suggests African American and Hispanic youths' possible selves are amenable to change from structured intervention, with positive effects lasting through the transition to high school. For American Indian youth, there is no evidence of the efficacy of structured intervention but there is evidence of the pernicious effects of stereotypes on salience of academic possible selves. Finally, there is some evidence that academic possible selves and strategies are related to cultural values – Individualism, Collectivism, and Racial/Ethnic Identity. This is an important tack for future research because it holds promise for development of culturally sensitive intervention.

REFERENCES

Aloise-Young, P., Hennigan, K. & Leong, C. (2001). Possible selves and negative health behaviors during early adolescence. *Journal of Early Adolescence, 21,* 158-181.

Anderman, E. M. &erman, L. H. & Griesinger, T. (1999). The relation of present and possible academic selves during early adolescence to grade point average and achievement goals. *Elementary School Journal, 100,* 3-17.

Anderman, E. M., Hicks, L. H. & Maehr, M. L. (1994, February). *Present and possible selves across the transition to middle grades school.* Paper presented at the biannual meeting of the Society for Research on Adolescence, San Diego, CA.

Anderman, E. M. & Midgley, C. (1997). Changes in achievement goal orientations, perceived academic competence, and grades across the transition to middle-level schools. *Contemporary Educational Psychology, 22,* 269-298.

Burack, J. H., Irby, D. M., Carline, J. D., Ambrozy, D. M., Ellsbury, K. E. & Stritter F. T. (1997). A study of medical students' specialty-choice pathways: Trying on possible selves. *Academic Medicine, 72,* 534-541.

Cantor, N. (1990). From thought to behavior: "Having" and "doing" in the study of personality and cognition. *American Psychologist, 45,* 735-750.

Carson, A. D., Madison, T. & Santrock, J. W. (1987). Relationships between possible selves and self-reported problems of divorced and intact family adolescents. *Journal of Early Adolescence, 7(2)*, 191-204.

Cross, S. & Markus, H. R. (1991). Possible selves across the life span. *Human Development, 34*, 230-235.

Curry, C., Trew, K., Turner, T. & Hunter, J. (1994). The effect of life domains on girls' possible selves. *Adolescence, 29*, 133-150.

Day, J., Borkowksi, J., Punzo, D. & Howsepian, B. (1994). Enhancing possible selves in Mexican American students. *Motivation and Emotion, 18*, 79-103.

Dunkel, C. (2000), Possible selves as a mechanism for identity exploration. *Journal of Adolescence, 23*, 519-529.

Erikson, E. (1968). *Identity, youth, and crisis.* New York: Norton.

Fryberg, S. A. & Markus, H. R. (2005). Cultural models of education in American Indian, Asian American, and European American contexts. *Unpublished manuscript.*

Fryberg, S. A., Markus, H. R., Oyserman, D. & Stone, J. M. (2005). Honor or harm? The impact of using American Indian mascots on American Indian selves.

James, W. (1890/1950). *The principles of psychology* (Vol. 1). New York: Dover.

Kao, G. (2000). Group images and possible selves among adolescents: Linking stereotypes to expectations by race and ethnicity. *Sociological Forum, 15*, 407-430.

Kemmelmeier, M. & Oyserman, D. (2001a). Gendered influence of downward social comparisons on current and possible selves. *Journal of Social Issues: Special Issue: Stigma: An insiders perspective, 57*, 129-148.

Kemmelmeier, M. & Oyserman, D. (2001b). The ups and downs of thinking about a successful other: Self-construals and the consequences of social comparisons. *European Journal of Social Psychology, 31*, 311-320.

Kemmelmeier, M., Oyserman, D. & Brosh, H. (2005). Gender, interdependence and the effects of upward comparison on self-concept" for review in Social Cognition. Unpublished manuscript. Ann Arbor, MI: *The University of Michigan.*

Kerpelman, J. & Pittman, J. (2001). The instability of possible selves: Identity processes within late adolescents' close peer relationships. *Journal of Adolescence, 24*, 491-512.

Kerpelman, J., Shoffner, M. & Ross-Griffin, S. (2002). African American mothers' and daughters' beliefs about possible selves and their strategies for reaching the adolescents' future academic and career goals. *Journal of Youth and Adolescence, 31*, 289-302.

Knox, M., Funk, J., Elliott, R. & Bush, E. G. (1998). Adolescents' possible selves and their relationship to global self esteem. *Sex Roles, 39*, 61-80.

Knox, M., Funk, J., Elliott, R. & Bush, E. (2000). Gender differences in adolescents' possible selves. *Youth and Society, 31*, 287-309.

Lee, J. & Cramdon, B. (1999). The positive effects of mentoring economically disadvantaged students. *Professional School Counseling, 2*, 172-178.

Leondari, A., Syngollitou, E. & Kiosseoglou, G. (1998). Academic achievement, motivation, and future selves. *Educational Studies, 4(2)*, 153-163.

Lips, H. (1995). Through the lens of mathematical/scientific self-schemas: Images of students' current and possible selves. *Journal of Applied Social Psychology, 25*, 1671-1699.

Lobenstine, L., Pereira, Y., Whitley, J., Robles, J., Soto, Y., Sergeant, J., Jimenez, D., Jimenez, E., Ortiz, J. & Cirino, S. (2001, month not listed). *Possible selves and pastels: A truly socially contextualized model of girlhood* [On-line]. Paper presented at "A New Girl Order: Young Women and Feminist Inquiry Conference", London, England. Retrieved August, 3, 2003, from http://whatkidscando.org/shorttakes/HolyokeGirlsPaperdoc.pdf

Markus, H. & Nurius, H. (1986). Possible selves. *American Psychologist, 41,* 954-969.

Marsh, H. (1990). Causal ordering of academic self-concept and academic achievement: A multivariate, longitudinal panel analysis. *Journal of Educational Psychology, 82,* 646-656.

Newberry, A. & Duncan, R. (2001). Roles of boredom and life goals in juvenile delinquency. *Journal of Applied Social Psychology: Special Issue, 31,* 527-541.

Oyserman, D. (2001). Self-concept and identity. In A. Tesser, and N. Schwarz (Eds.), *Blackwell Handbook of Social Psychology* (pp. 499-517). Malden, MA: Blackwell Press.

Oyserman, D. (2002). Values, psychological perspectives on. In N. Smelñ{r, and P. Baltes (Editors-in-chief), *International Encyclopedia of the Social and Behavioral Sciences* (Vol. 22, 16150-16153). *Developmental, Social, Personality, and Motivational Psychology* (N. Eisenberg, Volume Ed.). New York: Elsevier Science.

Oyserman, D., Bybee, D. & Mowbray, C. (2005). *When your mother has a mental health problem: Antecedents of mental health feared possible selves in adolescence.* Manuscript in preparation. Ann Arbor, MI: The University of Michigan.

Oyserman, D., Bybee, D., Terry, K. & Hart-Johnson, T. (2004). Possible selves as roadmaps. *Journal of Research in Personality, 38,* 130-149.

Oyserman, D., Bybee, D. and Terry, K. (2005). Possible selves, strategies, social identity and meta-cognitive experience. Unpublished manuscript. Ann Arbor, MI: The University of Michigan.

Oyserman, D., Coon, H. & Kemmelmeier, M. (2002). Rethinking Individualism and Collectivism: Evaluation of Theoretical Assumptions and Meta-Analyses. *Psychological Bulletin, 128,* 3-73.

Oyserman, D., Gant, L. & Ager, J. (1995). A socially contextualized model of African-American identity: Possible selves and school persistence. *Journal of Personality and Social Psychology, 69,* 1216-1232.

Oyserman, D. & Harrison, K. (1998). Implications of cultural context: African American identity and possible selves. In: J. Swim, & C. Stangor, (Eds.), *Prejudice: The target's perspective* (281-300). San Diego, CA: Academic Press.

Oyserman, D. & Markus, H. (1990a). Possible selves in balance: Implications for delinquency. *Journal of Social Issues, 46,* 141-157.

Oyserman, D. & Markus, H. R. (1990b). Possible selves and delinquency. *Journal of Personality and Social Psychology, 59,* 112-125.

Oyserman, D., Terry, K. & Bybee, D. (2002). A possible selves intervention to enhance school involvement. *Journal of Adolescence, 25,* 313-326.

Oyserman, D. & Markus, H. R. (1993). The Sociocultural self. In Jerry M. Suls (Ed.), *Psychological perspectives on the self: Vol. 4. The self in social perspective* (pp. 18-220). Hillsdale, NJ, England: Lawrence Erlbaum Associates.

Oyserman, D. & Saltz, E. (1993). Competence, delinquency, and attempts to attain possible selves. *Journal of Personality and Social Psychology, 65,* 360-374.

Ruvolo, A. & Markus, H. (1992). Possible selves and performance: The power of self-relevant imagery. *Social Cognition: Special Issue: Self-knowledge: Content, structure, and function, 10,* 95-124.

Sheldon, K. & Emmons, R. (1995). Comparing differentiation and integration within personal goal systems. *Personality and Individual Differences, 18,* 39-46.

Shepard, B. (2003). Creating selves in a rural community [On-line]. In W. M. Roth (Ed.), *Connections '03* (111-120). Retrieved August 3, 2003, from the University of Victoria, Faculty of Education Research Web Site: http://www.educ.uvic.ca/Research/conferences/connections2003/07Shepard102.pdf.

Shepard, B. & Marshall, A. (1999). Possible selves mapping: Life-career exploration with young adolescents. *Canadian Journal of Counselling, 33,* 33-54.

Stein, K. F., Roeser, R. & Markus, H. R. (1998). Self-schemas and possible selves as predictors and outcomes of risky behaviors in adolescents. *Nursing Research, 47(2),* 96-106.

Yowell, C. M. (2000). Possible selves and future orientation: Exploring hopes and fears of Latino boys and girls. *Journal of Early Adolescence, 20,* 245-280.

Yowell, C. M. (2002). Dreams of the future: The pursuit of education and career possible selves among ninth grade Latino youth. *Applied Developmental Science, 6,* 62-72.

In: Race and Ethnicity
Editor: Jonathan K. Crennan, pp. 137-158

ISBN: 978-1-60692-099-2
© 2010 Nova Science Publishers, Inc.

Chapter 4

CHALLENGES OF ETHNICITY IN ORGANIZATIONAL INTERACTION: THE ROLE OF LANGUAGE USE IN EXPATRIATE MANAGEMENT

Jakob Lauring[1] and David S. Guttormsen[2]

[1]Department of Management, Aarhus School of Business, Aarhus University, Denmark,
[2]Centre for International Business, Leeds University Business School,
University of Leeds, United Kingdom

ABSTRACT

Increasing globalization is forcing a growing number of organization members of different ethnic origins to interact across linguistic boundaries. And since language affects almost all aspects of everyday life, this calls for the attention of researchers and practitioners engaged with multiethnic organizations. Extant research has noted a strong association between ethnic identity and language use. However, while the link between language and ethnic identity is often perceived to be linear, this chapter takes a different approach. By drawing on anthropological theories on ethnicity and ethnic identity it is argued that the relation between language and identity is dynamic and dialectical due to the ways it is negotiated in interaction. In the empirical analysis the chapter focuses on the encounters between expatriates and local employees in two Danish subsidiaries – one in England and one in Saudi Arabia. We use ethnographic field study methodology relying on longitudinal participant observations and semi-structured interviews to collect data. The findings show that identity-making may be actualized by competition for resources and recognition. This can be done by investing certain objects such as the symbolic application of language with certain identifications. It is finally argued that the processes by which identifications develop can cause both polarization and accommodation in the relation between groups and individuals. It is recommended that the character of language as linked to social strategies is taken into account in expatriate management and management in multiethnic organizations. Ignoring the important role of language in these organizations may lead to loss of resources and hindrances to organizational and managerial development due to lack of communication.

INTRODUCTION

In today's increasing globalized world the ability to interact with individuals of different cultural, ethnical, and linguistic backgrounds becomes more important with each day passing (Henderson, 2005). Consequently, intercultural interaction becomes increasingly critical for the acquisition of competitive advantage (Griffith, 2002). This is particularly true in multiethnic organizations and in international organizations using subsidiaries in different countries (Tsai & Ghoshal, 1998).

One common strategy to guarantee communication between parent companies and subsidiaries is to use expatriates as mediators. During this function, the expatriates should engage in, for example, developing activities, creating social ties across cultural boundaries, and learning from the surroundings (Bennett, Aston & Colquhoun, 2000; Harris & Kumra, 2000). To achieve this, it is essential that the expatriate establishes a mutual dialogue with local employees and other actors (Minbaeva, 2005). Hence, when exercising the role as a communication mediator, the expatriate can assure the transfer of relevant knowledge between different international business units (Bonache & Brewster, 2001; Geppert, 2005; Park, Hwangt & Harrison, 1996). In this manner, expatriates are expected to maintain and develop social networks across national barriers and thus increase the probability that contacts within the network will be employed to gather relevant business information (Ghoshal, 1990; Hedlund, 1986; Makela, 2007).

Unfortunately, expatriates are not always able to communicate at a satisfactory level. A number of barriers can arise. In multiethnic organizations language can be described as both a necessary communication device and an obstacle to management processes (Gilsdorf, 1998; Victor, 1992). Hence, language both facilitates and impedes the processes of coordination and, as a result, it also influences the manager's ability to control international activities (Marschan-Piekkari, Welch & Welch, 1999). In other words, linguistic barriers can affect cross-cultural knowledge sharing, dialogue, relationship building and networking in the effort to manage international activities and to respond rapidly to the changing demands of the different markets (Bonache et al., 2001; Feely & Harzing, 2003). Accordingly, given its important role in international management, it is an important research assignment to outline in detail how expatriate managers may cope with language diversity issues in multiethnic organizations.

In this chapter language use is considered the way the linguistic medium is used in communication. To further define the concept, it is the main argument of the chapter that language use should be understood as a dynamic and dialectical communicative process involving both relationship-building and knowledge-sharing between different groups and individuals (Cooren, 2006). In addition, language is understood as socially and historically constituted in line with other human practices (Bourdieu, 1977; 1991). Language, then, is not only a means of understanding and communication but also an object of action (e.g. Austin, 1975; Taylor, 2006). The communicative process is then to be understood, in a broader sense, as the transfer of information as well as the organization of social relationships, thought patterns and actions (Robichaud, 2006).

This chapter will describe language use among expatriates in two Danish subsidiaries situated in England and Saudi Arabia. Through an ethnographic account of the relation between the control and coordination processes in the multinational subsidiaries, the chapter describes the role of language in expatriate management as a negotiated marker of identity and source of power.

LITERATURE REVIEW

Language is a resource that pervades daily practice and almost all other aspects of human life. Nevertheless, throughout history the structure and the function of language have often been looked upon as separate entities to be investigated independently (Gumperz, 1965). In 1957 Chomsky, however, triggered the era of generative grammar, holding the opinion that language structures should be viewed as internalized sets of rules contained in the mind (Chomsky, 1957). He thereby demonstrated the inability of existing taxonomic models to account for the properties of language as the speaker's ability to understand sentences he had not been confronted with in his past. As Chomsky (1992: 59) contended:

> "... the computational system of language that determines the forms and relations of linguistic expressions may indeed be invariant; in the sense, there is only one human language...'.

Hence, Chomsky argued that the goal of linguistic description should be to construct a theory that would account for the infinite number of sentences of a natural language (e.g. Searle, 1982). Even though trying to integrate the structures and the functions of language in a conceptual framework, Chomsky's cognitive approach was criticized by other linguists, but especially by social anthropologists for the conception that language should be studied as an autonomous system reproducing itself more or less independently of social and cultural structures of society (Hymes, 1996; Lakoff, 1987).

Since the beginning of the 20th century the theory of language in society has been an important issue in the field of social anthropology (Evans-Pritchard, 1951; Malinowski, 1922). While these studies did not focus so much on language use by itself but tried to relate different parts of cultural constructs to each other, social anthropologists and others have in more recent years developed an interest in linking the concept of language to the concept of ethnicity and identity (Keesing, 1972; SanAntonio, 1988; Smith, 1984).

Hymes (1964) was one of the first after Evans-Pritchard and Malinowski to reintroduce thoughts on language to the field of social anthropology. For completing such a project, there should, according to him, be a higher level of analysis in which linguistic forms were viewed also in terms of their social significance (Hymes, 1996). Until then anthropologically oriented linguists had been working with the assumption that language influenced speakers to include certain aspects of experience resulting mental representations (e.g. Sapir, 1921; Whorf, 1951). A growing body of literature, however, began to investigate the use of language as guided more or less by the same practices that also guided other forms of social activity (e.g. Halliday, McIntosh, & Strevens, 1964). This happened at a time where social anthropology was slowly moving toward more dynamic models of group interaction.

The Dynamics of Ethnic Groups and Boundaries

The focus of social anthropology is 'meaning', which emerged as an inherent quality of the discipline after its epistemological shift from positivism (function) to interpretivism (meaning) during the 1960s and 1970s. This had a strong impact on the wider social sciences, and reflects intellectual advancements resulting in calling off attempts at quantifying culture several decades ago (Chapman 1997). These developments have hardly diffused business and management studies where positivist oriented quantitative research permeates the predominant research paradigm (i.e. essentialist, reductionist, hypo-deductive cultural theories (see Bate 1997; Lowe 2002)). In regard to social and cultural boundaries, the emphasis is on how they are drawn and what upholds them through the attributed meaning of the boundaries, the dynamicity, and what happens inside them and what is excluded (Lamont & Molnar (2002).

In social anthropological theory ethnicity generally refers to relationships between groups whose members may consider themselves as different, and these groups may in some situations be ranked within a society – or an organization (e.g. Eriksen, 2002). In the anthropological debate it is often discussed whether more objectified features such as race, nationality, language group – or more subjective aspects such as individuals' conception of affinity to particular categories – determine the ethnicity of an individual (Comaroff, 1996). However, most scholars seem to agree that individuals use social categories to organize their social environment and to reduce the complexities of their surroundings (Gudykunst, 2004; Jenkins, 19961997a).

Today, social anthropology plausibly argues that ethnicity is based on a group's social categorization where differences to those excluded by cultural and social boundaries are accentuated. Thus, main focus is directed toward the categorization taking place (Barth 1971; Jenkins 1997a).

The particular contribution of social anthropology to the understanding of ethnicity is the notion that the formation of cultural groups is based on a continual, internal and external social categorization of certain individuals forming a unit that is differentiated from other groups of individuals (e.g. Barth, 1971). This means that the construction of the group is generally built on a categorization of 'us and them' in which, for example, individuals of other nationalities are described as different from the native group. As opposed to functionalist and primordial theories on culture – such as the ideas of Hofstede (1991) – it is, in the social-constructivist oriented anthropological tradition, argued that groups cannot exist without social categorization – neither ethnic, national nor other groups (Jenkins, 1997a). This implies that the researcher should focus particularly on the processes involved in categorizing individuals and groups as different, and should try to identify the motives, ideals and strategies behind the categorization. Hence, the focus of anthropology lies on the creation and maintenance of social boundaries instead of the objectified categories the group is ascribed to, such as nationality. Departing from this line of thought, Barth (1971) argues that researchers should direct their attention to boundary-spanning and recruitment processes rather than the 'cultural stuff', or what could be termed 'the collective values and norms' maintained by the group. Following this, social and cultural boundaries are to be viewed as constituted by continuous inclusion and exclusion through socialization and categorization of differences. Rather than reflecting the objectified cultural difference in itself, the relation between groups mirrors the social organization of those differences (Bourdieu, 2004;

Roosens, 1989). Hence, groups, whether ethnic or national, should not be perceived as entities and cast as actors. Rather, issues can be framed as either national or ethnical depending on the political or social context. Accordingly, the difference between what is ethnicized and what is nationalized is only historically and politically constituted (Taussig, 1993). Instead of thinking in objectified groups, researchers should be thinking in terms of categories (e.g. nationality, ethnicity, language commonality) that may have the potential basis for group formation, and the focus should be directed at social processes as dynamics of identity making through which categories get invested with 'groupness' (Brubaker, 2002). In this way, ethnic identifications are contextual and situated, deriving from social negotiations that do not necessarily build upon objective criteria or observable traits.

Language and Ethnic Identity

As a second barrier, language can be associated with social identity formation. In socio-psychological research identity theory is based on the assumption that individuals gain a feeling of belonging from group membership (Tajfel, 1982). When individuals identify with members of a group, they are more likely to view their group and its members more positively than other groups. Hence, group members are generally perceived as being more loyal, trustworthy, skilled and cooperative than outsiders. According to Giles and his associates (1981) language is one of the most characteristic markers of social identity. Therefore, relationships and interaction are argued to be directly linked to language boundaries.

In anthropological theory the organization of identities is constantly constructed and reconstructed in interactions. In this process, the 'imagining' of the community plays an important role (Anderson, 1990). Identity should thus be understood as a form that is actualized as necessary fiction of a group, depending on the situation. This may be aided by linguistic terms which create practices of self-representation (Pavlenko & Blackledge, 2004). This way, language provides the opportunity for engaging in social interaction and serves as the main agent of an individual's integration into a cultural and social group. In other words, shared symbolic expressions which are articulated through language are the means of socialization, and create an imagined and actualized social bond between individuals and groups, since the roles and social relations available in the greater community or organization are transmitted and internalized through language (Mueller, 1973).

Through processes of imagining, the symbolic use of language provides the context for interactions and social identifications, but is itself also shaped in these social processes (cf. Goodwin & Duranti, 1992; Gumperz, 1982). In other words, the use of language is tied to the social context, and the social practice of identifying is enacted, in part, through language (LePage & Tabouret-Keller, 1985). Hence, the relationship between language and identity is mutually constitutive in at least two ways. On the one hand, languages supply the linguistic means with which identities are constructed and negotiated. On the other hand, ethnic identifications guide ways in which individuals use linguistic resources to categorize their identities and to evaluate the use of linguistic resources by others (Pavlenko & Blackledge, 2004).

The anthropological approach explores ways in which language functions symbolically in the process of internal and external boundary creation and subsequently becomes invested in identity making. Identity is produced and reproduced during social interaction, constantly situated in the local context. In other words, language differences should not be a priori linked to the formation of social identity differences.

In summary, it is in the process of social organization of differences that language becomes an important factor in the categorization process (Usunier, 1998). Accordingly, differences in language have a tendency to be used also as markers of social differences, and groups tend to cluster together according to the use of language (Erez & Earley, 1993; Wright, Kumagai, & Bonney, 2001). Hence, language use may have a great effect on the definition of boundaries, relationship building and knowledge sharing between the groups in multiethnic organizations. However, language (as well as other categories) can also be strategically used as a symbolic tool in the formation of collective communities. Therefore, the existence of language differences within a group can lead to both polarization and to accommodation of social relationships depending on the context. The main contribution of this perspective to understanding expatriate management is that the outcome of identity-making processes is unpredictable in as much as the formation of social identity groups is not necessarily determined by differences in nationality or linguistic skills.

Proposition 1: Language can be used as a strategic object to be used in ethnic identification processes.

Language, Power and Social Structure

When language is linked to identity it can both unite and divide, as it may become an object of oppression and a means of discrimination. In this regard, those who are not speakers of the official language may be subject to symbolic domination. Labov (1972) argues that certain group members may be able to set the social norms in the speech community. Hymes (1977) shows that to be a member of a speech community, knowing how to say something appropriately may sometimes be just as important as knowing how to communicate understandably. According to Bourdieu (1991), the success of language use is linked to the social competencies and authority of the individuals in the situation. Consequently, some individuals are better positioned and have a better 'sense of the game' when creating and maintaining rules and regulations than others. These competent individuals will, in their own 'field of practice', be better equipped in the struggle for resources and recognition (Bourdieu, 2004). This also implies that some may be excluded from communication due to their lack of competence in acting in the social field (Bourdieu, 1991). Being a competent speaker of a certain language is to have the competences necessary to engage in the continuous transaction and negotiation of its form and purpose (Bourdieu, 1977; 1991). Further, Bourdieu points out that the social use of language should be seen in relation to the production of social differences (e.g. Bourdieu, 2004). The speaker's competence not only refers to the capability of speaking legitimate language but also to the ability to relate linguistic expression to a symbolic logic of distinction. To put it differently: On the one hand, language skills are resources that can be used in communication and, on the other hand, language skills can be applied by individuals or groups as a way to distinguish themselves in a particular setting. Accordingly, what counts as legitimate language use depends on the context. Hence, in understanding the relation between language and social organization, it can be useful to analyze the speech acts as a way in which individuals negotiate the production and reproduction of social structures and power relations (Cooren, 2006; Varey, 2006). In consequence, understanding the relation between the use of language as a social process of exclusion and inclusion is of great importance when dealing with language issues in international management.

Proposition 2: Language use can be invested with power relations.

RESEARCH METHODOLOGY

The chapter draws on the results of an exploratory, ethnographic fieldwork in two subsidiaries in England and Saudi Arabia affiliated with a Danish company here called Dan Firm. The objective of the study was to investigate the association between language and ethnic identity, and the role of language use during intercultural encounters between Danish expatriates and local staff. The Dan Firm Corporation is one of Denmark's largest companies employing more than 20,000 people in more than 20 countries. As many other international corporations, it has a vision of developing an overall international corporate culture. The top corporate management had formulated a policy describing the company's aim to utilize the potential in international transfer of valuable knowledge sharing and internationalization. In other words, the idea is for employees from Dan Firm to develop international competences through overseas stationing by *"getting acquainted with people holding different cultural values and norms and a way of living differing from everyday Danish lifestyle"* (Personnel Manual 2008). Those competences should mainly be understood as: improved language skills, local knowledge of markets and partners and generally a broader world view.

Ethnographic fieldwork as a research strategy is advantageous to employ when researching dynamic, fluid, and complex processes relating to human behavior (Hammersley 1990). Thus, it enables the researcher to investigate the more or less implicit ways in which ethnic relations are being defined and conceived by groups and individuals. Consequently, it is possible to map how informants talk and think about their own group as well as other groups, and how their implicit understanding of the situation is being created, maintained or contested (Eriksen, 2002). The inherent multi-method nature of ethnographic research assists in increasing internal validity of the study through the opportunity to triangulate data. Below are the main research techniques which were employed during a time frame of three months at each subsidiary.

Participant Observation

The use of participant observation in data collection was linked to the argument of this chapter that social structure should be experienced and mapped mainly through speech acts or events observed in the setting (Adler & Adler, 1994; Jorgensen, 1989). Through its use of longitudinal studies, the ethnographic fieldwork has the unique advantage that it generates data on social processes at the level of everyday interaction, which is where the communicative structures and boundaries of ethnic groups are created and recreated (Dewalt, Dewalt, & Wayland, 1998; Eriksen, 2002; Kunda, 1992).

Through a longer process of learning in the local setting, the researchers reach the ability to recognize and understand the social organization of interaction. This provides an opportunity to register processes producing and reproducing social categories applied at the scene (Brubaker, 2002). In this particular fieldwork, these processes could be observed in daily dialogues between organizational members, where the negotiation of internal and external categories was debated in a way that would not have been registered in a more formal interview situation. Furthermore, participant observation also allows registrations of group behavior such as socialization or boundary creation that is not directly available through interviews. Such group processes could be observed by mapping interaction patterns in the offices and in the canteen etc.

The researchers were allowed to move around with few restrictions at both subsidiaries. During frequent walks around the plants, the researchers gradually became familiar with a substantial part of the organization members, at all levels, and in all functions. However, since the researchers were not directly connected to any department, there was never any danger of becoming too much of a full member of any group. Altogether, the degree of participation during observation depended on the nature of the activities. During business meetings, a low level of participant observation took place. In the canteen and at social gatherings, however, the researchers exercised a high level of participation. In addition to direct observations, numerous conversations with the employees were scribbled down in a small notebook that the researchers kept in their pocket at all times. All such observations were coded in the same way as interview transcripts.

Interviews

The interviews took the form of an open dialogue between the researcher and the informants, as close to a normal conversation as possible (Bernard, 1995). During the course of the interview, questions centered around the relation and communication between expatriates and host country nationals, following up on previous statements or observations that had been integrated in the continuously developing interview guide (cf. Alvesson, 2003; Fontana & Frey, 1994).

In England, a total of 90 individual semi-structured interviews were conducted, including 28 with Danish expatriates and 62 with English host country nationals. 51 of the interviewed informants had managerial responsibilities. All interviews were conducted in the informants' native language, in order to register as many details as possible and capture nuances and meanings in the oral accounts as accurate as possible.

In Saudi-Arabia all 16 expatriates were interviewed formally as were 10 of the following spouses. Among third country nationals (TCN) formal interviews were made with six Indians, three Filipinos, three Egyptians, and one British employee. These last interviews were all in English.

Managers were interviewed in their offices while other employees (e.g. workers and secretaries) were interviewed in vacant team leader offices or meeting rooms. One of the researchers' Danish nationality may have influenced the relationship to the interviewees. The Danish organization members could well have conceived the researchers as in-group members whereas some native or TCN employees may have been more reluctant to reveal negative feelings toward a Dane. However, the researchers presented themselves as independent and a large number of local or TCN employees saw the interview as an opportunity to air disagreements in an anonymous context. Thereby the researcher became a means to communicate potential discontent with the situation to the top management. All interviews were taped and transcribed.

Analysis

Observations and interview material were analyzed by constructing taxonomies according to the guidelines of Spradley (1980). This implicates hand coding the collected data material - printed material as well as interview transcriptions and observation notes – and sorting it in different categories. From that a taxonomy tree could be constructed consisting of categories, subcategories and sub-subcategories. This process is subjective in the way that the placement of spoken statements or other pieces of information is not always unequivocal. Nevertheless, it is on the basis of these formed categories that the writing process departed, creating narratives as sequences of events (e.g. Clifford & Marcus, 1986; Geertz, 1988).

The process of data collection was concluded with a written report sent to all involved informants and gatekeepers. Informants were asked to comment on the conclusions and the comments were integrated into the final data material, in order to ensure that relevant topics had been addressed during the interviews and that the results coincided with the perceptions of the informants.

RESULTS

This section presents data from each of the Danish subsidiaries separately. Data and literature are juxtaposed in order to inductively analyze the data, as well as obtaining a rich and deep understanding of the interplay between language and ethnicity.

Case 1 - England: "What Is Unknown, We Fear" – Language and Suspicion

Dan Firm started to buy up dairies in England 15 years ago and has since grown to be one of England's largest dairy companies – not without difficulties, however. A few years after initiating business in England the subsidiary had lost all its net capital. Much of the trouble affecting the subsidiary arose as a result of the powerful positions of supermarket chains in England's highly competitive markets.

This led the parent company to formulate a plan in which a large number of Danish expatriates were sent to England to improve the situation. Around 35 Danes were stationed in the subsidiary holding 2000 employees at the time of the fieldwork. With these imposed changes there was a demand for establishing a more modern, flat – and Danish-style – organizational structure with less hierarchy and more openness, empowerment, and training. This created insecurity among the staff as sudden changes created mass lay-offs.

The sudden entrance of Danish employees into the organization gave rise to some uneasiness among the English employees, causing them to question their own personal employment status. As an English employee expressed it, "*Well, they are building a company in England to fill it with Danes and get the English people out as soon as there is an opportunity*". This tension gradually resulted in a polarization between the two nationalities. As an English manager described it,

> "*For me this company is very much the Danes and the English. The Danes seem to think they come with all the knowledge and if they weren't here there would be no company*".

Interestingly, the tension between the expatriates and the locals was linked to language as a marker of difference and power. However, in the meeting between the two speech communities, it was not the linguistic differences, as such, that created opposing identifications. Rather, it was the perceived power relations affiliated with the membership of a speech community that affected communication.

English was the dominating language, as it naturally was the language of the subsidiary. All Danes spoke English well enough to converse, and there was no doubt that it was the obvious language to use in everyday management. However, occasionally Danes would use their native language in communicating with each other. This made their English co-workers feel uneasy. As described by an English employee:

> "One thing which is really bad is when Danish people speak Danish when there are English people present. That is bad and it does happen. I have heard it on many occasions and just last week. It just makes you uncomfortable".

It was, however, not only the breaking of social norms that was the concern of the English employees. A large number of organizational members felt insecure about their position, and communication in an incomprehensible code increased their uncertainty. The suspicious feelings toward the Danes were expressed by the way English employees were afraid they were under surveillance by the Danes. There were theories of a wide, informal communication network based on the Danish language. This network was supposed to connect all Danes across levels, functions and departments. The English employees were afraid of "*all the stabbing in the back*" (Informant) that the Danes supposedly did.

> "For me it looks like they have put Danes in all the departments. Like the entire department in Leeds you have got all the marketing people and the marketing director and you have got the finance director and the production director. You have Danes in all the key positions. I think people are afraid they have a different communication system. I am just saying what it looks like to me" (English Manager).

According to Danish managers, such tales of secret networks were far from the truth. As they saw it, the only reason some English employees were laid off was their incompetence in changing to a more democratic and empowering management style. Language and nationality became a marker of difference - a catalyst triggering the dynamics of cultural clashes.

"I don't talk nearly as much to the Danes as the English think. It is this conspiracy theory. If you ask the Danes they would say that they saw me far too little – and it is on purpose. Every time I see a Danish manager I make sure to talk at least the same time to the English managers as well. I have never taken a decision about a Danish - or an English employee based on information from a Dane" (Danish Top Manager).

Language and nationality became markers of ethnic affiliation. And gradually individuals from the two groups came to see each other as opposing each other. To communicate efficiently with the English employees, the Danish expatriates needed to engage in socialization, meaning, for example, that they should not end a discussion in too abrupt a fashion, even when patience was running out or if they were struggling with the foreign language. The problem of the Danes can be described through the observation of the coaching of one of the Danish managers. An English consultant advised a manager to 'warm' the relationship to his employees, and the Dane responded by asking what tactics would be best for accomplishing this. This, among other things, was interpreted as a lack of interpersonal skills. Hence, specific traits of behavior were highlighted and similarities were ignored in the description of themselves and others. English employees explained how the Danes were thinking logically and structured, and that they were not good at dealing with people. An English manager formulated his opinions as follows:

The Danes are very capable of understanding their weaknesses. They have a very logical approach to that as well. They address it like mathematics - tell me exactly what I do wrong and how I can do it right (English Manager).

A colleague expressed his opinion about the role of emotions:

"The Danish tend to be less emotional. They are very well organized and rational. If it is an English person and you really want to pursue something - if it is a really important issue you tend to be really emotional about it and really argue and fight for it. Danes are not like that. If they really want something they will not get passionate about it but they would go for even more rational arguments. In that respect I guess they are a little like the Germans" (English Manager).

Even though the Danes obviously were more structured in their approach to other people, a number of English employees noticed that the expatriates did not use formal rules and guidelines to the same extent as they did themselves. Instead the Danish managers would show an example and expect workers to follow with the same enthusiasm and responsibility. The Danes would use training and empowerment of the subordinates and expect the English workers to do the work in the most 'rational' way with as little formal leadership as possible. Disagreements came up when the English workers did not always take the path that seemed rational in the eyes of the Danes. In these situations the Danish managers felt they needed to work out specific procedures for the workers to do things the right way – or the Danish way.

Accordingly, there was a tendency for the Danes to be gradually more direct whenever they felt their English subordinates did not understand the proper way of working. Sometimes the Danes would even lose their temper in a most inappropriate way in the eyes of the English employees. The Danish managers expected things to be done, if not on the workers' own initiative then at least according to the given guidelines. That was not always the case in England. When the English employees did not just do their job without being told continuously, the expatriate managers got frustrated and so impatient with matters that they, in opposition to their usual more democratic management style, started to give some very direct orders.

> "Danes that come here they tend to say I - Think - You - Are - Wrong - Because...and there are other ways to say that in English and English people use a lot of humor in the language which Danes don't do. In the beginning the Danes will be very abrupt, and that pisses people off and makes them do the opposite of what you request" (English Manager).

In that way the frustration of the perceived ignorance of the English workers and a lacking understanding of the more polite English way of communication made the Danes come across as very direct or autocratic. The disagreement arose because of the difficulties of certain Danish and English employees to realize that working results could be achieved in different ways, rather than being a result of inherent differences.

> "I have been working in Denmark and I find that the Danes are different from English people in their attitude to work. They expect the employees to do exactly the job they tell them but with us that is not the case. That is why people in Denmark don't have procedures as we do. They trust people to do things" (English Manager).

It could be rather difficult for the Danish expatriates to work in England, because they did not all understand the practice of creating and maintaining social relations or how to communicate in a less direct fashion – among other things through humor. Communication-wise, English humor seemed to level social hierarchies but, at the same time, upheld the formal relations. Many of the Danes did not fully understand that. To get through to the English employees they needed to play along on the games of socializing, meaning that they should not end a discussion in a too abrupt fashion even when patience was running out. The expatriates who did not master the more politically sensitive form of communication soon became classified as *German Danes*.

> "What we would be looking for are the more Anglo Danes, not the more Germanic type of people - the more autocratic people that think people will do something just because they tell them to. The people that would just expect that if I told them to do it they would do it, are more like the German *luft waffe*" (English Top Manager).

One of the Danish Top Managers commented on the "German" characterizations by his English counterpart:

> "The English hold a kaleidoscope centering a lot on Germans. If they meet anything that reminds them of Germans, like if you do not catch the irony fast enough... If you do not laugh at things. The English can be really harsh on people with no humor. If you can't laugh and make fun you will get in trouble, and if they meet someone that doesn't joke he per definition is a German Dane. Sometimes Danes come to the point where we say enough of all the

bullocks now we need to take a decision. That can be perceived as a German Dane as well" (Danish Top Manager).

Often Danes were perceived as very serious people, never smiling or joking. But some English employees had observed the tendency of some Danes to be just as joking and humorous as any English person outside working hours – at the pub or at a social gathering. In that way the Danes seemed to draw on different resources of communication in the private sphere in spite of possible language difficulties. Compared to the English, the Danish employees seemed to differentiate more between working hours and spare time. English managers would work from early morning till late at night, engaging in extensive socializing and talking in between working. On the contrary, Danish managers worked fast and efficiently to get working hours over with and get home to their family as early as possible. That was one reason for the Danes to not spend too much time socializing and building up relationships as well as creating alliances. It could be observed how the Danes would often leave their office at night almost without saying goodbye to colleagues and secretaries, even when going away on holiday. That was perceived by the English employees to be extremely rude, whereas the Danes found it natural to distinguish between friends and colleagues. The different patterns of social interaction made it more difficult to create relations with Danes on the job compared to English co-workers, widening the gap between the two groups. One way of explaining such patterns is that the groups draw up the boundaries of what constitutes work life and non-work life differently.

The polarization of the national groups became more apparent during the fieldwork period. Due to their communication style, the Danes were increasingly compared to Nazi Germans. The Danish reaction to the exclusion from the English community was to perceive the local English employees with contempt, and being even more direct in their approach, using harsh language, and using a more authoritarian managerial communication style. As it was commented by an English manager, *"that pisses people off and makes them do the opposite of what they request"*. This way, the English employees tried to obstruct what they perceived as 'Danish procedure', especially regarding hygiene. As an example, workers would wear dirty clothing entering the dairy machinery, or team leaders and managers would put on ties over their overalls. At the same time as the majority of Danes were perceived increasingly as German Danes, certain expatriates were described as *"more English than Danish"*. As one of the English managers put it, *"There are some sorts of very free thinking-out-of-the-box Danes around. But they are in the minority"*. Others described these few individuals as a bit more 'wacko'. Interestingly, the direct language use applied by these individuals was positively described as *"refreshingly freed of political agenda"* (English team leader), or *"right to the point"* (English worker). Hence, different individual and group characteristics came into play in complex interaction situations between expatriates and local employees. As one of the English top managers described the development:

"At first people considered the Danes to be very abrupt and not ignorant but unfriendly, cold. I think that has changed as the Danes have integrated more into the business. They have learned our funny silly ways and we have learned theirs. We are gradually coming together, understanding the language barrier and the jokes. You know when I tell a joke you might say what the hell is she on to? Silly things like that build up to a significant barrier (English Top Manager)".

This way it becomes apparent that small symbolic actions expressed in language use can lead to either polarization or accommodation.

In this case of the Danish subsidiary in England, it is evident how identity is actualized based on the nature of interaction between the Danish expatriates and English local staff. This way, language becomes a marker of how social and cultural boundaries are drawn. Hence, language and ethnicity are not constant, but always transforming in a dialectical relationship during interaction.

Case 2 Saudi Arabia: Language as a Powerful Segregation Tool

Expatriating Danish employees in the Dan Firms Corporation had many different purposes and not all of them were valued equally. The parent company had formally described how the firm, when sending expatriates to subsidiaries, aimed at utilizing the potential for knowledge sharing across cultural boundaries. The cross-cultural interaction was meant to develop international skills such as language competences and knowledge about the market and the way of conducting business. In spite of such general formulations, the Danish subsidiary in Saudi Arabia was mainly perceived as a sales company. The Danish expatriate management was evaluated exclusively on the basis of sales targets and market shares. Those evaluation criteria had a great effect on the daily running of the subsidiary in regard to cross-cultural communication and learning.

All the Danes lived together in a large compound. This created a very interdependent and tight-knit group structure. Thus, members of this group, including newcomers, socialized extensively with each other, which also greatly influenced how the Danes interacted with other nationalities at the workplace. A very exclusive Danish in-group emerged, and management decided to maintain such a "pure" Danish environment. This way, they felt that communication and decision-making would be much more effective due to sharing greater understanding amongst the Danish expatriates.

It had been decided to maintain the traditional Saudi Arabian organizational form in the subsidiary. The subsidiary, accordingly, was organized in what could be called an ethnically segregated hierarchy – nationality defined who were to hold a particular position throughout the organization. Hence, one had to be European to be a manager and Egyptian to be a supervisor. The Philippine employees often possessed good technical skills, and they were therefore generally employed in technical positions or vehicle maintenance. The Indians were ranked lowest in the hierarchy and worked mainly in the production. As one of the Danish managers expressed it

"To have an Indian boss for a Saudi worker, that is almost impossible. Same thing with an Egyptian worker and an Indian boss, that is difficult in many cases as well. There exists some sort of informal class division, which divides people hierarchically depending on where they come from (Danish Manager)".

The segregation could be said to somewhat ease the daily communication, because the different national groups were able to use their own native languages most of the time. In addition, it made the managerial process easier because managers did not have to confer or discuss business issues with subordinates. The managers needed only to communicate in simple

English terms to subordinates about what they were expected to do. As a result, members of the management team recommended the researcher to use imperatives only when addressing non-Danish employees because they would not understand long sentence structures in English. The researchers' impression, however, was that a large proportion of the non-European employees, such as Indians and some Egyptians, spoke significantly better English compared to most of the Danes.

The negative evaluation of the language competences of the national groups could, to a high extent, be related to the separation of nationalities into speech communities. As the single English manager expressed it: *"we have very much a situation where the Danes are divorced from the rest like feudal landlords"*. Hence, it was very uncommon to see employees of different nationality engaged in longer conversation, while the national groupings internally exercised an extensive informal socialization. But not only did the management not involve other nationalities in the discussion of business issues, they also went as far as to use the Danish language to protect the integrity and decision-making power of their own group. By using mostly Danish language in the daily interaction, information was kept strictly within the group of managers and excluded non-Danes from any productive contributions in this regard. As one of the Egyptian middle managers reported, *"If you want to work in this company, you have to be like those monkeys that cover their mouth and eyes and ears. We have to be their monkeys"*.

Even the English manager was kept out of the conversation and when attending social arrangements, he was totally excluded from the conversation. He did not understand the language and felt that the Danes were behaving so rudely that he did not want to participate in the *'embarrassing scene'*. As he said: *"Communication is only for the Danes. No question. Nothing has changed in that respect. As you have seen it here in formal or informal get-togethers inevitably the conversation moves to Danish"*.

Another example of the way the Danes excluded other nationalities from the communication channels and withheld information from the rest of the company was presented to the researcher by one of the Philippine employees. He once told the researcher that *'big guests'* would soon arrive, so we should dress accordingly for the next few days. The researcher asked him how he knew that, and was told that he had just seen the carpets being cleaned, and he had noticed that this happened every time 'big guests' arrived. At lunch with the Danes later that day it was confirmed that there was to be a board meeting a few days later. Such an event was never publicly announced or mentioned in other ways. Only through the internal Danish conversation (or from observing the floor being cleaned) could the information be acquired. There was no formal information system implemented in the company but messages were passed on orally – both between the Danish families in the compound where they lived and between the non-Danish members of the organization. Not even in eventful situations, such as a fatal car accident, formal information was disseminated and employees exclusive the Danish in-group had to rely on rumors and guesswork.

The Danish management was aware that information was spread informally and attempted to prevent other nationalities from acquiring knowledge of the business. They deliberately spoke Danish when other nationalities were present in the room, and the foreign secretaries were prohibited from reading incoming fax messages. This was done to stop information leaks, even though most of the information they tried to protect seemed quite harmless to share with the other employees – such as the knowledge of a coming board meeting. But the Danes generally were annoyed with the curiosity of the subordinates, feeling more confident when keeping information exclusive to the management group.

It was explained to the researcher by the General Manager that it was a deliberate strategy to keep the management team all Danish to increase the decision-making speed and not having to deal with cultural or linguistic barriers. The ethnical segregation strategy was applied by organizing the remaining part of the subsidiary for the same reasons – to limit the conflicts and misunderstandings in communicating across linguistic and cultural boundaries. Hence, the use of language was strategically applied to fulfill the personal aim of the expatriate managers. Through intensive internal socialization and recruitment of like-minded individuals, the Danes reproduced the social structure of ethnical stratification along with cultural and linguistic exclusion. In their opinion, at least, this was the most obvious way to run the subsidiary efficiently.

The maintained group structures between and within the nationalities created an environment where only very limited communication was directed across the cultural boundaries. Moreover, the Danish expatriates did not achieve the cultural learning they were formally sent out to experience. Instead, informal communication was very well developed within the group conversely. This demonstrates the link between language use and power structures.

CONCLUSION

The use of language has received little attention in the literature on expatriate management (Janssens et al., 2004; Marschan et al., 1997). To contribute to the area, this chapter has examined the implications of the social use of language in the specific practices employed in two Danish subsidiaries in England and Saudi Arabia. Though the field of language management in international and multiethnic organizations has yet to be fully investigated, scholars seem to agree that language use is essential to the creation of networks and to the management of knowledge sharing as a valuable contribution to organizational and managerial development (e.g. Bonache et al., 2001; Harris et al., 2000). The present account makes it clear that the management of language use should not be viewed as an outpost of expatriate management but as an integral element of the effective management of multiethnic operations (e.g. Marschan et al., 1997).

The two cases illustrate how identification happens in clashes often triggered or enhanced by issues such as competition for resources and recognition – not as a priori categories. In the English case, the process of ethnic identity-making led to the gradual actualization and enforcement of speech communities and the employment of language use as an object of expressing ethnicity. In this change process, linguistic boundaries, which under different circumstances would have little effect on the interaction, were either enhanced or, in certain examples, ignored. In conclusion, the case description suggests that the polarization/accommodation between individuals of different national origin is a variable to be explored rather than assumed and that the degree of inclusion into any particular community is best left as an empirical question.

In the Saudi Arabia case the field study presented describes the effects of language use in relation to the maintenance of a stratified social structure, and has highlighted how important this factor can be in the execution of long-term corporate strategies of international development. The Danish management team of the Saudi Arabian subsidiary strategically utilized their powerful position to reinforce a general practice of language use that excluded other nationalities from participating in the decision-making process. By this approach, the managers felt they had a better grasp of communication and could make fast responses to market changes. Furthermore, through this practice the position of the expatriates could not be challenged and decision-making was comfortably in the hands of the Danish managers. By using language to control access to information and participation, the Danes placed themselves in a totally dominant position.

This chapter has illustrated how the linguistic exchange that takes place depends on the structures of the social field and how the communicative actions are used in positioning actors within the field. Thereby language use becomes a specific expression of the power relations between the individuals and groups involved. Hence, language should not be treated only as a neutral communication device by international corporations when formulating their communication policies (e.g. Erez et al., 1993; Tajfel, 1982; Wright et al., 2001). Rather, language is to be seen as linked to other social structures facilitating the social categorization of groups and individuals (Bourdieu, 19912004; Jenkins, 1997b). In other words, language can be used in processes of both exclusion and inclusion of individuals, and differences in language use might form distinctions by which individuals and groups can be restrained from influence (Bourdieu, 1991; Janssens et al., 2004). To sum up, language is thus not only used for communication and information transfer since the speech act in itself also becomes a means in the ongoing negation of power, resources, recognition and influence (Varey, 2006). Thereby language can be actively used as a marker of identity and groupness leading to specific patterns of distribution resources and recognition.

In terms of practical implication some initial guideline can be outlined. Direct suggestions for multiethnic organizations of international firms sending expatriates to countries where they are faced with speaking a foreign language may be somewhat premature due to the exploratory character of the study. Nevertheless, increasing the awareness of social processes linking language use to social identity may be a first step toward avoiding polarization and promoting accommodation. The findings suggest that companies may want to closely. monitor and try to counteract negative outcomes of such opposing identifications. This may be crucial, since the disadvantages may otherwise over time become substantial and difficult to eliminate. Efficient counter-measures may include cross-cultural training and language training combined with group exercises especially focused on intercultural cooperation.

Moreover, it can be recommended that the dynamic role of language in the creation and maintenance of social structures should be integrated in the theories of expatriate management. If the target is to achieve cross-cultural development, networking and knowledge sharing, subsidiary managers should to a larger extent be held accountable for the management of communication (Welch, Welch, & Piekkari, 2005). It is also suggested that a communication policy motivating expatriates to learn and use foreign languages in order to facilitate cross-cultural communication should be considered if the targets of the corporation depend on cross-cultural networks and knowledge sharing. Firstly, such a policy could have a positive effect on the ongoing dialogue and relationship-building between nationalities and hence soften the hegemonic and impermeable position of the dominant expatriate group. Secondly, this could also invite language minorities to participate in knowledge sharing.

Finally, it might even keep ethnocentrically oriented expatriates from accepting the important subsidiary positions (e.g. Janssens et al., 2004). As it has been indicated, policies of language use should thus be part of a broad organizational approach to expatriate management, even in the selection, training, and positioning of personnel (Dowling & Welch, 2004).

There are several limitations in this qualitative study, such as the character of the two case studies with a limited number of informants and a limited time of observation. These limitations notwithstanding, the study advances theories of the relation between the use of language and ethnic identity by illustrating how the symbolical production and reproduction of social categories through language cannot always be predicted on the basis of linguistic skills or nationality. And that language can become invested with identity and power.

These suggestions have been made in the knowledge that there is a general need for more research on the management of language in multiethnic organizations. The analytical framework of this chapter has suggested an interrelation between language use and social strategy. Scholars in the field of expatriate management could use this notion as a point of departure in further studies on the influences of language on decision-making and performance as well as networking and knowledge sharing. In this chapter an inter-disciplinary approach combining anthropology, linguistics and business studies has been applied to understand language and expatriate management in a social setting. But other combinations of perspectives within the social studies might provide additional or complementary information on the use of language in an international managerial setting. Future research could consider applying a series of social network analyses to gain additional knowledge on the developments of interaction patterns in intercultural encounters. Such an approach could add interesting quantitative measures to the relations and social ties between different individuals and groups.

REFERENCES

Adler, P. A. & Adler, P. (1994). Observational techniques. In N. Denzin, & Y. Lincoln (Eds.), *Handbook of qualitative research,* 377-392. London: Sage.

Alvesson, M. (2003). Beyond neopositivists, romantics, and localists: A reflexive approach to interviews in organizational research. *Academy of Management Review, 28(1),* 13-33.

Anderson, B. (1990). *Imagined Communities: Reflections on the Origin and Spread of Nationalism.* London: Verso.

Austin, J. L. (1975). *How to do things with words.* Oxford: Oxford University Press.

Barth, F. (1971). *Ethnic Groups and Boundaries: The Social Organization of Cultural Difference.* Bergen: Universitetsforlaget.

Bartlett, C. & Ghoshal, S. (1990). Matrix management: Not a structure, a frame of mind. *Harvard Business Review,* July-August,: 138-147.

Bate, S. P. (1997). Whatever Happened to Organizational Anthropology? A Review of the Field of Organizational Anthropology and Anthropological Studies.. *Human Relations 50(9),* 1147-1175.

Bennett, R., Aston, A. & Colquhoun, T. (2000). Cross-cultural training: A critical step in ensuring the success of international assignments. *Human Resource Management, 39(2/3),* 239-241.

Bernard, R. H. (1995). *Research methods in anthropology: Qualitative and quantitative approaches*. Thousand Oaks: Sage.

Bonache, J. & Brewster, C. (2001). Knowledge Transfer and the Management of Expatriation. *Thunderbird International Business Review, 43(1)*, 3-20.

Bourdieu, P. (1977). *Outline of a Theory of Practice*. Cambridge: Cambridge University Press.

Bourdieu, P. (1991). *Language and symbolic power*. Cambridge: Polity Press.

Bourdieu, P. (2004). *Distinction: A social critique of the judgment of taste*. London: Routledge.

Brubaker, R. (2002). Ethnicity without groups. *European Journal of Sociology*, XLIII(2): 163-189.

Chapman, M. (1997). Social Anthropology, Business Studies, and Cultural Issues. *International Studies of Management & Organization, 26(4)*, 3-29.

Chomsky, N. (1957). *Syntactic structures*. The Hague: Mouton.

Chomsky, N. (1992). *Language and thought*. Wakefield: Moyer Bell.

Clifford, J. & Marcus, G. E. (1986). *Writing Culture: The Poetics and Politics of Ethnography*. Berkeley: University of California Press.

Comaroff, J. N. (1996). Ethnicity, Nationalism, and the Politics of Difference in an Age of Revolution. In: E. N. Wilmsen, & P. McAllister, (Eds.), *The Politics of Difference,* 162-184. Chicago: The University of Chicago Press.

Cooren, F. (2006). The organizational world as a plenum of agencies. In: F., Cooren, J. R. Taylor, & E. J. Van every, (Eds.), *Communication as Organizing*: 81-101. London: LEA.

Dalton, M. & Chrobot-Mason, D. (2007). A theoretical exploration of manager and employee social identity, cultural values and identity conflict management. *International Journal of Cross Cultural Management, 7(2)*, 169-183.

Dewalt, K. M., Dewalt, B. R. & Wayland, C. B. (1998). Participant observation. In: H. R. Bernard, (Eds.), *Handbook of methods in cultural anthropology*: 259-300. Walnut Creek: AltaMira.

Dhir, K. S. & Góké-Paríolá, A. (2002). The case for language policies in multinational corporations. *Corporate Communications: An International Journal, 7(4)*, 241-251.

Dowling, P. J. & Welch, D. E. (2004). *International human resource management: Managing people in a multinational environment*. London: Thomson Learning.

Erez, M. & Earley, P. C. (1993). *Culture, self-identity and work*. New York: Oxford University Press.

Eriksen, T. H. (2002). *Ethnicity and nationalism*. London: Pluto Press.

Evans-Pritchard, E. E. (1951). *Social Anthropology*. London: Cohen and West.

Feely, A. J. & Harzing, A. W. (2003). Language management in multinational companies. *International Journal of Cross Cultural Management, 10(2)*, 37-53.

Fontana, A. & Frey, J. H. (1994). Interviewing: The art of the science. In N. Denzin, & Y. Lincoln (Eds.), *Handbook of qualitative research,* 361-376. London: Sage.

Geertz, C. (1988). *Works and Lives: The Anthropologist as Author*. Standford: Standford University Press.

Geppert, M. (2005). Competence development and learning in British and German subsidiaries of MNCs Why and how national institutions still matter. *Personnel Review, 34(2)*, 155-177.

Ghoshal, S. (1990). *The innovative multinational: A differentiated network of organizational roles and management processes.*, Ann Arbor Michigan.

Giles, H. & Johnson, P. (1981). The Role of Language in Ethnic Group Relations. In: J. C. Turner, & H. Giles (Eds.), *Intergroup Behavior*: 199-243. Oxford: Blackwell.

Gilsdorf, J. W. (1998). Organizational Rules on Communicating: How Employees Are- and Are Note- Learning the Ropes. *Journal of Business Communication, 35(2)*, 173-201.

Goodall, K. & Roberts, J. (2003). Only connect: teamwork in the multinational. *Journal of World Business, 38*, 150-164.

Goodwin, C. & Duranti, A. (1992). Introduction, *Rethinking Context: Language as an Interactive Phenomenon*: 1-43. Cambridge: Cambridge University Press.

Griffith, D., A. (2002). The role of communication competencies in international business relationship development. *Journal of World Business, 37*, 256-265.

Gudykunst, W. B. (2004). *Bridging differences: Effective intergroup communication.* London: Sage.

Gumperz, J. (1982). *Language and social identity.* Cambridge: Cambridge University Press.

Gumperz, J. J. 1965. Language. *Biennial Review of Anthropology, 4*, 84-120.

Halliday, M. A. K., McIntosh, A. & Strevens, P. (1964). *The Linguistic Sciences and Language Teaching.* Bloomington: Indiana University Press.

Hammersley, M (1990). *Reading Ethnographic Research.* London: Longman.

Harris, H. & Kumra, S. (2000). International manager development. *Journal of Management Development, 19(7)*, 607-620.

Hedlund, G. (1986). The hypermodern MNC: A heterarchy? *Human Resource Management, 25(1)*, 9-35.

Henderson, J. K. (2005). Language diversity in international management teams. *International Studies of Management and Organization, 35(1)*, 66-82.

Herzfeld, M. (2005). *Cultural Intimacy: Social Poetics in the Nation-State.* New York: Routledge.

Hofstede, G. (1991). *Cultures and organizations: Software of the mind.* London: MCGraw publications.

Holden, N. J. (2002). *Cross-cultural management. A knowledge management perspective.* Dorset: Prentice Hall.

Hymes, D. (1964). *Language in Culture and Society.* New York: Harper.

Hymes, D. (1996). *Ethnography, linguistics, narrative inequality: Toward an understanding of voice.* Aresford: Taylor and Francis.

Hymes, D. H. (1977). *Foundations of Sociolinguistics: An Ethnographic Approach.* London: Tavistock.

Janssens, M., Lambert, J. & Steyaert, C. (2004). Developing language strategies for international companies: The contribution of translation studies. *Journal of World Business, 39*, 414-430.

Jenkins, R. (1996). *Social Identity.* New York: Routledge.

Jenkins, R. (1997a). *Categorization and Power.* England: Sage Publication.

Jenkins, R. (1997b). *Rethinking ethnicity: Arguments and explorations.* London: Sage Publications.

Joardar, A., Kostova, T. & Ravlin, E. C. (2007). An experimental study of the acceptance of a foreign newcomer into a workgroup. *Journal of International Management, 13(4)*, 513-537.

Jorgensen, D. L. (1989). *Participant observation: A methodology for human studies*. London: Sage.

Keesing, R. (1972). Paradigm Lost: The new Ethnography and the New Linguitics. *Southwestern Journal of Anthropology, 28(2)*, 299-332.

Kunda, G. (1992). *Engineering Culture*. Philadelphia: The University Press.

Labov, W. (1972). *Sociolinguitic Patterns*. Oxford: Basil Blackwell.

Lakoff, G. (1987). *Women, fire, and dangerous things: What categories reveal about the mind*. Chicago: University of Chicago Press.

LePage, R. B. & Tabouret-Keller, A. (1985). Acts of identity: Creole-based approaches to language and ethnicity. Cambridge: Cambridge University Press.

Lowe, S. (2002). The Cultural Shadows of Cross-Cultural Research: Images of Culture, *Culture and Organization, 8(1)*, 21-34.

Makela, K. (2007). Knowledge sharing through expatriate relationships: A social capital perspective. *International Studies of Management & Organization, 37(3)*, 108-125.

Malinowski, B. (1922). *Argonauts of the Western Pacific*. London: Routledge.

Marschan-Piekkari, R., Welch, D. E. & Welch, L. S. (1999). Adopting a common corporate language: IHRM implications. *The International Journal of Human Resource Management, 10(3)*, 377-390.

Marschan-Piekkaria, R., Welch, D. & Welch, L. (1999). In the shadow: the impact of language on structure, power and communication in the multinational. *International Business Review, 8*, 421-440.

Marschan, R., Welch, D. & Welch, L. (1997). Language: The forgotten factor in multinational management? *European Management Journal, 15(5)*, 591-598.

Minbaeva, D. B. (2005). HRM practices and MNC knowledge transfer. *Personnel Review, 34(1)*, 125-144.

Lamont, M. & Molnar, V. (2002). The Study of Boundaries in the Social Sciences, *Annual Review Sociology, 28*, 167-195.

Mueller, C. (1973). *The politics of communication: A Study in the Political Sociology of Language, Socialization, and Legitimation*. New York: Oxford University Press.

Park, H., Hwangt, S. D. & Harrison, J. K. (1996). Sources and Consequences of Communication Problems in Foreign Subsidiaries: the Case of United States Firms in South Korea. *International Business Review, 5(1)*, 79-98.

Robichaud, D. (2006). Steps toward a relational view of agency. In: F., Cooren, J. R. Taylor, & E. J. Van every, (Eds.), *Communication as Organizing*: 101-115. London: LEA.

Roosens, E. E. (1989). *Creating ethnicity*. London: Sage.

Sackmann, S. A. & Phillips, M. E. (2004). Contextual influences on culture research: Shifting assumptions for new workplace realities. *International Journal of Cross Cultural Management, 4(3)*, 370-390.

SanAntonio, P. M. (1988). Social Mobility and Language Use in an American Company in Japan. In: W. B. Gudykunst, (Eds.), *Language and Ethnic Identity*: 35-45. Clevedon: Clevedon, Multilingual Matters Ltd.

Sapir, E. (1921). *Language: An introduction to the study of speech*. New York: Harcourt, Brace.

Saussure, F. (2000). *Course in general linguistics*. London: Duckworth.

Searle, J. (1982). Chomsky's Revolution in Linguistics. In: G. Harman (Eds.), *On Noam Chomsky: Critical Essays*: 2-33. Amherst: University of Massachusetts Press.

Smith, S. J. (1984). Negotiating ethnicity in an uncertain environment. *Ethnic and Racial Studies, 7*, 360-372.

Spradley, J. P. (1980). *Participant observation*. New York: Holt Rinehart and Winston.

Søderberg, A. M. & Holden, N. (2002). Rethinking cross-cultural management in a globalising business world. *International Journal of Cross Cultural Management, 12(1)*, 103-121.

Tajfel, H. (1982). Social psychology of intergroup relations. *Annual Review of Psychology,, 33*, 1-39.

Taussig, M. (1993). *Mimesis and alterity: a particular history of the senses*. London: Routledge.

Taylor, F. (2006). Coorientation: a conceptual framework. In: F., Cooren, J. R., Taylor, & E. J. Van Every, (Eds.), *Communication as Organizing*: 141-157. London: LEA.

Taylor, J. R. & Cooren, F. (1997). What makes communication 'organizational'? How the many voices of a collectivity become the one voice of an organization. *Journal of Pragmatics, 27*, 409-438.

Tsai, W. & Ghoshal, S. (1998). Social capital and value creation: The role of intrafirm networks. *Academy of Management Journal, 41*, 464-476.

Usunier. (1998). *International and Cross-Cultural Management Research*. London: Sage Publications.

Varey, R. J. (2006). Accounts in interactions: Implications of accounting practices for managing. In: F., Cooren, J. R. Taylor, & E. J. Van every (Eds.), *Communication as Organizing*: 181-197.

Victor, D. (1992). *International business communication*. New York: Harper Collins Publishers.

Vaara, E., Risberg, A., Søderberg, A. M. & Tienari, J. (2003a). Nation talk: The construction of national stereotypes in a merging multinational. In A. Søderberg, & E, Vaara (Eds.), *Merging across borders: People, cultures and politics,* 61-86.

Vaara, E., Tienari, J., Piekkari, R. & Säntti, R. (2005). Language and the circuits of power in a merging multinational corporation. *Journal of Management Studies, 42(3)*, 595-623.

Vaara, E., Tienari, J. & Säntti, R. (2003b). The international match: Metaphors as vehicles of social identity-building in cross-border mergers. *Human Relations, 56(4)*, 419-451.

Welch, D., Welch, L. & Piekkari, R. (2005). Speaking in Tongues: The Importance of Language in International Management Processes. *International Studies of Management & Organization, 35(1)*, 10-27.

Whorf, B. L. (1951). *Language, thought, and reality*. Cambridge, MA: MIT Press.

Wright, C., Kumagai, F. & Bonney, N. (2001). Language and power in a Japanese transplant in Scotland. *Sociological Review, 49(2)*, 236-250.

Yoshikawa, M. J. (1987). The double-Swing Model of Intercultural Communication between the East and the West. In: D. L. Kincaid, (Eds.), *Communication Theory: Eastern and Western Perspectives*: 319-329. London: Academic Press inc. Harcourt Brace Jovanovich College Publishers.

In: Race and Ethnicity
Editor: Jonathan K. Crennan, pp. 159-177

ISBN: 978-1-60692-099-2

Chapter 5

SECOND GENERATION IMMIGRANT STUDENTS, SOCIOECONOMIC STATUS, CULTURAL ROLES AND NEW CHALLENGES

*Carol Schmid**
Guilford Technical Community College, Jamestown, NC, USA

ABSTRACT

In 2007 approximately 38 million immigrants resided in the United States. The large increase in contemporary immigration has given rise to a record number of children who are raised in immigrant families. Since the 1980s, a new generation of immigrants has populated the nation's schools. It is the fastest growing and the most ethnically diverse segment of America's child population. About one of every five individuals under 18 is either an immigrant or has parents who are immigrants. This population is certain to increase. The first section of the paper examines the role social class plays in academic achievement of second generation students. There is a significant debate between schools stressing the socioeconomic vs. sociocultural perspective on educational achievement. The second section of the paper analyzes the sociocultural perspective. Why do Asian children excel in school to a much greater extent than children from Latino families? To what degree is this disparity explained by socioeconomic class as opposed to the factors related to the culture of various ethnic groups? The third section of the paper will critically analyze variants of assimilation theory. What factors condition the adaptation process of second generation youth? The traditional assimilation framework of Gordon (1964) and his followers believe that a "foreign" group will with increasing contact overtime be absorbed in the 'mainstream' of American society. In contrast Portes and Rumbaut (2006) propose that a process of "segmented assimilation" better characterizes the experience of recent immigrants to the US and their children. Finally the last section of the paper will conclude with an examination of some of the major challenges of integrating immigrant and second generation students in the American mainstream. Factors such as poverty, segregation, and attitudes toward immigration will be discussed.

---

* Corresponding author: clschmid@gtcc.edu

Forty years of sustained immigration following the passage of the 1995 Immigration Act with large numbers of foreign born and their children has and will have a significant impact on the nation's schools and the job market. The children and young adults of American's immigrant are only beginning to capture the attention of public policy makers and social scientists in spite of their growing numbers. The social inclusion of the second generation is of critical importance. "A great deal of how tomorrow's social contract between natives and newcomers is worked out and how the commitment to democratic values of equity and inclusion is met will hinge on the mode of political incorporation and civic engagement of newcomer youth today" (Rumbaut 2008:108).

The large increase in contemporary immigration has given rise to a record number of children who are raised in immigrant families. Since the 1980s, a new generation of immigrants has populated the nation's schools. It is the fastest growing and the most ethnically diverse segment of America's child population. About one of every five individuals under 18 is either an immigrant or has parents who are immigrants. This population is certain to increase. In 1997 there were 3 million foreign-born children under 18, and nearly 11 million U.S.-born children under 18 living with at least one foreign-born parent (Alba, Massey and Rumbaut 1999). The Census Bureau estimates that between 1999 and 2050, the total numbers of foreign-born Americans will more than double, from 26 million to 53.8 million, to make up 13 percent of the population (Schmid 2001).

In 2007 approximately 38.1 million immigrants resided in the United States, which is about 12.6 percent of the US population (Terrazas and Batalova 2008). From 1970 to 2002 the foreign-born and their children increased to approximately 62 million or 22 percent of the US population (Schmidley and Richardson 2003). In contrast with the first surge in immigration in the early 1900s when the majority of immigrants were from Europe, the current immigrants are disproportionately from Mexico, Central America and Asia (Schmidley 2003).

The Asian-origin population has increased significantly in the decades after 1965. Asian born individuals are the second largest foreign-born population world region behind those from Latin America. The number of Asian born individuals in the US increased 986 percent between 1970 and 2007 from 1.4 million to 15.2 million. The Hispanic population accounted for the largest number of immigrants. The Hispanic population increased 337 percent between 1970 and 2007 from 9.6 million to 45.5 million (U.S. Census, 2005, 2008). First Hispanic generation immigrants accounted for 45 percent of the increase and the second generation added an additional 28 percent (Suro and Passel 2003). Concerns over the assimilation prospects and barriers of the new second generation have been raised by academic and policy makers.

This article examines determinants of educational achievement with special emphasis on the Asian and the Hispanic populations. Education is one of the most important stepping stones to job mobility and full integration into American life. The first section of the paper will examine the role social class plays in academic achievement of foreign-born and second generation students. There is a significant debate between schools stressing the socioeconomic vs. the sociocultural perspective on educational achievement. The second section of the papers analyzes educational achievement and ethnic cultures. Why do Asian students excel in school to a much greater extent than second generation Latino students? To what degree is this disparity explained by socioeconomic class as opposed to factors related to the culture of various ethnic groups? The third section of the paper will critically analyze variants of assimilation theory. What factors condition the adaptation process of second generation youth? The traditional assimilation framework of Gordon (1964) and his followers believe that a 'foreign' group will with increasing contact overtime be absorbed in the 'mainstream' of American society. In contrast Portes and Rumbaut (2006) propose that a process of "*segmented assimilation*" better characterizes the experience of recent immigrants to the US and their children.

Finally the last section of the paper will conclude with an examination of some of the major challenges of integrating immigrants and second generation students in the American mainstream. Factors such as poverty, segregation, attitudes toward education and programs designed to address the needs of the children of the foreign born will be discussed.

SOCIO-ECONOMIC FACTORS AND EDUCATIONAL ACHIEVEMENT

The link between academic performance, educational attainment and labor outcomes has been extensively documented in both the educational and social stratification literature. Koa and Thompson observe that (2003:431) "Parental education and family income is probably the best predictor of eventual academic outcomes among youth." Status-attainment research has established that among native children that parent's socioeconomic status (SES) has a strong and positive effect on children's achievement (see Blau and Duncan 1967; Featherman and Hauser 1978; Sewell and Hauser 1975). Children whose parents are better educated, make more money, have higher-status jobs, and live in two parent families tend to attain higher levels of education than do other children.

Human capital theory interprets the correlation between higher SES and educational achievement in a somewhat different way. According to this perspective, parents make choices about how much time and other resources to invest in their children on the basis of their objectives, resources, and constraints (Haveman and Wolf 1994). These investment decisions affect the students' taste for education (preferences) and cognitive skills (human capital), which in turn, affect their educational success.

According to Rumbaut in his study of the second generation over a four year period in the Miami-Dade and San Diego school systems, a more cohesive, stable, and resourceful home environment leads to higher educational attainment (Alba, Massey, and Rumbaut 1999). Family human capital, family composition and modes of incorporation continue to have significant power in shaping the lives of the second generation in the early years of adulthood (from 23 to 27 years old) (Portes, Fernandez-Kelly and Haller 2005). When the results are broken down by major nationalities the differences show remarkable continuity from earlier surveys taken in the adolescent years. Parents' human capital – the education, family structure and the way parents are incorporated into their communities continue to exert a significant influence on the lives of the second generation in young adulthood (Rumbaut 2006). In these respects children of immigrants are identical to findings on the native born (Portes and MacLeod 1996; Steinberg, Blinde and Chan 1984; Warren 1996). Children who come from intact immigrant families with both of the parents present have higher grade point averages, lower dropout rates, and higher aspirations than children raised in stepfamilies or single-parent families. Similar patterns were found to be evident for indicators of socioeconomic status such as parental education, homeownership, and poverty (Alba, Massey, and Rumbaut 1999).

This is also the case for undocumented students. Academic success of undocumented students in a study by Perez, Espinoza, Ramos, Coronado and Cortes (2009) was found to be related to both personal and 'environmental resources' such as supportive parents, friends, and participation in school activities. When the various resources were present, academic performance was generally positive, even in the presence of multiple risk factors such as living in poverty, low parental education and working long hours after school. Compared to the group who possessed more human capital, the high risk group without these factors exhibited lower levels of academic success.

Social class intervenes with other factors to influence educational attainment of the second generation. A study of the second generation in New York City of Dominicans, West Indians, South Americans, Chinese and Russians found that second generation immigrants do better than their parents and also surpass native Blacks and Puerto Ricans. Expectations of immigrant parents for their second generation children with respect to getting a higher education and their own level of educational attainment influenced the educational attainment of their children (Kasinitz, Mollenkopf, Waters and Holdaway 2008).

Families from different class and ethnic backgrounds have widely divergent ability to navigate the New York educational system. Chinese and Russian students consistently came out on top. More Chinese (64 percent) and Russian Jews (63 percent) attained a baccalaureate or higher in comparison to Dominicans (26 percent), West Indians (28 percent) and South Americans (26 percent). The school system was found to treat different groups in significantly different ways – these included reactions from teachers and academic expectations. Although both Dominicans and Chinese had poorly educated parents Chinese parents settled in mixed or formerly white areas with relatively good schools and invested their savings on their children's education. Chinese language media provided extensive information on the best public schools. There was also the model minority stereotype and teacher's expectations to do well. The cumulative effects of social class and human and social capital helped to explain the divergent outcomes in high school completion and college attendance (Kasinitz, Mollenkopf, Waters and Holdaway 2008). The New York study does not include second generation students from Mexico.

Smith (2006) in his extensive ethnographic study of Mexicans in New York City points to distress signs when considering education and income in New York City. For Mexicans without a high school education their income dropped from $17,495 in 1980 to $13,537 in 1990 and only increased slightly in 2000. Furthermore Mexicans had the highest rate of sixteen to nineteen-year-olds who were not in high school and had not graduated in New York City: 47 percent compared with 22 percent of Dominicans in 1990. This is related to the influx of less educated Mexican immigrants, especially teen immigrants since 1990.

Empirical evidence suggests that socioeconomic factors can explain the generally low educational achievement of the new second generation of Mexican American students. Using data from the 1990 Public Use Micro Samples, Warren (1996) in his study of educational inequality among white and Mexican-origin adolescents in the Southwest found that family background factors do the most to explain the educationally disadvantaged position of Mexican-origin relative to white adolescents. English-language ability and migration history, on the other hand, does relatively little to explain the gap in schooling outcomes between Mexican-origin and non-Hispanic white adolescents. However, even after SES, migration history, and language ability are taken into account, adolescents of Mexican origin still are at an educational disadvantage relative to their white counterparts in the final years of high school. Kao and Tienda (1995) using national data also found that SES provided the best explanation of the difference between grades and test scores between Latino immigrants and native students.

The low educational achievement of Hispanics is by far more complex than has often been painted. The United States government figures, covering the 1994-95 academic year conclude that Hispanic students have a higher dropout rate than either whites or blacks. The dropout rate is defined as the proportion of young adults (ages 16 to 24) who are not enrolled in a high school program and who have not completed high school. During the 1994/95 school year, 30 percent of Hispanic young adults were classified as dropouts, as compared to 8.6 percent of non-Hispanic whites and 12.1 percent of non-Hispanic blacks (McMillen, Kaufman and Klein 1997).

The dropout rate has continued to climb. Dropout rates for 2007 show that overall, 37 percent of Hispanic female and 48 percent of Hispanic male students will not graduate with a regular high school diploma in the standard, four-year time period in contrast with 18 percent of Asian female students and 24 percent of Asian male students (these were not broken down by generation) (National Women's Law Center 2007). It is significant that very few social science researchers analyze the second generation according to gender. The disparity between female and male high school graduates is particularly striking for Hispanics.

Among Hispanic adults dropout rates include many individuals who never enrolled in school. Several studies have shown that the relatively low in-school participation of Mexican immigrants of high school age is primarily due to their not "dropping in" to the school system in the first place rather than their "dropping out" of school. In a 2000 sample Oropesa and Landale (2009) found a significant difference whether one included the never-enrolled or not. Because the foreign-born make up a large share of Hispanic adolescents – perhaps 17 percent for this age group – many Mexican youth may have already completed their education by the time they migrated to the United States. They found that approximately 86 percent of Mexican youths aged 16-17 are in school for the ever-enrolled, however this figure drops to 70 percent when the never enrolled are included.

In the earlier study by McMillan, Kaufman, and Klein (1997) they found about one-third of the 30 percent dropout rate for Hispanic young adults was due to non-enrollees. The true dropout figure is about 20 percent. In 1990, one out of every four immigrants from Mexico in the 15-17 age group was not in school. By age 15 Mexican immigrants had already been out of school in Mexico for two years on average. The high rate of dropouts among Hispanics is related primarily to economic factors. Rumberger (1983) found that among Hispanic male dropouts only 4 percent said that the reason for dropping out was 'poor performance in school.' This compared to 8 percent of male non-Hispanic white students. Economic reasons were given by 38 percent of the Hispanic students in contrast to 22 percent of the non-Hispanic white students.

Several factors have been identified as predictors of dropping out among Hispanic students. These include lack of English language speaking ability, low socioeconomic class, and presence of only one parent, recent immigration, and lack of a family support system (in terms of monitoring homework). When these factors are controlled between racial and ethnic groups, there is no difference in dropout rates between Hispanics and other groups. The stark reality is that Hispanic children are much more likely to find themselves in dire economic conditions. Approximately 40 percent of Hispanic children live in poverty, compared to 15 percent of white non-Hispanic children, and only 45 percent live with parents who have completed high school, compared to 81 percent of non-Hispanic white children. Only 68 percent live with both parents, compared to 81 percent of non-Hispanic white children (Rumberger 1991, 1995).

In addition, generation has played a significant if conflicting role in predicting educational outcomes. The 'Immigrant Paradox' posits that second immigrant students have better educational outcomes than the third generation born in the United States with US born parents, despite similarly disadvantaged circumstances. Rong and Grant (1992) found a positive association between years of education and generation for Hispanics. Yet, generation may also play a negative role in affecting student outcomes. Controlling for SES narrowed but did not close the gap between the chances of graduating from high school of U.S.-born and Mexican-born students of Mexican origin (Warren 1996). Wojtkiewicz and Donato (1995) by differentiating Mexicans not only by their own place of birth, but also by their parents' place of birth found important differences among U.S.-born Mexicans with U.S.-born Mexican parents and U.S.-born Mexicans with foreign-born parents from Mexico. American-born Mexicans with both parents foreign born had significantly higher chances of completing high school than Mexican students with both parents U.S.-born. The Wojtkiewicz and Donato (1995) study documented that U.S.-born Mexican students had high school graduation rates comparable to whites; however, they established that this masked a strong difference according to the birthplace of the parents. Other studies have also confirmed this finding. Rumberger (1995) found that that second generation Mexican-Americans were less likely to drop out than their third generation counterparts, even though on the average their socioeconomic status was lower. Driscoll (1999) in her study of immigrant and native Hispanic youth also found that U.S.-born students of U.S.-born parents were more than twice as likely to drop out of high school as were U.S.-born students with foreign-born parents. Furthermore, in her sample third generation sophomores were almost three times as likely to drop out as immigrant sophomores.

Keller and Harker (2008) analyzed college attendance and generational differences. They concluded that there are several important differences between first and second-generation youth and their third-plus generation counterparts. Although immigrants disproportionately experience social, economic and political inequities they are just as likely to attend college as their native-born peers. Overall second generation Hispanic immigrant youth are academically out performing their third generation peers in high school. The beneficial effects are most significant among second-generation Chinese and first generation black immigrant youth.

The tensions between different paths of integration were analyzed in Suárez-Orozco and Suárez-Orozco's (1995) comparison of recent Mexican immigrants with U.S.-born Mexican Americans. According to the authors, who employ primarily qualitative data, first-generation immigrants often possess a "dual frame of reference," a dual orientation which contrasts their previous life before migration to their current life. Such a frame of reference enables recent Mexican immigrants to feel that their life in the United States is markedly better than the life they left behind. Children of immigrants, not having access to a dual frame of reference, do not see their current status as one of being better off; rather, the third generation see themselves as marginalized in comparison with the dominant culture. Mexican American youth revealed identification with the "dominant American paradigm of adolescent ambivalence" (Suárez-Orozco and Suárez-Orozco's 1995:188). In contrast they found that Mexican youth in Mexico and recent Mexican immigrants are comparatively more achievement-oriented then second-generation Mexicans and white American adolescents.

In general, the families' ability to invest in the education of their children is limited by their economic, social and human capital resources. Asian Americans students' performance is enhanced by their socioeconomic status. In an analysis of Asians, Hispanics, Afro-Americans and whites, Blair and Legazpi (1999) found that social class was the strongest predictor of academic performance for all groups. Overall, they concluded that Asian American student's academic success can be attributed to a combination of both cultural and class related attributes, but with the effects of the families' socioeconomic status being the stronger of the two sets of predictors. Much of the educational success of Asian American children in the United States can be attributed to their relatively high SES (Kao 1995). Asian Indian, Japanese, Chinese, Filipino, and Korean American adults surpass whites in average educational attainment (Hao and Bonstead-Bruns 1988). In California and Florida, second-generation Haitian, Mexican, Vietnamese, and Cuban students were found by Portes and MacLeod (1996) to be heavily influenced by their family's socioeconomic status and by the average socioeconomic levels of their schools. The national background of the new second generation also played a significant independent role

In contrast to socioeconomic factors, there is a body of literature that questions whether differences in SES are sufficient to explain the large gap in educational achievement among Latino American and Asian students. For example Rumbaut (1995) found that first and second-generation Mexican American students had significantly lower grades and test scores than did other immigrant students even after differences in English ability and family SES were controlled. Fejgin (1995) also reported that even when family income and parental educational levels were held constant, Asian and Jewish students performed academically better than other students. Thus, the socioeconomic approach does not account for all the variation in the academic performance of racial-ethnic groups.

A SOCIOCULTURAL PERSPECTIVE OF SCHOOL ACHIEVEMENT

Even after class differences are eliminated, according to this perspective significant differences in intellectual achievement remain. In a sociocultural perspective, school performance can be explained more fully in terms of factors related to the culture of various ethnic groups (Fejgin 1995; Ogbu 1992; Rumberger and Larson 1998, Zhou and Bankston 1998) and the context of reception in the United States. Among children of immigrants, there are very large differences by national origin. Rumbaut observes that this portends a significant ethnic segmentation of socioeconomic trajectories as youths make their transition into the adult labor force (Alba, Massey and Rumbaut 1999).

Several theories have been proposed to explain why some, notably Asian groups, have succeeded to a greater degree than most Hispanic groups, even when parental socioeconomic status and the quality and location of the schools the students attend is controlled.

Pedro Portes' (1999) analysis of data collected by the "Children of Immigrants" project in Miami and San Diego (see Portes and Schauffler 1996, Portes and Rumbaut 2006) found that the influence of cultural background remained and could not be disaggregated by key demographic, SES, and sociopsychological factors. However, he observed that the two groups found to excel in American schools, Asians and Cubans, have more established inroads in the community and therefore may be able to provide greater social and cognitive support. The lowest achievers, Mexicans and Haitians, were from groups that have the least support, encounter language problems in school, and felt most unwelcomed by the mainstream. One unresearched question concerning Mexicans and Haitians is the impact of parental illegal status on children's achievements.

Portes and MacLeod (1996) have refined the sociocultural theory; also emphasizing the importance of social incorporation and the context of reception in the United States (see also Portes and Rumbaut 2006). They observe that the Cuban and Vietnamese groups were products of communist take-overs in their respective countries, and most of the original members were political refugees. Both of the groups were treated sympathetically and received various forms of federal assistance. The Cubans and Vietnamese were able to use government and private resources to create solidarity and entrepreneurial communities. They tend to live in close-knit communities, in which academic achievement is encouraged. Cuban and Vietnamese immigrants are optimistic about their children's chances of attending college and have high expectations for their children.

The conditions of Haitian and Mexican communities, who are primarily "economic" immigrants, are quite different from "political" immigrants such as Cubans and Vietnamese studied by Portes and Leod (1996). The Haitian and Mexican communities contain large numbers of unauthorized immigrants. Both groups have been the subject of deportations, and have been less sympathetically received than Cubans and Vietnamese. Unlike Cubans, Haitians were considered economic immigrants and were routinely denied refugee status. Mexican immigrants, especially in California, have often experienced pervasive discrimination even when they have entered the United States legally. Neither Haitians nor Mexicans are eligible for federal assistance granted to Southeast Asian refugees. Because of the marginal jobs both groups tend to hold and their often-disputed status, Mexicans and Haitians have a more difficult time maintaining cohesive communities. They are also deprived of the economic subsidies granted to legal refugees.

The differences between the academic success of these four national groups may give rise to invidious comparisons among the cultures and the success of the second generation. Portes and MacLeod (1996) have cautioned against this conclusion. They observe that "the factors that account for the significant differences among these groups have to do with the human capital that immigrants bring with them from their countries of origin and the social context that receives them and shapes their adaptation in the United States" (Portes and MacLeod 1996:271). Inequalities in the situation of various immigrant national origin groups influence the academic success of the new second generation, indicating that both class and ethnic privilege are transmitted from generation to generation.

Zhou and Bankston (1998) embody the sociocultural perspective. They argue that ethnic-immigrant children who remain close to their family's culture do better than those who acculturate more rapidly. In Bankston's and Zhou's (1997) first person account of Versailles Village, a poor community in New Orleans, they analyzes how the immigrant community serves as an integrating device for second generation Vietnamese youth, demonstrating how a close identification with being Vietnamese is highly associated with success in local public schools. Strong associations are found between measures of Vietnamese language proficiency, ethnic identification, association with same-race peers, and values such as respect for elders, obedience, and belief in hard work that they attribute to Vietnamese culture (Zhou and Bankston 1998).

In analyzing the Chinese immigrant community in Los Angeles, Zhou (2009) observed that the academic success of second generation Chinese students is related to supplementary education. These intangible resources include reinforcing values on education in the home and community and ethnic after school programs to bolster academic success. In addition to teaching the Chinese language, those programs provide reinforcement of school lessons. While Latinos may live in the same neighborhoods as Chinese immigrants they do not have access to the same intangible resources such as private after school programs (Zhou 2009).

Further evidence of sociocultural influences is found in the research of Fejgin (1995). In her study of Asian and Jewish students she found that Asian and Jewish students perform better than do other students from similar socioeconomic backgrounds. Kasinitz, Mollenkopf, Waters and Holdaway (2008) found a similar result in their study of the second generation in New York City with the highest rate of college attendance among Chinese and Russian Jews. Kaufman (2004) in her ethnographic study of a working class 'relatively low income' High School located in the midst of a large and dense Chinese community in New Work City observed that Chinese immigrants were motivated to work hard and to value demanding teachers, a difficult curriculum and discipline. By the second generation Chinese students wanted more entertaining, knowledgeable teachers while still agreeing that effort determines school success. Although the second-generation students are more likely to accept American beliefs and norms, they have Chinese-immigrant parents and relatives who encourage hard-work and school success (Kaufman 2004:1294).

It is significant that Asians also attain higher academic achievement in other immigrant societies. A national sample in Canada found large group differences in university attendance among children of immigrants. While fathers' education and two-parent households made a significant difference, parental education could not account for the higher academic achievement of Asians (with the exception of Filipinos). The fact that human and social capital factors could not account for the advantages of Asian groups suggests that cultural explanations may play a significant role – such as obligation to parents, and an emphasis on self-reliance and achievement (Araba, Hou and Ram 2009).

Among community college students there are major differences in racial/ethnic persistence rates. Two year institutions enroll over 40 percent (43 percent) of African Americans and Asian (45 percent) undergraduate students and over half of Hispanic (52 percent) and Native American (52 percent) undergraduates. Eight years after students said their goal was to transfer and obtain a 4-year degree only 4 percent of native blacks, 10 percent of Hispanics, 17 percent of whites, but 30 percent of Asians completed a Bachelor Degree (in contrast 49 percent of blacks, 38 percent of Hispanics, 67 percent of whites and 73 percent of Asians who began their education at a public 4-year college completed their B.A. /B.S in eight years (Schmid 2010). At every level of education Asians are more likely to complete their education than the white majority.

Fejgin concludes that racial-ethnic differences in school performance "should not be reduced to class differences. Different ethnic groups, even within the White category that we researchers tend to view as unitary, have distinct values and attitudes related to schoolwork and use different socialization patterns to encourage or discourage academic performance" (Fejgin 1995:28). The findings on the salience of cultural traits appear to hold true for both white ethnic groups and racial minorities in the United States. In a study of the Irish, Italian,

Jewish, and African Americans in Providence, Rhode Island, Perlman (1988) found that even when family background was held constant, ethnic differences in levels of schooling and economic attainment persisted in the second and later generations.

The sociocultural approach places it major emphasis on the values and cultural baggage that interacts with societal reception of new immigrant groups. The socioeconomic approach according to Goyette and Xie (1999) is unsatisfactory as a general framework for explaining the educational achievement of Asian American children. Goyette and Xie (1999) explored why distinct Asian groups have higher educational expectations than do whites. In order to explain Asian academic success three factors were analyzed: socioeconomic and background characteristics, demonstrated academic ability, and parent's high expectations. They found the explanatory power of the three sets of factors varied across different Asian groups. Socioeconomic factors explained much of the difference between the educational expectations of well-assimilated Asian groups, for example, Filipinos, Japanese, and South Asians, but none of the difference in expectations of the Chinese, Koreans, and Southeast Asians. Ability explains some of the high expectations of the Chinese and Koreans, and Southeast Asians, but none of those of the Filipinos or Japanese. Perhaps the most significant finding by Goyette and Xie (1999) was that parental expectations play an important role in explaining the Asian-white gap for all the major Asian national groups.

Ogbu (1991, 1992) and Ogbu and Matute-Bianchi (1986) classified ethnic and national origin immigrant groups into two types. The first group was called "voluntary minorities" such as European and recent Asian Americans, who came to the United States voluntarily. The second group they labeled "involuntary minorities," such as African Americans and early Mexican Americans, who were brought to the United States against their will, either through forced immigration or domination. Because of their different reception and treatment in the United States they have had different trajectories with respect to integration in the labor market and the success of their children. They also have different identities that have aided or impeded their success, which is conditioned on their treatment in the society.

> Voluntary minorities seem to bring to the United States a sense of who they are from their homeland and seem to retain this different but non-oppositional social identity, at least during the first generation. Involuntary minorities, in contrast, develop a new sense of social or collective identity that is in opposition to the new social identity of the dominant group after they have become subordinated. They do so in response to their treatment by White Americans in economic, social, psychological, cultural, and language domains (Ogbu 1992:9).

Whereas voluntary immigrants and their children do not perceive learning the attitudes and behaviors required for school success as threatening, in fact they generally encompass these behaviors; involuntary minorities often see these same behaviors in a negative light. Ogbu (1974, 1991) concluded that voluntary immigrant groups frequently promoted upward mobility. To achieve this goal high value was placed on education. Ogbu's (1989) research on Chinese-American students in Oakland, California found that in spite of cultural and language differences and relatively low socioeconomic status, the students maintained very high grade point averages. Cultural values such as a tradition of respect for teachers may also have aided the positive value held for education (Zhou 1997). "Accommodation and acculturation without assimilation" has also led to the success of U.S-born Punjabi children in spite of the relatively low socioeconomic status of their parents. The Punjabi parents wanted their children to acquire competence in the dominant culture but not at the expense of their Indian identity. Cultural values aided the academic success of Punjabis. The children became skillful in the dominant culture, but at the same time held strongly to their ethnic identity (Gibson 1998).

Involuntary minorities, on the other hand, according to Ogbu (1992) may be unable or unwilling to separate their attitudes and behaviors from other symbols of assimilation to the dominant white majority. Success in school is seen as "selling out" to the dominant culture. Although Ogbu's (1992) dichotomy between voluntary and involuntary minorities appears to fit Asians and Cubans as opposed to Black Americans, recent Mexican Americans provide a more difficult case. Most post-1965 Mexicans have arrived voluntarily in the United States.

Ogbu and Maute-Bianchi (1986) argue that Mexican Americans tend to behave more like involuntary minorities. Because their treatment is more like native-born Mexican Americans, who have been subject to considerable discrimination, they do not have the same expectations as other voluntary minorities. One of the problems of this theory is that it fails to differentiate between Mexican immigrants that come with high aspirations for educational success and those who equate academic success with giving up one's own ethnic identity to the dominant group.

SEGMENTED ASSIMILATION RE-ASSESSED

Concerns with the prospects of the second generation and the different pathways to assimilation of various ethnic groups led Portes and Zhou (1993) to argue that the children of today's immigrants will assimilate in three major ways – as opposed to the single straight line path of assimilation supposedly followed by the earlier great wave of immigration at the beginning of the 20th century. The three major discernable patterns are: 1) upward mobility and acculturation and economic integration into the mainstream of middle class America. Immigrants give up old-world values, norms and behavioral patterns; 2) downward mobility pattern of acculturation and integration into the margins of American society. This is the pattern of adopting 'oppositional subculture' associated with lower class native racial minorities; 3) socioeconomic integration into the mainstream with selective acculturation and deliberate preserving of ethnic institutions, norms and values (Zhou 2009).

Portes and Zhou (1993) argue that how the first generation adapts to living in the United States creates differential opportunities and social capital in the form of ethnic jobs, networks, and values that in turn create different types of pulls on the second generation. For immigrant groups that face societal discrimination and reside in close proximity to American minorities, the second generation is more likely to develop the "adversarial stance" that American minorities such as poor blacks and Hispanics hold toward the dominant white society. For some groups the different pulls inherent in the second generation are less clear. The distinctiveness of skin color, especially those who are deemed phenotypically black may exert a powerful influence on assimilation and school achievement.

An important and largely unanswered question is to what degree "segmented assimilation" is a new phenomenon. Socioeconomic class, cultural values, structural constraints and societal reception appear to have played an important role in each new wave of immigrants and their children. The segmented aspirations and performance in education is not a new one, especially for newcomers from rural and less privileged backgrounds. Rothstein (1998:102-103) observed that "Test after test in the 1920s found that Italian immigrant students had an average IQ of about 85, compared to an average for native-born students of 102...The challenge of educating Italian immigrant children was so severe that New York established its first special education classes to confront it. A 1921 survey disclosed half of all special education children in New York had Italian-born fathers."

A number of popular myths and images, according to Foner (2000, 2006); have grown up about the massive immigration to New York City around the turn of the twentieth century. The belief that the earlier wave of immigrants that brought more than 23 million immigrants to the United States made rapid upward progress and achieved success with remarkable ease and speed is a myth. Foner in her book *From Ellis Island to JFK* (2000) observes that many exclusionary barriers were erected by more privileged Americans in educational institutions and in residential areas. While there was considerable second generation progress the ascent up the socioeconomic ladder was more difficult and less rapid than Portes and his colleagues (Portes and Zhou 1993, Portes and Rumbaut 2006, Portes, Ferdandez-Kelly and Halter 2005) make out. Even for the successful Jewish immigrants, the ascendency to the professions was generally a third or fourth generation phenomenon. It took almost 100 years from the time of the mass education of the Italians, many of whom had peasant roots, before it became clear they would make it educationally and occupationally into the American mainstream (Foner 2000, 2006).

Gratton (2002:74) cautions again the "rush among scholars to reject assimilation and embrace the new segmented assimilation models". He observes that during the earlier wave of immigration scientific racial theories graded white people hierarchically with Italians and Poles further at the bottom of the ladder than Germans and the recently elevated Irish. During the first large wave of immigration xenophobia theories passed as science explicitly stating that some ethnicities, those closest to the white Protestant mainstream could assimilate while those further away from the mainstream could not. "This view has intriguing parallels with contemporary segmented assimilation theory, which proposed that certain immigrants are destined to fail, albeit by force of discrimination against them rather than via inherent characteristics" (Gratton 2002:78).

Research on the immigrant second generation in the United States has been very influenced by the segmented assimilation theory. The contention has been challenged that the children of immigrants, specifically Hispanics, are at risk of downward mobility into a 'new rainbow underclass" by several social scientists. Quantitative studies by Waldinger and Feliciano (2004) of the 1996-2001 Current Population Survey come to a more nuanced and less pessimistic conclusion. They focus on the experience of Mexicans, the largest second generation group who are predominantly of working class or lower-class origins. While low skilled immigrants are entering an economy that provides few rewards for workers with modest education, Waldinger and Feliciano (2004) found little support that the offspring of working class immigrants will experience 'downward mobility.' The evidence shows that the experience of the current second generation is consistent with the earlier pattern, in which children of immigrants progressed by moving ahead in the working class.

In their study of the second generation in New York, Kasinitz and associates (2008) concluded that while 'ethnic capital' benefited many second generation youth, there is mixed evidence that maintaining ethnicity or in the words of Portes and Rumbaut (2006) "consonant assimilation" helped the second generation achieve more education. While the Chinese often went to Chinese schools as a form of child care they rarely learned the Chinese language or were very familiar with the Chinese culture. However, parents did attempt to enroll their children in the best public schools in New York City. There was also a significant generation gap between the immigrant and second generation. These finding do not appear to support the hypothesis of segmented assimilation which involves socioeconomic integration into the mainstream with selective acculturation and deliberate preserving of ethnic institutions, norms and values (Kasinitz, Mollenkopf, Waters and Holdaway 2008).

The Dominicans were the most likely to live in ethnically concentrated neighborhoods. However, they were not helped by holding closely to their ethnic kin and dividing available funds between the new and old country. Rather living in ethnic enclaves confined them to the worst schools. In examining consonant assimilation in New York City Kasinitz, Mollenkopf, Waters and Holdaway (2008) conclude that ethnic solidarity can work in positive or negative ways depending on the resources, norms, and information available to an immigrant group.

Mexican second generation children initially come with high expectations for education. St.-Hilaire's (2002) sample of eighth and ninth-grade students in California were nearly unanimous in professing positive values toward formal education. The students' length of residence in the United States, however, is negatively associated with educational aspirations. Fluent bilingualism in Spanish and English is positively correlated with educational aspirations and expectation. Before entering high school Mexican-origin students profess positive educational values, aspirations and expectations. The conclusion of this study seems to belie the high drop-out rates of Mexican high-school students. The findings reveal mixed and inconclusive evidence of segmented assimilation among the second generation of Mexican immigrants. The belief in formal education is almost universally held in the middle school years. Gandara and Contreras (2009) call this the 'paradox of high aspiration and low school effort'. The discrepancy between beliefs in the American dream of second generation Mexican youth and upward mobility through education and the reality of large number of high school drop-outs is a critical gap in the study of second generation immigrants.

The evidence of segmented assimilation is mixed. The jury is still out on the degree to which segmented assimilation will characterize today's second generation immigrant children and youth. Assimilation may take four or more generations before a group reaches the mainstream of American society depending on the characteristics and human and social capital it takes with it from the old country. Most empirical research on the second generation has been conducted long before assimilation is complete so it cannot provide a definitive answer about the progress of assimilation. The recent research does, however, shed light on particular problems and challenges of the second generation.

CONCLUSION

Immigrants, Immigrant Students and New Challenges

Of the record 38 million immigrants who lived in the United States in 2007, Mexican-immigrants accounted for almost a third of all foreign born, by far the largest immigrant group in the United States (Terrazas and Batalova 2008, Pew Hispanic Center 2009). For this reason I will analyze some of the major problems of this large population of first and second generation immigrants.

One of the major challenges to Mexican immigrants and their children is the large percentage of undocumented. More than half (55 percent) of the Mexican immigrants in the United States are unauthorized. The number of immigrants is also large in relationship to the Mexican population – about 11 percent of everyone born in Mexico is currently living in the United States (Pew Hispanic Center 2009). The precarious position of the large Mexican population is certainly translated to the second generation. This may be the source of lowered expectation after middle school.

Mexicans are more likely to perceive discrimination than other immigrant groups. Thirty-two percent say there is a great deal of discrimination against immigrants in comparison to only 1 percent of East Asians. On the other hand, when asked if they have personally experienced a great deal of discrimination there is no difference between Mexican (7 percent) and East Asians (9 percent). Despite their low income and education levels Mexican immigrants say they are extremely happy in the US (40 percent vs. 35 percent for East Asians) (Bittle and Rochkind 2009).

Initially, Mexicans come with high expectations but poor performing schools, poverty, unfamiliarity with the education system, language difficulties, and need for more income has perpetuated the crisis in education. Mexicans low levels of human and social capital including education, income and disputed status make it difficult to obtain parity with other Americans. Mexican immigrants are distinguished by their historically low levels of education. Second generation students complete less formal schooling and have a higher drop out (or stop-out) rate than any other demographic group. They are less likely to be U.S. citizens than other immigrants, partially because there is a large percentage of unauthorized. In addition they have lower incomes and are more likely to work in lower-skilled occupations.

The Mexican second-generation is making slow progress over the first generation. They are better educated and second generation men find better paid and more stable jobs in the working class (Telles and Ortiz 2008, Waldinger and Reichl 2006, Waldinger, Lim and Cort 2007). Telles and Ortiz observe that there has been a very gradual breaking down of Mexican American ethnic boundaries over the last 100 years. However, three disturbing trends in recent years could slow or reverse the prospects for further integration: labor polarization, worsening public education, and significant numbers of undocumented immigrants. Immigration reform and school reform are therefore imperative to lift the prospects of the second and subsequent generations of Mexican Americans.

The gender disparity between Hispanic males and females has hardly been addressed. Since the early 1980s Latinas have completed high school at a much higher rate than Latino males and since the 1990s they have entered and completed college at significantly higher rates than their male counterparts (Gandara and Contreras 2009). Unfortunately there is comparatively little literature on gender roles among the second generation. The experience of immigrants and their children certainly differs by gender as well as race and ethnicity (Boyd and Gieco 2003, Foner 2000).

In many ways today's immigrants and their children bear a striking resemblance to the first generation of immigrants who moved at very different rates into the American mainstream. The first generation still has a positive perception of the United States. When asked if they would come again to the United States if they had an opportunity – 75 percent of Mexican and 74 percent of East Asian first generation immigrants answered affirmatively.

Over 70 percent of all the immigrant groups – South and East Asians, Middle Easterners, Central and South Americans and Mexicans said that it took five years or less before they felt comfortable and part of the community (Bittle and Rochkind 2009). For many immigrants the American dream is still alive. However, it remains to be seen how long the ethnic-identified second generation will link themselves with their parents' optimism. In the end this may be more dependent on their reception by the dominant society than their own judgments.

REFERENCES

Abada, T., Hou, F. & Ram, B. (2009). "Ethnic Differences in Educational Attainment among the Children of Canadian Immigrants." *Canadian Journal of Sociology 34*, 1-28.

Alba, R., Massey, D. S. d Rumbaut, R. G. (1999). *The Immigration Experience for Families and Children*. Washington, D.C.: American Sociological Association.

Bankston, C. L. & Zhou, M. (1995). Effects of Minority-Language Literacy on the Academic Achievement of Vietnamese Youths in New Orleans." *Sociology of Education 68*, 1-17.

Bittle, Scott and Rochkind. (2009). A Place to Call Home: What Immigrants Say Now about Life in America. *Public Agenda*. September. http://www.publicagenda.org/files/pdf/Immigration.pdf.

Blau, P. & Duncan, O. D. (1967). *The American Occupational Structure*. New York: John Wiley & Sons.

Blair, S. L. & Legazpi, M. C. (1999). "Racial/ethnic Differences in High School Students' Academic Performance: Understanding the Interweave of Social Class and Ethnicity in the Family Context." *Journal of Comparative Family Studies 30*, 539-555.

Boyd, M. & Gieco, E. (2003). "Women and Migration: Incorporating Gender into International Migration Theory." *Migration Information Source*. March 1. http://www.migrationinformation.org.

Driscoll, A. K. (1999). "Risk of High School Dropout among Immigrant and Native Hispanic Youth. *International Migration Review 33*, 857-876.

Featherman, D. L. & Hauser, R. M. (1978). *Opportunity and Change*. New York: Academic Press.

Fejgin, N. (1995). "Factors Contributing to the Academic Excellence of American Jewish and Asian Students." *Sociology of Education 68*, 18-30.

Foner, N. (2000). *From Ellis Island to JFK: New York's Two Great Waves of Immigration*. New Haven: Yale University Press.

Foner, N. (2006). "Than and Now or Then to Now: Immigration to New York in Contemporary and Historical Perspective." *Journal of American Ethnic History* (Winter/Spring), 33-47.

Gandara, P. & Contreras, F. (2009). *The Latino Education Crisis*. Cambridge: Harvard University Press.

Gibson, M. A. (1998). "Promoding Academic Success among Immigrant Students: Is Acculturation the Issue? *Educational Policy 12*, 615-633.

Gordon, M. (1964). *Assimilation in American Life: The Role of Race, Religion and National Origins*. New York: Oxford University Press.

Goyette, K. & Xie, Y. (1999). "Educational Expectations of Asian American Youths: Determinants and Ethnic Differences." *Sociology of Education 72*, 22-36.

Gratton, B. (2002). "Race, the Children of Immigrants, and Social Science Theory." *Journal of American Ethnic History* (Summer), 74-84.

Hao, L. & Bonstead-Bruns, M. (1998). "Parent-Child Differences in Educational Expectations and the Academic Achievement of Immigrant and Native Students." *Sociology of Education 71,* 175-198.

Haveman, R. & Wolfe, B. (1994). *Succeeding Generations: On the Effects of Investments in Children.* New York: Russell Sage Foundation.

Kasinitz, P., Mollenkopf, J., Waters, M. & Holdaway, J. (2008). *Inheriting the City: The Children of Immigrants Come of Age.* Cambridge: Harvard University Press and Russell Sage Foundation.

Kaufman, J. (2004). "The Interplay between Social and Cultural Determinants of School Effort and Success: An Investigation of Chinese Immigrant and Second-Generation Chinese Students' Perception toward School." *Social Science Quarterly 85,* 1276-1298

Keller, U. & Tillman, K.H. (2008). "Post-secondary Education Attainment of Immigrant and Native Youth." *Social Forces 87,* 121-152.

Kao, G. (1995). "Asian-Americans as Model Minorities? A Look at Their Academic Performance." *American Journal of Education 103,* 121-59.

Kao, G. & Tienda, M. (1995). "Optimism and Achievement: The Educational Performance of Immigrant Youth." *Social Science Quarterly 76,* 1-19.

Kao, G. & Thompson, J.S. (2003). "Racial and Ethnic Stratification in Educational Achievement and Attainment." *Annual Review of Sociology 29,* 417-442.

McMillan, M., Kaufman, P. & Klein, S. (1997). *Dropout Rates in the United States: 1995.* NCES 97-473. Washington, D.C.: United States Department of Education.

National Women's Law Center. (2007). "When Girls Don't Graduate We All Fail." Washington, DC. http://www.nwlc.org

Ogbu, J. U. (1974). *The Next Generation.* New York: Academic Press.

Ogbu. J. U. (1991). "Immigrant and Involuntary Minorities in Comparative Perspective." In: M. A. Gibson, & U. John, J. U. Ogbu, (Eds.), *Minority Status and Schooling: A Comparative Study of Immigrant and Involuntary Minorities,* (3-33). New York: New Press.

Ogbu, J. U. (1992). "Understanding Cultural Diversity and Learning." *Educational Researcher, 21,* 5-14.

Ogbu, J. U. & Matute-Bianchi, M. E. (1986). "Understanding Sociocultural Factors: Knowledge, Identity, and School Adjustment." Bilingual Education Office (Ed.) *Beyond Language: Social and Cultural Factors in Schooling Language-Minority Students,* (73-142) California State Department of Education. Los Angeles.

Oropesa, R. S. & Landale, N. S. (2009). "Why do Immigrant Youth who Never Enroll in U.S. Schools Matter? School Enrollment among Mexicans and Non-Hispanic Whites." *Sociology of Education 82,* 240-266.

Perlmann, J. (1988). *Ethnic Differences: Schooling and Social Structure among the Irish, Jews, and Blacks in an American City, 1888-1935.* New York: Cambridge University Press.

Perez, W., Espinoza, R., Ramos, K., Coronado, H. & Cortes, R. (2009). "Academic Resilience among Undocumented Latino Students. *Hispanic Journal of Social Science 31,* 149-181.

Pew Hispanic Center. (2009). *"Mexican Immigrants in the United States, 2008."* April 15.

Portes, A., Ferdandez-Kelly, P. & Halter, W. (2005). "Segmented Assimilation on the Ground: The New Second Generation in Early Adulthood." *Ethnic and Racial Studies 28,* 1000-1040.

Portes, A. & MacLeod, D. (1996). "Educational Progress of Children of Immigrants: The Roles of Class, Ethnicity, and School Context." *Sociology of Education 69,* 255-275.

Portes, A. & Rumbaut, R. (2006). *Immigrant America.* 3rd ed. Berkeley: University of California Press.

Portes, A. & Schauffler, R. (1996). "Language and the Second Generation: Bilingualism Yesterday and Today." In: A. Portes *The New Second Generation.* (8-29). New York: Russell Sage Foundation.

Portes, A. & Zhou, M. (1993). "The New Second Generation: Segmented Assimilation and its Variants among Post-1965 Immigrant Youth." *Annals of the American Academy of Political and Social Science 530,* 74-96.

Portes, P. R. (1999). "Social and Psychological Factors in the Academic Achievement of Children of Immigrants: A Cultural Puzzle." *American Research Education Journal 36,* 489-507.

Rong, X. L. & Grant, L. (1992). "Ethnicity, Generation, and School Attainment of Asians, Hispanics, and non-Hispanic Whites." *Sociological Quarterly, 33,* 624-636.

Rothstein, Richard. (1998). *The Way We Were? The Myths and Realities of America's Student Achievement.* New York: The Century Foundation Press.

Rumbaut, R. G. (1995). "The New Californians: Comparative Research Findings on the Educational Progress of Immigrant Children." In: R. G., Rumbaut, & W. A., Cornelius (Eds.), *California's Immigrant Children: Theory, Research and Implications for Educational Policy.* (17-70). La Jolla, CA: Center for U.S.-Mexican Studies, University of California, San Diego.

Rumbaut, R. G. (2006). "The Second Generation in Early Adulthood: New Findings from the Children of Immigrant Longitudinal Study." *Migration Information Source.* October 1. http://www.migrationinformation.org.

Rumbaut, R. G. (2008). "Reaping What You Sow: Immigration, Youth, and Reactive Ethnicity." *Applied Development Science 12,* 1008-111.

Rumberger, R. (1983). "Dropping out of High School: The Influence of Race, Sex, and Family Background. *American Educational Research Journal, 20,* 199-200.

Rumberger, R. (1991). "Chicano dropouts: A review of research and policy issues." In R. Valencia, *Chicano School Failure and Success.* (64-89). New York: Falmer Press.

Rumberger, R. (1995). Dropping out of middle school: A multilevel analysis of students and schools. *American Educational Research Journal, 32,* 583-625.

Rumberger, R. W. & Larson, K. A. (1998). "Toward Explaining Differences in Educational Achievement among Mexican American Language-Minority Students." *Sociology of Education, 71,* 69-93.

Schmid, C. L. (2001). "Educational Achievement, Language-Minority Students, and the New Second Generation." *Sociology of Education, 74,* (Extra Issue):74-87.

Schmid, C. L. (2010). "Inequalities in Higher Education: Access and Success of Community College Students in the United States." In G. Goastellec (Ed.), *Understanding Inequalities in and by Higher Hducation*, Rotterdam: Sense Publishers.

Schmidley, D. (2003). The Foreign-Born Population in the United States: March 2002. *Current Population Reports*, P20-539. Washington, DC: US Census Bureau.

Schmidley, D. & J. Richardson, G. (2003). "Measuring the Foreign Born Population in the United States with the Current Population Survey: 1994-2002. *Population Working Paper Series No., 73.,* Washington, DC: US Census Bureau

Sewell, W. & Hauser, R. (1975). *Education, Occupation, and Earnings: Achievement in the Early Career.* New York: Academic Press

Smith, R. C. (2006). *Mexican New York: Transnational Lives of New Immigrants.* Berkeley: University of California Press.

St-Hilaire, A. (2002). "The Social Adaption of Children of Mexican Immigrants: Educational Aspirations Beyond Junior High School." *Social Science Quarterly, 83,* 1026-1043.

Steinberg, L., Blinde, P. & K. Chan, K. (1984). "Dropping out among Minority Youth." *Review of Educational Research, 54,* 113-132.

Suarez-Orozco, C. & Suarez-Orozco, M. (1995). *Transformations: Migration, Family Life, and Achievement Motivation among Latino Adolescents.* Stanford: Stanford University Press.

Suro, R. & Passel, J. S. (2003). The Rise of the Second Generation: Changing Patterns in Hispanic Population Growth. *Pew Hispanic Center.* October 12.

Telles, E. E. & Otiz, V. (2008). *Generations of Exclusion.* New York: Russell Sage Foundation.

Terrazas, A. & Batalova, J. (2008). "The Most Frequently Requested Statistics on Immigrants in the United States." *Migration Information Source.* December ·12. http://www. migrationinformation.org.

U. S. Census. (2008). "U.S. Hispanic Population Surpasses 45 Million, Now 15 Percent of Total." Press Release, May 1. Washington, D.C.: U.S. Department of Commerce.

U. S. Census. (2005). Table A-1. Race and Hispanic Origin for the United States: 1790 to 1990. Washington, D.C.: Government Printing Office. http://www.census.gov/population.

Waldinger, R. & Feliciano, C. (2004). "Will the New Second Generation Experience 'Downward Assimilation'? Segmented Assimilation Re-assessed." *Ethnic and Racial Studies, 27,* 376-402.

Waldinger, R. & Reichl, R. (2006). "Second Generation Mexican: Getting Ahead or Falling Behind." *Migration Information Source*, March. http://www.migrationinformation.org

Waldinger, R., Lim, N. & Cort, D. (2007). "Bad Jobs, Good Jobs, No Jobs? The Employment of the Mexican American Second Generation." *Journal of Ethnic and Migration Studies, 33,* 1-35.

Warren, J. R. (1996). "Educational Inequality among White and Mexican-Origin Adolescents in the American Southwest: 1990." *Sociology of Education, 69,* 142-158.

Wojtkiewicz, R. A. & Donato, K. M. (1995). "Hispanic Educational Attainment: The Effects of Family Background and Nativity." *Social Forces, 74,* 559-574.

Zhou, M. (1997). "Segmented Assimilation: Issues, Controversies, and Recent Research on the New Second Generation." *International Migration Review, 31,* 975-1008.

Zhou, Min. (2009). *Contemporary Chinese America: Immigration, Ethnicity, and Community Transformation*. Philadelphia: Temple University Press.

Zhou, M. & Bankston, C. L. (1998). *Growing Up American: How Vietnamese Children Adapt to Life in the United States*. New York: Russell Sage Foundation.

In: Race and Ethnicity
Editor: Jonathan K. Crennan, pp. 179-196

ISBN: 978-1-60692-099-2
© 2010 Nova Science Publishers, Inc.

Chapter 6

RACIAL DISPARITIES IN THE MEDICAL CARE OF WOMEN WITH BREAST CANCER

M. S. Simon,[1,2,] N. Petrucelli,[1] and T. L. Albrecht,[1,3]*

[1]Division of Hematology and Oncology, Karmanos Cancer Institute at Wayne State University, Detroit, MI, USA
[2]Population Studies and Prevention Program, Karmanos Cancer Institute at Wayne State University, Detroit, MI, USA
[3]Communication and Behavioral Oncology Program, Karmanos Cancer Institute at Wayne State University, Detroit, MI, USA

ABSTRACT

Breast cancer incidence rates are higher among white than African-American (AA) women in the USA, although mortality rates from breast cancer are higher among AA women. Many published studies have shown trends towards younger age at diagnosis, worse prognostic features and lower survival rates for AA and other ethnic minority women with breast cancer compared with white women. Other studies have reported on racial and ethnic differences in patterns of care for women with breast cancer, suggesting that unequal access to care may in part explain the noted disparity in survival. While debate continues as to the relative degree in which tumor biology vs. socioeconomic factors influence racial differences in survival, cultural and behavioral differences play at least some role, and can partially explain the noted disparity in breast cancer survival seen among different racial and ethnic groups. Approximately 5 to 10% of all breast cancer in this country is associated with known hereditary mutations in the *BRCA1* and *BRCA2* genes, meaning nearly 22,000 breast cancer cases diagnosed per year are due to mutations in these cancer susceptibility genes. Hereditary breast cancer is more common among women with early age at diagnosis and is also more common among certain ethnic groups. While AA women are more likely to develop breast cancer at a younger age than white women, cancer risk assessment and testing for hereditary breast cancer syndromes

* Corresponding author: Professor of Medicine and Oncology, Barbara Ann Karmanos Cancer Institute, Room 4221 HWCRC, 4100 John R, Detroit MI, 48201, (313) 576-8727 – office, (313) 576-8764 – fax, Simonm@ karmanos.org

is underutilized among AA women compared to non-minority women. It is incumbent on health care professionals to help develop solutions to the inequities in access to medical care for women with breast cancer in order to decrease the gap in breast cancer outcomes seen in this country. One way to achieve this is to improve access to screening and cancer risk assessment for all eligible women, and to make state of the art cancer treatment available for all women affected with breast cancer.

INTRODUCTION

Compared to whites, at every point of their life-span, AAs have greater morbidity and mortality from all causes of disease [1-7]. Cancer is a significant cause of morbidity and mortality in the AA population with AAs sharing a disproportionate share of the cancer burden in this country [5;8;9]. Recent statistics show higher death rates among AA men and women for the four major causes of cancer compared to any other racial or ethnic group studied [10].

Breast cancer is the most common cause of cancer among women in the US. While breast cancer incidence is higher among white than AA women, mortality due to breast cancer is higher among AA women [10;11]. Many published reports have shown trends towards younger age at diagnosis, worse prognostic features and lower survival rates for AA women with breast cancer compared with white women [12]. Other reports have documented racial and ethnic differences in patterns of care, suggesting that unequal access may in part explain the noted disparity in survival [13]. While debate continues as to the relative degree in which tumor biology vs. socioeconomic factors influence survival differences, cultural and behavioral differences play at least some role in access to care, and can partially explain the noted racial disparity in breast cancer survival. For society as a whole, health inequalities are a leading indicator of worsening social and economic quality of life, suggesting that racial disparities in breast cancer treatment and survival should be a matter of high priority for the public health agenda in this country [14].

The Effect of Race and Age on Breast Cancer Incidence and Mortality

According to the American Cancer Society (ACS) 1 in 3 women in the US will develop cancer sometime during their lifetime [15]. In 2005 there were an estimated 211,240 newly diagnosed cases of invasive female breast cancer, and 40,410 deaths from breast cancer in the US, making breast cancer the most common cause of cancer, and second leading cause of cancer related death among women [16]. As reported in the National Cancer Institute's (NCI) Surveillance Epidemiology and End Results (SEER) Program, there are noted racial differences in breast cancer rates, with higher incidence seen among white women, and higher mortality among AA women [17]. Between 1996 and 2000, age-adjusted breast cancer incidence rates (per 100,000 women) were 140.8 for white women and 121.7 for AA women, resulting in a 14 percent higher overall incidence among white women. During the same time period, age adjusted mortality rates (per 100,000 women) were 27.2 for white women compared to 35.9 for AA women resulting in a 25 percent greater mortality from breast cancer among AA women [18].

According to the SEER data, between 1990 and 2002, there were no significant changes in breast cancer incidence rates for both white and AA women, and for the same time period, mortality rates have dropped presumably due to improvements in available treatments. On closer evaluation though, the gap in mortality for white and AA women has widened over time, and higher mortality rates first seen among AA women in the early 1980's, have increased for the subsequent two decades. From 1990 through 2002 mortality due to breast cancer had dropped by 2.4 percent among white women, and only by 1.0 percent among AA women [15;19]. This racial discrepancy in mortality was also seen in a study of women treated in the US Department of Defense Healthcare system [20].

While mortality from breast cancer is higher among AA women for all reported age groups, there is a reversal in incidence rates by race beginning at about age 40, with incidence slightly higher among AA than white women younger than age 35 at diagnosis, and increasingly higher for white than AA women after age 40 [17]. This cross-over in incidence in the mid-to late 30's was also seen in reports of breast cancer risk based on data from two large case-control studies [21;22]. It is unclear why an age-related cross-over in incidence occurs. Possible explanations include age related differences in childbearing [23], other risk factor patterns related to age [24;25] or other socio-cultural influences [26]. In an analysis of risk-factor patterns among white and AA participants in the population based Carolina Breast Cancer Study, multiparity was associated with an increased risk of cancer among younger AA women but not younger white women. There was also noted to be racial variability in the presence of other reproductive variables (age at first full-term pregnancy and nulliparity) both of which have an influence on breast cancer risk [24].

Based on SEER data collected between 2000 and 2002, a woman's estimated lifetime risk of developing invasive breast cancer through age 80 is 13.2 percent or 1 in 8 [15]. Gail et al utilized data collected through the Breast Cancer Detection and Demonstration Project and computed lifetime breast risk estimates based on age, family history, prior breast biopsies and reproductive history initially only for white women [27;28], and later expanded to include AA women [29]. Claus et al utilized data from the Cancer and Steroid Hormone (CASH) Study to estimate lifetime breast cancer risks for both white and AA women with a family history of breast cancer [22]. These risk estimates were based on family history information collected from a population that consisted of female relatives of index cases diagnosed between the ages 20 and 54 years of whom only 10% (490) were AA. From a genetic analysis of the CASH data based on white participants [30], Claus et al. published lifetime breast cancer risk estimates stratified by the number and types of affected relatives and ages at diagnosis of those relatives [31]. More recently cancer risk estimates for both white and AA women with a family history of breast cancer were analyzed using information derived from the National Institute of Child Health and Human Development's (NICHD) Women's Contraceptive and Reproductive Experiences (CARE) Study [21]. This population-based case-control study was conducted among women aged 35 to 64 years and over-sampled AA women in order to permit sufficient numbers to address race-specific questions (30% AA). Based on CARE data, white women with a family history of breast cancer have a cumulative life-time risk of 22.4% (S.E. 1.25) compared to 14.5% (1.45) for AA women. These statistics highlight the importance of understanding differences in the etiology of breast cancer by race.

The Impact of Race on Breast Cancer Survival

A number of population-based studies using SEER data [32-45] as well as studies of smaller populations from hospitals and/or other health care systems [20;46-51] and data from randomized controlled trials [52], have revealed worse prognostic features and lower survival rates for AA and other ethnic minority women with breast cancer compared with white women. A recent meta-analysis of 20 studies all which utilized some measure of socioeconomic status (SES) in their analytic models, found that AA women with breast cancer had a considerably significant excess risk of overall death (mortality hazard, 1.27; 95% CI, 1.18 to 1.38) and death due to breast cancer (mortality hazard, 1.18; 95% CI, 1.19 to 1.29) [12]. According to SEER, overall survival trends for women with breast cancer have slowly improved over the past several decades, although disparities by race remain, with recent 5-year adjusted survival for AA women with breast cancer reported as 76 percent, compared to 90 percent for white women [17]. The degree to which racial differences in survival are due to inherent biologic and/or genetic differences, versus social economic differences and/or factors related to quality of medical care received remains to be determined [53].

The majority of reports which have evaluated breast cancer survival indicate that that AA compared to white women are more likely to be diagnosed at a younger age, more advanced stage, and with prognostic features associated with more aggressive disease [33-39;41-43;47;54] [20;45;48-52;55]. As reported in an analysis of 9,321 incident cases of female invasive breast cancer diagnosed between 1988 and 1992 in the Detroit Metropolitan Area [33], AA women were more likely than white women to be diagnosed at a younger age (33% of AA women diagnosed at age 50 or less, compared to 24% of white women (p< 0.001)), to have larger diameter tumors at the time of diagnosis (almost twice as many AA vs. white had tumors greater than 5 cm in greatest diameter, p< 0.001) and to present with tumor involvement of the axillary lymph nodes (36% of AA compared with 31% of white, p< 0.001). AA women were also more likely than white women to have poorly differentiated tumors (26% vs. 16% p< 0.001), ER negative tumors (17% vs. 9% p< 0.001) and PR negative tumors (20% vs. 14% p< 0.001).

A number of studies have reported on racial differences in the patterns of care received among women with breast cancer [33;35;38;39;42;43;45;48;51;52;54;56;57] [13]. In the analysis conducted among women diagnosed in the Detroit metropolitan area [33], AA women were more likely than white women to undergo mastectomy (69% of AA women compared to 66% of white women p<0.001) and less likely to have gone through breast conserving surgery (29% of AA women had lumpectomy vs. 32% of white women p<0.001). Only 18% of the AA women underwent lumpectomy followed by radiation compared to 22% of white women (p< 0.001). Other reports have shown similar findings. Li et al [42] reported that AA and other ethnic minority women were less likely than white women to receive a first course of surgical and radiation treatment that met current standards of care. In another SEER based analysis, AA women were similarly less likely to receive breast radiotherapy [38]. In two prior reports of treatment utilization in the Detroit Metropolitan area, AA women were less likely to undergo lumpectomy and radiation therapy [57], or lumpectomy alone [56]. These findings suggest that AA women are more likely than white women to receive more aggressive treatment (i.e. mastectomy), and less likely to receive lumpectomy or radiation following lumpectomy.

Other studies have evaluated the effect of various measures of socioeconomic differences among women with breast cancer [21;35;43;45;48;50-52;54] [58]. In the context of a population based study, SES is generally not available on an individual basis, but rather a measure of SES is derived for a particular geographic region and used as a proxy for individual-specific SES. One methodology used to develop an aggregate SES measure is to utilize a person's address at the time of diagnosis to derive a SES Group variable. This methodology involves a geo-coding process that first assigns each individual in the study to a census block-group number [55;59].

Variables which have been used to estimate SES Groups include occupation, poverty status, educational attainment and age. The U.S. Census Bureau utilized 13 occupational categories of which 5 are defined as "professional" and the remaining 8 identified as "working class". Professional block-groups are defined as those geographic areas where 34% or more of employed persons have supervisory or executive positions. Working-class block-groups are defined as those areas in which 66% or more of employed persons report a working class occupation, such as administrative support or laborer. In regards to poverty status, poor block-groups are defined as those in which 20% or more of the population is below the poverty level. The poverty level in 1990 (corresponding to the 1990 census) is defined as an income of $12,674 for family of four. Educational attainment has been defined as whether a block group includes at least 75% or more of the individuals age 25 and older who have completed at least a high school education (educated block group) vs. an undereducated block groups defined as those with < 75% completed a high school.

In the Detroit SEER study [33], the SES Groups used for the analysis were computed for each individual woman according to the method of Krieger et al [60]. Women were assigned to one of four SES Groups which included: 1) Working, Poor (WP); 2) Working, Non-poor, Undereducated (WNP-UE); 3) Working, Non-poor, Educated (WNP-E); and 4) Professional (P). This analysis revealed that AA women were more likely to reside in a census area that had a higher proportion of individuals categorized as WP and a lower proportion categorized as P (62% of AA women resided in a WP census block and 19% resided in P census block). In contrast, 8% of CA women resided in a WP block, and 46% resided in a P block (p< 0.001). While grouped census data only serves as a proxy for individual SES, others have argued that neighborhood SES also functions as a predictor of access to care [61].

In the Detroit analysis [33] the unadjusted HR (95% CI) of death for AA compared to white women with breast cancer was 1.28 (1.15-1.44) for local, and 1.45 (1.30-1.61) for regional stage disease. After taking into account age, tumor size, axillary lymph node involvement, SES, and treatment, the multivariable adjusted HR (95% CI) of death for AA vs. white women was not significantly different for women with local stage breast cancer 1.07 (0.90-1.27), and was still greater but attenuated for AA vs. white women with regional stage disease 1.27 (1.10-1.46). Of note, women who lived in a census block group ranked as WP or WNP-UE compared to women who resided in a P census block group had the greater risk of death (HR (95% CI) 1.34 (1.13-1.6) and 1.18 (1.03-1.35) respectively for local stage disease, and 1.24 (1.06-1.45) and 1.20 (1.05-1.36) respectively for regional stage disease).

Other investigators have also found that access to care and other socio-demographic factors account at times for a large component of the survival differences seen among AA and white women with breast cancer. Chu et.al. found racial differences in survival for younger women compared with women aged 65 and older, concluding that access to Medicare allowed for better survival among older women with breast cancer [39]. Other studies have shown that adjustment for prior mammography use [47], treatment [38] or SES [32;35;44;45;50;52] account for a significant component of the racial or ethnic differences in survival. Because SES is known to be a significant predictor of stage at diagnosis [55], and stage at diagnosis is a strong predictor of survival, it is not surprising that the results of survival studies have found an attenuation of racial differences in survival after adjustment for SES. These results suggest that known prognostic and predictive factors as well as SES account for at least some of the racial differences in survival.

In order to evaluate racial differences in treatment and survival among a group of women who because of where they were treated, should have all had equal access to state of the art medical care, we evaluated patterns of care and outcomes among women with breast cancer treated at a single large NCI funded Comprehensive Cancer Center [54]. The results of this analysis showed no racial differences in treatment utilization as assessed by the use of surgery, radiation therapy, chemotherapy, hormonal therapy, or in the overall costs of treatment (AA women were slightly more likely than white women to undergo lumpectomy). After adjustment for age, stage and hormone receptor status, and the presence of other co-morbid conditions, there were no significant racial differences in breast cancer survival. These results suggest that equal access to care results in comparable survival outcomes. Improvement in screening, early detection and access to good medical care can have a significant on survival among women with breast cancer. Further research is needed to better quantify the impact of SES on breast cancer survival and to evaluate interventions at the community level which might have an impact on racial and SES differences in cancer mortality.

Hereditary Breast and Ovarian Cancer: Racial Differences in Utilization of Genetic Counseling and Testing

Estimates from population-based studies suggest that in 5% to 10% of women with breast cancer, and 10% to 15% of women with ovarian cancer, cancer risk is associated with germ line mutations in highly penetrant susceptibility genes such as *BRCA1* (breast cancer gene 1) and *BRCA2* (breast cancer gene 2). Inherited mutations in *BRCA1* or *BRCA2* confer a significantly increased risk of both breast and ovarian cancer. Women harboring a mutation in either gene have up to an 87% lifetime risk of developing breast cancer, and a 40% lifetime risk of ovarian cancer for *BRCA1* mutation carriers, and greater than 20% lifetime risk for *BRCA2* carriers [62]. In addition, breast cancer survivors with an inherited mutation in *BRCA1/2* are at a substantial risk to develop a second breast cancer, as well as an ovarian cancer and other types of cancer. Men who carry *BRCA1/2* mutations are at increased risk to develop breast, prostate, and pancreatic cancer [63-65].

Genetic testing to identify deleterious *BRCA1* and *BRCA2* mutations became available in 1996, and can provide individual information about breast and ovarian cancer risk, and thus can influence decisions about risk reduction strategies. For example, prophylactic mastectomy has been demonstrated to reduce the risk of breast cancer, by more than 90 percent [66]. It has also been shown that prophylactic oophorectomy in *BRCA1/2* carriers reduces the risk of ovarian cancer by as much as 96%, and if performed pre-menopausally reduces the risk of breast cancer risk by 53% [67]. Prophylactic oophorectomy has also been shown to extend life expectancy by more than 3 years, and has been found to be widely acceptable to women with *BRCA1/2* mutations who have completed childbearing [68;69]. In addition to medical management implications for the person undergoing genetic testing, the identification of a *BRCA1/2* mutation within a family enables other family members to better define their own cancer risk secondary to the autosomal dominant fashion in which these mutations are inherited.

Predictive genetic testing for hereditary breast and ovarian cancer is not without risks or limitations. Mutations in the *BRCA1/2* genes are rare and explain only about 7 to 10 percent of all cases of breast and ovarian cancer. While the presence of a *BRCA1/2* mutation does not guarantee that an individual will develop cancer, it is impossible to predict if and/or when cancer will develop. Moreover, testing is expensive and therefore, may be inaccessible to individuals with few financial resources. Concerns about genetic discrimination exist however there are no well-documented cases of genetic discrimination in regards to cancer genetic testing [70]. Finally, the psychosocial ramifications of genetic testing have been recognized, in both the genetics and oncology communities. Accordingly, not all women with a family history of breast and/or ovarian cancer will choose to undergo genetic counseling to discuss the risks, benefits, and limitations of *BRCA1/2* testing.

Genetic counseling and testing may be especially beneficial for AA women who are at a greater risk of developing early-onset breast cancer and have higher breast cancer mortality rates when compared to their white counterparts [71]. This may result in added benefits from prevention and early detection in the AA community. Thus, there is no clear clinical rationale why utilization of genetic counseling and testing should differ for AA and white women with a family history of breast or ovarian cancer. Furthermore, although the published data are sparse, several studies have suggested that the prevalence of *BRCA1/2* mutations in AA hereditary breast cancer families may be similar to that in white hereditary breast cancer families [72]. Therefore, racial differences in the use of *BRCA1/2* counseling and testing cannot be directly attributed to differences in the clinical utility of testing.

Little is known about the determinants of the use of genetic testing in the general population, including racial differences and disparities in interest and utilization. To assess the association between race and use of genetic counseling for *BRCA1/2* testing among women at risk of carrying a *BRCA1/2* mutation, Armstrong et al conducted a case-control study of 408 women with a family history of breast or ovarian cancer [73]. It was found that white women had almost 5 times the chance of undergoing *BRCA1/2* cancer genetic counseling as AA women. The noted disparity in utilization of counseling was not explained by differences in a woman's predicted probability of carrying a *BRCA1/2* mutation, SES, cancer risk perception and worry, attitudes about the risks and benefits of *BRCA1/2* testing, or primary care physician discussions regarding *BRCA1/2* testing. Other studies have demonstrated racial differences in attitudes about genetic testing, as well as racial differences in cancer risk perception, and interest in education and counseling about *BRCA1/2* testing in a research setting [74-77]. A number of studies have reported that AA women have more concerns about the limitations and risks of testing compared to white women, with a greater proportion of AA women reporting worry that testing would be too difficult to handle emotionally and might have a significant effect on family members [74] [78]. Other studies have found that AA women had more concerns regarding confidentiality of test results [78;79]. There is evidence that AA women who declined *BRCA1/2* counseling were more likely to anticipate that they would feel ashamed, singled out, and that others would view them negatively if they were found to carry a *BRCA1/2* mutation, compared to women who accepted counseling [80]. The Armstrong study; however, provides some of the first empirical evidence of a racial disparity in utilization of genetic testing in clinical practice, but the authors conclude that other variables may be contributing to this disparity.

There are several empiric reasons to believe that racial disparities in the use of predictive genetic testing are likely to exist. Disparities have been demonstrated in many areas of health care and may be most significant when new technologies such as genetic testing are being considered. In a report entitled *"Unequal Treatment: Understanding Racial and Ethnic Disparities in Health Care"* published by the Institute of Medicine [81], the authors emphasize that the advent of new technologies has the potential to increase health care disparities even more than what already exists. The use of genetic counseling and testing for primary cancer prevention is yet another area of health care in which racial and ethnic disparities may be predicted to intensify.

Health care related-distrust has been demonstrated to be higher among AA than white women and may serve as a major barrier to use of medical care. As an example, AA men and women have been the targets of selective testing for genetic traits such as mass screening for sickle cell trait as part of the National Sickle Cell Anemia Control Act of 1972 [82] [83]. While this legislation was originally intended to increase the availability of medical services to AA who carry this trait, this mass screening program has resulted in further discrimination and reinforcement of unfavorable racial stereotypes resulting in insurance and job discrimination. This historical legacy may at least partially contribute to suspected trepidation experienced among AA women with a family history of breast or ovarian cancer in regards to genetic technology, even when a better understanding of hereditary cancer risk may have significant health implications.

Some populations may be particularly likely to distrust genetic testing because of prior attempts to label certain racial groups as genetically inferior. Others may feel that the assessment of genetic risk may defy one's basic religious belief that medical conditions or predispositions are viewed as part of "God's plan" and that new technology may disrupt this plan [82]. There is evidence that when queried, AA compared to white women are more likely to agree that genetic testing is used to show that their ethnic group is not as good as others, to interfere with the way God meant for people to be, and to interfere with the natural order of life [84]. These same women were more likely compared to white women to agree that genetic testing allows scientists and doctors to "play God". The impact of religious beliefs on the utilization of genetic services is an area which needs further exploration.

Racial disparities in the use of *BRCA1/2* counseling and testing may also reflect differences in the characteristics of the primary care physicians who take care of AA and white women rather than differences in the characteristics of the women themselves. It has been shown that AAs are less likely to be cared for by primary care physicians that are board certified and are more likely to be cared for by physicians that report difficulty in their ability to deliver high quality medical care [85]. In a recent study Freedman et al [86] found that 51% of 1,251 physicians in the USA felt qualified to recommend genetic counseling to their patients. Among primary care physicians, only 40% felt qualified to recommend genetic counseling. Therefore, the role of the physician in identifying and referring high-risk women for cancer genetic counseling and testing cannot be underestimated.

Explanations for racial disparities in the use of cancer genetic testing may be further explained by the results of the 2000 National Health Interview Survey [87]. The results indicated that in regards to their perceived risk of breast cancer and ovarian cancer that AA controls had consistently lower scores than their white counterparts indicating that a greater proportion reported "less than average" risk. In the National Health Interview Survey, investigators found that 49.9% of white women had reported that they had ever heard of genetic testing for cancer susceptibility compared to only 32.9% of AA participants. These findings suggest that the average AA woman underestimates her risk of breast cancer and are generally less aware of genetic testing technology as a way of assessing personal risk.

In a focus group session conducted at the University of Chicago, Matthews AK et al [88] found that virtually half (48%) of their AA participants with a strong family history of cancer reported rarely discussing cancer-related issues with their family members, and that none had prior awareness of breast cancer genetics, genetic counseling, or of the *BRCA1/2* genes. These findings of poor personal knowledge of risk, and limited information regarding cancer genetics are likely related to the lower utilization of genetic services by AAs. Until efforts are made to improve the racial, ethnic, and socioeconomic disparities that contribute to unequal access and utility of preventive medical care, the benefits gained from cancer risk assessment, genetic counseling and testing will not be fully realized. Only by advancing our ability to identify and characterize cancer risk in all Americans can steps be taken to effectively reduce racial disparities in health outcomes.

Sociodemographic Influences on Racial Disparities

Low rates of participation in cancer screening and treatment protocols including early termination of chemotherapy by the patients themselves [89] contribute directly to health disparities experienced by urban AAs, particularly those aged 55 and older, as does lack of access to newer medical treatments [90]. This group is characterized by relatively higher rates of poverty and co-morbid medical conditions as well as lower overall SES [91]. AA women are also less likely to engage in primary prevention behaviors such as exercise, smoking cessation, and maintaining a healthy weight [92], important because smoking and lack of physical activity are both associated with cancer risk [93]. Relative to whites, AAs take greater risks with their health [94]. AA breast cancer patients are also less likely to seek cancer related information from sources such as the Internet [95].

Disparities also exist among women who survive breast cancer. AA breast cancer survivors report significantly more pain, other symptomotology, and basic functional difficulties [96]. AA women with invasive breast cancer still have significantly lower survivorship rates even when they report having access to care and adequate insurance [97]. Genetic testing for breast cancer among AA relatives poses further difficulties. Families, though large, are often geographically separated and attitudes, beliefs and lack of social support mitigate against the motivation to undergo genetic testing and obtain information about genetic predisposition [98]. As a result of poorer health care across a lifetime, combined with documented and perceived barriers to care, older AA women and men distrust much of the health system. This lack of trust directly affects rates of participation in health research, including community screening and treatmen. Specifically, AAs are more suspicious about medical testing [77], and are more likely to harbor misconceptions about medical treatments, and procedures [99].

Racial Disparities in Mammography Screening

Studies show that active and sustained engagement in screening programs appears to occur as part of a set of preferred health practices for healthy AA and healthy white women alike. Having recent contact with a physician and participation in other secondary prevention activities (e.g., pap smears, dental checkups) together with the belief that annual breast screening for early detection improves health status was associated with maintaining a schedule for routine mammograms [90]. Conversely, lack of screening has been correlated with self-reported poor health [90], lack of access to health insurance [100], fear of mastectomy [101], fatalism or belief that a breast cancer diagnosis inevitably results in death, as well as drug and domestic abuse [102;103] [104].

Church-based education programs have been touted as economically effective for increasing mammography usage among rural AA women, given that barriers to mammography reported by this group of women included lack of a perceived need for early detection, a view of mammography as "embarrassing", and religious beliefs related to mortality and "God's Will" [105]. Religious beliefs also accounts for the past refusal by AA women to participate in a breast cancer prevention trial, asserting that faith was more important for preventing cancer than taking drugs [106]. Finally, under-representation of AA women in mammography screening programs is a factor in disparities regarding late stage at diagnoses. The fact that race was found to be a significant and independent predictor of the lack of medical follow-up after an abnormal screening result is particularly disturbing [107].

Racial Disparities in Regards to Provider-Patient Communications

A more complicated and controversial source of health disparities is based in the breadth and quality of interactions between AA breast cancer patients and their physicians or other health providers. The disparate treatment accorded patients may range from a relatively straightforward question of whether or not the physician is recommending screening, to the extent to which providers are reassuring survivors in ways that enhance their cognitive and emotional well being, to dynamics that involve stereotyping or other biases that result in unequal treatment [108] [109].

Physician recommendations are known to influence behavior, whether it concerns screening, treatment, or accrual to clinical trials [110;111]. A recent study by Garber and Chiasson [112] showed that AA women who reported receiving a recommendation from their physician for breast cancer screening were eight times more likely to have actually obtained a mammogram. However, the investigators also found that U.S.-born AA women as opposed to those born in the Caribbean were more likely to report receiving a recommendation, clearly a potential source of disparity.

The reason for health disparities across diseases that was given the most attention in the report of the Study Committee of the Institute of Medicine (IOM) [109] was that quality of health care provided to AA and other racial/ethnic minorities is inferior to that provided to white patients. The conclusion in the report was that "in almost every identifiable respect the quality of health care provided to ethnic minorities was poorer and less effective than that provided to the European-American majority". The Committee argued that one way this was manifested was that providers may be treating "majority group" and "minority group" patients differently, with minorities disadvantaged in the level of health care received.

The Committee identified ways in which providers' can engage in "discriminatory patterns of healthcare." These include holding biases against minorities, and engaging in stereotypes about the behavior or health of minorities. Health providers may react differently to AA and white patients, according to the report [113]. Cline and McKenzie [114] reviewed the literature on physician-patient communication and strongly suggested that this occurs in physician-patient interactions. For example, van Ryn and Burke [115] found that physicians believe AA are less likely to comply with treatment recommendations and more likely to behave in ways that will interfere with their recovery.

To the extent that these processes are implicit or explicit in patient-provider encounters is likely a fundamental source of breast cancer disparities. Interactions with providers span the spectrum of women's health, including primary prevention (physical activity, diet), secondary prevention (routine and regular breast exams and mammography) to diagnostic follow-up, treatment decision making, medical care, and survivorship. If any or all of these points of contact are disrupted, particularly for AA women, either by lack of communication, system breakdowns, or interpersonal biases/stereotypes, it is clear that affected patients will disproportionately suffer.

CONCLUSIONS

Although breast cancer is more common among white than AA women, AA women are more likely to die as a result of breast cancer and are somewhat more likely to develop breast cancer at a younger age. AA women are more likely than white women to present with more aggressive and more advanced stage breast cancer and despite adjustment for stage, survival rates are generally worse among AA women. Much of the disparities in survival are due to lack of access to necessary health care resources. Genetic counseling and genetic testing for hereditary breast and ovarian cancer has the potential to identify individuals at higher risk for both breast and ovarian cancer, although these services are underutilized in the AA community in part due to lack of trust in the health care system. Much of the work in health care disparities centers on socioeconomic differences and the lack of availability of adequate resources. Central to the proper care of women with breast is the relationship between provider and patient. To the extent that miscommunication based on ethnic differences may disrupt this relationship there may be a major impact on how medical care is delivered. Further work is needed to have a better understanding of how health care providers can decrease disparities experienced by women with breast cancer who come from different ethnic or racial backgrounds.

REFERENCES

Health issues in the black community. San Francisco: Jossey-Bass, 2006.

Freeman, VL; Durazo-Arvizu, R; Keys, LC; Johnson, MP; Schafernak, K; Patel, VK. Racial differences in survival among men with prostate cancer and comorbidity at time of diagnosis. *Am J Public Health*, 2004, 94(5), 803-808.

Life in black America. Newbury Park: Sage Publications, 1991.

Jackson, JS; Sellers, S. African American health over the life course: A multidimensional framework. In: Kato PM; Mann T; editors. *Handbook of diversity issues in health psychology*. New York: Plenum Press, 1996, 301-317.

LaVeist, TA. African Americans and health policy: Strategies for a multiethnic society. In: Jackson JS; editor. *New directions: African Americans in a diversifying nation*. Washington, DC: National Policy Association, 2000, 144-161.

Rauscher, GH; Earp, JA; O'Malley, M. Relation between intervention exposures, changes in attitudes, and mammography use in the North Carolina Breast Cancer Screening Program. *Cancer Epidemiol Biomarkers Prev*, 2004, 13(5), 741-747.

Yabroff, KR; Breen, N; Vernon, SW; Meissner, HI; Freedman, AN; Ballard-Barbash, R. What factors are associated with diagnostic follow-up after abnormal mammograms? Findings from a U.S. National Survey. *Cancer Epidemiol Biomarkers Prev*, 2004, 13(5), 723-732.

Merrill, RM; Weed, DL. Measuring the public health burden of cancer in the United States through lifetime and age-conditional risk estimates. *Ann Epidemiol*, 2001, 11(8), 547-553.

Glanz, K; Croyle, RT; Chollette, VY; Pinn VW. Cancer-related health disparities in women. *Am J Public Health*, 2003, 93(2), 292-298.

Weir, HK; Thun, MJ; Hankey, BF; Ries, LA; Howe, HL; Wingo, PA; et al. Annual report to the nation on the status of cancer, 1975-2000, featuring the uses of surveillance data for cancer prevention and control. *J Natl Cancer Inst*, 2003, 95(17), 1276-1299.

Gloeckler Ries, LA; Reichman, ME; Lewis, DR; Hankey, BF; Edwards, BK. Cancer survival and incidence from the Surveillance, Epidemiology, and End Results (SEER) program. *Oncologist*, 2003, 8(6), 541-552.

Newman, LA; Griffith, KA; Jatoi, I; Simon, MS; Crowe, JP; Colditz, GA. Meta-analysis of survival in African American and white American patients with breast cancer: ethnicity compared with socioeconomic status. *J Clin Oncol*, 2006, 24(9), 1342-1349.

Shavers, VL; Brown, ML. Racial and ethnic disparities in the receipt of cancer treatment. *J Natl Cancer Inst*, 2002, 94(5), 334-357.

Miringoff, M; Miringoff, ML. *The social health of the nation: How American is really doing.*, New York: Oxford University Press, 1999.

American Cancer Society. *Breast Cancer Facts and Figures* 2005-2006. 3. 2005. Atlanta, Georgia, American Cancer Society Inc. Ref Type: Report.

Jemal, A; Murray, T; Ward, E; Samuels, A; Tiwari, RC; Ghafoor, A; et al. Cancer statistics, *CA Cancer J Clin*, 2005, 55(1), 10-30.

SEER Cancer Statistics Review, 1975-2002. Ries LAG, Eisner MP, Kosary CL, editors. 2005. Bethesda, MD, National Cancer Institute. Ref Type: Report

Ries, LAG; Reichman, ME; Lewis, DR; Hankey, BF; Edwards, BK. Cancer survival and incidence from the Surveillance, Epidemiology, and End Results (SEER) program. *Oncologist*, 2003, 8(6), 541-552.

Surveillance, Epidemiology, and End Results (SEER) Program (www.seer.cancer) SEER*Stat Database: Mortality-All COD, public-Use with State, total U.S. for expanded races (1990-2002). 2005. National Cancer Institute, DCCPS, Surveillance Research PRogram, Cancer Statistics Branch. Ref Type: Report

Jatoi, I; Becher, H; Leake, CR. Widening disparity in survival between white and African-American patients with breast carcinoma treated in the U. S. Department of Defense Healthcare system. *Cancer*, 2003, 98(5), 894-899.

Simon, MS; Korczak, JF; Yee, CL; Malone, K; Ursin, G; Bernstein, L; et al. Breast cancer risk estimates for relatives of Caucasian and African American women with breast cancer in the Women's Contraceptive and Reproductive Experiences (CARE) Study. *J Clin Oncol*, 2006, 24(16), 2498-2504.

Claus, EB; Risch, NJ; Thompson, WD. Age at onset as an indicator of familial risk of breast cancer. *Am J Epidemiol*, 1990, 131(6), 961-972.

Palmer, JR; Wise, LA; Horton, NJ; Adams-Campbell, LL; Rosenberg, L. Dual effect of parity on breast cancer risk in African-American women. *J Natl Cancer Inst*, 2003, 95(6), 478-483.

Hall, IJ; Moorman, PG; Millikan, RC; Newman, B. Comparative analysis of breast cancer risk factors among African-American women and White women. *Am J Epidemiol*, 2005, 161(1), 40-51.

Mayberry, RM. Age-specific patterns of association between breast cancer and risk factors in black women, ages 20 to 39 and 40 to 54. *Ann Epidemiol*, 1994, 4(3), 205-213.

Krieger, N. Social class and the black/white crossover in the age-specific incidence of breast cancer: a study linking census-derived data to population-based registry records. *Am J Epidemiol*, 1990, 131(5), 804-814.

Gail, MH; Brinton, LA; Byar, DP; Corle, DK; Green, SB; Schairer, C; et al. Projecting individualized probabilities of developing breast cancer for white females who are being examined annually. *J Natl Cancer Inst*, 1989, 81(24), 1879-1886.

Benichou,. J; Gail, MH; Mulvihill, JJ. Graphs to estimate an individualized risk of breast cancer. *J Clin Oncol*, 1996, 14(1), 103-110.

Euhus, DM. Understanding mathematical models for breast cancer risk assessment and counseling. *Breast J*, 2001, 7(4), 224-232.

Claus, EB; Risch, N; Thompson, WD. Genetic analysis of breast cancer in the cancer and steroid hormone study. *Am J Hum Genet*, 1991, 48(2), 232-242.

Claus, EB; Risch, N; Thompson, WD. Autosomal dominant inheritance of early-onset breast cancer. Implications for risk prediction., *Cancer*, 1994, 73(3), 643-651.

Simon, MS; Severson, RK. Racial differences in survival of female breast cancer in the Detroit metropolitan area., *Cancer*, 1996, 77(2), 308-314.

Simon, MS; Banerjee, M; Crossley-May, H; Vigneau, FD; Noone, A; Schwartz, K. Racial differences in breast cancer survival in the Detroit Metropolitan area. *Breast Cancer Res Treat*, 2005.

Edwards, MJ; Gamel, JW; Vaughan, WP; Wrightson, WR. Infiltrating ductal carcinoma of the breast: the survival impact of race. *J Clin Oncol*, 1998, 16(8), 2693-2699.

O'Malley, CD; Le, GM; Glaser, SL; Shema, SJ; West, DW. Socioeconomic status and breast carcinoma survival in four racial/ethnic groups: a population-based study., *Cancer*, 2003, 97(5), 1303-1311.

Clegg, LX; Li, FP; Hankey, BF; Chu, K; Edwards, BK. Cancer survival among US whites and minorities: a SEER (Surveillance, Epidemiology, and End Results) Program population-based study. *Arch Intern Med*, 2002, 162(17), 1985-1993.

Shavers, VL; Harlan, LC; Stevens, JL. Racial/ethnic variation in clinical presentation, treatment, and survival among breast cancer patients under age, 35. *Cancer* 2003, 97(1), 134-147.

Joslyn, SA. Racial differences in treatment and survival from early-stage breast carcinoma., *Cancer* 2002, 95(8), 1759-1766.

Chu, KC; Lamar, CA; Freeman, HP. Racial disparities in breast carcinoma survival rates: Seperating factors that affect diagnosis from factors that affect treatment., *Cancer*, 2003, 97(11), 2853-2860.

Joslyn, SA. Hormone receptors in breast cancer: racial differences in distribution and survival. *Breast Cancer Res Treat*, 2002, 73(1), 45-59.

Joslyn, SA; West, MM. Racial differences in breast carcinoma survival., *Cancer*, 2000, 88(1), 114-123.

Li, CI; Malone, KE; Daling, JR. Differences in breast cancer stage, treatment, and survival by race and ethnicity. *Arch Intern Med*, 2003, 163(1), 49-56.

Grann, V; Troxel, AB; Zojwalla, N; Hershman, D; Glied, SA; Jacobson, JS. Regional and racial disparities in breast cancer-specific mortality. *Soc Sci Med*, 2005.

Delgado, DJ; Lin, WY; Coffey, M. The role of Hispanic race/ethnicity and poverty in breast cancer survival. *P R Health Sci J*, 1995, 14(2), 103-116.

Bradley, CJ; Given, CW; Roberts, C. Race, socioeconomic status, and breast cancer treatment and survival. *J Natl Cancer Inst*, 2002, 94(7), 490-496.

Du, W; Simon, MS. Racial disparities in treatment and survival of women with stage I-III reast cancer at a large academic medical center in Metropolitan Detroit. *Breast Cancer Res Treat*, 2005.

Wojcik, BE; Spinks, MK; Stein, CR. Effects of screening mammography on the comparative survival rates of African American, white, and Hispanic beneficiaries of a comprehensive health care system. *Breast J*, 2003, 9(3), 175-183.

Gwyn, K; Bondy, ML; Cohen, DS; Lund, MJ; Liff, JM; Flagg, EW; et al. Racial differences in diagnosis, treatment, and clinical delays in a population-based study of patients with newly diagnosed breast carcinoma., *Cancer* 2004, 100(8), 1595-1604.

Mancino, AT; Rubio, IT; Henry-Tillman, R; Smith, LF; Landes, R; Spencer, HJ; et al. Racial differences in breast cancer survival: the effect of residual disease. *J Surg Res*, 2001, 100(2), 161-165.

Yood, MU; Johnson, CC; Blount, A; Abrams, J; Wolman, E; McCarthy, BD; et al. Race and differences in breast cancer survival in a managed care population. *J Natl Cancer Inst*, 1999, 91(17), 1487-1491.

Ansell, D; Whitman, S; Lipton, R; Cooper, R. Race, income, and survival from breast cancer at two public hospitals., *Cancer*, 1993, 72(10), 2974-2978.

Gordon, NH; Crowe, JP; Brumberg, DJ; Berger, NA. Socioeconomic factors and race in breast cancer recurrence and survival. *Am J Epidemiol*, 1992, 135(6), 609-618.

Jones, BA; Kasl, SV; Howe, CL; Lachman, M; Dubrow, R; Curnen, MM; et al. African-American/White differences in breast carcinoma: p53 alterations and other tumor characteristics., *Cancer* 2004, 101(6), 1293-1301.

Du, W; Simon, MS. Racial disparities in treatment and survival of women with stage I-III breast cancer at a large academic medical center in metropolitan Detroit. *Breast Cancer Res Treat*, 2005, 91(3), 243-248.

Schwartz, KL; Crossley-May, H; Vigneau, FD; Brown, K; Banerjee, M. Race, socioeconomic status and stage at diagnosis for five common malignancies. *Cancer Causes Control*, 2003, 14(8), 761-766.

Simon, MS; Severson, RK. Racial differences in breast cancer survival: the interaction of socioeconomic status and tumor biology. *Am J Obstet Gynecol*, 1997, 176(6), S233-S239.

Chuba, PJ; Simon, MS. Trends in primary surgical and radiation therapy for localized breast cancer in the Detroit Metropolitan area 1973-1992. *Int J Radiat Oncol Biol Phys*, 1997, 38(1), 103-107.

Baquet, CR; Commiskey, P. Socioeconomic factors and breast carcinoma in multicultural women. *Cancer,* 2000, 88(5 Suppl), 1256-1264.

US Census Bureau. Census of Population and Housing (1990) Summary Tape File 3 TEchnical Documentation. 1991. Washington DC, US Census Bureau. Ref Type: Report.

Krieger, N; Quesenberry, C; Jr., Peng, T; Horn-Ross, P; Stewart, S; Brown, S; et al. Social class, race/ethnicity, and incidence of breast, cervix, colon, lung, and prostate cancer among Asian, Black, Hispanic, and White residents of the San Francisco Bay Area, 1988-92 (United States). *Cancer Causes Control*, 1999, 10(6), 525-537.

Diez-Roux, AV; Kiefe, CI; Jacobs, DR; Jr., Haan, M; Jackson, SA; Nieto, FJ; et al. Area characteristics and individual-level socioeconomic position indicators in three population-based epidemiologic studies. *Ann Epidemiol*, 2001, 11(6), 395-405.

Hughes, C; Fasaye, GA; LaSalle, VH; Finch, C. Sociocultural influences on participation in genetic risk assessment and testing among African American women. *Patient Educ Couns*, 2003, 51(2), 107-114.

Ford, D; Easton, DF; Bishop, DT; Narod, SA; Goldgar, DE. Risks of cancer in BRCA1-mutation carriers. *Breast Cancer Linkage Consortium. Lancet*, 1994, 343(8899), 692-695.

Cancer risks in BRCA2 mutation carriers.The Breast Cancer Linkage Consortium. *J Natl Cancer Inst*, 1999, 91(15), 1310-1316.

Thompson, D; Easton, DF. Cancer Incidence in BRCA1 mutation carriers. *J Natl Cancer Inst*, 2002, 94(18), 1358-1365.

Rebbeck, TR; Friebel, T; Lynch, HT; Neuhausen, SL; van, V; Garber, JE; et al. Bilateral prophylactic mastectomy reduces breast cancer risk in BRCA1 and BRCA2 mutation carriers: the PROSE Study Group. *J Clin Oncol*, 2004, 22(6), 1055-1062.

Rebbeck, TR; Lynch, HT; Neuhausen, SL; Narod, SA; Van't Veer, L; Garber, JE; et al. Prophylactic oophorectomy in carriers of BRCA1 or BRCA2 mutations. *N Engl J Med*, 2002, 346(21), 1616-1622.

Grann, VR; Jacobson, JS; Thomason, D; Hershman, D; Heitjan, DF; Neugut, AI. Effect of prevention strategies on survival and quality-adjusted survival of women with

BRCA1/2 mutations: an updated decision analysis. *J Clin Oncol*, 2002, 20(10), 2520-2529.

Lerman, C; Hughes, C; Croyle, RT; Main, D; Durham, C; Snyder, C; et al. Prophylactic surgery decisions and surveillance practices one year following BRCA1/2 testing. *Prev Med*, 2000, 31(1), 75-80.

Hall, MA; Rich, SS. Laws restricting health insurers' use of genetic information: impact on genetic discrimination. *Am J Hum Genet*, 2000, 66(1), 293-307.

Royak-Schaler, R; deVellis, BM; Sorenson, JR; Wilson, KR; Lannin, DR; Emerson, JA. Breast cancer in African-American families. Risk perception, cancer worry, and screening practices of first-degree relatives. *Ann N Y Acad Sci*, 1995, 768:281-285.

Olopade, OI; Fackenthal, JD; Dunston, G; Tainsky, MA; Collins, F; Whitfield-Broome, C. Breast cancer genetics in *African Americans. Cancer*, 2003, 97(1 Suppl), 236-245.

Armstrong, K; Micco, E; Carney, A; Stopfer, J; Putt, M. Racial differences in the use of BRCA1/2 testing among women with a family history of breast or ovarian cancer. *JAMA*, 2005, 293(14), 1729-1736.

Hughes, C; Gomez-Caminero, A; Benkendorf, J; Kerner, J; Isaacs, C; Barter, J; et al. Ethnic differences in knowledge and attitudes about BRCA1 testing in women at increased risk. *Patient Educ Couns*, 1997, 32(1-2), 51-62.

Hughes, C; Lerman, C; Lustbader, E. Ethnic differences in risk perception among women at increased risk for breast cancer. *Breast Cancer Res Treat*, 1996, 40(1), 25-35.

Lerman, C; Hughes, C; Benkendorf, JL; Biesecker, B; Kerner, J; Willison, J; et al. Racial differences in testing motivation and psychological distress following pretest education for BRCA1 gene testing. *Cancer Epidemiol Biomarkers Prev*, 1999, 8(4 Pt 2), 361-367.

Peters, N; Rose, A; Armstrong, K. The association between race and attitudes about predictive genetic testing. *Cancer Epidemiol Biomarkers Prev*, 2004, 13(3), 361-365.

Donovan, KA; Tucker, DC. Knowledge about genetic risk for breast cancer and perceptions of genetic testing in a sociodemographically diverse sample. *J Behav Med*, 2000, 23(1), 15-36.

Durfy, SJ; Bowen, DJ; McTiernan, A; Sporleder, J; Burke, W. Attitudes and interest in genetic testing for breast and ovarian cancer susceptibility in diverse groups of women in western Washington. *Cancer Epidemiol Biomarkers Prev*, 1999, 8(4 Pt 2), 369-375.

Thompson, HS; Valdimarsdottir, HB; Duteau-Buck, C; Guevarra, J; Bovbjerg, DH; Richmond-Avellaneda, C; et al. Psychosocial predictors of BRCA counseling and testing decisions among urban African-American women. *Cancer Epidemiol Biomarkers Prev*, 2002, 11(12), 1579-1585.

Unequal Treatment: Understanding Racial and Ethnic Disparities in Health Care. 2002. Institute of Medicine, The National Academic Press. Ref Type: Report.

Telfair, J; Nash, KB. African American culture. In: N. L., Fisher, editor. *Cultural and ethnic diversity: a guide for genetic professionals.* Baltimore: The John Hopkins University Press, 2000, 37-59.

Bowman, JE. Technical, genetic, and ethical issues in screening and testing of African-Americans for hemochromatosis. *Genet Test*, 2000, 4(2), 207-212.

Thompson, HS; Valdimarsdottir, HB; Jandorf, L; Redd, W. Perceived disadvantages and concerns about abuses of genetic testing for cancer risk: differences across African American, Latina and Caucasian women. *Patient Educ Couns*, 2003, 51(3), 217-227.

Bach, PB; Pham, HH; Schrag, D; Tate, RC; Hargraves JL. Primary care physicians who treat blacks and whites. *N Engl J Med*, 2004, 351(6), 575-584.

Freedman, AN; Wideroff, L; Olson, L; Davis, W; Klabunde, C; Srinath, KP; et al. US physicians' attitudes toward genetic testing for cancer susceptibility. *Am J Med Genet*, 2003, 120(1), 63-71.

Wideroff, L; Vadaparampil, ST; Breen, N; Croyle, RT; Freedman, AN. Awareness of genetic testing for increased cancer risk in the year 2000 National Health Interview Survey. *Community Genet*, 2003, 6(3), 147-156.

Matthews, AK; Cummings, S; Thompson, S; Wohl, V; List, M; Olopade, OI. Genetic testing of African Americans for susceptibility to inherited cancers: Use of focus groups to determine factors contributing to participation. *Journal of Psychosocial Oncology*, 2000, 18(2), 1-19.

Hershman, D; McBride, R; Jacobson, JS; Lamerato, L; Roberts, K; Grann, VR; et al. Racial disparities in treatment and survival among women with early-stage breast cancer. *J Clin Oncol*, 2005, 23(27), 6639-6646.

Jatoi, I; Anderson, WF; Rao, SR; Devesa, SS. Breast cancer trends among black and white women in the United States. *J Clin Oncol*, 2005, 23(31), 7836-7841.

Maloney, N; Koch, M; Erb, D; Schneider, H; Goffman, T; Elkins, D; et al. Impact of race on breast cancer in lower socioeconomic status women. *Breast J*, 2006, 12(1), 58-62.

Dowda, M; Ainsworth, BE; Addy, CL; Saunders, R; Riner, W. Correlates of physical activity among U.S. young adults, 18 to 30 years of age, from NHANES III. *Ann Behav Med*, 2003, 26(1), 15-23.

Bernstein, L; Patel, AV; Ursin, G; Sullivan-Halley, J; Press, MF; Deapen, D; et al. Lifetime recreational exercise activity and breast cancer risk among black women and white women. *J Natl Cancer Inst*, 2005, 97(22), 1671-1679.

Rosen, AB; Tsai, JS; Downs, SM. Variations in risk attitude across race, gender, and education. *Med Decis Making*, 2003, 23(6), 511-517.

Talosig-Garcia, M; Davis, SW. Information-seeking behavior of minority breast cancer patients: an exploratory study. *J Health Commun*, 2005, 10 Suppl 1:53-64.

Deimling, GT; Sterns, S; Bowman, KF; Kahana, B. The health of older-adult, long-term cancer survivors. *Cancer Nurs*, 2005, 28(6), 415-424.

Field, TS; Buist, DS; Doubeni, C; Enger, S; Fouayzi, H; Hart, G; et al. Disparities and survival among breast cancer patients. *J Natl Cancer Inst Monogr*, 2005, (35), 88-95.

Lee, R; Beattie, M; Crawford, B; Mak, J; Stewart, N; Komaromy, M; et al. Recruitment, genetic counseling, and BRCA testing for underserved women at a public hospital. *Genet Test*, 2005, 9(4), 306-312.

Margolis, ML; Christie, JD; Silvestri, GA; Kaiser, L; Santiago, S; Hansen-Flaschen, J. Racial differences pertaining to a belief about lung cancer surgery: results of a multicenter survey. *Ann Intern Med*, 2003, 139(7), 558-563.

Rosenberg, L; Wise, LA; Palmer, JR; Horton, NJ; Adams-Campbell, LL. A multilevel study of socioeconomic predictors of regular mammography use among African-American women. *Cancer Epidemiol Biomarkers Prev*, 2005, 14(11 Pt 1), 2628-2633.

Fernandez, ME; Palmer, RC; Leong-Wu, CA. Repeat mammography screening among low-income and minority women: a qualitative study. *Cancer Control*, 2005, 12 Suppl 2, 77-83.

Green, BL; Lewis, RK; Wang, MQ; Person, S; Rivers, B. Powerlessness, destiny, and control: the influence on health behaviors of African Americans. *J Community Health*, 2004, 29(1), 15-27.

Moy, B; Park, ER; Feibelmann, S; Chiang, S; Weissman, JS. Barriers to repeat mammography: cultural perspectives of African-American, Asian, and Hispanic women. *Psychooncology*, 2005.

Russell, KM; Perkins, SM; Zollinger, TW; Champion, VL. Sociocultural context of mammography screening use. *Oncol Nurs Forum*, 2006, 33(1), 105-112.

Husaini, BA; Emerson, JS; Hull, PC; Sherkat, DE; Levine, RS; Cain, VA. Rural-urban differences in breast cancer screening among African American women. *J Health Care Poor Underserved*, 2005, 16(4 Suppl A), 1-10.

Paterniti, DA; Melnikow, J; Nuovo, J; Henderson, S; DeGregorio, M; Kuppermann, M et al. "I'm going to die of something anyway": women's perceptions of tamoxifen for breast cancer risk reduction. *Ethn Dis*, 2005, 15(3), 365-372.

Jones, BA; Dailey, A; Calvocoressi, L; Reams, K; Kasl, SV; Lee, C; et al. Inadequate follow-up of abnormal screening mammograms: findings from the race differences in screening mammography process study (United States). *Cancer Causes Control*, 2005, 16(7), 809-821.

Clayton, MF; Mishel, MH; Belyea, M. Testing a model of symptoms, communication, uncertainty, and well-being, in older breast cancer survivors. *Res Nurs Health*, 2006, 29(1), 18-39.

Unequal treatment: Confronting racial and ethnic disparities in health care. Washington, D.C.: The National Academies Press, 2002.

Albrecht, TL; Blanchard, C; Ruckdeschel, JC; Coovert, M; Strongbow, R. Strategic physician communication and oncology clinical trials. *J Clin Oncol*, 1999, 17(10), 3324-3332.

Katz, SJ; Lantz, PM; Janz, NK; Fagerlin, A; Schwartz, K; Liu, L; et al. Patient involvement in surgery treatment decisions for breast cancer. *J Clin Oncol*, 2005, 23(24), 5526-5533.

Garbers, S; Chiasson, MA. Breast cancer screening and health behaviors among African American and Caribbean Women in New York City. *J Health Care Poor Underserved*, 2006, 17(1), 37-46.

Cooper, LA; Roter, DL. Patient-provider communication: The effect of race and ethnicity on process and outcomes of healthcare. In: Smedley BD, editor. *Unequal treatment: Confronting racial and ethnic disparities in health care*. Bethesda: Institute of Medicine, 2003, 552-593.

Cline, RJ; McKenzie, NJ. The many cultures of health care: Taling social structures, talking medical outcomes. In: LD; Jackson, BK; Duffy, editors. *Health communication research: A guide for developments and direction*. Westport: Greenwood Publishing Company, 1998, 57-74.

van Ryn, M; Burke, J. The effect of patient race and socio-economic status on physicians' perceptions of patients. *Soc Sci Med*, 2000, 50(6), 813-828.

In: Race and Ethnicity   ISBN: 978-1-60692-099-2
Editor: Jonathan K. Crennan, pp. 197-216   © 2010 Nova Science Publishers, Inc.

Chapter 7

RACIAL/ETHNIC DISPARITIES IN HYPERTENSION AND DIABETES ASCRIBED TO DIFFERENCES IN OBESITY RATE

Ike S. Okosun[1] and John M. Boltri[2]†*

[1]Institute of Public Health, Georgia State University,
Atlanta, Georgia. USA
[2]Department of Family Medicine, Mercer University School of Medicine,
Macon, Georgia, USA

ABSTRACT

Context

American ethnic minorities, particularly those of African and Hispanic descent have a greater risk of developing hypertension and type 2 diabetes compared to American Whites. Despite the consistency of the epidemiologic evidence of the racial/ethnic variation for these diseases, relatively little is known with confidence about the causes of the non-White dilemma.

Objective

To determine how much of the relative difference in the rates of hypertension and type 2 diabetes between high-risk Blacks and Hispanics and low-risk Whites is attributable to their differences in obesity.

---

* Phone: (404) 651-4249: Fax: (404) 651-1559: Email: iokosun@gsu.edu
† Phone: (478) 633-5758: Fax: (478) 784-5496: Email: Boltri.john@mccg.org

Methods

Data (n=5531) from the 1999-2002 U.S. National Health and Nutrition Examination Surveys were utilized for this analysis. Gender-specific proportions of White to non-White differences in odds of hypertension and diabetes that were due to their relative differences in the prevalence of obesity were estimated using relative attributable risk derived from multiple logistic regression modeling. Statistical adjustment was made for age, education, alcohol intake, education, and physical activity.

Results

50.2% and 30.6% of differences in odds of hypertension between White men and Black men and between White men and Hispanic men, respectively, are attributable to their differences in rates of obesity. The analogous values for diabetes were 70.7% and 57.4% for Black men and Hispanic men. Also, 30.6 % and 13.4% of differences in odds of hypertension between White women and Black women and between White women and Hispanic women, respectively, are associated with their differences in rates of obesity. The analogous values for diabetes are 62.2% and 83.7% for Black women and Hispanic women when compared with White women.

Conclusion

The magnitude of racial/ethnic differences in hypertension and diabetes due to their differences in obesity provides an encouraging reason to continue to implement public health obesity prevention programs in the United States' minority groups. Aggressive programs to reduce obesity and increase physical activity in Blacks and Hispanics may prove useful in reducing racial/ethnic disparities in hypertension and diabetes.

INTRODUCTION

American ethnic minorities, particularly those of African and Hispanic descent have greater risks of developing hypertension and non-insulin dependent diabetes mellitus (type 2 diabetes) compared to American Whites [1-6]. Despite the consistency of the epidemiologic evidence of the racial/ethnic variation for these diseases, relatively little is known with confidence about the causes of the non-White dilemma. The two most common factors explaining racial/ethnic disparities for these diseases are access to health care and treatment [7-8]. However, healthcare access and treatment disparities do not totally explain racial/ethnic differences for these diseases. Understanding reasons for the non-White disadvantage for these diseases is critical for developing effective public health programs in eliminating racial/ethnic disparities as proposed by the United States Healthy People 2010 objective [9].

Racial/Ethnic Differences in Hypertension

The prevalence of hypertension in African Americans is among the highest in the world [10]. The prevalence of hypertension is estimated to be about 37% for African Americans, compared with 20%-25% for non-Hispanic whites [1-2, 10]. African Americans have earlier age of onset and increased rates of consequences of hypertension, including stroke, cardiovascular disease, and renal failure compared to Whites [11]. The estimated prevalence of hypertension is about 28.7% for Hispanic Americans [13]. A review of the recent studies of genetic epidemiology has not exposed unique genotypes that explain hypertension or the disparate impact endured by African and Hispanic Americans [13]. However, the emerging consensus is that environmental factors predominate in their effect and are mutable [3]. Epidemiologic literature has shown that racial/ethnic minorities with hypertension receive less aggressive treatment for their high blood pressure compared to Whites. Indeed, a recent review of medical records of about 1200 patients who had a minimum of two hypertension-related outpatient visits to one of twelve general internal medicine clinics during one year period showed that 80.3% Whites were likely to have therapy intensified compared with 71.5% Latinos [14]. The ethnic differences in therapy intensification from the study were largely due to differences in frequency of clinic visits and in the prevalence of diabetes [14]. The U.S. Veterans Administration study to investigate the contribution of differential access to health care to lower blood pressure control rates in African American compared with White hypertensive patients showed that the ethnic disparity in blood pressure control between Blacks and Whites was approximately 40% less at VA than at non-VA health care sites (6.2% vs 10.2%; P<.01) [4].

Racial/Ethnic Differences in Type 2 Diabetes

Type 2 diabetes in the United States is increasing in adolescents, young adults and in the elderly and there are significant disparities in diabetes with Whites having the lowest rates [15-19]. The prevalence of diabetes is estimated to be 8.4-8.7% for non-Hispanic Whites, 13.3-15.0% for non-Hispanic Blacks, and 9.5-13.8% for Mexican Americans [16, 17]. Diabetes is estimated to be 1.7 to 1.8 times as prevalent in Hispanics and blacks, compared to whites [16]. There is also evidence that Whites with diabetes have better control of their illness compared with Blacks and Hispanics as evidenced by hemoglobin A1c levels [20].

Racial/Ethnic Differences in Obesity

Obesity is increasing dramatically in the United States and most likely contributes substantially to the burden of many chronic health conditions. The National Health and Nutrition Examination Survey (NHANES) data indicate continuing disparities between U.S. adults of racial/ethnic groups in the prevalence of obesity. A similar increasing prevalence of overweight has been observed in U.S. children and adolescents [21]. The prevalence of overweight in US children, defined as a body mass index exceeding the 95th percentile for age and sex increased between 1986 and 1998 [21]. Between the study periods of 1986 and 1998, overweight prevalence increased to 21.5% among African Americans, 21.8% among Hispanics, and 12.3% among non-Hispanic whites [21]. The trends in increased obesity in the US as demonstrated in this study may be due to the shift of energy intake, food portion size and snacking patterns at the population level [22].

Explanatory Power of Obesity for Racial/Ethnic Variations in Hypertension and Diabetes

Obesity has consistently been shown as an important risk factor for racial/ethnic differences in hypertension, since mean body mass index (BMI) levels are higher among these American minorities compared to American Whites [23-29]. In a multi-state screening project examining the relationship between obesity and cardiovascular risk factors in the United States, compared to non-overweight respondents, SBP increased by 13.2 mmHg for severely obese (p < 0.001); by 8.9 mmHg for obese (p < 0.001), and by 5.2 mmHg (p < 0.001) for overweight respondents, respectively [12]. Increases in diabetes have also been observed in conjunction with the rise in obesity [30-32]. The decrease in many cardiovascular risk factors, including high blood cholesterol and high blood pressure at all BMI levels that have been observed in the US is not applicable to what has been observed for diabetes [33]. Unlike these cardiovascular risk factors, the prevalence of diabetes has increased in Whites, Blacks and Hispanics, for the periods between 1976 and 2000 [34]. The increase was concentrated among individuals with BMI of 35 or greater in whom the proportion of cases that were diagnosed increased from approximately 41% to 83% [34].

METHODOLOGIC ISSUES ASSOCIATED WITH STUDYING OBESITY AND RACIAL/ETHNIC VARIATIONS IN DISEASES

The basic methodological issues that are associated with studying racial/ethnic differences in the association of obesity with diseases include lack of consensus in three ways; (1) how to measure and quantify obesity, (2) how to quantify the association of obesity with diseases, and (3) how to measure the impact of obesity on diseases.

Obesity Measurement

One of the unsettled methodological areas in comparing obesity across racial/ethnic groups is the lack of agreement of the BMI cutpoint for obesity. BMI is a height adjusted measure of generalized obesity. It is an anthropometric surrogate measure of body fat that is easy to measure and interpret. Although its cutpoint is critical for triggering public health or clinical action on obesity, the current cutpoint for obesity (BMI of 30 kg/m2 or greater) is somewhat subjective. A BMI of 30 or higher has a different meaning for body fat across racial/ethnic groups [35]. Hence comparing the association of obesity defined by BMI of 30 kg/m^2 or greater with various disorders such as hypertension and diabetes is a subject of disagreement [36]. Indeed, many studies have shown differential predictive values of BMI of 30 kg/m^2 or greater for many cardiovascular and coronary disease risk factors [35, 37]. However, BMI is highly correlated with body fat determined using other methods such as underwater weighing, deuterium dilution, dual-energy X-ray absorptiometry, magnetic resonance and computed tomography [38].

Quantifying Obesity Risk

Studies quantifying the association of obesity risk with diseases are not consistent. Odds ratios and relative risks are the most common statistics seen in epidemiologic literature. In retrospective designs, odds ratios often approximate relative risks if the disease under study is rare. For hypertension that is relatively common in the US, the use of odds ratio in estimating relative risk is questionable. In cross-sectional studies, prevalence odds ratios are often used to quantify the association of obesity with hypertension.

Estimation of odds ratio

The odds ratio compares whether the probability of a certain event is the same for two groups (cases and controls). An odds ratio of 1 implies that the event is equally likely in both groups. An odds ratio that is greater than one implies that the event is more likely in the first group. An odds ratio less than one implies that the event is less likely in the first group. For a dichotomous response variable with outcomes event and nonevent, a dichotomous risk factor variable X takes the value 1 if the risk factor is present and 0 if the risk factor is absent. According to the logistic regression model, the log odds function, $g(X)$, is given by:

$$g(X) = \log \Pr(event \mid X) \div \Pr(noevent \mid X) = \beta_0 + \beta_1 X \qquad [1]$$

The odds ratio φ is defined as the ratio of the odds for those with the risk factor $(X=1)$ to the odds for those without the risk factor $(X=0)$. The log of the odds ratio is given by:

$$\log(\varphi) = \log(\varphi(X=1, X=0)) = g(X=1) - g(X=0) = \beta_1 \qquad [2]$$

The parameter, β_1, associated with X represents the change in the log odds from $X = 0$ to $X = 1$. Thus, the odds ratio is obtained simply by exponentiation of the value of the parameter that is associated with the risk factor. The odds ratio indicates how the odds of the event changes when X changes from 0 to 1. For instance, an odds ratio of 3 means that the odds of an event when $X=1$ is three times the odds of an event when $X=0$.

Estimation of relative risk

In a cohort study individuals with differing exposures to a risk factor are identified and then observed for the occurrence of outcomes over some time period. The incidence rates of the disease of interest are measured and related to estimated exposure levels. Incidence can be measured as a proportion or rate. When measured as a proportion, incidence is identical with risk. It is often regarded as absolute risk. Incidences from two groups can be contrasted in absolute terms (subtracting one incidence from the other) or in relative terms (by division). The absolute comparison of incidence proportions is termed the risk difference while the relative comparison of incidences is called the risk ratio. In simple terms, proportions from two independent groups can be compared using notation for a cross tabulation:

	Disease+	Disease-	Total
Exposure+	A_1	B_1	N_1
Exposure -	A_0	B_0	N_0
Total	M_1	M_0	N

where, A indicates "case" and B indicates "noncase." Subscript 1 denotes "exposed" and subscript 0 denotes "nonexposed." For example, A1 indicates the number of exposed cases, A0 indicates the number of nonexposed cases, and so on. There are N1 exposed subjects and N0 nonexposed subjects. There are N subjects.

To determine the risk ratio, let P_1 represent the incidence proportion (risk) estimate in the exposed group, and let P_0 represent the risk estimate in the nonexposed group. Thus,

$$P_1 = A_1/N_1 \text{ and } P_0 = A_0/N_0 \qquad [3]$$

The risk ratio (RR), also called relative risk is calculated as:

$$RR = P_1/P_0 \qquad [4]$$

RR represents the incidence rate in the exposed group divided by the incidence rate in the unexposed group. The above RR formula can be applied to prevalences, and hence the prevalence ratio can be calculated. The prevalence ratio is equal to the risk ratio when the average duration of disease is the same in the groups, the disease is rare, and the disease does not influence the presence of the exposure.

The risk ratio is a multiplier of risk. For example, a risk ratio of 3.99 is about 4, indicating that the risk in the exposed group is 4 times that of the non-exposed group. The risk ratio can also be viewed as measuring the effect of the exposure in relative terms. The risk ratio above (or below) 1 quantifies the relative increase (or decrease) in risk associated with the exposure. Cohort studies can either be performed prospectively or retrospectively from historical records.

Quantifying Obesity Impact

Population Attributable Risk

The most commonly used statistical and epidemiologic measure of impact of a risk factor on an outcome is population attributable risk [39]. Population attributable (PAR) risk is defined as a population's disease rate that would not occur if the risk factor(s) of interest had been absent [39-41]. Population attributable risk is the portion of the incidence of a disease in the population (exposed and nonexposed) that is due to exposure. The PAR is calculated by subtracting the incidence in the unexposed (Iu) from the incidence in total population (exposed and unexposed) (Ip):

$$PAR = Ip - Iu \qquad [5]$$

Population attributable risk percent (PAR%) is the percent of the incidence of a disease in the population (exposed and nonexposed) that is due to exposure. It is the percent of the incidence of a disease in the population that would be eliminated if exposure were eliminated. The PAR% is calculated by dividing the PAR by the incidence in the total population and then multiplying the product times 100 to obtain a percentage:

$$PAR\% = \frac{Ip - Iu}{Ip} * 100, \text{ or } \frac{PAR}{Ip} \tag{6}$$

In a retrospective study, population attributable risk is often estimated as [40, 41]:

$$\frac{P_E (OR-1)}{1+P_E (OR-1)} * 100 \tag{7}$$

where P_E is the prevalence of risk factor, and OR is the odds ratio comparing individuals with disease with those who do not have disease. The analogous formula for a prospective study is:

$$\frac{I_E (RR-1)}{1+I_E (RR-1)} * 100 \tag{8}$$

where I_E is the incidence of the risk factor, and RR is the relative risk comparing individuals with the disease with those who do not have the disease. Indisputably, estimating the population attributable risk is necessary because it provides the basis for public health disease prevention programs.

Relative attributable risk

An important but often overlooked question in determining the contribution of risk factors to racial/ethnic differences in diseases is, "What fraction of the difference in the rates of disease between high-risk and low-risk groups is due to their differences in the prevalence of the risk factor?" The answer to this question requires the use of a rarely used statistical measure called the relative attributable risk (RAR). First described by Cornfield [42], and subsequently by Breslow and Day [43], RAR is defined as the proportion of the excess disease rate in the high-risk group that would disappear if the high-risk group had the same prevalence of risk factor(s) as the low risk population. RAR is based on the assumption that the relationship between the risk factor(s) and the disease in the high-risk population is causal [42-45]. RAR as a percentage can be estimated using the following formula [44-45]:

$$RAR = \frac{[AR_2 - AR_1] \div [1 - AR_1]}{[R - 1] \div [R]} * 100 \tag{9}$$

where AR_2 and AR_1 denote attributable risks of disease in the high-risk and the low-risk group, respectively. R is the overall prevalence rate of disease and is calculated as:

$$R = [\lambda_2 \sum_{i=0}^{k} P_{2k} \Gamma_k] \div [\lambda_1 \sum_{i=0}^{k} P_{1k} \Gamma_k] = R_0 w \tag{10}$$

where λ_1 and λ_2 are prevalence rates of the disease for the non-exposed in low and high risk populations, respectively. $\Gamma_0 = 1$, $\Gamma_1, \ldots \Gamma_k$ denotes the associated odds ratio which is assessed to apply equally to the high risk and the low risk populations. P_{1k} is the proportion of the low risk population exposed to the risk factor, and P_{2k} for the high risk population. The ratio may be decomposed into the product of t terms, the ratio of rates, $R_0 = [\lambda_2] \div [\lambda_1]$, which would persist if the high and low risk populations have the same pattern of exposure, and a multiplicative factor $w = [\sum P_{2k} \Gamma_k] \div [\sum P_{1k} \Gamma_k]$, which denotes how much R_0 is changed by exposure differences. Termed as a confounding risk ratio, w measures the degree to which the effect of one factor on the prevalence of disease is confounded by the effects of the other factors [46-48].

OBJECTIVE OF STUDY

Many studies investigating the contribution of obesity to racial/ethic differences in deaths or diseases such as hypertension and type 2 diabetes are often restricted to conceptual frameworks where population attributable risks are often estimated in quantifying the role of obesity [49-50]. To our knowledge the use of relative attributable risk to quantify the contribution of obesity to racial/ethnic variation in hypertension and diabetes is rare. Hence, this study sought to determine how much of the relative difference in the rates of hypertension and type 2 diabetes between Blacks and Hispanics and Whites is attributable to differences in their obesity rates.

METHODS

Data from the 1999-2001 National Health and Nutrition Examination Survey (NHANES) collected by the National Center for Health Statistics of the Center for Disease Control and Prevention (CDC) were used for this analysis. The measurement and sampling procedures have been previously described [51-52]. Briefly, the NHANES 1999-2001 is a national, cross-sectional, multistage probability sample of the US civilian, non-institutionalized population, selected using a complex, stratified, multistage probability cluster sampling design. This sample is considered to be highly representative of the U.S. civilian population. Consent was obtained from all subjects for the interview (which included collection of demographic data) and for the physical examination and laboratory testing.

Variables that are used for this analysis include race/ethnicity, age, height, weight, waist circumference, diastolic and systolic blood pressures, total cholesterol, physical activity and alcohol use status. Only adults who were identified as non-Hispanic White, non-Hispanic Black and Hispanic Americans between 18 to 85 years old were included in this investigation. Height, weight, diastolic (DBP) and systolic (SBP) blood pressures were measured and laboratory samples were obtained in the mobile examination center [53]. All techniques and equipment were standardized. Height was measured in meters to the nearest 0.1 cm using a stadiometer against a vertical wall with a rigid headboard and an inelastic tape measure [53]. Weight was measured in the upright position using a Toledo self-zeroing scale (Seritex, Carlstadt, New Jersey) and recorded to the 0.01 kg. Waist measurements were made at the natural waist midpoint between the lowest aspect of the rib cage and highest point of the iliac crest, and to the nearest 0.1 cm. The technique used to obtain blood pressure was similar to the latest recommendations of the American Heart Association [54]. Three and sometimes four blood pressure measurements were taken on all eligible individuals using a mercury sphygmomanometer. Participants who are 50 years and older who were unable to travel to the mobile examination units were offered an abbreviated examination in their homes. Total cholesterol was measured enzymatically in serum or plasma in a sequence of coupled reactions that hydrolyze cholesteryl esters and oxidize the 3-OH group of cholesterol [53]. The concentration of total cholesterol is proportional to the color intensity of the reaction.

Definition of Terms

Diabetes was defined based on the answer to the question: *Has a doctor ever told you that you have diabetes? Hypertension* was defined as SBP $\geq$ 140 or DBP $\geq$ 90 mmHg, or current use of anti hypertension medication. *Education* reported in years of schooling was classified as less than high school, high school and greater than high school for this analysis. Questions on alcohol use in NHANES covered lifetime and recent (past 12 months) use of alcohol. In this analysis alcohol use was defined as current if the subject indicated having used alcohol for at least one time in the past 12 months. Subjects who reported moderate *physical activity* over the past 30 days were classified as those who are currently engaged in physical activity. In terms of variables we did not consider for our analysis, those who were excluded due to missing variables of interest were not different from the population examined in our study.

Statistical Analysis

Statistical programs available in SAS for Windows [55] and SUDAAN [56] were utilized for this analysis. To account for disproportionate probabilities of selection, over sampling, and non-response, appropriate sample weights provided by NHANES were used for the analysis. Estimates of standard errors were computed using the SUDAAN statistical program by means of the delete 1 jackknife method, partitioning the sample into 52 replicates by deleting one unit at a time [57].

Racial/ethnic differences in continuous and categorical variables were evaluated using one-way analysis of variance (ANOVA) and chi-squared statistics, respectively. Prevalences of hypertension and diabetes were age-adjusted by direct methods using the 2000 U.S. population census data. Gender-specific associations of obesity with hypertension and diabetes was determined using odds ratios from the logistic regression analysis in which dummy variables were used to compare Whites with non-Whites. In the regression models statistical adjustments were made for age, education, alcohol use, total cholesterol, and physical activity. In order to determine whether obesity had the same effect for hypertension and diabetes in the three racial/ethnic groups, we fitted the gender-specific interaction term between obesity and race/ethnicity (Model II) in the logistic regression model.

Public health consequences of hypertension and diabetes were quantified using population attributable risk (PAR) expressed as a percentage (Model I) using odds ratio comparing individuals with the disease (hypertension and diabetes) with those who do not have the disease.

To estimate the fraction of White to non-White differences in the rates of the disease (hypertension and diabetes) that was due to their relative differences in the prevalence of obesity, we estimated the RAR. In all analyses, P <0.05 and 95% confidence intervals were used to indicate statistical significance.

RESULTS

The basic characteristics of men (n=2626) and women (n=2905) who were eligible for this study are shown in Tables 1 and 2, respectively. Overall, there were significant racial/ethnic differences for all variables studied (P <.05). White men and women were older than their Black and Hispanic counterparts (P <.01). White men had larger waist girth and higher prevalences of abdominal obesity, physical activity and alcohol use than Black and Hispanic men (P <.001). Black men had higher mean values of BMI and DBP compared with their White and Hispanic counterparts. Black men also had higher prevalences of hypertension, diabetes and obesity compared to White and Hispanic men (P <.001). Black women had larger waist girth and had higher mean values of DBP and SBP than White and Hispanic women (P <.001). Black women also had higher prevalences of abdominal obesity, hypertension and diabetes compared with White and Hispanic women (<.001). The mean values of serum cholesterol and the prevalences of physical activity and alcohol intake were higher in White women compared to Black and Hispanic women (P <.001).

Table 1. Characteristics of studied variables in men.

Variables	Whites	Blacks	Hispanics	P-value
n	1414	575	637	
Age (years)	52.1 ± 20.7	43.2 ± 18.9	40.6 ± 18.7	<.001
Weight (kg)	86.4 ± 18.1	84.6 ± 20.7	79.2 ± 17.6	<.001
Height (cm)	176.4 ± 7.4	176.9 ± 6.9	169.7 ± 7.2	<.001
Body mass index (kg/m^2)	24.8 ± 5.3	27.8 ± 6.2	27.4 ± 5.3	.019
Waist circumference (cm)	100.4 ± 14.3	93.6 ± 17.2	95.9 ± 13.7	.003
Blood Pressures (mmHg)				
Diastolic	71.4 ± 14.4	73.6 ± 16.3	68.9 ± 13.5	<.001
Systolic	125.0 ± 17.4	128.2 ± 19.0	128.2 ± 19.0	<.001
Total Cholesterol (mg/dl)	196.6 ± 45.5	192.7 ± 43.6	196.8 ± 41.8	.040
Prevalences (%)				
Abdominal obesity	67.8	42.1	49.8	<.001
Hypertension	38.6	43.7	41.8	<.001
Type 2 diabetes	8.0	9.6	9.4	<.001
Obesity	22.8	29.4	26.1	<.001
Physical activity	55.1	37.5	32.0	<.001
Alcohol intake	82.2	75.1	75.2	<.001

Table 2. Characteristics of studied variables in women.

Variables	Whites	Blacks	Hispanics	P-value
n	1613	628	664	
Age (years)	51.1 ± 21.7	43.6 ± 19.6	40.4 ± 18.8	<.001
Weight (kg)	72.9 ± 18.2	79.9 ± 21.7	70.2 ± 16.2	<.001
Height (cm)	162.5 ±6.8	162.9 ±6.3	157.2 ±6.4	<.001
Body mass index (kg/m2)	27.6 ±6.6	30.0 ±7.8	28.5 ±6.2	<.001
Waist circumference (cm)	93.2 ± 15.6	95.9 ± 17.2	93.9 ± 14.5	.003
Blood Pressures (mmHg)				
Diastolic	68.4 ± 13.3	70.7 ± 14.9	67.1 ± 12.2	<.001
Systolic	124.1 ± 23.4	125.9 ± 23.5	118.8 ± 21.3	<.001
Total Cholesterol (mg/dl)	208.8 ± 42.1	197.5 ± 42.8	197.8 ± 43.3	<.001
Prevalences (%)				
Abdominal obesity	24.4	29.4	22.7	<.001
Hypertension	35.9	43.6	40.0	<.001
Type 2 diabetes	5.6	10.0	8.3	<.001
Obesity	31.2	45.5	34.1	<.001
Physical activity	56.5	34.2	35.7	<.001
Alcohol intake	91.2	80.8	83.1	<.001

The association of obesity with hypertension and diabetes in men as determined from multiple logistic regression models is shown in Table 3 (Model I). As shown, obesity was associated with increased odds of hypertension (OR: 2.22; 95% CI: 1.77-2.77) and diabetes (OR: 2.04; 95% CI: 1.46-2.87), adjusting for age, education, alcohol intake, education, physical activity and race/ethnicity. Compared with Whites, Black race/ethnicity was associated with 112% increased odds of hypertension and 129% increased odds of diabetes. Compared with Whites, Hispanic race/ethnicity was associated with 37% decreased odds of hypertension and 135% increased odds of diabetes. Table 3 (Model II) also shows multiple logistic regression models of the associations of obesity with hypertension and diabetes that included fitting the interaction between race/ethnicity and obesity. As shown, there were significant interactions between race/ethnicity and obesity in models testing the association of obesity with hypertension and diabetes.

The association of obesity with hypertension and diabetes in women as determined from multiple logistic regression models is shown in Table 4 (Model I). As revealed, obesity was associated with increased odds of hypertension (OR: 2.46; 95% CI: 1.96-3.09) and diabetes (OR: 3.28; 95% CI: 1.32-4.63), adjusting for age, education, alcohol intake, education, physical activity and race/ethnicity. Similar to the findings in men, being a Black woman was associated with 133% increased odds of hypertension and 111% increased odds of diabetes. Relative to White, Hispanic race/ethnicity was associated with 21% decreased odds of hypertension and 192% increased odds of diabetes. As shown (Model II), by significant interaction terms in regression models, the responses of obesity for hypertension and diabetes in women are different across race/ethnicity.

Table 3. Multivariate odds ratio for association of obesity with hypertension and type 2 diabetes in men.

	Model I			Model II			Model I			Model II		
	Hypertension						Type 2 diabetes					
Variables	OR	95%	CI	OR	95%	CI	OR	95%	CI	OR	95%	CI
Obesity	2.22	1.77	2.77	1.93	1.44	2.58	2.04	1.46	2.87	3.83	2.37	6.19
Age	1.05	1.04	1.06	1.05	1.04	1.06	1.05	1.04	1.06	1.06	1.04	1.07
Education												
High school	0.73	0.55	0.98	0.72	0.54	0.97	1.07	0.68	1.68	1.15	0.73	1.81
College	0.65	0.50	0.85	0.65	0.50	0.84	0.81	0.53	1.20	0.83	0.55	1.26
Alcohol intake	1.89	1.21	2.94	1.87	1.20	2.90	3.73	1.13	12.24	3.88	1.18	12.76
Total cholesterol	1.00	0.99	1.01	1.01	0.99	1.02	0.99	0.98	1.00	0.99	0.98	1.00
Physical activity	1.04	0.85	1.29	1.04	0.84	1.28	1.14	0.81	1.61	1.16	0.83	1.64
Race**												
Black	2.12	1.62	2.76	1.75	1.27	2.40	2.29	1.49	3.51	3.56	2.06	6.17
Hispanic	0.63	0.46	0.83	0.62	0.44	0.88	2.35	1.51	3.64	4.17	2.43	7.16
Race* obesity												
* Black	--	--	--	1.95	1.10	3.46	--	--	--	0.36	0.15	0.83
* Hispanic	--	--	--	0.99	0.56	1.77	--	--	--	0.21	0.14	0.53

OR, Odds ratio; CI, Confidence intervals from the logistic regression analysis; **, Reference group is White.

Table 4. Multivariate odds ratio for association of obesity with hypertension and type 2 diabetes in women.

	Model I			Model II			Model I			Model II		
	Hypertension						Type 2 Diabetes					
Variables	OR	95%	CI	OR	95%	CI	OR	95%	CI	OR	95%	CI
Obesity	2.46	1.96	3.09	3.03	2.21	4.16	3.28	1.32	4.63	3.89	2.31	6.57
Age	1.08	1.07	1.09	1.08	1.07	1.09	1.05	1.04	1.06	1.05	1.04	1.06
Education												
High school	0.92	0.67	1.27	0.91	0.67	1.27	0.92	0.58	1.45	0.92	0.58	1.45
College	0.75	0.57	1.00	0.75	0.57	1.00	0.73	0.48	1.10	0.72	0.47	1.10
Alcohol intake	1.25	0.82	1.88	1.26	0.84	1.89	0.82	0.45	1.50	0.83	0.45	1.52
Total cholesterol	1.00	0.99	1.01	1.00	0.99	1.01	0.99	0.98	1.00	0.99	0.98	1.02
Physical activity	0.99	0.78	1.24	1.00	0.80	1.26	1.02	0.71	1.46	1.02	0.71	1.47
Race**												
Black	2.33	1.75	3.11	2.67	1.83	3.90	2.11	1.35	3.29	2.63	1.34	5.18
Hispanic	0.79	0.59	1.08	0.99	0.68	1.44	2.92	2.87	4.56	3.31	1.81	6.06
Race*obesity												
* Black	--	--	--	0.72	0.42	1.24	--	--	--	0.69	0.29	1.62
* Hispanic	--	--	--	0.57	0.32	1.00	--	--	--	0.79	0.30	1.71

OR, Odds ratio; CI, Confidence intervals from the logistic regression analysis; **, Reference group is White.

Table 5. Racial/ethnic specific association of obesity with odds of hypertension and type 2 diabetes in men.

Variables	White		Black		Hispanic		White		Black		Hispanic	
	Hypertension						Type 2 Diabetes					
	OR	95% CI	OR	95% CI	OR	95% CI	OR	95% CI	OR	95% CI	OR	95% CI
Obesity	1.89	1.42 - 2.83	3.76	2.25 -6.28	1.98	1.18 -2.31	2.46	2.19 -3.47	3.21	1.03 - 2.99	2.78	1.33 -3.00
Age	1.05	1.04 - 1.06	1.06	1.04 -1.07	1.06	1.05 -1.09	1.04	1.02 -1.06	1.08	1.01 - 1.11	1.09	1.05 -1.10
Education												
High school	0.81	0.54 - 1.23	0.67	0.37 -1.29	0.63	0.31 -1.27	0.91	0.47 - 2.30	1.82	0.75 – 4.44	1.04	0.35 -3.08
College	0.76	0.52 - 1.09	0.47	0.27 -0.81	0.59	0.32 -1.07	0.63	0.35 - 1.81	1.09	0.44 - 2.41	0.39	0.17 -1.91
Alcohol intake	1.60	0.81 – 3.15	2.08	0.96 -4.02	1.97	0.76 -5.10	1.12	0.22 - 1.43	1.24	0.25 - 6.11	0.99	0.98 -1.06
Total cholesterol	1.00	0.99 - 1.01	1.00	0.99 -1.01	1.00	0.99 -1.01	0.95	0.98 - 1.01	0.99	0.98 -1.01	0.99	0.98 -1.01
Physical activity	0.94	0.72 – 0.98	1.13	0.71 -1.82	1.35	0.81 -2.24	0.96	0.62 - 0.98	1.02	0.98 -3.38	1.20	0.60 -2.44

OR, Odds ratio; CI, Confidence intervals from the logistic regression analysis.

Table 6. Racial/ethnic specific association of obesity with odds of hypertension and type 2 diabetes in women.

Variables	White		Black		Hispanic		White		Black		Hispanic	
	Hypertension						Type 2 Diabetes					
	OR	95% CI	OR	95% CI	OR	95% CI	OR	95% CI	OR	95% CI	OR	95% CI
Obesity	3.00	2.18 - 4.14	2.12	1.25 -3.35	1.72	1.05 -2.78	3.98	2.33 -6.08	2.48	1.36 - 4.86	3.33	1.81 -6.26
Age	1.08	1.07 - 1.09	1.08	1.06 -1.10	1.08	1.07 -1.10	1.06	1.04 -1.08	1.03	1.01 - 1.05	1.06	1.04 -1.08
Education												
High school	0.98	0.61 - 1.59	0.66	0.35 -1.22	0.96	0.49 -1.90	0.99	0.47 - 2.40	0.91	0.38 - 1.81	0.86	0.36 -2.06
College	0.72	0.47 - 1.18	0.66	0.38 -1.12	1.03	0.59 -1.80	0.83	0.43 - 1.72	1.06	0.50 - 2.23	0.39	0.17 -0.90
Alcohol intake	1.21	0.62 - 2.35	1.58	0.82 -3.05	0.95	0.40 -2.26	0.40	0.15 - 1.68	1.25	0.44 - 3.56	1.11	0.34 -3.56
Total cholesterol	1.00	0.99 - 1.01	1.00	0.99 -1.01	1.00	0.99 -1.01	0.99	0.98 - 1.01	0.99	0.98 -1.00	0.99	0.98 -1.01
Physical activity	0.98	0.72 - 0.99	1.14	0.70 -1.85	0.90	0.54 -1.51	0.96	0.56 - 0.98	0.73	0.34 -1.55	1.39	0.73 -2.66

OR, Odds ratio; CI, Confidence intervals from the logistic regression analysis.

Because of the significant interaction between race and obesity we fitted race/ethnic specific multiple logistic regression models for men and women in Table 5 and Table 6, respectively. In men obesity was associated with increased odds of hypertension in Whites (OR: 1.89; 95% CI: 1.42-2.83), Blacks (OR: 3.76; 95% CI: 2.25-6.28) and Hispanics (OR: 1.98; 95% CI: 1.18-2.31), adjusting for age, education, alcohol intake, education, and physical activity. In men obesity was also was associated with an increased odds of diabetes in Whites (OR: 2.46; 95% CI: 2.19-3.47), Blacks (OR: 3.21; 95% CI: 1.03-3.99) and Hispanics (OR: 2.78; 95% CI: 1.33-3.00), after adjusting for the independent variables. In women obesity was associated with increased odds of hypertension in Whites (OR: 3.00; 95% CI: 2.18-4.14), Blacks (OR: 2.12; 95% CI: 1.25-3.35) and Hispanics (OR: 1.72; 95% CI: 1.05-2.78), adjusting for the other independent variables. In women obesity was also was associated with an increased odds of diabetes in Whites (OR: 3.98; 95% CI: 2.33-6.08), Blacks (OR: 2.48; 95% CI: 1.36-4.86) and Hispanics (OR: 3.33; 95% CI: 1.81-6.26), after adjusting for the other independent variables. Moderate physical activity was associated with decreased odds of hypertension and obesity in both White men and White women.

Population attributable risks for hypertension and diabetes that are associated with obesity in Whites, Blacks and Hispanics are shown in Table 7. As shown, proportions of odds of hypertension explained by obesity in men were 16.9%, 44.8% and 20.4%, for Whites, Blacks and Hispanics, and 25%, 26.2% and 31.7% for diabetes, respectively. In women, proportions of odds of hypertension explained by obesity were 38.4%, 33.8% and 19.7%, for Whites, Blacks and Hispanics, and 48.2%, 40.2% and 44.3% for diabetes, respectively.

Table 7 also shows relative attributable risks for hypertension and diabetes in Blacks and Hispanics that are associated with their differences in the rates of obesity as compared with Whites. As shown. 50.2% and 4.9% of the differences in odds of hypertension between White men and Black men and between White men and Hispanic men, respectively, are attributed to their differences in rates of obesity. The analogous values for diabetes were 30.6% and 13.4% for comparing Black men and Hispanic men with White men, respectively. Also, 70.7% and 57.4% of differences in odds of hypertension between White women and Black women and between White women and Hispanic women, respectively, are due to higher rates of obesity in non-Whites. The analogous values for diabetes were 602.2% and 83.7% for Black women and Hispanic women when compared with White women.

DISCUSSION

Higher prevalences of hypertension and diabetes among Blacks and Hispanics have been documented since the early part of the last century. In the United States, the prevalence of hypertension between 1988 and 2000 increased by 3.1% and 4.6% for Whites and Blacks, respectively [58]. Recent reports also show that the number of persons with diabetes has increased in the United States in the same time period [59-60].

Although Blacks and Hispanics are socioeconomically disadvantaged compared to Whites based on measures of income and education [61-63], these measures alone, do not completely explain their excesses in hypertension and diabetes. Obesity which is more common in Blacks and Hispanics than Whites, [19, 52, 64] may have explanatory power for the higher prevalences and risks of hypertension and diabetes in these minority groups. Indeed, rates of hypertension and diabetes have risen sharply with increasing obesity in recent years among Blacks and Hispanics in the United States [52, 65-68]. The prevalence of obesity in adults has risen from 13% to 31% in the past 25 years [52]. In the period between 1999 and 2002, the prevalence of obesity among adults with diagnosed diabetes was 57.9% for non-Hispanic whites, 63.0% for non-Hispanic blacks, and 59.5% for Mexican Americans [19]. Hence, there is a need to completely clarify the role of obesity in racial/ethnic variations for diseases, including hypertension and diabetes.

Table 7. Population and relative attributable risks for hypertension and type 2 diabetes associated with obesity.

	Men			Women		
	White	Black	Hispanic	White	Black	Hispanic
Population attributable risk (%)						
Hypertension	16.9	44.8	20.4	38.4	33.8	19.7
Type 2 diabetes	25.0	26.2	31.7	48.2	40.2	44.3
Relative attributable risk (%)						
Hypertension	Reference	50.2	4.9	Reference	70.7	57.4
Type 2 diabetes	Reference	30.6	13.4	Reference	62.2	83.7

In this study we used a different approach to examine the contribution of the excess rates of obesity in Blacks and Hispanics that are associated with their higher prevalences for hypertension and diabetes. We utilized the 1999-2001 United States National Health and Nutrition Examination Surveys. These surveys are highly respected because the sampling schemes are representative and national in scope. The training program and quality control measures that were instituted in the surveys provide an added level of credibility to the data.

The results of this analysis showed significant racial/ethnic differences in the odds of hypertension and diabetes attributable to rates of obesity. In men, obesity was associated with increased odds of 89%, 276% and 98% for hypertension and 146%, 221% and 178% increased odds of diabetes in Whites, Blacks and Hispanics, respectively. The population attributable risk of hypertension due to obesity in these groups were 16.9%, 44.8% and 20.4%, and 25%, 26.2% and 31.7% for diabetes in Whites, Blacks and Hispanics, respectively. In women, obesity was associated with increased odds of 200%, 112% and 72% for hypertension and 298%, 148% and 233% increased odds of diabetes in Whites, Blacks and Hispanics, respectively. The population attributable risk of hypertension due to obesity in women were 38.4%, 33.8% and 19.7%, and 48.2%, 40.2% and 44.3% for diabetes in Whites, Blacks and Hispanics, respectively.

The results of this study also showed that in both men and women the relative differences in the odds of hypertension and diabetes between Whites and non-Whites are attributable to their differences in the prevalence of obesity. Approximately 50% and 31% of the differences in odds of hypertension and diabetes, respectively, between White men and Black men are due to their differences in the rates of obesity. The corresponding values comparing White women and Black women were approximately 71% and 62% for hypertension and diabetes, respectively. Also, approximately 5% and 13% of the differences in odds of hypertension and diabetes, respectively, between White men and Hispanic men are due to their differences in the rates of obesity. The corresponding values comparing White women and Hispanic women with White women were approximately 57% and 84%, respectively.

PUBLIC HEALTH IMPLICATIONS OF FINDINGS

The results of this study have significant implications in terms of obesity prevention at population-based levels. In this study, the prevalence of obesity in White men, Black men and

Hispanic men were 22.8%, 29.4% and 26.1%, respectively. The corresponding values in White women, Black women and Hispanic women were 31.2%, 45.5% and 34.1%, respectively. Accordingly, if the prevalences of obesity in Blacks and Hispanics were reduced to the levels seen in Whites, hypertension and diabetes rates would also be reduced to rates seen in Whites. This has significant implications for racial/ethnic disparities in the prevalence of hypertension and diabetes between Blacks, Hispanics and Whites. These results suggest that much of disparity could be reduced by reducing obesity in Blacks and Hispanics. However, a major limitation of this study must be taken into account in the interpretation of results from this study. As a cross-sectional study, directionality of the associations of obesity with hypertension and diabetes cannot be clearly established. The replication of this study using a prospective epidemiologic approach is needed to add credibility to the result of this study.

CONCLUSION

The contribution of obesity to racial/ethnic variations for the prevalence odds of hypertension and diabetes in this study is noteworthy, and may provide an explanation for racial/ethnic differences for hypertension and diabetes. The results of this study indicate that there would be a significant reduction in hypertension and diabetes if obesity prevalence in minority groups is reduced to the levels seen in Whites. This indicates that obesity reduction strategies in ethnic minorities should be a major health policy imperative in addressing racial/ethnic disparities for hypertension and diabetes in the United States. There is a need to investigate the role of obesity in racial/ethnic variations for other obesity-associated sequalae.

REFERENCES

[1]   Centers for Disease Control and Prevention (CDC). Racial/ethnic disparities in prevalence, treatment, and control of hypertension--United States, 1999-2002. *MMWR* 2005, 54, 7-9.

[2]   Burt, VL; Cutler, JA; Higgins, M; Horan, MJ; Labarthe D; Whelton P; Brown C; Roccella EJ. Trends in the prevalence, awareness, treatment, and control of hypertension in the adult US population. Data from the health examination surveys, 1960 to 1991. *Hypertension.* 1995, 26:60-69.

[3]   Cooper, RS; Liao, Y; Rotimi, C. Is hypertension more severe among U.S. blacks, or is severe hypertension more common? *Ann Epidemiol.,* 1996, 6, 173-180.

[4]   Rehman, SU; Hutchison, FN; Hendrix, K; Okonofua, EC; Egan, BM. Ethnic differences in blood pressure control among men at Veterans Affairs clinics and other health care sites. *Arch Intern Med.,* 2005, 165, 1041-1047.

[5]   Harris, MI; Flegal, KM; Cowie, CC; Eberhardt, MS; Goldstein, DE; Little, RR; Wiedmeyer, HM; Byrd-Holt, DD. Prevalence of diabetes, impaired fasting glucose, and impaired glucose tolerance in U.S. adults. The Third National Health and Nutrition Examination Survey, 1988-1994. *Diabetes Care.,* 1998, 21, 518-524.

[6]   Ahluwalia, IB; Mack, KA; Murphy, W; Mokdad, AH; Bales, VS. State-specific prevalence of selected chronic disease-related characteristics--Behavioral Risk Factor Surveillance System, 2001. *MMWR Surveill Summ.,* 2003, 52, 1-80.

[7]   Adams, AS; Zhang, F; Mah, C; Grant, RW; Kleinman, K; Meigs, JB; Ross-Degnan, D. Race Differences in Long-Term Diabetes Management in an HMO. *Diabetes Care.,* 2005, 28, 2844-2849.

[8]   Lin, SX; Larson, E. Does provision of health counseling differ by patient race? *Fam Med.,* 2005, 37, 650-654.

[9]   US Department of Health and Human Services. Healthy people 2010: understanding and improving health. 2nd ed. Washington, DC: US Department of Health and Human Services, 2000.

[10]   Kearney, PM; Whelton, M; Reynolds, K; Whelton, PK; He, J. Worldwide prevalence of hypertension: a systematic review. *J Hypertens.,* 2004, 22, 11-19.

[11]   Gadegbeku, CA; Lea, JP; Jamerson, KA. Update on disparities in the pathophysiology and management of hypertension: focus on African Americans. *Med Clin North Am.,* 2005, 89, 921-33.

[12]   Joshi, AV; Day, D; Lubowski, TJ; Ambegaonkar, A. Relationship between obesity and cardiovascular risk factors: findings from a multi-state screening project in the United States. *Curr Med Res Opin.,* 2005, 21, 1755-1761.

[13]   Fields, LE; Burt, VL; Cutler, JA; Hughes, J; Roccella, EJ; Sorlie, P. The burden of adult hypertension in the United States 1999 to 2000: a rising tide. *Hypertension.,* 2004, 44, 398-404.

[14]   Hicks, LS; Shaykevich, S; Bates, DW; Ayanian, JZ. Determinants of racial/ethnic differences in blood pressure management among hypertensive patients. *BMC Cardiovasc Disord.,* 2005, 5, 16.

[15]   Brown, AF; Gregg, EW; Stevens, MR; Karter, AJ; Weinberger, M; Safford, MM; Gary, TL; Caputo, DA; Waitzfelder, B; Kim, C; Beckles, GL. Race, ethnicity, socioeconomic position, and quality of care for adults with diabetes enrolled in managed care: the Translating Research Into Action for Diabetes (TRIAD) study. *Diabetes Care.,* 2005, 28, 2864-2870.

[16]   National Institute of Diabetes and Digestive and Kidney Diseases. National Diabetes Statistics: Total prevalence of diabetes by race/ethnicity among people aged 20 years or older United States, 2005. [monograph on the Internet]. Bethesda, MD: National Diabetes Information Clearinghouse.http://diabetes.niddk.nih.gov/dm/pubs/statistics/index.htm#10.

[17]   Lethbridge-Cejku, M; Vickerie, J. Summary health statistics for U.S. adults: National Health Interview Survey. 2003. National Center for Health Statistics. Tables 7 and 8. *Vital Health Stat,* 2005, 10(225), 28-31.

[18]   Center for Disease Control and Prevention. Prevalence of Diabetes and Impaired Fasting Glucose in Adults-United States, 1999-2000. *MMWR,* 2003, 52, 833-7.

[19]   Eberhardt, MS. Prevalence of overweight and obesity among adults with diagnosed diabetes--United States, 1988-1994 and 1999-2002. *MMWR,* 2004, 53, 1066-1068.

[20]   Boltri, J; Okosun, I; Davis-Smith, Y; Vogel, R. Hemoglobin A1c levels in diagnosed and undiagnosed Black, Hispanic, and White persons with diabetes: results from NHANES 1999-2000. *Ethnicity and Disease, 2005,* 15, 562-567.

[21] Strauss, RS; Pollack, HA. Epidemic Increase in Childhood Overweight, 1986-1998. *JAMA.,* 2001, 286, 2845-2848.

[22] McCrory, MA; Suen, VM; Roberts, SB. Biobehavioral influences on energy intake and adult weight gain. *J Nutr,* 2002, 132, 3830S-3834S.

[23] Okosun, IS. Racial differences in rates of type 2 diabetes in American women: how much is due to differences in overall adiposity? *Ethn Health.,* 2001, 6, 27-34.

[24] Okosun, IS; Chandra, KM; Choi, S; Christman, J; Dever, GE; Prewitt, TE. Hypertension and type 2 diabetes comorbidity in adults in the United States: risk of overall and regional adiposity. *Obes Res.,* 2001, 9, 1-9.

[25] Bermudez, OI; Tucker, KL. Total and central obesity among elderly Hispanics and the association with Type 2 diabetes. *Obes Res.,* 2001, 9, 443-451.

[26] Resnick, HE; Valsania, P; Halter, JB; Lin, X. Differential effects of BMI on diabetes risk among black and white Americans. *Diabetes Care.,* 1998, 21, 1828-1835.

[27] Flegal, KM; Carroll, MD; Ogden, CL; Johnson, CL. Prevalence and Trends in Obesity Among US Adults, *1999-2000 JAMA,*2002, 288, 1723 -1727.

[28] Hedley, AA; Ogden, CL; Johnson, CL; Carroll, MD; Curtin, LR; Flegal, KM. Prevalence of Overweight and Obesity Among US Children, Adolescents, and Adults, *1999-2002 JAMA,* 2004, 291, 2847-2850.

[29] David, S. Freedman, Laura Kettel Khan; Mary K. Serdula; Deborah A. Galuska; William H. Dietz. Trends and Correlates of Class 3 Obesity in the United States From 1990 Through 2000. *JAMA,* 2002, 288, 1758 - 1761.

[30] Laurencin, MG; Goldschmidt, R; Fisher, L. Type 2 diabetes in adolescents. How to recognize and treat this growing problem. *Postgrad Med.,* 2005, 118, 31-36.

[31] Centers for Disease Control and Prevention (CDC), Prevalence of diabetes and impaired fasting glucose in adults-United States, 1999–2000, *MMWR,* 2003, 52, 833-837.

[32] Brosnan, CA; Upchurch, S; Schreiner, B. Type 2 diabetes in children and adolescents: an emerging disease. *J Pediatr Health Care.,* 2001, 15, 187-193.

[33] Gregg, EW; Cheng, YJ; Cadwell, BL; Imperatore, G; Williams, DE; Flegal, KM; et al., Secular trends in cardiovascular disease risk factors according to body mass index in US adults, *JAMA,* 293 (2005) (15), 1868-1874.

[34] Gregg, EW; Cadwell, BL; Cheng, YJ; Cowie, CC; Williams, DE; Geiss, L; Engelgau MM; Vinicor FTrends in the Prevalence and Ratio of Diagnosed to Undiagnosed Diabetes According to Obesity Levels in the U.S. *Diabetes Care, 2004,* 27, 2806-2812.

[35] Henderson, RM. The bigger the healthier: are the limits of BMI risk changing over time? *Econ Hum Biol.,* 2005, 339-366.

[36] Deurenberg, P; Yap, M; van Staveren, WA. Body mass index and percent body fat: a meta analysis among different ethnic groups. *Int J Obes Relat Metab Disord.,* 1998, 22, 1164-1171.

[37] Shiwaku, K; Anuurad, E; Enkhmaa, B; Nogi, A; Kitajima, K; Yamasaki, M; Yoneyama, T; Oyunsuren, T; Yamane, Y. Predictive values of anthropometric measurements for multiple metabolic disorders in Asian populations. *Diabetes Res Clin Pract.,* 2005, 52-62.

[38] Bhansali, A; Nagaprasad, G; Agarwal, A; Dutta, P; Bhadada, S. Does Body Mass Index Predict Overweight in Native Asian Indians? A Study from a North Indian Population. *Ann Nutr Metab.,* 2005, 50, 66-73.

[39] Dictionary of Epidemiology. Last JM (ed). *International Epidemiological Association* 2001, Oxford University Press, New York, NY.

[40] Leon Gordis. *Epidemiology.* Elsevier Saunders Publishing, 2004.

[41] Encyclopedia of Epidemiologic Methods. Gail MH; and Benichou J (eds.)., 2000. John Wiley & Son, Ltd. New York, NY.

[42] Cornfield, J. A method of estimating comparative rates from clinical data. Applications to cancer of the lung, breast and cervix. *J National Cancer Institute,* 1951, 11, 1269-1275.

[43] Breslow, NE; Day, NE. Statistical Methods in Cancer Research. Vol 1-Analysis of case-control studies. IARC Scientific Publications, Lyon, France, 1980.

[44] Lele, C; Whittemore, AS. Different disease rates in two populations: how much is due to differences in risk factors? *Stat Med,* 1997, 16, 2543-2554.

[45] Gefeller, O. Relative attributable risks. *Epidemiology,* 1996, 7, 217-218.

[46] Mietiinen, OS. Component of crude odds ratio. *American Journal of Epidemiology.* 1972, 96, 168-172.

[47] Eyigou, A; McHugh, R. On the factorization of the crude relative risk. *American Journal of Epidemiology.,* 1977, 106, 188-193.

[48] Schlesselman, JJ. Assessing the effect of confounding variables *American Journal of Epidemiology.,* 1982, 108, 3-8.

[49] Mark, DH. Deaths attributable to obesity. *JAMA.,* 2005, 293, 1918-1919.

[50] Flegal, KM; Graubard, BI; Williamson, DF; Gail, MH. Excess deaths associated with underweight, overweight, and obesity. *JAMA.,* 2005, 293, 1861-1867.

[51] Williams, DE; Cadwell, BL; Cheng, YJ; Cowie, CC; Gregg, EW; Geiss, LS; Engelgau, MM; Narayan, KM; Imperatore, G. Prevalence of impaired fasting glucose and its relationship with cardiovascular disease risk factors in US adolescents, 1999-2000. *Pediatrics.,* 2005, 11, 1122-1126.

[52] Gregg, EW; Cheng, YJ; Cadwell, BL; Imperatore, C; Williams, DE; Flegal, KM; Narayan, KM; Williamson, DF. Secular Trends in Cardiovascular Disease Risk Factors According to Body Mass Index in U.S. Adults. *Obstet Gynecol Surv.,* 2005, 60, 660-661

[53] www.cdc.gov/nchs/nhanes.

[54] Pickering, TG; Hall, JE; Appel, LJ; Falkner, BE; Graves, JW; Hill, MN; Jones, DH; Kurtz, T; Sheps, SG; Roccella, EJ; Council on High Blood Pressure Research Professional and Public Education Subcommittee, American Heart Association. Recommendations for blood pressure measurement in humans: an AHA scientific statement from the Council on High Blood Pressure Research Professional and Public Education Subcommittee. *J Clin Hypertens (Greenwich).,* 2005, 7, 102-109.

[55] SAS Release 8.02. SAS Institute, Cary, NC.

[56] Shah, BV; Barnwell, BG; Bieler, GS; Sudaan User's manual. Research Triangle Institute. Research Triangle Park, NC.

[57] Wolter, KM. Introduction to variance estimation. Springer-Verlag, New York, NY 1990.

[58] Hajjar, I; Kotchen, TA. Trends in prevalence, awareness, treatment, and control of hypertension in the United States, 1988-2000. *JAMA.,* 2003, 290, 199-206.

[59]   Mokdad, AH; Bowman, BA; Ford, ES; Vinicor, F; Marks, JS; Koplan, JP. The Continuing Epidemics of Obesity and Diabetes in the United States. *JAMA*, 2001, 286: 1195-1200.

[60]   Cowie, CC. Prevalence of Diabetes and Impaired Fasting Glucose in Adults—United States, 1999-2000. *JAMA*, 2003, 290, 1702-1703.

[61]   Chang, VW; Lauderdale, DS. Income disparities in body mass index and obesity in the United States, 1971-2002. *Arch Intern Med.*, 2005, 165, 2122-2128.

[62]   Lewis, TT; Everson-Rose, SA; Sternfeld, B; Karavolos, K; Wesley, D; Powell, LH. Race, education, and weight change in a biracial sample of women at midlife. *Arch Intern Med.*, 2005, 165, 545-551.

[63]   Gordon-Larsen, P; Adair, LS; Popkin, BM. The relationship of ethnicity, socioeconomic factors, and overweight in US adolescents. *Obes Res.*, 2003, 11, 121-129.

[64]   Boardman, JD; Saint Onge, JM; Rogers, RG; Denney, JT. Race differentials in obesity: the impact of place. *J Health Soc Behav.*, 2005, 46, 229-243.

[65]   Kimm, SY; Barton, BA; Obarzanek, E; McMahon, RP; Sabry, ZI; Waclawiw, MA; Schreiber, GB; Morrison, JA; Similo, S; Daniels, SR. Racial divergence in adiposity during adolescence: The NHLBI Growth and Health Study. *Pediatrics.*, 2001, 107, E34.

[66]   Liao, Y; Tucker, P; Okoro, CA; Giles, WH; Mokdad, AH; Harris, VB. REACH 2010 Surveillance for Health Status in Minority Communities – United States, 2001-2002. *MMWR Surveill Summ.*, 2004, 53, 1-36.

[67]   Klein, DJ; Aronson Friedman, L; Harlan, WR; Barton, BA; Schreiber, GB; Cohen, RM; Harlan, LC; Morrison, JA. Obesity and the development of insulin resistance and impaired fasting glucose in black and white adolescent girls: a longitudinal study. *Diabetes Care.*, 2004, 27, 378-383.

[68]   Qureshi, AI; Suri, MF; Kirmani, JF; Divani, AA. Prevalence and trends of prehypertension and hypertension in United States: National Health and Nutrition Examination Surveys 1976 to 2000. *Med Sci Monit.*, 2005, 11, 403-409.

In: Race and Ethnicity
Editor: Jonathan K. Crennan, pp. 217-231

ISBN: 978-1-60692-099-2
© 2010 Nova Science Publishers, Inc.

Chapter 8

THE IMPACT OF THE INTERNET FOR THOSE WITH CANCER AND FROM RACIAL/ETHNIC GROUPS AND/OR LOW LITERACY POPULATIONS

Joshua Fogel[*]

Brooklyn College of the City University of New York, Department of Economics,
218A, 2900 Bedford Avenue, Brooklyn, NY 11210, USA

ABSTRACT

This chapter reviews the empirical literature related to cancer topics among those of racial/ethnic populations and/or low literacy groups. A comprehensive search of databases retrieved 23 relevant articles. These articles were classified into five overall groups of topics pertaining to characteristics of Internet users, attitudes toward Internet use, psychological aspects of Internet use, health attitudes and Internet use, and readability and the Internet. Some points concluded include that those of racial/ethnic populations are less likely to use the Internet than whites. Also, Internet websites would be of greater interest and relevance to those of racial/ethnic populations if there is tailoring of the websites to their cultural interests. Lastly, there are potential mental and physical health benefits for using the Internet. However, among the racial/ethnic group of African Americans, they are unlikely to use the Internet for health information and are less interested in online support groups. Also, the websites are often written at 10th grade or higher levels.

INTRODUCTION

Internet use is increasingly becoming more common among many in the United States. In data collected by the Pew Internet and American Life Project in 2005, 70% of urban and suburban individuals used the Internet with rural Internet use only a few percentage points

---

[*] Corresponding author: Phone: (718) 951-3857, Fax: (718) 951-4867, e-mail: joshua.fogel@gmail.com

behind at 62% (Burns, 2006a). In data collected in the same time period in 2005 by Ipsos Insight, they report Internet use at an overall 71% rate. Internet users in the United States use the Internet for an average of 11.4 hours online each week (Burns, 2006b).

With regard to use of the Internet for health purposes, the results vary and are reported at lower rates than general Internet use with use ranging from 40% to 55% (Baker, Wagner, Singer, & Bundorf, 2003; Fox & Rainee, 2004). As these data were not collected in 2005, it is entirely possible that Internet use rates have increased since the time these nationally representative surveys were conducted. With regard to Internet use for information about cancer topics, breast cancer has been one of the areas most commonly studied. Among women with breast cancer, Internet use ranges from 40% to 49%, based upon data published from before 2004 (Fogel, Albert, Schnabel, Ditkoff, & Neugut, 2002a; Satterlund, McCaul, & Sandgren, 2003).

Although there are overall high rates of Internet use, there are differences that are often attributed to the "digital divide," where certain groups are deemed to have greater access to Internet use. The digital divide is quite common based upon age, education, and race/ethnicity. Data collected in 2005 is consistent and provides support for this digital divide approach. With regard to age, only 26% of older Americans above age 65 use the Internet, while the age group of 50-64 has 67% use. The highest Internet use among adults is among those ages 18-29, with use at 84%. Education is an important factor differentiating Internet users from non-users. Only 29% of those without a high school degree use the Internet, this increases to 61% for high school graduates, and is at 89% use for college graduates. Race/ethnicity too is an important differentiating factor. For example, only 57% of African Americans use the Internet as compared to 70% of whites (Fox, 2005).

In 2003, a review article on cancer topics reviewed the existing eight scientific articles published on Internet health information use among those of racial/ethnic groups or low literacy populations (Fogel, 2003). Since that time many more individuals have researched and published on Internet use. Also, Internet use research has expanded to not only information but also services provided through the Internet such as support groups and Internet based treatments. In this chapter, a comprehensive review is conducted on all the scientific articles published on cancer topics as it relates to any use of the Internet health among those of racial/ethnic groups and/or low literacy populations.

METHOD

Inclusion and Exclusion Criteria

All inclusion and exclusion criteria were determined a-priori before performing the database searches. Studies were included if they were 1) articles with empirical data (either qualitative or quantitative analytic approaches) discussing Internet use among those of racial/ethnic populations and/or low literacy groups in North America, and 2) information about cancer or prevention of cancer, and 3) discussed Internet topics for a) consumers/patients or b) both consumers/patients and health care professionals.

Studies were excluded if they were 1) theoretical articles, 2) anecdotal information, or 3) non-peer reviewed journals, or 4) Internet use intended for health care professionals (i.e., training, continuing education).

Search Strategy

On January 23, 2006, a number of databases were searched for all the relevant studies from the year of 1990 to that date. The search strategy below consisting of three sets of terms was included in each search. All terms were searched in both the subject heading and also for text words. The search strategy was: (Internet OR web OR www. OR www OR cyber* OR cyber) AND (cancer OR neoplasms OR cancers OR neoplasm OR neoplast* OR oncology OR metasta* OR metastatic OR neoplastic OR neoplast) AND (culture OR ethnic OR race OR racial OR black OR blacks OR African OR Africans OR African American OR African Americans OR Hispanic OR Hispanics OR Hispanic American OR Hispanic Americans OR Latino OR Latinos OR Latina OR Latinas OR Asian OR Asians OR Asian American OR Asian Americans OR Indian OR Indians OR North American OR North Americans OR racial/ethnic OR literacy OR cultural diversity OR diverse OR cross-cultural OR cross-cultural comparison OR attitude to health/ethnology OR ethnology OR health behavior/ethnology)

Databases searched included Medline and Pre-Medline using the PubMed interface, PsycInfo using Ebsco, and CINAHL using Ebsco. Finally, a search was done by reading the relevant articles in order to determine if there were any other relevant articles of interest. No additional articles were found from this article review.

RESULTS

The search retrieved 198 hits with PubMed, 12 hits with PsycINFO, and 85 hits with CINAHL. These were not all unique hits, as there was some overlap in the retrieved articles from these databases. Overall 23 different articles were deemed relevant and were included in the review.

The Table summarizes some details about the 23 reviewed articles. Although the articles were published from the years of 2001 to 2006, data collection ranged from as early as 1995 to only as recent as 2004. Also, 9 (39.1%) did not have the date when the data were collected. With regard to Internet use, this is potentially important as new technology takes time to develop and use patterns can rapidly change within only a few years. Almost all the studies were quantitative studies with only 5 (21.7%) being either completely qualitative or having a qualitative component. Minority populations as the focus of the study includes African American (n = 15), Hispanic American (n = 10), American Indian (n = 4), Asian American / Pacific Islander (n = 5), and non-Caucasian (n = 1). Studies were conducted in 13 states plus one region of the "southeastern United States." This corresponds to representation as defined by the Census Bureau (Census Bureau, 2000) from the four broad regions in the United States of the Northeast, Midwest, South, and West. However, based upon region division breakdown, the divisions of West North Central, East South Central, and West South Central did not have any studies conducted in these areas.

Below are brief summaries about all the included and reviewed articles. They are grouped into five broad categories based upon the primary emphasis of the article. These categories include characteristics of Internet users, attitudes toward Internet use, psychological aspects of Internet use, health attitudes and Internet use, and readability and the Internet.

Table. Description of 23 Studies Reviewed Regarding Internet Use

Study Author / Date Publication	Date Data Collection	Study Type	Minority Population	Location
Abdullah et al., 2005	2003	quantitative	Non-Caucasian	IN
Buller et al., 2001	1998, 2000	qualitative, quantitative	AA, HA	NY
Changrani & Gany, 2005	unknown	quantitative	AA	NY
Fogel et al., 2002b	2000	quantitative	AA, HA	NY
Fogel, 2003	2000	quantitative	AA, HA	NY
Fogel et al., 2005	2000	quantitative	AA, HA, AAPI	NY
Friedman et al., 2004	2002	quantitative	Not Applicable	Not Applicable
Gustafson, McTavish, Stengle, Ballard, Hawkins et al., 2005	2001-2003	quantitative	AA	MI, WI
Haughton et al., 2005	2000	quantitative	AA	MO
Helft et al., 2005	unknown	quantitative	AA, HA	IN
Henderson & Fogel, 2003	unknown	qualitative, quantitative	AA	Southeastern US
Im et al., 2005	2003	quantitative	AA, HA, AAPI	Not Applicable
Kahn et al., 1999	unknown	qualitative	AA, HA	MA
Kakai et al., 2003	unknown	qualitative, quantitative	AAPI	HI
Kaphingst et al., 2006	2003	quantitative	Not Applicable	Not Applicable
McTavish et al., 2003	1995-1997	quantitative	AA, AAPI, AI	IL, IN, WI
Monnier et al., 2002	unknown	quantitative	AA	SC
Nguyen et al., 2005	2003	quantitative	AA, HA, AAPI	CA
Roubidoux, 2005	2004	qualitative	AI	MI
Smith et al., 2003	unknown	quantitative	AA	PA
Talosig-Garcia & Davis, 2005	unknown	quantitative	AA, HA	CA
Wilson et al., 2000	1997-1998	quantitative	Not Applicable	Not Applicable
Zimmerman et al., 2003	unknown	quantitative	HA, AI	CO, NM

Note: Minority Population Column: AA = African American, AAPI = Asian American Pacific Islander, AI = American Indian, HA = Hispanic American.

Location Column: CA = California, CO = Colorado, HI = Hawaii, IL = Illinois, IN = Indiana, MA= Massachusetts, MI = Michigan, MO = Missouri, NM = New Mexico, NY = New York, PA = Pennsylvania, SC = South Carolina, WI = Wisconsin.

Characteristics of Internet Users

Fogel, Albert, Schnabel, Ditkoff, & Neugut (2002b) conducted a survey in New York City during 2000. The sample of women with breast cancer included 79% whites (n = 143) and 21% non-whites (n = 37) of either African American or Hispanic American race/ethnicity. In their logistic regression analyses with Internet health information use as the outcome variable, the non-whites had an odds ratio of 0.39 indicating lesser odds for using the Internet for health information, as compared to the reference group of whites. This approached significance with a p-value of 0.08. Also, in the overall sample, higher income level and higher education level were both significantly related to Internet use.

Monnier, Laken, & Carter (2002) surveyed 319 cancer patients, caregivers, and others in Charleston, South Carolina using convenience sampling regarding their interest in Internet-based cancer services. No year for the study was provided. This sample included 25% African Americans (n = 79), 68% whites (n = 216), <1% Hispanic Americans (n = 1), and 7% "others" (n = 23). Whites were compared to minority group members. Minority group members differed from whites in that they were less likely to use the Internet, less likely to have a family member who used the Internet, less likely to have home Internet access, less likely to know where else besides home they could access the Internet, and less likely to use the Internet for cancer-related services (e.g., conversing with a variety of health-care professionals, use of online support groups). They found no differences between minority group members and whites on items inquiring about the likelihood to use the Internet to access cancer-related services (e.g., sending results of tests to physicians, sending prescriptions to the pharmacy by the Internet), or for home healthcare delivered by a personal computer. A study limitation is that they collapsed two important areas into one area. Online conversations with health care professionals are quite distinct from using online support groups. It could be that the results are influenced by one of the categories within that group of items.

Buller et al. (2001) conducted surveys in 1998 in Colorado and New Mexico with 200 individuals comprised of 63% whites (n = 126), 30% Hispanic Americans (n = 60), 2% American Indians (n = 4), 1% African Americans (n = 2), 0.5% Asian Americans (n = 1), 1.5% other (n = 3), and 2% refused to answer (n = 4). They also conducted focus groups in 2000 in New Mexico with 43 individuals comprised of 44% Hispanic Americans (n = 19), 33% American Indians (n = 14), and 23% mixed whites and Hispanic Americans (n = 10) regarding implementing a web based nutrition program for primary prevention of cancer. In the survey results they found that nearly all the participants were aware of the Internet. Significantly fewer Hispanic Americans owned a computer (32%) as compared to whites (59%) and also that there was a significantly lower rate of Internet use among Hispanic Americans (40%) as compared to whites (58%). In the focus group results, they studied the cultural relevance of an existing nutrition website from a different cancer prevention research group. They found that this nutrition website was not culturally relevant to the American Indians as it did not include traditional American Indian foods. Also, it was not culturally relevant to Hispanic Americans whose primary language was Spanish, as it only included a minimal amount of Spanish language.

Abdullah et al. (2005) conducted a survey among a convenience sample of 416 cancer patients in Indiana during March and April 2003. This included those from both urban (n = 186) and rural (n = 230) areas. Almost all of the 47 "non-Caucasians" were from the urban area (n = 44). They compared access of e-mail and Internet by ethnicity. Among the non-Caucasians, 57% had e-mail and Internet access while 56% of the Caucasians had e-mail and Internet access, with no significant differences between the groups. They did not report data specific for ethnic group for overall predictors of Internet use, although in their overall sample they found that younger age, current employment, greater income levels, and greater education levels were predictors of e-mail/Internet access. They report from the overall sample that the major reason for non-access was that greater than half reported non-interest. Also, cost of Internet services was not a reason for non-access. They recommended that placement of computers in waiting rooms with links to cancer-related websites and that contain potentially beneficial educational or problem solving content may help encourage interest. They also recommended that educational programs about the benefits of Internet use may also be helpful to increase Internet use.

Kakai, Maskarinec, Shumay, Tatsumura, & Tasaki (2003) interviewed 140 cancer patients in Hawaii comprised of 24% Japanese Americans (n = 33), 30% non-Japanese Asian Americans and Pacific Islanders (n = 42), and 46% whites (n = 65) about the types of health information used since their cancer diagnosis. No date was provided. Percentages for use of Internet health information were for whites (26.2%), Japanese Americans (12.1%), and non-Japanese Asian Americans and Pacific Islanders (14.3%). Among whites, Internet use was ranked tied for third among 9 sources of health information. Among Japanese Americans it was ranked tied for sixth among 9 sources of health information. Among non-Japanese Asian Americans and Pacific Islanders it was the sixth among 9 sources of health information. In their analyses of the coded qualitative interview data using "correspondence analysis," a technique similar to principal components analysis, they found an association of Internet health information use for whites but not for either Japanese Americans or non-Japanese Asian Americans and Pacific Islanders.

Haughton, Kreuter, Hall, Holt, & Wheetley (2005) surveyed 1,227 adult African American women from St. Louis, Missouri in 2000 who were participating in a study of behavior and cultural tailoring of women's health magazines to promote mammography and increased fruit and vegetable use. Median income was in the $10,001-$20,000 category, with 23.7% earning less than $5,000 and only 13.1% earning greater than $30,000. When providing contact information, participants were asked to provide e-mail addresses. Only 112 (9.1%) provided it, while 320 (26.1%) provided cell phone or pager information. Logistic regression analyses showed that those of younger age, with more years of education, and with higher income levels were predictors of e-mail use. The authors write that this e-mail use is much less than what is reported for African American Internet use. This could be because this was a low income population. They caution that this e-mail use question may only be a proxy for measuring Internet use. Also, it is possible that not providing an e-mail address may have just been a preference for wanting to be contacted through other ways rather than e-mail, so this may not be indicative of low e-mail use. It is also possible to have Internet access but not have an e-mail account.

Smith et al. (2003) surveyed 295 consecutive patients undergoing radiotherapy for prostate cancer from three different hospitals in the Philadelphia, Pennsylvania area. The racial/ethnic composition included 175 whites (59.3%), 113 African Americans (38.3%), and 7 from other race/ethnicities (2.4%). The date of survey administration was not mentioned. They found significant differences in home computer ownership between whites (62%) and African Americans (17%). Whites significantly used the Internet to access information (47%)

more than African Americans (11%). Even when analyzing only those who owned computers, there were still significant differences in Internet use between whites (61%) and African Americans (32%), which indicate that computer access is not a confounding factor.

Talosig-Garcia & Davis (2005) surveyed 287 Hispanic American and African American women diagnosed with breast cancer in 2000-2001 from the Sacramento region of California. Their response rate was 74% and interviews were conducted in either English or Spanish. Of the 53% that provided income information, almost all had household income below $60,000. With regard to information at the time of diagnosis, almost 75% reported that the information received was either "adequate" or "very adequate." Less than 1% reported that this information was information from the Internet. Among the approximately 25% (n = 73) subset of participants who searched for information after diagnosis, the source of information choices were first for "doctor, nurse, other health care professional (29.9%)," second for "books, brochures, pamphlets (18.6%)," and third for the Internet (13.4%). In general, the cancer-related information sources used (including multiple responses from participants) were "books, brochures, pamphlets (98%)," "doctor, nurse, other health care professional (97%)," "spouse/partner, family members/friends (62%)," "newspapers/magazines (46%)," "the Internet (39%)," "television/radio (32%)," "toll-free information service (20%)," "face-to-face support groups (18%)," and "support groups on the Internet (0%)." In general, approximately one third of participants or someone in their household used a computer. Only 15% used e-mail. Only 17% used the world wide web. The two major reasons reported for non-Internet use were lack of computer access (65%) and that the Internet was "too complicated to use" (55%). Only 15% reported using the Internet to obtain cancer information for themselves or others. The top three types of information searched for on the Internet included "breast cancer information, diagnosis, and prognosis (35%)," "risk factors and family risk and causes (25%)," and "standard treatment options (22%)." This percentage dropped to 12% when asked if the Internet was used to obtain information about one's "own" cancer. Popular websites accessed while searching for one's own cancer diagnosis included the American Cancer Society (www.cancer.org), Susan G. Komen, and WebMD. Over 50% did not remember the websites accessed. No one reported using the National Cancer Institute website (www.cancer.gov). The authors report as a study limitation that the survey was conducted 1 to 2 years after diagnosis, so there may have been recall bias among the participants.

Attitudes toward Internet Use

Kahn et al. (1999) used qualitative analysis consisting of focus groups and semi-structured interviews with 15 adolescents comprised of 53.3% African Americans (n = 8), 13.3% Hispanic Americans (n =2) and 33.3% whites (n =5). This was done in Boston, Massachusetts and no date for the study was provided. They inquired about a number of attitudes about Papanicolaou smears regarding perceived benefits, perceived barriers, perceived susceptibility to abnormal Papanicolaou smears/cervical cancer, and information seeking after an abnormal Papanicolaou smear. One question received a response regarding using the Internet to obtain information. The question of, "Where could Lisa go to get more information about her abnormal Papanicolaou smear?," elicited responses from 2 respondents (ethnicity unknown) that they could conduct their own research through information obtained from the Internet.

Changrani & Gany (2005) discuss their approach for creating a culturally-sensitive cancer website for English speaking black immigrant women to the United States from the Caribbean. These were from a number of Caribbean countries including Jamaica, Trinidad, Barbados, Antigua, Grenada, Bahamas, and Guyana. They conducted website review groups with 60 women who were recruited from the community in New York City. No previous knowledge or exposure to the Internet was required. Each review session was with a small group of 4-7 individuals for a duration of 2.5 hours. Participants ages ranged from 19 to 60 years. Half had annual income of less than $39,000. Eighty-seven percent had Internet access (n = 52). Of the Internet users, 39% accessed it daily and 40% weekly. Although more than half were either "extremely" or "quite" confident using the Internet, only 2 (3%) individuals had used the Internet for obtaining health information in the past 6 months. Many of the users chose not to enter websites with long website addresses (URLs). These individuals did not consider differently the information from edu, gov, com, org, or net URL suffixes. A few individuals when searching for breast cancer topics viewed pornography websites. Toggling between pages was challenging, especially when websites had directed individuals to external links or to print information. Participants preferred less information content on each page. They also preferred communication tools including question and answer, slide shows, and audio and video content, rather than just pure text. Even so, participants mentioned some drawbacks with this approach of not being able to listen to the Internet audio content and also page printing limits at the library, a place where they would typically access the Internet. The authors emphasize that this use for health information is much less than the reported 62% of individuals in the general population searching for health information over the past 6 months. As a lot of the sample were active Internet users, the authors believe that there is a great need for culturally appropriate Internet websites so that these individuals will search for and use this information. The one area not addressed in this study is that perhaps there is an actual cultural approach of not searching for health information among immigrant blacks from the Caribbean. Creating culturally relevant websites may not encourage this change in health information seeking behavior.

Nguyen, Hara, & Chlebowski (2005) conducted a survey among a multiethnic mostly minority sample of 59 cancer patients with reported ethnicities of Hispanic American (42%), white (25%), African American (19%), and Asian American / Pacific Islander (11%). Almost half did not have a primary language of English. The survey was administered in 2003 in California. Spanish language surveys were administered as appropriate. They found that those whose primary language was not English had less Internet access than those whose primary language was English. These results were maintained even when stratifying for age, gender, or income. Their survey evaluated websites from the two major cancer organizations of People Living with Cancer from the American Society of Clinical Oncology (ASCO) and the Breast Cancer Info website from the Susan G. Komen Cancer Foundation (SKF). Greater percentages for those whose primary language was not English (as compared to those whose primary language was English) reported that the website information would be more useful in pamphlet form than on the web (ASCO 90% versus 55%, p = 0.01; SKF 86% versus 45%, p = 0.004) and also that the information on the website would be more useful as a printed pamphlet in their own language. Although these differences exist and it is most likely among the Hispanic Americans who were surveyed in Spanish, there was no mention of analyses among those whose primary language was Spanish.

Roubidoux (2005) describes the creation of a computer game for information on breast cancer screening for Native Americans that can be used either through the Internet or through a CD. She discusses that although there is no information on home access for Native American women of breast cancer screening age, there is computer availability along with broadband access at almost all of the Indian Health Service clinics. Her game used culturally appropriate content, language, and graphics. Learning objectives were created and the player reads the case scenario and chooses from multiple choice answers. Culturally specific Native American graphics were incorporated. The style of the game is similar to Jeopardy. Individuals could play with another person or choose to play with one or two players who are part of the game package. She has initially tested it with focus groups. She emphasized that the scientific literature supports game use for health education. Also, specifically among Native Americans there is an historical tradition of teaching concepts through games. She did not report any specific data from this focus group. As this is an initial report and appears promising, data and further testing is necessary to determine the effectiveness of this game.

Helft, Eckles, Johnson-Calley, & Daugherty (2005) used convenience sampling and interviewed 200 oncology patients ages 18 or greater in Indianapolis, Indiana. Participants included 102 whites (51%), 90 African Americans (45%), 5 Hispanic Americans (3%), and 3 other (1%). The date of survey administration was not mentioned. The sample was described as from a disadvantaged lower income population, although no income data were provided. Only 10% of all participants used the Internet themselves to search for cancer information. Also, 21% who did not use the Internet themselves reported that proxies searched the Internet to provide them cancer information. Race was not associated with using the Internet for cancer information. In a question asking individuals to evaluate the accuracy of Internet information with 1=inaccurate and 7= accurate, African Americans had a mean value of 4.6 which was significantly lower than the mean value of whites (white mean value was not provided). The authors suggest that African Americans rated the Internet information as less accurate possibly because of a general African American suspicion of the medical establishment and of medical information.

Psychological Aspects of Internet Use

Fogel, Albert, Schnabel, Ditkoff, & Neugut (2003) surveyed 180 women with breast cancer using the Internet for breast health information. This sample is described above in the study of Fogel et al. (Fogel et al., 2002b). They found that comparisons of Internet use between racial/ethnic minorities and whites resulted in significantly greater levels of overall, appraisal, and tangible social support for the racial/ethnic minorities. However, there were no differences between minority and white participants with regard to belonging or self-esteem social support. These social support categories represent the following constructs (Cohen & Hoberman, 1983). The appraisal subscale measures the perceived availability of someone to talk to about one's problems. The belonging subscale measures the perceived availability of people with whom one can do things. The self-esteem subscale measures the perceived availability of a positive comparison when comparing oneself to others. The tangible subscale measures the perceived availability of material aid. Also, comparisons were made for perceived stress, depressive symptoms, loneliness, and coping. No differences were found between minorities and whites.

Henderson & Fogel (2003) studied 43 African American women with breast cancer participating in African American centered breast cancer support groups. They found that these women used a number of different support networks. However, using the Internet was least common. Support networks (including multiple responses) included God (n=22), family (n=19), friends (n=11), health care professionals (n=8), and the Internet (n=2). The Internet support reported was health information (i.e., informational support) and not participation in Internet support groups.

McTavish, Pingree, Hawkins, & Gustafson (2003) used the Comprehensive Health Enhancement Support System (CHESS), a specialized information and support program installed on one's computer. There was also an option of participating in an online bulletin-board support group that was available at all times of the day. Between 1995 and 1997 they recruited women aged 60 years or below with early and late stage breast cancer from a number of communities in the Midwestern portion of the United States (Madison, Chicago, and Indianapolis). Among those assigned to the CHESS treatment group, there were whites (n = 86), African Americans (n = 23), Native Americans (n = 2) and Asians (n = 2). Everyone besides the whites was grouped into a "women of color" group for the analyses. Whites posted a significantly greater average number of messages than the women of color group (19.16 versus 3.28) and also spent an average of significantly more minutes in the discussion group as compared to the women of color (2,397 versus 445). Almost all (92%) of the messages from the women of color were posted during the first three months. In analyses of message content, there were significant differences where women of color posted a greater proportion of messages about breast cancer (i.e., treatment and coping with side effects) and a lesser proportion about daily life than whites. There were no differences in disclosure of personal information in the messages. However, whites were significantly more likely to offer support than women of color (47% versus 16%). They noticed a time pattern in use. Initially message content was similar for both groups. However as time progressed, white women wrote more about daily issues and less about breast cancer issues while women of color had the opposite pattern where they wrote more about breast cancer issues and less about daily issues.

Gustafson, McTavish, Stengle, Ballard, Hawkins et al. (2005) recruited individuals from 2001 to 2003 (see Gustafson, McTavish, Stengle, Ballard, Jones et al., 2005). Whites were from rural Wisconsin (n = 154) and African Americans (n = 77) from Detroit, Michigan. Individuals were either diagnosed with breast cancer within the past year or had metastatic breast cancer. These individuals were given the CHESS program to use for 4 months. Also, peer advocates were provided to assist either by telephone or e-mail. Pre- and post-tests were conducted on a number of measures. An objective measure of web use included a web browser that tracked user's time and recorded the URLs visited. In every week except for the first 2 weeks, whites accessed CHESS significantly more than the African American women; however overall time for use did not differ between the groups. For a number of the weeks, there was overall more time spent in the different categories depending upon the ethnic group. There were four overall categories defined as Communication services (discussion group, ask an expert, and My Friend - a personal bulletin board for study participants and their peer advocates), Information services (questions and answers, instant library, resource guide, resource directory, web links, personal stories, video gallery and dictionary), Analysis services (decision notebook, action plan, health tracking, assessment, journaling, and learning from others), and Training services (services that helped the users learn how to use CHESS or the Internet; user guide, basic web skills, evaluating web information, and about CHESS). African Americans significantly spent more time in information services and analysis services while whites spent more time in communication services. No differences were reported for training services. In analyses for CHESS overall, they compared the current results to ethnic matched groups from a control group of data collected from a different study. In analyses of whites to whites, the CHESS user group had greater scores than the control group on variables measuring participation in health care, information competence, functional well-being, perceived social support, and negative emotion but not emotional well-being, additional breast cancer concerns, and barriers to information. In analyses of African Americans to African Americans, the CHESS user group had greater scores than the control group only on variables measuring participation in health care and information competence but not for any of the other six measures. It appears that since the African Americans used the discussion group much less than whites, they did not report any of the differences related to psychological variables such as social support and negative emotions.

Im, Chee, Tsai, Lin, & Cheng (2005) searched in 2003 with the five search engines of yahoo.com, msn.com, google.com, aol.com, and acor.org for Internet cancer support groups. There were a total of 546 Internet cancer support groups. Only 8 were specifically for African Americans, 8 specifically for Asian Americans, 0 specifically for Hispanic Americans, and 8 specifically for diverse ethnic groups. It is worth noting that this is overall only 4.4% of the support groups, while minority groups comprise a much greater percentage of the population than 4.4%.

Health Attitudes and Internet Use

Fogel, Morgan, & Davis (2005) surveyed women with breast cancer. The sample of 161 individuals is a subset of the sample described in the studies of Fogel et al. (Fogel et al., 2002b, 2003). There were 121 whites and 39 non-whites including 18 Hispanic Americans, 15 African Americans, and 6 Asian Americans. They studied the relationship of self-rated health to Internet health information use. In the analyses among whites, fair/poor self-rated health had an odds ratio of 5.3 that was associated with increased odds of using the Internet. On the other hand, for the analyses for minorities, the odds ratio was 0.04, indicating a decreased association with Internet use. So the minorities that potentially would benefit the most due to their fair/poor health status are not using the Internet for health information.

Readability and the Internet

Zimmerman, Akerelrea, Buller, Hau, & Leblanc (2003) conducted a series of three usability testing studies among mostly Hispanic Americans and American Indians in the states of New Mexico and Colorado for a website intended for primary prevention of cancer. No date was provided, but this took place after Microsoft Word 2000 was in use, as that computer program was used for the readability analyses. The third usability testing study was conducted for their "almost final" version of their website. This included 31 individuals consisting of 42% Hispanic Americans (n = 13), 35% American Indians (n = 11), and 23% whites (n = 7). The website had a Flesch-Kincaid readability score of grade 6.8. Among the participants, 83% rated it as very interesting, 74% as useful, and 55% as easy to read. Some of the reported difficulties even after this third usability testing study included unclear web links, small text size, and the practice of placing a dead link as a temporary feature where a future featured link would be placed.

Wilson, Baker, Brown-Syed, & Gollop (2000) studied the readability and cultural aspects of information on CancerNet from webpages downloaded in 1997 and 1998. They analyzed 49 documents retrieved from the "Patients and the Public" section of CancerNet. Using the Flesch-Kincaid readability approach, they found an overall 12th grade readability level. The beginning paragraphs were easier to read than those paragraphs in the middle or end portions. They also conducted a separate cultural focused sub-sample (n = 17) analysis of documents titled with the word "ethnic." They did not find any culturally tailored content, although English and Spanish language options were provided. Specifically, although there were inquiries based upon ethnic category, the individual information contained upon completing these searches were the same for someone who indicated an Asian American racial/ethnic category as for someone indicating a Hispanic American racial/ethnic category.

Kaphingst, Zanfini, & Emmons (2006) in 2003 analyzed a total of 19 colorectal websites. They included the first five unique links from searches in yahoo, msn, and google, along with four other specific websites. The SMOG reading level was 12.8, indicative of a bit more than 12th grade reading level, with 63% of the websites requiring a college-level reading ability. They also assessed the websites with the Suitability Assessment of Materials (SAM) instrument, a measure that examines 22 factors relevant to reading difficulty. This instrument showed that 53% of the websites were "not suitable." Reasons for poor scores included 1) poor content scores including a poor focus on behavioral content and poor review of key ideas, and 2) not enough illustrations to explain the key ideas.

Friedman, Hoffman-Goetz, & Arocha (2004) analyzed 55 websites in 2002 on the topics of breast cancer, colon cancer, and prostate cancer. They assessed readability with the SMOG reading level, the Flesch-Kincaid (F-K) grade level, and the Flesch Reading ease (FRE) score. The mean SMOG score was grade 13.7, the mean F-K score was grade 10.9, and the mean FRE score was 41.6, a score indicating a difficult reading style. All three readability measures indicated that breast cancer websites were easier to read than the colon and prostate cancer websites.

CONCLUSION

This chapter reviews the scientific empirical literature on Internet use among those of racial/ethnic populations and/or low literacy groups. There are a number of studies describing characteristics of Internet users. The clear message from the reviewed studies is that those of racial/ethnic populations are less likely to use the Internet. The reasons for less use are not clear. Is it due to the existence of a digital divide? Is it due to the fact that the websites are not culturally sensitive?

There are a number of studies that review attitudes toward Internet use. African Americans do not necessarily trust everything on the Internet the same way as do whites. Hispanic Americans find the information useful, but prefer it in a more traditional medium of printed pamphlets. The importance of cultural training to teach individuals how to use the Internet and also tailoring of websites to be of greater interest and relevance to those of racial/ethnic populations is emphasized. Have there been changes since these studies have been conducted to allow websites to be more appealing to those of racial/ethnic populations? It is unknown at this time.

The studies that focus on the psychological aspects of Internet use show two points. First, for those who use the Internet there are greater potential benefits for using it that among those of whites. Unfortunately, at least among the reviewed studies regarding African Americans, they are unlikely to use the Internet for health information. They also are less interested in online support groups. The key area to focus upon is how to increase interest in the Internet among racial/ethnic populations, as they can potentially benefit a lot from this medium but yet are not doing so.

Only one study discusses health aspects and Internet information use. At least from this study, one understands that among those of racial/ethnic populations, those who could benefit the most from Internet information due to their fair/poor health condition are less likely to use the Internet for health information. The question to be addressed is what can be done so that the Internet appeals to those of racial/ethnic populations? It may be that the questions above regarding the digital divide, attitudes towards use, and the psychological aspects of Internet use first need to be addressed before focusing on this topic.

With regard to readability of websites, the reviewed studies show that unless there is a special emphasis on creating a website with readability levels at lower grade levels, the typical website assumes a high grade level of at least 10th grade. This approach can make it difficult for those with lower education levels to benefit from the wealth of information on the Internet.

There are also a number of areas which have not been studied among those of racial/ethnic populations that have been studied among whites. For example, is the Internet useful for decision-making for those of racial/ethnic populations (Diefenbach et al., 2002)? Are there gender differences among the different racial/ethnic groups with regard to the support they receive from the Internet (Seale, Ziebland, & Charteris-Black, 2006)?

In summary, this review found five broad areas studied regarding Internet use among those of racial/ethnic populations. A number of questions remain unanswered based upon this review. Further research is needed to better understand the impact of the Internet among those of racial/ethnic populations and/or low literacy groups.

REFERENCES

Abdullah, M., Theobald, D. E., Butler, D., Kroenke, K., Perkins, A., Edgerton, S., et al. (2005). Access to communication technologies in a sample of cancer patients: An urban and rural survey. *BMC Cancer, 5,* 18.

Baker, L., Wagner, T. H., Singer, S. & Bundorf, M. K. (2003). Use of the Internet and E-mail for health care information: Results from a national survey. *JAMA, 289(18),* 2400-2406.

Buller, D. B., Woodall, W. G., Zimmerman, D. E., Heimendinger, J., Rogers, E. M., Slater, M. D., et al. (2001). Formative research activities to provide Web-based nutrition education to adults in the Upper Rio Grande Valley. *Family and Community Health, 24(3)*, 1-12.

Bureau, C. (2000). *Census regions and divisions of the United States.* Retrieved May 10, 2006, from http://www.census.gov/geo/www/us_regdiv.pdf.

Burns, E. (2006a). *Global Internet adoption slows while involvement deepens.* Retrieved May 7, 2006, from http://www.clickz.com/stats/sectors/demographics.

Burns, E. (2006b). *Rural America slow to adopt broadband.* Retrieved May 7, 2006, from http://www.clickz.com/stats/sectors/demographics.

Changrani, J. & Gany, F. (2005). Online cancer education and immigrants: Effecting culturally appropriate websites. *Journal of Cancer Education, 20(3)*, 183-186.

Cohen, S. & Hoberman, H. M. (1983). Positive events and social supports as buffers of life change stress. *Journal of Applied Social Psychology, 13(2)*, 99-125.

Diefenbach, M. A., Dorsey, J., Uzzo, R. G., Hanks, G. E., Greenberg, R. E., Horwitz, E., et al. (2002). Decision-making strategies for patients with localized prostate cancer. *Seminars in Urologic Oncology, 20(1)*, 55-62.

Fogel, J. (2003). Internet use for cancer information among racial/ethnic populations and low literacy groups. *Cancer Control, 10*(5 Suppl), 45-51.

Fogel, J., Albert, S. M., Schnabel, F., Ditkoff, B. A. & Neugut, A. I. (2002a). Internet use and social support in women with breast cancer. *Health Psychology, 21(4)*, 398-404.

Fogel, J., Albert, S. M., Schnabel, F., Ditkoff, B. A. & Neugut, A. I. (2002b). Use of the Internet by women with breast cancer, *Journal of Medical Internet Research, 4,* e9.

Fogel, J., Albert, S. M., Schnabel, F., Ditkoff, B. A. & Neugut, A. I. (2003). Racial/ethnic differences and potential psychological benefits in use of the internet by women with breast cancer. *Psycho-Oncology, 12(2)*, 107-117.

Fogel, J., Morgan, P. D. & Davis, B. L. (2005). Consumers of Internet health information and self-rated health status: Breast care disparities issues. *Journal of Multicultural Nursing and Health, 11*, 35-40.

Fox, S. (2005). *Digital divisions.* Retrieved May 9, 2006, from http://www.pewinternet.org/pdfs/PIP_Digital_Divisions_Oct_5_2005.pdf

Fox, S. & Rainee, L. (2004). *The online health care revolution: How the Web helps Americans take better care of themselves.* Retrieved February 16, 2005, from http://www.pewinternet.org/pdfs/PIP_Health_Report.pdf.

Friedman, D. B., Hoffman-Goetz, L. & Arocha, J. F. (2004). Readability of cancer information on the internet. *Journal of Cancer Education, 19(2)*, 117-122.

Gustafson, D. H., McTavish, F. M., Stengle, W., Ballard, D., Hawkins, R., Shaw, B. R., et al. (2005). Use and impact of eHealth system by low-income women with breast cancer. *Journal of Health Communication, 10 (Suppl 1)*, 195-218.

Gustafson, D. H., McTavish, F. M., Stengle, W., Ballard, D., Jones, E., Julesberg, K., et al. (2005). Reducing the digital divide for low-income women with breast cancer: a feasibility study of a population-based intervention. *Journal of Health Communication, 10 (Suppl 1)*, 173-193.

Haughton, L. T., Kreuter, M., Hall, J., Holt, C. L. & Wheetley, E. (2005). Digital divide and stability of access in African American women visiting urban public health centers. *Journal of Health Care for the Poor and Underserved, 16(2)*, 362-374.

Helft, P. R., Eckles, R. E., Johnson-Calley, C. S. & Daugherty, C. K. (2005). Use of the internet to obtain cancer information among cancer patients at an urban county hospital. *Journal of Clinical Oncology, 23(22)*, 4954-4962.

Henderson, P. D. & Fogel, J. (2003). Support networks used by African American breast cancer support group participants. *ABNF Journal, 14(5)*, 95-98.

Im, E. O., Chee, W., Tsai, H. M., Lin, L. C. & Cheng, C. Y. (2005). Internet cancer support groups: A feminist analysis. *Cancer Nursing, 28(1)*, 1-7.

Kahn, J. A., Chiou, V., Allen, J. D., Goodman, E., Perlman, S. E. & Emans, S. J. (1999). Beliefs about Papanicolaou smears and compliance with Papanicolaou smear follow-up in adolescents. *Archives of Pediatric and Adolescent Medicine, 153(10)*, 1046-1054.

Kakai, H., Maskarinec, G., Shumay, D. M., Tatsumura, Y. & Tasaki, K. (2003). Ethnic differences in choices of health information by cancer patients using complementary and alternative medicine: An exploratory study with correspondence analysis. *Social Science and Medicine, 56*, 851-862.

Kaphingst, K. A., Zanfini, C. J. & Emmons, K. M. (2006). Accessibility of web sites containing colorectal cancer information to adults with limited literacy (United States). *Cancer Causes and Control, 17(2)*, 147-151.

McTavish, F. M., Pingree, S., Hawkins, R. & Gustafson, D. (2003). Cultural differences in use of an electronic discussion group. *Journal of Health Psychology, 8*, 105-117.

Monnier, J., Laken, M. & Carter, C. L. (2002). Patient and caregiver interest in internet-based cancer services. *Cancer Practice, 10(6)*, 305-310.

Nguyen, K. D., Hara, B. & Chlebowski, R. T. (2005). Utility of two cancer organization websites for a multiethnic, public hospital oncology population: Comparative cross-sectional survey. *Journal of Medical Internet Research, 7(3)*, e28.

Roubidoux, M. A. (2005). Breast cancer detective: a computer game to teach breast cancer screening to Native American patients. *Journal of Cancer Education, 20*(1 Suppl), 87-91.

Satterlund, M. J., McCaul, K. D. & Sandgren, A. K. (2003). Information gathering over time by breast cancer patients, *Journal of Medical Internet Research, 5,* e15.

Seale, C., Ziebland, S. & Charteris-Black, J. (2006). Gender, cancer experience and internet use: A comparative keyword analysis of interviews and online cancer support groups. *Social Science and Medicine, 62(10)*, 2577-2590.

Smith, R. P., Devine, P., Jones, H., DeNittis, A., Whittington, R. & Metz, J. M. (2003). Internet use by patients with prostate cancer undergoing radiotherapy. *Urology, 62(2)*, 273-277.

Talosig-Garcia, M. & Davis, S. W. (2005). Information-seeking behavior of minority breast cancer patients: An exploratory study. *Journal of Health Communication, 10 (Suppl 1)*, 53-64.

Wilson, F. L., Baker, L. M., Brown-Syed, C. & Gollop, C. (2000). An analysis of the readability and cultural sensitivity of information on the National Cancer Institute's Web site: CancerNet. *Oncology Nursing Forum, 27(9)*, 1403-1409.

Zimmerman, D. E., Akerelrea, C. A., Buller, D. B., Hau, B. & Leblanc, M. (2003). Integrating usability testing into the development of a 5 a day nutrition website for at-risk populations in the American Southwest. *Journal of Health Psychology, 8(1)*, 119-134.

In: Race and Ethnicity

Editor: Jonathan K. Crennan, pp. 233-248

ISBN: 978-1-60692-099-2

© 2010 Nova Science Publishers, Inc.

Chapter 9

ETHNICITY, CULTURAL ROLES AND THEIR RELEVANCE FOR CLINICAL PSYCHOLOGY: THE EXAMPLE OF POSTTRAUMA ADJUSTMENT AND PSYCHOPATHOLOGY

Birgit Kleim[1,2] *and Laura Jobson*[3]

[1]King's College London, United Kingdom
[2]University of Basel, Switzerland
[3]University of East Anglia, United Kingdom

ABSTRACT

Clinical psychology is concerned with the diagnosis and treatment of mental disorder, such as anxiety or depression (e.g., Davison & Neale, 2000). Despite some cross-cultural differences in the exact prevalence of psychological disorders, most disorders are common across the world, to all cultures and ethnic groups (e.g., Kleinman, 2004; Merikangas et al., 1998). A key point is that such disorders cause substantial distress across cultures, and pose a significant social and economical challenge by affecting hundreds of millions of people worldwide. The World Health Organisation Global Burden of Disease Survey estimates that mental disease will be the second leading cause of disabilities worldwide by the year 2020 (WHO, 2009). This calls for a better understanding of the development and maintenance of psychological disorders in order to be able to treat them effectively. Many treatments have been shown to be effective for a range of different psychological disorders, for instance cognitive behavioural treatments (CBT) for anxiety and depression (e.g., Steward & Chambless, 2009, Butler et al., 2006). However, despite their clinical effectiveness, questions remain about dissemination in various contexts, and about a considerable proportion of patients who drop out of therapy or do not benefit from CBT (Shafran et al., 2009, Barlow, 2002). Hence, there are current efforts to refine CBT and advance further the underlying theory and current practice. Ethnicity and cultural roles are key factors that may play a large role in how psychological disorders are developed, why they are maintained, and, in turn, how patients respond to treatment. More specifically, cultural beliefs, attitudes, values, expectations and assumptions, such as cultural differences in beliefs about psychological health and disorders, help-seeking, and recovery, impact on the course of psychological disorders. Additionally, wider cultural differences, such as views regarding power distribution, self-understanding, masculinity, religion, and acceptance of uncertainty (Hofstede & Hofstede, 2004), may also impact on the processes involved in the development, expression and maintenance of psychological disorders (Draguns & Tanaka-Matsumi, 2003). In practice, however, this relation between ethnicity and mental disorders is not simple and may often be indirect and multifaceted. A better understanding of this relationship is of vital importance for at least two reasons. First, recent reports have highlighted the reality of health disparities and unequal treatment of different cultures and ethnic minorities. A recent study on psychiatric treatment, for instance, of primary care patients reported that only about half of the patients with anxiety disorders received mental health treatment at the time, and that members of ethnic minority groups were less likely to receive mental health treatment (Weisberg et al., 2007). Second, an individual's ethnicity and his or her cultural role/orientation seem to have a wide-ranging influence on the development and maintenance of psychological disorders, such as anxiety or depression. The present chapter will focus on both of these issues and explore the impact of ethnicity on mental disorders in detail. This is done using the example of posttraumatic stress disorder (PTSD), a common anxiety disorder following trauma with a particularly cultural influence. First, we aim to suggest ways in which theories of PTSD could be adapted in order to incorporate ethnicity and cultural roles. Second, we present preliminary data on the role of ethnicity in autobiographical memory, appraisals and posttrauma adjustment, demonstrating that there are important differences in the way Caucasian and Non-Caucasian trauma survivors perceive and appraise their trauma, and how they later make meaning of it. Towards the end of the chapter, implications for theory and clinical practice, i.e., treatment and prevention programs for PTSD and other disorders, are discussed.

DRAWING MODELS OF PTSD INTO THE CULTURAL SPHERE

PTSD is an anxiety disorder that can develop following exposure to traumatic events. Trauma survivors who develop PTSD experience symptoms of repeated and unwanted re-experiencing of the event, hyperarousal, emotional numbing and avoidance (*Diagnostic and Statistical Manual of Mental Disorders-IV*; American Psychiatric Association, 1994). Research indicates that up to 14% of people will at some point in their life suffer PTSD. While accumulating research indicates PTSD to be a universal phenomenon(e.g. Figueira et al., 2007; Paunovic & Ost, 2001; Pham, Weinstein & Longman, 2004), it remains substantially unknown whether the processes implicated in the aetiology and maintenance of PTSD are culturally similar.

PTSD Models

In recent years there have been major advances in the theoretical models of PTSD. These models account well for the development and maintenance of PTSD and have guided treatment. As relatively recent review articles (e.g., Brewin & Holmes, 2003; Dalgleish, 2004) provide excellent accounts of these models, this chapter will not review these models but rather highlight several psychological processes suggested by these models to be involved in PTSD. Such processes include autobiographical memory (e.g., Brewin, Dalglesih, &

Joseph, 1996; Conway & Pleydell-Pearce, 2000; Dalgleish, 2004; Ehlers & Clark, 2000; Rubin, Berntsen, & Bohni, 2008), appraisals (e.g., Ehlers & Clark, 2000), assumptions, schema and meaning and belief systems (e.g., Dalgleish, 2004; Foa & Riggs, 1993; Horowitz, 1997; Janoff-Bulman, 1992), emotion (e.g., Dalgleish, 2004; Foa & Rothbaum, 1998), motivation and goals (e.g., Conway, 2005; Dalgleish, 2004; Ehlers & Clark, 2000; Horowitz, 1997), identity, social roles and role transitions (e.g., Berntsen & Rubin, 2006, 2007), and self (e.g., Berntsen & Rubin, 2006, 2007; Conway, 2005; Ehlers & Clark, 2000). This list is by no means exhaustive but is sufficient to commence a discussion about the need for current PTSD models to consider cultural differences in self. Despite these impressive theoretical advances, these models have been developed independently of recent findings indicating culture impacts on, and in numerous cases govern, many of these psychological processes. Therefore, current models of PTSD may be limited in the context of cultural differences, both theoretically and clinically.

The Influence of Cultural Sphere on Components of PTSD Models

Theorists (e.g. Markus & Kitayama, 1991, 1994) posit that different cultures hold remarkably divergent construals of the self, others and the interdependence between the two. In individualistic cultures (typically Western) the self is perceived as an independent entity, while in collectivistic cultures (typically non-Western) the self is perceived as an interdependent entity. The independent self is bounded, unitary and stable, and private internal aspects of self (such as abilities, thoughts and emotion) are valued. The independent self aims to be unique, express the self, realize internal attributes and promote own goals (Markus & Kitayama, 1991). In contrast, the interdependent self is flexible and variable and external, public aspects of the self (such as social roles, relationships and status) are important. The interdependent self aims to belong, fit-in, occupy one's proper place, engage in appropriate action and promote other's goals (Markus & Kitayama, 1991). While variation exists to which individuals exhibit an independent versus interdependent orientation within and between cultures and situations (e.g., Lee & Zane, 1998), normative differences between collectivistic and individualistic cultures are marked (e.g., Fiske, Kitayama, Markus, & Nisbett, 1998, Kagitcibasi, 1996). Such culturally diverging self construals have been found to impact on, and in many circumstances govern, the very nature of individual experience, including behavior, cognition and emotion. The influence of culturally diverging self construals on some psychological process will now be explored.

Autobiographical Memory

Cultural differences in self-understanding have been found to influence the emergence of autobiographical memory (Nelson & Fivush, 2004). Research has shown that mothers from collectivistic cultures engage their children in reminiscing that encourages on-going relationships and model to the children to construct personal stories that give way to social interactions and collectivity (e.g., Wang, 2007; Wang & Fivush, 2005; Nelson & Fivush, 2004; Mullen & Yi, 1995). In contrast, mothers from individualistic cultures invite children to actively participate in the creation of their own life story (Wang & Fivush, 2005). There is also considerable support for cultural differences in child and adult autobiographical memories. Moreover, self-revealing, self-focused, emotionally elaborate, lengthier accounts of specific, one-point-in-time personal events are more prevalent among individualistic cultures than collectivistic cultures. In contrast, collectivistic cultures tend to focus on collective activities, social interactions and significant others, general routines, emotionally neutral events, and social and historical events (e.g. Jobson & O'Kearney, 2008a; Pillemer, 1998; Wang & Conway, 2004; Wang, 2008). As Wang (2001) claims, in individualistic cultures an elaborate, coherent, well-integrated life story with the individual cast as the "lead" is vital as it provides self-understanding, self-continuity and affirmation of the self as an autonomous unit, whereas in collectivistic cultures, collective activities are often esteemed over this unique life story. These findings suggest that the content, quality and mechanisms of autobiographical memory are culturally distinct and instrumental in reaffirming the culturally sanctioned self (Wang & Conway, 2004).

Appraisals

Research has demonstrated that cultural differences in self-construal impact on the way in which events, situations, and life encounters are appraised (e.g. Mauro, Sato, & Tucker, 1992; Mesquita & Ellsworth, 2001; Mesquita & Markus, 2004; Mesquita & Walker, 2003). Mesquita and Walker (2003) claim that cultural differences in self-construal "facilitate and render desirable certain appraisals of events, while making the occurrence of others less likely and less valued" (p. 784) and "foster culture-specific appraisal tendencies that are reflected in culturally distinct patterns of emotional experience" (p. 784). Markus and Kitayama (1991) claim individualistic cultures appraise success through independent, personal accomplishment and a personal sense of control, while in collectivistic cultures, "agency is differently instantiated...or is not valued as much" (Mesquita & Walker, 2003, p. 785) but rather fate, secondary control, adjustment to the situation, multi-determination of events and the interdependence of an individual and their social environment are stressed (e.g., Fiske et al., 1998; Nisbett, Peng, Choi, & Norenzayan, 2001). Studies have also found that those from individualistic cultures, when compared to those from collectivistic cultures, are more likely to judge the dimension of responsibility to be applicable to emotional situations, and personal responsibility and control have been found to predict positive emotion in individualistic cultures but not in collectivistic cultures (e.g., Matsumoto, Kudoh, Scherer, & Wallbott, 1988; Mesquita & Karasawa, 2002). Additionally, Mesquita and Walker (2003) note that while in the West, an appraised lack of personal control contributes to sadness, worry and fear, it remains less known whether personal control is equally important in other cultures.

Identity

Markus and Kitayama (1991) propose that in individualistic cultures identity is derived from a set of internal personal attributes, whereas in collectivistic cultures identity is derived from others, and relationships with others, in specific contexts. This has been demonstrated in numerous studies (e.g., Cousins, 1989; Gur-Yaish & Wang, 2006; Jobson & O'Kearney, 2008b) using the Twenty Statements Test (Kuhn & McPartland, 1954) which asks people to respond to the question "Who am I?" It is repeatedly shown that those from individualistic cultures provide responses related to private inner aspects of self (e.g., I am friendly, I am kind, etc.), while those from collectivistic cultures provide responses associated with public aspects of the self or social roles (e.g., I am a mother, I am Chinese, etc.).

Motivation and Goals

Cultural variations in self translate into cultural differences in motivation and goals. Based on empirical findings, Mesquita and Walker (2003) claim that those from individualistic cultures hold goals of being distinct from others, standing out and personally achieving, whereas those from collectivistic cultures aim to meet social responsibilities and obligations to maintain group harmony. Events in turn are created and promoted to allow goal obtainment. Lee, Aaker, and Gardner (2000) found that individualistic cultures emphasize the approach of positive outcomes, whereas collectivistic cultures focus on the avoidance of bad outcomes. This is thought to align with cultural differences in self as individualistic cultures emphasize strengthening good qualities and in turn become autonomous and unique, whereas collectivists desire to live up to obligations and responsibilities and thus, the aim is to avoid bad outcomes (Mesquita & Walker, 2003). Such motivations and goals could be important in terms of trauma consequences and post-trauma adjustment.

Schema, Assumptions and Emotion

Markus and Kitayama (1991) hypothesize that the independent versus interdependent construals of self are among the most overarching schema of the individual's self-system. They suggest that these construals engage and organize the more specific self-regulatory schemata. Hence, they suggest that the precise organization of many self-relevant processes and their outcomes relies essentially on whether these processes are rooted in an independent or interdependent construal of the self. Markus and Kitayama note that in the process of giving meaning and coherence to the world it is known that people show an increased sensitivity to self-relevant stimuli. For those with an independent self-construal, this includes information relevant to one's self-defining attributes but for those with an interdependent self-construal, such stimuli would include information about significant others within the person's social context or information about the self in relation to another person. Research supports cultural differences in self impact on schema (e.g., Aaker & Scmitt, 2001; Eagle, 2005; Takata, 1999; Schwartz & Kim, 2002).

Liem, Lim, and Liem (2000) claim that the "centrality of independence versus interdependence to one's sense of self is thought to influence one's affective response to life encounters" (p. 25). Mesquita and Walker (2003) theorize that cultural differences in self-construal can impact on differences in antecedent events, perceived significance of events, perceived focus of attention during an event and differences in appraisals, which all impact on emotional outcome. Research has identified that other-focused emotions (emotions that have another as the primary referent) are more common in collectivistic cultures and ego-focused emotions (emotions centered on the individual and involve experiences such as self-affirmation, blocked autonomy or threat to one's integrity) are more prevalent in individualistic cultures (e.g., Liem et al., 2000). Feldman Barrett and Russell (1999) found cultural differences in emotion valence.

PTSD Models and the Cultural Sphere

The PTSD Models section above highlighted a range of psychological processes, such as autobiographical memory, appraisals, identity, motivation and goals, schema, assumptions and belief systems, thought to be involved in the development and maintenance of PTSD. The Cultural Sphere section demonstrated that cultural differences in self have been found to impact on these concepts fundamental to the models of PTSD. Specifically, diverging construals have been found to impact on, often to the extent of governing, the very nature of individual experience, including autobiographical memory, appraisals, identity, motivation and goals, schema and assumptions and emotion; elements deemed to be fundamental in PTSD. However, the PTSD models have thus far not considered this literature and thus, it remains unknown whether these models are bound to western, individualistic approaches to the self or whether they are flexible enough to accommodate these cultural differences. In light of this, significant questions need to be addressed, such as; Are there cultural differences in the autobiographical memory of trauma and if so, what do these differences mean for the development and maintenance of PTSD? What impact do cultural differences in appraisals have on the proposed role of appraisals in PTSD? Given trauma memory can become central to personal identity, what is the influence of cultural variation in self-construal on the relationship between trauma and identity? How do cultural differences in emotion impact on the development and maintenance of PTSD? It is these questions that can draw our PTSD models into the cultural realm. Namely, it is uncertain whether cultural variations in self impact on these concepts in the event of trauma in a similar way to that found in general everyday events. The following section will give examples of investigations into the impact of culture on autobiographical memory, and differences in appraisals, posttrauma adjustment and PTSD.

ETHNICITY, CULTURE AND AUTOBIOGRAPHICAL MEMORY

There is accumulating evidence (e.g., Trafimow, Triandis, & Goto, 1991; Wang & Ross, 2005) suggesting that regardless of culture, temporary primes, situations and events can call forth a particular orientation of the self. By its nature a traumatic event challenges goals to survive, to protect personal safety, and to personally control and master the situation (i.e., goals of autonomy, control and self-determination) (e.g., Dalgleish, 2004). Additionally, from an evolutionary perspective, it seems plausible to suggest that across all cultures, humans, when faced with trauma, focus on personal survival. Therefore, applying these proposals to the empirical evidence indicating events can call forth a particular orientation of self, it was hypothesized that while there will be cultural differences in levels of autonomous orientation in the everyday memory, the trauma memory may contain culturally similar levels of autonomous orientation. To examine this hypothesis, trauma survivors from individualistic and collectivistic cultures provided everyday and trauma narratives. Narratives were scored for autonomous orientation (an index of participants' tendency to express autonomy and self-determination in their memories) and interdependence (an index of participants' tendency to refer to social interactions and significant others). The findings (Jobson, 2009a; Jobson & O'Kearney, 2006) supported the hypothesis. Despite cultural variation in levels of autonomous orientation in autobiographical remembering of everyday events, cultural variation in levels of autonomous orientation were not evident in the autobiographical memory of trauma. The everyday narratives of trauma survivors from individualistic cultures were significantly more autonomously oriented than the narratives of those from collectivistic cultures. For the trauma narratives, however, collectivistic and individualistic cultures provided equally autonomously oriented autobiographical memories (Jobson, 2009-a). Additionally, however, there were some cultural differences; trauma survivors from collectivistic cultures had higher levels of interdependence in both their everyday and trauma memories (Jobson, 2009-a) and provided less specific memories (Jobson, 2009-b) than trauma survivors from individualistic cultures. It was also of interest to investigate the influence of culture on the relationship between autobiographical remembering and PTSD. It was found (Jobson, 2009-a) that trauma survivors from individualistic cultures with PTSD had *lower* levels of autonomous orientation in their autobiographical remembering than trauma survivors from individualistic cultures without PTSD. In contrast, trauma survivors from collectivistic cultures with PTSD had *higher* levels of autonomous orientation in their autobiographical remembering than trauma survivors from collectivistic cultures without PTSD. Hence, the findings suggest that there were both cultural similarities and differences in the autobiographical remembering of trauma and that the cultural distinction in self has an influence on the relationship between the nature of autobiographical remembering and posttraumatic psychological adjustment, an issue that will be discussed further below.

ETHNICITY, CULTURE AND TRAUMA-RELATED APPRAISALS

Ehlers and Clark (2000) emphasize the role of self-relevant appraisals of the trauma experience and/or its sequelae in the maintenance of PTSD. There has been ongoing examination of four theoretical-derived cognitive appraisal domains in particular; mental defeat, control strategies, permanent change and alienation (e.g. Dunmore, Clark and Ehlers, 2001; Ehlers, Clark et al., 1998; Ehlers, Maercker and Boos, 2000; Ehlers, Mayou and Bryant, 1998). There is acknowledgment (Ehlers and Clark, 2000; Kleim et al., 2007) that the relative importance of specific appraisal factors may be influenced by several "background" factors, in particular characteristics of the trauma and the person's previous experiences and beliefs. It proposed, therefore, that there were very good conceptual and empirical reasons to suggest that cultural differences in the nature of self and self-construal may play an important role in determining the relative importance of appraisal domains in PTSD. All four of these appraisals either focus on the self and one's actions, autonomy and consistency across time (e.g. "I was weak", "I deserved for this to happen", "I am incompetent, inferior, unworthy", "I am permanently damaged"), or on self in relationship to others (e.g. "Others can know that I am a trauma survivor", "I will always be alone and no one understands", "Others think I cannot cope"). Ehlers and Clark posit that appraisals centered round the self maintain PTSD as survivors continue to perceive current situations as threatening and dangerous and themselves as inadequate and unable to cope in current situations. They suggest that appraisals about others and interpersonal relationships maintain PTSD because they are instrumental in withdrawal from social interactions and reduce opportunities to receive social support and to correct negative beliefs about themselves and others (Ehlers et al., 2000). It is this inclusion of appraisal of self and self-in-relationship that brings Ehlers and Clark's model into the cultural sphere. As outlined above, research (e.g. Mesquita & Walker, 2003) has shown that cultural differences in self-construal influence how events are appraised and associated affective responses (Mesquita and Karasawa, 2002; Mesquita and Walker, 2003). It was predicted that trauma appraisals that focus on the self, independence, control and agency (i.e. mental defeat, control strategies and permanent change) would have greater impact on post-trauma psychological adjustment of trauma survivors from independent cultures than for trauma survivors from interdependent cultures. Hence, the difference in these appraisals between those with and without PTSD will be significantly more pronounced for trauma survivors from independent cultures than for trauma survivors from interdependent cultures. On the other hand, trauma appraisals that focus on the self in relation to others and interdependence (i.e. alienation) will have a greater impact on the psychological adjustment of those from interdependent cultures than those from independent cultures. Thus, the difference in these appraisals between those with and without PTSD will be significantly more pronounced for trauma survivors from interdependent cultures than for trauma survivors from independent cultures. Trauma survivors with PTSD and without PTSD from independent and interdependent cultures provided trauma narratives. Narratives were coded for negative cognitive appraisals (mental defeat, control strategies, alienation and permanent change). In line with Ehlers and colleagues' work, trauma survivors with PTSD from independent cultures reported more mental defeat, alienation, permanent change and less control strategies than non-PTSD trauma survivors from independent cultures. In contrast, for those from interdependent cultures, only alienation appraisals differentiated between trauma survivors with and without PTSD. Those with PTSD had more alienation appraisals than those without PTSD. The findings suggest cultural differences in self impact on the relationship between appraisals and posttraumatic psychological adjustment.

ETHNICITY, CULTURE AND POSTTRAUMA ADJUSTMENT

Survivors of traumatic events may not only develop psychological problems such as posttraumatic stress disorder, but also report positive changes in their lives as a consequence of the trauma (e.g., Frazier et al., 2001, 2004; Tedeschi & Calhoun, 2004). Paradoxically, the shattering of previous beliefs can be seen as a starting point for posttraumatic growth in that it promotes the development of new perspectives, and a sense that valuable lessons have been learned (Calhoun & Tedeschi, 2006). These include a feeling of strength, becoming closer to family and friends, or a greater appreciation of life. Such perceived positive changes are summarized in the concept of posttraumatic growth (PTG). PTG has been observed after a range of traumatic events, such as traumatic bereavement (Davis, Nolen-Hoeksema & Larson,

1998), combat (Schnurr, Rosenberg & Friedman, 1993), or man-made disasters (McMillen et al., 1997). A recent theoretical model explained positive changes after trauma as the result of a number of factors, such as characteristics of the person and of the challenging situation, management of emotional distress, and rumination (Calhoun & Tedeschi, 2006). These authors argued that the more an individual needs to work through a traumatic event and its aftermath, the more he or she will subsequently benefit from the experience (Tedeschi & Calhoun, 2004). As suggested above, cultural roles, ethnicity and religiousness may have an important impact on the extent to which trauma survivors successfully make meaning from their experience (i.e., experience posttraumatic growth, find life meaningful, and restore beliefs in a just world), which may, in turn, influence psychological adjustment. African American sexual assault survivors (Kennedy, Davis & Taylor, 1998) and African American HIV patients (Milam, 2004), for instance, reported more posttraumatic positive change than white Americans. A recent meta-analysis also found that ethnic minorities are more likely to report growth, and associations between growth and well-being have been greatest in studies that consisted of a larger percentage of ethnic minority participants (Helgeson et al., 2006).

In a longitudinal study of over two-hundred recent assault survivors, Kleim and Ehlers (2009) examined predictors of posttraumatic growth, and found that being Non-Caucasian was associated to more perceived growth at 6 months following the assault.

Table 1. Posttraumatic growth in Caucasian and Non-Caucasian assault survivors at 6 months post-trauma.

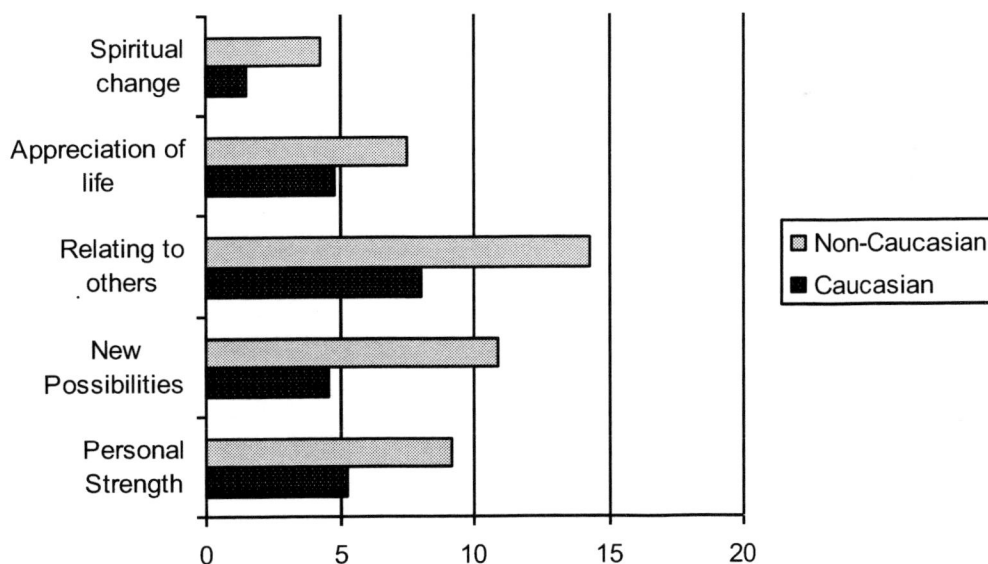

As shown in Table 1, Non-Caucasians reported most changes in relating to others, as well as in their perceived new possibilities and personal strength. Moreover, they felt that they appreciated life more since their trauma, and that they had changed spiritually. Taken together, they reported larger amounts of positive change since the assault than their Non-Caucasian counterparts. Interestingly, however, Non-Caucasians had also higher initial acute stress disorder symptoms, an anxiety disorder diagnosed in the first weeks following a traumatic event, and reported more symptoms of PTSD in a clinical interview 6 months later. Religious trauma survivors also reported more growth than those not observing any religion. More research is required in order to confirm these findings and test further mechanisms. In accord with the above mentioned cultural influences on different processes in the development and maintenance of PTSD, however, it is conceivable that Non-Caucasian trauma survivors processed the trauma somewhat differently than Caucasians, i.e. they may have felt greater shame and humiliation, or more fear during the assault, which was predictive of later growth. Moreover, post-trauma adaptation is likely to be different in these groups, which in turn, affects whether posttraumatic growthis experienced and reported. The findings raise the question whether, and in what ways, posttraumatic growth and psychopathology are related in different ethnic groups. Scholars have recently raised the question whether "finding something good in the bad is always good"? (Tomich & Helgesson, 2004). Non-Caucasians reporting high growth levels may reflect attempts to reassure themselves that the outcome of the trauma is less catastrophic than they think and to minimize symptoms. This subgroup may also have been more prone to denial, avoidance, or wishful thinking, which, in turn, may promote growth. Future research should investigate whether and when Non-Caucasians more often respond with a mildly distorted positive perception of themselves, an exaggerated sense of personal control, and unrealistic optimism (see also Davis & McKearney, 2003) and when they develop "true" posttraumatic growth. Hobfoll and colleagues (2007) have recently proposed that action is essential to true growth, and that PTG may index positive adaptation when accompanied by actions, not solely by cognitive processes. It is conceivable that some Non-Caucasian participants may not have been able to turn growth cognition into action, for example., by becoming socially or politically active in response to being assaulted, or by actively engaging in getting therapy or socialising with others, and may thus not have experienced the protective effect of PTG and showed more psychopathology. Taken together, research on adjustment and posttraumatic growth also highlights some important differences between different cultural groups that are likely to be directly related to a survivor's recovery trajectory, affect course and severity of the disorder, and are likely to influence engagement in treatment.

IMPLICATIONS FOR THEORY AND CLINICAL PRACTICE

Findings from these studies point to important cultural considerations both in the aetiology of PTSD and in its maintenance, which are not part of current psychological models of PTSD, such as the ones outlined initially. The findings challenge PTSD models to articulate how the cultural self aligns with their accounts and to be more explicit regarding the impact of the cultural self on the processes involved in the development and maintenance of PTSD. In response to this, and in light of the findings outlined above, a working model, the Threat to the Conceptual Self (TCS) model (see Jobson, 2009-c) was developed. The TCS model offers a method for accounting for the relationship between trauma and the conceptual self in the etiology and maintenance of PTSD. This model will not be discussed in detail in this chapter but rather the point to be emphasized here is that theoretical models of PTSD need to be extended to consider cultural differences in self.

There are also a number of important clinical implications. The majority of trauma survivors globally are from non-western cultures (Onyut, Neuner, Ertl, Schauer, Odenwald, & Elbert, 2009) . It is therefore imperative to understand those from non-western culture's responses to trauma through models which take into account cultural differences. This in turn will inform mental health care. Cross-cultural clinical psychology remains exceptionally under-researched. Less than 6% of mental health research and less than 1% of clinical intervention research is conducted using non-Western populations (Arrindell, 2003). This has the potential to result in ethnic groups often receiving sub-optimal mental health services (Dana, 2000).

The fact that there are differences in autobiographical memory, post-trauma appraisals and posttrauma adjustment is crucial and calls for culturally adapted procedures in trauma-focused therapies, such as trauma-focused cognitive behavioral therapy. For instance, the above findings suggest that for those with an independent self, treatment may need to focus on increasing autonomous orientation in clients with PTSD. Practically, this may involve exposure work that highlights and focuses on autonomous aspects of the memory. It may also involve clients repeatedly re-telling the trauma event with increased autonomous orientation. However, for those with PTSD from collectivistic cultures, a primary focus on agency and autonomous orientation may be less relevant. Instead the focus of therapy may need to center on re-framing and/or reducing the level of autonomous orientation and increasing levels of relatedness. This may translate to a downplaying of autonomous aspects of the memory during exposure work and clients re-telling the trauma event with decreased autonomous orientation and/or increased emphasis on relatedness aspects of the memory.

Similarly, new studies suggest that culture influences the integration of the trauma memory into current self-knowledge (Jobson & O'Kearney, 2006, 2008-b), negative appraisals (Jobson & O'Kearney, 2009), belief and meaning systems (Jobson, 2009-c), and a survivor's recovery trajectory, affect course and severity of the disorder (Kleim & Ehlers, 2009). Exposure and cognitive therapy target the elaboration and contextualization of the trauma memory, and the interpretation and meaning of trauma and trauma sequelae. If culture influences these elements, this calls again for taking into account culture. Currently, the National Institute for Clinical Excellence (2006) guidelines for PTSD mention culture in terms of considering the language and cultural background of the patient. However, the guidelines (presumably due to a lack of research) do not provide guidance on the influence of culture on assessment and treatment of PTSD. Additionally, from a service perspective countries, such as the United Kingdom, have recognized this need and the Department of Health has recently emphasised the need to improve mental heath services for Black and Ethnic Minority groups.

SUMMARY

As stated initially, anxiety disorders are thought to be amongst the most common psychological disorders worldwide. Research on ethnic and cultural impact on the development and maintenance of these disorders, as well as on their treatment, is needed to provide culturally appropriate and effective services to a diverse population. More specifically, as discussed in the outset of this chapter, patients' values, beliefs and behaviours, as well as their attitudes towards the respective illness within his or her community are likely to influence a patient's recovery trajectory and engagement in treatment and may thus, be a crucial factor that affects course and severity of the disorder.

This chapter has investigated the impact of cultural differences in self-construal on the psychological processes implicated by PTSD models. Clinically, it was suggested to expand current elements of cognitive behavior therapy for PTSD by including considerations of public and communal aspects of the self. This area of research is very new and thus, the empirical work has merely scratched the surface. Further research is required to explore cultural differences in structural, perceptual, biological, cognitive, and emotional processes involved in PTSD and other psychological disorders. Future research needs to investigate what methods other cultures use in the treatment of trauma responses. Research should examine whether trauma type (i.e., an individualistic trauma such as a motor vehicle accident versus a collectivistic trauma such as a natural disaster moderates the impact of cultural differences in self on autobiographical remembering of trauma). Further, these processes are by no means unique to our PTSD models. These processes can also be seen in our depression and anxiety models. Therefore, research needs to investigate the influence of cultural differences in self on the processes in these other disorders. Finally, cultural differences in self, is only one cultural dimension. The impact of other cultural factors needs to be examined.

REFERENCES

Aaker, J. & Schmitt, B. (2001). Culture-dependent assimilation and differentiation of the self: preferences for consumption symbols in the United States and China. *Journal of Cross-Cultural Psychology, 32*, 561-576.

American Psychiatric Association. (1994). *Diagnostic and statistical manual of mental disorders* (4th ed.). Washington DC: Author.

Arrindell, W. A. (2003). Cultural abnormal psychology, *Behaviour Research and Therapy, 41,* 749-753.

Barlow, D. (2002). *Anxiety and its disorders: the nature and treatment of anxiety and panic* (2nd ed.), The Guilford Press, New York (2002).

Berntsen, D. & Rubin, D. C. (2006). The centrality of event scale: A measure of integrating a trauma into one's identity and its relation to posttraumatic stress disorder symptoms. *Behaviour Research and Therapy, 44*, 219-231.

Berntsen, D. & Rubin, D. C. (2007). When trauma becomes a key to identity: Enhanced integration of trauma memories predicts posttraumatic stress disorder symptoms. *Applied Cognitive Psychology, 21,* 417- 431.

Brewin, C. R., Dalgleish, T. & Joseph, S. (1996). A dual representation theory of post traumatic stress disorder. *Psychological Review, 103*, 670-686.

Brewin, C. R. & Holmes, E. A. (2003). Psychological theories of posttraumatic stress disorder. *Clinical Psychology Review, 23,* 339-376.

Butler, A. C., Chapman, J. E., Forman, E. M. & Beck, A. T. (2006). The empirical status of cognitive-behavioral therapy: a review of meta-analyses. *Clinical Psychology Review, 26,* 1, 17-31

Calhoun, L. G. & Tedeschi, R. G. (2006). The foundations of posttraumatic growth. In L.G. Calhoun & R.G. Tedeschi (Eds), *Handbook of Posttraumatic Growth* (pp. 1-23). Mahwah, NJ. Lawrence Erlbaum.

Calhoun, L. G. & Tedeschi, R. G. (2004). The foundations of posttraumatic growth: New considerations. *Psychological Inquiry, 15*, 93-102.

Conway, M. A. (2005). Memory and the self. *Journal of Memory and Language, 53*, 594-628.

Conway, M. A. & Pleydell-Pearce, C. W. (2000). The construction of autobiographical memories in the self-memory system. *Psychological Review, 107*, 261-288.

Cousins, S. D. (1989). Culture and self-perception in Japan and the United States. *Journal of Personality and Social Psychology, 56*, 124-131.

Dana, R. H. (Eds.) (2000). *Handbook of cross-cultural and multicultural personality assessment*. Mahwah, NJ: LEA.

Dalgleish, T. (2004). Cognitive approaches to posttraumatic stress disorder: The evolution of multirepresentational theorizing. *Psychological Bulletin, 130*, 228-260.

Davison, G. C. & Neale, J. M. (2000). *Abnormal Psychology*. Wiley.

Draguns, J. G. & Tanaka-Matsumi, J. (2003). Assessment of psychopathology across and within cultures: issues and findings. *Behaviour Research and Therapy, 41*, 755-776.

Dunmore, E., Clark, D. M. & Ehlers, A. (2001). A prospective investigation of the role of cognitive factors in persistent posttraumatic stress disorder (PTSD) after physical or sexual assault. *Behaviour Therapy, and Research, 39*, 1063-1084.

Eagle, G. T. (2005). Therapy at the cultural interface: Implications for African cosmology for traumatic stress intervention. *Journal of Contemporary Psychotherapy, 35*, 199-209.

Ehlers, A. & Clark, D. M. (2000). A cognitive model of posttraumatic stress disorder. *Behaviour Research & Therapy, 38*, 319-345.

Ehlers, A., Clark, D. M., Dunmore, E., Jaycox, L., Meadows, E. & Foa, E. B. (1998). Predicting response to exposure treatment for PTSD: The role of mental defeat and alienation. *Journal of Traumatic Stress, 11*, 457-471.

Ehlers, A., Maercker, A. & Boos, A. (2000). Posttraumatic stress disorder following political imprisonment: The role of mental defeat, alienation, and perceived permanent change. *Journal of Abnormal Psychology, 109*, 45-55.

Ehlers, A., Mayou, R. A. & Bryant, B. (1998). Psychological predictors of chronic PTSD after motor vehicle accidents. *Journal of Abnormal Psychology, 107*, 508-519.

Feldman Barrett, L. & Russell, J. A. (1998). Independence and bipolarity in the structure of current affect. *Journal of Personality and Social Psychology, 74*, 967-984.

Figueira, I., Luz, M., Braga, R. J., Cabizuca, M., Coutinho, E. S. F. & Mendlowicz, M. (2007). The increasing internationalization of mainstream posttraumatic stress disorder research: a bibliometric study. *Journal of Traumatic Stress, 20*, 89-95.

Fiske, A. P., Kitayama, S., Markus, H. R. & Nisbett, R. E. (1998). The cultural matrix of social psychology. In D. T. Gilbert, S. T. Fiske, & G. Lindzey (Eds.), *The handbook of social psychology,* (Vol. 4, pp. 915-981). Boston, WA: McGraw Hill.

Foa, E. B. & Riggs, D. S. (1993). Post-traumatic stress disorder in rape victims. In: J. Oldham, M. B. Riba, & A. Tasman (Eds.), *American Psychiatric Press Review of Psychiatry*, Vol. *12*. (273-303)Washington, DC: American Psychiatric Press.

Foa, E. B. & Rothbaum, B. O. (1998). *Treating the trauma of rape: cognitive behavioral therapy for PTSD*. New York: Guilford Press.

Frazier, P., Conlon, A. & Glaser, T. (2001). Positive and negative life changes following sexual assault. *Journal of Consulting and Clinical Psychology, 69*, 1048-1055.

Frazier, P., Tashiro, T., Berman, M., Steger, M. & Long, J. (2004). Correlates of levels and patterns of positive life changes following sexual assault. *Journal of Consulting and Clinical Psychology, 72*, 19-30.

Gu-Yaish, N. & Wang, Q. (2006). Self-knowledge in cultural contexts: the case of two western cultures. In: A. P. Prescott, (Eds.), *The concept of self in psychology* (129-143). New York: Nova Science Publishers.

Helgeson, V. S., Reynolds, K. A. & Tomich, P. L. (2006). A meta-analytic review of benefit finding and growth. *Journal of Consulting and Clinical Psychology, 74*, 797-816.

Hofstede, G. & Hofstede, G. J. (2004). *Cultures and organizations: Software of the mind: Intercultural cooperation and its importance for survival.*, New York: McGraw-Hill.

Horowitz, M. J. (1997). *Stress response reactions* (2nd ed.). Northvale, NJ, Aronson. Janoff-Bulman, R. (1992). *Shattered assumptions: Towards a new psychology of trauma.* New York: Free Press.

Jobson, L. (2009-a). *Cultural differences in levels of autonomous orientation in autobiographical remembering in posttraumatic stress disorder*. Manuscript submitted for publication.

Jobson, L. (2009-b). A brief report on cultural differences in specificity of autobiographical memories: Implications for asylum decisions. *Psychology, Psychiatry and Law, 16*, 453-457.

Jobson, L. (2009-c). Drawing current posttraumatic stress disorder models into the cultural sphere: The development of the 'threat to the conceptual self' model. *Clinical Psychology Review, 29*, 368-381.

Jobson, L. & O'Kearney, R. T. (2009). Impact of cultural differences in self on cognitive appraisals in posttraumatic stress disorder. *Behavioural and Cognitive Psychotherapy, 37*, 249-266.

Jobson, L. & O'Kearney, R. T. (2008-a). Cultural differences in retrieval of self-defining memories. *Journal of Cross-Cultural Psychology, 39*, 75-80.

Jobson, L. & O'Kearney, R. T. (2008-b). Cultural differences in personal identity in posttraumatic stress disorder. *British Journal of Clinical Psychology, 47*, 1-16.

Jobson, L. & O'Kearney, R. T. (2006). Cultural differences in the autobiographical memory of trauma. *Clinical Psychologist, 10*, 89-98.

Kagitcibasi, C. (1996). *Family and human development across cultures: A view from the other side.* Hillsdale, NJ: Erlbaum.

Kennedy, J. E., Davis, R. C. & Taylor, B. G. (1998). Changes in spirituality and well-being among victims of sexual assault. *Journal for the Scientific Study of Religion, 37*, 322-328.

Kleim, B. & Ehlers, A. (2009). Evidence for a curvilinear relationship between posttraumatic growth and posttrauma depression and PTSD in assault survivors. *Journal of Traumatic Stress, 22*, 1, 45-52.

Kleim, B., Ehlers, A. & Glucksman, E. (2007). Early predictors of chronic post-traumatic stress disorder in assault survivors. *Psychological Medicine, 37*, 1457-1467.

Kleinman, A. (2004). "*Culture and Psychiatric Diagnosis and Treatment.*" The Trimbos Lecture. Harvard University. October, *31*.

Kuhn, M. H. & McPartland, T. S. (1954). An empirical investigation of self-attitudes. *American Sociological Review, 19*, 68-76.

Lee, A. Y., Aaker, J. L. & Gardner, W. L. (2000). The pleasures and pains of distinct self-construals: The role of interdependence in regulatory focus. *Journal of Personality and Social Psychology, 78(6)*, 1122-1134.

Lee, L. C. & Zane, N. W. S. (1998). *Handbook of Asian American Psychology.* Thousand Oaks, CA: Sage.

Liem, R., Lim, B. A. & Liem, J. H. (2000). Acculturation and emotion in among Asian Americans. *Cultural Diversity and Ethnic Minority Psychology, 6,* 13-31.

Markus, H. R. & Kitayama, S. (1991). Culture and the self: Implications for cognition, emotion, and motivation. *Psychological Review, 98,* 224-253.

Markus, H. R. & Kitayama, S. (1994). A collective fear of the collective: Implications for selves and theories of selves. *Personality and Social Psychology Bulletin, 20,* 568-579.

Matsumoto, D., Kudoh, T., Scherer, K. R. & Wallbott, H. (1988). Antecedents of and reactions to emotions in the United States and Japan. *Journal of Cross-Cultural Psychology, 19*(3), 267-286.

Mauro, R., Sato, K. & Tucker, J. (1992). The role of appraisal in human emotions: A cross-cultural study. *Journal of Personality and Social Psychology, 62(2)*, 301-317.

Merikangas, K. R., Mehta, R. L., Molnar, B. E., Walters, E. E., Swendsen, J. D., Aguilar-Gaziola, S., Bijl, R., Borges, G., Caraveo-Anduaga, D. J., Dewit, D. J., Kolody, B., Vega, W., Wittchen, H.. U. & Kessler, R. C. (1998). Comorbidity of substance use disorders with mood and anxiety disorders: Results of the international consortium in psychiatric epidemiology. *Addictive Behaviors, 23,* 6, 893-907.

Mesquita, B. & Ellsworth, P. C. (2001). The role of culture in appraisal. In: K. R. Scherer, & A. Schorr, (Eds.), *Appraisal processes in emotion: Theory, methods, research* (233-248). New York: Oxford University Press.

Mesquita, B. & Karasawa, M. (2002). Different emotional lives. *Cognition and Emotion, 16(1)*, 127-141.

Mesquita, B. & Markus, H. R. (2004). Culture and emotion: Models of agency as sources of cultural variation in emotion. In: N. H., Frijda, A. S. R. Manstead, & A. H. Fischer, (Eds.), *Feelings and emotions: The Amsterdam symposium*, Cambridge, MA: Cambridge University Press.

Mesquita, B. & Walker, R. (2003). Cultural differences in emotions: A context for interpreting emotional experiences. *Behaviour Research and Therapy, 41,* 777-793.

Milam, J. E. (2004). Posttraumatic growth among HIV/ AIDS patients. *Journal of Applied Social Psychology, 34,* 2353-2376.

Mullen, M. K. & Yi, S. (1995). The cultural context of talk about the past: Implications for the development of autobiographical memory. *Cognitive Development, 10,* 407-419.

National Institute for Clinical Excellence (2006). Post-traumatic stress disorder. The management of PTSD in adults and children in primary and secondary care

Nelson, K. & Fivush, R. (2004). The emergence of autobiographical memory: A social cultural developmental theory. *Psychological Review, 111*, 486-511.

Nisbett, R. E., Peng, K., Choi, I. & Norenzayan, A. (2001). Culture and systems of thought: Holistic vs analytic cognition. *Psychological Review, 108,* 291-310.

Onyut, P. L., Neuner, F., Ertl, V., Schauer, E., Odenwald, M. & Elbert, T. (2009). Trauma, poverty and mental health among Somali and Rwandese refugees living in an African refugee settlement - an epidemiological study. *Conflict and Health, 3,* 6.

Paunovic, N. & Ost, L. G. (2001). Cognitive-behavior therapy vs. exposure therapy in the treatment of PTSD in refugees. *Behaviour Research and Therapy*, *39*, 1183-1197.

Pillemer, D. B. (1998). *Momentous events, vivid memories*. Cambridge, MA, Harvard University Press.

Pham, P. N., Weinstein, H. M. & Longman, T. (2004). Trauma and PTSD symptoms in Rwanda: implications for attitudes toward justice and reconciliation. *JAMA*, *292*, 602-612.

Rubin, D. C., Berntsen, D. & Bohni, M. K. (2008). A memory-based model of posttraumatic stress disorder: evaluating basic assumptions underlying the PTSD diagnosis. *Psychological Review*, *115*, 985-1011.

Schwartz, B. & Kim, M. (2002). Honor, dignity, and collective memory: Judging the past in Korea and the United States. In K.A. Cerulo (Ed.), *Culture in mind: Toward a sociology of culture and cognition* (209-226). New York, NY: Routledge.

Steward, R. E. & Chambless, D. L. (2009). Cognitive-behavioral therapy for adult anxiety disorders in clinical samples: a meta-analysis of effectiveness studies. *Journal of Consulting and Clinical Psychology, 77*, 595-606.

Shafran, R., Clark, D. M., Fairburn, C. G., Arntz, A., Barlow, D. H., Ehlers, A., Freestone, M., Garety, P. A., Hollon, S. D., Salkovskis, P. A,, Wilson, G. T. & Williams, J. M. (2009). Mind the gap: Improving the dissemination of CBT. *Behaviour Research and Therapy*, epub, ahead of print.

Takata, T. (1999). Development of independent and interdependent self-construal in Japanese culture: cross-cultural and cross-sectional analysis. *Japanese Journal of Educational Psychology*, *47*, 480-489.

Tedeschi, R. G. & Calhoun, L. G. (2004). Posttraumatic growth: Conceptual foundations and empirical evidence. *Psychological Inquiry*, *15*, 1-18.

Trafimow, D., Triandis, H. & Goto, S. (1991). Some tests of the distinction between the private and collective self. *Journal of Personality and Social Psychology, 60,* 649-655.

Wang, Q. (2001). Culture effects on adults' earliest childhood recollection and self-description: Implications for the relation between memory and the self. *Journal of Personality and Social Psychology, 81*, 220-233.

Wang, Q. (2007). "Remember when you got the big, big bulldozer?" Mother-child reminiscing over time and cultures. *Social Cognition*, *25*, 455-471.

Wang, Q. & Conway, M. A. (2004). The stories we keep: Autobiographical Memory in American and Chinese Middle-Aged Adults. *Journal of Personality, 72,* 911-938.

Wang, Q. & Fivush, R. (2005). Mother-child conversations of emotionally salient events: Exploring the functions of emotional reminiscing in European-American and Chinese families. *Social Development, 14,* 473-495.

Wang, Q. & Ross, M. (2005). What we remember and what we tell: The effects of culture and self-priming on memory representations and narratives. *Memory, 13,* 594-206.

WHO, *Disorders Management, Depression and Anxiety* (2009), accessed online at www.who.int, on February, *8*.

In: Race and Ethnicity
Editor: Jonathan K. Crennan, pp. 249-266

ISBN: 978-1-60692-099-2
© 2010 Nova Science Publishers, Inc.

Chapter 10

RACE MATTERS: MALTREATMENT IDENTIFICATION AND IMPACT AMONG HIGH-RISK ADOLESCENTS

Omar G. Gudiño, Lisa L. Liu and Anna S. Lau
University of California, Los Angeles, CA, USA

ABSTRACT

This chapter describes recent empirical findings on maltreatment identification and impact in a diverse high-risk sample of adolescents involved in public sectors of care. A set of three related research questions is addressed. The first research question concerns the extent to which race matters in the institutional identification of maltreatment and need for protection. Secondly, we address the question of whether race matters in whether youngsters view specific parenting behaviors as abusive. The final research question focuses on whether there are racial differences in the impact of maltreatment-related experiences. In each, we center our focus on youngsters' own perceptions of their personal histories in the context of maltreatment identification. The findings reviewed suggest that matters of race in maltreatment identification are complex, as there appear to be racial differences in whether certain parent behaviors are labeled by adolescents as abusive, and in the institutional identification of maltreatment victimization. However, punitive parent behaviors, whether or not they are labeled as abusive, are strongly associated with psychological distress across racial groups. Thus, racial variability in the labeling and identification of maltreatment does not necessarily translate into differential impact of adverse family experiences on youth.

INTRODUCTION

It is commonly believed that distinct cultural communities may hold differing views on what constitutes child maltreatment (Korbin, 1994). Cross-cultural research has documented examples of controversial parental behaviors that are considered to be abusive in some cultures, but are considered to be normative or even essential as a parental duty in other cultures (see Korbin, 1994). As such, considerable attention has been paid to cultural competence in child welfare practices. Child welfare professionals are continually faced with the task of sensitively demarcating the line between culturally sanctioned child-rearing practices and state defined abuse (Fontes, 2002; Terao, Borrego, and Urquiza, 2001). Individuals from different racial and ethnic communities may hold different views on where these lines should be drawn. For example, some research indicates that ethnic minority parents including African Americans, Asian Pacific Islanders, and Hispanic Americans acknowledge more physically punitive acts toward their children than Non-Hispanic White parents (Straus and Gelles, 1990; Straus, Hamby, Finkelhor, Moore and Runyan, 1998; Ferrari, 2002) and endorse greater acceptance and use of corporal punishment in child rearing (Hong and Hong, 1991; Kelley and Tseng, 1992; Corral-Verdugo, Frias-Armenta, Romero and Munoz, 1995; Deater-Deckard, Dodge, Bates and Petit, 1996; Chen et al., 1998; Jambunathan, Burts and Pierce, 2000; Pinderhughes, Dodge, Bates, Pettit and Zelli, 2000; Ferrari, 2002). Indeed, ethnic minority families may bring a diverse range of cultural traditions in child rearing that may shape definitions of abusive parenting.

Along these lines, racial differences in the identification or labeling of maltreatment have been examined. For instance, some investigators have used vignette studies to determine whether racial background influences whether respondents deem certain parental actions as abusive (Giovannoni and Becerra, 1979; Hong and Hong, 1991; Ferrari, 2002). Giovannoni and Becerra (1979) reported that Hispanics and African Americans judged maltreatment vignettes more seriously than Non-Hispanic Whites. Similarly, other investigators have reported that ethnic minority parents perceive some forms of child neglect as more serious than do their Non-Hispanic White counterparts (Dubowitz, Klockner, Starr and Black, 1998; Rose and Meezan, 1996). However, Hong and Hong (1991) found that Chinese Americans displayed increased tolerance for physical beating as a disciplinary strategy compared to Non-Hispanic Whites and Hispanics. More recently, Ferrari (2002) found that neither race nor cultural values were systematically associated with parents' ratings of the seriousness of maltreatment vignettes. Yet, race was related to parents' self-reported use of physically and emotionally abusive child-rearing tactics, with Hispanic and African American parents endorsing greater use than Non-Hispanic White parents.

Thus, there is some mixed support for the notion that certain minority groups may hold different thresholds of tolerance for parental acts that may be characterized as abusive by authorities. These data may have implications for public education, outreach, and preventive programs. Ultimately, however, culturally competent *child protection* decisions should not necessarily be based on group-specific norms about what constitutes abuse. These decisions must function to promote child wellness across communities. Therefore, research must investigate both how race influences maltreatment identification and how race may influence the impact of maltreatment exposure, variously defined. The previously mentioned research eliciting adult judgments about whether hypothetical parental behaviors constitute maltreatment is limited since it tells us little about the actual experiences of families and nothing about the impact of adverse experiences on youth. This chapter describes recent empirical findings regarding maltreatment identification and its impact in a diverse high-risk sample of adolescents involved in public sectors of care. A set of three related research questions are addressed. In each, we highlight the importance of assaying youngsters' own perceptions of their personal histories to arrive at conclusions about exposure to abusive parenting.

The first research question concerns the extent to which race matters in the institutional identification of maltreatment and need for protection. Here we are concerned with whether children's perceptions of their personal maltreatment histories are related to their history of involvement in the child welfare system in a similar way across racial groups. Given that children from diverse socio-cultural backgrounds may hold different views about what constitutes abuse, children's own subjective appraisals of their experience may or may not correspond with identification of maltreatment victimization by child protective services (CPS). Previous research suggests that institutional and community factors may conspire to identify more children from certain ethnic minority groups as maltreated and in need of child protective services while others are kept with their families and out of the system (Chand, 2000; Garland, Ellis-Macleod, Landsverk, Ganger, and Johnson, 1998; Jenkins and Diamond, 1985).

There is compelling evidence that race influences the likelihood of maltreatment reporting (Chasnoff, Landress and Barrett, 1990). For example, even when socioeconomic status and the severity of the abuse incident are controlled, maltreatment reports are more likely to be filed when an African American family is involved (e.g., Hampton and Newberger, 1985). Moreover, race is associated with the likelihood of substantiation of maltreatment reports (Eckenrode, Powers, Doris, Munsch, and Bolger, 1988), placement in out-of-home care (Goerge, Wulczyn and Harden, 1994; Mech, 1983), and re-entry into foster care following attempts at family reunification (Courtney, 1995). At each stage of the process, children from African American, Hispanic American, and Native American families appear to be more likely than Non-Hispanic Whites to be identified as being in need of protection. In contrast, there has been some speculation that Asian American families may be less likely to make contact with CPS, as community norms regarding reporting may differ. For example, investigators have noted that South and East Asian parents are reluctant to contact CPS to intervene when there is a concern about physical or sexual abuse (Maiter, Alaggia and Trocmé, 2004; Okamura et al., 1995). Rather, these families felt that such problems could be resolved privately with friends and family, rather than involving outside agencies.

Thus, children with a similar maltreatment history may be more or less likely to come to the attention of CPS depending on their racial background. Given the same family history, African American children may be more likely than Non-Hispanic Whites to be officially categorized as victims of abuse and neglect in need of CPS intervention, while Asian Americans may be less likely to receive such attention. As a corollary, it is possible that there may be racial differences among children in CPS in their perceptions of whether they have actually been victimized warranting the state's actions to protect them. Therefore, the first research question addresses whether or not there are racial differences in the association between a history of CPS involvement and youth self-reports of maltreatment history.

Similarly, the second research question concerns whether race matters in whether youngsters view their family experiences as abusive. Here we are interested in whether specific parental actions are similarly labeled as abusive among youth from diverse racial or cultural backgrounds. Given the same exposure to harsh or punitive parental behaviors, would youth from a range of racial groups be equally likely to subjectively identify themselves as being victims of physical or emotional abuse? If indeed physically and emotionally punitive parenting practices are more normative among certain ethnic communities, these parental actions may be less likely to be labeled as or understood to be abusive. This may be especially true in cultural traditions where physically and emotionally punitive parenting practices are commonly associated with positive parent-child relationship qualities. For example, among African American families, firm parental control involving physical restraint and punishment has been found to occur in the context of affectively warm parent-child relationships (Brody and Flor, 1998). Likewise, firm parental control in Asian American groups is also noted to be coupled with warmth and closeness (Chao, 1994), and physical control in Hispanic American families is tied to parental sensitivity (Carlson and Harwood, 2003). Thus, youth growing up in families with these child-rearing traditions may not associate the same parental actions with the notion of victimization. Thus, we examined whether race influences the relationship between adolescents' reports of specific parental punitive behaviors and the likelihood that they consider themselves to be victims of abuse.

Yet even if there exists cultural variability in how youngsters label their experiences as abusive or normative, it may nonetheless be possible that the same sets of parental behaviors lead similarly to distress or poor outcomes across racial or cultural groups. Thus, the third research question focuses on whether there are racial differences in the impact of maltreatment-related experiences. While research in this area has produced mixed results, there has been some support found for the influence of race and culture on a victim's emotional response to sexual abuse. For example, Hispanic girls appear to have higher levels of depression and anxiety following sexual abuse compared to African American and Non-Hispanic White victims (Mennen, 1995; Phillips-Sanders et al., 1995). Additionally, Rao et al. (1992) found that Asian Americans who were abused were least likely to display inappropriate sexual behaviors and anger, but were often suicidal in comparison to Non-Hispanic Whites and African Americans. Racial differences also appear to exist in the developmental consequences of harsh physical discipline. For example, longitudinal evidence reported by Deater-Deckard, Dodge, Bates and Pettit (1996) indicates that harsh physical punishment is related to later externalizing behavior problems among Non-Hispanic White children, but no such association was found among African American children. These findings do not demonstrate that there are racial differences in the effects of physical abuse, but they do suggest that the meaning of harsh physical discipline may differ between groups. If a youngster's racial or cultural background influences the extent to which s/he perceives punitive parental behaviors to be abusive and the extent to which this treatment is associated with distress, then this would provide cause to caution the use of uniform practices in the delivery of child protection interventions across diverse cultural communities. Understanding how race matters in the association between parental actions, youth perceptions of victimization, and resultant youth distress can be instrumental in guiding culturally competent child welfare practices.

MALTREATMENT IN THE PATTERNS OF CARE STUDY

The current chapter presents recent empirical findings on the associations between officially identified maltreatment, youth reports of specific parental behaviors, and youngster's self-identification as victims of abuse. These findings were all based on data gathered for the Youth Patterns of Care Study (POC), which surveyed a large representative sample ($N = 1,715$) of youth ages 6 to 17 years who had active cases in at least one public sector of care in San Diego County (alcohol/drug treatment, child welfare, juvenile justice, mental health, and public school services for youth with a Serious Emotional Disturbance [SED]) in the second half of fiscal year 1996-1997. In juvenile justice, only adjudicated delinquents were included, and in child welfare, only court-ordered dependents were included. The final sample of 1,715 youth was selected by simple random sampling techniques and was stratified by race/ethnicity and level of restrictiveness of placement. A post-stratification weighting procedure (Henry, 1990) was used to ensure that the data reflect the characteristics of the total population of service users. Garland and colleagues (2001) provide a full description of the sampling process and results.

The studies reviewed below were conducted using a subsample of 1,045 youth from the POC study who were age 12 to 17 (mean age of 15.6 years) and completed the measures of interest. Due to incomplete measures, there is slight variation in the final sample size for individual research questions (N ranges from 1, 010 to 1,045). Participants in this subsample were 700 males and 345 females and consisted of 37.6% Non-Hispanic Whites ($n = 393$), 22.4% African Americans ($n = 234$), 30.2% Hispanic Americans ($n = 316$), and 9.8% Asian Pacific Islanders ($n = 102$). The median household income for the sample at large was between $19,000 and $19,999 per year.

Interviews for the POC study were completed between September 1997 and February 1999. Parents/primary caregivers were interviewed about their child's demographic characteristics, psychological symptomatology, child service-use history, and exposure to risk or protective factors. Youths provided reports of their emotional/behavioral problems, parenting behaviors and support in the last year, maltreatment history, and service-use history. Parents and youths were interviewed separately and every effort was made to ensure the privacy of both respondents and the independence of their responses. All measures used in the studies reviewed below were administered by trained interviewers.

STUDY 1: RACE AND THE INSTITUTIONAL IDENTIFICATION OF MALTREATMENT

To study the association between race and the institutional identification of maltreatment and need for protection, Lau and colleagues (2003) analyzed youth self-reported maltreatment history and the association between self-reported maltreatment history and foster care placement history in this diverse sample of youth receiving public services. Retrospective youth self-report of maltreatment history was obtained using the Childhood Trauma Questionnaire, Short Form (CTQ; Bernstein and Fink, 1998), which produces five scales: Physical abuse, physical neglect, emotional abuse, emotional neglect, and sexual abuse as well as a total maltreatment scale. Cutoffs scores for the five scales and total maltreatment score have been established to demarcate moderate and severe levels of maltreatment (Bernstein and Fink, 1998). Foster care placement history was assessed utilizing the variable indicating lifetime use of foster care reported by the caregiver or youth on the Services Assessment for Children and Adolescents (SACA; Horwitz et al., 2001).

As shown in Table 1, self-reports of maltreatment were fairly common in this high-risk sample of adolescents, with 51.1% of youth reporting at least one type of maltreatment reaching a moderate level and 31.5% of youth reporting a history of severe maltreatment of at least one type. However, when examining mean scale scores, no racial/ethnic differences were found for any of the maltreatment subscales or total maltreatment score. When examining rates of moderate and severe levels of maltreatment, racial/ethnic differences were generally not found. The only significant finding of racial differences indicated that Non-Hispanic White youth were more likely to report severe levels of emotional abuse compared to the other race/ethnic groups ($F = 3.27$, $p = .02$).

Additional analyses were conducted to examine the association between race/ethnicity and moderate and severe levels of any type of maltreatment by the public sector from which the youth was sampled. Again, no ethnic/racial differences in the proportion of youth endorsing maltreatment in the alcohol and drug, mental health, special education (SED) and juvenile justice sectors were found. However, a significant association between race/ethnicity and self-reported maltreatment was found in the child welfare sector. African American youth appeared to report moderate and severe levels of maltreatment at lower rates than other racial/ethnic groups in child welfare.

Logistic regression models including race/ethnicity, family income, gender and age as predictor variables and six dichotomous criterion variables (emotional abuse, physical abuse, sexual abuse, emotional neglect, physical neglect and any moderate maltreatment) were then constructed to test the associations between these demographic variables and youth-reported maltreatment of at least a moderate severity. Results suggested that girls were more likely to report moderate levels of all types of abuse. Furthermore, age was positively associated with reports of moderate levels of emotional abuse, physical abuse, sexual abuse and physical neglect. Given that the study assessed lifetime history of abuse, it makes logical sense that older children would report higher levels of victimization. Family income was not associated with youths' reports of maltreatment history, but it is important to note that the sample consisted of low-income families involved with public-service systems of care. As in the analyses reviewed above, few effects of race/ethnicity emerged in these analyses. In the six logistic regression models, only one marginally significant effect of race/ethnicity emerged, with African Americans being less likely to endorse moderate levels of emotional neglect relative to Non-Hispanic Whites (O.R. = .59, $p = .047$).

Next, the investigators examined the association between self-reported maltreatment history and lifetime history of foster care placement using a logistic regression model (see Table 2). Youth who reported a history of maltreatment of at least moderate severity were three times as likely to have a history of foster care placement as children who did not report a history of maltreatment (O.R. = 3.11, $p = < .001$). However, after controlling for socio-demographic variables and maltreatment history, African Americans were more than 12 times more likely to have had a history of foster care placement (O.R. = 12.66, $p = <.001$). The interaction between African American group membership and youth-reported maltreatment also significantly predicted foster care placement history ($\beta = -1.01$, $p = .018$). Results from subsequent chi-square analyses, displayed in Table 3, indicated that the expected positive association between maltreatment history and foster care placement was evident for all groups except African Americans, who were instead equally likely to have a history of foster care placement, irrespective of maltreatment history.

Table 1. Maltreatment Subtypes (mean scale scores and prevalence rates) by Race/Ethnicity.

Maltreatment Subscales	Race/Ethnicity				Total Sample	R/E Effects p<.05
	NHW n=393	AA n=204	HA n=316	API n=102		
Emotional Abuse	9.41	8.41	8.49	9.29	8.87	ns
Moderate	23.0%	18.9%	19.0%	24.6%	20.9%	ns
Severe	14.6%	8.5%	7.2%	6.4%	10.0%	NHW > API, AA, HA
Physical Abuse	8.26	8.82	8.01	8.20	8.30	ns
Moderate	23.7%	28.3%	21.6%	22.0%	23.9%	ns
Severe	18.1%	19.1%	14.8%	16.4%	17.1%	ns
Sexual Abuse	6.82	6.44	6.76	6.39	6.68	ns
Moderate	19.2%	15.0%	15.3%	12.6%	16.4%	ns
Severe	8.9%	7.5%	10.9%	10.3%	9.4%	ns
Emotional Neglect	11.40	10.38	10.94	11.63	11.04	ns
Moderate	24.6%	17.6%	22.0%	30.5%	22.7%	ns
Severe	15.0%	11.9%	15.1%	14.8%	14.3%	ns
Physical Neglect	8.04	7.82	7.48	7.78	7.78	ns
Moderate	24.9%	27.7%	21.6%	26.6%	24.6%	ns
Severe	13.4%	11.3%	9.9%	7.5%	11.2%	ns
Any Maltreatment						
Moderate	53.8%	50.1%	48.3%	53.3%	51.1%	ns
Severe	34.9%	29.2%	28.7%	34.4%	31.5%	ns

Table 2. Multiple Logistic Regression Predicting Lifetime History of Foster Care Placement.

Independent Variable	B	S.E.B	t	p	O.R.
Gender [a]	.86	.20	4.34	<.001	2.36
Age	-.15	.05	-2.72	.007	.86
Family Income	.03	.02	1.80	.07	1.03
Moderate Maltreatment Any Subtype	1.13	.24	4.63	<.001	3.11
African American [b]	2.54	.69	3.66	<.001	12.66
Hispanic American [b]	.32	.25	1.26	.21	1.38
Asian Pacific Islander [b]	-.30	.38	-0.78	.43	.74
African American [b] X Moderate Maltreatment	-1.01	.43	-2.36	.018	.36

[a] Male = 1, Female = 2

[b] Reference Group = Non-Hispanic White

STUDY 2: RACE AND THE SUBJECTIVE IDENTIFICATION OF ABUSE

To examine whether adolescents experience, perceive and label parental actions as abusive similarly across racial groups, Lau and colleagues (in press) tested the hypothesis that high-risk minority youth would be less likely to subjectively identify as victims of physical or emotional abuse, given the same exposure to harsh parental behaviors, when compared to adolescents from the majority group. Subjective self-identification of physical and emotional abuse was assessed using the items, "I believe that I was physically abused" and "I believe that I was emotionally abused," from the Childhood Trauma Questionnaire, Short Form (Bernstein and Fink, 1998). Harsh physical discipline, hereafter referred to as physical parental behavior, was assessed using the nine items from the minor and severe assault scales of the Parent-Child Conflict Tactics Scale (Straus et al., 1998). Youth reports of emotionally punitive parental behavior, hereafter referred to as emotional parental behavior, were assessed using the six relevant items form 10-item Mother/Father Support Questionnaire (UNOCCAP Workgroup, 1996). It was expected that a more relativistic approach to defining maltreatment would be supported if an adolescent's racial background strongly influenced the extent to which s/he perceived harsh parental treatment as abusive.

Table 3. Moderate Maltreatment History and Foster Care History by Race/Ethnicity.

Non-Hispanic White Youth $\chi^2 = 9.78$, p=.002		Maltreatment		
		.No	Yes	
Foster Care	No	162	142	304
	% within Foster	53.3%	46.7%	
	Yes	29	60	89
	% within Foster	32.6%	67.4%	
		191	202	393

African American Youth $\chi^2 = 0.71$, p=.400		Maltreatment		
		No	Yes	
Foster Care	No	76	67	143
	% within Foster	53.1%	46.9%	
	Yes	45	46	91
	% within Foster	49.4%	50.6%	
		121	113	234

Hispanic American Youth $\chi^2 = 12.41$, p=.0004		Maltreatment		
		.No	Yes	
Foster Care	No	130	116	246
	% within Foster	52.8%	47.1%	
	Yes	16	54	70
	% within Foster	22.8%	77.1%	
		146	170	316

Asian Pacific Islander Youth $\chi^2 = 4.82$, p=.028		Maltreatment		
		.No	Yes	
Foster Care	No	44	44	88
	% within Foster	50.0%	50.0%	
	Yes	3	11	14
	% within Foster	21.4%	78.6%	
		47	55	102

Table 4. Study 2 Sample Characteristics by Race.

	Race				F(3,1007) Or $\chi^2(3)$
	NHW (n=403)	AA (n=197)	HA (n=319)	API (n=91)	
Parent Behavior Reports					
Emotional mean score[a] (SD)	2.76 (1.3)	2.67 (1.5)	2.70 (1.3)	2.92 (1.3)	.902
Any Minor Assault[b] (%)	90.1%	80.3%	88.9%	85.1%	13.86[†]
Any Severe Assault[b] (%)	58.8%	48.3%	61.1%	63.4%	11.46[†]
Self-labeled Abuse					
Emotional Abuse[c] (%)	32.9%	22.2%	25.3%	29.4%	9.85[*]
Physical Abuse[c] (%)	24.8%	19.7%	22.7%	24.5%	2.35

* p<.05, † p<.01.

[a] Emotional parent behavior reported by youth on a 1 to 7 Likert type scale.

[b] Endorsement of the past year occurrence of any CTSPC item on minor or severe physical assault scales.

[c] Dichotomized responses on the CTQ contrasting response of 'never true' to responses of 'rarely true', 'sometimes true', 'often true', or 'very often true' in response to self-labeling item 'I believe I was physically/emotionally abused'.

Given that past year severe assault rates of 5% to 15% based on parent reports (Straus and Hamby, 1997; Straus et al., 1998) and 5% based on youth reports (Finkelhor and Dzuiba-Leatherman, 1994) have been previously cited in studies of nationally representative samples, youths in the POC sample were at high risk of maltreatment. Past year reports of severe assault ranging from 48.3% among African Americans to 63.4% among Asian Pacific Islander youth were found in the current sample drawn from public service sectors of care. However, when examining the descriptive statistics presented in Table 4, no significant racial differences in youth ratings of emotional parent behaviors were found. However, Non-Hispanic Whites did self-label as emotionally abused more often when compared to African American and Hispanic youth. There were significant, but inconsistent, racial differences in the endorsement of physical parental behaviors depending on whether minor or severe assault was examined. However, no significant racial differences emerged when examining self-labeled physical abuse.

To examine whether race moderated the association between youth reports of parent behaviors and the subjective identification of abuse, multiple regression analyses were conducted utilizing self-labeled emotional abuse and physical abuse as criterion variables. Each model included demographic control variables (age, gender, and family income), three dummy coded variables contrasting the three minority groups with the Non-Hispanic White reference group, youth reports of the relevant parental behavior (emotional of physical), and the interaction terms between the race dummy variables and youth reports of parent behavior. The results of each model are presented in Table 5.

As expected, youth ratings of physical parent behaviors were related to self-labeled physical abuse ($\beta = .47$, $p < .001$). While race was not associated with self-labeled physical abuse, there was a significant interaction between Asian Pacific Islander race and physical parent behaviors in predicting self-labeled physical abuse. As seen in Figure 1a, the association between physical parent behaviors and self-labeled physical abuse was stronger in Non-Hispanic Whites than in Asian Pacific Islanders ($\beta = -.15$, $p < .01$). The magnitude of the association between physical parental behaviors and self-labeled abuse did not differ significantly for African Americans and Hispanics when compared to Non-Hispanic Whites.

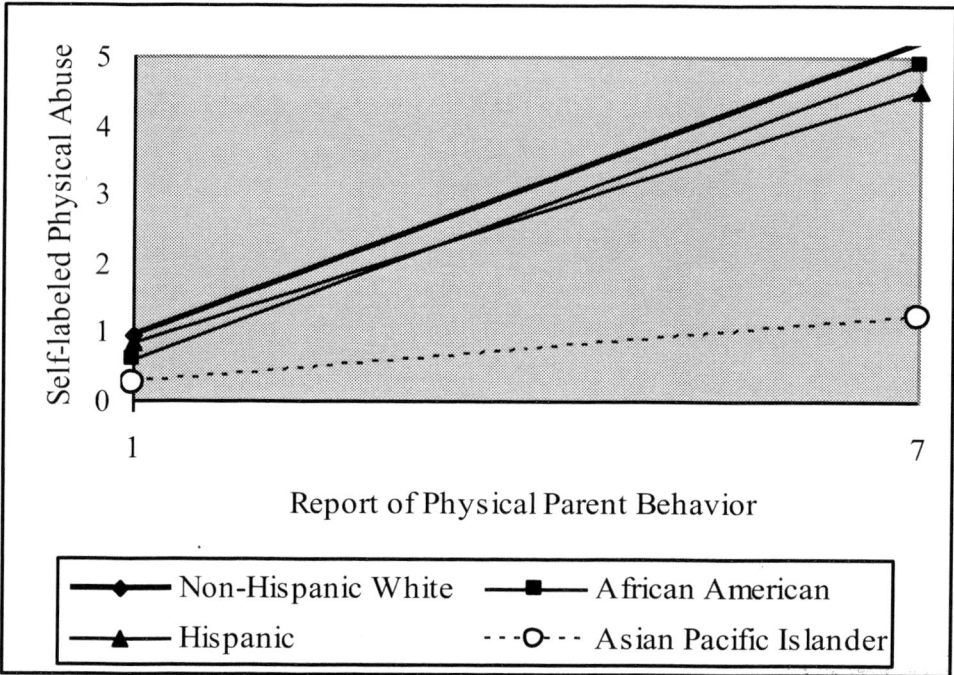

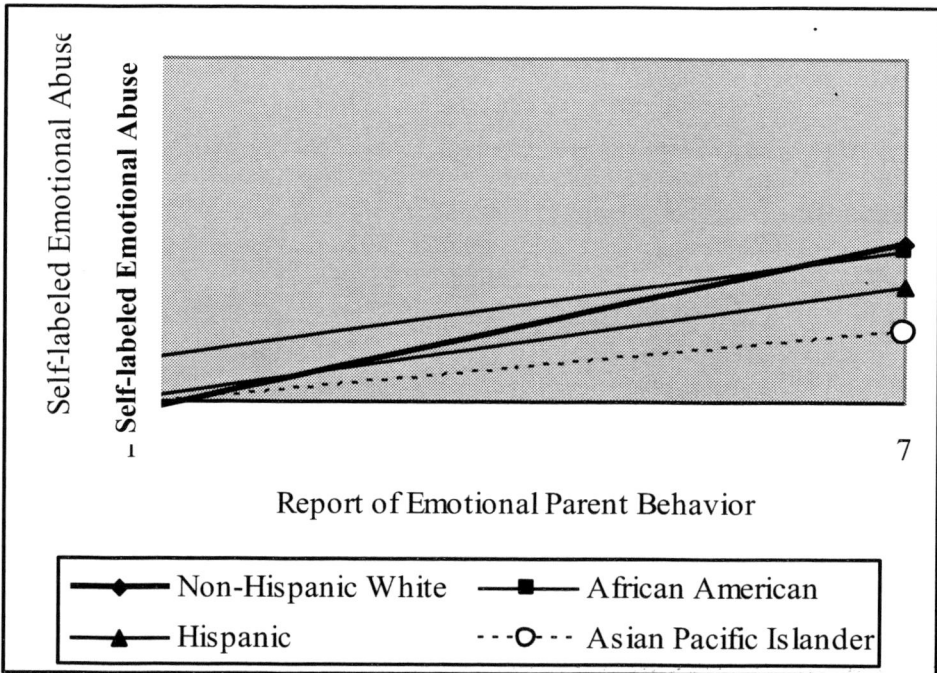

Figure 1a. Self-labeled physical abuse as a function of race and report of physical parental behavior. (b). Self-labeled emotional abuse as a function of race and report of emotional parental behavior.

When examining emotional abuse, youth ratings of emotional parent behaviors were strongly associated with self-labeled emotional abuse ($\beta = .42$, $p < .001$). However, race emerged as a moderator of this association. Specifically, Asian Pacific Islander race interacted with emotional parent behaviors to predict self-labeled emotional abuse ($\beta = -.17$, $p <.05$). Furthermore, the interaction between Hispanic race and emotional parent behaviors in the prediction of self-labeled emotional abuse was marginally significant ($\beta = -.16$, p <.08). As seen in Figure 1b, the association between emotional parent behaviors and self-labeled emotional abuse was stronger in Non-Hispanic Whites than in Asian Pacific Islanders ($\beta = -.15$, $p < .01$). The magnitude of the association between emotional parental behaviors and self-labeled abuse did not differ significantly for African Americans and Hispanics when compared to Non-Hispanic Whites.

Table 5. Regression Predicting Self-Labeled Abuse from Reports of Parent Behaviors.

Variable	Self-labeled PA regressed on physical parent behaviors			Self-labeled EA regressed on emotional parent behaviors		
	B	SE B	β	B	SE B	β
Youth's age	.04	.02	.08[*]	.05	.02	.08[*]
Youth's gender [a]	.42	.07	.18[‡]	.62	.08	.26[‡]
Total household income	-.01	.01	-.07[*]	-.01	.00	-.08[*]
African American [b]	-.07	.12	-.03	.07	.21	.03
Hispanic American [b]	-.16	.11	-.07	.03	.19	.03
Asian Pacific Islander [b]	.03	.16	.01	.26	.31	.07
Reports of Parent Behavior	.88	.11	.47[‡]	.06	.01	.42[‡]
Afr Am X Parent Behavior	-.009	.16	-.003	-.02	.01	-.13
Hisp Am X Parent Behavior	-.08	.15	-.03	-.02	.01	-.16†
API X Parent Behavior	.56	.18	-.15[†]	-.03	.02	-.17[*]
	Adjusted $R^2 = .23$			Adjusted $R^2 = .19$		

[a] Male = 1, Female = 2; [b] Reference group = Non-Hispanic White.
† p<.08, [*] p<.05, [†] p<.01, [‡] p<.001.

STUDY 3: RACE AND THE IMPACT OF MALTREATMENT

One may reasonably expect that an adolescent's interpretation of parental actions as maltreatment would be more likely to be associated with affective responses than actions that are not so labeled. Previous research indeed suggests that childhood experiences are associated with depression when individuals label those experiences as abusive (Carlin et al., 1994). Additionally, emotional and physical maltreatment are frequently associated with internalizing symptoms, such as depression and anxiety (Kaplan, Pelcovitz and Labruna, 1999). Lau and colleagues (in press) examined the relative impact of self-labeled abuse and reports of specific parental behaviors on adolescents' internalizing distress and explored race as a potential moderator of these associations. To test the hypothesis that the self-labeling of abuse victimization may be important in understanding internalizing distress over and above the experience of specific forms of harsh parental behavior, Lau and colleagues (in press) assessed emotional parental behavior, physical parental behavior, and self-labeled emotional and physical abuse in the same manner described above (Study 2). Internalizing symptom distress was assessed using the internalizing broadband scale score (including symptoms of depression, anxiety, social withdrawal and somatic complaints) from the Youth Self-Report (YSR; Achenbach, 1991).

Lau and colleagues (in press) first conducted hierarchical multiple regression analyses to determine the relative impact of youth reports of parental behaviors and self-labeled abuse on youth internalizing symptoms. When predicting internalizing distress utilizing physical abuse variables, internalizing symptoms increased as ratings of physical parent behaviors increased (β = .12, p <.001). However, the addition of self-labeled physical abuse did not significantly contribute to the prediction of internalizing problems. Similarly, when predicting internalizing distress utilizing the emotional abuse variables, internalizing symptoms increased as ratings of emotional parent behaviors increased (β = .33, p <.001). Again, the addition of self-labeled abuse, emotional abuse in this case, did not contribute to the prediction of internalizing symptoms. The authors carried out parallel analyses, with the order of parental behaviors and self-labeled abuse reversed; in order to confirm that variance in internalizing scores was best explained by the unique contribution of reports of parental behaviors. These analyses confirmed that the degree to which adolescents' labeled parental acts as abusive did not contribute to the prediction of internalizing symptoms over and above youth reports of specific parental behaviors.

Table 6. Regression Predicting Internalizing Symptoms from Reports of Parent Behaviors.

Variable	Internalizing Problems regressed on Physical Parent Behavior			Internalizing Problems regressed on Emotional Parent Behavior		
	B	SE B	B	B	SE B	B
Youth's age	.37	.22	.06	.08	.22	.01
Youth's gender [a]	3.14	.87	.12[‡]	3.72	.87	.14[‡]
Total household income	.02	.06	.01	-.03	.06	-.02
African American [b]	-2.39	1.50	-.08	.09	2.45	.00
Hispanic American [b]	-4.15	1.38	-.16[**]	-6.34	2.24	-.25[**]
Asian Pacific Islander [b]	2.11	2.07	.05	-8.63	3.51	-.20[*]
Parent behavior	4.20	1.37	.20[**]	.43	.09	.28[‡]
Afr Am X Parent behavior	4.53	1.94	.14[*]	-.01	.13	-.01
Hisp Am X Parent behavior	4.13	1.81	.14[*]	.28	.12	.20[*]
API X Parent behavior	.71	2.23	.02	.58	.18	.27[**]
	Adjusted R^2 = .14			Adjusted R^2 = .17		

[a] Male=1, Female=2; [b] Reference group = Non-Hispanic White.
* p<.05, ** p<.01, ‡ p<.001.

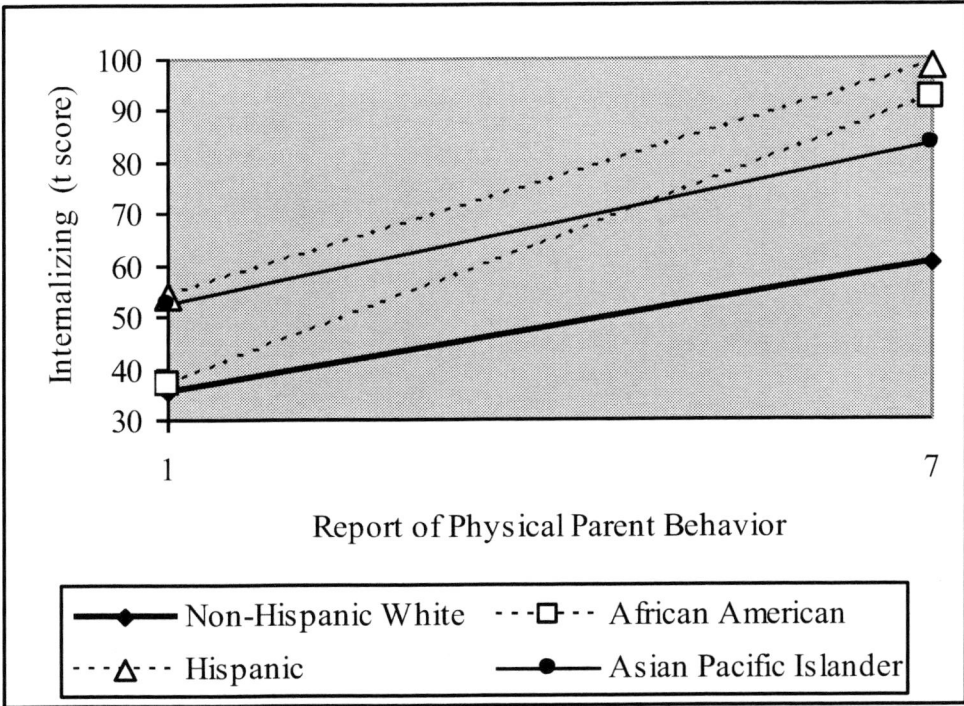

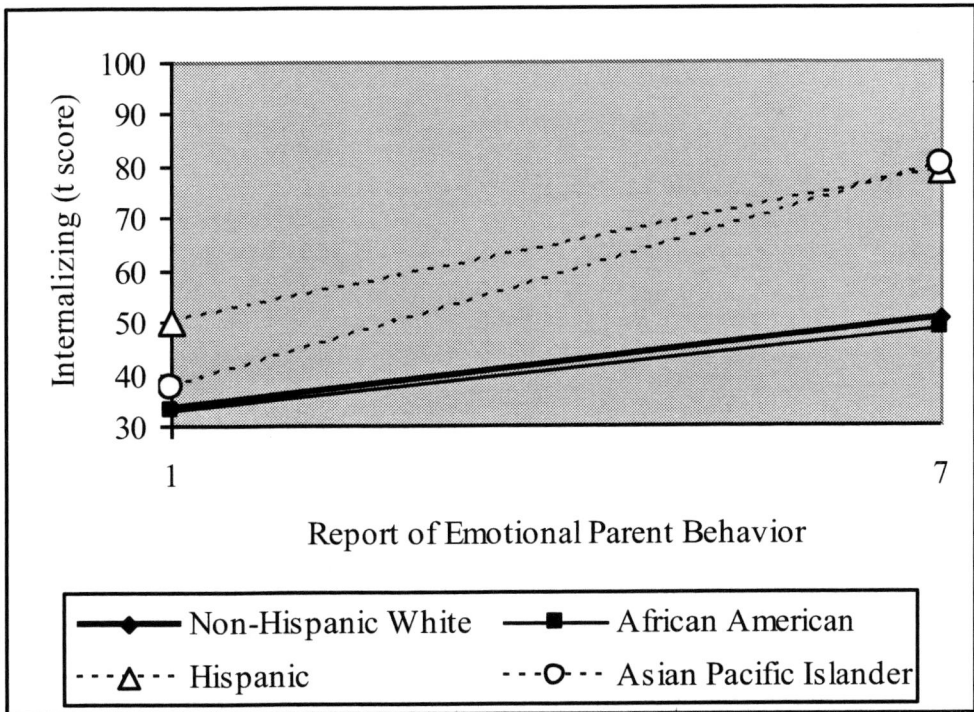

Figure 2a. Youth-reported internalizing problems as a function of race and report of physical parental behavior. (b). Youth-reported internalizing problems as a function of race and report of emotional parental behavior.

Since self-labeled abuse was not significantly associated with internalizing distress beyond reports of parenting behavior, remaining analyses examined race as a moderator in the association between parent behavior (i.e., emotional or physical) and internalizing distress. Results of these analyses indicated significant race by parent behavior interactions (Table 6). Compared to Non-Hispanic White youth, there appeared to be a stronger association between physical parent behaviors and internalizing symptoms in African American ($\beta = .14$, $p < .05$) and Hispanic youth ($\beta = .14$, $p < .05$; see Figure 2a). When considering emotional parent behavior, there appeared to be a stronger association between emotional parent behaviors and internalizing symptoms in Hispanic youth ($\beta = .20$, $p < .05$) and Asian Pacific Islander youth ($\beta = .27$, $p < .01$) when compared to Non-Hispanic White youth (see Figure 2b).

CONCLUSION

Across four major racial groups, youth self-reports of maltreatment history were examined in relation to child welfare involvement. When assessing need for protection based on youths' own reports of maltreatment victimization, there appeared to be racial disparities in institutional identification of maltreatment vis-à-vis child welfare placement. Findings suggested that African American youth may be disproportionately identified as maltreated and taken into protective custody, even when experiencing levels of maltreatment similar to children from other racial groups. These findings support the concern that there may still exist systematic institutional or community level biases in the processes of maltreatment investigation, identification, substantiation, and protective services intervention in CPS systems, such that African American families are scrutinized more closely than families from other backgrounds. This finding can be placed in the context of other evidence of racial disparities in child welfare, including longer stays in foster care, with fewer family reunifications and more re-entries into care among African Americans compared to Non-Hispanic Whites (e.g., Wells and Guo, 1999). Also of concern are findings suggesting that once in the child welfare system, African American children are less likely than Non-Hispanic Whites to receive mental health services even when level of need is controlled (Leslie, Hurlburt, Landsverk, Barth, and Slymen, 2004; Garland et al., 2000). The finding that African American youth who have had stays in foster care are less likely than others to identify themselves as victims of maltreatment may fuel the arguments of some that child welfare practice and policy result in intervention decisions influenced heavily by race and class rather than child protection from parental inadequacy (Roberts, 2003).

However, race-based discrimination is only one potential explanation for racial differences in perceptions among youth in the child welfare system. It is also possible that youth from diverse cultural backgrounds have divergent perspectives on what constitutes abuse. That is, adolescents raised within certain cultural child-rearing traditions may view the same set of parental behaviors quite differently. Indeed, the next set of findings suggested that race influenced the likelihood that youth would associate specific punitive parenting behaviors with the experience of being abused. The evidence indicated that Asian Pacific Islander youth, in particular, may be less likely to label emotionally and physically punitive parental acts as abusive. Thus, there was some indication of socio-cultural differences in the set of meanings attached to punitive parenting practices for children reared in diverse communities.

Ultimately, however, whether parental behaviors are cognitively or affectively labeled by youth as abusive may not matter if the consequences of these parental behaviors for youth adjustment are uniformly deleterious. Following up on the previous analyses, the associations between reports of specific punitive parent behaviors, self-labeled abuse and psychological distress were examined across racial groups. Interestingly, reports of punitive parent behaviors were more strongly related to concurrent symptoms of distress among ethnic minority youth compared to Non-Hispanic White youth. Further, youth reports of specific parental behaviors were more predictive of youth distress than were youth appraisals regarding whether they had been victims of abuse. Therefore, it did not seem to matter how punitive parental practices were labeled; they had negative consequences across groups, and were associated with greatest distress among minority youth.

Taken together, these findings suggest that matters of race in maltreatment identification are complex. There appear to be racial differences in whether certain parent behaviors are labeled by adolescents as abusive, and in the likelihood of institutional identification of maltreatment victimization. Given the same set of experiences, some minority youth may be less likely to self-identify as victims of maltreatment, yet they may be more likely to be identified as victims by institutions. Nonetheless, punitive parent behaviors, whether or not they are labeled as abusive, are strongly associated with psychological distress across racial groups. Thus, racial variability in maltreatment identification does not necessarily reflect differential impact. Cultural competence in child protective services should not mean holding families to different standards of protection from harm. However, those charged with child welfare reform are faced with the task of ensuring that African American families, in particular, are served in a manner that assures parity in protection while avoiding disparities in outcome.

REFERENCES

Achenbach, T. M. & Edelbrock, C. (1991). *Manual for the Child Behavior Cheklist/4-18 and Profile.* Newbury Park, CA: Sage Publications.

Bernstein, D. P. & Fink, L. (1998). *Childhood Trauma Questionnaire: A retrospective self-report.* San Antonio, TX: The Psychological Corporation.

Brody, G. H. & Flor, D. L. (1998). Maternal resources, parenting practices, and child competence in rural, single-parent African American families. *Child Development, 69,* 803-816.

Carlin, A. S., Kemper, K., Ward, N. G., Sowell, H., Gustafson, B. & Stevens, N. (1994). The effect of differences in objective and subjective definitions of childhood physical abuse in estimates of incidence and relation to psychopathology. *Child Abuse and Neglect, 18,* 393-399.

Carlson, V. J. & Harwood, R. L. (2003). Attachment, culture, and the caregiving system: The cultural patterning of everyday experiences among Anglo and Puerto Rican mother-infant pairs. *Infant Mental Health Journal, 24,* 53-73.

Chand, A. (2000). The over-representation of Black children in the child protection system: Possible causes, consequences and solutions. *Child and Family Social Work, 5*, 67-77.

Chao, R. K. (1994). Beyond parental control and authoritarian parenting style: Understanding Chinese parenting through the cultural notion of training. *Child Development, 65*, 1111-1119.

Chasnoff, I. J., Landress, H. J. & Barrett, M. E. (1990). The prevalence of illicit-drug or alcohol use during pregnancy and discrepancies in mandatory reporting in Pinellas County, Florida. *New England Journal of Medicine, 322*, 1202-1206.

Chen, X., Hastings, P. D., Rubin, K. H., Chen, H., Cen, G. & Stewart, S. L. (1998). Child-rearing attitudes and behavioral inhibition in Chinese and Canadian toddlers: A cross-cultural study. *Developmental Psychology, 34*, 677-686.

Corral-Verdugo, V., Frias-Armenta, M., Romero, M. & Munoz, A. (1995). Validity of a scale measuring beliefs regarding the "positive" effects of punishing children: A study of Mexican mothers. *Child Abuse and Neglect, 19*, 669-679.

Courtney, M. E. (1995). Reentry to foster care of children returned to their families. *Social Service Review, 69*, 226-241.

Deater-Deckard, K., Dodge, K. A., Bates, J. E. & Pettit, G. S. (1996). Physical discipline among African American and European American mothers: Links to children's externalizing behaviors. *Developmental Psychology, 32*, 1065-1072.

Dubowitz, H., Klockner, A., Starr, A., Jr. & Black, M. M. (1998). Community and professional definitions of child neglect. *Child Maltreatment, 3*, 235-243.

Eckenrode, J., Powers, J., Doris, J., Munsch, J. & Bolger, N. (1988). Substantiation of child abuse and neglect reports. *Journal of Consulting and Clinical Psychology, 56*, 9-16.

Ferrari, A. M. (2002). The impact of culture upon child rearing practices and definitions of maltreatment. *Child Abuse and Neglect, 26*, 793-813.

Finkelhor, D. & Dzuiba-Leatherman, J. (1994) Children as victims of violence: A national survey. *Pediatrics, 84*, 413-420.

Fontes, L. A. (2002). Child discipline and physical abuse in immigrant Latino families: Reducing violence and misunderstandings. *Journal of Counseling and Development, 80*, 31-40.

Garland, A. F., Ellis-Macleod, E., Landsverk, J. A., Ganger, W. & Johnson, I. (1998). Minority populations in the child welfare systems: The visibility hypothesis reexamined. *American Journal of Orthopsychiatry, 68*, 142-146.

Garland, A. F., Hough, R. L., Landsverk, J. A., McCabe, K. M., Yeh, M., Ganger, W. C. & Reynolds, B. J. (2000). Racial and ethnic variations in mental health care utilization among children in foster care. *Children's Services: Social Policy, Research and Practice, 3*(3), 133-146.

Garland, A. F., Hough, R. L., McCabe, K. M., Yeh, M., Wood, P. A. & Aarons, G. A. (2001). Prevalence of psychiatric disorders in youths across five sectors of care. *Journal of the American Academy of Child and Adolescent Psychiatry, 40*, 409-418.

Giovannoni, J. & Becerra, R. (1979). *Defining Child Abuse*. New York: The Free Press.

Goerge, R. M., Wulczyn, F. H. & Harden, A. (1994). Foster care dynamics: California, Illinois, Michigan, New York and Texas: A first year report from the multi-site state foster care data archive. Chicago: Chapin Hall Center for Children, University of Chicago.

Hampton, R. L. & Newberger, E. H. (1985). Child abuse incidence and reporting by hospital: Significance of severity, class, and race. *American Journal of Public Health, 75*, 56-60.

Henry, G. T. (1990). *Practical sampling.* Newbury Park, CA: Sage.

Hong, G. K. & Hong, L. K. (1991). Comparative perspectives on child abuse and neglect: Chinese versus Hispanics and Whites. *Child Welfare, 70*, 463-475.

Horwitz, S., Hoagwood, K., Stiffman, A. R., Summerfield, T., Weisz, J. R., Costello, E. J., et al. (2001). Reliability of the Services Assessment for Children and Adolescents. *Psychiatric Services, 52*, 1088-1094.

Jambunathan, S., Burts, D. C. & Pierce, S. (2000). Comparisons of parenting attitudes among five ethnic groups in the United States. *Journal of Comparative Family Studies, 31*, 395-406.

Jenkins, S. & Diamond, B. (1985). Ethnicity and foster care: Census data as predictors of placement variables. *American Journal of Orthopsychiatry, 55*, 267-276.

Kaplan, S.J., Pelcovitz, D. & Labruna, V. (1999). Child and adolescent abuse and neglect research: A review of the past 10 years. Part I: physical and emotional abuse and neglect. *Journal of the American Academy of Child and Adolescent Psychiatry, 38*, 1214-1222.

Kelley, M. L. & Tseng, H. (1992). Cultural differences in child rearing: A comparison of immigrant Chinese and Caucasian American mothers. *Journal of Cross-Cultural Psychology, 23*, 444-455.

Korbin, J. (1994). Sociocultural factors in maltreatment. In G. Melton, and F. Berry (Eds.), *Protecting children from abuse and neglect: Foundations for a new national strategy* (pp. 182-223). New York, NY: Guilford Press.

Lau, A.S., Huang, M.M., Garland, A.F., McCabe, K.M., Yeh, M. & Hough, R.L. (in press). Racial variation in self-labeled child abuse and associated internalizing symptoms among high-risk adolescents. *Child Maltreatment.*

Lau, A. S., McCabe, K. M., Yeh, M., Garland, A. F., Hough, R. L. & Landsverk, J. (2003). Race/ethnicity and rates of self-reported maltreatment among high-risk youth in public sectors of care. *Child Maltreatment, 8*(3), 183-194.

Leslie, L. K., Hurlburt, M. S., Landsverk, J., Barth, R. & Slymen, D. J. (2004). Outpatient mental health services for children in foster care: A national perspective. *Child Abuse and Neglect, 28*(6), 697-712.

Maiter, S., Alaggia, R. & Trocmé, N. (2004). Perceptions of child maltreatment by parents from the Indian subcontinent: Challenging myths about culturally based abusive parenting practices. *Child Maltreatment, 9*, 309-324.

Mech, E. V. (1983). Out-of-home placement rates. *Social Service Review, 57*, 659-667.

Mennen, F. E. (1995). The relationship of race/ethnicity to symptoms in childhood sexual abuse. *Child Abuse and Neglect, 19*(1), 115-124.

Okamura, A., Heras, P. & Wong-Kerberg, L. (1995). Asian, Pacific Island, and Filipino Americans and sexual child abuse. In L. A. Fontes (Ed.), *Sexual abuse in nine North American cultures: Treatment and prevention* (pp. 67-96). Thousand Oaks, CA: Sage Publications, Inc.

Phillips-Sanders, K., Moisan, P. A., Wadlington, S., Morgan S., et al. (1995). Ethnic differences in psychological functioning among Black and Latino sexually abused girls. *Child Abuse and Neglect, 19*(6), 691-706.

Pinderhughes, E. E., Dodge, K. A., Bates, J. E., Pettit, G. S. & Zelli, A. (2000). Discipline responses: Influences of parents' socioeconomic status, ethnicity, beliefs about parenting, stress, and cognitive-emotional processes. *Journal of Family Psychology, 14,* 380-400.

Rao, K., DiClemente, R. J. & Ponton, L. E. (1992). Child sexual abuse of Asians compared to other populations. *Journal of the American Academy of Child and Adolescent Psychiatry, 31*(5), 880-886.

Roberts, D. (2003). *Shattered Bonds: The Color of Child Welfare.* New York, NY: Basic Books.

Rose, S. J. & Meezan, W. (1996). Variations in perceptions of child neglect. *Child Welfare, 75,* 139-160.

Straus, M. and Gelles, R. (Eds.). (1990). *Physical violence in American families: Risk factors and adaptations to violence in 8,145 families.* New Brunswick, NJ: Transaction Publishers.

Straus, M. & Hamby, S. L. (1997). Measuring physical and psychological maltreatment of children with the Conflict Tactics Scale. In: G. Kaufman Kanot, & J. Jasinski, (Eds.), *Out of the darkness: Contemporary research perspectives on family violence* (pp. 119-135). Thousand Oaks, CA: Sage.

Straus, M. A., Hamby, S. L., Finkelhor, D., Moore, D. W. & Runyan, D. (1998). Identification of child maltreatment with the parent-child conflict tactics scales: Development and psychometric data for a national sample of American parents. *Child Abuse and Neglect, 22,* 249-270.

Terao, S. Y., Borrego, J. & Urquiza, A. J. (2001). A reporting and response model for culture and child maltreatment. *Child Maltreatment, 6,* 158-168.

Use, Needs, Outcomes, and Costs in Child and Adolescent Populations [UNOCCAP] Work Group (1996). Mother/Father Support. Unpublished measure.

Wells, K. & Guo, S. (1999). Reunification and reentry of foster children. *Children and Youth Services Review, 21(4)*, 273-294.

In: Race and Ethnicity
Editor: Jonathan K. Crennan, pp. 267-283

ISBN: 978-1-60692-099-2
© 2010 Nova Science Publishers, Inc.

Chapter 11

Addressing Mental Health Disparities: A Preliminary Test of the Multicultural Assessment Intervention Process (MAIP) Model

Glenn Gamst, [1] Richard Rogers,[1] Aghop Der-Karabetian[1] and Richard H. Dana[2]*

[1]University of La Verne, La Verne, CA, USA
[2]Regional Research Institute, Portland State University, Portland, OR, USA

ABSTRACT

Racial and ethnic disparities in American health and healthcare are becoming increasingly apparent and are garnering a growing body of research attention (e.g., La Viest, 2005). These disparities are particularly problematic regarding mental health service delivery to multicultural populations (Snowden and Yamada, 2005; U.S. Department of Health and Human Services, 2001). The present study explores a variety of key parameters associated with the Multicultural Assessment Intervention Process (MAIP) model proposed by Dana (1993, 1998, 2000) and Dana, Aragon, and Kramer, (2002). This model provides a mental health agency and its practitioners with the necessary conceptual scaffolding and theoretical clarity to address service delivery disparities by positing that mental health consumers are best served when factors such as (1) consumer-provider ethnic/racial match, (2) consumer acculturation status and/or ethnic/racial identity, and (3) provider cultural competence are assessed and factored into the treatment process and clinical outcome. Toward this end, a sample of 123 university counseling center consumers was measured on the 4 previous independent variables (i.e., ethnic/racial match, acculturation status, ethnic identity, and staff cultural competence). Five clinical outcome dependent measures were assessed including Global Assessment of Function (GAF) pre and post treatment differences, and 4 subscales of the Brief

---

[*] Corresponding author: Department of Psychology, University of La Verne, 1950 Third Street, La Verne, CA 91750 (e-mail: gamstg@ulv.edu).

Psychiatric Rating Scale (BPRS): Thinking Disturbance, Withdrawal/Retardation, Hostile-Suspicious, and Anxious-Depression, all of which served as dependent variables. A 2 x 2 x 2 x 2 factorial between-subjects multivariate analysis of covariance (MANCOVA) indicated a statistically significant multivariate interaction effect between Ethnic Match x Client Acculturation x Client Ethnic Identity for the BPRS-thinking disturbance measure. Implications for the MAIP model with this college student population are discussed.

INTRODUCTION

The issue of health disparities or inequality in the United States is receiving more attention from researchers, practitioners, and politicians. The National Institutes of Health (cited by LaViest, 2005, p. 108) operationalize the concept of health disparities as "differences in the incidence, prevalence, mortality and burden of diseases and other adverse health conditions that exist among specific population groups in the United States".

A recent groundbreaking monograph by the Institute of Medicine (2002) titled *Unequal treatment: Confronting Racial and Ethnic Disparities in Health Care*, documented a considerable body of evidence demonstrating that White Americans receive better quality of health care than do people of color. This report aptly contextualized the poor clinical outcomes, underutilization of services, and low levels of service satisfaction that racial/ethnic minorities experience as part of the historical legacy of racism and discrimination people of color continue to cope with.

In the realm of mental health, these same concerns regarding disparities were echoed in the 2001 U.S. Surgeon General's supplemental report titled *Mental Health: A Report of the Surgeon General* (U.S. Department of Health and Human Services, 2001). In this report, it is argued that the U.S. mental health system may be ill prepared to meet the mental health needs of racial/ethnic groups due to deficiencies in the level of cultural competence among service providers of all types (e.g., psychiatrists, therapists, case managers) (see also, Gamst, et al., 2004). Cultural competence deficiencies are exacerbated by the unique cultural differences displayed by racial/ethnic groups with regard to coping styles, utilization of services, help-seeking attitudes and behaviors, and the use of family and community as resources (U.S. Department of Health and Human Services, 2001).

RACIAL /ETHNIC GROUP RISK FACTORS

While not meant to be a comprehensive compilation, below is a brief overview of some significant and unique mental health challenges and needs of the four underserved racial/ethnic groups in the United States.

African Americans

Evidence indicates that African Americans may be at a higher risk of mental disorders than White Americans due to socioeconomic differences (Reiger, et al.,1993) and perceived racism (Dana, 2002). African Americans tend to be underrepresented in outpatient treatment, yet overrepresented in inpatient treatment facilities at the rate of twice that for White Americans (Snowden and Cheung, 1990; Snowden, 1999). Additionally, African Americans are more likely to utilize emergency room services for mental health problems than White Americans (Snowden, 1999).

Native American Indians

A genuine paucity of epidemiological survey research exists currently on the incidence of mental disorders or the mental health needs of this population. High levels of poverty, poor general health and mental health are disproportionately associated with Native Americans (Manson, 2000). Depression and alcohol abuse continue to be a significant problem for many Native American Indians, along with increasing suicide rates (see Novins, Duclos, Martin, Jewett, and Manson, 1999).

Asian Americans/Pacific Islanders

It is difficult to assess this population's mental illness prevalence rates due to methodological challenges such as lack of adequate population sub-sampling. In general, Asian Americans/Pacific Islanders tend to not seek help for mental health problems (Leong and Lau, 2001), and underutilize both outpatient and inpatient treatment because of perceived stigma, and language barriers (Leong, 2001).

Latino Americans

The Epidemiologic Catchment Area Study (ECA) (Robins and Reiger, 1991) found similar rates of psychiatric disorders between Mexican Americans and White Americans, however, higher rates of depression and phobias were reported among acculturated Latino Americans in comparison to White Americans. Differential needs among Latino subgroups have been identified (U.S. Department of Health and Human Services, 2001). Specifically, Central American immigrants who have experienced trauma in their country of origin may have the greatest mental health needs. Exacerbating these problems is the fact that over one-third of Latino Americans have no health insurance (National Center for Health Statistics, 2003).

Clearly, the mental health needs and challenges of these racial and ethnic minority groups is real, immediate, and growing. To address these needs, the U.S. Surgeon General's Supplemental Report has encouraged the development and evaluation of culturally responsive evidence-based mental health treatment services. For example, this report notes that "culture and language affect the perception, utilization, and potentially, the outcomes of mental health services. Therefore, the provision of culturally and linguistically appropriate mental health services is a key ingredient for any programming design to meet the needs of diverse racial and ethnic populations" (U.S. Department of Health and Human Services, 2001, p. 166). The development of the Multicultural Assessment Intervention Process (MAIP) model is one attempt to address mental health disparities within a comprehensive system.

THE MULTICULTURAL ASSESSMENT INTERVENTION PROCESS (MAIP) FRAMEWORK

The MAIP has its roots in a multicultural historical trichotomy that includes issues of social justice, multicultural training and assessment, and large-scale mental health systems of care models. Persistent public sector mental health services disparities are addressed with the MAIP by routinely probing client preference for ethnic, gender, or linguistic match with their provider, using culturally appropriate social etiquette and service delivery styles, with culturally competent mental health providers, evaluating client acculturation status and ethnic identity, and determining the beneficial application of cultural formulations and ethnic-specific services.

The MAIP developed essentially as a multiculturally sensitive assessment model for mental health consumer populations (Dana, 1993, 1998, 2000), and was one of six models recently reviewed by Ponterotto, Gretchen, and Chauhan, (2000). The most recent iteration of the MAIP (see, Dana, Aragon, and Kramer, 2002) and its component parts can be seen in Figure 1.

In its bare essence, The MAIP can be construed as a funnel that routes a diverse mental health consumer clientele to a limited amount of agency resources. As can be seen in Figure 1, this is accomplished in a seven-step process. First, clients are screened, presenting problems and personal history are evaluated, client matching preferences are noted, preliminary diagnosis, Global Assessment of Function (GAF), and other initial clinical outcome and cultural assessments are made. Second, cultural, linguistic, and gender client preferences and needs are addressed, with the overall aim of achieving a balance between the client goals and the available agency human resources. Recent evidence indicates that client requests for specific ethnic/cultural matches range between one-fourth and one-third of community mental health populations. For example, Gamst et al. (2003) reported that 24.2% of their Asian American sample requested a cultural match. Similarly, Gamst et al. (2002) reported 32.9% of their Latino Americans requested a cultural match. Third, determining acculturation status of ethnic/racial minority clients through standard classification procedures (e.g., acculturated, bicultural, marginal, traditional) and assessing ethnic identity status of all clients (e.g., high or low ethnic identity) provides crucial information in the treatment planning and service delivery process. Fourth, to this point the model has focused on the mental health consumer. However, the MAIP also postulates that we scrutinize the cultural competence of the mental health provider. Due to differences in training and clinical experience, providers vary in their cultural knowledge, skills, and abilities (Gamst et al., 2004). Hence, cultural competence of all mental health providers must be routinely assessed and the results of that assessment incorporated into the client disposition or resource allocation process. Fifth, these differences in staff cultural competencies will drive the allocation of multicultural training resources (Dana et al., 2006). Sixth, based on the previous steps, a determination is made as to the viability and usefulness of providing the client with a culture/ethnic-specific clinical intervention. Most clients neither seek nor desire ethnic-specific services. The key question then becomes which clients would benefit from these ethnic-specific services and which clients might be engaged alternatively with more standard culture-general treatment interventions? The MAIP model weighs in on this fundamental resource allocation question by suggesting that traditional (unacculturated) clients may need to be linguistically and ethnically matched with culturally competent providers using specialized cultural formulations and interventions. Conversely, many acculturated clients do not expect or require mental health services from an ethnically matched provider or a culture-specific intervention.

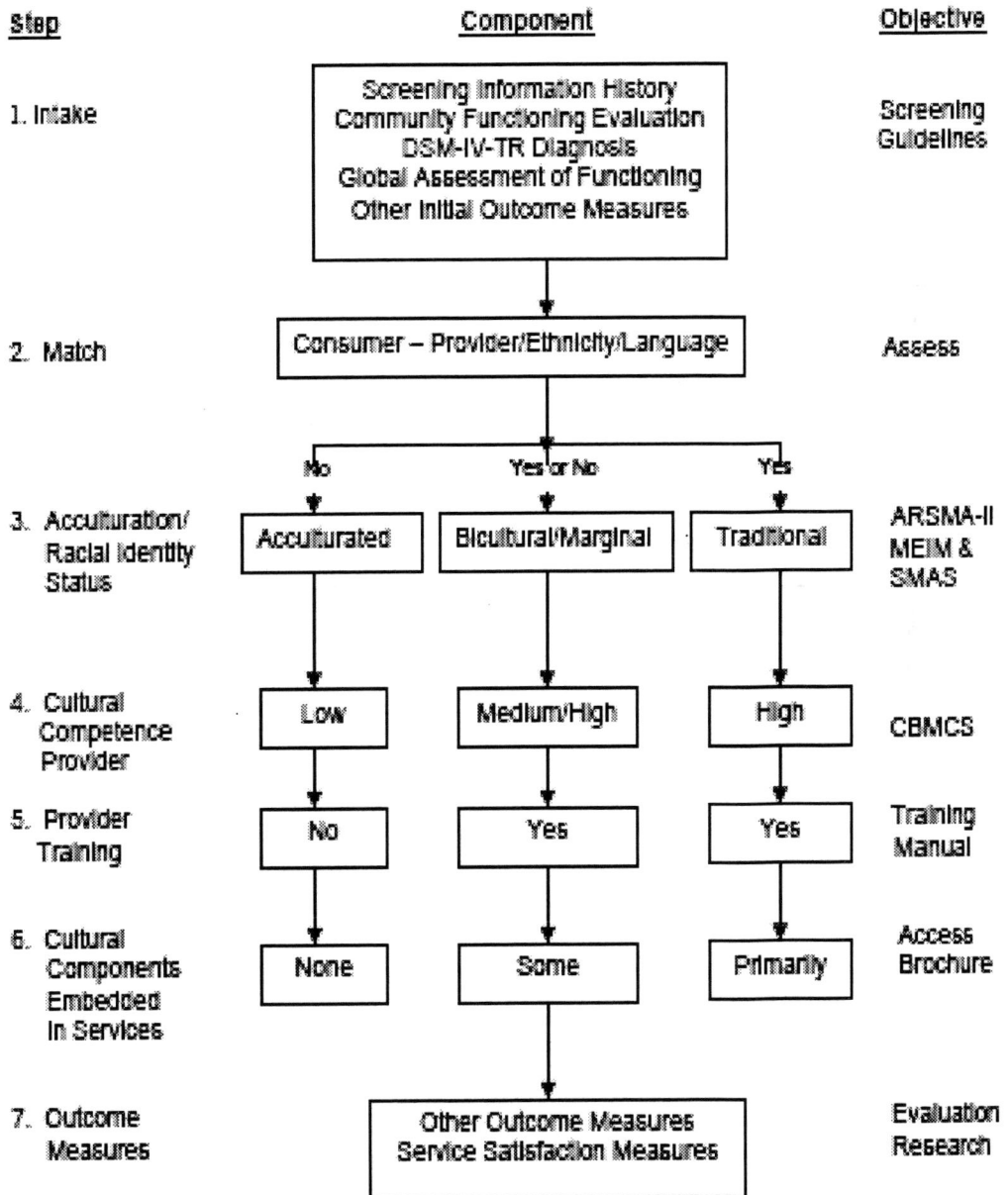

Step	Component	Objective
1. Intake	Screening Information History Community Functioning Evaluation DSM-IV-TR Diagnosis Global Assessment of Functioning Other Initial Outcome Measures	Screening Guidelines
2. Match	Consumer – Provider/Ethnicity/Language	Assess
	No / Yes or No / Yes	
3. Acculturation/ Racial Identity Status	Acculturated / Bicultural/Marginal / Traditional	ARSMA-II MEIM & SMAS
4. Cultural Competence Provider	Low / Medium/High / High	CBMCS
5. Provider Training	No / Yes / Yes	Training Manual
6. Cultural Components Embedded In Services	None / Some / Primarily	Access Brochure
7. Outcome Measures	Other Outcome Measures Service Satisfaction Measures	Evaluation Research

Figure 1. Schematic Flow Chart of MAIP Model Components.

However, the MAIP model does prescribe that all mental health consumers be treated with dignity and respect, including provider service delivery styles and social etiquette that acknowledge and embrace such consideration. The seventh and final step of the MAIP model is the client/provider completion of a variety of posttest outcome measures of the client's functioning at the end of treatment or at annual review. Consumer service satisfaction measures would also be completed at this juncture.

Clearly, the MAIP model as depicted in Figure 1 proscribes or argues against the typical community mental health practice of connecting a mental health consumer to the first available mental health provider resource. Rather, this model encourages a thoughtful and careful evaluation of the client as a cultural being in a multicultural milieu. By injecting a multicultural focus and formulation into the therapeutic process, the MAIP should increase consumer satisfaction and attitudes toward the counseling process. These beneficial attitudes should, in turn, reduce the client "churn" or dropout rate after the first session, thereby, reducing mental health disparities.

Present Study

The present study examined key parameters of the MAIP (e.g., client-provider ethnic match, client acculturation, client ethnic identity, and provider cultural competence) on the clinical outcome of a sample of college students seeking mental health services at a university counseling center. The basic question under study is to what extent do the MAIP variables interact with each other, and contribute to clinical outcome?

Method

The population under study included all students who received mental health services at a southern California, private university counseling center between September 2004 and May 2005. The process of assigning students to mental health providers was a random process, driven primarily by staff caseloads and occasionally the special needs or preferences of the student. Client and provider ethnicity were based on self-report. The racial composition of the sample data reflect a complete census of university students who received mental health services at an university counseling center during the course of Academic Year 2004-2005. Twenty clients were eliminated from the present study (8 African American, 6 bi-racial, 4 Asian American, 2 other) due to small sub-sample sizes. The final total sample of 123 clients included 66 (53.7%) White American and 57 (46.3%) Latino American clients.

Clients received culture-general services from nine mental health providers, 8 of whom were female. The ethnic breakdown of the providers was 4 White Americans, 3 Latino Americans, 1 Asian American, and 1 bi-racial provider. Provider degree status was as follows: 1 Psy.D, 4 Psy.D 3rd year graduate students, 2 Psy.D 2nd year graduate students, and 2 Marriage and Family Counseling 2nd year graduate students. Clients received a variety of outpatient services including individual therapy, group therapy, and case management.

Variables

Four main independent variables were used in this study: client ethnicity, client-provider ethnic match, client ethnic identity, and client acculturation status. Two additional variables served as covariates to adjust the dependent variables: client-provider gender match, and provider cultural competence. Client ethnicity was dichotomized as White American, and Latino American (coded 1, or 0, respectively).

Client-provider ethnic match was dichotomized as match or no match (coded as 1, or 0, respectively) and followed the operationalization offered by Gamst, Dana, Der-Karabetian, and Kramer, (2004), who considered that an ethnic match existed when the provider who made the admission evaluation of functioning had the same ethnicity as the client.

Client ethnic identity was dichotomized as either high or low (coded as 1, or 0, respectively), and was based on the 12-item Multigroup Ethnic Identity Measure (MEIM) (Phinney, 1992; Roberts et al., 1999). This measure is composed of two subscales (ethnic identity search, and affirmation, belonging, and commitment). Internal consistency as measured by Cronbach's alpha was computed on all clients who completed the MEIM. High reliability was observed for both subscales: Ethnic identity search (alpha = .79) and affirmation, belonging, and commitment (alpha = .92). Because the present study found strong positive correlation ($r = .52$) between the two MEIM subscales, only one (affirmation, belonging, and commitment) was used as a measure of ethnic identity.

Likewise, client acculturation was measured using the 32-item Stephenson Multigroup Acculturation Scale (SMAS) (see, Stephenson, 2000). This measure is composed of two subscales (ethnic society immersion, and dominant society immersion). Internal consistency as measured by Cronbach's alpha was again high for both subscales: Ethnic society immersion (alpha = .82) and dominant society immersion (alpha = .86). Again, the present study discovered strong positive correlation between the two SMAS subscales ($r = .79$) indicating considerable conceptual and empirical overlap, thus only one of the subscales (dominant society immersion) was used as our measure of client acculturation status. This measure was dichotomized as high or low (coded as 1, or 0, respectively) and was based on a median split of the dominant society immersion subscale of the SMAS. The correlation observed between the composite SMAS and MEIM scales was $r = -.32$, indicating that the two scales were measuring separate constructs.

Two dichotomous covariates were used to adjust the dependent variables. Gender match between client and provider was defined as either gender match or no gender match (coded as 1, or 0, respectively). Provider cultural competence was based on the California Brief Multicultural Competence Scale (CBMCS) developed by Gamst et al. (2004). This 21-item scale is composed of four subscales that include multicultural knowledge, awareness of cultural barriers, sensitivity and responsiveness to consumers, and sociocultural diversities. For purposes of the present study, a median split was computed on the entire 21-item scale which classified providers as being either high or low in overall cultural competence (coded as 1, or 0, respectively).

Clinical Outcome Variables

Five dependent variables were used in the present study. One dependent measure was the Global Assessment of Functioning (GAF) Axis V rating of the *Diagnostic and Statistical Manual of Mental Disorders*, fourth edition (DSM-IV; American Psychiatric Association, 1994). The GAF was completed by the mental health provider at intake, and again at termination, and a computed difference score examined all phases of the treatment process. GAF scale values can range from 1 (severe impairment) to 100 (good general functioning). GAF-difference scores were computed for each client by means of subtraction (e.g., GAF at time 2 minus GAF at time 1). A positive GAF-difference score indicated a more positive clinical assessment by the counselor at termination; conversely, a negative GAF-difference score indicated a more pessimistic clinical assessment by the mental health provider at termination. Adequate reliability and validity have been reported using this subjective measure (e.g., Jones, Thornicroft, Coffey, and Dunn, 1995).

Four additional dependent measures were developed from the 18-item Brief Psychiatric Rating Scale (BPRS; Overall and Gorham, 1988). Following the factor analytic work with this scale by Hedlund and Vieweg, (1980), four subscales were computed by summing the individual items comprising the subscale. These subscales (dependent measures) included: Thinking disturbance (three items, alpha = .44), withdrawl/retardation (two items, alpha = .32), hostile/suspiciousness (three items, alpha = .55), and anxious/depression (three items, alpha = .72). Clients were evaluated on the BPRS at intake and at termination. A difference score was computed on the sums of each BPRS subscale (i.e., time 2 minus time 1). A negative subscale value indicates improvement in client functioning. A positive value indicates a more pessimistic appraisal of the client by the mental health provider at termination. The relatively weak internal consistency of several of the BPRS subscales is possibly due to the paucity of items making up each individual subscale, and also may indicate a lack of sensitivity among these BPRS subscales in discriminating client functioning among college students seeking mental health services.

Sample Characteristics

A breakdown of sample characteristics by client ethnicity can be seen in Table 1. Of the 123 students who received mental health services, 57 (46.3%) were Latino Americans and 66 (53.7%) were White Americans. The mean age of the clients was 24 years and nearly three-fourths were female. Over eight of ten of the clients were single, never married. Roughly, four of ten clients were ethnically matched with a mental health provider. Gender matches occurred for about seven of ten clients, primarily for the females. High ethnic identity was found in half of the Latino Americans and in about four of ten White Americans. High acculturation was twice the level for Latino Americans (70.2%) as for White Americans (35.6%).

Analysis Strategy

Two sets of statistical analyses were computed with several independent and dependent variables. First inter-item correlations were computed among all independent, dependent, and covariate measures in this study. Second, one four-way between-subjects multivariate analysis of covariance (MANCOVA) was conducted using client ethnicity (2 levels), ethnic match (2 levels), client acculturation (2 levels), and client ethnic identity (2 levels) as independent variables and GAF-difference, and four BPRS subscales (thinking disturbance, withdrawl/retardation, hostile/suspiciousness, anxious/depression) served as dependent measures.

Table 1. Sample Characteristics by Client Ethnicity.

	Total	Latino American	White American
Sample size	123	57	66
Mean age	24.0	23.8	24.2
Percentage female	74.0	77.2	71.2
Percentage single marital status	84.6	86.0	83.3
Percentage ethnic match	43.9	35.1	51.5
Percentage gender match	69.9	71.9	68.2
Percentage high ethnic identity	45.3	50.9	40.0
Percentage high acculturation	52.6	70.2$_a$	35.6$_b$

Note. Tests of statistical significance of difference between proportions is used for variables summarized by percentages. Variables represented by means are evaluated with analysis of variance. Percentages or means in the same row with subscripts that differ are statistically significantly different at the .01 level of significance. The ethnic identity measure is based on a median split of the affirmation, belongingness, and commitment subscale of the MEIM. The acculturation measure is based on a median split of the dominant society immersion subscale of the SMAS.

Table 2. Pearson Correlations Among Independent and Dependent Variables and Covariates.

Variables	1	2	3	4	5	6	7	8	9	10	11
1. Ethnic match	--	.17	-.17	-.13	.01	.08	.05	-.23*	.03	-.09	.11
2. Client ethnicity		--	-.35*	-.11	.06	-.04	.05	-.14	.17	-.12	.13
3. Client acculturation			--	-.14	.07	.04	.01	.02	-.15	.08	-.25*
4. Client ethnic identity				--	-.03	-.14	-.05	.14	.15	.15	-.18
5. Provider cultural competence					--	.15	.12	-.13	-.17	21*	.01
6. Gender match						--	-.07	-.12	-.19	-.12	-.05
7. GAF-difference							--	-.29*	-.19	-.07	-.37*
8. BPRS-TD								--	.14	.20*	.10
9. BPRS-WR									--	.29*	.32*
10. BPRS-HS										--	-.05
11. BPRS-AD											--

N=123

* p<.01

BPRS-TD=Brief Psychiatric Rating Scale-Thinking Disturbance, BPRS-WR=Brief Psychiatric Rating Scale-Withdrawal/Retardation, BPRS-HS=Brief Psychiatric Rating Scale-Hostile/Suspiciousness, BPRS-AD=Brief Psychiatric Rating Scale-Anxious/Depression.

Two covariates were used to adjust the five dependent variables in the MANCOVA model. These covariates were gender match and provider cultural competence. The first covariate has been found in previous research (see, Gamst et al., 2000; 2001; 2003) to provide significant adjustment.

RESULTS

As can be seen in Table 2, Pearson correlations among the covariates and independent and dependent variables in the study generated low to moderate correlation. Specifically, client ethnicity was negatively correlated with client acculturation. Ethnic match produced a low negative correlation with the BPRS- thinking-disturbance measure. The GAF-difference measure was found to be negatively correlated with the BPRS thinking disturbance and anxious/depression measures.

Multivariate Analysis of Covariance Model

A 2 x 2 x 2 x 2 between-subjects multivariate analysis of covariance (MANCOVA) was performed on five dependent measures associated with client outcomes: GAF-difference, BPRS-thinking disturbance, BPRS-withdrawl/retardation, BPRS-hostile/suspiciousness, BPRS-anxious/depression. Adjustment was made for two covariates: gender match and provider cultural competence. Independent variables were client ethnicity (White American, Latino American), ethnic match (match, no match), client acculturation (high, low), and client ethnic identity (high, low).

SPSS General Linear Model: Multivariate was used for this analysis. Total $N = 123$ cases with no cases eliminated due to missing data. There were no univariate or multivariate within-cell outliers at $\alpha = .01$. Evaluation of cases for multivariate assumptions was satisfactory, and covariates were considered reliable for covariate analysis.

Due to a statistically significant Box's M Test of equality of covariance matrices ($p < .001$), Pillai's Trace was used as the multivariate test statistic (see, Meyers, Gamst, and Guarino, 2006). Using Pillai's criterion, the combined dependent variables were statistically significantly related to ethnic match $F (5, 75) = 2.24$, $p < .05$, partial $\eta^2 = .13$, client acculturation $F (5, 75) = 2.69$, $p < .03$, partial $\eta^2 = .15$, and the multivariate interaction effects of, Ethnic Match x Client Acculturation $F (5, 75) = 2.41$. $p < .04$, partial $\eta^2 = .14$, Ethnic Match x Client Ethnicity $F (5, 75) = 3.08$, $p < .01$, partial $\eta^2 = .17$, and Ethnic Match x Client Acculturation x Client Ethnic Identity $F (5, 75) = 3.04$, $p < .01$, partial $\eta^2 = .17$.

Neither covariate (gender match or provider cultural competence) significantly adjusted the dependent measures ($p > .05$). While five multivariate main and interaction effects were found in the present study, we will focus on interpreting the multivariate triple interaction of Ethnic Match x Client Acculturation x Client Ethnic Identity, since it takes interpretive precedence over the other statistically significant effects.

Univariate three-way between-subjects analyses of covariance (ANCOVAs), followed by simple-simple effects analyses, were conducted on each dependent measure separately to determine the locus of the statistically significant multivariate triple interaction effect. Only the BPRS-thinking disturbance dependent variable reached statistical significance, F (1, 79) = 11.34, $p < .001$, partial $\eta^2 = .13$. Table 3 displays the means for the BPRS-thinking disturbance triple interaction effect.

Table 3. Adjusted Means and Standard Errors for BPRS-Thinking Disturbance by Ethnic Match, Client Acculturation, and Client Ethnic Identity

Ethnic Match	Acculturation	Ethnic Identity	M	SE
Match	Low	Low	-.27	.34
		High	-.04	.27
	High	Low	-.04	.25
		High	-.57	.54
No Match	Low	Low	1.86	.47
		High	-.01	.26
	High	Low	-.18	.20
		High	.44	.25

Note. A Negative BPRS-Thinking Disturbance Mean indicates an improvement in client functioning between intake and termination as assessed by the mental health provider. A positive value indicates a more pessimistic appraisal between Time 1 and Time 2.

Due to the fact that after adjusting for differences on the covariates, only the univariate Ethnic Match x Client Acculturation x Client Ethnic Identity interaction effect was found to be statistically significant, a simple-simple effects analysis (see Levine, 1991) collapsed across each level of ethnic match and client acculturation was conducted ($p < .05$). No statistically significant differences were observed among the ethnic match treatment conditions ($p > .05$). However, clients in the no match, low acculturation, and low ethnic identity conditions ($M = 1.86$, $SE = .47$)' garnered more pessimistic appraisals from their mental health providers than did their no match, low acculturation, and high ethnic identity counterparts ($M = -.01$, $SE = .26$). This result produced the multivariate triple interaction effect for the BPRS-thinking disturbance measure.

DISCUSSION

The present study examined relationships among client ethnicity, client-provider ethnic match, client acculturation, and client ethnic identity on five types of clinical outcome, while controlling for client-provider gender match and provider cultural competence with college student clients. Results, adjusted for the effects of the covariates, indicated a statistically significant multivariate triple interaction effect among the client-provider ethnic match, client acculturation, and client ethnic identity variables. Subsequent univariate analyses indicated the locus of the multivariate effect to be with the BPRS-thinking disturbance dependent measure. Specifically, this dependent measure indicated poorer outcome or lack of clinical progress (between initial intake and termination of services) among clients who were not ethnically matched, and were unacculturated, and indicated low ethnic identity. This finding provides limited support for the MAIP model in that poorer clinical outcomes are predicted among college student clients who are culturally marginalized, have low ethnic identity, and who do not experience mental health services from providers who are culturally similar to them.

Surprisingly, the independent variables produced a statistically significant impact on only one of the five dependent measures (BPRS-thinking disturbance). This finding suggests that the GAF-difference and other three BPRS subscales may not be sensitive enough to capture variability for this particular college student population.

This study underscores the importance of including salient independent variables (e.g., matching, acculturation, ethnic identity, cultural competence), identified by the MAIP model during the course of mental health assessment and intervention.

Recent reviews of the ethnic/racial matching literature (e.g., Karlsson, 2005; Maramba and Hall, 2002; Shin et al., 2005) indicate the importance of client-provider matching in the context of the other MAIP variables. Additional empirical evidence demonstrating the importance of ethnic matching to clinical outcome, and analogous to the present findings, can be found with adult African American, Latino American, and White American community mental health consumers (e.g., Gamst, Dana, Der-Karabetian, and Kramer, 2000), Adult Asian American community mental health consumers (Gamst et al., 2003; Gamst, Dana, Der-Karabetian, and Kramer, 2001), and African American, Latino American, and White American child and adolescent community mental health consumers (Gamst, Dana, Der-Karabetian, and Kramer, 2004). Some of the variability in the previous match literature may be affected by the unspecified professional identities of public sector mental health providers. An additional source of variability is that match is almost always confounded by provider cultural competence.

The role of acculturation or adaptation of a group to a host culture has garnered a great deal of attention in the theoretical (Dana, 1993; 1998;Van de Vijver, and Phalet, 2004) and empirical (e.g., Marin, Balls Organista, and Chun, 2003) literature. Many acculturation scales are ethnic-specific (e.g., Cuellar, Arnold, and Maldonado, 1995), while some profess to be ethnic-general (e.g., Stephenson, 2000). Currently, a paucity of empirical research exists concerning the use of ethnic-specific versus general acculturation devices with mental health consumer populations. The present study employed the Stephenson (2000) ethnic-general (SMAS) acculturation instrument with good success. One benefit of using this instrument is that it provides the researcher with a cost effective means of measuring acculturation with a diverse client base. Conversely, employment of such a measure may not be sensitive enough to address acculturative stress and transformation issues of each cultural group.

Like acculturation, ethnic and racial identity research is also expanding at a rapid rate (Dana, 1993; Trimble, Helms, and Root, 2003). Identity issues have been successfully explored for specific cultural groups and also in the multigroup domain. The present research successfully employed the Phinney (1992) multigroup measure (MEIM) with this college student population. The finding of an elusive triple interaction of ethnic match, acculturation, and ethnic identity supports the MAIP model contention of both the complexity and value of disentangling these cultural factors in allocating scarce mental health human resources. The present interaction effect parallels somewhat the acculturation and ethnic identity effects found by Gamst et al., (2002) with Latino Americans. This finding underscores the multicultural complexity that identity and acculturation manifest themselves in the real world.

The issue of a mental health provider's cultural competence has also garnered a tremendous amount of historical (e.g., Sue et al., 1982; Sue, Arredondo, and McDavis, 1992) and recent (e.g., Pope-Davis, Coleman, Liu, and Toporek, 2003) attention in the literature. Currently, six instruments have been developed that purport to measure aspects of the original 11 and later 31 specific competencies identified in the Sue et al. (1982; 1992) publications. These instruments included the Cross-Cultural Counseling Inventory-Revised (CCCI-R; LaFromboise et al., 1991), the Multicultural Awareness, Knowledge, Skills Survey (MAKSS; D'Andrea et al., 1991), the Multicultural Counseling Knowledge and Awareness Scale (MCKAS; Ponterotto, and Potere, 2003), the Multicultural Counseling Inventory (MCI; Sodowski, Kuo-Jackson, Richardson, and Corey, 1998), the Multicultural Competency and Training Survey (MCCTS; Holcomb-McCoy, 2000), and the California Brief Multicultural Competence Scale (CBMCS; Gamst et al., 2004). The present study employed the CBMCS, an amalgamation of four of the above instruments, due to its brevity and good reliability and validity among a large number of mental health practitioners. The dichotomized CBMCS variable was used as a covariate in the present study and not an independent variable due to the small number (9) of providers who rendered mental health services to our sample. While this covariate (as well as the gender match covariate) failed to statistically significantly adjust the dependent measures, we believe its measurement is crucial in implementing human resource allocations governed by the MAIP model. Specifically, mental health providers' scores on the CBMCS four subscales can demarcate essential staff multicultural training needs and future training interventions (e.g., Dana et al., 2006).

Some obvious limitations to the present study should be noted. First, due to the relatively small sample size, an examination of the present independent variables' *simultaneous* impact on the dependent measures (e.g., through structural equation modeling) was not conducted in the present study. Recent structural equation modeling of MAIP variables with a large adult community mental health sample has supported many of the MAIP postulates (e.g., Gamst, Dana, Der-Karabetian, Meyers, and Guarino, 2006). Second, this study is based on a relatively small sample of college students who sought help for mental health issues, and thus, may not be generalizable to the adult mental health consumer (non-student) population. Third, clients and providers were paired on the basis of availability, rather than a deliberate allocation process based on the MAIP model. Fourth, for the most part, all clients received culture-general clinical intervention, which may have impacted the clinical outcomes used in this study. Fifth, clients' responses to some of the BPRS subscales achieved relatively low reliability, and may not have been sensitive enough to detect any group differences.

CONCLUSION

The MAIP model affords a community mental health agency, or as in the present case, a university counseling center, with opportunities to integrate culturally responsive and evidence-based treatments and outcomes. The MAIP helps focus management attention on the critical question of who should provide what services to whom? The answer to this query is multifaceted and constrained by organizational human resource limitations and shaped ultimately by an organization's cultural competence.

The strength of the MAIP model lies in its empirical basis and flexibility in conducting culturally sensitive client assessments, clinical interventions, client outcome evaluation, and the targeting of provider multicultural competence in-service training needs. The MAIP premise of examining client ethnic identity and acculturation status provides researchers and practitioners with empirical tools for pondering consumer within-group differences. Such scrutiny, by MAIP model proponents should provide exciting and practical mental health payoffs over time for agencies providing services to diverse communities.

Future research with the MAIP would be enhanced by examining, simultaneously, MAIP variables in a variety of mental health contexts (e.g., university counseling center consumers, adult community mental health consumers, child/adolescent community mental health consumers, etc.). Systematic assessment of the most cost-effective instruments for measuring cultural identity needs to be undertaken. Ways of engaging MAIP methodology (see, Gamst and Dana, 2006) in the context of public-sector managed systems of care will surely garner increasing attention from researchers, practitioners, and mental health care and university counseling center administrators.

ACKNOWLEDGMENTS

The authors acknowledge the helpful comments of Chris Liang (Department of Psychology, University of La Verne) on an earlier draft of this chapter.

REFERENCES

American Psychiatric Association. (1994). *Diagnostic and statistical manual of mental disorders* (4th ed.). Washington, DC: Author.

Cuellar, I., Arnold, B. & Maldonado, R. (1995). The Acculturation Rating Scale for Mexican Americans-II (ARSMA-II): A revision of the original ARSMA scale. *Hispanic Journal of Behavioral Sciences, 17(3),* 275-304.

Dana, R. H. (2002). Mental health services for African Americans: A cultural/racial perspective. *Cultural Diversity and Ethnic Minority Psychology, 8(1),* 3-18.

Dana, R. H. (Eds.). (2000). An assessment-intervention model for research and practice with multicultural populations. In: R. H. Dana, (Eds.), *Handbook of cross-cultural and multicultural personality assessment* (6-16). Mahwah, NJ: Erlbaum.

Dana, R. H. (1998). *Understanding cultural identity in intervention and assessment.* Thousand Oaks, CA: Sage Publications.

Dana, R. H. (1993). *Multicultural assessment perspectives for professional psychology.* Needham Heights, MA: Allyn and Bacon.

Dana, R. H., Aragon, M. & Kramer, T. (2002). Public sector mental health services for multicultural populations: Bridging the gap from research to clinical practice. In: M. N. Smyth, (Eds.), *Health care in transition* (Vol. 1, pp.1-13). Hauppauge, NY: Nova Science Publishers.

Dana, R. H., Gamst, G., Der-Karabetian, A., Arellano-Morales, L., Endriga, M., Huff-Musgrove, R., Morrow, G. (2006). *The California Brief Multicultural Training Program: A manual for trainers.* La Verne, CA: University of La Verne Press.

D'Andrea, M., Daniels, J. & Heck, R. (1991). Evaluating the impact of multicultural counseling training. *Journal of Counseling and Development, 70,* 143-150.

Gamst, G. and Dana, R. H. (2006). Testing the MAIP model: A proposed method for assessing culturally sensitive mental health service delivery for adults and children. Unpublished manuscript, University of La Verne.

Gamst, G., Dana, R. H., Der-Karabetian, A. & Kramer, T. (2004). Ethnic match and treatment outcomes for child and adolescent mental health center clients. *Journal of Counseling and Development, 82,* 457-465.

Gamst, G., Dana, R. H., Der-Karabetian, A., Aragon, M., Arellano, L., Morrow, G. & Martenson, L. (2004). Cultural competency revised: The California Brief Multicultural Competence Scale. *Measurement and Evaluation in Counseling and Development, 37,* 163-183.

Gamst, G., Aguilar-Kitibutr, A., Herdina, A., Hibbs, S., Krishtal, E., Lee, R., Roberg, R., Ryan, E., Stephens, H. & Martenson, L. (2003). Effects of racial match on Asian American mental health consumer satisfaction. *Mental Health Services Research, 5,* 197-208.

Gamst, G., Dana, R. H., Der-Karabetian, A., Aragon, M., Arellano, L. & Kramer, T. (2002). Effects of Latino acculturation and ethnic identity on mental health outcomes. *Hispanic Journal of Behavioral Sciences, 24,* 479-505.

Gamst, G., Dana, R. H., Der-Karabetian, A. & Kramer, T. (2001). Asian American mental health clients: Effects of ethnic match and age on global assessment and visitation. *Journal of Mental Health Counseling, 23(1),* 57-71.

Gamst, G., Dana, R. H., Der-Karabetian, A. & Kramer, T. (2000). Ethnic match and client ethnicity effects on global assessment and visitation. *Journal of Community Psychology, 28(5),* 547-564.

Gamst, G., Dana, R. H. , Der-Karabetian, A., Meyers, L. S. & Guarino, A. J. (2006, May). Assessing the validity of the Multicultural Assessment Intervention Process (MAIP) model for mental health consumers. Poster presented at the Western Psychological Association Meeting, Palm Springs, CA.

Hedlund, J. L. & Vieweg, B. W. (1980). The Brief Psychiatric Rating Scale (BPRS): A comprehensive review. *Journal of Operational Psychiatry, 11,* 48-65.

Holcomb-McCoy, C. C. (2000). Multicultural counseling competencies: An exploratory factor analysis. *Journal of Multicultural Counseling and Development, 28,* 83-97.

Institute of Medicine. (2002). *Unequal treatment: Confronting racial and ethnic disparities of health care.* Washington, DC: National Academies Press.

Jones, S. H., Thornicroft, G., Coffey, M. & Dunn, G. (1995). A brief mental health outcome scale: Reliability and validity of the global assessment of functioning. *British Journal of Psychiatry, 166,* 654-659.

Karlsson, R. (2005). Ethnic matching between therapist and patient in psychotherapy: An overview of findings, together with methodological and conceptual issues. *Cultural Diversity and Ethnic Minority Psychology, 11,* 113-129.

LaFromboise, T. D., Coleman, H. L. K. & Hernandez, A. (1991). Development and factor structure of the Cross-Cultural Counseling Inventory-Revised. *Professional Psychology: Research and Practice, 22,* 380-388.

LaVeist, T. A. (2005). *Minority populations and health: An introduction to health disparities in the United States.* San Francisco, CA: Jossey-Bass.

Leong, F. T. L. (2001). Guest editor's introduction to the special issue: Barriers to providing effective mental health services to racial and ethnic minorities. *Mental Health Services Research, 3,* 179-180.

Leong, F. T. L. & Lau, A. S. L. (2001). Barriers to providing effective mental Health services to Asian Americans. *Mental Health Services Research, 3,* 201-211.

Levine, G. (1991). *A guide to SPSS for analysis of variance.* Hillsdale, NJ: Lawrence Erlbaum Associates, Publishers.

Manson, S. M. (2000). Mental health services for American Indians: Need, use, and barriers to effective care. *Canadian Journal of Psychiatry, 45,*617-626.

Maramba, G. G. & Hall, G. C. N. (2002). Meta-analyses of ethnic match as a predictor of dropout, utilization, and level of functioning. *Cultural Diversity and Ethnic Minority Psychology, 8 (3),* 290-297.

Marin, G., Balls Organista, P. & Chun, K. M. (2003). Acculturation research: Current issues and findings. In: G., Bernal, J. E., Trimble, A. K., Burlew, & F. T. L. Leong, (Eds.), *Handbook of racial and ethnic minority psychology* (208-219). Thousand Oaks, CA: Sage Publications.

Meyers, L. S., Gamst, G. & Guarino, A. (2006). *Applied multivariate research: Design and interpretation.* Thousand Oaks, CA: Sage Publications.

National Center for Health Statistics. (2003). *Health, United States,* Hyattsville, MD: Author, Centers for Disease Control and Prevention, U.S. Department of Health and Human Services.

Novins, D. K. , Duclos, C. W., Martin, C., Jewett, C. S. & Manson, S. M. (1999). Utilization of alcohol, drug, and mental health treatment services among American Indian adolescent detainees. *Journal of the American Academy of Child and Adolescent Psychiatry, 38,* 1102-1108.

Overall, J. E. & Gorham, D. R. (1988). The Brief Psychiatric Rating Scale (BPRS): Recent developments in ascertainment and scaling *Psychopharmocology Bulletin, 24,* 97-99.

Phinney, J. S. (1992). The Multigroup Ethnic Identity Measure: A new scale for use with diverse groups. *Journal of Adolescent Research, 7,* 156-176.

Ponterotto, J. G. & Potere, J. C. (2003). The Multicultural Counseling Knowledge and Awareness Scale (MCKAS): Validity, reliability, and user guidelines. In: D. B. Pope-Davis, H. L. K., Coleman, W. Ming Liu, & R. L. Toporek (Eds.), *Handbook of multicultural competencies in counseling and psychology.* Thousand Oaks, CA: Sage Publications.

Ponterotto, J. G., Gretchen, D. & Chauhan, R. V. (2000). Cultural identity and multicultural assessment: Quantitative and qualitative tools for the clinician. In: L. A. Suzuki, J. G. Ponterotto, & P. J. Meller, (Eds.), *Handbook of multicultural assessment: Clinical, psychological, and educational applications* (2nd ed., 67-100). San Francisco, CA: Jossey-Bass.

Pope-Davis, D. B., Coleman, H. L. K., Liu, W. M. & Toporek, R. L. (Eds.) (2003). *Handbook of multicultural competencies in counseling and psychology.* Thousand Oaks, CA: Sage Publications.

Reiger, D. A., Narrow, W. E., Rae, D. S., Manderscheid, R. W., Locke, B. Z. & Goodwin, F. K. (1993). The de facto U.S. mental and addictive disorders service system. Epidemiologic Catchment Area prospective 1-year prevalence rates of disorders and services. *Archives of General Psychiatry, 50,* 85-94.

Roberts, R., Phinney J., Masse, L., Chen, Y., Roberts, C. & Romero, A. (1999). The structure of ethnic identity in young adolescents from diverse ethnocultural groups. *Journal of Early Adolescence, 19,* 301-322.

Robins, L. & Reiger, D. A. (1991). *Psychiatric disorders in America: The Epidemiologic Catchment Area Study.* New York: The Free Press.

Shin, S. M., Chow, C., Camacho-Gonsalves, Levy, R. J., Allen, I., E. & Leff, H. S. (2005). A meta-analytic review of racial-ethnic matching for African American and Caucasian American clients and clinicians. *Journal of Counseling Psychology, 52,* 45-56.

Snowden, L. R. (1999). African American service use for mental health problems. *Journal of Community Psychology, 27,* 303-313.

Snowden, L. R. & Yamada, A.-M. (2005). Cultural differences in access to care. *Annual Review of Clinical Psychology, 1,* 143-166.

Snowden, L. R. & Cheung, F. K. (1990). Use of inpatient mental health services by members of ethnic minority groups. *American Psychologist, 45,* 347-355.

Sodowsky, G. R., Kuo-Jackson, P. Y., Richardson, M. F. & Corey, A. T. (1998). Correlates of self-reported multicultural competencies: Counselor multicultural social desirability, race, social inadequacy, locus of control, racial ideology, and multicultural training. *Journal of Counseling Psychology, 45,* 256-264.

Stephenson, M. (2000). Development and validation of the Stephenson Multigroup Acculturation Scale (SMAS). *Psychological Assessment, 12,* 77-88.

Sue, D. W., Arredondo, P. & McDavis, R. J. (1992). Multicultural counseling competencies: A call to the profession. *Journal of Multicultural Counseling and Development, 20,* 64-88.

Sue, D. W., Bernier, J. E., Durran, A., Feinberg, L., Pedersen, P., Smith, E. J., et al. (1982). Position paper: Cross-cultural counseling competencies. *The Counseling Psychologist, 10,* 45-52.

Trimble, J. E., Helms, J. E. & Root, M. P. P. (2003). Social and psychological perspectives on ethnic and racial identity. In G. Bernal, J. E. Trimble, A. K. Burlew, F. T. L. and Leong (Eds.), *Handbook of racial and ethnic minority psychology* (pp.239-275). Thousand Oaks, CA: Sage Publications.

U.S. Department of Health and Human Services. (2001). *Mental health: Culture, race, and ethnicity—a supplement to mental health: A report of the Surgeon General.* Rockville, MD: Author.

Van de Vijver, F. J. R. & Phalet, K. (2004). Assessment in multicultural groups: The role of acculturation. *Applied Psychology: An International Review, 53 (2),* 215-236.

In: Race and Ethnicity
Editor: Jonathan K. Crennan, pp. 285-301

ISBN: 978-1-60692-099-2
© 2010 Nova Science Publishers, Inc.

Chapter 12

INFLUENCE OF PHYSICAL AND SEDENTARY ACTIVITY PREFERENCES ON BODY MASS INDEX FOR URBAN AFRICAN AMERICAN YOUTH

Michelle B. Stockton, Barbara S. McClanahan
and Nicole Saffer
The University of Memphis, Department of Health and Sport Sciences,
Memphis, TN, USA

ABSTRACT

Background

The high incidence and increased prevalence of childhood obesity has led to multiple efforts for intervention specifically aimed at increasing levels of physical activity (PA). Preferences for physical activities and sedentary activities have been linked as potential mediators to objectively measured PA participation. However; little research has evaluated whether these preferences are related to Body Mass Index (BMI), particularly in African American children. The purpose of this study was to explore the relationships among BMI and preferences for physical activities and sedentary activities in urban African American youth, a population at increased risk for obesity related heatlh problems.

Methods

Cross-sectional data were analyzed from 75 10- to 16-year-old African American children who were attending the local chapter of the National Youth Summer Program. Of the participants, 53.3% were male and 46.7% were female. The mean age of study participants was 12.29 (± 1.86) years old. Participants mean grade level was 7.27 (± 1.93). Eleven children and adolescents (14.6%) were at risk for becoming overweight and seventeen children and adolescents (21.2%) were overweight according to age-sex specific percentile BMI guidelines of the Centers for Disease Control (Kuczmarski et al.,

2000). Due to age interaction, four separate multiple linear regression models were analyzed based on age category. Preadolescents were defined as 10-12 year olds and adolescents were defined as 13-16 year olds. The dependent variable was age- and gender-specific body mass index percentile. Independent variables were childrens' self-reported preferences for physical activities or sedentary activities with gender as a covariate. Preferences for physical activities and sedentary activities are represented via two scales with higher scores indicating higher preferences.

Results

For preadolescents (n = 43) preference for physical activities significantly explained 16.4% of the variance in BMI ($p = .028$) after controlling for gender. A lower BMI was related to a higher preference for physical activities ($\beta = -32.82$, p = .01), mainly soccer and outdoor play. Also for preadolescents, preference for sedentary activities significantly explained 17.9% of the variance in BMI ($p = .020$) after controlling for gender. A lower BMI was related to a higher preference for sedentary activities ($\beta = -31.25$, p = .01). The major sedentary activities that were contributors were watching television, watching movies or videos on a VCR or DVD, playing video games, and listening to the radio, tapes or CDs. However, there were no significant relationships found among preferences and BMI for adolescent children (n =32).

Conclusions

These results add to a growing body of literature explaining the potential influences of activity preference on BMI among African American youth; a high-risk, understudied population. More specifically, preadolescence might be an ideal time for obesity prevention in that the encouragement of activities could lead to increased activity levels. for African Americans.

INTRODUCTION

Participation in regular physical activity, an integral part of a healthy lifestyle, is an essential component in preventing overweight and obesity. Physical inactivity is a health risk that has been directly linked to a number of serious and life-threatening conditions, such as obesity (NCHS, 2005; Sulemana, Smolensky, & Lai, 2006), heart disease (Williams et al., 2002), diabetes (HSPH, 2004), and cancer (Byers et al., 2002; Friedenreich, 2001; NCHS, 2005). Participating in physical activity has been shown to reduce these risks and consequences (NCHS, 2005). However, during adolescence studies have consistently shown a decrease in physical activity (Allison, Adlaf, Dwyer, Lysy, & Irving, 2007; Hallal, Victoran, Azevedo, Wells, 2006; Kimm, et al., 2002; Nelson, Neumark-Stzainer, Hannan, Sirard, & Story, 2006; Trost et al., 2002). Moreover, both physical activity beliefs and patterns (Hallal, Victoran, Azevedo, Wells, 2006; Malina, 2001; Sagatun, Kolle, Anderssen, Thoresen, &Søggard, 2008) and overweight status (Gordon-Larsen, Adair, Nelson & Popkin, 2004; Matton et al., 2006) track into adulthood. These factors coupled with the continued rise of obesity prevalence in adolescents lead to the importance of exploring the influences of physical activity and obesity among children and adolescents in order to promote participation in physical activity during these pivotal years.

Although significant efforts are necessary to promote the establishment and maintenance of active lifestyles, current trends show that children are participating less in physical activities and more in sedentary activities (Kimm et al., 2002). The current recommendation for physical activity in children is a minimum of 60 minutes per day, at least 5 days per week of moderate to vigorous physical activity (CDC, 2006; Surgeon General, 2004). Yet, nearly one half of the United State's youth, ages 12-21 are not engaged in any type of vigorous physical activity on a daily basis (CDC, 2006). It is clear that children are not meeting the current physical activity recommendations. Decreases in physical activity participation appear to begin during the adolescent years (CDC, 2004a), especially in girls (Goran, Gower, Nagy & Johnson, 2002). In the National Longitudinal Study of Adolescent Health the majority of adolescents did not participate in moderate physical activity five or more times per week (Gordon-Larsen et al., 2004). Moreover, in a study of high school students, 9th grade males experienced a 23.8% inactivity level. This level increased to 32.1% in the 12th grade. The increased prevalence was similar for females, where 32.7% 9th grade females were inactive compared to 48.4% inactive 12th graders (CDC, 2004b). Overall, females had lower physical activity levels (40.1%) than males (26.9%). African American children are at the highest risk for inactivity and sedentary living (Kimm et al., 2002; Taylor et al., 2002; Tershakovec, Kuppler, Zemel, & Stallings, 2002). Population data in 2003 indicate that African American adolescents have the highest level of participation in insufficient physical activity at 42%, as compared to their Hispanic (36.5%) and White (31.0%) counterparts (CDC, 2004a). Studies have found that girls are less active than boys and that African American girls are less active than Caucasian girls (CDC, 2006). In summary, physical inactivity is a primary risk factor for the development of obesity and its co-morbidities, and African Americans appear to be at increased risk for obesity, therefore it is important to identify factors which may affect activity behaviors in this priority population. Developing a physically active lifestyle at a young age is key to living a life of optimal health, therefore; identifying barriers or obstacles to being active is essential.

Physical Activity Barriers

Today there are a number of challenges to a physically active lifestyle among children and adolescents. Advancements in technology, changes in the education system, and changes in the environment have all influenced activity behaviors. First, the increased popularity of predominately sedentary technology emerges as a direct competitor of physical activity. Television, computers, portable hand held devices and video games are accessible and attractive to most youth, enticing them to adopt a sedentary way of life. Researchers have found that adolescents who spend significant amounts of time watching television are less likely to be physically active than their peers who watch little or no television (Hanley et al., 2000; HSPH, 2004; Pate et al., 1997; Surgeon General, 2004). In 1997, Pate and colleagues reported that children who watch television three or more hours per day are less likely to be physically active than children who watch less than three hours of television per day. Similarly, Hanley et al. (2000) found that children who watch television five or more hours a day are two and a half times more likely to be overweight than children who watch television less than five hours a day. In 2004 the Surgeon General released a report stating that 43% of America's adolescents watch two or more hours of television per day. Others have also found associations between television watching and disease. In a report released by the Harvard School of Public Health [HSPH] (2004) it was reported that children who watch two or more hours of television each day have a 14% increase in the risk of developing Type II diabetes. While the risk of spending a large amount of time watching television is generally accepted, some studies have failed to uncover a relationship between time spent watching television and obesity (De Bourdeaudhuij et al., 2005; Robinson et al., 1993).

As technology attracts youth to sedentary activities, accessible outlets for physical activity, such as physical education classes, are becoming scarce, adding to the difficulty to adapt to being physically active. The American Heart Association (n.d.) reported a 17% decrease in the number of children who participated in physical education classes on a daily basis between the years 1991 and 1995. In 2003, only 22 states mandated that physical education be part of the school curriculum (Bryne, 2003). Of those 22 states, only 11 required physical education credit for high school graduation (Bryne, 2003). Unfortunately, the decline in participation in physical education classes is most significant among schools with high African American student populations (CDC. 2003a).

Environmental factors also contribute to the lack of physical activity behavior in children and adolescents. Availability of facilities has been cited as an environmental factor that interferes with children's physical activity levels (Kohl III and Hobbs, 1998; Pate et al., 1997). Other environmental issues such as neighborhood safety, crime, and an increase in motor vehicle traffic have also been cited as reasons for decreased physical activity and increased sedentary behaviors in children and adolescents (CDC 2002; CDC, 2003b, Cecil-Karb & Grogan-Kaylor, 2009). In fact, in a survey conducted in 1999 about healthy lifestyles, parents reported that traffic danger was a major barrier to walking or biking to school for about 40% of children (CDC, 2002). Morevoer, the Youth Media Campaign Longitudinal Survey indicated hat neighborhood safety, transportation, and opportunities within the area were concerns among the non-Hispanic black and Hispanic parents more so than non-Hispanic white parents when it came to environmental barriers to physical activity for their children (CDC, 2003b).

Influences on Physical Activity

Technology, physical education and environmental barriers to exercise pose considerable threats to the health of America's children and adolescents today, specifically within the African American population. However, successful attempts to address these threats have been futile. It is clear that the decision to be physically active is influenced by various factors at multiple levels. Therefore, researchers have explored potential activity influences from various frameworks. An approach based on Bandura's Social Cognitive Theory (SCT) appears to be particularly applicable to increasing understanding of activity behaviors.

SCT describes learning as a reciprocal interaction between the individual's environment, cognitive processes, and behavior. It places reinforcement as an important part of learning (McKenzie, Neiger & Smeltzer, 2005). Self-efficacy, social support, and activity preference are three potential influences on participation in physical activity. Self-efficacy and social support have been have been widely studied as mediators for behavior change, whereas physical activity preference has not been studied as thoroughly. More specifically, SCT has been used as a tool to understand and explain self-efficacy of physical activity in the context of obesity (Cole, Waldrop, D'Auria, Garner, 2006; Petosa, Hortz, Cardina, & Suminski,

2005; Sallis, Prochaska & Taylor, 2000). In other words, the belief is that if one feels competent to participate in physical activity, then they would be more likely to engage in that activity. A number of researchers have reported successful outcomes in studies which used specific strategies to improve self-efficacy for physical activity (Benight & Bandura, 2004; Dishman et al., 2004; Netz & Raviv, 2004). Social support (family and peer support/reinforcement) have also been linked to increased physical activity (Sallis, Prochaska & Taylor, 2000; De Bourdeaudhuij et al., 2005; McGuire et al., 2002; Thompson et al., 2003).

Physical Activity Preference. Preference for physical activity is a potential mediator that has not been studied as extensively (Dishman et al., 2004; Sallis, Alcaraz, McKenzie, & Hovell, 1999). This mediator implies that an individual prefers a particular physical activity because that individual perceives a certain level of confidence in performing that particular activity. In a study conducted by Dishman et al. (2004) they indirectly illustrated this point while studying the affect of self-efficacy in relation to physical activity participation. Study researchers designed an intervention for 9th grade females participating in physical education classes. The goal of the study was to use self-efficacy as a mediator variable within the physical education classroom in order to increase physical activity levels outside of the classroom. The physical education teachers chose physical activities that the girls would be most likely to participate in and feel confident participating in within the class time (i.e. dance, aerobics, weight training, and self defense). Results indicated that the girls were able to increase self-efficacy within the PE classroom which resulted in the increased levels of physical activity outside of the classroom. From these results, it is logical to assume that a relationship may exist between physical activity preference and self-efficacy because the activities chosen were based on preference. The results of this study suggest that physical activity preference could be an important mediating factor in increasing self-efficacy and levels of physical activity, especially among females, and needs to be studied further.

Another study explored whether physical activity preference could predict actual physical activity behaviors in girls and boys (Sallis, Alcaraz, McKenzie, & Hovell, 1999). The researchers found that physical activity preferences predicted a positive change in physical activity, but only among girls with lower body fat. Specific modes of activity preferred were not revealed in this study. Participation in physical activity has also been studied in relation to interest in physical activity (De Bourdeaudhuij et al., 2005). Interest is very closely related to physical activity preference in that both are factors in the decision to engage in physical activity. A large study of 11-19 year old adolescents (n = 6,078) in Belgium found that interest in physical activity (or lack of interest) was the greatest barrier to participation within physical activity (De Bourdeaudhuij et al., 2005). They also found that the overweight group had lower levels of self-efficacy than the normal weight group when asked about perceived confidence in their ability to participate in a sport or physical activity that would last longer than 30 minutes per day.

Summary

The increased prevalence of childhood obesity has led to multiple efforts for prevention and intervention. Increasing levels of physical activity helps prevent obesity related problems and diseases (NCHS, 2005; Sulemana, Smolensky, & Lai, 2006). However, children, in particular African American children, show a decrease in levels of physical activity as they age which in turn can have a negative impact on weight. Studies are needed to delineate the potential influences on obesity for African American youth. It seems logical that a preference for a particular physical activity will positively influence the decision to participate in that and similar activities and will ultimately lead to decreased sedentary behaviors and increased health status. While this appears to be a logical assumption, little data are available to explain the relationship between activity preference and BMI in this at-risk population. Therefore, the purpose of this study was to explore the relationships among activity preferences and BMI in African American preadolescents and adolescents.

METHOD

Participants

Cross-sectional data were obtained from 113 10- to 16-year-old African American children who were attending the local chapter of the National Youth Summer Program. Eligibility criteria required that all participants turn in a signed parental consent form. The informed consent was signed by the parent and the child. Exclusionary criteria included conditions limiting participation in the assessments (e.g. unable to speak English) an inability or failure to provide informed consent. All protocols were approved by the University of Memphis Institutional Review Board. A total of 75 participants who had complete data on the measures were utilized for this study.

Physical Measures

Prior to the start of camp, all campers received a mandated physical examination by a medical doctor. At this time, body weight was assessed using a beam scale by camp physicians in pre-camp physicals. Height was obtained using a stadiometer attached to the scale. Body mass index (BMI) was calculated (BMI = weight (kg)/height (m)^2) and then converted into percentiles representing BMI-for-age and -gender as defined by the Center for Disease Control (Kuczmarski et al., 2000).

Assessment of Activity Preference

The existing camp allowed research staff to administer the preference survey to the participants during a two-hour time slot after lunch. Study participants were separated from camp staff and completed the survey as directed by trained research staff.

Preference for physical activities and sedentary activities were assessed using a 37-item paper-pencil questionnaire which was modified from the Stanford Obesity Prevention in Pre-Adolescent trial. A variety of both physical and sedentary activities were listed and both boys and girls were asked to respond to options such as (1) "I've never done it", (2) Don't like it",

(3) "Like it a little", or (4) "Like it a lot". The response "I've never done it" was recorded as missing. Preference for physical activities and sedentary activities were determined via two scales with higher scores indicating a greater preference for that type of activity.

Statistical Analyses

Analyses for this study were conducted with SPSS version 15.0 for Windows (SPSS for Windows, Rel. 15.0.1., 2006). Preliminary analyses included examining frequencies, distributions, histograms and box-plots to evaluate potential outliers. The outcome of these examinations indicated that all participants reported variables of interest within a plausible range. Descriptive statistics using means, standard deviations, and frequencies were conducted. Bivariate correlations were also examined. Multiple linear regression analyses were performed to identify significant independent activity preference predictors of BMI while controlling for gender. Models were tested to determine potential confounders of age and gender. Due to age interaction, four separate multiple linear regression models were analyzed based on age. Preadolescents were defined as 10-12 year olds and adolescents were defined as 13-16 year olds. The dependent variable was age- and gender-specific body mass index percentile. Independent variables were children's self-reported preferences for physical activities or sedentary activities with gender as a covariate. Preferences for physical activities and sedentary activities are represented via two scales with higher scores indicating higher preferences.

RESULTS

Of the original 113 participants, 38 participants were eliminated from the final data analysis. Twenty seven participants had incomplete data or no data to compare to measures of body mass index (BMI). Four participants had obvious patterns in their responses to the survey which could lead to misleading results. Four participants did not have an official height or weight recorded from the physician physicals provided by the NYSP camp. Lastly, three participants did not supply a date of birth so calculation of BMI percentile could not be determined. . Of the 75 participants, 53.3% were male and 46.7% were female. The mean age of study participants was 12.29 (± 1.86) years old (See Table 1). Overall average BMI percentile was 68.5 (sd = 29.1). BMI percentile by age category is presented in Table 2 verifying that over 44% of the preadolescent participants were above the 85th percentile for BMI. The majority of the adolescents (28.1%) were between the 76th and 85th percentile for BMI followed by approximately 22% falling above eh 85th percentile.

Multiple Linear Regressions

The assumptions underlying the application of multiple linear regression were analyzed. Results indicated that there were no severe departures from independence, normality, heteroschedasticity, and linearity. In addition, multicollinearity was not present as indicated by the largest variation inflation factor for all regressions being 1.18 (well below 10). An alpha of 0.05 was used for all statistical tests.

Table 1. Descriptive Statistics on Study Participants (*n* = 75).

		Frequency	%	Min	Max	Mean	Std. Deviation
BMI Percentile		75	100.0	0.10	99.52	68.5	29.12
Gender	Males	40	53.3	1.00	2.00	1.47	0.50
	Females	35	46.7				
Race*	African American	74	100	1.00	4.00	1.04	0.35
	Caucasian	0	0				
	Asian	0	0				
	Other	0	0				
Age	10	17	22.7	10.00	16.00	12.29	1.86
	11	13	17.3				
	12	13	17.3				
	13	11	14.7				
	14	8	10.7				
	15	10	13.3				
	16	3	4.0			.	
Grade	Third	1	1.3	3.00	11.00	7.27	1.93
	Fourth	3	4.0				
	Fifth	12	16.0				
	Sixth	13	17.3				
	Seventh	11	14.7				
	Eighth	15	20.0				
	Ninth	9	12.0				
	Tenth	7	9.3				
	Eleventh	4	5.3				
*Missing data from one participant. However, all participants were observed to be African American.							

Table 2. BMI Percentile and Frequency by Age.

	Preadolescents (n = 43)			Adolescents (n = 32)	
BMI %	Frequency	Percentage of occurrence	Frequency	Percentage of occurrence
0-25	7	16.3%	2	6.3%
26-50	5	11.6%	7	21.9%
51-75	8	18.6%	6	18.8%
76-85	4	9.3%	9	28.1%
86-94	6	14.0%	4	12.5%
≥ 95	13	30.2%	3	9.4%

Table 3a. Correlations, Means, and Standard Deviations for Preadolescents.

Subscale	1	2	3
1. BMI	—		
2. Gender	0.136	—	
3. Prefers Physical Activities	-0.349**	0.187	—
Means	69.03	1.42	2.22
Standard Deviations	31.60	0.50	0.37

*p ≤ 0.05; **p ≤ 0.01

Table 3b. Correlations, Means, and Standard Deviations for Preadolescents.

Subscale	1	2	3
1. BMI	—		
2. Gender	0.136	—	
3. Prefers Sedentary Activities	-0.368**	0.184	—
Means	69.03	1.42	2.49
Standard Deviations	31.60	0.50	0.41

*p ≤ 0.05; **p ≤ 0.01

Table 3c. Influences on BMI Percentile for Preadolescents Physical Activity Preferences.

Variables	b	Beta	t
Gender	13.22	.209	1.42
Prefers Physical Activities	-32.82	-.388	-2.64*
R^2 = .164*			

*p ≤ 0.05; **p ≤ 0.01

Table 3d. Influences on BMI Percentile for Preadolescents Sedentary Activity Preferences.

Variables	b	Beta	t
Gender	13.4	.211	1.45
Prefers Sedentary Activities	-31.25	-.407	-2.79**
R^2 = .179*			

*p ≤ 0.05; **p ≤ 0.01

For preadolescents (n = 43) preference for physical activities significantly explained 16.4% of the variance in BMI (p = .03) after controlling for gender. A lower BMI was related to higher preferences for physical activities (β = -.388, p = .01). Also for preadolescents, preference for sedentary activities significantly explained 17.9% of the variance in BMI (p = .02) after controlling for gender. A lower BMI was related to a higher preference for sedentary activities (β = --.407, p = .01).

However, there were no significant relationships found among physical activity preferences and BMI nor sedentary activity preferences and BMI for adolescent children (n =32).

Table 4a. Correlations, Means, and Standard Deviations for Adolescents.

Subscale	1	2	3
1. BMI	—		
2. Gender	0.169	—	
3. Prefers Sedentary Activities	0.091	0.301*	—
Means	67.78	1.53	2.66
Standard Deviations	25.90	0.51	0.31

*$p \leq 0.05$; **$p \leq 0.01$

Table 4b. Correlations, Means, and Standard Deviations for Adolescents.

Subscale	1	2	3
1. BMI	—		
2. Gender	0.169	—	
3. Prefers Physical Activities	-0.084	-.077	—
Means	67.78	1.53	2.26
Standard Deviations	25.90	0.51	0.38

*$p \leq 0.05$; **$p \leq 0.01$

Table 4c. Influences on BMI Percentile for Adolescents Physical Activity Preferences.

Variables	b	Beta	t
Gender	10.62	.207	1.08
Prefers Physical Activities	4.93	.074	0.39
$R^2 = .048$			

*$p \leq 0.05$; **$p \leq 0.01$

Table 4d. Influences on BMI Percentile for Adolescents Sedentary Activity Preferences.

Variables	b	Beta	t
Gender	10.37	.202	0.97
Prefers Sedentary Activities	.80	.009	0.05
$R^2 = .042$			

*$p \leq 0.05$; **$p \leq 0.01$

Table 5. Correlations between BMI percentile and Activity Preferences.

Activity	Preadolescent BMI %ile (r)	Adolescent BMI %ile (r)
Sedentary Activity Preference		
Watching Television (not including videos on a VCR or DVD)	-0.466**	-0.104
Watching movies or videos on a VCR or DVD	-0.382*	0.088
Playing video games (like Nintendo or Sega)	-0.413**	-0.106
Using a computer	-0.280	0.155
Listening to the radio, tapes or CDs	-0.313*	-0.080
Arts and crafts	-0.178	0.209
Playing board games	0.003	0.286
Homework, reading	0.143	-0.003
Talking on the phone	-0.095	0.080
Physical Activity Preference		
Bicycling	-0.043	-0.057
Swimming laps	-0.018	-0.009
Gymnastics like bars, beam, tumbling, trampoline	-0.220	-0.105
Exercises like push-ups, sit-ups, jumping jacks	-0.261	0.125
Basketball	-0.060	-0.223
Baseball/Softball	0.198	-0.123
Football	-0.003	-0.008
Soccer	-0.412**	0.229
Volleyball	-0.250	0.048
Racket sports like badminton, tennis	-0.360*	0.028
Ball playing like four square, dodge ball, kickball	-0.296	-0.098
Games like chase, tag, hopscotch	-0.296	0.099
Outdoor play like climbing trees, hide and seek	-0.394**	-0.262
Water play like swimming pool, ocean, lake	0.032	-0.265
Jump rope	-0.280	-0.004
Dance	-0.162	-0.078
Outdoor chores like mowing, raking	0.039	-0.113
Indoor chores like moping, vacuuming, sweeping	-0.004	0.160
Walking	-0.207	0.333
Running or jogging	-0.288	-0.207
Rollerblading, roller skating, or ice skating	-0.227	0.197
Martial arts like karate, judo	-0.076	0.219
Physical Education class at school	0.004	0.062
Climbing on playground equipment	-0.277	0.002
Hiking	-0.269	0.017
Weight lifting or strength training	-0.097	-0.217
Yoga	-0.118	0.235
Cheerleading	-0.055	0.099

$*p \leq 0.05; **p \leq 0.01; ***p \leq 0.001$

Next, each activity was individually correlated with BMI percentile using a bivariate correlation analysis in order to highlight some of the item-by-item correlations for preadolescents and adolescents (see Table 5). For preadolescents, there were several activities statistically significantly correlated with BMI percentile. Soccer ($r = -0.412$, $p =\leq .01$) and outdoor play ($r = -0.394$; $p =\leq .01$) were negatively associated with BMI percentile meaning that those preadolescents who had a higher preference for soccer and outdoor play had a lower BMI. In addition, for sedentary activities, watching television (not including videos on a VCR or DVD); $r = -0.466$ $(p \leq 0.01)$, watching movies or videos on a VCR or DVD; $r = -0.382$ $(p \leq 0.05)$, playing video games (like Nintendo or Sega); $r = -0.413$ $(p \leq 0.01)$, and listening to the radio, tapes or CDs; $r = -0.313$ $(p \leq 0.05)$ were negatively correlated with BMI percentile for preadolescents. There were no significant bivariate correlations between the individual activity items and BMI for adolescents.

DISCUSSION

The purpose of this study was to examine the relationship among physical activity preferences and sedentary activity preferences on body mass index (BMI) for urban African American youth. Participants were categorized into preadolescents and adolescents. Several children and adolescents in this study were found to be at risk for overweight (14.6%) or overweight (21.2%) according to CDC recommended BMI guidelines. We had hypothesized that both physical activity preferences and sedentary activity preferences significantly influenced BMI percentile for both preadolescents and adolescents. Hypotheses were that physical activity preference would have an inverse relationship to BMI percentile and sedentary activity preference would have a positive relationship to BMI percentile.

As hypothesized, physical activity preference was significantly inversely related to BMI percentile for preadolescents and had a significant amount of influence. Soccer and playing outside were the main contributors to this influence. That is to say that, BMI percentile was lower among those preadolescents who had higher physical activity preferences specifically for playing soccer and playing outside. Although not comparable to BMI, this is consistent with findings that suggest physical activity preference affects physical activity participation (Sallis, Alcaraz, McKenzie, and Hovell, 1999).

Results indicated that sedentary activity preference had a positive relationship with BMI indicating that the higher the preference for sedentary activities the higher the BMI percentiles among preadolescents. This was contradictory to what was expected. Specifically, watching television, watching movies or videos, playing video games, and listening to music all had statistically significant inverse relationships to BMI. Therefore, the more TV watched, movies or videos watched, video games played, or music listened to the lower the BMI scores across this population. These results suggest that children can prefer sedentary activities and still have low BMI percentile scores. De Bourdeaudhuij et al (2005) found similar results when they looked at normal weight children and overweight children aged 11 to 19 years old in relation to physical activity. They attributed these results to the possibility that children can prefer sedentary activities but still be physically active enough during the day to stay within a healthy BMI. We suggest that kids that are active in general may participate in more activities throughout the day regardless of whether these activities are sedentary or active. Another study by Robinson et al (1993) also supports this idea. They found a that television viewing had a low association with the increased risk of becoming overweight and less physically active. Clearly, more in-depth research is needed to explore the true relationship of activity preference to BMI percentiles among children and adolescents in this population.

As children get older it has been found that physical activity participation decreases. This decrease in physical activity participation is seen across gender as well as age, with older females being the least physically active group (CDC, 2004; NCHS, 2005). Within the literature, age as well as gender have been found to be confounders of activity participation in respect to psychosocial constructs such as self-efficacy, barriers to participation, and attitude toward participation (Sallis, Prochaska & Taylor, 2000). Interestingly, we found that both sedentary activity preference and physical activity preference for adolescents did not significantly influence BMI. This could be attributed to adolescents overall decrease in physical activity as they age (Allison, Adlaf, Dwyer, Lysy, & Irving, 2007; Hallal, Victoran, Azevedo, Wells, 2006; Kimm, et al., 2002; Nelson, Neumark-Stzainer, Hannan, Sirard, & Story, 2006; Trost et al., 2002). However, in this study and different from the literature, gender had no interaction on BMI percentile so was only controlled for in the analyses. Reasons for these findings with adolescents are unclear and provide a fertile ground for future research. Perhaps girls' preference for being physically active is overshadowed by other influences (lack of support, lack of facilities, time, etc.).

Constructs of the Social Cognitive Theory such as self-efficacy and perceived barriers to physical activity have been used to predict participation in exercise and physical activity (Dishman, 1994). A limitation of this study is that data were not collected on the physical activity levels within the study population in order to observe the predictive power of physical activity preference in relation to physical activity level and this could account for the low correlation coefficients that were found. The preference for a particular physical activity could be a strong correlate of physical activity in children and adolescents and could also be a mediating variable in relation to self-efficacy, a very well known correlate of physical activity (Sallis, Prochaska & Taylor, 2000). In other words, it is reasonable to assume that if a child has a particular preference for a physical activity then the child is more self-efficacious in that activity and is therefore more likely to engage in that activity. Thus, a recommendation is to examine this assumption in future research.

Although a major strength of this study is that we are studying an at-risk population and are aware that ethnicity is associated with differences in attitudes, beliefs and behaviors and that these cultural influences are important to evaluate, the results of this study are limited to African American youth. Therefore, findings are unique to perceptions and behaviors of this group and do not generalize to broader populations. The cross-sectional nature of the data is a limiting factor in the study. Future research into correlates of BMI in African American youth would benefit from obtaining longitudinal data and also exploring potential direct and indirect paths by which activity preferences may be related to physical activity behaviors.

In conclusion, these results add to a growing body of literature explaining the potential influence of activity preference on BMI among African American youth. In particular, preadolescence might be an ideal time for obesity prevention in that the encouragement of activities could lead to increased activity levels as children age. Adopting and maintaining beneficial levels of physical activity are essential to reverse current trends in childhood obesity. This is a multi-layered undertaking and further success in increasing physical activity participation could be gained by addressing additional mediating variables such as activity preference.

REFERENCES

Allison, K. R., Adlaf, E. M., Dwyer, J. J., Lysy, D. C. & Irving, H. M. (2007). The decline in physical activity among adolescent students: a cross-national comparison. *Can J Public Health, 98,* 97-100.

American Heart Association (2004). [AHA]. (n.d.). Physical Education is "on the move" in many states. Retrieved on December 5, 2004 from http://www.americanheart.org/presenter.jhtml?identifier=3011064.

Benight, C. C. & Bandura, A. (2004). Social cognitive theory of posttraumatic recovery: the role of perceived self-efficacy. *Behavior Research and Therapy, 42,* 1129-1148.

Boreham, C. & Riddoch, C. (2001). The physical activity, fitness and health of children. *J Sports Sci, 19,* 915-929.

Bryne, D. (2003). *Physical Education.* Health Policy Tracking Service, National Conference of State Legislature. Retrieved on November 30, 2004, from http://ncsl.org/programs/health.

Byers, T., Nestle, M., McTiernan, A., Doyle, C., Currie-Williams, A., Gansler, T. & Thun, M. (2002). American Cancer Society Guidelines on Nutrition and Physical Activity for Cancer Prevention: Reducing the Risk of Cancer with Healthy Food Choices and Physical Activity. *CA: A Cancer Journal for Clinicians, 52,* 92-119. Retrieved on April 25, 2006, from http://caonline.amcanceroc.org/cgi/content/52/2/92.

Cecel-Karb, R. & Grogan-Kaylor, A. (2009). Childhood body mass index in community context: neighborhood safety, television viewing, and growth trajectories of BMI. *Health Social Work, 34(3),* 169-77

Centers for Disease Control and Prevention [CDC]. (2000). *Executive Summary: Healthy Weight, Physical Activity, and Nutrition: Focus Group Research with African American, Mexican American, and White Youth.* Retrieved on April 4, 2004, from http://www.cdc.gov/nccdphp/dnpa/physical/pdf/exec_summary_2000.pdf.

Centers for Disease Control and Prevention [CDC]. (2002). Barriers to Children Walking and Biking to School --- United States, 1999. *Morbidity and Mortality Weekly Report [MMWR], 51(32),* 701-704. Retrieved on April 13, 2004, from http:// www.cdc.gov/mmwr/ preview/mmwrhtml/mm5132a1.htm.

Centers for Disease Control and Prevention [CDC]. (2003a). Tennessee: (2003). *Youth Risk Behavior Survey (YRBS) Results.* Retrieved on November 30, 2004, from http://www.cdc.gov/HealthyYouth/yrbs/pdfs/statefacts/tennessee.pdf

Centers for Disease Control and Prevention [CDC]. (2003b). Physical Activity Levels Among Children Aged 9-13 Years --- United States, 2002. *Morbidity and Mortality Weekly [MMWR], 52(33),* 785-788. Retrieved on April 13, 2004, from http://www.cdc.gov/mmwr/preview/mmwrhtml/mm5233a1.htm

Centers for Disease Control and Prevention [CDC]. (2004a). Obesity Still a Major Problem, New Data Show. Retrieved on November 15, 2004, from http://www.cdc.gov/nchs/pressroom/04facts/obesity

Centers for Disease Control and Prevention [CDC]. (2004b). Youth Risk Behavior Surveillance --- United States, 2003. *Morbidity and Mortality Weekly Report [MMWR], 53(SS-2)*, 21-29. Retrieved on November 30, 2004, from http://www.cdc.gov/mmwr/ PDF/ss/ss5302.pdf.

Centers for Disease Control and Prevention [CDC]. (2006). Physical Activity for Everyone: *Recommendations: Are there special recommendations for young people?* Retrieved on May 9, 2006, from http://www.cdc.gov/nccdphp/dnpa/physical/recommendations/young. htm.

Cole, K., Waldrop, J., D'Auria, J. & Garner, H. (2006). An integrative research review: effective school-based childhood overweight interventions. *J Spec Pediatr Nurs, 11(3)*, 166-177.

De Bourdeaudhuij, I., Lefevre, J., Deforche, B., Wijndaele, K., Matton, L. & Philippaerts, R. (2005). Physical Activity and Psychosocial Correlates in Normal Weight and Overweight 11 to 19 Year Olds. *Obesity Research, 13(6)*, 1097-1105. Retrieved on May 9, 2006, from http://www.obesityresearch.org/cgi/reprint/13/6/1097.

Dishman, R. K. (Eds.). (1994). *Advances in Exercise Adherence.* Champaign: Human Kinetics.

Dishman, R. K.; Motl, R. W.; Saunders, R., Felton, G., Ward, D. S., Dowda, M. & Pate, R. R. (2004). Self-efficacy partially mediates the effect of a school-based physical-activity intervention among adolescent girls. *Preventive Medicine, 38*, 628-636.

Friedenreich, C. M. (2001). Physical Activity and Cancer Prevention: From Observational to Intervention Research. *Cancer Epidemiology, Biomarkers & Prevention, 10*, 287-301. Retrieved on May 9, 2006, from http://cebp.aacrjournals.org/cgi/reprint/10/4/287.

Goran, M. I., Gower, B. A., Nagy, T. R. & Johnson, R. K. (1998). Developmental Changes in Energy Expenditure and Physical Activity in Children: Evidence for a Decline in Physical Activity in Girls Before Puberty. *Pediatrics, 101*, 887-891. Retrieved on February 13, 2005, from http://www.pediatrics.org/cgi/content/full/101/5/887.

Gordon-Larsen, P., Adair, L. S., Nelson, M. C. & Popkin, B. M. (2004). Five year obesity incidence in the transition period between adolescence and adulthood: the National Longitudinal Study of Adolescent Health. *American Journal of Clinical Nutrition, 80*, 569-575.

Hallal, P. C., Victora, C. G., Azevedo, M. R. & Wells, J. C. (2006). Adolescent physical activity and health: a systematic review. *Sports Med.; 36*, 1019-1030.

Hanley, A. J. G., Harris, S. B., Gittelsohn, J., Wolever, T. M. S., Saksvig, B. & Zinman, B. (2000). Overweight among children and adolescents in a Native Canadian community: prevalence and associated factors. *American Journal of Clinical Nutrition, 71*, 693-700.

Harvard School of Public Health [HSPH]. (2004). *Diabetes.* Retrieved on April 17, 2004, from http://www.hsph.harvard.edu/nutritionsource/diabetes.html.

Kimm, S. Y., Glynn, N. W., Kriska, A. M., Barton, B. A., Kronsberg, S. S., Daniels, S. R., Crawford, P. B., Sabry, Z. I. & Liu, K. (2002). Decline in physical activity in black girls and white girls during adolescence. *N Engl J Med, 347*, 709-715.

Kohl, III, H. W. & Hobbs, K. E. (1998). Development of Physical Activity Behaviors Among Children and Adolescents. *Pediatrics, 101*, 549-554. Retrieved on April 28, 2006, from http://www.pediatrics.org/cgi/content/full/101/3/S1/549

Koplan, J. P., Liverman, C. T. & Kraak, V. I. (2005). Committee on Prevention of Obesity in Children and Youth. Preventing childhood obesity: health in the balance: executive summary. *Journal of American Dietetic Associaiton, 105(1)*, 131-8.

Kuczmarski, R. J., Ogden, C. L., Grummer-Strawn, L. M., Flegal, K. M., Guo, S. S., Wei, R., Curtin, L. R., Roche, A. F. & Johnson, C. L. (2000). *CDC Growth Charts: United States. Advance data from vital and health statistics, no. 314.* Hyattsville, Maryland: NCHS. Retrieved on May 10, 2006, from http://www.cdc.gov/nchs/data/ad/ad314.pdf.

Malina, R. M. (2001). Physical activity and fitness: pathways from childhood to adulthood. *Am J Hum Biol.,* 2001, *13,* 162-172.

Matton, L., Thomis, M., Windaele, K., Duvigneaud, N., Beunen, G., Claessens, A. L., Vanreusel, B., Philippaerts, R. & Lefevre, J. (2006). Tracking of Physical Fitness and Physical Activity from Youth to Adulthood in Females. *Medicine and Science in Sports and Exercise, 38(6),* 1114-1120.

McGuire, M. T., Hannan, P. J., Neumark-Sztanier, D., Falkner Cossrow, N. H. & Story, M. (2002). Parental Correlates of Physical Activity in a Racially/Ethnically Diverse Adolescent Sample. *Journal of Adolescent Health, 30,* 253-261.

McKenzie, J. F., Neiger, B. L. & Smeltzer, J. L. (2005). *Planning, Implementing & Evaluating Health Promotion Programs: A Primer (4th ed.).* San Francisco: Pearson Benjamin Cummings.

National Center for Health Statistics [NCHS]. (2005). *Health, United States, With Chartbook on Trends in the Health of Americans.* Hyattsville, Maryland. Retrieved on May 10, 2006, from http://www.cdc.gov/nchs/data/hus/hus05.pdf.

Nelson, M. C., Neumark-Stzainer, D., Hannan, P. J., Sirard, J. R. & Story, M. (2006). Longitudinal and secular trends in physical activity and sedentary behavior during adolescence. *Pediatrics., 118,* 1627-1634.

Netz, Y. & Raviv, S. (2004). Age Differences in Motivational Orientation Toward Physical Activity: An Application of Social-Cognitive Theory. *The Journal of Psychology, 138(1),* 35-48.

Pate, R. R., Trost, S. G., Felton, G. M., Ward, D. S., Dowda, M. & Saunders, R. (1997). Correlates of Physical Activity Behavior in Rural Youth. *Research Quarterly for Exercise and Sport, 68(3),* 241-248. Retrieved on April 28, 2006, from http://find.galegroup.com/itx/retrieve.do.

Petosa, R. L., Hortz, B. V., Cardina, C. E. & Suminski, R. R. (2005). Social cognitive theory variables associated with physical activity among high school students. *International Journal of Sports Medicine, 26(2),* 158-163.

Robinson, T. N., Hammer, L. D., Killen, J. D., Kraemer, H. C., Wilson, D. M., Hayward, C. & Taylor, C. B. (1993). Does Television Viewing Increase Obesity and Reduce Physical Activity? Cross-sectional and Longitudinal Analyses Among Adolescent Girls. *Pediatrics, 91(2),* 273-280. Retrieved on April 28, 2006, from http://www.pediatrics.org.

Sallis, J. F., Alcaraz, J. E., McKenzie, T. L. & Hovell, M. F. (1999). Predictors of Change in Children's Physical Activity Over 20 Months: Variations by Gender and Level of Adiposity. *American Journal of Preventive Medicine, 16(3),* 222-229.

Sallis, J. F., Prochaska, J. J. & Taylor, W. C. (2000). A review of correlates of physical activity of children and adolescents. *Medicine and Science in Sports and Exercise, 32(5),* 963-975.

Sagatun, A., Kolle, E., Anderssen, S. A., Thoresen, M. & Søgaard, A. J. (2008). Three-year follow-up of physical activity in Norwegian youth from two ethnic groups: associations with socio-demographic factors. *BMC Public Health, 8,* 419. SPSS for Windows, Rel. 15.0.1. 2006. Chicago: SPSS Inc.

Sulemana, H., Smolensky, M. H. & Lai, D. (2006). Relationship between Physical Activity and Body Mass Index in Adolescents. *Medicine and Science in Sports and Exercise, 38(6),* 1182-1186.

Surgeon General. (2004). Surgeon General's Call to Action to Prevent and Decrease Overweight and Obesity: Overweight in Children and Adolescents. *Overweight and Obesity Fact Sheet.* Retrieved on April 10, 2004, from http://www.surgeongeneral. gov/ topics/obesity/calltoaction/fact_adolescents.htm

Taylor, W., Chan, W., Cummings, S., Simons-Morton, B., Day, R., Sangi-Haghpeykar, H.,

Pivarnik, J., Mueller, W., Detry, M., Wei, I., Johnson-Masotti, A. & Hsu, H. (2002). Healthy growth: Project description and baseline finding. *Ethnic Diseases, 12,* 567-577.

Tershakovec, A., Kuppler, K., Zemel, B. & Stallings, V. (2002). Age, sex, ethnicity, and body composition, and resting energy expenditure of obese African American and white children and adolescents. *American Journal of Clinical Nutrition, 75,* 867-71.

Thompson, V. J., Baranowski, T., Cullen, K. W., Rittenberry, L., Baranowski, J., Taylor, W. C. & Nicklas, T. *(*2003). Influences on Diet and Physical Activity among Middle-Class African American 8- to 10-Year-Old Girls at Risk of Becoming Obese. *Journal of Nutrition Education and Behavior, 35(3),* 115-123.

Trost, S. G., Pate, R. R., Dowda, M., Ward, D. S., Felton, G. & Saunders, R. (2002). Psychosocial Correlates of Physical Activity in White and African American Girls. *Journal of Adolescent Health, 31,* 226-233.

Trost, S. G., Pate, R. R., Sallis, J. F., Freedson, P. S., Taylor, W. C., Dowda, M. & Sirard, J. (2002). Age and gender differences in objectively measured physical activity in youth. *Med Sci Sports Exerc., 34,* 350-355.

Williams, C. L., Hayman, L. L., Daniels, S. R., Robinson, T. N., Steinberger, J., Paridon, S. & Bazzarre, T. (2002). Cardiovascular Health in Childhood: A Statement for Health Professionals from the Committee on Atherosclerosis, Hypertension, and Obesity in the Young (AHOY) of the Council on Cardiovascular Disease in the Young, American Heart Association. *Circulation, 106,* 143-160. Retrieved on April 25, 2006, from http://www.circulationaha.org.

In: Race and Ethnicity
Editor: Jonathan K. Crennan, pp. 303-317

ISBN: 978-1-60692-099-2
© 2010 Nova Science Publishers, Inc.

Chapter 13

AN UNDERSTANDING OF HEALTH, CULTURE AND ETHNICITY WITHIN THE CONTEXT OF HISTORY

Faisal Aboul-Enein

College of Nursing, Texas Woman's University, Houston, Texas, USA

"The success or failure of mankind depends not upon the outcome of economic growth, but upon the appearance or non-appearance of pestilence." – Anonymous, 1915

INTRODUCTION

It is understood that diseases have been the biggest killers of people; they have also been decisive shapers of history (Diamond, 1997). There is no doubt that Malaria, Yellow Fever, and related diseases had a direct impact on history and outcome of society's social and economic development. Yellow Fever could not be distinguished from Malaria, Dengue and other plagues that confronted sailors, soldiers, and colonists in tropical areas on both sides of the Atlantic (Bres, 1986). What is astonishing is how the mosquito played a significant role in determining the course of history.

The growth of tropical medicine stemmed from needs of imperial powers around the early 1900's to further extend its colonial holdings, each competing to enlarge their stakes in Africa, Asia, and the Americas. Disease control was central to imperialism. Long before the germ theory, European colonizers established sanitary camps for their troops on the miasmatic theory that disease was caused by emanations from the earth (Platt, 2003). Numerous efforts have documented mankind's battle against infectious diseases; this is especially true among uniformed personnel (Hospenthal, 2005). Until World War II, more victims of war died of war-borne microbes than of battle wounds (Diamond, 1997). Efforts to preserve the fighting strength of armies and society as a whole have included development of vaccines, therapeutics such as antibiotics, vector control agents such as the use of chemical sprays, pseudo-intellectual theories on race and other preventive strategies (Diamond, 1997).

The first decades of the twentieth century saw profound changes in both the scientific knowledge and medical advances in understanding disease causation, particularly among vector-borne diseases. However, Yellow Fever is, for most practicing physicians today, a medical oddity—a vaccine-preventable disease, briefly mentioned in medical school, never expected to be seen in modern practice. Reports continue to surface occasionally from distant tropical nations.

Interestingly, throughout the 19th century, Yellow Fever was central to the debate about contagion, the germ theory, and public health practice (Humphries, 1992). While this was ongoing, such diseases posed a very real and terrifying threat to any populace. The core of this discussion will examine how these infectious diseases impacted history and further reveal the significance disease plays in better understanding patterns of human development throughout the course of history.

During the mid-seventeenth century, Dutch slave traders brought Yellow Fever and diseases to the Americas from Africa. For the next two and a half centuries, the disease terrorized seaports throughout the Americas. Proof of the mosquito hypothesis was delayed because of two aspects of the disease: patients were viremic only during the first several days of clinical illness, and most mosquitoes require about 2 weeks of viral incubation before becoming infectious (Bryan et al, 2003). European conquest of the Americas starting with Columbus's 1492 voyage could not be told without revealing the fact that numerous natives died of microbes brought on by Europeans. Equally instructive is the decimation of would-be European occupiers in the African and Asian tropics also known as *"White Man's Graveyard."* The spread of disease played a significant impact on the outcome of history.

Firsthand knowledge of the etiology of Yellow Fever would be illustrative. Like all species, a microbe evolves and spreads more effectively creating more victims and opportunities for dissemination by natural selection. It is an acute infectious viral disease that is transmitted by the bite of a female mosquito. There are two recognized forms of the disease: an urban form carried by the *Aedes. aegypti* mosquito and the jungle form transmitted by the *Hemagogus* species mosquito from canopy-dwelling monkeys. Humans are considered the primary host among the *Aedes. Aegypti and are secondary* hosts in the jungle cycle (Bres, 1986).

Attacks from Yellow Fever can range from mild to fatal. One can expect flu-like symptoms leading towards severe forms of internal bleeding, liver and kidney damage. Jaundice was a common feature hence the name "Yellow" fever. In the Americas, it was named *el vómito negro*, the black vomit. The case fatality rate range from 5% of the infected population in endemic areas to 50% among native populations during epidemic which will be examined later as attributing to the further spread of this disease (Chin, 2000).

For instance, based on historical accounts within the United States, from 1702-1800 the disease appeared at least 35 times, in the spring and ending in the fall season. Epidemics developed slowly which then spread through the population. The apparent randomness of the infection caused terror and panic. In the book *The Microbe Hunters,* Paul DeKriuf wrote, with a touch of hyperbole *"….when folks of a town began to turn yellow and vomit black…the only thing to do was get out of that town."*

HISTORICAL CONTEXTS

Knowledge of history can strengthen a public health practitioner understanding in confronting upcoming pathogenic threats and broad patterns correlated with history. Understanding history reduces fear, and provides a firm understanding of a disease's continuity. This appreciation provides a productive and fascinating explanation of historical contexts. The modern challenge in public health is to understand the lessons and events which pathogens have plagued much of history. Such lessons can provide a clearer perspective on how to eradicate or contain diseases especially when facing emerging threats such as SARS or the Ebola virus outbreak. The following takes into account various events in history illustrating the impact mosquito-borne diseases and other pathogens had on the event and geographical areas:

Darien Scheme (1690-1700)

Around the 17th century, Scotland was in the midst of organizing itself as another colonial power equally competing against England. It wanted to share in the riches of the New World from Darien's advantageous position astride the Pacific and Atlantic trade routes (McSherry, 1982). The Scottish leadership led by James VI of Scotland established a company to conduct overseas trade around 1680-1690. Scotland established high ambitions by forming its own equivalent "East India Company" and its own colonies like England. At the time, the Scotts traveling overseas were treated in English colonies as foreigners until the Union of Scotland and England in 1707.

The Darien region is out of most geographic domains of any English efforts, it was claimed by the Spanish but never settled. This region is today the Isthmus of Panama located in Central America. Furthermore, the Spanish saw the British as enemies so it was natural to allow the Scotts to have the Darien region. For economic and political reasons, the Scottish company competed directly with English colonial presence and so they had to settle elsewhere.

The first settlers arrived in October 1698, named their town and fort New Edinburgh. From the very onset, numerous problems faced the new Scottish settlers, namely diseases. There were good reasons why the Spanish decided not to settle in that location since they were early colonialists to this region. The Scottish company attempts to settle Darien were significant financial deals for the Scottish treasury. People all over Scotland invested money in the enterprise. The eventual failure of both, the company and Scotland, was a fatal blow that led to the Union of 1707 of England and Scotland.

Darien Scheme illustrates the significant impact diseases can wreak havoc on a nation's ambition and in the course of history. The entire campaign was a severe blow to Scotland's national pride and, more importantly, financial status. Early expectations of the Darien expedition did not result in major migrations although it was expected that they would be. The expedition illustrates how poor planning, ignorance of the topography, and lack of understanding of the diseases facing a geography from past settlers such as the Spanish led to the collapse of Scottish colonial power and its union with the English in 1707.

Continental Army and Smallpox- (1775)

Smallpox was another serious problem for the new Continental Army, especially during the first two years of the war (Glynn, 2004). The American invasion of Canada in 1775 failed in large part due to the smallpox outbreak among the ranks of the Continental Army. The British troops did not suffer from smallpox, because they had either survived smallpox in childhood or had been inoculated when they joined the military. The degree of exposure to the disease has been shown to be the main determinant of mortality; that is, exposure to certain contagious diseases at an early age such as Smallpox or Typhoid, would confer immunity and thereby reduce the risk of dying while in the military (Cirillo, 2008).

Since the majority of the colonists to America came from sparsely populated areas, they had little exposure to the variola virus before the Revolutionary War and were not immunized until 1777 when General George Washington made smallpox inoculation compulsory in the Continental Army. Even President Washington became infected with smallpox as a young man was able to fully appreciate its dangers as a survivor. On April 13, 1777, he wrote to Governor Patrick Henry that smallpox "is more destructive to an Army than the Enemy's sword (Gillett 1981)." Mandatory inoculation was the most significant medical success of the Revolutionary War that contributed significantly to America's victory (Cirillo, 2008).

Mexican-American War (1847)

Mexico claimed ownership of Texas as a breakaway province. The war was initiated in the wake of the 1845 annexation of Texas. Political consequences of the war were the terms of surrender in which the Mexican territories of Alta California and New Mexico were ceded to the United States. Diseases played a major role in the mortality and morbidity of soldiers. Both sides of the conflict were acutely aware of this, but the medical establishment did not understand the disease etiology facing them. The Mexicans called Yellow Fever, *La Vomito*, due to the victim's symptoms of vomiting, fever, chills, and headache. All that medical corps staff can do is offer clinical support of the symptoms and hope for the best. Yellow Fever played a role in tactical and operational planning of numerous campaigns; one particularly astute of this was Major General Winfield Scott who was appointed to command the invasion of Veracruz.

The campaign to invade Veracruz was chosen to begin during the winter season and push his Scott's forces west of the "Yellow Fever Line" into the Sierra Madres before *La Vomito* season starts. General Winfield Scott and his field commanders understood the important role health of his brigades meant to winning. While the Americans did not suffer a major debilitating yellow fever epidemic, diseases exacted a terrible toll on the whole dynamic of this war. *La Vomito*, diarrhea, dysentery, smallpox, and syphilis claimed lives due to the poor sanitation of the camps and limited understanding of the medical communities on how best to treat these diseases. Disease claimed a greater proportion of victims than bullets and war-related trauma. It is worth noting that Scott and many other military leaders on both sides of the battle sought to avoid adding to the count of victims from unseen enemies like microbes.

Spanish-American War (1898)

The 1898 Spanish-American War was a powerful stimulus for the U.S government to consider reform, particularly, the typhoid outbreak during this event. The Spanish-American War gave the U.S a permanent base in the Caribbean and at the same time an opportunity to confront the tropical illnesses facing soldiers and immigrants. It was long suspected that Yellow Fever attacking U.S cities, especially seaports, originated in the Caribbean with Cuba being the main focal point. During that time, it was thought Yellow Fever to be a deadly consequence of commerce thus the prevalent practice to inspect and quarantine incoming ships carrying people and goods was the standard.

The U.S had to deal with this disease affecting many people. An often repeated quote made by the wife of Major Gorgas was, *"The man who conquers Yellow Fever would be the real conqueror of Cuba."* Gorgas, trusting in the fomite theory, wrote, *"Let me give Havana a good scouring and a bath…and Yellow Fever and other diseases will disappear.* "The fomite theory stated that anything a victim touched was potentially contagious. Gorgas did his job well; having made Havana orderly, as clean and civilized in its appearance as Fifth Avenue (Gorgas et al, 1935)." Yellow Fever did subside at first but then came back with a vengeance, in large part due to the influx of newly arrived immigrants and soldiers to the island of Cuba.

One cannot discuss this particular war without putting it into context of the time. Infectious diseases claimed more lives of U.S soldiers, sailors and marines than did battle injuries. Even in minor battles, microbes proved more deadly than bullets. For example, the Second Seminole War (1835-1842) brought a 75% death rate due chiefly to Malaria (Smith 1994). In addition, the limited knowledge of hygiene and infection control even among physicians complicated the matter further. Surgeons explored gunshots wounds with unwashed fingers and unsterilized probes both having pernicious consequences. Furthermore, Malaria/Yellow Fever and other related diseases played a significant role in the mortality and morbidity of competing armies, the confederates and union troops, during the American Civil War (1861-1865). Statistics from that time suggest the magnitude of diseases were equivalent with two soldiers died of disease (primarily, dysentery, malaria, typhoid, and yellow fever) for every one soldier killed in battle.

The epidemic outbreaks during the Spanish-American War revealed the importance of preventive medicine to preserve the fighting strength of an army and its populace. The rapid rise in disease was partly due to an increase in mobilization, overcrowding, and poor camp and field sanitation. Improper disposal of human and animal waste led to a proliferation of houseflies and mosquitoes, all potent vectors for the spread of pathogens. Statistics from the United States Army illustrate the magnitude, nearly 75% of deaths from diseases occurred among raw volunteer units in camps from the U.S Army (Cirillo, 2004b).

Malaria/Yellow Fever and the Panama Canal (1904-1906)

Major William C Gorgas of the US Army was scrubbing centuries of filth away from the streets of Havana, Cuba, certain he was scrubbing Malaria and Yellow Fever. Interestingly, Gorgas was discouraged by his work initially, but his inquisitive mind would eventually defeat the disease both in Havana and the Panama Canal (Byerly, 2005; Cirillo 2004b). The medical community in most of the 19th and early 20th century was powerless against invisible microbial foes that proved far more lethal than any enemy bullet or bayonet. More importantly, they did not know what they did not know. Gorgas can be credited for shifting his tactic from "population-based hygiene only measures" towards a more comprehensive approach to eradicating the mosquitoes causing the Yellow Fever by using measures such as insecticide, eliminating standing water and oiling ponds. This was a key observation worth noting; in their "ignorance" great discoveries had been made. Dr. Giuseppe Sanarelli, an Italian-trained bacteriologist who was the director of the Institute of Experimental Hygiene at the University of Montevideo in Uruguay, discovered what he was sure it was the Yellow Fever bacteria; and named it *Bacillus icteroides*. Sanarelli's pathogen turned out to be the common hog cholera bacillus. However, the tracking of micro-organisms was a major source in thinking about the origins of disease.

Yellow Fever and other infectious diseases in the Panama Canal were rampant and destroyed the valiant French effort to build the Panama Canal in the 1880s. Non-immune workers in the Canal Zone developed febrile illness which heralded the later complications of jaundice, mucosal hemorrhage, "black vomit", shock and inevitably death. Fully loaded ships dropped off equipment for the canal excavation and returned fully loaded with caskets of dead canal workers, most of who died of yellow fever or malaria. The French effort was abandoned in 1889 after enormous financial losses, estimated to be in excess of $300 million (in today's dollars) and loss of 22,000 workers to yellow fever.

The U.S military's involvement in Yellow Fever began in 1897, with the establishment by President McKinley of a scientific commission to study its causes. The commission made the decision to examine transmission instead of etiology. Army Surgeon General George Sternberg appointed a young officer, Major Walter Reed to head this commission. Although Walter Reed was convinced that a bacterial etiology (i.e. Sanarelli's *Bacillus icteroides* hypothesis) was unlikely, actual viral etiology of Yellow Fever was decades away.

After gaining independence from Colombia, the Panama Canal became an American-controlled territory by treaty in 1903, providing the United States the opportunity to complete the task abandoned earlier by the French. Predictably, the Americans faced the same challenges as the French with regards to Yellow Fever, malaria and other diseases. As in Cuba, later aggressive vector-control program proved their efficacy; within 16 months, Gorgas and his team of inspectors eliminated Yellow Fever from the Canal Zone. Some evidence suggests the Americans researched the experience of the French in building the Panama Canal and the Suez Canal. Immediately after Gorgas's success in Havana, he wrote the Surgeon General anticipating the start of the Panama Canal work, offering his services to control malaria and Yellow Fever. The U.S government delayed his appointment and sent him to Paris to look at the medical records there so they could have some idea of the tropical disease problem in Panama and the French medical intervention during the Suez Canal construction.

However, before one strikes this as conclusive, it is important to illustrate that initially numerous hypotheses concerning Yellow Fever transmission centered on fomites or airborne "miasmas" related to poor sanitation and was widely held among the medical establishment at that time. Carlos Finlay, a Cuban physician, first suggested that Yellow Fever was driven by mosquitoes in 1881. His work was questioned and hampered due to experimental limitations and his peers not convinced of his hypothesis. Meanwhile, Reed thought the mosquito theory had merit. The commission decided to replicate Finlay's study and obtain human subjects to test this theory. Concurrently, the initial phase of Gorgas's work involved educational campaigns to drain any standing water, improving hygiene practices, and executing a pipeline sewage system to safely carry human waste from the population and implement quarantine efforts. Vector control came later in his campaign.

CONCLUSION

Infectious diseases like Malaria and Yellow Fever posed serious obstacles to European colonization of the tropics, and can explain why the European colonial partitioning of Africa was not accomplished until nearly 400 years after European partitioning of the "New World" began (Diamond, 1997). Furthermore, once Malaria and Yellow Fever did become transmitted to the Americas by ship traffic, they emerged as major impediment to colonization of the New World tropics as well. A good example the role these two diseases had was in the abortion of French efforts to construct the Panama Canal, and nearly aborting the ultimately successful American effort, to construct the Panama Canal (Diamond, 1997).

Yellow Fever and other infectious diseases continue to be a major public health problem, affecting up to 200,000 persons with up to 30,000 deaths each year (Bryan et al, 2004). Most occur in Africa, especially West Africa due to breakdown in vaccination and mosquito control programs. This is usually a corollary to a break down in civil order in areas like Liberia or the Democratic Republic of the Congo. As a zoonosis (any agent able to be transmitted to humans from animals), Yellow Fever cannot be eradicated. As a continuing threat to humans including the potential use as a bioterrorism agent, such pathogens cannot be forgotten.

The various historical accounts discussed support the view that microbes are as deserving of a place in history texts as kings, presidents, and generals. In the classic treatise on this subject, Hans Zinsser noted "...*epidemics...have often determined victory or defeat before the generals knew where they were going to (base their) headquarters' mess* (Zinsser, 1934)." Public health professionals in all fields fundamentally must appreciate microbes such as Yellow Fever or Malaria and other pathogens not just from a scientific viewpoint, but its imprint on economics, literature, sociology, and virtually every aspect of human society. In the end, disease has altered the course of human history.

"*Guns, Germs and Steel,* " by Diamond (1997) illustrates how European civilization conquered other areas and maintained dominance through a disproportionate distribution of power vis-à-vis superior weapons, the migration of diseases brought by the Europeans to local populations, and organizing central (often brutal) governmental systems. It is worth mentioning that diseases had no particular selection of race or ethnicity, it was a two way attack in which Europeans were equally devastated by local diseases in which natives were immune from. The book offers a perspective which places disease as an important variable worth analyzing in any final calculus.

Since the earliest records began, malaria and other similar fevers have imposed enormous human and economic costs despite significant effort to control the diseases, such as the use of DDT chemical sprays (Dichloro-Diphenyl-Trichloroethane) and other man-made strategies to tackle natural challenges. It is clear that man's economic and disease control strategies played a far larger impact in the incidence of disease. A historical examination of how our predecessors dealt with these scourges by furnishing examples, both good and bad, illustrate how we should react in the face of frustration and uncertainty; the history of Yellow fever and other infectious diseases remains instructive, as we face an ever increasing encroachment on areas of the globe previously untouched by human habitation.

REFERENCES

Anonymous. (2001). Introduction: Yellow Fever Before 1900. *Military Medicine, 166*, 3-4.

Bres, P. L. J. (1986). A century of progress in combating yellow fever. *Bull. World Health Organization, 64*, 775-786

Bryan, C. S., Moss, S. W. & Kahn, R. J. (2004). Yellow fever in the Americas. *Infectious Disease Clinics of North America, 18*, 275-292.

Byerly, C. R. (2005). Fever of war: The influenza epidemic in the U.S. *Army during World War I*. New York: New York University Press.

Chin, J. (2000). Control of Communicable Diseases Manual. 17th edition. Washington, DC, *American Public Health Association*.

Cirillo, V. J. (2008). Two Faces of Death: fatalities from disease and combat in America's principal wars, 1775 to present. *Perspectives in Biology and Medicine, 51*, 121-133.

Cirillo, V. J. (2004). Bullets and bacilli: The Spanish-American *War and military medicine*. New Brunswick: Rutgers University Press.

DeKriuf, P. (1985). *The Microbe Hunters*. New York, Washington Square Press.

Diamond, J. (1997). *Guns, Germs, and Steel*. New York, W.W. Norton Publishers.

Gillet, M. C., (1981). The Army Medical Department 1775-1818. Washington, DC: GPO.

Gorgas, M. D. & Burton, H. J. (1935). *William Crawford Gorgas, His Life and Work*. Garden City, NY, Doubleday, Doran and Company.

Humphries, M. (1992). *Yellow fever and the South*. New Brunswick, NJ, Rutgers University Press.

Insh, G. P. (1924). Papers Relating to the Ships and Voyages of the Company of Scotland Trading to Africa and the Indies, 1696-1707, Scottish History Society, Edinburgh University Press.

McSherry, J. A. (1982). Some medical aspects of the Darien Scheme: was it dengue? *Scottish Medical Journal, 27*, 183-184.

Platt, D. (2003). The Social Impact of Medicine. *Delaware Medical Journal, 75*, 461-464.

Zinsser, H. (1934). Rats, lice and history, 152. Little, Brown & Co., Boston.

AN APPRECIATION OF "FOLK BELIEFS" CONCERNING DISEASE CAUSATION IMPACTED, FOR BETTER OR WORSE, BEHAVIORS THAT WAS ASSOCIATED WITH TRYING TO AVOID OR PREVENT MALARIA/YELLOW FEVER

Introduction

In most historical accounts, a broadly shared view across most cultures defines the behavior regarding disease causation. This interpretation within a culture provides the context within which diseases spread or were contained. By understanding human behavior within the context of a disease such as Malaria/Yellow Fever one can explain the state of knowledge at the time and what ideas communities have regarding illness causation, such as, ideas like the imbalances in the hot-cold energy of the body, bad vapors "miasma," rituals and amulets to ward away illness. These ideas come from an underlying psychological and cultural orientation of a group.

Wide variations exist among indigenous beliefs and practices associated with health promotion, disease prevention regarding the causation of diseases in their attempt to augment or improve one's own health when one is sick or ill. However, health is considered a treasure in all cultures. To illustrate the high value given to health, a quote from the 19th century Indian philosopher Rabindranath Tagore said, *"The emancipation of our physical nature is in attaining health, of our social being in attaining goodness, and of our self in attaining love."* To examine broadly held beliefs one can divide cultural "folk" beliefs into four overlapping groups:

1. Beneficial- to be supported and adopted into health teaching.
2. Harmless- no scientific value and best left alone.
3. Uncertain- difficult to assess as different interpretations may be possible and therefore need to be observed and researched further.
4. Harmful- belief and practices that should be tackled by health education through persuasion and convincing demonstration (Jelliffe, 1963).

In "An Integrated Theory of Disease: Ladino-Mestizo Views of Disease in the Chiapas Highlands," a case in point illustrating the study of disease concepts and illness behavior of folk and nonliterate communities can teach us characteristics of human function during illness. Fabrega eloquently states that "a *society's theory of disease is not only an explanation of how a person (body, mind, behavior) is changed during a phase of life we may define as illness...it is also a map or blueprint that provides the outline of what members of a culture accept as real."*

All "folk beliefs" serve to create a context of meaning within which the person can make sense of his or her experience. An understanding of the context for illness usually reflects core cultural values, and allows one to bring order in an uncertain phase in life defined as illness. This paper will discuss different events and traditions using folk belief as our "lens" to better understand how behavior, for better or worse, was used to avoid or prevent Malaria/Yellow Fever and other infectious diseases.

Palestine, Smallpox, the British Mandate

Palestine was a distant part of the Ottoman Empire at the early part of the 20th century. Infectious diseases were high and the Ottoman government did not put sufficient resources to adequately address the needs of residents in Palestine. High infant mortality rates, as well as infectious diseases such as cholera, dysentery, malaria, and tuberculosis, had a strong impact on daily life (Sufian, 2002).

On multiple dimensions, Palestine served as the right environment for illness and disease. The geography did not provide an easy living, comprising a relatively small area with both swamps and deserts. The geography provided a transient route for Islamic pilgrims to cross through Palestine, from Egypt, Sudan and Libya, in route to Mecca, Saudi Arabia. This annual influx provided an opportunity for diseases to be transmitted.

During the Ottoman rule and British occupation, local populations relied mainly on "traditional" medicine which included herbal (plant) medicine, bone-setting, cauterization, blood-letting, leeching, cupping, as well as amulet writers. Even to this day, a parallel medical system exists in conjunction with Westernized medicine in this part of the world.

When the British entered Palestine in 1917, their first priority was to embark on installing new sewage and drainage systems. In addition, major investments were made in hygiene education campaigns and a school hygiene service was established. However, against a backdrop of limitations in resources and tension within the British budget to govern this region restricted any real improvement in health to the local population. Smallpox outbreaks have been recorded in Palestine during the 19th and early 20th centuries. The British forces discovered few relics of any preexisting government health services (Sufian, 2002).They were faced with a poverty and disease stricken population.

Local populations relied on "folk beliefs" that surrounded two broad categories: personalistic and naturalistic. In the personalistic approach, illness was believed to be caused by the intervention of a supernatural being (a deity or Jinn i.e. spirits). The sick person would ask for a religious healer to come to one's house and recite specific Quranic (divine religious text of Islam) verses to expel the illness such as smallpox from one's body. The Arab culture offers a rich tapestry of superstitious tales and religion intertwined to create the explanation that one who is ill has transgressed moral and or spiritual order.

The afflicted person would believe that the possession of evil spirits would be the cause of illness brought on by one bad misfortune or in the Arab culture "the evil eye," which results in illness or calamity. Religious healers and mystics were considered malevolent who can manipulate secret rituals and charms to rebalance one's affliction through reciting Quranic verses interspersed with dance, incense burning. Although such practices mentally can make the ill person feel well. Smallpox patients were not treated appropriately since the populace was unaware that it was a viral pathogen.

In the naturalistic approach the Palestinians context viewed disease causation as a state of disharmony between human being and the environment, when upset, illness resulted. Naturalistic approach can be widely found in India, Asia, China and the Americas. The issue was to bring balance through appropriate attention to diet, activity and the use of various herbal and mineral intakes to bring the body back to harmony with the environment.

Cupping, blood-letting and use of herbal plant medicine in the form of tea were used by practitioners to treat the afflicted. This created infection control problems and often led to further infection since the practice was made in sub-hygienic standards. Medical asepsis and cleanliness was often not practiced as it is understood today.

Sudanese *Zar (Healing Cult)*

The *Zar* is best described as a "healing cult" utilizing dance, drums, and human voice that allow the participant to go into a state of trance. The *Zar* should not be defined as type of "exorcism" as many describe it because the spirit is often accommodated and placated (Harding, 1996). The subject is advised to "be continually attentive to their inner self, perform such daily work as they require, avoid dirt, and refrain from negative emotion." Failure to do this may result in a relapse. The fact that this advice is as valid for modern western women as it is for *Zar* patients is proof to the practical nature of the *Zar* experience (Harding, 1996).

The *Zar* is a well established ceremony found in numerous parts of Africa, most notably in Sudan and Egypt. Even though it is technically prohibited in Islam, it continues to be practiced as an essential ceremony to dispel a subject considered ill or "possessed by spirits." The folklore belief is an essential practice that provides relief to women in strict patriarchal societies such as North Africa and the Middle East. Its function serves to share knowledge and execute a dance process leftover from old African deities, a variant from what we consider as "voodoo" in the Americas. Most leaders and participants of *Zar* are women. Men play a role in assisting with the drumming or slaughter of a ritual animal. The sacrificial animal is an optional matter that may or may not be a part of this modern ceremony.

The *Zar* ceremony involves women moving to the pulse of a drum. The sick subject often moves with intensity and speed with eyes half closed. The ceremony often allows the dancers and sick person to abandon their bodies to the pulse of the dance. The chief musical instruments used are the tar, a kind of tambourine, and the *tabla* (drum). The number of "helpers" ranges from three to six and provide rhythmic backup. During the *Zar* ceremonies the various spirits are summoned by their own distinctive drum beat (or "thread") (Harding, 1996). In the context of *Zar* it is permissible to flail about, speak out loudly, and drink blood and alcohol. The leader of a *Zar* is often called an *Umiya* or *Shayka* (leader) who is herself possessed and has come to terms with her spirit. Heredity regarding leadership qualification is an important requirement often passed from mother to daughter.

From a folk belief model, what behavior can be learned from the *Zar* experience? The *Zar* ritual is a cathartic and multisensory dimension, which serves as psychotherapy in western culture. It involves several critical aspects which contribute to its success as therapy. The patient is the focus of attention, and receives the help of friends and relatives. Experience and feelings are recognized as valid (Harding, 1996). As dance therapist Claire Schmais (1996) explains, "It is community based, followers and members are not sent away to be cured....it creates a sense of community while it heals, embracing the individual within a community."

The *Zar* provides a multisensory experience with sights, sounds and smells for all who participate. These rituals include an altar, the smell of incense, and costumes. Songs are rhythmically chanted and drums play trance-like rhythms. In addition, the ritual sharing of food creates communion in all cultures and times. Thus, it is important to understand these rituals in the context of the total experience (Harding, 1996).

The major elements of the *Zar* experience offer potential benefits to women or men in our culture to create more meaningful life experiences which impacts positively on one's health, in whatever ritual context they prefer. This could be done either as religious or secular context. Through the sense of "moving together", a sense of closeness builds between members of the group. Furthermore, the experience of being the center of attention is, in itself, a therapeutic experience, when surrounded by friends (Harding, 1996). Ultimately, this form of folk belief provides a foundation within which cultures understand disease, namely India and the Middle East.

Disease Causation: Chinese Context

An understanding of Chinese folk belief can facilitate an appreciation among health care professionals in phrasing curative and preventive measures. Five disease causation theories in the Chinese context includes severe exercise after a meal causes appendicitis, diabetes arises from eating too much sugar, exposure to cold and wetness causes rheumatism/arthritis, and gallstones are the result of long term consumption of foods contaminated with sand and dirt. These types of "folk" theories are not exclusive to China alone but parallel similar traditional understandings in many cultures in the world.

Health behavior within the Chinese context tended to be derived from cosmological beliefs which emphasized the importance of balancing "hot" and "cold" forces within the body, also known as the "Ying-Yang Model." For example, there is a prevalent fear among Chinese in the Hong Kong area that a high fever could "burn out" the nervous system, and therefore result in neurological disorders like polio and mental retardation.

The concepts of treatment around such vector-driven agents are centered on dietary changes and seeking mystical healers who can manipulate body energy through the use of acupuncture, herbal teas, and other "traditional remedies." It is instructive to point out that over the course of time, an increased recognition that "the relationship of the person to his or her total environment determines health," was understood by folk theories. Western medicine has incorporated this understanding within the field of epidemiology by examining "risk factors" associated with a pathogen.

Malaria and Folk Beliefs

Two central issues in most anthropological studies regarding vector-borne diseases revolve first, around how communities connect a mosquito bite with disease causation and secondly, the communities understanding of whether a fever and other associated symptoms are connected with Malaria. In addition, understanding of Malaria can differ widely within the same geographical region. This paper discusses several examples illustrating the significance folk beliefs play in understanding and designing programs to control disease.

In Tanzania, a study by Muela and colleagues (1998) found that the majority of people interviewed believed that mosquito bites caused Malaria. Many concurrently held the belief that other modes of transmission, such as drinking "dirty" water or being exposed to intense sun can cause Malaria. In the cultural context of this particular sample conducted in Tanzania, the concept of fever had broader meaning and implications for the victim. The understanding of fever in relations to climate plays a major role in understanding modes of transmission. In rainy seasons, fever was associated with the mosquito since the vector prefers damp and hot environments. In the dry season, fever was more attributable to exposure to sun or "hard work."

In Egypt, a folk belief model with fever is understood as being a symptom and disease. Fever was associated with being possessed by spirits known as *Jinns*. In the Arab culture, it is understood and shared throughout the Middle East that a parallel universe exists in the same context or plain as humans on earth. Interestingly, the association of fever with *Jinns* can be partly explained because as the temperature of the human body increases this raises the probability of delirious mental behavior expressed by the victim. This can now be explained by biomedicine. However, in many parts of the Arab World both in urban and rural areas, the victim would be brought to a religious mystic who would read Quranic verses to expel the "*Jinn*" within the human body.

In India, a study by Lobo and Kazi (1997) discovered different folk models of fever, and of the causes of Malaria. In this study, it was found to be a disease and symptom. The study found 30 different types or definitions of fever in the Gujarat state. A wide interpretation existed in villager's description of fever in regards to cause and treatment modalities.

Folk Belief within Health Professionals

A tacit assumption has been made between social scientists and health professionals that a clear-cut dichotomy exists between folk and scientifically-based beliefs. Indeed, the terminology often found in the literature refer to belief systems typically including words such as *orthodox, objective, professional, and evidence-based practice* as contrasted with the words *unorthodox, lay, subjective* (Demers et al, 1984; Weidman, 1979; Tripp-Reimer, 1982). This contextual discussion serves to illustrate that even health professionals may hold some beliefs that could be described as "folk" health.

A study by Roberson (1987) sampled 97 nurses and 23 physicians in a southern U.S locale and found that over half responding to a 25 item Likert-type scale positively agreed to statements that included major folk health beliefs related to disease causation and health restoration such as "*Someone who sits or sleeps in a draft is likely to come down with a cold.*" Even though conventional understanding shows a clear cut line has been drawn between the two, folk and scientific base in modern medicine today, one cannot draw any clear conclusions. It does suggest that health professionals should have an open and receptive integration of both, folk and scientific systems, and prudently value the degree to which they draw on either or both.

CONCLUSION

It is important to understand the biology of disease causation as part of a larger paradigm, equally important are local traditions and "folk beliefs" regarding the treatment of infectious disease such as malaria. Positive or negative behaviors discussed in this paper illustrate how powerful these rituals and traditions are in treating the afflicted. The modalities include but are not limited to traditional healers, rituals, herbal treatments, and other related behaviors. It is of interest to point out that self-treatment versus seeking attention are both types modalities that have to be considered for any successful program to be locally implemented.

Any public health professional must take into account local folk beliefs about disease and not generalize even within the same town or geographical area. Contemporary understanding of disease causation, however bad or good, must be accepted by a public health practitioner as reality among a particular group. It is sobering to note that an effective program must be flexible in approach to take into account locally held folk beliefs and traditions to better understand which behavior is productive or counterproductive in propagating disease. Furthermore, a thorough analysis of what is considered a myth or stigma associated with disease can provide a broader knowledge of how communities view a disease. Incorporating locally held belief and understanding of disease causation clearly has positive short-term and long-term implications any public health practitioner must comprehend in reducing behavioral misconceptions and ultimately promote the health of a community.

REFERENCES

Demera, R. Y., Altamore, R., Mustin, H., Kleinman, A. & Leonardi, D. (1980). An exploration of the dimensions of illness behavior. *Journal of Family Practice, 11(7)*, 1086-1096.

Engle, G. L. (1973). Personal Theories of Disease as Determinants of Patient-Physician Relationships. *Psychosomatic Medicine, 35*, 3, 184-186.

Fabrega, H., Jr. & Manning, P. R. (1973). An integrated theory of disease: Ladino-Mestizo views of disease in the Chiapas Highlands. *Psychosomatic Medicine, 35*, 223-239.

Geertz, C. (1973). *The interpretation of cultures*. New York: Basic Books.

Harding, K. (1996). The Zar Revisited. *Crescent Moon*, (July-Aug. 1996), 9-10.

Jelliffe, D. B. (1963). Customs and child health in Buganda. *Tropical geography & Medicine, 15*, 121-123.

Lobo, L. & Kazi, B. (1997). *Ethnography of malaria in Surat*. Surat: Centre for Social Studies.

Muela, S. H., Ribera, J. M. & Tanner, M. (1998). Fake malaria and hidden parasites- the ambiguity of malaria. *Anthropological Medicine., 5(1)*, 43-61.

Roberson, M. (1987). Folk Health Beliefs of Health Professionals. *Western Journal of Nursing Research, 9(2)*, 257-263.

Sufian, S. (2002). *An introduction to the history of Arab health care during the British mandate*, 1920-1947. Westport (CT) and London: Praeger.

Tripp-Reimer, T. (1982). Barriers to health care: Variations in interpretation of Appalachian client behavior by Appalachian and non-Appalachian health professionals. *Western Journal of Nursing Research, 4(2)*, 179-191.

Tripp-Reimer, T. (1984). Reconceptualizing the construct of health: Integrating emic and etic perspectives. *Research in Nursing Research, 7*, 101-109.

Weidman, H. H. (1979). The transcultural view: prerequisite to interethnic (intercultural) communication in medicine. *Social Science & Medicine, 13B*, 85-87.

In: Race and Ethnicity   ISBN: 978-1-60692-099-2
Editor: Jonathan K. Crennan, pp. 319-334   © 2010 Nova Science Publishers, Inc.

Chapter 14

THE LIBERALISM OF AMERICAN JEWS

David Verbeeten
Pembroke College, University of Cambridge, United Kingdom

ABSTRACT

The relative liberalism of American Jews is a phenomenon of enduring interest to specialists and laypeople alike. The ongoing American Jewish attachment to liberal politics and the Democratic Party defies rational-choice models and intuitive understandings of political orientation. Other groups with the same socioeconomic status as American Jews tend to be more conservative and/or Republican.

This essay begins (§I) with a description of the dimensions of American Jewish liberalism. It proceeds (§II) to a discussion of the more common theories that seek to explain the phenomenon, noting the deficiencies of each. It concludes (§III) that American Jewish liberalism is best viewed as an expression of "lived religion"; this expression functions to fulfill American Jews' self-definition and thereby to impede ethnic dissolution in an atomizing society.

Of the phenomenon of American Jewish liberalism, the sociologist Milton Himmelfarb, in a 1969 article in *Commentary* magazine, rather famously quipped that Jews earn like Episcopalians yet vote like Puerto Ricans. Just in case the surprising strangeness of this point was lost on any of his readers, he clarified whom he meant by Puerto Ricans: "—the poor, the racial minorities" (Himmelfarb 1969: 33-34). Several years later, in a 1985 article in the same venue, Himmelfarb slightly revised his assessment, declaiming that "Jews vote like Hispanics, *only more so*" (Himmelfarb 1985: 40). By 1985, moreover, Jewish individuals had surpassed Episcopalians, indeed all other religious and ethnic groups, in their individual affluence (Lipset 1990: 4; Medoff 1981: 79).

Himmelfarb gets right to the heart of why the Jewish case is of such enduring interest, both to specialists and laypeople alike. It seems very clearly to defy rational-choice models and intuitive understandings of political orientation, which emphasize "objective" or "rational" socioeconomic factors like status and wealth. By such factors, Jews, like other white American of their level of affluence, ought to be rather more conservative or at least

Republican (Gelman 2008: 46-57), but they are decidedly not. The political orientation of American Jews is also of interest because, despite their small size—from just under five per cent of the American population at the beginning of the twentieth century to around half that by the end—they are involved and influential in the political process, the media, academia, and the national elite (Lipset and Raab 1995: 138).

I

That American Jews have been a liberal group, by most definitions and indicators of what has typically been regarded as liberal or left-wing in the United States throughout the twentieth century, is well-established. While there is a sizeable, often confusing and confused, academic literature on the exact nature and dimensions of American Jewish liberalism – with surveys and polls differing from year to year in their particular results or emphases – the general proclivity is not in doubt. A glance at the voting habits of American Jews since 1916 gives an immediate indication of the basic tendencies.

Figure 1 demonstrates that Jews have for decades favoured Democrats over Republicans by wide margins. With the exception of 1920, when over a third of the Jewish vote went to the socialist candidate, Eugene Debs, there were no presidential elections from 1916 in which more Jews voted for a Republican candidate than a Democratic one. The curved trendlines give a good sense of the overall, longstanding party preferences of American Jews.

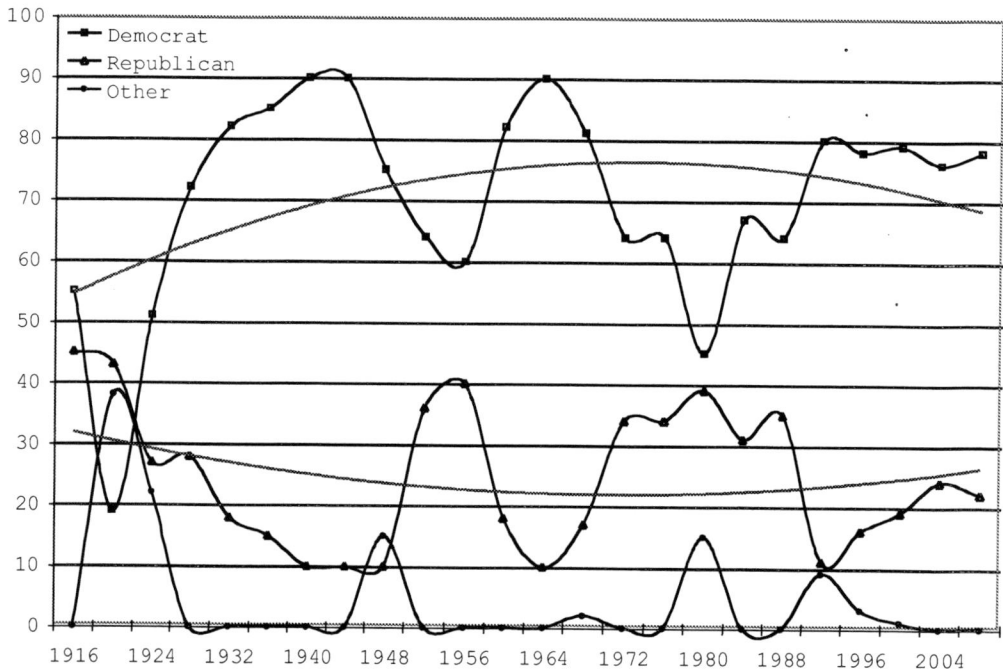

Source: Forman 2004: 153.

Figure 1. Jewish Voting Patterns in Presidential Elections, 1916-2008, by percentage.

The extent of American Jewish political distinctiveness becomes more immediately apparent when comparing the Jewish vote with the general vote, which includes Jews yet is not greatly affected by their small numbers. A comparative plotting of voting data of the Jewish and the general population is portrayed in Figure 2, from which representation of third-party votes has been removed for the sake of visual clarity.

The trendlines on this graph, which are for the voting preferences of the general population (solid lines) rather than the Jewish population (dotted lines), are virtually indistinguishable from one another.

American Jews have not simply voted for the Democratic party out of partisan habit. Lobbyist and author, Benjamin Ginsberg, maintained almost twenty years ago that "Jews are Democrats more than they are liberals" and that "Jewish liberalism is more an *institutional* than an *attitudinal* phenomenon" (Ginsberg 1993: 142-143). The data have suggested otherwise, with American Jews tending to support liberal Republicans in contests against conservative Democrats. Notably, in the 1956 presidential election, in which Dwight D. Eisenhower received almost 40 per cent of the Jewish vote—an unprecedented achievement for a Republican candidate in forty years—sociographer Lawrence H. Fuchs noted that it was quite possible "that Jewish voters for Eisenhower were something other than a manifestation of illiberalism. Literally dozens of Jewish voters indicated in their replies to open-end questions that they thought Eisenhower was a liberal himself" (Fuchs 1955: 393). This (mis)perception did not extend to Richard Nixon in his bid against John F. Kennedy in 1960.[*]

American Jews have self-identified as liberals and espoused principles and policies that are typically liberal more often than other white Americans of their socioeconomic background, more often than Hispanics, and, on issues of social rather than economic liberalism, more often than African-Americans. A majority of American Jews believes in or supports abortion, gay marriage, and a strict separation between church and state (Greenberg and Wald 2004: 171-183). American Jews have historically demonstrated greater sympathy for blacks and other disadvantaged groups, even when controlled for education and socioeconomic status (Glaser 1997: 446). Indeed, it is on this issue that American Jews regard Democrats as having the greatest positive margin over Republicans, as indicated in the table below.

Table 1. Democrat Margin over Republicans, Jews and non-Jews, 2001

Party trusted to do better job at...	Jews	Non-Jews	Non-Jewish Democrats
Sympathizing with disadvantaged	+67	+29	+62
Protecting individual rights	+42	+9	+46
Encouraging higher moral standards	+6	-19	+11
Promoting self-reliance	-4	-20	+10

Source: Greenberg and Wald 2004: 174.

---

[*] There is some recent evidence that Jews may increasingly be voting according to partisan habit rather than normative commitment to contemporary American liberalism *per se*. In a study before the 2008 presidential election, several sociographers conducted surveys that seemed to support this contention. Whatever the present state of affairs, however, this pattern has not obviously pertained in the past (Cohen, Abrams and Veinstein 2008: 7-24).

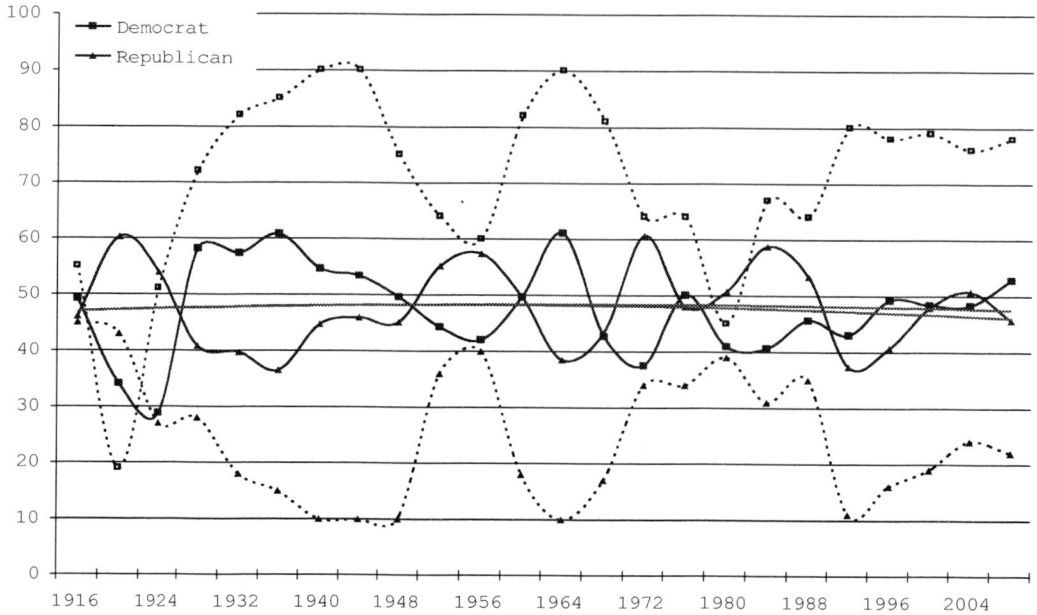

Figure 2. Jewish versus General Voting Patterns in Presidential Elections, 1916-2008, by percentage.

The only cause on which American Jews have not been unduly more liberal than other Americans is capital punishment—a majority of Jews as non-Jews believe that convictions of murder should be punished by death (Greenberg and Wald 2004: 178). All the same, even when Jews from the 1980s and 1990s are compared against a select control group of Americans who belong to self-styled liberal Protestant churches (which is rather like stacking the deck), there is a narrowing and even closing of statistical gaps on certain issues, but Jews remain more liberal in key areas: their self-identification as Democrats, their strict views on the separation of church and state, their acceptance of permissive social codes, and their support for domestic spending on education, the environment, urban renewal, and health care (Cohen and Liebman 1997: 419-420).

American Jewish elites, intellectuals and activists—i.e., those individuals who have been most committed to political ideas and events in their everyday lives—have often been more liberal or left-wing than the average Jewish man or woman. There is a fascinating history of involvement by American (as well as European) Jewish individuals in radical movements in the twentieth century, although Jewish prominence in these movements has declined in recent decades (Lerner, Nagai and Rothman 1989: 335-343). The role of American Jews in the "Old Left" of the interwar period and the "New Left" of the postwar 1960s was substantial (Lichter and Rothman 1982: 81). American Jewish youths and organizations were disproportionately involved in the black civil rights movement of the 1960s as well as the anti-Vietnam war movement of the 1970s, although estimates of numbers vary and lack precision (Liebman 1979). Jewish faculty tended to be more sympathetic than their gentile peers to the student protest movements of the 1960s and 1970s, which also had a significant Jewish component, especially amongst the leadership (Lichter and Rothman 1981: 347-348). These Jewish academics "played an important role in persuading a much larger public of the merits of the 1960s student activists" (Lichter and Rothman 1982: 104).

II

For all that the relative liberalism of American Jews is well-established, the reasons for it are not. The main issue that requires explanation is not why Jews are liberal, but why they are disproportionately liberal by comparison with the population as a whole and with other select groups. After all, there are millions if not tens of millions of Americans who are typically liberal yet not Jewish. There are also some American Jews who are quite conservative in their political orientation; while these Jews are of great interest to scholars seeking to understand their more liberal peers, their numbers are relatively small. On the main issue there is no agreement among the specialists as to the etiology. Political scientist Geoffrey B. Levey, an astute observer, insisted that "none of the existing theories of American Jewish liberalism can withstand scrutiny"—the phenomenon "continues to elude explanation" (Levey 1996: 371, 400).

The most common explanation for the relative liberalism of American Jews insists that liberalism was in the Jews' objective social and economic self-interest as a poor ethnic and religious minority that suffered from discrimination and that knew a history of persecution. In short, the left was friendly to the Jews and their causes, the right was not. There are various different versions of this theory. Some focus on the circumstances that Jews found in America; others seek continuity between the Jewish experience in Europe and their political behaviour in America.

Those who focus on American circumstances maintain that Jews became a hard-pressed, ghettoized, working-class population upon their arrival in the United States during the period of the great migration from 1881 to 1924, and that the policies of the New Deal appealed to them as it did others in their difficult straits. Moreover, the administration of F. D. Roosevelt provided Jews with unique opportunities on the American "national scene" that were not offered by his Republican rivals (Ginsberg 1993: 140). Roosevelt brought Jews, especially those who had voted for Eugene Debs in 1920, into the mainstream of American politics (Mendelsohn 1993: 89-90). He afforded them vehicles for social mobilization and social expression. He "gave specific instructions for recruitment in New York, where generations of Jews had begun to spill into the legal and academic professions" (Lipset and Raab 1995: 142). This unprecedented overture to the Jewish community in conjunction with a promotion of their socioeconomic interests resulted in a profound attachment to the party of the New Deal and Roosevelt, which persisted even after Jewish socioeconomic interests ceased to be obviously aligned with the Democratic party after the Second World War (Dawidowicz and Goldstein 1974: 300).

It is true that Roosevelt "appointed more Jews to public office than all previous presidents combined" and that these appointments were part of a much larger incorporation of Jews into government at the time (Dalin 2004: 35-37). This fact, however, was a reflection of the general expansion of the state in the 1930s and the preexisting support of American Jews for the socialistic New Deal rather than of Republican indifference to them or their concerns. The Democratic machine rewarded Jews for their intense loyalty, whereas Republicans, especially at the federal level, "neither owed nor paid many debts to the East Side" (Howe 1976: 383). Prior to the New Deal, Republicans, many of whom were associated with Progressive politics, had appointed more (German) Jews to office, especially at the local level in New York, and had made vociferous statements against the persecution of Jews in Eastern

Europe and Russia (Howe 1967: 382-383; Forman 2004: 152). This did not preclude the mass Jewish movement into the Democratic party, which, as shown in Figure 1, preceded the New Deal by ten years. Nor did the fact that the Democratic party was home to some of the most antisemitic elements in the country: Catholic immigrants and African-Americans (Dinnerstein 1994: 112-122, 132-133, 203).[*]

Further, American Jews of the interwar period were neither unduly impoverished nor unduly ostracized. The 1910s and 1920s were not decades of want, but decades of new prosperity and economic growth, hence F. Scott Fitzgerald's novels on American decadence. To a greater extent than other immigrant groups from the turn of the century, broad segments of American Jewry were moving decidedly into the middle classes by the interwar period and were on their way to that exalted socioeconomic position that would define them as a group after the Second World War (Kahan 1978: 235-251). It was not an easy ascent, but it was real. The persistence of a sizeable Jewish working-class was in large part due to successive waves of new immigrants taking the places of those who were leaving manual labour for white-collar occupations. Jews did suffer from discrimination and exclusion, but so did Irish and Italians immigrants as well as blacks and Asians (Dinnerstein and Reimers 1975: 40). None of these groups "clung so tenaciously to the liberal wing of the Democratic Party" and none, with exception of blacks, for so long (Whitfield 1986: 12-13).

America was a land of opportunity and tolerance for Jews unlike anything they had known in Europe, especially Eastern Europe. Due to these exceptional American circumstances, which were not characterized by oppression, there are those who attempt to explain the relative liberalism of American Jews by emphasizing European conditions. According to this view, Jews arrived in the United States as established partisans of the left, because in Europe, ever since the time of the French Revolution, Jews "had no alternative but to side with those of the left," which promoted Jewish emancipation and equality even as conservative forces opposed Jewish admission into civil society (Cohn 1958: 614-626).

This view is in part supported by the historical record, but it is superficial and simplistic. First, although the European left did tend to support Jewish emancipation more so than conservatives, the Jewish response to emancipation was itself varied and often ambivalent, especially as many liberal emancipators envisioned and demanded the total assimilation (and hence dissolution) of corporate Jewish identity (Trigano 1990: 171-190). English Jews, who were secure in life and property, largely regarded efforts in the mid-nineteenth century to achieve formal emancipation and political equality as immaterial, the goal of plutocrats to gain entry into parliament (Endelman 2002: 104-105). French Jews' way of life and self-image did not undergo significant change until a generation or more after the Revolution, before which they remained a traditional community that was materially and spiritually devastated by the upheaval of the Revolution and the anti-religious persecution of Jacobins (Berkovitz 1995: 78-86). Most German Jews remained orthodox and allied to conservative and loyalist forces until the New Era around 1858; an ultra-orthodox newspaper admonished that "Above all emancipation emancipates the Jews from Judaism" (Pulzer 1992: 82). Among the great pious mass of Polish Jewry as late as the 1930s, a "nostalgic view of pre-modern

---

[*] Jewish support for the 'Catholic' party was also replicated in Canada, even during the Second World War, when the Liberal party implemented petty policies against the admission of Jewish refugees in large part to placate the Catholic vote, on which it relied, especially in the province of Quebec; this led one Jewish leader to dismay that Canadian Jews would support the Liberals 'through hell and high water' (Abella and Troper 1991: 19, 134-135, 142, 162, 262).

Jewish life was the prevailing sentiment of the east European rabbis and presumably of the laity too" (Shapiro 1999: 41).

Second, and more importantly, the vast majority of American Jews did not come from Western Europe where the "dialectic of emancipation" pertained. Most did not arrive in America with socialist or even liberal beliefs or sympathies (Burgin 1914: 80-81). They arrived as a traditional or at least quasi-traditional and largely quietist group. There were activists among them, and indeed these activists had often had training in the radical movements that opposed tsarist autocracy, but they did not gain prominence or a mass following until the advent of the second generation in the 1910s and 1920s. This generational divide is reflected in the sales of the different dailies of the Yiddish press. The orthodox, conservative *Tageblatt* dominated the Yiddish-reading public into the 1900s. The secular, populist, social-democratic *Forverts* only gained a larger (and eventually the largest) circulation after 1910, and for years thereafter it had to contend with the orthodox, pro-Republican *Morgen Zhurnal* (Howe 1976: 528, 545).

In America, the "dialectic of emancipation" had little of the kind of relevance that it may have had in Germany or France—Jews were not granted civic equality as a concession by a rationalizing state or as contingent upon their so-called "reformation". Religious freedom was American *per se* and not an allowance to Jews. In America (as indeed in much of Europe), the Jewish attachment to the left did not follow chronologically from dilemmas of emancipation so much as from secularization, which was effected not so much by emancipation as by modernization and the disintegration of traditional lifestyles and rabbinical authority that it engendered with or without formal processes of emancipation. Notably, while the Catholic hierarchy reestablished its authority in the New World, the rabbinate failed to do so (Cantor 1995: 227; Goren 1970). Orthodox Judaism disintegrated in the new reality of the New World. Jews had come to America to work, not to pray.

Antisemitism does not seem to have been the decisive factor in the political orientation of the average American Jewish man or woman, which is not to deny that it was at times a significant if not very significant presence in Jewish life. Some individuals were obviously greatly perturbed and motivated by it, and some of these became left-wing radicals (Wistrich 1976).[*] All the same, the relationship between antisemitism and the relative liberalism of American Jews is simply not clear.

It is true that more American Jews have viewed conservatives and Republicans as more likely to be antisemitic than liberals and Democrats, but the majority has considered neither most Republicans nor most Democrats to be antisemitic. Further, if Republicans are more often viewed as antisemitic in surveys, then that is in part because more Jews are Democrats. Indeed, American Jews have tended to regard their party of choice as being less antisemitic than its rival: Democratic Jews believe Republicans are more antisemitic; Republican Jews believe Democrats are more antisemitic (Cohen 1984: 29; Cohen 1989: 41). Thus, perceptions have been mediated by preexisting political commitments. They have also been subject to considerable volatility from year to year. In all, contemporary American Jewry's perceptions of antisemitism bear "no relation to any objective evidence" (Lipset and Raab 1995: 107); they are a manifestation of a general sense of foreboding about the Jewish place in society (Rawidowicz 1986).

---

[*] The rage and pain over antisemitic violence is clear in the stories and articles written by the famous Russian-Jewish radical author, Isaac Babel (2002).

There is no conclusive evidence that antisemitism or the insecurity that it may cause induces greater liberalism. There have been a variety of responses to such things. Some studies have indicated that American Jews who feel most subordinate because of their Jewishness are in fact less tolerant of political non-conformity and less altruistic toward disadvantaged groups. In a study of Jewish males in an eastern city in 1961, Edgar Litt discovered that "Feelings of true minority status reduce the sense of effectiveness in external political affairs and reduce the amount of political activity" (Litt 1961: 282). In his more recent history of American Jewry and their political behaviour, Marc Dollinger described a tendency for American Jews who felt threatened—as during the Holocaust or when they lived in the segregated South—to avoid social activism (Dollinger 2000). A coming-to-terms with the Holocaust after the Second World War rendered the American Jewish community, or at least important segments thereof, less, not more, liberal (Feingold 1987: 38-39).

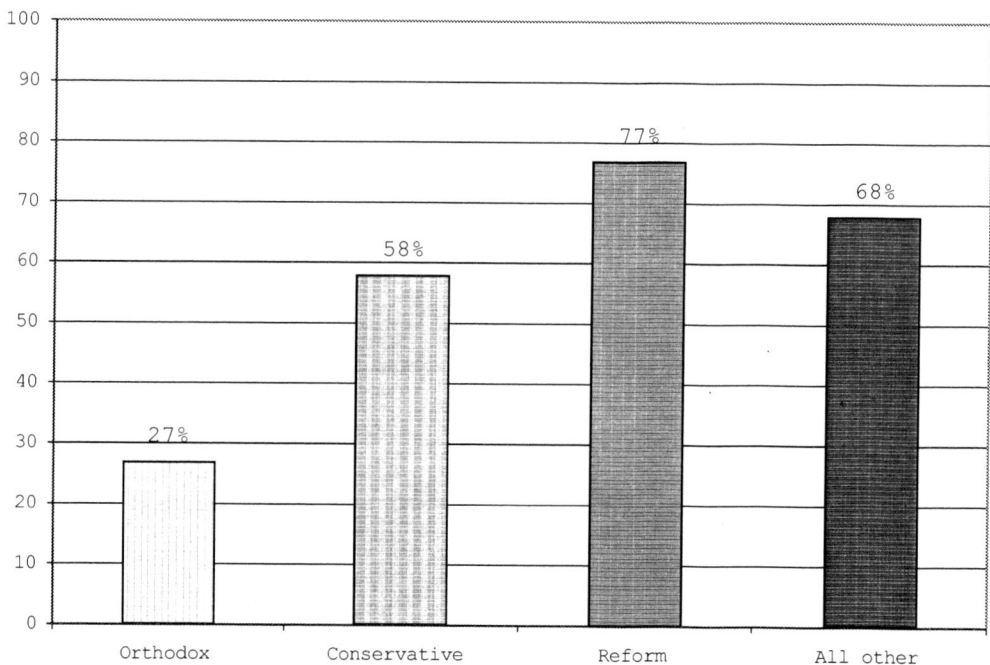

Source: Cohen, Abrams and Veinstein 2008: 7-24.

Figure 3. Intention to vote for Obama in the 2008 election, by Jewish denominational identity, by percentage.

That there is an ambiguous relationship between antisemitism and liberalism or the left in general is underscored by comparing the political preferences of the world's two largest Jewish communities during the crucial interwar period. In the 1920s and 1930s, Jews in the United States became overwhelmingly Democrats and fervent New Dealers, and a minority in New York City made up the electoral and financial mainstay of minor, leftist third parties, as they would continue to do into the 1940s and early 1950s (Dubofsky 1968: 365; Spinrad 1957-1958: 550). In the same period, the set-upon Jews of Poland—impoverished, harassed and persecuted—voted most often for ultra-conservative religious parties or specifically Jewish (Zionist) parties (Mendelsohn 1983: 51), even though secular intellectuals of Jewish origin were disproportionately involved in the leadership of the far left (Schatz 2004: 21; Bauman 1996: 576). Despite the slanderous and hateful association between East European Jews and communism, few Polish Jews voted for the communist party even at the peak of its popularity in the 1920s, when many Polish Ukrainians and Belarusians, the other large national minorities, were doing so (Kopstein and Wittenberg 2003: 105). After 1935, the Bund, a Jewish workmen's party, achieved strong support in local elections; this revival reflected not a sudden attachment to Marxism among the Jewish masses, but rather the desperation and sense of futility that had overcome a doomed community (Polonsky 1997: 191-192; Johnpoll 1967: 260).

A large part of Polish Jewish society in the interwar period was orthodox and rather anti-modern; this community comprised a conservative constituency, as manifested as much in elections as in daily life. In America, as in Poland and elsewhere in the diaspora, a similar pattern pertained. American Jews who have been more orthodox have tended to be more conservative than those, by far the majority, who have belonged to more relaxed denominations—viz. Reform Judaism—or those who have been more secular (Figure 3) (Gelman 2008: 78). This fact has often been cited to discount those theories on the relative liberalism of American Jews that seek to explain the phenomenon as a consequence of Judaism *per se* (Liebman 1973: 140; Lichter and Rothman 1982: 112).

III

Most data do suggest that the correlation between Judaism and liberalism is negative. Nonetheless, that there is a connection between the two has not only been the intuitive view of many scholars of liberal Jews (L. H. Fuchs 1956: 178), but also the view of literally countless liberal (and more left-wing) Jews themselves (Mendes-Flohr 1991: 15; Sorin 1985). If for this reason alone, it demands closer attention rather than curt dismissal. Authors who have related Judaism to liberalism have often done so in an unconvincing manner, half apologia, half self-congratulation. The rejection of the relation, however, has proceeded from a narrow conception of religion and an unwillingness or inability to perceive the ways in which Judaism in the United States has been a lived reality within Jewish communities and among Jewish individuals. Indeed, a sociology of religion does much to elucidate the nature of the relative liberalism of American Jews.

The historian, Michael Alexander, has expounded upon American Jewish liberalism as part of a lived religion. He describes lived religion as that which "manifest[s] commonly held understandings of the way the world is, as well as one's rightful place in that world, into ideological and behavioral forms" (Alexander 2001: 180). In his award-winning book, *Jazz Age Jews*, Alexander notes that as the second generation of Jews came of age in interwar America, they encountered a world that had little resemblance to the remembered worlds of their Russian or Polish parents. This second generation did not live in enforced alienation or poverty.

> Yet as this generation took its place among other middle-class groups in American society, some of its members displayed a peculiar behavior that did not correspond to their new social positions: They acted as though they were increasingly marginalized. What is more, many identified themselves with less fortunate individuals and groups, people who

remained in America's economic, political, and cultural margins.... As Jews moved up, they identified down (Alexander 2001: 1).

No other group, Alexander insists, engaged in this "outsider identification" to the same extent as Jews.

To bolster his contention, Alexander looks at three major Jewish figures from interwar New York, who "marked themselves off from American society and were celebrated by their Jewish peers for doing so." They "*intentionally* impair[ed] their economic, political, and cultural relations with gentiles" so as to be true to themselves as Jews and to retain racial fellow-feeling in a country that was diverse, dynamic, and atomizing (Alexander 2001: 8). Thus, Arnold Rothstein became king of the gambling underworld, and as such was "exalted" by the Yiddish press "for being a transgressive power," and excused by the Anglo-Jewish press "by finding sources for the behavior in the oppression of Jews in Eastern Europe." Felix Frankfurter became the most vocal legal activist and champion for the anarchical terrorists, Nicola Sacco and Bartolomeo Vanzetti, who "were political outsiders, and thus became a Jewish cause," much more so than an Italian one. Finally, Al Jolson and other East European Jews revived blackface and ragtime in American theatre and cinema to great popular enthusiasm, "depicting African-Americans...for their own ends" so as "to see in African-American life their own story of exile and slavery" (Alexander 2001: 59, 74-75, 136-137).

Diasporic existence, with all its vicissitudes and travails, has been justified by Jews to themselves and others as communal exile from Israel and the world for having a covenant with God as a chosen people with a special mission. These basic theological concepts pervade all of Jewish culture and thought, which have had an obvious messianic dimension (Kavon 2009: 19-23; Frankel 1991). In his best-seller from several decades ago, *World of Our Fathers*, Irving Howe wrote on the messianic fervour that permeated Jewish culture and thought, and the minute ways in which it impinged upon Jewish life and psychology—like the intergenerational tension over the rightful place of sport:

> Decades would have to go by before the sons and daughters of the immigrants could shake off – if they ever could! – this heritage of discomfort before the uses and pleasures of the body. What they were struggling for was nothing less than the persuasion that they had as much right as anyone else to feel at home on this earth, and what their parents were saying was no, Jews could not feel at home on this earth. Seemingly trivial or comic disputes over matters like playing baseball released profound clashes of world view, perhaps nothing less than whether Jewish messianism still mattered in the new world (Howe 1976: 182-183).

As Howe's passage indicates, the age-old Jewish self-definition, which had been corroborated by most European experience, was confounded by American conditions, especially the realization of rapid social mobility within a tolerant setting: Jews seemed to have ceased to be in exile and to have begun to be at home. For Orthodox Jews, the issue was not acute: they had faith and fulfilled themselves *qua* Jews by fulfillment of God's commandments. For non-observant Jews, however, a self-fulfillment *qua* Jews was met by re-enactment of exile, self-marginalization, or romanticized alienation, as emulation of remembered and re-constructed European experience. This transmutation took political expression in liberalism, with a particular emphasis on outsider identification as a surrogate for Jewish exile and chosenness. The Jews were still in a state of exile if others were. The effect or function of this transmutation was to express a certain Jewish identity and thereby preserve it.

It is not difficult to find anecdotal corroboration of this impulse in the explicit statements of American and other Jews (Mendes-Flohr and Reinharz 1995; Staub 2002). Isaac Deutscher, who was born in Poland, spent the war in London, and became a professor at Berkeley, wrote in his essay, "Who is a Jew?", that he was not a Jew by race (whose existence he denied), religion, or national sentiment, but he was "a Jew by force of my unconditional solidarity with the persecuted and exterminated" (Deutscher 1968: 51). Deutscher did not relate his self-definition to anti-assimilation, but many others did so. Thus, Leo Pfeffer, an important figure in the American Jewish Congress, proclaimed in 1965:

> I believe that ultimately there is no justification for Jewish survival unless there is that separateness, that outsidedness, that being the goad of the universal conscience. I don't think, realistically, that theology itself will long be adequate to maintain Jewish survival. To justify his survival as Jew the Jew should be the radical, the malcontent, the one who sparks revolutions. That, for better or for worse, is his mission in society (in Staub 2002: 84).

Paul Cowan, a young American Jewish civil rights activist, was very explicit about his politics and his resistance to assimilation. He described his civil rights activism as a form of "secular messianism" and "a lifelong debt to the six million dead", and he insisted: "*That* is my own way of resisting assimilation" (in Staub 2002: 87)

In 1986 in Philadelphia, at a Jewish-organized forum on sanctuary for illegal aliens, the connection between the exile of Jews and the exile of others was explicitly made by Rabbi Joseph Weizenbaum of Tuscon, Arizona.

> [He] reminds his audience of the Holocaust and the Jews who sought sanctuary but found none. Heads nod with saddened recognition. The Rabbi continues, "The same drama takes place today," he says, "but the Jews aren't the Jews anymore. Who are the Jews? The Guatemalans. The Salvadorans. They're the ones in pain. They're the ones suffering. They're the ones like unto us" (Coyne 1986: 1).

That neither Guatemalans nor Salvadorans faced a Holocaust did not mitigate the rabbi's emotional impulse toward outsider identification as a fulfillment and so assertion of Jewish identity.

There are hundreds if not thousands of such testimonies and stories. The general statistical evidence, to be sure, is also in accord with the view of liberalism as a Jewish lived religion and as assertion of Jewish identity against the pressures of assimilation. The most liberal Jews are not those who are most removed from Judaism (as many scholars have claimed), but those who exist between the two poles of communal orthodox commitment and assimilated non-affiliation, which tend to be more conservative. Thus, they are Jews, especially in the Reform movement, who are exposed to basic theological concepts and historical narratives, yet who are relaxed or basically secular in their observance – that is, the majority of American Jews. This is what Geoffrey B. Levey has described as the statistically "curvilinear" pattern to American Jewish political expression, which is partially represented in Figure 3 (Levey 1996: 397).

The conflation of liberalism with Jewishness has not been without its critics and challenges. First, most Orthodox Jews reject contemporary liberalism as antithetical to normative Judaism and regard it as insufficient to ensure Jewish continuity. Second, the outsiders with whom Jews have so often identified have tended to be more antisemitic than ostensible insiders. This was as true of the European working classes whom many European Jews regarded as fellow victims, outsiders, and hence allies, as it was of the African-Americans on whose behalf so many American Jews devoted so much energy and emotion (King and Weiner 2007: 60-67; Mühlberger 2003: 50, 79-80).[*] Jews have perceived themselves, as per their secularized theological self-definition and sacralized historical memory, as exiled and ostracized, whereas the unsuccessful have tended to view Jews as an elite because of their education and affluence.[**] Finally, Zionism undermines outsider identification, for it rejects or at least redefines exile, respecting power rather than powerlessness, and existing within history rather than beyond it. Indeed, as shown in Figure 4, there is an inverse relationship between Zionism and liberalism among American Jews. Zionism is an alternative to liberalism for the construction and expression of a Jewish identity. There is also a recurrent ideological tension between Zionism and contemporary liberalism.

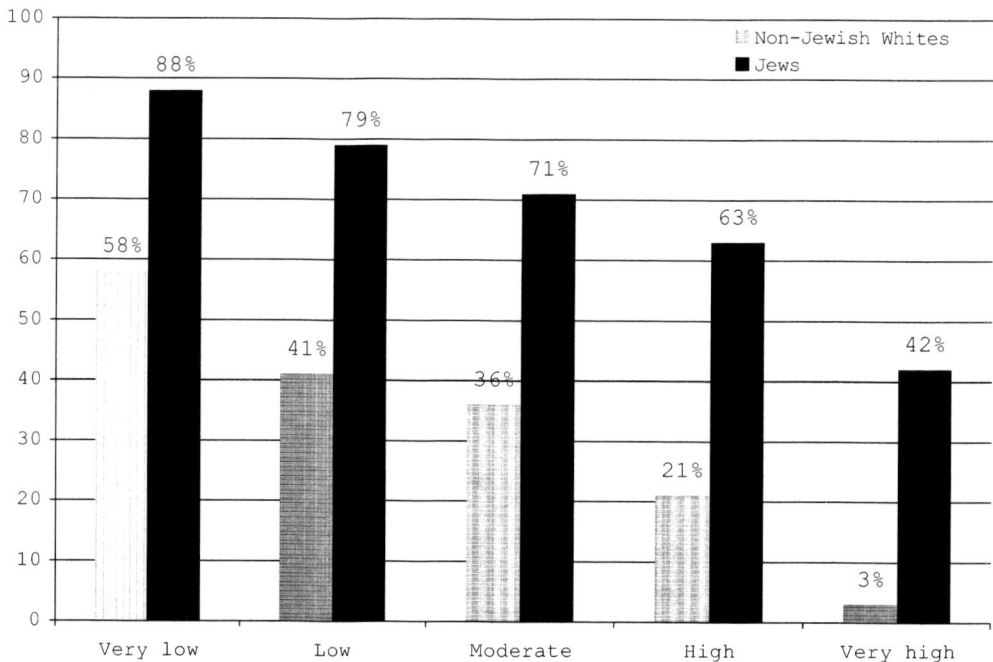

Source: Cohen, Abrams, and Veinstein 2008: 7-24.

Figure 4. Intention to vote for Obama, by importance of Israel (mean scores), by percentage.

---

[*] In the Polish provinces of imperial Russia, the detested tsarist government was often the only staying force between the Jews and the violently antisemitic, repressed Polish masses. See Weeks 1998: 233-249.

[**] The socialist movement in pre-WWI Austria-Hungary was never sure whether Jews were victims of capitalism or capitalist victimizers. Those who were of the latter persuasion often became proto-fascists in the form of Christian socialists. Wistrich 1982: 175-298.

Jewish resistance to assimilation has often been overlooked in the historiographical literature, which has tended to portray Jewish aspirations in the modern period as geared toward this very goal, often by an undue focus on German Jews and the German-Jewish experience. It is of course true that Jews have sought economic opportunity and cultural integration as well as the removal of antisemitism and discrimination from the public space. To seek to achieve these things, however, does not imply the desire for corporate dissolution. The American Jewish resistance to assimilation has been expressed in myriad ways, the most important of which may have been liberalism or more left-wing politics. As outsider identification, concern for the disadvantaged, and preoccupation with social justice, liberalism afforded secular or non-observant American Jews a vehicle for the expression of an identity that was distinctly informed by secularized theological concepts and a sacralized historical experience.[*]

The resistance to assimilation via liberalism has not been a complete success. Many authors have noted the gradual disappearance of the American Jewish community through intermarriage, indifference, and ignorance of Judaism (Dershowitz 1997). The strategy, however, has not been a complete failure. After all, "the Jews continue to maintain a measure of cohesion and identity in a nation whose other European ethnic groups are now largely indistinguishable" (Ginsberg 2004: 26). The very fact that Jews have retained a distinct political profile against all expectations is indicative of the strength of their attachment to their separate and unique identity.

REFERENCES

Abella, I. & Troper, H. (1991). *None Is Too Many: Canada and the Jews of Europe, 1933-1948*. Toronto: Lester Publishing.

Abrams, N. (2008). Kosher Beefcakes and Kosher Cheesecakes: Jews in Porn – An Overview. In N. Abrams (Ed.), *Jews and Sex* (147-168). Nottingham: Five Leaves.

Alexander, M. (2001). *Jazz Age Jews*. Princeton: Princeton University Press.

Babel, I. *The Complete Works of Isaac Babel*. N. Babel (Ed.). P. Constantine (Trans.). New York: W.W. Norton and Company.

Bauman, Z. (1996). Assimilation into Exile: The Jew as a Polish Writer. *Poetics Today, 17(4)*, 569-597.

Berkovitz, J. R. (1995). The French Revolution and the Jews: Assessing the Cultural Impact. *AJS Review, 20(1)*, 25-86.

Burgin, H. (1914). *History of the Jewish Workers Movement*. New York University: Archives of the Tamiment Library, in TAM 249, Box 1, Folder 1.

Cantor, N. (1995). *The Sacred Chain: A History of the Jews*. New York: Harper Perennial.

Cohen, S. M. (1984). *The 1984 National Survey of American Jews: Political and Social Outlooks*. New York: American Jewish Committee, Institute of Human Relations.

Cohen, S. M. (1989). *The Dimensions of American Jewish Liberalism*. New York, American Jewish Committee, Institute of Human Relations.

---

[*] Another has been ethnic wit and humour (Reik 1962). Another has been a repudiation of gentile manners as hypocrisy (Cuddihy 1974). Still another has been a rebellion against established sexual mores (Abrams 2008).

Cohen, S. M. & Abrams, S. & Veinstein J. (2008). *American Jews and the 2008 Presidential Election: As Democrat and Liberal as Ever?* New York: New York University Wagner, Berman Jewish Policy Archive.

Cohen, S. M. & Liebman, C.S. (1997). American Jewish Liberalism: Unraveling the Strands. *The Public Opinion Quarterly, 61(3)*, 405-430.

Cohn, W. (1958). The Politics of American Jews. In M. Sklare (Ed.), *The Jews: Social Patterns of an American Group* (614-626). Glencoe, IL: Free Press, 1958.

Coyne, D. (1986). Agenda Promotes Sanctuary Work – Rabbis on Speaking Tour. *Agenda, 19.* At New York University, Cooper Union: Archives of the Tamiment Library, in TAM 183, Box 13.

Cuddihy, J. M. (1974). *The Ordeal of Civility: Freud, Marx, Lévi-Strauss, and the Jewish Struggle with Modernity.* New York: Basic Books.

Dalin, D. G. (2004). At the Summit: Presidents, Presidential Appointments, and Jews. In L. S. Maisel (Eds.), *Jews in American Politics* (30-47). Lanham, MD: Rowman and Littlefield.

Dawidowicz, L. S. & Goldstein, L. J. (1974). The American Jewish Liberal Tradition. In M. Sklare (Ed.), *The Jewish Community in America* (285-300). New York: Behrman House.

Dershowitz, A. M. (1997). *The Vanishing American Jew: In Search of Jewish Identity for the Next Century.* Boston: Little Brown.

Deutscher, I. (1968). Who is a Jew?. In T. Deutscher (Ed.), *The Non-Jewish Jew and Other Essays.* London: Oxford University Press.

Dinnerstein, L. (1994). *Anti-Semitism in America.* New York: Oxford University Press.

Dollinger, M. (2000). *Quest for Inclusion: Jews and Liberalism in Modern America.* Princeton and Oxford: Princeton University Press.

Dubofsky, M. (1968). Success and Failure of Socialism in New York City, 1900-1918: A Case Study. *Labor History, 9(3)*, 361-375.

Endelman, T. M. (2002). *The Jews of Britain, 1656 to 2000.* Berkeley: University of California Press.

Feingold, H. L. (1987). American Jewish Liberalism and Jewish Response. *Contemporary Jewry, 9(1)*, 19-45.

Forman, I. N. (2004). The Politics of Minority Consciousness. In: L. S., Maisel (Eds.), *Jews in American Politics* (142-159). Lanham, MD: Rowman and Littlefield.

Frankel, J. (Eds.). (1991). *Jews and Messianism in the Modern Era: Metaphor and Meaning*: Vol. *12. Studies in Contemporary Jewry.* Oxford: Oxford University Press.

Fuchs, L. H. (1955). American Jews and the Presidential Vote. *American Political Science Review, 49(2)*, 385-401.

Fuchs, L. H. (1956). *The Political Behaviour of American Jews.* Glencoe, IL: Free Press.

Gelman, A. (2008). *Red State, Blue State, Rich State, Poor State: Why Americans Vote the Way They Do.* Princeton, NJ: Princeton University Press.

Ginsberg, B. (1993). *The Fatal Embrace: Jews and the State.* Chicago: Chicago University Press.

Ginsberg, B. (2004). Identity and Politics: Dilemmas of Jewish Leadership in America. In L. S. Maisel (Ed.), *Jews in American Politics.* Lanham, MD: Rowman and Littlefield.

Glaser, J. M. (1997). Toward an Explanation of the Racial Liberalism of American Jews. *Political Research Quarterly, 50(2)*, 437-458.

Goren, A. A. (1970). *New York Jews and the Quest for Community: The Kehillah Experiment,* 1908-1922. New York: Columbia University Press.

Greenberg, A. & Walk, K. D. (2004). Still Liberal After All These Years? In L. S. Maisel (Ed.), *Jews in American Politics* (162-193). Lanham, MD: Rowman and Littlefield.

Himmelfarb, M. (1969). Is American Jewry in Crisis? *Commentary*, March, 33-42.

Himmelfarb, M. (1985). Another Look at the Jewish Vote. *Commentary*, December, 39-44.

Howe, I. (1976). *World of Our Fathers: The Journey of East European Jews to America and the Life They Found and Made*. New York: Simon and Shuster.

Johnpoll, B. K. (1967). *The Politics of Futility: The General Jewish Workers Bund of Poland, 1917-1943*. Ithaca, NY: New York University Press.

Kahan, A. (1986). Economic Opportunity and Some Pilgrims' Progress: Jewish Immigrants from Eastern Europe in the United States, 1890-1914. *The Journal of Economic History*, *38(1)*, 235-251.

Kavon, E. (2009). Abraham Geiger and Abraham Isaac Kook: Messianism's Return to History. *Midstream*, *55(1)*, 19-23.

King, R. D. & Weiner, M. F. (2007). Group Position, Collective Threat, and American Anti-Semitism. *Social Problems*, *54(1)*, 47-77.

Kopstein, J. S. & Wittenberg, J. (2003). Who Voted Communist? Reconsidering the Social Bases of Radicalism in Interwar Poland. *Slavic Review*, *62(1)*, 87-109.

L. Dinnerstein, L. & Reimers, D. M. (1975). *Ethnic Americans: A History of Immigration and Assimilation*. New York: Dodd, Mead and Company.

Lerner, R. & Nagai, K. & Rothman, S. (1989). Marginality and Liberalism Among Jewish Elites. *The Public Opinion Quarterly.*, *53(4)*, 330-352.

Levey, G. B. (1996). The Liberalism of American Jews – Has It Been Explained? *British Journal of Political Science*, *26(3)*, 369-401.

Lichter, R. S. & Rothman, S. (1982). *Roots of Radicalism: Jews, Christians, and the New Left*. New York: Oxford University Press.

Lichter, R. S. & Rothman, S. (1981). Jews on the Left: The Student Movement Reconsidered. *Polity*, *14(2)*, 347-366.

Liebman, A. (1979). *Jews and the Left*. New York: John Wiley and Sons.

Liebman, C. S. (1973). *The Ambivalent American Jew: Politics, Religion and Family in American Jewish Life*. Philadelphia: Jewish Publication Society of America.

Lipset, S. M. (1990). A Unique People in an Exceptional Country. *Society*, *28(1)*, 4-13.

Lipset, S. M. & Raab, E. (1995). *Jews and the New American Scene*. Cambridge, MA: Harvard University Press.

Litt, E. (1961). Ethnic Status and Political Perspectives. *Midwest Journal of Political Science*, *5(3)*, 276-283.

Medoff, M. B. (1981). Note: Some Differences between the Jewish and General White Male Population in the United States. *Jewish Social Studies*, *43(1)*, Winter 1981, 75-80.

Mendelsohn, E. (1983). *The Jews of East Central Europe between the World Wars*. Bloomington: Indiana University Press.

Mendelsohn, E. (1993). *On Modern Jewish Politics*. New York: Oxford University Press.

Mendes-Flohr, P. (1991). *Divided Passions: Jewish Intellectuals and the Experience of Modernity*. Detroit: Wayne State University Press.

Mendes-Flohr, P. & Reinharz, J. (1995). *The Jew in the Modern World: A Documentary History*. Oxford: Oxford University Press.

Mühlberger, D. (2003). *The Social Bases of Nazism, 1919-1933*. Cambridge, Cambridge University Press.

Polonsky, A. (1997). The Bund in Polish Political Life, 1935-1939 [1988]. In E. Mendelsohn (Eds.), *Essential Papers on Jews and the Left* (166-197). New York: New York University Press.

Pulzer, P. (1992). *Jews and the German State: The Political History of a Minority, 1848-1933*. Oxford: Blackwell.

Rawidowicz, S. (1986). *Israel, the Every-Dying People and Other Essays*. B. C. I. Ravid (Eds.). Cranbury, NJ: Associated University Presses.

Reik, T. (1962). *Jewish Wit*. New York: Gamut Press.

Schatz, J. (2004). Jews and the Communist Movement in Interwar Poland. *Dark Times, Dire Decisions: Jews and Communism*: Vol. *20. Studies in Contemporary Jewry*. J. Frankel (Ed.). Oxford: Oxford University Press.

Shapiro, M. B. (1999). *Between the Yeshiva World and Modern Orthodoxy: The Life and Works of Rabbi Jehiel Jacob Weinberg*. Oxford: Littman Library of Jewish Civilization.

Sorin, G. (1985). *The Prophetic Minority: American Jewish Immigrant Radicals, 1880-1920*. Bloomington: Indiana University Press.

Spinrad, W. (1957-1958). New York's Third Party Voters. *The Public Opinion Quarterly, 21(4)*, 548-551.

Staub, M. E. (2002). *Torn at the Roots: The Crisis of Jewish Liberalism in Postwar America*. New York: Columbia University Press.

Trigano, S. (1990). The French Revolution and the Jews. *Modern Judaism, 10(2)*, 171-190.

Weeks, T. R. (1998). Polish-Jewish Relations 1903-1914: The View from the Chancellery. *Canadian Slavonic Papers, 40(3/4)*, 233-249.

Whitfield, S. J. (1986). The Jewish Vote. *Virginia Quarterly Review, 62(1)*, 1-20.

Wistrich, R. S. (1982). *Socialism and the Jews: The Dilemmas of Assimilation in Germany and Austria-Hungary*. London and Toronto: Associated University Presses.

Wistrich, R. S. (1976). *Revolutionary Jews from Marx to Trotsky*. London and New York: Harrap, Barnes and Noble.

In: Race and Ethnicity   ISBN: 978-1-60692-099-2
Editor: Jonathan K. Crennan, pp. 335-348   © 2010 Nova Science Publishers, Inc.

Chapter 15

ETHNIC DIFFERENCES IN CULTURAL AND FAMILY PROCESSES IN MEXICAN, CHICANO, CUBAN, PUERTO RICAN AND CENTRAL SOUTH AMERICAN FAMILIES LIVING IN THE UNITED STATES

Judith C. Baer and MiSung Kim

Rutgers, The State University of New Jersey, New Brunswick, NJ 08902, USA

ABSTRACT

Contemporary research on families and their adolescent offspring has been shaped by contextualism which underscores the importance of phenomena such as ethnicity, social class and family processes. Given current demographic trends, especially for Latinos, contextualism and the topic of ethnicity have gained impetus among researchers. Latinos currently comprise the largest group of immigrants in the United States, representing approximately 44 million people, with Mexicans alone representing 64% of this number (Census Bureau, 2009). Latinos are not only the fastest growing ethnic group, they are also relatively young. In the two decades beginning in 1980 and ending in 1999, the proportion of Latino children in the United States increased from 9% to 16%. This represents the highest growth rate of any racial or ethnic group (Hobbs & Stoops, 2002; Ramirez & De la Cruz, 2002).

In light of these trends and the importance of research on Latinos, this chapter explores the study of culture in family processes in Latino families with adolescent offspring. We are especially interested in within group Latino diversity and subgroup differences on familismo a phenomenon central to Latino family life. The importance of familismo is underscored by its protective mechanisms. For example it is believed to provide a buffering effect for high stress situations such as those that occur during acculturation and adjustment to a new country as well as stress related to developmental change typical during adolescence. Given the importance of familismo as a protective factor and ethnic signifier, this chapter explores Latino subgroup differences and changes in aspects of familismo which may occur as a function of acculturation and generational status.

LATINO POPULATIONS IN THE U.S.

Beginning in 2003 the Latino population became the largest minority in the U.S. (CDC, 2009). This increase in population consists of immigrants from all of the primary countries of origin. There is a marked difference in the age distribution of those who were U.S. born and those who were born outside of the U.S. Native born have a much younger age distribution. Nearly 20% of the U.S. born Latinos were less than 10 years of age, while about 2% of the foreign born were in that group. Immigrants tend to be older and in the work force. Future projections for 2050 indicate that the Latino population will triple, while the non-Hispanic White population will increase by 8% (CDC, 2009).

The overall economic status of the Latino population living in the U.S. is lower than that of Euro-Americans. For example, for Latino men age 65 and over, 21% live in poverty compared to 6% of Euro-American men. For women age 65 and over, the percent in poverty is 26% for the Latinos, and 12% for Euro-Americans. Measures of wealth accumulation show large average differences, with Euro-American households (male or couple-headed) of over $300,000 while those of Mexican origin show less than $100,000. Moreover, recent data from the U.S. Census Bureau (2005) indicates that the percent of the population (age 51 – 61) with no health insurance is less than 10% for Euro-Americans, and more than 40% for those of Mexican origin.

A number of studies have suggested that Latinos, who reside in the United States, are at increased risk for mental health problems. According to the Hispanic Health and Nutrition Examination Survey (HHANES), the Epidemiologic Catchment Area Study (ECA), and the National Co-morbidity Survey (NCS), Latinos are at high risk for depressive episodes within their lifetimes. According to NCS 17.7% of Latinos will suffer from major depression in their lifetime (Hough, Landsverk & Karno, 1987). Data from the Mexican American Prevalence and Services Survey (MAPSS), when compared to eight other sites of the International Consortium of Psychiatric Epidemiology (ICPE), demonstrate that Mexican American females and males ranked first and second, respectively, in likelihood to have reported a major depressive episode within the previous 12 months.

These trends generalize to Latino youth as well. A meta-analysis conducted by Twenge and Nolen-Hoeksema (2002) reported that youth from various Latino subgroups had significantly elevated scores on commonly used indices compared with their peers who were of European American decent. Additionally, epidemiological studies of Mexican American adolescents have reported high rates of depression and anxiety for this group compared with Non-Hispanic white adolescents (Roberts, Roberts, & Chen, 1997; Swanson, Linskey, Quintero-Salinas, Pumariega, & Holzer, 1992; Glover, Pumariega, Holzer, Wise, & Rodriguez, 1999).

While these findings are disturbing, there are a number of questions about the quality of the prevalence estimates. It remains unclear whether theories about the etiology of mental illness as well as symptom presentation, developed with primarily Euro-American samples, apply in the same way to Latino groups. These Euro-centric theories shape what is counted as disease. As noted by Weiss and Kleinman in 1988, the development and expression of internalizing disorders is shaped and affected by cultural context. Thus, the experience of the phenomenon and the expression of symptoms will vary across cultures and ethnic groups.

This has resulted in problems with both over estimating and underestimating along with misdiagnosing data reporting (National Council of LaRaza, 2005).

There are also a number of barriers which affect both the diagnosis and treatment of Latinos, especially those who have limited English proficiency. Latinos are vulnerable to the challenges of accessing medical and psychiatric care, and they are more likely to have greater difficulties communicating about problems with a provider (National Council of LaRaza, 2005). At times language barriers impede Spanish-speaking Latinos from accurately understanding instructions and written information from a doctor's office. According to The Commonwealth Fund (2003) nearly half of Spanish-speaking Latinos had problems communicating with their physicians or health care providers and close to half also reported difficulty understanding instructions and written information, much of which was provided only in English.

Furthermore, people from different cultures express symptoms of depression in a variety of ways. Unlike their Euro-American counterparts, Latinos generally experience depression somatically in the form of bodily aches and pains such as stomach aches, backaches, or headaches. Depression is often described as feeling nervous or tired (HealthyPlace, 2004). This somatic symptomotology is known to occur in cultures which have high degrees of collectivism. It is postulated that somatic symptoms are shaped in part by the cultural value of simpatia defined as agreeableness, politeness, and respect of others (Varela et al., 2004).

In sum, these trends, the large population growth and economic disadvantage all have important implications for Latino health and family functioning. While emigrants who leave their country tend to be healthier than those left behind, it is critical to understand how this status can be maintained. So studies concerning ways in which new immigrants can maintain mental as well as physical health are imperative.

ACCULTURATION AND IMMIGRATION

Acculturation has a long history in the social and behavioral sciences and most scholars agree that it consists of multidimensional, complex social and psychological processes at both the individual and family levels (Cabrera et al., 2006; Miranda et al., 2000). There are important contextual influences as well such as differences in socio-political contexts and situational factors in both the exiting and host cultures. While there are changes in the cultural patterns of both the host and the immigrating groups, studies generally focus on modifications and adaptations of indigenous practices in response to host culture exposure (Rumbalt, 1994).

A distinguishing feature of Latino populations is wide variation of immigration and acculturation experiences. Since culture shapes beliefs and behaviors it is a key determinant of social and psychological resources. The transition of Latino populations from one culture to another provides an avenue to describe and understand the processes and consequences of cultural change. Outcomes of immigration vary in degrees of both benefit and harm.

Acculturative stress and the stress experienced upon immigration to the U.S. is reported to be pervasive, and have a life-long influence on Latinos' psychological adjustment, decision-making abilities, occupational functioning, and overall physical and mental health (Smart & Smart, 1995). Complicating acculturative stress are factors such as language barriers, lack of coping resources, and loss of family cohesion (Miranda & Matheny, 2000).

Cultural distance often contributes to a sense of alienation and isolation, leading to acculturative stress and depression (Bhugra, 2003).

Although data show that immigrants tend to fare better than their non-immigrant peers in terms of mental health issues, the stress experienced by those who are separated from their families and the subsequent loss of social support is significant. Latinos' experience of acculturative stress has been associated with fatalistic thinking (Ross, Mirowsky & Cockerham, 1983), decreased feelings of self-efficacy, depression, and low social interest (Miranda, 1995). The acculturative stress which recent immigrants suffer is believed to be related to major changes in lifestyle, and environment, loss of social support (Gonzalez, Haan & Hinton, 2001), as well as the effects of marginalization, a concomitant of living within a host culture.

A related complicating factor is the degree to which immigrants are expected to gradually relinquish their cultural values and adapt to those of the host culture. When acculturation is interpreted as a one-dimensional and unidirectional process, it more accurately resembles assimilation. A key issue in the conceptualization of acculturation has been dimensionality, and scholars have generally adopted a bidimensional or multidimensional perspective. Such a perspective consists of dimensions such as assimilation, integration, separation and marginalization (Berry, 2003; Ryder et al., 2000). Padilla's (1980b) definitions of acculturation focused on the importance of cultural awareness and ethnic loyalty. By cultural awareness he means the knowledge of one's cultural heritage, which includes the values, language, and life styles. Ethnic loyalty refers to the preference for the native culture over the host culture. Padilla suggests that cultural knowledge is cognitive and preference for one's ethnic group is affective. Phinney (1990) also defines an affective component to acculturation as evidenced by the strengths of feelings about one's ethnic group and the host society. A core feature to understanding the acculturative processes is the level of preference a person has for his or her native heritage and identity versus preference for the host culture (Berry, 2003).

Research on the complex processes of acculturation, including the components of cultural adaptation is important to study. These processes influence the psychological consequences of living in a society with different norms. Studies about the ways in which they operate are important because illumination of the dynamics of change can lead to the identification of modifiable factors which can be the target of interventions to ameliorate or maintain positive functioning.

THE ROLE OF AUTONOMY IN THEORIES OF ADOLESCENT DEVELOPMENT

Autonomy is an important construct in theories of adolescent development. Studies of adolescence have examined the role of emotional distancing from parents as a part of the adolescents' move toward greater autonomy, although it is well understood that the dynamic emotional bonds between adolescents and their parents consist of a set of complex interrelations (Schmitz & Baer, 2001). Historically there have been a number of debates stemming from conceptual issues about whether emotional distancing from parents was a form of autonomy or unhealthy detachment from the family. The concept of emotional distancing from parents was based on the work of Douvan and Adelson (1966) and Peter Blos (1962), theorists who were grounded in drive theory and who conceptualized adolescent development as a process whereby the adolescent reduces parental dependency and relinquishes omnipotent ideas about parents in favor of more mature and balanced ones (Blos, 1962; Douvan & Adelson, 1966). It was postulated that libido, which was invested in the parents prior to adolescence was withdrawn from the parents so that it could be reinvested in the service of new family formation.

Other theorists, such as Ryan and Lynch (1989) proposed that adolescent development was facilitated by parental attachment, emotional closeness and a sense of support. Detachment was considered harmful and a maladaptive reluctance by the adolescent to rely on parents. They concluded, "The more 'emotional autonomy' teenagers or young adults express, the less connected or secure they feel within the family, the less they experience their parents as conveying love and understanding, and the less they report willingness to draw upon parental resources" (Ryan & Lynch, 1989, p. 353). Thus detachment represented a pseudo independence which deprived the adolescents with needed parental support and guidance.

For Latino adolescence, these concepts of emotional distancing and independence so heavily emphasized in the U.S. host culture may be highly incongruent with the Latino value of familismo. Such distancing would be especially problematic for adolescents, who are highly stressed due to acculturating and at the same time experiencing the stressful biopsychosocial changes inherent in puberty and development. For Latinos, the press for adaptation to values of independence in the host culture would be diametrically opposed to the strong familial and intergenerational values of familismo. Furthermore, both adolescent development and the acculturative process involve risk and protective pathways that involve aspects of intergenerational relational processes. Theories that define adolescent psychosocial development as a process of emotional distance and independence have been debated by scholars (Chilman, 1993; Harrison, Wilson, Pine, Chan, & Buriel, 1990), and the United States has been characterized as being preoccupied with self-reliance and independence when contrasted with other countries especially those that are more collective (Marin, 1993; Silverberg & Gondoli, 1996).

A review of the empirical literature shows that there has been a disruption in the adaptive functioning of parents as well as in the power structure in some acculturating families (Santisteban et al., 1997; Santisteban, Szapocznik, Kurtines, & Perez-Vidal, 1996). At the same time, high levels of family bonding have been shown to provide important protection from the stresses related to both adolescent development and acculturation.

Ethnicity and Familismo

Ethnicity involves a sense of belongingness with a group of people that share a common historical origin, common behaviors and values. Both ethnic and minority identity have as their basis the grouping or banding together, for promoting a sense of connectedness to others for comfort and for survival. Minority cultures are often described as relational cultures because their members characteristically give significant importance to the quality of relationships with significant others, especially family members. Relational factors present nuanced, unspoken powerful messages that influence behavior. Cultural values such as familismo and level of acculturation often operate as moderators or mediators of the effect between an environmental condition and a health or mental health outcome.

Familismo is a cognitive construct which represents an emotional support system for individual family members and concerns the importance an individual places on the family, as well as dependence or reliance on others and an obligation to others (Marin, 1993). Familismo consists of at least three dimensions: structural, behavioral, and attitudinal (Valenzuela & Dornbusch, 1994). The structural dimension consists of the spatial and social boundaries within which behaviors occur and attitudes acquire meaning (Valenzuela & Dornbusch, 1994). The presence or absence of nuclear and extended family define these boundaries. The behavioral dimension of familism consists of the behaviors associated with feelings and attitudes about the family (Sabogal, Marin, Otero-Sabogal, & Marin, 1987). This dimension is signified by behaviors such as visiting family members and maintaining telephone contact. The attitudinal dimension was first defined in the sociological literature and is often referred to as familialism, family solidarity, family integration, or intergenerational solidarity (Lugo Steidel & Contreras, 2003). Attitudinal familismo theoretically aligns with attitudes towards family members (Cuellar, Arnold, & Gonzalez, 1995), specifically to feelings of loyalty to the family, solidarity, and attachment among family members (Alvarez, 2007; Cuellar, Arnold, & Gonzalez, 1995; Keefe, 1980; Marin, 1993). Attitudinal familism includes dependence on other family members for emotional support, along with a sense of responsibility and obligation to other (Cuellar, Arnold, Gonzalez, 1995). In sum it is a normative commitment to family members and to family relationships, which supersedes the individual (Luna et al., 1996).

Aims

We conducted a small study on the relationship between acculturation and levels of family caring and communication by Latino subgroups. We hypothesized that the acculturation process would be different for Puerto Ricans because they are U.S. citizens by birth, although they have a very dynamic ethnic milieu. We also thought that Cubans would be different because they have a higher socioeconomic status in general of all the Latino groups. Another hypothesis was that levels of familismo would decline with time in the U.S. such that first generation Latinos would have the higher levels than second or third generation across all groups.

METHODOLOGY

Sample and Study Design

Data used in this study were from Waves I and Waves III of The Longitudinal Study of Adolescent Health (Add Health) which encompassed data collected between 1994 and 1995 (Wave 1) and 2001 and 2002 (Wave III). The primary sampling frame consisted of systematic sampling and implicit stratification of 80 high schools selected as representative of US schools with respect to region of the country, urbanicity, size, type, and ethnicity. Eligible high schools included an 11th grade and enrolled more than 30 students. More than 70 percent of the originally sampled high schools participated. Each school that declined to participate was replaced by a school within the stratum.

Participating high schools identified feeder schools, which included a 7th grade and sent at least five graduates to that high school. There were 132 schools in the core study. We used the in-home samples which consisted of a nationally representative sample of adolescents in grades 7 through 12 in the US in the 1994-95 school year. Students in each school were stratified by grade and sex. About 17 students were randomly chosen from each stratum so that a total of approximately 200 adolescents were selected from each of the 80 pairs of schools to equal the total core sample (N = 12,105). The Latino sample consisted of a special oversampled group consisting of Mexican-Americans (n = 1,702), Cubans (n = 538), Puerto Ricans (n = 633), Central/South American (n = 403), Chicano (n = 152), Hispanic other (n = 320). For information about the parents, we used the Parent Questionnaire which consisted of a parent, mostly the resident mother of each adolescent respondent. The parent completed an interviewer-assisted, op-scanned questionnaire. Table 1 shows the Sociodemographic descriptors of the sample.

Analyses

To determine level of acculturation, we conducted a Latent Class Analysis (LCA). Acculturation is a complicated process and difficult to measure. We conceptualized acculturation as latent because latent variables are not observed directly, but are studied via their manifestations or observed indicators. The basic premise is that the covariation actually observed among the manifest variables is due to each observed variable's relationship to the latent variable such that the latent variable "explains" the relationships between the observed variables (McCutcheon, 1987). The latent class probabilities describe the distribution of classes (levels) of the latent variable. There are two important aspects of the latent class probabilities: the number of classes and the relative sizes of these classes. Thus, for example, if the latent variable has two classes, the population can be described as being either two "types" or two levels of an underlying (latent) continuum. The relative size of the classes provides information for the interpretation of the latent class probabilities. For example, the population may be relatively evenly distributed among the classes or some of the classes may represent relatively large segments of the population while other classes represent relatively small segments. The conditional probabilities are comparable to the factor loading in factor analysis. Within each of the latent classes, the conditional probabilities indicate whether observations in a class are likely or unlikely to have characteristics of each of the observed variables (McCutcheon, 1987).

We considered the latent class analysis to be exploratory because we several measures which we believed are parts of a common complex. The conditional probabilities represent a measure of the degree of association between each of the observed variables and each of the latent classes. The conditional probabilities indicate the probability that an individual in a latent class will score a particular way on an observed measure. Therefore, the conditional probabilities provide a way to interpret the nature of the classes of the latent variable.

We then used the classes to predict the levels of communication and caring adolescents' reported about their relationship with their parents. Using an ethnic-homogeneous Latino group consisting of individuals who self identified as Mexican, Chicano, Cuban Puerto Rican, Central/South American, and Other ((consisting of parents one of which was from one subgroup (i.e., Mexican) and the parent was from another group (i.e., Central/South American) or the country of origin was not listed)) we attempted to describe the characteristics of each subgroup.

Measures

Observed indicators of acculturation that we used to determine probabilities of class membership were: language used with family (Spanish or English); language used with friends; buy music in non-English; Use media in non-English. First, second and third generation was identified with a nominal variable with three categories. Aspects of familismo were captured using the following indicators: How close to you feel to your mother? How much do you think she cares about you? How close do you feel to your father? How much do you think he cares about you? These items were assessed using a 5-point Likert scale with 1 = not close at all to 5 = very close. Did you talk with your mother about someone you're dating? Did you talk to your mother about a personal problem you're having? Did you have a serious argument with your mother about your behavior? Did you talk to your mother about your school work? Did you talk about other things you're doing in school? Did you talk with your father about someone you're dating? Did you talk to your father about a personal problem you're having? Did you have a serious argument with your father about your behavior? Did you talk to your father about your school work? Respondents answer yes or no to these items.

Results

Characteristics of the sample are shown in Table 1. Given that the figures represent U.S. demographic characteristics of the Latino groups, Mexican-Americans are the largest group in all three generations followed by Central/South Americans in the first generation category and Puerto Ricans in the third generation category. Most first generation speak Spanish with their family and as is shown, and well documented, this declines significantly by the third generation. From first to third generation almost all of the groups speak English with their friends.

As stated earlier, we attempted to capture levels of acculturation by hypothesizing a latent factor. We then determined the classes via posterior probabilities of responses from the sample. This method is radically different from imposing categories onto the data. What were the characteristics of the two types of classes of respondents identified in our analysis? The first class, the more acculturated group consisted of 52% of the Mexicans, 72% of the Chicanos, 25% of the Cubans, 83% of the Puerto Ricans, 46% of the Central/South Americans and 60% of the Hispanic Other group (see Table 2). Most of the adolescents in class 1 reported that they spoke English with their family, and English with their friends.

However, the Chicano group in class 1 reported that they spoke English with friends and Spanish with family. Also, most adolescents in class 1 did not listen often to non-English music, except for the Chicanos and Central/South Americans, who reported that they listened more often to non-English music. For class 2, the less acculturated group spoke Spanish with their family and English with their friends, except for the Chicanos, who spoke English with their family and English with their friends. Also all of the less acculturated stated that the often listened to non-English music except for Chicanos.

When we entered the variables about caring for family members and levels of communication the less acculturated class predicted slightly higher scores, but the differences were not statistically significant. We also examined how much control parents gave to their children about who to make friends with. As is shown in the graphs, the trends were similar and parents gave the most control by the third generation with first generation most often exerting the most control.

Finally, we examined religious or spiritual experiences that adolescents' reported. Spirituality is known to be important to Latinos and is also considered an important buffer for the stress and strain of life. Although Roman Catholicism is the dominant religion throughout most of Latin America, it varies in practice and form by region and is mixed with other traditions. This variety is exemplified for example, in the Virgin of Guadalupe who is an important icon in Mexico, but is of little interest to Cubans or Puerto Ricans. Additionally some Latinos believe in the evil eye, miracles, faith healing, and witchcraft. Santeria, the worship of African gods clothed in Catholic dogma, is popular with Cubans and Puerto Ricans, but not Mexicans. Latinos in the United States also show variation in preference for patron saints, special days of observance as well as ritual. While most Latinos in Latin American and the U.S. practice Catholicism, evangelical Protestantism has gained popularity.

As is displayed in Table 3, our data indicate that about 24% of the sample reported having a significant religious or spiritual experience that changed their life. This trend was fairly stable across the different subgroups. About 6% of the respondents reported being involved in organized religion and this trend was consistent across the three generations and across gender.

DISCUSSION

This has been a study of Latino subgroups who reside in the United States. These groups often straddle two cultures both of which are composed of highly variable systems of meanings which shape life and the meanings of events (Rohner, 1984). According to Triandis (1989) subjective culture includes elements such as social norms, roles, beliefs, and values. These include family roles, communication patterns, affective styles, and values regarding personal control, individualism, collectivism, spirituality and religiosity. Given the pervasiveness of these cultural factors in shaping life it is easy to see what a difficult and overwhelming process it is to be confronted with new, varying and at times incongruent cultural referents.

While we expected to find significant subgroup differences, our findings suggest that there are probably more within group differences than between group differences in the subgroups. Previous research also supports this conclusion. Studies indicate that differences between individuals within the same group account for more than 84% of the variance than between group differences (Zuckerman, 1990). Ethnicity is associated with culture and it is generally used in reference to groups such as those in our study that share a common nationality, culture, or language. While cultural background can be a determinant of ethnic identity or affiliation, ethnic group membership also determines culture (Betancourt, & Lopez 1993). It is a well-known fact that culture is transmitted intergenerationally in families and ethnic groups. According to Berry (1995) ethnic groups interact with each other and consequently influence each other. Therefore, he says that it is important in comparative studies of ethnic groups to identify and measure cultural variables which are attributed to observed differences before saying that the differences are due to culture. This is especially important in the United States because interethnic communications occur frequently through the mass media and such communications can be confounding. This is probably the case throughout Latin America as well.

Other significant confounders of culture and ethnicity are socioeconomic factors. Prevalence studies which indicated that Latinos had more significant levels of depressive symptoms than other ethnic groups were shown to be insignificant when controlling for SES-related variables such as employment and family income. This led some researchers to conclude that ethnicity and culture have little significance on rates of depression, whereas economic strain is very significant (Frerich, Aneshensel, & Clark, 1981).

On the other hand when controlling for SES, the variance due to culture is also removed and this may lead to the erroneous conclusion that culture does not play a significant role. Moreover, groups within different social strata also generate norms and values. So when social classes are compared within the same ethnic groups, cultural elements typical of the social strata may be attributed to SES when in fact they are subcultural elements.

There were a number of limitations to our study. Given that this was a secondary analysis, we did not directly assess cultural values or beliefs nor did we directly assess acculturative stress. Therefore, it is difficult to establish precision about the heterogeneity of our sample between these variables. Moreover, the analyses were cross sectional and have temporal limitations

Cultural meanings influence what events count as problems or illness and these meanings also influence contextual factors. Thus the role of culture in the study of healthy functioning and psychopathology cannot be understated. Large epidemiological studies which have reported high prevalence rates of mental disorders among Latinos has come under criticism following subsequent examinations of cultural influences (Lopez et al, 1992). Additionally clinicians have documented that Latinos frequently have the experience of hearing voices, which is reflective of a high degree of spirituality or religiosity and is not indicative of psychosis (Abad, Ramos, & Boyce, 1977; Torrey, 1972). Based on these clinical observations, Lopez et al. (1992) proposed that relative to Euro-Americans Mexicans report more evidence of auditory hallucinations, a symptom associated with schizophrenia. Moreover, they hypothesized that these were due to religiosity typical of this ethnic group. Consistent with their hypotheses, significant differences were found among Latinos of Mexican origin (U.S. born and Mexican born) and Euro-Americans. With regard to auditory hallucinations, more Mexican-born Latinos reported this symptom (2.3%) than U.S. born Latinos (1.6%). One conclusion was that auditory hallucinations are related to spiritual beliefs independent of organized religious affiliation. In sum these findings are consistent with the idea that cultural elements or values and beliefs that individuals hold shape the manner in which psychological distress and disorders are manifest.

On a final note, we assumed that because the groups were from distinct countries that they differed from each other on key cultural dimension. This however, was not the case.

REFERENCES

Abad, V., Ramos, J. & Boyce, E. (1977). Clinical issues in the psychiatric treatment of Puerto Ricans. In E. Padilla & A. Padilla (Eds.), *Transcultural psychiatry: An Hispanic perspective* (Monograph No. 4, 23-24). Los Angeles: Spanish Speaking Mental Health Research Center.

Adelson, J. (1966). *The adolescent experience.* New York: Wiley.

Alvarez, L. (2007). Derecho u Obligacion? Parents' and youths' understanding of parental legitimacy in a Mexican origin familial context. *Hispanic Journal of Behavioral Sciences, 29(2),* 192-208.

Betancourt, H. & Lopez, S. R. (1993). The study of culture, ethnicity, and race in American Psychology. *American Psychologist, 48(6),* 29-637.

Berry, J. W. (2003). Conceptual approaches to acculturation. In: K. M., Chun, P. B. Organista, & G. Marin, (Eds.), *Acculturation.* Washington, DC: American Psychological Association.

Bhugra, D. (2003). Migration and depression. *Scandinavica Acta Psychiatrica, 108(418),* 67-72.

Blos, P. (1962). *On adolescence: A psychoanalytic interpretation.* Glencoe, IL: Free Press.

Buriel, R. (1993). Childrearing orientations in the Mexican-American families: The influence of generation and sociocultural factors. *Journal of Marriage and Family, 55,* 987-1000.

Cabrera N. J., West H., Shannon, J. D. & Brooks-Gunn, J. (2006). Parental interactions with Latino infants: Variation by country of origin and English proficiency. *Child Development, 77,* 1190-1207.

Centers of Disease Control. Hispanics in the U.S., Puerto Rico, and U.S. Virgin Islands: Issued June 2009. Population Division Working Paper No. 84.

Chilman, C. S. (1993). Hispanic families in the United States: Research perspectives. In H.P. McAdoo (Ed.), *Family ethnicity: Strength in diversity* (141-163). Newbury Park: Sage.

Cuellar, I. A., Arnold, B. & Gonzalez, G. (1995). Cognitive referents of acculturation: Assessment of cultural constructs in Mexican-Americans. *Journal of Community Psychology, 23,* 339-356.

Frerichs, R. R., Aneshensel, C. S. & Clark, V. A. (1981). Prevalence of depression in Los Angeles County. *American Journal of Epidemiology, 113,* 691-699.

Glover, S. P., Pumariega, A. J., Holzer, C. E. III, Wise, B. K. & Rodriguez, M. (1999). Anxiety symptomatology in Mexican-American adolesdents. *Journal of Child and Family Studies,* 47-57.

Gonzalez, H. M., Haan, M. N. & Hinton, L. (2001). Acculturation and the prevalence of depression in older Mexican Americans: Baseline results on the Sacramento area Latino Study on Aging. *Journal of the American Geriatrics Society, 49(7),* 948-953.

Harrison, A. O., Wilson, M. N., Pine, C. J., Chan, S. Q. & Buriel, R. (1990). Family ecologies of ethnic minority children. *Child Development, 61*, 347-362.

Healthy Place (2004). *Depression Community Fact Sheet.* Retrieved on July 8, 2009. http://www.healthyplace.com/communities/Depression/index.asp.

Hobbs, F. & Stoops, N. (2002). Demographic trends in the 20th century. U.S. Census Bureau, Census 2000 special reports, Series CENSR-4 Retrieved July 4, 2009 from the World Wide Web: http//:www.census.gov/prod/2002pubs/censr-4.pdf.

Hough, R. L., Landsverk, .A. & Karno, M. (1987). Utilization of health and mental health services by Los Angeles Mexican-American and non-Latino whites. *Archives of General Psychiatry, 44*, 702-709.

Keefe, S. (1980). Acculturation and the extended family among urban Mexican Amerians. In A. M. (Eds.), *Acculturation: Theory, models, and some new findings* (85-110). Boulder, CO: Westview.

Lopez, S. R., Hurwicz, M., Karno, M. & Telles, C. A. (1992). Schizophrenic and manic symptoms in a community sample: A sociocultural analysis. Unpublished manuscript.

Lugo Steidel, A. G. & Contreras, J. M. (2003). A new familism scale for use with Latino populations. *Hispanic Journal of Behavioral Sciences, 25*, 312-330.

Marin, G. (1993). Influence of acculturation on familialism and self-identification among Hispanics. In M. B. (Eds.), *Ethnic identity: Formation and transmission among Hispanics and other minorities* (181-196). New York: State University of New York Press.

Miranda, A. O. (1995). Adlerian life styles and acculturation as predictors of the mental health of Hispanic adults. Unpublished doctoral dissertation. Georgia State University, Atlanta.

Miranda, A. O. & Matheny, K. B. (2000). Socio-psychological predictors of acculturative stress among Latino adults. *Journal of Mental Health Counseling, 22(4)*, 306-317.

McCutcheon, A. L. (1987). *Latent Class Analysis*: A Sage University paper #64. Newbury Park: Sage.

Padilla, A. M. (1980). The role of cultural awareness and ethnic loyalty in acculturation. In: A. M. Padilla (Eds.), *Acculturation theory: Models and some new findings.* 47-84. Boulder, CO: Westview.

Phinney, J. S. (1991). Ethnic identity and self-esteem: A review and integration. *Hispanic Journal of Behavioral Sciences, 13(2)*, 193-203.

Ramirez, R. R. & D la Cruz, G. P. (2002). *The Hispanic population in the United States: March* 2002. pp20-545. Washington, DC: U.S. Bureau of Census, 2003.

Roberts, R. R., Roberts, C. R. & Chen, Y. R. (1997). Ethnocultural differences in prevalence of adolescent depression. *Journal of Community Psychology, 46*, 95-110.

Rohner, R. P. (1984). Toward a conception of culture for cross-cultural psychology. *Journal of Cross-Cultural Psycholgy, 15*, 111-138.

Ross, C. E., Mirowsky, J. & Cockerham, W. C. (1983). Social class, Mexican culture, and fatalism. Their effects on psychological distress. *American Journal of Community Psychology, 11*, 383-399.

Rumbaut, R. G. (1994). The crucible within: Ethnic identity, self-esteem, and segmented assimilation among children of immigrants. *International Migration Review, 28(4)*, 748-794.

Ryan, R. M. & Lynch, J. H. (1989). Emotional autonomy versus detachment: Revisiting the vicissitudes of adolescence and early adulthood. *Child Development, 60*, 340-356.

Ryder, A. G., Alden, P. E. & Paulhus, D. L. (2000). Is acculturation unidimensional or bidimensional? A head-to-head comparison in the prediction of personality, self-identity, and adjustment. *Journal of Personality and Social Psychology, 79*, 49-65.

Sabogal, F., Marin, G., Otero-Sabogal, R. VanOss Marin, B. B. & Perez-Stable, E. J. (1987). Latino familism and acculturation: What changes and what doesn't? *Hispanic Journal of Behavioral Sciences, 9*, 397-412.

Santisteban, D. A., Coatsworth, J. D., Perez-Vidal, A., Mitrani, V., Jean-Gilles, M. & Szapoeznik, J. (1997). Brief structural strategic family therapy with African American and Hispanic high risk youth: A report of outcome. *Journal of Community Psychology, 25*, 453-471.

Santisteban, D. A., Szapocznik, J., Kurtines, W. & Perez-Vidal, A. (1996). Efficacy of interventions for engaging youth/families into treatment and some factors that may contribute to differential effectiveness. *Journal of Family Psychology, 10*, 35-44.

Schmitz, M. F. & Baer, J. C. (2001). The vicissitudes of measurement: A confirmatory factor analysis of the Emotional Autonomy Scale. *Child Development, 72*, 207-219.

Silverberg, S. B. & Gondoli, D. M. (1996). Autonomy in adolescence: A contextualized perspective. In: G. R. Adams, R. Montemayor, & T. Gullotta, (Eds.), *Psychosocial development during adolescence: Progress in developmental contextualism* (12-61). Thousand Oaks, CA:Sage.

Smart, I. F. & Smart, D. W. (1995). Acculturative stress of Hispanics: Loss and challenge. *Journal of Counseling and Development, 73*, 390-396.

Swanson, J. W., Linsky, A. O., Quintero-Salenas, R., Pumariega, A. J.& Holzer, C. E. (1992). A binational school survey of depressive symptoms, drug use, and suicidal ideation. *Journal of the American Academy of Child & Adolescent Psychiatry, 31*, 669-678.

Szapocznik, J., Perez-Vidal, A., Brickman, A., Foote, F. H., Santisteban, D. A. & Hervis, O. (1988). Engaging adolescent drug abusers and their families into treatment: A strategic structural systems approach. *Journal of Consulting and Clinical Psychology, 56*, 552-557.

Torrey, E. F. (1972). *The mind game: Witch doctors and psychiatrists*. New York: Emerson Hall.

Triandis, H. (1989). The self and social behavior in differing cultural contexts. *Psychology Review, 96*, 506-20.

Twenge, J. M. & Nolen-Hoeksema, S. (2002). Age, gender, race, socioeconomic status, and birth cohort differences on the Children's Depression Inventor: A meta-analysis. *Journal of Abnormal Psychology, 222*, 578-588.

Valenzuela, A. Dornbusch, S. M. (1994). Familism and social capital in the academic achievement of Mexican origin and Anglo adolescents. *Social Science Quarterly, 75*, 18-36.

Varela, R. E., Vernberg, E. M., Sanchez-Sosa, J., Riveros A., Mitchell, M. & Mashunkashey, J. (2004). Anxiety reporting and culturally associated interpretation biases and cognitive schemas: A comparison of Mexican, Mexican-American, and European American families. *Journal of Clinical Child and Adolescent Psychology, 33*, 237-247.

Weiss, M. & Kleinman, A. (1988). Depression in cross-cultural perspective: Developing a culturally informed model. In: J. B. P. R. Dasen, (Eds.), *Health and cross-cultural psychology: Toward applications* (pp. 197-206). Newbury Park, CA:Sage.

Zuckerman, M. (1990). Some dubious premises in research and theory on racial differences: Scientific, social , and ethical issues. *American Psychologist, 45,* 1297-1303.

In: Race and Ethnicity   ISBN: 978-1-60692-099-2
Editor: Jonathan K. Crennan, pp. 349-361   © 2010 Nova Science Publishers, Inc.

Chapter 16

THE EFFECT OF ETHNICITY ON THE INCIDENCE OF FOOT COMPLICATIONS IN DIABETES MELLITUS IN EGYPT

Mamdouh El-Nahas[1], Hanan Gawish[1], Manal Tarshoby[1], Omnia State[1] and Nesrene Omar[2]

[1]Diabetic Foot Team, Diabetes and Endocrinology Unit,
Internal Medicine Department, Mansoura University, Egypt.
[2]Medical Microbiology and Immunology Department,
Mansoura University, Egypt.

ABSTRACT

Regional differences in clinical presentation of diabetic foot syndrome had been reported. The Eurodiale study, revealed considerable differences among diabetic foot ulcer (DFU) patients in different European centers. Although ethnicity sometimes becomes difficult to define but it can capture something that genes cannot. These include aspects of culture, behavior, environment, and social status. Objective: To study the presentation of diabetic foot syndrome in Egypt and point out the differences from what is reported from Western countries. Egypt is an African country but part of its territories lies in Asia. It could also be considered as a Mediterranean country. We found that the majority of the studied diabetic patients (93.8%) didn't receive any prior education about proper foot care. Tinea pedis, dry skin and calluses were found in 43.6%, 44.6% and 5.7% of patients. Inappropriate footwear was used by 61.6% of patients. Most of diabetic foot ulcers were neuropathic (93.8%), while neuroischaemic and ischaemic ulcers were much less frequent (4.1% and 2.1% respectively). The majority of DFUs (80.7%) were of 3 months duration or longer (16.1 $\pm$ 13.6 months). Most of ulcers (85.6%) were located on the plantar surface of the foot. The distribution of ulcer location was as follow; plantar forefoot (35.3%), plantar toes (34 %), inerdigital and dorsal toes (9.2%), plantar hindfoot (9.8 %), plantar midfoot (6.5%) and dorsal or lateral aspect of the foot (5.2%). Bacterial pathogens associated with infected diabetic foot ulcers were also to some extent different. S. aureus was the most common species (21.1%) isolated from infected DFU. However, it is much less prevalent than what is reported from Western countries. MRSA represented 42.8 % of the isolated Staphylococci.

It is concluded that, in Egypt, there are major differences in the presentation of diabetic foot syndrome than data reported from Western countries. These differences could lead to regional variation in the outcome and the management strategies. It could also help to elucidate the impact of social, cultural and environmental factors on the pathogenesis of the diabetic foot syndrome.

INTRODUCTION

The term ethnicity refers to common cultural traditions, geography, ancestry, religion, and history. The term comes from the Greek word "ethnos", which means "nation" or "people" (Oldroyd et al 2005). Doyle (2006) suggested that despite the fluid nature of the concept, self-identified race and ethnicity can capture something that genes cannot, namely, aspects of culture, behavior, diet, environment, and features of social status.

The effect of ethnicity on the incidence of foot complications in diabetes mellitus had been previously suggested but the results are to large extent contradictory. Lavery et al (1996) reported elevation in risk of amputation in USA diabetic patients of African descent compared with USA whites. Whereas, in UK , amputation risk was reduced in diabetic African-Caribbean men by about two-thirds compared with UK whites (Leggetter et al 2002). The prevalence of foot ulceration in diabetic patients of African descent was also reported to be different from European or Asian populations. Abbott et al (2005) reported lower risk of foot ulcers for African Caribbeans diabetic patients (2.7%) than for Europeans (5.5%). Lower neuropathy was the main contributor to the reduced African-Caribbean ulcer rate, particularly in men. Leggetter et al (2002) also found lower level of neuropathy in African Caribbeans in UK that could, in part, explain the reduced amputation rate in such population. However, data on the prevalence of neuropathy in different ethnic populations are very limited. Also, there are very few prevalence studies comparing peripheral arterial disease (PAD) between different ethnic groups. Hobbs et al (2003) suggested that Blacks and Asians have a tendency towards more distal occlusive disease, while abdominal aortic aneurysms appear to be predominantly a disease of Caucasians.

Most of the research that study the effect of ethnicity on diabetic foot syndrome entirely depends upon studying ethnic minority groups living in Western countries. As ethnicity is a complex concept which has both socio-cultural and biological components (Anand 1999), we suggest that ethnicity will has greater impact on the socio-cultural components rather than the biological component. The large nature of Africa continent that include diverse populations together with the possible effect of environmental and cultural factors on racial differences, make it plausible to study African patients in their original countries. Although Egypt is one of the African countries, part of its territories lies in Asia and it is also considered as a Mediterranean country.

The aim of this work was to study the presentation of diabetic foot syndrome in Egypt and point out the differences from what is reported from Western countries..

Subjects and Methods

Data for this chapter came from three studies. The first was to screen randomly selected diabetic patients for foot ulceration and their risk factors. The study included 1220 diabetic patients randomly selected from diabetes outpatient clinics of Specialized Medical Hospital, Mansoura University, Egypt in the period from February 2005 to January 2006. The second study included all consecutive diabetic foot ulcer patients (145 patients) presented to Mansoura Diabetes Foot Clinic during the same period of the first study. The third was a bacteriological study of all swabs (242 samples) taken from clinically infected diabetic foot ulcers presented to Mansoura Diabetes foot clinic in the period from February 2005 to May 2008.

Mansoura university lies in the middle of the Nile Delta in a heavily populated area and serve more than 4 governorates that include both rural and urban populations.

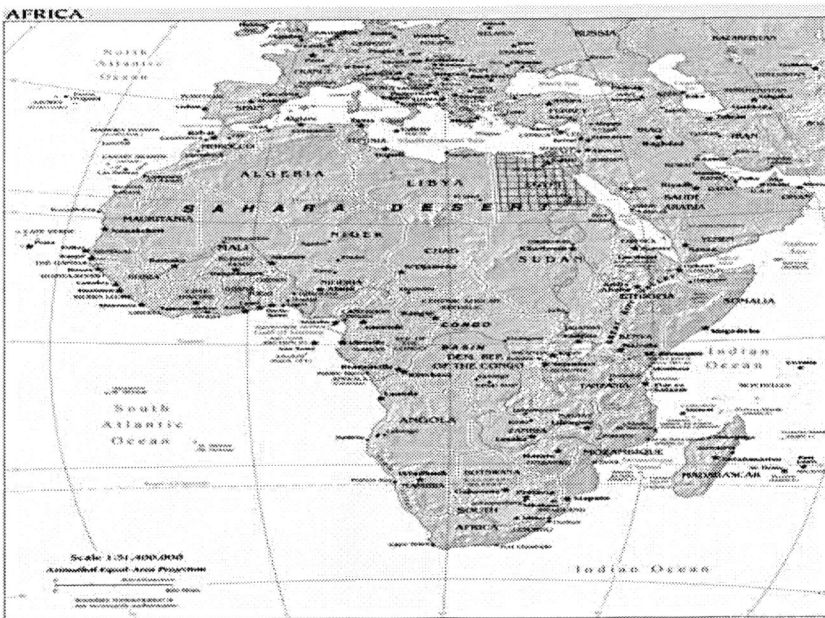

Egypt Map (Photo).

Data of all participants were collected including demographic data e.g. the age of patients and gender. Health risk factors included smoking habits, height and degree of adiposity. Patients were asked about the known duration of diabetes and treatment received (oral hypoglycemic, insulin or the combination of both oral hypoglycemic and insulin). History of receiving prior foot care education or having any previous knowledge about foot problems in diabetes were also taken.

All patients underwent a complete bilateral lower extremity evaluation including examination for PAD, loss of protective sensation as well as any preulcerative pathology. Loss of protective sensation was defined as the inability to sense a 10-g Semmes-Weinstein monofilament at two or more sites on each foot. Peripheral arterial status was assessed by palpating the dorsalis pedis and posterior tibial pulses on both feet. PAD was diagnosed if 2 or more of pedal pulses were absent. The diagnosis of PAD was further confirmed by measuring ankle pressure (Dopplex; Bidop ES-100 V3 Hadeco, Inc. Japan) and calculation of ankle brachial pressure index. Values less than 0.9 were considered abnormal. The feet were thoroughly examined for deformities such as hallux valgus, claw/hammer toes, prominent metatarsal heads and flat foot. The skin of the foot were examined for dryness, thickness, fissures, calluses, maceration, redness and warmth. A foot ulcer was defined as a full thickness skin break at least to Wagner stage 1, occurring distal to the malleoli. The nails were also thoroughly examined for thick, ingrown, badly cut nails and for the presence of fungal infection of nails.

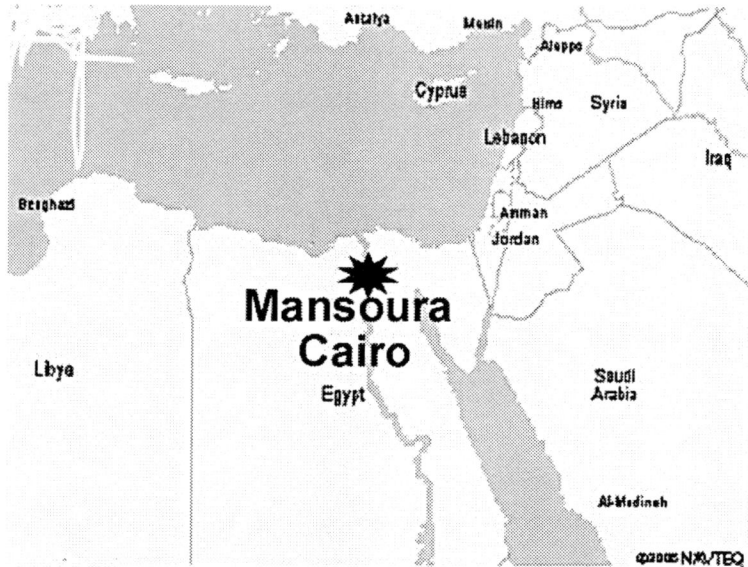

Mansoura Map (Photo).

Assessment of footwear had also been done. We considered the footwear inappropriate if there is any inappropriate characteristic related to the size, shape, heel, shock-absorbing capacity of the insole or the method of fixing the shoe to the foot.

Swabs were taken from all clinicaly dignosed infected foot ulcers. The swabs were obtained from the depth of the wound, using aseptic precautions. The samples were cultured using aerobic microbiological techniques to determine the bacterial pathogens and their antimicrobial susceptibility. The tested organism was uniformly seeded over the Mueller-Hinton agar surface and exposed to a concentration gradient of antibiotic diffusing from antibiotic-impregnated paper disk into the agar medium.

RESULTS

Screening of 1220 randomly selected Egyptian diabetic patients revealed that previous amputations were found in 14 patients (1.15%). Ten patients (0.8 %) had underwent minor amputations, and four patients (0.33 %) had major amputations. Active foot ulceration was identified at screening in 15 patients (1.2 %), whereas 70 patients (5.7 %) give history of past ulceration. Therefore, the overall DFU prevalence (present and past) was 6.9 %.

Insensate neuropathy was diagnosed in 113 patients (9.3 %). Whereas only 38 patients (3.1%) had absent foot pulses that proved by Doppler ultrasound to have reduced ankle brachial pressure index. The prevalence of Hallux valgus, hammer toe and flat foot was 23.4, 10.2 and 2.1 % respectively. Dry skin and calluses were recorded in 544 patients (44.6%) and 69 patients (5.7%) respectively. Tinea pedis was found in 532 patients (43.6%). Thick nails and badly cut nails were found in 215 (17.6%) and 376 (30.8%) respectively. The shoes were inappropriate in 751 patients (61.6%) and 1145 patients (93.8%) didn't receive any prior foot education.

Demographic data of DFU patients were compared to 1191 diabetic patients screened for foot complications after excluding patients with amputations and active foot ulceration. The mean age of DFU patients was not significantly different from non-ulcer patients (52.5 ± 9.2 vs 51.5 ± 9.6 yrs). Height, weight and mean duration of diabetes were significantly higher in DFU patients than in non-ulcer patients (165.5±9.4 vs 160.3± 8.2 cm; 94.5 ±17.9 vs 89.3 ± 15.9 Kg and 13.2 ± 8.1 vs 7.8 ± 5.8 yrs respectively). Higher prevalence of male gender, insulin usage and smoking were also found in DFU patients in comparison to non-ulcer patients.

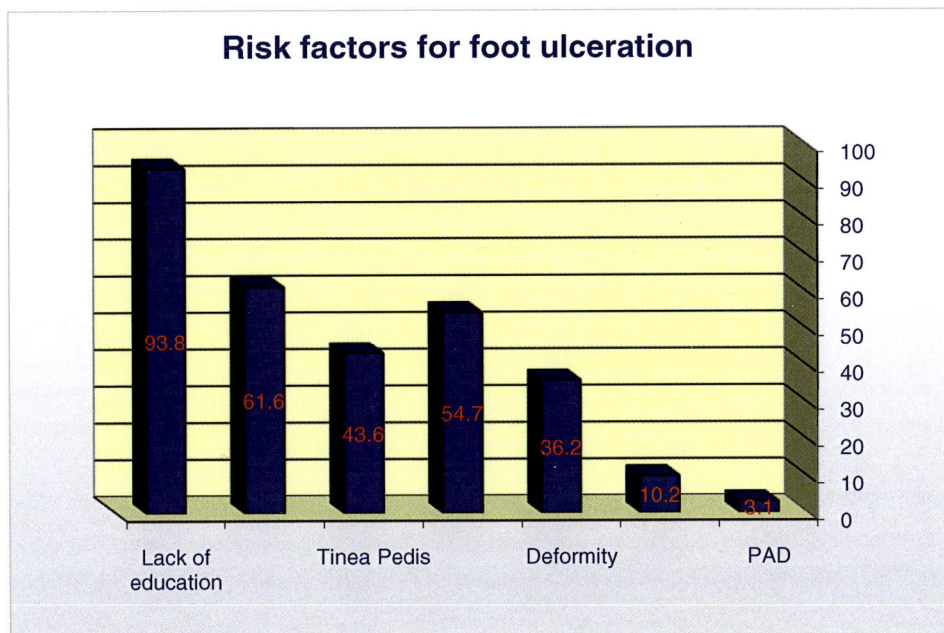

Figure 1. Risk factors for foot ulceration in patients with diabetes.

The majority of ulcers (93.8%) were neuropathic, while neuroischaemic and ischaemic ulcers were much less frequent (4.1% and 2.1% respectively). The total number of foot ulcers were 153 as 6 patients (4.1%) presented with more than one ulcer. The majority of DFUs (80.7%) were of 3 months duration or longer (mean 16.1 ± 13.6 months). Most of ulcers (85.6%) were located on the plantar surface of the foot. The location for ulcers were plantar forefoot (35.3%), plantar toes (34 %), inerdigital and dorsal toes (9.2%), plantar hindfoot (9.8 %), plantar midfoot (6.5%) and dorsal or lateral aspect of the foot (5.2%) (Figure 2).

Table 1. Characteristics of DFU patients in comparison to non-ulcer patients.

	DFU patients	Non-ulcer diabetic patients
Number	145	1191
Age of patients	52.493 ± 9.275	51.548 ± 9.583
Gender (M/F)	77/68 *	386/805
Duration of diabetes	13.2 ± 8.1 *	7.8 ± 5.8
Weight	94.496 ±17.7 *	89.328 ± 15.9
Height	165.475±9.4 *	160.329 ± 8.2164
BMI	34.269±6.3	34.896 ±6.4
Smoking (Smok./nonsmok)	50/95*	168/1023
Treatment (OHA/Insulin/combined)	25/94/26 *	647/302/242
Past history of foot ulcer (+/-)	89/56 *	55/1136

* p < 0.05

Ulcer site

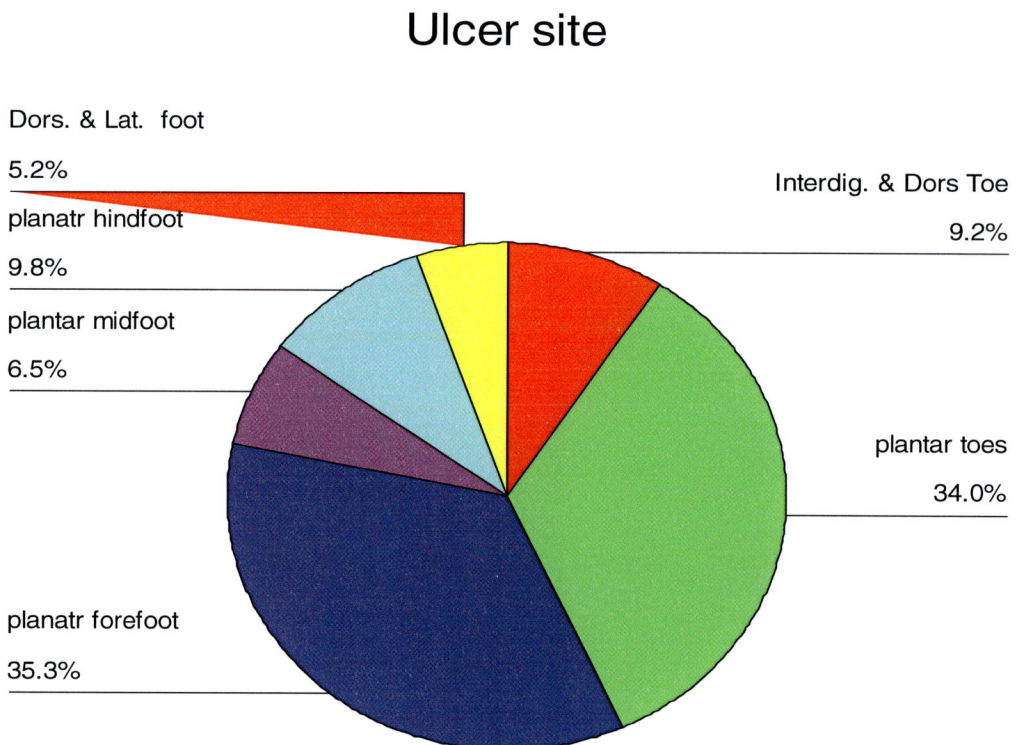

Figure 2. Ulcer location.

Culture of swabs taken from clinically infected diabetic foot ulcers were done to determine the bacterial pathogens and their antimicrobial susceptibility. Forty seven (19.4%) samples yield no growth, single isolate was detected among 157 (64.9%) and polymicrobial growth among 38 (15.7%) cases . The most common isolates were *S. aureus* (21.1%) with MRSA representing 42.8 % of the isolated *Staphylococci*. Each of *K. pneumoniae* and *P.mirabilis* were 14.5%, *Ps.aeruginosa* 12.4% and 8% for each of *S.epidermidis, E. coli* , and *P.mirabilis*. The least common were species of *Enterococci* , *Candida* and *Citrobacter* by 1.7% followed by *Streptococci spp* by 3.3% . Both of Gram- positive and Gram –negative bacterial isolates were sensitive to imipenem and Ceftazidime , while vancomycin showed good activity against Gram-positive bacteria. The least effective antibiotics for *S. aureus*, *Ps.aeruginosa* and *Proteus* were amoxicillin and amoxicillin/clavulanate.

Table 2. The antibiotic susceptibility results for Gram positive bacteria.

	Enterococci	Staphylococcus aureus	Staphylococcus epidermidis	Streptococcus spp
Amoxycillin	100.0%	64.3%	75.0%	100.0%
Amoxicillin/ clavulanate	100.0%	64.3%	75.0%	100.0%
Cefazoline	75.0%	89.3%	95.0%	100.0%
Ceftriaxone	75.0%	96.4%	100.0%	100.0%
Cefipime	100.0%	100.0%	100.0%	100.0%
Ciprofloxacin	75.0%	92.9%	95.0%	100.0%
Doxycycline	100.0%	96.4%	90.0%	100.0%
Cephalexin	100.0%	78.6%	85.0%	100.0%
Levofloxacin	75.0%	89.3%	85.0%	60.0%
Meropnem	100.0%	96.4%	100.0%	100.0%
Trimethoprim	75.0%	53.6%	90.0%	80.0%
Vancomycin	100.0%	100.0%	100.0%	100.0%
Tetracycline	100.0%	85.7%	75.0%	80.0%
Imipenem	100.0%	100.0%	100.0%	100.0%
Ceftazidime	100.0%	100.0%	100.0%	100.0%

Table 3. The antibiotic susceptibility results for Gram negative bacteria.

	E. coli	Ps. Aeruginosa	Proteus	Citrobacter
Gentamicin	73.7%	83.3%	65.7%	100%
Amoxycillin	63.2%	33.3%	40.0%	75%
Amoxicillin/clavulanate	63.2%	33.3%	40.0%	75%
Cefazoline	78.9%	73.3%	48.6%	100%
Ceftriaxone	89.5%	70.0%	65.7%	75%
Cefipime	100.0%	86.7%	100.0%	100%
Ciprofloxacin	94.7%	83.3%	91.4%	100%
Doxycycline	100.0%	100.0%	97.1%	100%
Cephalexin	100.0%	100.0%	91.4%	100%
Levofloxacin	89.5%	66.7%	88.6%	100%
Meropnem	94.7%	93.3%	94.3%	100%
Piperacillin	94.7%	76.7%	80.0%	100%
Trimethoprim	63.2%	86.7%	51.4%	75%
Vancomycin	100.0%	100.0%	100.0%	100%
Amikacin	78.9%	66.7%	74.3%	75%
Imipenem	100.0%	96.7%	94.3%	100%
Ceftazidime	100.0%	96.7%	100.0%	100%

CONCLUSION

Despite the low prevalence of insensate neuropathy and PAD in diabetic patients the prevalence of DFU is still high in Egypt. Active foot ulceration was identified in 15 patients (1.2 %) of randomly selected diabetic patients. The prevalence of past ulceration was 5.7 % (70 of 1220). Therefore, the overall DFU prevalence was 6.9%. Abbott et al (2005) demonstrated that the prevalence of diabetic foot ulcers (past or present) in Asians (1.8%) and African Caribbeans (2.7%) was significantly lower than for Europeans (5.5%). Thus the prevalence of DFU in Egypt is higher than that reported for all ethnic groups living in UK.

Insensate neuropathy was found in 113 patients (9.3%) of 1220 diabetic patients. It is very difficult to know how these rates compare to European populations as methods of neuropathy detection vary widely. However, Gregg et al (2004) using the same diagnostic criteria (inability to feel monofilament) reported much higher prevalence (28.5 %) of neuropathy in US diabetic population Although peripheral neuropathy is an important contributor to diabetic foot ulceration and amputation, there are very limited data available of the prevalence of neuropathy in different ethnic populations. Few studies suggested low prevalence of neuropathy in African patients. The U.K. Prospective Diabetes Study found lower prevalence of abnormal vibration sensation in African-Caribbean patients with newly diagnosed diabetes than for Europeans (UKPDS 1994). Abbott et al (2005) attributed the reduced ulcer risk in African Caribbeans men to lower neuropathy levels. They found that abnormal vibration sensation was twofold less prevalent for African Caribbeans, than Europeans, however, other neuropathy differences were generally less pronounced.

It was found that, only 38 patients (3.1%) of diabetic patients had absent foot pulses that proved by Doppler ultrasound to have PAD. We admit that the higher the sensitivity of the screening method the greater will be the number of detected cases. However, Abbott et al (2005) using the same diagnostic criteria reported absent foot pulses in 20.3% [75 of 370] of African Caribbeans diabetic patients living in UK. Kumar et al (2007) also reported high prevalence of PAD (29.3%) in rural black subjects living in South Africa. The lower prevalence of PAD found in this study is unlikely to be due to the effect of age as the mean age of our patients was 50.5 ± 10.9 years. But we disclose that the more the population aging the more will be the prevalence of PAD. Several factors could explain the low prevalence of PAD in our country. Egypt is actually one of the African countries, but, the majority of people belong to the Caucasian rather than black race. The term Caucasian race had been used to describe the entire population of Europe, North Africa and West Asia. Being one of the Mediterranean countries could point to the possible beneficial effect of dietary patterns usually used in this area. Mediterranean diets are characterized not only by high consumption of olive oil, but with high consumption of fruits and vegetables, cereal products, fish, legumes, in combination with little meat. Mediterranean dietary pattern had been reported to have a protective role against PAD and the use of butter increased the risk of PAD even in patients regularly consuming olive oil (Ciccarone et al 2003). Also, other factors could be responsible for reduced prevalence of PAD such as higher physical activity level that is expected in developing countries. There is strong evidence suggesting that cardiovascular disease is largely a disease associated with physical inactivity. Epidemiological investigations showed approximately half the incidence of CAD in active compared to sedentary persons (Prasad and Das 2009).

The high prevalence of DFU in Egypt appears paradoxical with the low prevalence of two principal risk factors: insensate neuropathy and PAD. As, DFU result from different physiopathological mechanisms, therefore, other risk factors should be incriminated. We previously reported that the high prevalence of skin and nail pathology, the lack of knowledge regarding diabetic foot problems, and the frequent use of inappropriate footwear could explain this paradox (El-Nahas et al 2008). Understanding the physiopathological mechanisms that lead to foot ulceration is crucial to reduce their incidence, provide early care, allow targeted management for high risk patients and appropriate allocation for resources. Lavery et al (2008) suggested that there is a finite number of key factors that, if identified and addressed with appropriate intervention strategies, may reduce the risk for the cascade of events towards ulceration and subsequent amputation. The results of the cluster analysis showed four consistent, dominant clusters: (i) neuropathy, deformity, callus and elevated peak pressure; (ii) peripheral vascular disease; (iii) penetrating trauma and (iv) Ill-fitting shoe gear.

Dry skin and calluses were recorded in 544 patients (44.6%) and 69 patients (5.7%) respectively. Tinea pedis was found in 532 patients (43.6%). The importance of callus as a precipitating factor for DFU has been previously confirmed (Thomas et al 2003). Previous studies suggested that diabetic patients with known foot disease had more often callosities and dry skin compared to diabetic patients without foot disease (Bresater et al 1996). Bristow (2008) reported that fungal infection is a very common foot problem and if left untreated can threaten tissue viability in the diabetic foot leading to secondary bacterial infection and cellulitis. Foot deformities could also play a role in the high prevalence of DFU in our patients. We found Hallux valgus, hammer toe and flat foot in 23.4, 10.2 and 2.1 % respectively of diabetic patients. Bus et al (2005) showed that claw/hammer toe deformity is associated with a distal-to-proximal transfer of load in the forefoot and elevated plantar pressures at the MTHs in neuropathic diabetic patients. Distal displacement of the plantar fat pad is suggested to be the underlying mechanism in this association and increase the risk for plantar ulceration.

The diabetic foot problems could also be exacerbated by socio-cultural factors such as the lack of knowledge regarding diabetic foot complications, the inappropriate footwear. We found that 751 patients (61.6%) used inappropriate footwear and 1145 patients (93.8%) didn't receive any prior foot education. Otieno et al (2005) reported that patients' inadequate knowledge of self-care, unique socio-economic and socio-cultural characteristics are contributors to the barriers that compound sub-optimal foot care in developing countries. A comparative study examining diabetic patients in Tanzania and Sweden found that Only 13.8% Tanzanians reported carrying out self-inspections of their feet, while 71% Swedes reported doing so (Smide 2009). Appropriate footwear is very important for prevention of diabetic foot complications. Unfortunately, even in developed countries using inappropriate foot wear remains a problem. Harrison et al (2007) assessed the feet and footwear of one-hundred patients with diabetes who were attending the general diabetic clinic in UK to determine whether they are wearing the correct-sized shoes. They concluded that many patients with diabetes wear shoes that do not fit, particularly, shoes that are too narrow for their foot width.

Activity level could be another factor that need consideration. Diabetic subjects in developing countries are expected to do much more manual work than their counterparts in developed country. Unfortunately, the design of this work didn't provide information to evaluate this risk factor. Armstrong et al (1997) suggested that a primary etiologic factor for amputation in most diabetic patients is an infected neuropathic ulceration brought about or exacerbated by increased activity. Rapid change in activity level may have an effect on cumulative stress and the risk of ulcer recurrence (Lott et al 2005).

Demographic data of DFU patients revealed that the mean age of DFU patients was not significantly different from non-ulcer patients. Height, weight and mean duration of diabetes were significantly higher in DFU patients than in non-ulcer patients. Higher prevalence of male gender, insulin usage and smoking were also found in DFU patients in comparison to non-ulcer patients. Morbach et al (2004) found similarities in different regions of the world among people with diabetes suffering foot lesions include a predominance of males and patients with Type 2 diabetes, as well as a high frequency of diabetic neuropathy. However, differences concerning age, diabetes duration, peripheral vascular disease, and precipitating factors contributing to injury are also observed. Diabetes of long duration had been suggested to be one of the risk factors for foot ulcers (Leymarie et al 2005), most likely due to other risk factors such as PNP and PAD developing with time (Merza and Tesfaye 2003). However, regional differences in the average diabetes duration until the onset of the initial foot lesion were reported between Germany (14 years), India (12 years) and Tanzania (5 years) (Morbach et al 2004). Greater height had been suggested to be a risk factor for developing foot ulcer (Boyko et al 1999). Height has a marked influence on quantitative sensory, nerve-conduction, and clinical indices of diabetic peripheral neuropathy (Gadia et al 1987). Peripheral insensate neuropathy was significantly higher among tall patients (Cheng et al 2006).

We found that most of diabetic foot ulcers were neuropathic, while neuroischaemic and ischaemic ulcers were much less frequent. The majority of DFUs were also of long duration. Most of ulcers were located on the plantar surface of the foot. The distribution of ulcer location was as follow; plantar forefoot (35.3%), plantar toes (34 %), inerdigital and dorsal toes (9.2%), plantar hindfoot (9.8 %), plantar midfoot (6.5%) and dorsal or lateral aspect of the foot (5.2%). Regional differences in clinical presentation of diabetic foot ulceration (DFU) had been reported. The prevalence of peripheral arterial disease varied from 22 to 73% among DFU patients in different European centers (Pompers et al 2007). The Eurodiale study, also revealed that non-plantar foot ulcers were more common than plantar ulcers. Gershater et al (2009) identified a complexity of factors related to outcome of DFUs, of which co-morbidity, duration of the disease, extent of tissue involvement and extent of PAD were strongly related to probability of primary healing. The EURODIALE Study reveled that predictors of healing differ between patients with and without PAD, suggesting that diabetic foot ulcers with or without concomitant PAD should be defined as two separate disease states (Pompers et al 2008).

Culture of swabs taken from clinically infected diabetic foot ulcers revealed no bacterial growth in forty seven samples (19.4%). Single isolate was detected among 157 (64.9%) and polymicrobial growth among 38 (15.7%) cases . The most common isolates were *S. aureus* (21.1%) with MRSA representing 42.8 % of the isolated *Staphylococci*. Most recent studies of the microbiology of diabetic foot infections have stemmed from Asian and African countries (Omar et al 2008). The majority of these have shown that S. aureus remains the single most commonly isolated species, albeit accounting for a considerably lower proportion of all isolates (14–39%) (El-Tahawy 2000, Abdulrazak et al 2005, Gadepalli et al 2006) than in studies from Western countries (70–80%) (Dang et al 2003). The decreased proportion of isolates that are S. aureus is offset by greater numbers of Gram-negative bacteria and anaerobes. There is no clear explanation for the apparent differences in the microbiological findings between developed and developing countries. We previously suggested some reasons to explain the difference e.g. patients presenting to medical services later in developing countries, differences in the pattern of wound exposure to microorganisms or differences in microbiological techniques (Omar et al 2008).

A significant proportion of bacterial isolates were resistant to Amoxicillin and Amoxicillin/clavulanate while resistance to Vancomycin was low. Vancomycin- resistant gram-positive cocci have emerged as an increasingly problematic cause of diabetic foot infections worldwide. Vancomycin-resistant enterococci infections have a negative impact with respect to mortality, length of hospital stay and costs, in comparison with infections due to vancomycin-susceptible enterococci (Lode 2009). In this study, none of the bacterial isolates were resistant to vancomycin possibly due to the limited use of the drug in Egypt. These findings will be important to guide the initial selection of antibiotic especially as the choice of antibiotic treatment for diabetic foot infection usually start empirically.

It is concluded that, in Egypt, there are major differences in the presentation of diabetic foot syndrome than data reported from Western countries. These differences could lead to regional variation in the outcome and the management strategies. It could also help to elucidate the impact of social, cultural and environmental factors on the pathogenesis of the diabetic foot syndrome.

REFERENCES

Abbott, C. A., Garrow, A. P., Carrington, A. L., Morris, J., Van Ross, E. R. & Boulton, A. J. (2005). Foot Ulcer Risk Is Lower in South-Asian and African-Caribbean Compared With European Diabetic Patients in the U.K.:The North-West Diabetes Foot Care Study. *Diabetes Care, 28*, 1869-1875.

Abdulrazak, A., Bitar, Z. I., Al-Shamali, A. A. & Mobasher, L. A. (2005). Bacteriological study of diabetic foot infections. *J Diabetes Complications., 19*, 138-41.

Anand, S. S. (1999). Using ethnicity as a classification variable in health research: perpetuating the myth of biological determinism, serving socio-political agendas, or making valuable contributions to medical sciences? *Ethn Health., 4(4)*, 241-4.

Armstrong, D. G., Lavery, L. A., van Houtum, W. H. & Harkless, L. B. (1997). Seasonal variations in lower extremity amputation. *J Foot Ankle Surg., 36(2)*, 146-50.

Boyko, E. J., Ahroni, H. J., Stensel, V., Forsberg, R. C., Davignon, D. R. & Smith, D. G. (1999). A prospective study of risk factors for diabetic foot ulcer. The Seattle Diabetic Foot Study. *Diabetes Care., 22(7)*, 1036-42.

Bresater, L. E., WelinL, & Romanus, B. (1996). Foot pathology and risk factors for diabetic foot disease in elderly men. *Diabetes Res Clin Pract., 32(1-2)*, 103-9.

Bristow, I. (2008). Non-ulcerative skin pathologies of the diabetic foot. *Diabetes Metab Res Rev., 24(1)*, S84-9.

Bus, S. A., Maas, M., de Lange, A., Michels, R. P. J. & Levi, M. (2005). Elevated plantar pressures in neuropathic diabetic patients with claw/hammer toe deformity. *Journal of Biomechanics, 38*, 1918-25.

Cheng, Y. J., Gregg, E. W., Kahn, H. S., Williams, D. E., De Rekeneire, N., Venkat Narayan, K. M. (2006). Peripheral Insensate Neuropathy--A Tall Problem for US Adults?. *Am J Epidemiology.*, *164(9)*, 873-80.

Ciccarone, E., Di Castelnuovo, A., Salcuni, M., Siani, A., Giacco, A., Donati, M. B., De Gaetano, G., Capani, F., Iacoviello, L. & Gendiabe Investigators (2003). A high-score Mediterranean dietary pattern is associated with a reduced risk of peripheral arterial disease in Italian patients with Type 2 diabetes. *J Thromb Haemost.*, *1(8)*, 1744-52.

Dang, C. N., Prasad, Y. D., Boulton, A. J. & Jude, E. B. (2003). Methicillin-resistant Staphylococcus aureus in the diabetic foot clinic: a worsening problem. *Diabet Med.*, *20*, 159-61.

Doyle, J. M. (2006). What race and ethnicity measure in pharmacologic research. *J Clin Pharmacol.*, *46(4)*, 401-4.

El-Nahas, M., Gawish, H., Tarshoby, M., State, O. & Boulton, A. J. M. (2008). The prevalence of risk factors for foot ulceration in Egyptian diabetic patients. *Practical Diabetes International.*, *25(9)*, 362-366.

El-Tahawy, A. T. (2000). Bacteriology of diabetic foot. *Saudi Med J.*, *21*, 344-7.

Gadepalli, R., Dhawan, B., Sreenivas, V., Kapil, A., Ammini, A. C. & Chaudhry, R. (2006). A clinico-microbiological study of diabetic foot ulcers in an Indian tertiary care hospital. *Diabetes Care.*, *29*, 1727-32.

Gardia, M. T., Natori, N., Ramos, L. B., Ayyar, D. R., Skyler, J. S. & Sosenko, J. M. (1987). Influence of height on quantitative sensory, nerve-conduction, and clinical indices of diabetic peripheral neuropathy. *Diabetes Care.*, *10(5)*, 613-6.

Gershater, M. A., Londahl, M., Nyberg, P., Thorne, J. et al (2009). Complexity of factors related to outcome of neuropathic and neuroischaemic/ischaemic diabetic foot ulcers: a cohort study. *Diabetologia.*, *52(3)*, 398-407.

Gregg, E. W., Sorlie, P., Paulose-Ram, R., Gu, Q., Eberhardt, M. S., Wolz, M., Burt, V., Curtin, L., Engelegau, M. & Geiss, L. (2004). 1999-2000 national heath and nutrition examination survey: Prevalence of lower-extremity disease in the US adult population >=40 years of age with and without diabetes: 1999-2000 national health and nutrition examination survey. *Diabetes care.*, *27(7)*, 1591-7.

Harrison, S. J., Cochrane, L., Abboud, R. J. & Leese, G. P. (2007). Do patients with diabetes wear shoes of the correct size?. *Int J Clin Pract.*, *61(11)*, 1900-4.

Harrison, S. J., Cochrane, L., Abboud, R. J. & Leese, G. P. (2007). Do patients with diabetes wear shoes of the correct size? *Int J Clin Pract.*, 61(11), 1900-4.

Hobbs, S. D., Wilmink, A. B. M. & Bradbury, A. W. (2003). Ethnicity and Peripheral Arterial Disease. Review. *Eur J Vasc Endovasc Surg*, *25*, 505-512.

Kumar, A., Mash, B. & Rupesinghe, G. (2007). Peripheral arterial disease - high prevalence in rural black South Africans. *S Afr Med J.*, *97(4)*, 285-8.

Lavery, L. A., Ashry, H. R., van Houtum, W., Pugh, J. A., Harkless, L. B. & Basu, S. (1996). Variation in the incidence and proportion of diabetes-related amputations in minorities. *Diabetes Care*, *19*, 48-52.

Lavery, L. A., Peters, E. J. & Armstrong, D. G. (2008). What are the most effective interventions in preventing diabetic foot ulcers?. *Int Wound J.*, *5(3)*, 425-33.

Leggetter, S., Chaturvedi, N., Fuller, J. H. & Edmonds, M. E. (2002). Ethnicity and risk of diabetes-related lower extremity amputation: a population-based, case-control study of African Caribbeans and Europeans in the United Kingdom. *Arch Intern Med*, *162*, 73-78.

Leymarie, F., Richard, J. L. & Malgrange, D. (2005). Factors associated with diabetic patients at high risk for foot ulceration. *Diabetes Metab., 31(6)*, 603-5.

Lode, H. M. (2009). Clinical impact of antibiotic-resistant gram-positive pathogens. *Clin Microbiol. Infect., 15(3)*, 212-7.

Lott, D. J., Maluf, K. S., Sinacore, D. R. & Mueller, M. J. (2005). Relationship between changes in activity and plantar ulcer recurrence in a patient with diabetes mellitus. *Phys Ther., 85(6)*, 579-88.

Merza, Z. & Tesfaye, S. (2003). The risk factors for diabetic foot ulceration. *The Foot., 13*, 125-129.

Morbach, S., Lutale, J. K., Viswanthan, V., Mollenberg, J., Ochs, H. R., Rajashkar, S., Ramachandran, A. & Abbas, Z. G. (2004). Regional differences in risk factors and clinical presentation of diabetic foot lesions. *Diabet Med., 21(1)*, 91-5.

Oldroyd, J., Banerjee, M., Heald, A. & Cruickshank, K. (2005). Diabetes and ethnic minorities. *Postgraduate Medical Journal., 81*, 486-90.

Omar, N., El-Nahas, M. & Gray, J. (2008). Novel antibiotics for the management of diabetic foot infections. Review. *International Journal of Antimicrobial Agents., 31*, 411-419.

Otieno, C. F., Nyamu, P. M. & Atieno-Jalango, G. (2005). Focus on delay as a strategy for care designs and evaluation of diabetic foot ulcers in developing countries: a review. *East Afr Med J., 82(12)*, S204-8.

Pompers, L., Huijberts, M., Apelqvist, J., Jude, E. et al. (2007). High prevalence of ischaemia, infection and serious comorbidity in patients with diabetic foot disease in Europe. Baseline results from the Eurodiale study. *Diabetologia., 50(1)*, 18-25.

Pompers, L., Schaper, N., Apelqvist, J., Edmonds, M., Jude, E. et al (2008). Prediction of outcome in individuals with diabetic foot ulcers: focus on the differences between individuals with and without peripheral arterial disease. The EURODIALE Study. *Diabetologia., 51(5)*, 747-55.

Prasad, D. S. & Das, B. C. (2009). Physical inactivity: a cardiovascular risk factor. *Indian J Med Sci., 63(1)*, 33-42.

Smide, B. (2009). Outcome of foot examinations in Tanzanian and Swedish diabetic patients, a comparative study. *J Clin Nurs., 18(3)*, 391-8.

Thomas, V. J., Patil, K. M., Radhakrishnan, S., Naravanamurthv, V. B. & Parivalavan, R (2003). The role of skin hardness, thickness, and sensory loss on standing foot power in the development of plantar ulcers in patients with diabetes mellitus--a preliminary study. *Int J Low Exterm Wounds., 2(3)*, 132-9.

Ukpds (1994). UK Prospective Diabetes Study. XII: Differences between Asian, Afro-Caribbean and white Caucasian type 2 diabetic patients at diagnosis of diabetes: UK Prospective Diabetes Study Group. *Diabet Med, 11*, 670-677.

In: Race and Ethnicity

Editor: Jonathan K. Crennan, pp. 363-371

ISBN: 978-1-60692-099-2

© 2010 Nova Science Publishers, Inc.

Chapter 17

CANCER GENERATED FACIAL DISFIGUREMENT: ETHNICITY, CULTURE AND SOCIAL CHALLENGES

Alessandro Bonanno[1] and Bita Esmaeli[2]

[1]Distingusished Professor and Chair, Department of Sociology, Sam Houston State University, Huntsville, Texas, USA

[2]Professor, Section of Ophthalmology, Department of Head and Neck Surgery, The University of Texas M. D. Anderson Cancer Center, Houston, Texas, USA

ABSTRACT

The face is one of the most important elements defining social interaction. Once the normal appearance of the face is altered, individuals encounter significant social problems. This is a situation that involves the facially disfigured but also those who interact with them. Due to medical advancements, patients who are facially disfigured because of cancer, related surgical procedures, and other treatments can now survive for an extended period of time. This survivorship is often accompanied with stigmatization as cancer survivors are viewed, and treated, differently because of their altered facial appearance. Despite its growing importance, the theme of the social consequences of cancer generated facial disfigurement has received limited scientific attention. Research tends to focus on patients' functional limitations and the manner in which they cope with their disfigurement. Less attention is placed on the social dimension of cancer generated facial disfigurement. In particular, limited research is available on the ways in which different social settings and groups affect the interaction of cancer patients who are facially disfigured. In this chapter, current research on these topics is reviewed underscoring findings in interaction patterns and outcomes. It is indicated that cultural and ethnic variations affect collective perceptions of, and responses to, cancer and disfigurement. The chapter concludes by stressing the importance of including cultural and ethnic components in the study of cancer generated facial disfigurement, the training of professionals, and development of pertinent protocols.

INTRODUCTION

The objective of this chapter is to illustrate the social problems experienced by patients who are facially disfigured because of cancer of the head and neck. These patients now survive for a number of years after the cancer is detected and later surgically removed (Mood 1997; Davis, Wingo and Parker 1998; Davis, Roumanas and Nishimura 1997; Dropkin 1999). While surgical procedures to correct alterations of the face are common along with the availability of increasingly sophisticated prostheses, often results do not rectify notable differences from the "normal" face (Davis, Roumanas and Nishimura 1997). Because of the cultural importance of the face both as an instrument for interaction and a symbol of personal identity, facially disfigured individuals are stigmatized and experience difficulties when interacting with other segments of society (Bull and Stevens 1981; Callahan 2004:75; Furness, Garrud, Faulder, and Swift 2006; Hawkesworth 2001; Hughes 1998; Kent 2000; Macgregor 1974; 1990). The importance of this topic is apparent, yet research on the social problems associated with cancer generated facial disfigurement remains limited (Clarke, Rumsey, Collin, Wyn-Williams 2003; Hughes, 1998; Kish and Lansdown 2000; Newell 1999; Pruzinsky, Levine, Persing, Barth, Obrecht 2006; Thompson and Kent 2001). In particular, research is lacking on the manner in which culturally and ethnic based behavior affects the interaction of facially disfigured cancer patients.

Cancer and Facial Disfigurement: Salient Literature

Stigma is a mark of disgrace attached to people who are considered different. As indicated by Goffman (1963), difference is socially constructed and is the outcome of discrepancies between an individual virtual social identity (expectations about what that individual ought to be) and his/her actual social identity (the attributes he/she actually posses) (Goffman 1963:2). When the actual social identity is perceived as departing from normality, the individual is "reduced in our minds from a whole and usual person to a tainted, discounted one. Such an attribute is a stigma" (Goffman 1963:3). Stigma is attached to an individual's feature "that is deeply discrediting" and that separates that person from the group of the normals. However, its actual genesis is not linked to attributes but, rather, is generated by the interaction between the stigmatized person and other members of society. "Relationships, not attributes" are at the origin of the problem, Goffman states (Goffman 1963:3). Stigma is generated by the existence of a number of blemishes. There are those of individual character such as homosexuality, dishonesty, imprisonment, radical political behavior, and addiction. There are those of tribal stigma that are related to a person's religion, ethnicity or race. And there are those of "abominations of the body" that refer to physical abnormalities. Goffman includes facial disfigurement in this category (Goffman 1963:52). In the case of cancer generated facial disfigurement there is a convergence of at least two types of blemishes: physical abnormality and ethnic-based behavior and responses to it (tribal stigma). As it will be indicated below, the manner in which culture and ethnicity affect interaction is relevant.

Following the work of Erving Goffman, social stigma has been widely studied and this production includes works such as those on stigma generated from diseases (i.e., cancer and AIDS) (Fife and Wright, 2000), physical disabilities (Cahill and Eggleston, 1995; Susman

1994), and mental health (Angermeyer and Matschinger 1994; Corrigan and Penn 1999). In spite of this wealth of contributions, stigma caused by facial disfigurement has been the subject of only a relatively small number of works (Clarke 1999; Clarke et al. 2003; Kent, 2000; Kish and Lansdown 2000; Hughes, 1998; Pruizinsky et al. 2006). These analyses stress the social importance of the face and the problems that affect those who display visible facial blemishes (Furness et al. 2006; Goffman 1963; Hawkesworth 2001; Hughes, 1998; Macgregor 1974). In a society in which individuals are fully clothed for virtually all of their social activities, the face represents one of the most notable physical attributes and a significant source of social information prior to, and during, social interaction (Anderson and Franke 2002; Cole 1998; Jackson 2002; Synnott 1989). Accordingly, people possessing an attractive face are better treated by others than less attractive members of society and often viewed as endowed with intellectual and emotional characteristics that are unrelated to their physical appearance (Feingold 1992; Kish and Lansdown 2000; Macgregor 1990; Bull and Rumsey 1988; Cash and Pruzinsky 2002). Lacking some of these physical attributes, facially disfigured individuals commonly engender negative responses by other members of society. Stigmatized and socially excluded, their ability to interact is often distorted and interaction is the source of problems including verbal and physical abuse, ridicule, hostile behavior, and isolation (Callahan, 2004; Hagedoorm and Molleman, 2006: Kish and Lansdown 2000).

Cancer patients experience less social and psychological problems than individuals who have been disfigured because of trauma (Rybarczyk and Behel 2002:389-90). However, cancer patients' "fear of dying is immense" (van Doorne et al. 1994:325; Macgregor 1974:151). This situation affects these individuals and their family members' perception of disfigurement (Bonanno and Choi 2009). In this context, patients are more preoccupied with the evolution of their cancer than with the social consequences of the scars that the disease left on their faces (Bonanno and Choi 2009; Pruzinsky et al. 2006:130). As this fear of dying diminishes, however, the process of dealing with the deformity affects both patients and family members (Bonanno and Choi 2009; van Doorne, van Waas and Bergsma 1994). The association of cancer and disfigurement is persistent. In effect, therapy almost inevitably mandates surgical removal of cancer-affected parts of the face making it an undesirable consequence of successful medical intervention (Callahan 2004; Millsopp, Brandom, Humphris, and Lowe 2006; Valente 2004). While the social perception of cancer has changed in recent decades, this disease engenders a wide variety of attitudes and responses that differentiate it from other pathological situations (Mosher and Danoff-Burg 2007). Often, these attitudes and responses are stigmatizing (Beremberg 1989; Bloom and Kessler 1994). However, differences have been recorded between reactions to forms of cancer that are perceived as "uncontrollable" – such as breast cancer – and those that are perceived as "controllable" – such as lung cancer due to smoking. Because the latter are seen as deriving from the patient's voluntary actions, more stigmatizing reactions are expected (Weiner, Perry and Magnusson 1988).

Among the limits of this otherwise important literature is the lack of attention paid to the social context within which the consequences of facially disfigurement emerge (Kent 2000:199; Clarke 1999; Furness et al., 2006; Thompson and Kent 2001). Theoretically, research is often conceptualized in terms of the ability and skills of the individual to adapt to his/her new and stigmatized condition. This psycho-functional approach (i.e. emphasis on individual adaptation) downplays "the everyday experience of the disfigured population in social settings" (Clarke, 1999:140; Bull and Ramsey, 1988; Hagedoorm and Molleman, 2006;

Kent, 2000; Partridge, 1998; Thompson and Kent, 2001). In this context, also downplayed is the "interaction process" through which disfigurement is recognized and stigmatization takes place. Usually, interaction is viewed in terms of the importance of individual behavior as predictor of successful outcomes in social situations (Bull and Ramsey, 1988: Clarke, 1999; Partridge, 1998). In particular, limited attention is paid to the fact that disfigurement and stigmatization are socially constructed and generated through processes of interaction that involve multiple actors and take different forms according to the settings in which they unfold (Kent, 2000).

When discussed, interaction is viewed in terms of the exchange of meanings between the disfigured individual and society. Attention is paid to the characteristics of the individual and their variability. Accordingly, the individual is conceptualized as endowed with an array of social and psychological features that affect his/her ability to achieve and maintain a satisfactory quality of life and adapt to the consequences of disfigurement and the existence of stigmatization. As these characteristics vary, their identification allows for the recognition of specific patterns of actions and outcomes.

The individual remains the research focus also in studies on the relationship between cancer-generated facial disfigurement and stigmatization (Bonanno, Choi and Esmaeli, 2008). Indeed, research on stigma has been "decidedly individualistic in focus" (Link and Phelan 2001:366). Accordingly, the ways in which interaction between the facially disfigured and the "normals" unfolds in different realms of society has been understudied. As Thompson and Kent put it "Most studies have examined the 'view form the inside,' with little work [carried out] on the social and the 'view form the outside'" (2001:677).

In the case of society, it is largely conceptualized in homogenous terms. It is viewed as a place that engenders stigmatization regardless of how, where, and when interaction takes place. Because of the overwhelming negative responses that facially disfigured individuals receive, a differentiation among types of interaction and the settings within which they are contained is normally absent. Accordingly, there is a general disregard for the heterogeneous nature of social situations and the different patterns of stigmatization that they carry with them. This is a limitation that new research is attempting to overcome. Yet, an established body of knowledge on the social settings and contexts in which interaction unfolds is not available. This situation includes the important variables of culture and ethnicity. Established sociological research has stressed the centrality of culture and ethnicity in determining the development and outcome of social interaction (Griswold 2003; Hitchcock 2003). Yet, these dimensions have not been explored in regard to head and neck cancer patients who have been disfigured because of their disease and in terms of their interaction within and between different cultural and ethnic enclaves.

The Family and friends

In this literature, the interaction of disfigured individuals with family members and friends has been privileged over than with stranger and acquaintances (Macgregor 1974; Hughes 1998; Bonanno, Choi and Esmaeli 2008). In particular, the spheres of the "family" and "caregivers" are portrayed as social settings in which the disfigured find more comfortable terms of interaction. The family is seen both as a "safer place" in which the disfigured feel protected and supported and the "institution" that provides them with alternative messages than the stigmatizing ones coming from society and its strangers (Hughes, 1998: 24-25, 277; Macgregor, 1974: 8-13; 15-18; 50-53; 120-125134-135; 196-

208). The family is usually seen as consisting of two dimensions. The first refers to the disfigured individuals' accounts of the family as a "safer place." The second consists of the actions that various members of the family and the family as a unit undertake in response to social events engendered by the facial deformities of their family members. It is concluded that in both cases the family provides alternative and supportive messages for the facially disfigured (Hughes, 1998: 24-25; Macgregor, 1974: 8-13; 196-208). Again, this literature on the role of the family in the interaction with the facially disfigured does not include cultural and ethnic variables despite the fact that it is easy to argue that these variables might have an impact on the interaction process.

An alternative view of the role of the family is provided by Goffman (1963). Goffman argues that there is empirical evidence demonstrating that familiarity may not reduce acceptance of people who are "different" (Goffman, 1963:53). Using the example of someone's wife, he contends that, while biography affects the relationship between husband and wife, there exist a full array of "socially standardize expectations" about the behavior of a wife that do not place her outside society (Goffman, 1963: 53). This means that the outcome of the intimate relationship between husband and wife does not exclude stigmatization but, in fact, it needs to be problematized by opening it to scrutiny. He stresses that "whether we interact with strangers or intimate, we will feel that the finger tips of society have reached into the contact, even here putting us in our place" (Goffman, 1963:53). Also in the case of Goffman, the family and society are not viewed in a terms of ethnicity. However, for Goffman culturally established patterns of actions define the manners in which diversity is established and with it stigmatization.

Strangers and acquaintances

The same literature indentifies interaction with "strangers" as negative. Strangers often intrude into the lives of the facially deformed through "staring, remarks, and questions, or obvious eye avoidance (Macgregor, 1974:56). They also negate that "civil inattention" normally granted to other members of society (Macgregor, 1974: 60). These groups constitute the "popular mind" (Macgregor 1974:77) that produces "generalized prejudice" (Macgregor, 1974: 94). The social settings where strangers are found are viewed as generating stigmatization as people deal "differently with those who have undergone facial surgery" (Hughes, 1998:277) and engender "fear" to the disfigured (Hughes, 1998: 235-237). Ultimately, society is the source of generalized stigmatization through widespread stereotyping that allows the "...unsightly face [to be] utilized as a visible symbol or a personification of evil, disease, criminality, or mental deficiency" (Macgregor, 1974:77). This process of stigmatization is so pervasive that it is viewed as if it is conducted uniformly throughout society regardless of actors and settings (Hughes 1998:190-193; Macgregor, 1974: 60, 77; 94). While evidence indicates that society is the primary source of stigmatization (Callahan, 2004; Hagedoorm and Molleman, 2006: Kish and Lansdown 2000; Pruzinsky et al. 2006; van Doorne et al. 1994:325), the manner in which this stigmatization is experienced in different spheres of society is understudied (Bonanno, Choi and Esmaeli 2008). Employing data from patients at a Northern European cancer center, van Doorne and his associates (van Doorne et al 1994), maintain that interaction patterns between patients and members of their immediate family, and patients and strangers are well understood. The formers setting provide patients with strong support. Strangers, conversely, are consistently the source of stigmatization. They contend, though, that further investigation is needed to ascertain the manner in which non-immediate family members and acquaintances react to facially disfigured patients. Addressing the problem underscored by van Doorne and his associates, additional literature indicates that interaction with professionals and acquaintances in some settings can be problematic and affected by culturally based behaviors. Interaction with caregivers is one of these settings. According to some, interaction with caregivers, and in particular those between surgeons, social workers and disfigured patients, is comfortable (Hughes, 1998:279). According to others, though, the lack of training that surgeons receive in regard to the social and cultural dimensions of facial disfigurement is a source of problems (Macgregor, 1974: 152-156). It is argued that caregivers – and surgeons in particular – tend to view medical decisions as purely technical matters. Underplayed is the cultural and ethnically-based dimensions that might affect these decisions. Accordingly, cultural and ethnic differences have not been taken into consideration in the analysis of interaction processes that take place in the hospital (Macgregor, 1990).

RECENT RESEARCH

In recent years, research has been carried out to study interaction with stranger and acquaintances. In particular, three general types of behavior have been identified as relevant in the interaction of facially disfigured cancer patients and strangers and acquaintances. The first of these behaviors is unsolicited attention, the second is unsolicited support, and the third consists of lack of special attention. When interacting individuals pay unsolicited attention to patients, ask unwanted questions, make unwelcome remarks, stare, or otherwise make their unspoken curiosity felt, patients feel uncomfortable regardless of whether the interaction take place in the crowd or in a small group. When people provide unsolicited "support" for patients, a number of outcomes are common. When interaction takes place among members of a small group, display of support often engenders comfortable interaction. It also shapes positive interaction in large groups as it is employed to construct advantageous conditions for patients. Instrumentally, support is used even in situations in which such assistance is not needed. Patients feel uncomfortable, however, when support suggests that disfigurement is a problem for patients. This is particularly the case when support creates a situation in which the patient is accorded what she/he perceives as undeserved attention. Finally, when interacting individuals do not pay particular attention to patients, both positive and stigmatizing outcomes are possible in small groups. In large groups, patients are comfortable when others do not pay particular attention to them. A large group allows patients to pass unnoticed among strangers.

Differences among settings underscore the centrality of culture and ethnicity in the determination of interaction patterns and outcomes. While understudies, these are variables that are relevant both in the interaction with family members and friends and with strangers and acquaintances. In the case of some ethnic groups, it has been documented that the perception of cancer is experienced in different ways. In selected ethnic enclaves, cancer is viewed as a stigma and a condition that should not be disclosed to friends and strangers alike. It is an approach that has negatively impacted programs to assist cancer patients (Deng 2009).

CONCLUSIONS

The analysis presented in this chapter stresses that social difference is a relevant factor in the establishment and determination of successful interaction between facially disfigured cancer patients and members of other groups. Accordingly, attention to difference is an important tool for improving the quality of life of cancer patients and those who interact with them. Simultaneously, the study of the impact of culture and ethnicity on interaction and its outcomes is significant but also clearly understudied. This lack of attention to, and limited knowledge of, the cultural and ethnic components of interaction generate consequences that need to be addressed. First, research on this topic should be promoted. This is an action that should be undertaken involving both medical institutions and universities working in cooperation. Second, because this research's evident interdisciplinary nature, cooperation between members of salient disciplines should constitute the context within which such research is carried out. Third, the result of this research as well as current social knowledge on culturally and ethnically based interaction should be incorporated in the training of pertinent medical personnel including surgeons. While progress in this direction has been made in recent years, currently, surgeons treating patients with head and neck cancer continue to have a relatively limited exposure during training and later in the development of their medical practices to the results of social studies. Finally, this knowledge should be employed to develop protocols for the treatment of head and neck patients. These protocols should address needed actions not only in regard to patients but also in terms of family members, friends and the general public. In this respect, further investigation is needed on the manner in which such knowledge can be successfully translated into protocols.

REFERENCES

Anderson, R. C. & Franke, K. A. (2002). "Psychological and Psychosocial Implications of Head and Neck Cancer." *Internet Journal of Mental Health, 1(2)*, 55-64.

Angermeyer, M. & Matschinger, H. (1994). "lay beliefs about schizophrenic disorder: the results of a population study in Germany."*Acta Psychiatrica Scandinavica., 89*, 39-45.

Berremberg, J. L. (1989). "Attitudes towards cancer as a function of experience with the disease: A test of three models. *Psychology and Health, 3*, 233-243.

Bloom, J. & Kessler, l. (1994). "Emotional Support Following Cancer: A test of the Stigma and Social Activity Hypothesis." *Journal of Health and Social Behavior, 35*, 118-133.

Bonanno, A. & Choi, J. Y. (2009). "Psychosocial aspects of orbitofacial disfigurement in cancer patients." In: B. Esmaeli, (Eds.), *Ophthalmic Oncology*. Norwell, MA: Springer.

Bonanno, A., Choi, J. Y. & Esmaeli, B. (2008). "*The contradictions of medical sociology understanding of stigma in facially disfigured individuals.*" Paper presented at the Annual Meeting of the Southwest Social Science Association. Las Vegas, NV. March 13-15.

Bonanno, A. & Esmaeli, B. (2008). "Social Challenges of Cancer Patients with Orbitofacial Disfigurement." Paper presented at the American Society of Ophthalmic Plastic and Reconstructive Surgery. Atlanta, GA. November 12-13.

Bull, R. & Rumsey, N. (1988). *The social psychology of facial appearance*. New York: Springer Vale.

Bull, R. & Stevens, J. (1981). "The effects of facial disfigurement on helping behavior." *The Italian Journal of Psychology, 8(1)*, April.

Cahill, S. & Eggleston, R. (1995). Reconsidering the Stigma of Physical Disability: Wheelchair use and Public Kindness. *The Sociological Quarterly, 36(4)*, 681-698.

Callahan, C. (2004). Facial disfigurement and sense of self in head and neck cancer. *Social Work in Health Care, 40(2)*, 73-87.

Cash, T. F. & Pruzinsky, T. (eds.) (2002). *Body Image. A handbook of theory, research, and clinical practice*. New York: The Guilford Press.

Clarke, A. (1999). "Psychosocial aspects of facial disfigurement: problems, management and the role of a lay-led organization." *Psychology, Health and Medicine, 4(2)*, 127-142.

Clarke, A., Rumsey, N., Collin, J. R. O. & Wyn-Williams, M. (2003). "Psychological distress associated with disfiguring eye conditions." *Eye, 17*, 35-40.

Cole, J. (1998). *About face*. Cambridge: The MIT Press.

Davis, K., Wingo, P. & Parker, S. (1998). Cancer statistics by race and ethnicity. *CA Cancer J Clin, 1*, 31-47.

Davis, K., Roumanas, E. D. & Nishimura, R. D. (1997). "Prosthetic-surgical collaboration in the rehabilitation of patients with head and neck defects." *Otolaryngologic Clinics of North America* Vol., *30(4)*, 631-645.

Deng, F. (2009). *"The Role of Community-Based Participatory Research in Reducing Health Disparities: The Experience of Asian Community in Houston."* Paper Presented at the Annual Conference Medicine and the Social Sciences and Humanities. Huntsville, TX. April 17.

Dropkin, M. J. (1999). "Body image and quality of life after head and neck cancer surgery." *Cancer Practice* November/December, *7(6)*, 309-313.

Fife, B. L. & Wright, E. R. (2000). The dimensionality of stigma: A comparison of its impact on the self of persons with HIV/AIDS and cancer. *Journal of Health Social Behavior, 42*, 50-67.

Furness, P., Garrud, P., Faulder, A. & Swift, J. (2006). "Coming to terms. A grounded theory of adaptation to facial surgery in adulthood." *Journal of Health Psychology, 11(3)*, 453-466.

Goffman, Erving. (1963). *Stigma. Notes on the management of spoiled identity*. New York: Simon & Shuster.

Griswold, W. (2003). *Culture and Societies in a Changing World*. Thousand Oaks, CA: Pine Forge Press.

Hagedoorm, M. & Molleman, E. (2006). "Facial disfigurement in patients with head and neck cancer: The role of social self-efficiency." *Health Psychology, 25(5)*, 643-647.

Hawkesworth, M. (2001). "Disabling spatialities and the regulation of a visible secret." *Urban Studies, 38(2)*, 299-318.

Hitchcock, J. (2003). *Lifting the White Veil: An Exploration of White Culture in a Multiracial Context*. Roselle, NJ: Crandall Dostie & Douglass Books.

Hughes, Michael. (1998). *The social consequences of facial disfigurement*. Aldershot: Ashgate.

Kent, G. (2000). "Understanding the Experiences of People with Disfigurements: An Integration of Four Models of Social and Psychological Functioning." *Psychology, Health & Medicine, 5(2)*, 117-129.

Kish, V. & Lansdown, R. (2000). "Meeting the psychosocial impact of facial disfigurement: developing a clinical service for children and families." *Clinical Child Psychology and Psychiatry, 5(4)*, 497-512.

Link, B. G. & Phelan, J. C. (2001). "Conceptualizing Stigma." *Annual Review of Sociology, 27*, 363-85.

Macgregor, F. (1990). "Facial disfigurement: problems and management of social interaction and implication for mental health." *Aesthetic and Plastic Surgery, 14(4)*, 249-257.

_____. (1974). *Transformation and Identity: The Face and Plastic Surgery*. New Your: Quadrangle/The New York Times Book Co.

Millsopp, L. & Brandom, L., Humphris, G. & Lowe, D. (2006). "facial appearance after operations for oral and oropharyngeal cancer: A comparison of casenotes and patient-completed questionnaire." *British Journal of Oral and Maxillofacial Surgery, 44*, 358-363.

Mood, D. W. (1997). "Cancers of the Head and Neck." 271-283 In: C. Varricchio, (Eds.) *A Cancer Source Book for Nurses*. Sudbury, MA: Jones and Bartlett Publishers.

Mosher, C. & Danoff-Burg, S. (2007). "Death anxiety and cancer related stigma: A terror management analysis" *Death Studies, 31*, 855-907.

Newell, R. J. (1999). "Altered Body Image: A Fear-Avoidance Model of Psycho-Social Difficulties Following Disfigurement." *Journal of Advanced Nursing, 30(5)*, 1230-38.

Partridge, J. (1998). Changing faces: taking up Macgregor's challenge. *Journal of Burn Care and Rehabilitation, 19*, 174-180.

Pruzinsky, T., Levine, E., Persing, J. A., Barth, J. T. & Obrecht, R. (2006). "Facial trauma and facial cancer." Pp.125-143 In: D. B., Sarwer, T., Pruzinsky, T., Cash, R. M., Goldwyn, & J. A., Persing. *Psychological Aspects of Reconstructive and Cosmetic Plastic Surgery: Clinical, Empirical and Ethical Perspectives* Philadelphia PA: Lippincott Williams.

Rybarczyk, B. D. & Behel, J. M. (2002). "Rehabilitation medicine and body image." 387-393 In: T. F. Cash, & T. Pruzinsky, (Eds.) Body Image. *A Handbook of Theory, Research, and Clinical Practice*. New York: The Guilford Press.

Thompson, A. & Kent, G. (2001). "Adjusting to disfigurement: process involved in dealing with being visibly different." *Clinical Psychology Review, 21(5)*, 663-682.

Susman, J. (1994). Disability, stigma and deviance. *Social Science and Medicine, 38*, 15-22.

Valente, S. (2004). "Visual disfigurement and depression." *Plastic Surgical Nursing, 24(4)*, 14-146.

van Doorne J. M., van Waas, M. A. & Bergsma, J. (1994). "Facial disfigurement after cancer. resection: a problem with an extra dimension." *Journal of Investigative Surgery* Vol., 7 (4), 321-326.

Weiner, B., Perry, R. P. & Magnusson, J. (1988). "An attributional analysis of reaction to stigma." *Journal of Social Issues, 35(1)*, 120-55.

In: Race and Ethnicity
Editor: Jonathan K. Crennan, pp. 373-379

ISBN: 978-1-60692-099-2
© 2010 Nova Science Publishers, Inc.

Chapter 18

RACE-BASED STUDIES: THE SLIPPERY SLOPE OF PHARMACOGENETICS?

Yvonne C. Lee and Elizabeth W. Karlson

Division of Rheumatology, Immunology and Allergy, Brigham and Women's Hospital, 75 Francis Street, PBB-B3, Boston, MA, USA

ABSTRACT

Race serves an important, yet controversial, role in many pharmacogenetic studies. The 2005 FDA approval of BiDil (isosorbide dinitrate/hydralazine), the first drug with a race-specific indication, fueled the debate regarding the risks and benefits of race-based studies. Proponents of BiDil contended that this drug's race-specific development and approval was appropriate and necessary. By focusing on African Americans, researchers were able to target a subgroup of patients who were more likely to respond to the drug, thereby increasing the likelihood of success and decreasing the time to market. They argued that race is a reasonable substitute for specific genetic information, yielding valuable information regarding relevant biological pathways. Critics, however, stated that race represents more than genetic information, often reflecting social and environmental factors. They argued that race-based studies perpetuate racism and lead to inferior care for populations that are considered inappropriate markets by the pharmaceutical industry. After considering these arguments, we believe there is a role for race-based studies in pharmacogenetics. However, these studies must be designed and interpreted cautiously. Researchers must be aware of the social and ethical implications of their studies, and policy makers should prioritize research funding for studies involving financially disadvantaged populations.

INTRODUCTION

In the age of the Human Genome Project and HapMap, more researchers are joining the "pharmacogenetics bandwagon," searching for genetic polymorphisms that can explain and predict differences in treatment response. In this environment, race has become a significant component of many studies. In some cases, it serves as a surrogate for genetic polymorphisms; in other cases, it is used to identify a homogeneous population in which genetic polymorphisms can be studied. While most scientists view race as a necessary element of their studies, there has been concern that the use of race in scientific studies may perpetuate racist ideas, inequalities, and, in fact, be an inaccurate reflection of genetics. In this chapter, we explore the benefits and risks of race-based studies in pharmacogenetics. We will provide a definition of pharmacogenetics and the role of race in this field. We will then discuss the case of BiDil, an example of race-based therapeutics. This example will be used as a springboard for discussion regarding race, pharmacogenetics and future studies.

THE HISTORY AND DEFINITION OF PHARMACOGENETICS

Pharmacogenetics is the study of genetic variation and its impact on treatment response. The ultimate goal of pharmacogenetics is to predict drug efficacy and toxicity based on genetic information. This information will hopefully enable clinicians to offer "individualized therapy," tailored to each patient based on genetic profile and lifestyle factors.

Some of the earliest pharmacogenetic observations were race-based. For example, scientists noted that primaquine-induced hemolysis occurred predominantly in African American soldiers. This adverse effect was linked to a glucose-6-phosphate dehydrogenase (G6PD) mutation found in 10% of African Americans [1]. Another example is the "Asian flush," a flushing reaction that occurs after alcohol consumption. This reaction was linked to polymorphisms in alcohol dehydrogenase that are commonly found in Asian populations [1].

To explore genetic diversity and better define its impact on disease and treatment response, the International HapMap Project was begun in 2002. The intent of the HapMap Project was to enable researchers "to find genes that affect health, disease and individual responses to medications and environmental factors" [2]. Four populations, the Yoruban people from Nigeria, the Han Chinese, the Japanese and a group of Americans with European ancestry, were included [2].

Since its inception, the HapMap Project has contributed to many new discoveries regarding the relationship between genes and drug response; however, due to lack of technology, knowledge and/or financial reimbursement, clinicians have not been able to incorporate many genetic tests into their routine assessment of drug response or toxicity. Studies using race as a proxy for genetic information, however, have been used to support the use of one medication over another. This practice has been encouraged by federal institutions such as the Food and Drug Administration (FDA), which, in 2003, recommended that specific race and ethnicity information be collected in clinical trials to facilitate the assessment of drug response in different racial and ethnic groups [3].

THE BIDIL SAGA

The use of race as a predictor of treatment response has been controversial. A particularly well-publicized case involves the 2005 FDA approval of BiDil (isosorbide dinitrate/hydralazine) as the first drug with a race-specific indication. The combination of isosorbide dinitrate and hydralazine was initially studied in 1980-1985, as a part of the Vasodilator Heart Failure Trial (V-HeFT). In this study, isosorbide dinitrate/hydralazine was effective in reducing mortality from heart disease in the study population, which consisted of both Caucasians and African Americans. Based on this information, isosorbide dinitrate/hydralazine was patented as a treatment for heart failure in the general population [4].

The race-specific effects of isosorbide dinitrate/hydralazine were reported in 1999 when a retrospective analysis of V-HeFT data showed that isosorbide dinitrate/hydralazine was associated with lower death rates in African American patients but not Caucasian patients [5]. In 2000, seven years before the original patent was scheduled to expire, a new patent application was filed for the use of isosorbide dinitrate/hydralazine for the treatment of heart failure in African Americans. Despite objections, a 20-year patent was approved. The FDA also assured NitroMed, the company developing BiDil, that BiDil would be approved to treat heart failure in African Americans if the results of a confirmatory study showed similar results. This trial, the African American Heart Failure Trial (A-HeFT) compared isosorbide dinitrate/hydralazine or placebo plus standard therapy for the treatment of heart failure in African American patients [6]. Results showed that patients receiving isosorbide dinitrate/hydralazine and standard therapy had lower death rates than patients given placebo and standard therapy. In fact, the trial was stopped early due to significantly higher mortality rates in the placebo group [6].

This trial and the subsequent FDA approval of BiDil for heart failure treatment in African Americans were highly criticized. Critics claimed that the hype surrounding BiDil as an "African American drug" took advantage of a minority group's desire for justice in the historically unfair world of American healthcare, and many viewed the use of race as exploitation of a minority population for the purposes of financial gain [7]. They argued that BiDil was already available as a treatment for heart failure. In fact, isosorbide dinitrate and hydralazine, the medications composing BiDil, were both commercially available, generic drugs that could be purchased at cheaper prices [7, 8].

In addition, there was little evidence that BiDil worked solely for African Americans [9]. A-HeFT, the study which led to FDA approval, only included African Americans, so no information could be obtained regarding the efficacy of this medication for Caucasian patients [7, 8]. The previous study that had suggested a differential effect between African Americans and Caucasians was a retrospective analysis of clinical trial data and subject to bias [5].

Furthermore, the definition of African American in A-HeFT was based only on self-identification. Participants with mixed ancestry were included in this study as long as they identified themselves as black. As such, the population was both phenotypically and genetically heterogeneous, leading to potentially flawed inferences between race and genetics. Even if the population had only consisted of participants with pure African/African American ancestry, the large amount of genetic diversity among people with African ancestry would have made genetic inferences problematic [10].

Supporters of A-HeFT, however, state that it would have been scientifically irresponsible not to perform this trial among African Americans because retrospective analyses of V-HeFT data showed that self-identified African American participants on isosorbide dinitrate/hydralazine plus standard therapy had lower mortality rates than African American participants on placebo plus standard therapy. The beneficial effect of isosorbide dinitrate/hydralazine was not seen in Caucasian participants [5]. Thus, performing the trial in a mixed population of African Americans and Caucasians could have resulted in unbalanced randomization, which would have biased the observed treatment effect toward the null. A null result in this study may have deprived African Americans, an already underserved population, from a potentially important, efficacious medication [11].

Although specific genetic data were not analyzed as a part of the original A-HeFT study, the results of A-HeFT have been used to suggest a genetic basis for the difference in treatment response between African Americans and Caucasians. Subsequent studies, including the Genetic Risk of Heart Failure in African Americans (GRAHF) study, a sub-study of the original A-HeFT study, are investigating the genetic polymorphisms responsible for this difference [12]. This pattern, beginning with a race-based study and then progressing to more specific analysis of genetic polymorphisms, has become more common as the interest in pharmacogenetics has increased. It has provided scientists with a way to stratify patients based on presumed genetic differences without specific genotypic information.

BENEFITS OF RACE-SPECIFIC RESEARCH

Ideally, pharmacogenetics and race-based therapeutics have the potential to improve efficacy while decreasing toxicity. By providing physicians with more information regarding the likelihood of response, better treatment decisions can be made, decreasing the amount of switching between medications, decreasing exposure to potential toxic side effects and decreasing time to maximal therapy [13]. The higher efficacy of treatment and the lower rate of side effects could also increase patient confidence in their healthcare provider, leading to increased compliance.

Many scientists predict that as the field of genetics advances, race will no longer be necessary because everything will be based on specific genetic polymorphisms rather than phenotypic differences [14, 15]. Currently, however, specific genetic tests are not available for most complex diseases. As such, when results are translated to physicians' clinics, knowledge about specific genetic polymorphisms and their effect on treatment response may actually be less informative than information about race and its impact on treatment response.

In research, race can also be a helpful, albeit imperfect, proxy for genetic information, especially when this information is not obtainable due to expense or lack of samples [16, 17]. Race may even serve as a surrogate for complex genetic and environmental interactions that would not otherwise be captured because researchers do not have enough information to expect and test these interactions [14].

On a societal level, race-based studies may lead to greater justice in clinical research and treatment of disease. As in the case of BiDil, pharmaceutical companies will want to identify populations that can benefit from their drugs [13]. Current costs of bringing a drug to market are approximately $880 billion, so it is advantageous for pharmaceutical companies to define populations that will respond well to medications and not experience adverse effects [13]. If study populations are enriched for participants who are likely to respond to treatment, phase II and phase III trials may require smaller sizes, decreasing costs and shortening recruitment times [16]. Targeting appropriate populations would also enable companies to salvage drugs that have toxic side effects in one population but important benefits in other populations [13]. Historically underserved minority groups, such as African Americans, may benefit from new opportunities to participate in clinical trials. These studies could yield important advances in the treatment of diseases in minorities.

RISKS OF RACE-BASED RESEARCH

Opponents of race-based research state that these studies oversimplify the relationship between genetics and race [14, 17]. These studies may also lead to scientific rationalization of race and racism, leading to a violation of the ethical principles of justice and non-maleficence. While much attention is focused on the association between genetics, race and treatment response, environmental effects, such as diet and socioeconomic factors, may be overlooked [7, 18].

In fact, many of the associations between race and treatment response are confounded by environmental exposures. Compared to Caucasians, African Americans and American Indians have a higher incidence of nearly every disease. Many of these correlations are likely due to environmental effects, such as poor access to healthcare and differences in diet rather than specific genetic polymorphisms [14]. The assumption that the effects of race are more closely tied to genetics rather than environment may be faulty and could direct attention away from deserving studies that would work towards minimizing socioeconomic disparities [9, 18].

Studies focusing on racial differences may also lead to inferior care for racial minorities. From a market-based perspective, pharmaceutical companies may not have the incentive to fund research in financially disadvantaged populations, populations that harbor rare alleles or groups deemed as "non-responders" [19]. Without research in these populations, there would be little information to guide physicians regarding treatment options. Faced with this dearth of information, physicians might be forced to use drugs tested in other populations and assume that they will also work in these populations. This could lead to ineffective treatment and an increased risk of side effects, especially if the medication was brought to market based on studies excluding populations at high risk [19]. Insurance companies may also refuse to cover these drugs for certain populations if they have not been tested and proven to be effective in these groups.

The overriding concern about race-based studies is that they may perpetuate racism. Polymorphisms that confer lower disease risk or better treatment response may be viewed as more desirable than others. Races with a high frequency of beneficial alleles may be considered better than those with a high frequency of risk alleles. Rather than deconstructing racism by linking phenotype directly to genotype, race-base studies may be used to validate the belief that some groups are "superior" to others [13, 19].

CONCLUSION

Based on the example of BiDil and an analysis of the risks and benefits of race-based therapeutics, we believe there is a role for race-based studies in pharmacogenetics. However, there is also an urgent need for increased awareness of its potential implications on basic ethical principles such as justice and non-maleficence.

To promote justice, databases such as HapMap should be expanded to include other groups such as populations in the Middle East, South Asia and other areas of Africa. Information regarding allele frequencies in populations with more closely related or mixed ancestries may provide more insight into the differences and similarities between these populations [13]. Data from these populations would also help researchers develop therapeutic agents that are beneficial to these populations, as opposed to just Caucasians and African Americans.

To ensure justice and prevent maleficence, government agencies should regulate the amount of funds appropriated to research in minorities and financially disadvantaged groups. The definition of minority should include groups who carry rare alleles as opposed to only groups defined strictly by race. This type of legislation is needed so that pharmaceutical companies developing new drugs do not abandon minority and financially disadvantaged groups [13]. Further governmental support could also include grants to independent researchers to provide funding for research on drug development for minority populations.

Finally, education is crucial. Researchers should explore and understand the potential social and ethical implications of their studies. The reasons for using race as a proxy for genetic information should be provided to research participants as well as to the community at large. A better understanding of the relationship between race, genetics and the environment may help avoid misconceptions about the role of race in pharmacogenetic studies and may help prevent the rationalization of racism.

REFERENCES

[1]   Weber, W. W. (1999). Populations and genetic polymorphisms. *Mol Diagn.* Dec; *4(4)*, 299-307.

[2]   International HapMap Project. (2007). http://www.hapmap.org.

[3]   U.S. Department of Health and Human Sevices. (2007). U.S. Food and Drug Administration. http://www.fda.gov.

[4]   Cohn, J. N. & Johnson, G. (1990). Heart failure with normal ejection fraction. The V-HeFT Study. Veterans Administration Cooperative Study Group. *Circulation*, *81*(2 Suppl), III48-53.

[5]   Carson, P., Ziesche, S., Johnson, G. & Cohn, J. N. (1999). Racial differences in response to therapy for heart failure: analysis of the vasodilator-heart failure trials. Vasodilator-Heart Failure Trial Study Group. *J Card Fail*, *5(3)*, 178-87.

[6]   Taylor, A. L., Ziesche, S., Yancy, C., Carson, P., D'Agostino, R., Jr., Ferdinand, K., et al. (2004). Combination of isosorbide dinitrate and hydralazine in blacks with heart failure. *N Engl J Med*, *351(20)*, 2049-57.

[7]   Bibbins-Domingo, K. & Fernandez, A. (2007). BiDil for heart failure in black patients: implications of the U.S. Food and Drug Administration approval. *Ann Intern Med*, *146(1)*, 52-6.

[8]   Kahn, J. (2007). Race in a bottle. Drugmakers are eager to develop medicines targeted at ethnic groups, but so far they have made poor choices based on unsound science. *Sci Am, 297(2)*, 40-5.

[9]   Duster, T. (2007). Medicalisation of race. *Lancet, 369(9562)*, 702-4.

[10] Bloche, M. G. (2004). Race-based therapeutics. *N Engl J Med, 351(20),* 2035-7.

[11] Cohn, J. N. (2006). The use of race and ethnicity in medicine: lessons from the African-American Heart Failure Trial. J Law *Med Ethics, 34(3),* 552-4.

[12] McNamara, D. M., Tam, S. W., Sabolinski, M. L., Tobelmann, P., Janosko, K., Taylor, A. L., et al. (2006). Aldosterone synthase promoter polymorphism predicts outcome in African Americans with heart failure: results from the A-HeFT Trial. *J Am Coll Cardiol, 48(6),* 1277-82.

[13] Lee, S. S. (2005). Racializing drug design: implications of pharmacogenomics for health disparities. *Am J Public Health, 95(12),* 2133-8.

[14] Jones, D. S., Perlis, R. H. (2006). Pharmacogenetics, race, and psychiatry: prospects and challenges. *Harv Rev Psychiatry, 4(2),* 92-108.

[15] Tutton, R., Smart, A., Martin, P. A., Ashcroft, R. & Ellison, G. T. (2008). Genotyping the future: scientists' expectations about race/ ethnicity after BiDil. *J Law Med Ethics, 36(3),* 464-70.

[16] Temple, R., Stockbridge, N. L. (2007). BiDil for heart failure in black patients: The U.S. Food and Drug Administration perspective. *Ann Intern Med, 146(1),* 57-62.

[17] Reverby, S. M. (2008). Special treatment": BiDil, Tuskegee, and the logic of race. *J Law Med Ethics, 36(3),* 478-84.

[18] Kahn, J. (2004). How a drug becomes "ethnic": law, commerce, and the production of racial categories in medicine. *Yale J Health Policy Law Ethics, 4(1),* 1-46.

[19] Smart, A., Martin, P. & Parker, M. (2004). Tailored medicine: whom will it fit? The ethics of patient and disease stratification. *Bioethics, 18(4),* 322-42.

In: Race and Ethnicity
Editor: Jonathan K. Crennan, pp. 381-385

ISBN: 978-1-60692-099-2
© 2010 Nova Science Publishers, Inc.

Chapter 19

ETHNICITY, HISTORY AND MENTAL HEALTH IN BRAZIL

J. R. M Oliveira [1,2] *and M. B. R. Souza* [1*]

[1]Keizo Asami Laboratory (LIKA) – Federal University of Pernambuco,
Recife-PE, Brazil
[2]Neuropsychiatry Department - Federal University of Pernambuco,
Recife-PE, Brazil

ABSTRACT

There is little data concerning medical reports about the first Brazilian habitants, after the first Portuguese expeditions at the XVI Century. However, some historical records mention a variable expression of behavioral disturbances amongst some descendents from European Caucasians, Native Indians from the Brazilian coast and Africans brought to work as slaves. The mixing of these three groups during decades of miscegenation generated a wide spectrum of cultural, behavioral and genetic variants and to study this issue is crucial to understand how their biological and cultural idiosyncrasies might have influenced the present Brazilian neuroepidemiology. On the other hand, the current ethnical profile in Brazil presents an unusual and unique distribution across the country, with highly mixed groups living at the coast, contrasting with a scattered distribution of high inbreeding clusters found at the country side, were almost 30% of the population lives. The natural consequence is the often manifestation of recessive disorders in rural areas, several of them with major neuropsychiatric symptoms and other with important psychological consequences due to general life quality impairment. There are, in part, geographic reasons for this pattern, in cases of families living in isolated regions, but there are also intriguing cultural aspects. Some poor families own significant, but barren and desolated pieces of land, and some of them are recognized as wealthy, compared to their neighbors. Actually they avoid to "mix" themselves with other kindred, avoiding splitting their property with subjects other than their own siblings. Additional studies are crucial for the full understanding of the connection between the past

---

[*] Corresponding author: Federal University of Pernambuco, Av. Prof. Moraes Rego, 1235 - Cidade Universitária, Recife - PE - CEP: 50670-901, Brazil João.ricardo@ufpe.br

Psychopathology of the first "Brazilians" and the nowadays neuropsychiatric profile at the general population.

There is little data concerning medical records about the first components of the Brazilian habitants after the first Portuguese expeditions at the XVI Century.

However, some historical proceedings mention a variable expression of behavioral disturbances amongst some descendents from European Caucasians, Native Indians from the Brazilian coast and Africans brought to work here as slaves.

The mixing of these three ethnicities groups during decades of miscegenation generated a wide spectrum of cultural, behavioral and genetic variants, forming the first "Brazilians". In order to start a discussion about this issue is crucial understand how their biological and cultural idiosyncrasies might have influenced the present Brazilian neuroepidemiology.

To analyze these manifestations is crucial for understanding the Psychopathology of the first subjects and populations with mental disorders that were originated by various ethnical groups and that latter started one of the largest populations at the American Continent.

The work of three major Brazilian Historians and Anthropologists interested in this period was analyzed in search of reports of behavioral changes compatible to the nowadays notions of Psychiatric symptoms (Freyre, 2003; Mello, 1996; Ribeiro, 1995).

The first Portuguese administrators sent to explore the Brazilian resources started slavering Native Indians in order to make them help exploiting, initially wood and latter minerals. However, the tribes were rebellious towards slavering and it was common the episodes of some subjects whom intentionally starved to death, laying down in hammocks indefinitely, resembling contemporary depressive patients in asylums, before the advent of antidepressant medication. (Ribeiro, 1995).

The Negroids brought from The East cost of Africa fitted better the intentions of the Portuguese Crown. However, a feeling of homesickness was common (called *Banzo*), inducing episodes compatible with major depression, mainly characterized by apathy, lethargy and indifference. Some of these subjects would be taken as rebels and punished to death while others would kill themselves by eating earth (suffocation), hanging or poisoning. Others would develop addictions to alcohol and *Cannabis sativa* (Freyre, 2003).

The most precise records about this issue are from European Caucasians, especially New-Christians (crypto-Jews) who migrated to Brazil after the Inquisition and Dispersion of Sephardic Jews during the first half of the XVI century. The study of a famous kindred, derived from Branca Dias and Diogo Fernandes, owners of a sugar-cane plantation in Pernambuco, Northeast region, shows the presence of some siblings displaying behavioral disturbances similar to what we would label today as mental retardation or maybe negative symptoms of schizophrenia. (Mello, 1996)

Curiously, we note a variety of expression of behavioral disturbances between the three Ethnical groups reported and we wonder if their cultural idiosyncrasies might influence the way these three different populations might face systematic violence, aggressiveness, emigration, prejudice and hostility.

Obviously that Mental Disorder was already a reality to these groups of Humans and here we intend to report the Colonization process, and various stressful aspects involved with it, as an important trigger to behavioral changes at the dawn of the XVI Century in Colonial Brazil in three different ethnical groups.

However, the current ethnical profile in Brazil presents an unusual and distinctive distribution across the country, with different ethnical groups living on the coast, in contrast with a unique cluster of high inbreeding groups in the rural areas, where almost 30% of the Brazilian population live. This specific group works mainly in agriculture and crafts, often in small towns or farms, in conditions of limited access to health care, transportation and family planning, often with large offspring, often with consanguineous marriages (www.ibge. gov. br)

The natural consequence is the common occurrence of recessive disorders, several with major neuropsychiatric symptoms and others with important psychological consequences such as: Pendred syndrome, Berardinelli-Seip lipodystrophies, Waardenburg syndrome, Tay-Sachs disease, juvenile parkinsonism, Knobloch syndrome, primary microcephaly, Ellis Van Creveld disease, familial dwarfism, Gaucher's disease, limb girdle muscular dystrophies and recently a new form of spastic paraplegia with neuropathy and optic atrophy. It was from some of these families that the responsible genes were first identified. (Bond J et al, 2005; Chien et al, 2006; Fu et al, 2004; Macedo-Souza et al, 2005; Nigro et al, 1994; Passos-Bueno et al, 1996; Rozemberg et al, 2004; 2006; Rui-Perez et al 2003; Salvatori et al, 1999; Sertié et al, 2000).

Other families with autossomal recessive conditions have been reported with Pycnodysostosis and Neuronal ceroid lipofuscinoses, but they lacked a further molecular investigation (Fonteles et al, 2007; Gama et al, 2007).

During the last two decades, the first molecular studies localized candidate regions and genes for various recessive syndromes in families from the Brazilian Northeast but this information was not provided in most of the articles and a nosological geography of these families is import to correlate the kindred's origin and the local inbreeding rate.

Fifty years ago, Newton Freire Maia established a milestone at the study of inbreeding across the Brazilian territory and the northeast region presented the highest rates known so far, especially at the countryside (Freire-Maia, 1957).

The low demographic density and the high inbreeding rates found at the Brazilian Northeast resemble the situation of others genetics isolates.

Various humans groups became isolated, for different reasons. Sometimes because of cultural isolation, geographical isolation or founder effect but often due to a combination of different reasons. The studies of population isolates were crucial for the identification of various genes and loci responsible for genetic disorders, especially the ones with autossomal recessive pattern of inheritance. The best examples are the Old Order Amish, Finnish, Sardinian, Hutterians and Jewish communities, with all of them presenting high inbreeding rates. The study of genetic isolates are scarce in South America and the best know example is the Paisa community from Colombia, mostly at the state of Antioquia. (Arcos-Burgos and Muenke, 2002).

There are, in part, geographic reasons for families living in isolated regions, but there are also intriguing cultural aspects. In our case, some poor families own significant, but barren and desolated pieces of land, and others are recognized as being wealthy, compared to their neighbors. In practice they do not want to "mix" themselves with other families to avoid splitting their property with people other than their own siblings.

Additional studies are crucial for the full understanding of the connection between the past Psychopathology of the first "Brazilians" and the nowadays neuropsychiatric profile at the general population.

REFERENCES

Bond, J., Roberts, E., Springell, K., Lizarraga, S. B., Scott, S., Higgins, J., Hampshire, D. J., Morrison, E. E., Leal, G. F., Silva, E. O., Costa, S. M., Baralle, D., Raponi, M., Karbani, G., Rashid, Y., Jafri, H., Bennett, C., Corry, P., Walsh, C. A. & Woods, C. G. (2005). A centrosomal mechanism involving CDK5RAP2 and CENPJ controls brain size. *Nat Genet, 37(4)*, 353-5.

Chien, H. F., Rohé, C. F., Costa, M. D., Breedveld, G. J., Oostra, B. A., Barbosa, E. R., Bonifati, V. (2006). Early-onset Parkinson's disease caused by a novel parkin mutation in a genetic isolate from north-eastern Brazil. *Neurogenetics., 7(1)*, 13-9.

Fu, M., Kazlauskaite, R., Baracho Mde, F., Santos, M. G., Brandão-Neto, J., Villares, S., Celi, F. S., Wajchenberg, B. L. & Shuldiner, A. R. (2004). Mutations in Gng3lg and AGPAT2 in Berardinelli-Seip congenital lipodystrophy and Brunzell syndrome: phenotype variability suggests important modifier effects. *J Clin Endocrinol Metab., 89(6)*, 2916-22.

Jorge, A. A., Menezes Filho, H. C., Lins, T. S., Guedes, D. R., Damiani, D., Setian, N., Arnhold, I. J. & Mendonça, B. B. (2005). [Founder effect of E180splice mutation in growth hormone receptor gene (GHR) identified in Brazilian patients with GH insensitivity]. *Arq Bras Endocrinol Metabol., 49(3)*, 384-9.

Macedo-Souza, L. I., Kok, F., Santos, S., Amorim, S. C., Starling, A., Nishimura, A., Lezirovitz, K., Lino, A. M. & Zatz, M. (2005). Spastic paraplegia, optic atrophy, and neuropathy is linked to chromosome 11q13. *Ann Neurol., 57(5)*, 730-7.

Nigro V., de Sá Moreira, E., Piluso, G., Vainzof, M., Belsito, A., Politano, L., Puca, A. A., Passos-Bueno, M. R. & Zatz, M. (1996). Autosomal recessive limb-girdle muscular dystrophy, LGMD2F, is caused by a mutation in the delta-sarcoglycan gene. *Nat Genet., 14(2)*, 195-8.

Passos-Bueno, M. R., Moreira, E. S., Marie, S. K., Bashir, R., Vasquez, L., Love, D. R., Vainzof, M., Iughetti, P., Oliveira, J. R., Bakker, E., Strachan, T., Bushby, K. & Zatz, M. (1996). Main clinical features of the three mapped autosomal recessive limb-girdle muscular dystrophies and estimated proportion of each form in 13 Brazilian families. *J Med Genet., 33(2)*, 97-102.

Rozenberg, R., Martins, A. M., Micheletti, C., Mustacchi, Z. & Pereira, L. V. (2004). Tay-Sachs disease in Brazilian patients: prevalence of the IVS7+1g>c mutation. *J Inherit Metab Dis., 27(1)*, 109-10.

Rozenberg, R., Kok, F., Burin, M. G., Sá Miranda, M. C., Vasques, C., Henriques-Souza, A. M., Giugliani, R., Vainzof, M. & Pereira, L. V. (2006). Diagnosis and molecular characterization of non-classic forms of Tay-Sachs disease in Brazil. *J Child Neurol., 21(6)*, 540-4.

Ruiz-Perez, V. L., Tompson, S. W., Blair, H. J., Espinoza-Valdez, C., Lapunzina, P., Silva, E. O., Hamel, B., Gibbs, J. L., Young, I. D., Wright, M. J. & Goodship, J. A. (2003). Mutations in two nonhomologous genes in a head-to-head configuration cause Ellis-van Creveld syndrome. *Am J Hum Genet., 72(3)*, 728-32.

Salvatori, R., Hayashida, C. Y., Aguiar-Oliveira, M. H., Phillips, J. A. 3rd., Souza, A. H., Gondo, R. G., Toledo, S. P., Conceicão, M. M., Prince, M., Maheshwari, H. G., Baumann, G., Levine, M. A. (1999). Familial dwarfism due to a novel mutation of the growth hormone-releasing hormone receptor gene. *J Clin Endocrinol Metab.*, *84(3)*, 917-23.

Sertié, A. L., Sossi, V., Camargo, A. A., Zatz, M., Brahe, C. & Passos-Bueno, M. R. (2000). Collagen XVIII., containing an endogenous inhibitor of angiogenesis and tumor growth, plays a critical role in the maintenance of retinal structure and in neural tube closure (Knobloch syndrome).*Hum Mol Genet. 9(13)*, 2051-8.

Baldwin, C. T., Hoth, C. F., Amos, J. A., da-Silva, E. O. & Milunsky, A. (1992). An exonic mutation in the HuP2 paired domain gene causes Waardenburg's syndrome. *Nature*, *355(6361)*, 637-8.

Ribeiro, (1995). Darcy-O povo brasileiro: a formação e o sentido do Brasil (*The Brazilian People: The Formation and Meaning of Brazil*). Editora: Cia das Letras, 2ª Edição.

Freyre, (2006). Gilberto-Casa-Grande e Senzala (*The Masters and the Slaves)*. Editora: Global, 51ª Edição.

Mello, (1996). José *Antônio Gonsalves* - Gente da Nação: *Cristãos-Novos e Judeus em Pernambuco*. Editora: Massangana, 2ª edição. *Instituto Brasileiro de Geografia e Estatística.* Disponível em: www.ibge.gov.br. Acesso em: 2009.

Gama, R. L., Nakayama, M., Távora, D. G., de Lara Alvim, T. C., Nogueira, C. D. & Portugal (2007). [Neuronal ceroid lipofuscinosis: clinical and neuroradiological findings] *Arq Neuropsiquiatr.*, *65(2A)*, 320-6.

Fonteles, C. S., Chaves, C. M., Jr, Da Silveira, A., Soares, E. C., Couto, J. L. & de Azevedo, M., de F. (2007). Cephalometric characteristics and dentofacial abnormalities of pycnodysostosis: report of four cases from Brazil. *Oral Surg Oral Med Oral Pathol Oral Radiol Endod.*, *104(4)*, 83-90.

Arcos-Burgos, M. & Muenke, M. (2002). Genetics of population isolates. *Clin Genet.*, *61(4)*, 233-47.

Baldwin, C. T., Hoth, C. F., Amos, J. A., da-Silva, E. O. & Milunsky, A. (1992). An exonic mutation in the HuP2 paired domain gene causes Waardenburg's syndrome. *Nature*, *355(6361)*, 637-8.

Freire-Maia, N. (1957). Inbreeding in Brazil. *Am J Hum Genet.*, *9(4)*, 284-98.

INDEX

B

D

G

M

Q

R

S

T